# CODE

## SECOND BASE OF TRIPLET CODE

| ADENINE | GUANINE | THIRD BASE OF TRIPLET CODE |
|---|---|---|
| Tyrosine UAU ⎫ Tyr | Cysteine UGU ⎫ Cys | URACIL |
| Tyrosine UAC ⎭ | Cysteine UGC ⎭ | CYTOSINE |
| UAA ⎫ End Chain | UGA     End Chain | ADENINE |
| UAG ⎭ | Tryptophan UGG ⎫ Try | GUANINE |
| Histidine CAU ⎫ His | Arginine CGU | URACIL |
| Histidine CAC ⎭ | Arginine CGC | CYTOSINE |
| Glutamine CAA ⎫ Gln | Arginine CGA ⎫ Arg | ADENINE |
| Glutamine CAG ⎭ | Arginine CGG ⎭ | GUANINE |
| Asparagine AAU ⎫ Asn | Serine AGU ⎫ Ser | URACIL |
| Asparagine AAC ⎭ | Serine AGC ⎭ | CYTOSINE |
| Lysine AAA ⎫ Lys | Arginine AGA ⎫ Arg | ADENINE |
| Lysine AAG ⎭ | Arginine AGG ⎭ | GUANINE |
| Aspartic Acid GAU ⎫ Asp | Glycine GGU | URACIL |
| Aspartic Acid GAC ⎭ | Glycine GGC | CYTOSINE |
| Glutamic Acid GAA ⎫ Glu | Glycine GGA ⎫ Gly | ADENINE |
| Glutamic Acid GAG ⎭ | Glycine GGG ⎭ | GUANINE |

*The Macmillan Biology Series*
*General Editor: Norman H. Giles*

# The Science of Genetics
## An Introduction to Heredity

[OVERLEAF] Model of a molecule of DNA, the genetic material. (*Photo courtesy of Sloan-Kettering Institute for Cancer Research, New York City.*)

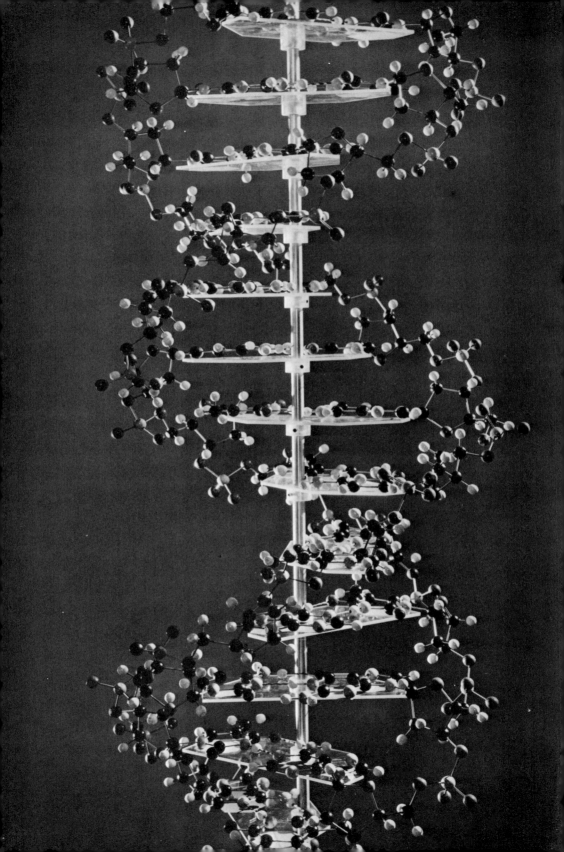

# The Science of GENETICS

## An Introduction to HEREDITY

*SECOND EDITION*

### George W. Burns

Ohio Wesleyan University

The Macmillan Company · NEW YORK

Collier-Macmillan Limited · LONDON

THE MACMILLAN COMPANY
866 Third Avenue, New York, New York 10022
COLLIER-MACMILLAN CANADA, LTD., Toronto, Ontario

*Library of Congress catalog card number*: 70-158173

First Printing

# Preface

THE very rapid progress in genetics, especially at the molecular level, has dictated preparation of this second edition of *The Science of Genetics* only a few years after the appearance of the first. As before, the problem approach is followed, frequently using the work of some of the men and women who have contributed most to the development of the science. Topics are developed inductively, from observation to explanation to principle. Examples are drawn from animal, plant, bacterial, and viral genetics, wherever a particular point is best illustrated. Because of the importance and interest attached to human genetics, applications to and illustrations from the genetics of man have been freely included.

Organization of *The Science of Genetics* is built on experience gained from nearly twenty-five years of teaching. Its sequence of topics, starting with "classical" genetics, then progressing to molecular genetics, gene regulation, and the question of cytoplasmic inheritance, follows in general the chronological development of the science.

Work of the past few years has necessitated a number of changes in this second edition. The entire portion on molecular genetics has been almost completely rewritten, as well as expanded by including the more important recent work in this field. Here, rapid expansion of the frontiers of the science has been reflected, for example, in separating a more detailed account of protein synthesis and the operation of the genetic code into two chapters. The status of our knowledge concerning chromosomal aberrations in man, with particular reference to the possible effects of various drugs, has been brought up to date and increased in coverage. Discussion of the genetics of human blood groups has been widened. Treatment of nondisjunction, both in man and in experimental animals, has been expanded as has also the discussion of sex chromosome anomalies such as the *XYY* human male. The chapter on mapping has been rewritten, and additional topics have been included in the chapter on population genetics; in both, the mathematics has been kept simple without sacrificing depth. More problems have been included, and many new references, most of them of very recent publication, have been added. Almost all of these are referred to within the chapters themselves, but a few significant, general references have also been included. The possible future application of genetics to the betterment of mankind has also been considerably broadened in the light of recent and ongoing research.

This book is intended for undergraduates who have had a previous college course in one of the life sciences. However, salient points of cell structure and behavior are reviewed briefly where needed. A series of appendixes contains answers to problems, life cycles of animals and plants used in genetic research, structural formulas of the biologically important amino acids, a summary of mathematical formulae, ratios and statistical tests which have been developed in the text, a table of metric values, and a list of general references and journals. The glossary has been considerably enlarged.

The help of many persons who have made this book possible is gratefully acknowledged. A number of professional associates have reviewed all or part of the manuscript and offered helpful suggestions; others have been most generous in permitting use of valuable illustration material (acknowledged with each figure). In particular, I am indebted to the Literary Executor of the late Sir Ronald A. Fisher, F.R.S., and to Oliver and Boyd, Ltd., Edinburgh, for their permission to reprint Table 3 from their book *Statistical Methods for Research Workers*. The editors and artists of The Macmillan Company are due especial thanks for their creative assistance during preparation of this second edition. Finally, to the students who have made the teaching of genetics an exciting and rewarding experience, this book is affectionately dedicated.

G.W.B.

# Contents

*Men love to wonder, and that is the seed of our science*

—EMERSON

# CHAPTER 1

# Introduction

**C**ERTAINLY one of the most exciting fields of biological science, if not of all science, is genetics. This is the study of the mechanisms of heredity by which traits or characteristics are passed from generation to generation. Not only has modern genetics had a compact history, being essentially a product of the twentieth century, but it has made almost explosive progress from the rediscovery in 1900 of Mendel's basic observations of the 1860s to a fairly full comprehension of underlying principles at the molecular level. As our knowledge of these operating mechanisms developed, it became apparent that they are remarkably similar in their fundamental behavior for all kinds of organisms, whether man or mouse, bacterium or corn. But geneticists' quest for truth and understanding is far from completed; as in other sciences, the answer to one question raises new ones and opens whole new avenues of inquiry.

Genetics is personally relevant to everyone. Man is a genetic animal; each of us is the product of a long series of matings. People differ among themselves with regard to the expression of many traits; one has some inherited characteristics of his father and certain ones of his mother, but often, as well, some not exhibited by either parent. Familiar examples abound in persons of your own acquaintance—hair or eye color, curly or straight hair, height, intelligence, and baldness, to list but a few. Less obvious genetic traits include such diverse ones as form of ear lobes (Fig. 1-1), ability to roll the tongue (Fig. 1-2), ability to taste the chemical phenylthiocarbamide (PTC), red-green color blindness, hemophilia or "bleeder's disease," extra fingers or toes, or ability to produce insulin (lack of which results in diabetes). Note that some of these characteristics seem purely morphological, being concerned primarily with form and structure, whereas others are clearly physiological. Look about you at your friends and family for points of difference or similarity. Many of these characteristics have genetic bases.

Although a survey of man's long interest in heredity is outside the scope of this book, it is well established that as much as six thousand years ago he kept records of pedigrees of such domestic animals as the horse or of crop plants like rice. Because certain animals and plants were necessary for his survival and culture, man has, since the beginning of recorded history at least, attempted to develop improved varieties. But the story of man's concern with heredity during his lifetime on this planet has been,

**1**

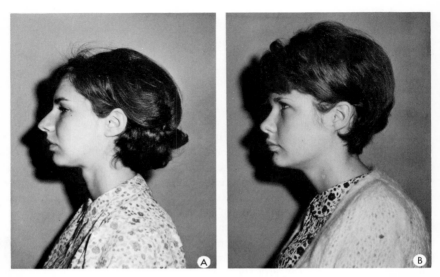

FIGURE 1-1. *Inherited difference in form of ear lobe. (A) Free ear lobe, the result of a dominant gene. (B) Attached ear lobe, caused by a recessive allele.*

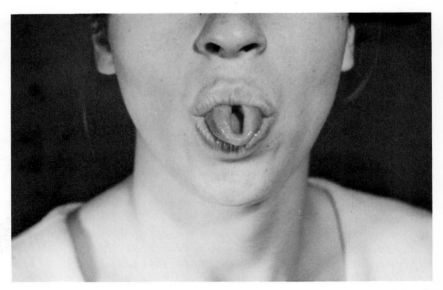

FIGURE 1-2. *Ability to roll the tongue, a trait which depends on presence of a dominant gene for its expression. A less commonly encountered character, ability to fold the tip of the tongue back toward its base, is caused by another dominant gene.*

FIGURE 1-3. *Homunculus, "little man in a sperm cell."*
[Drawing by N. Hartsoecker, *Journal des Scavans,* Feb. 7,
1695.]

until recently, one of interest largely in results rather than in fundamental
understanding of the mechanisms involved.

As one examines the development of ideas relating to these mechanisms,
he finds the way replete with misconceptions, many of them naïve in the
light of modern knowledge. These theories may be divided roughly into
three categories: (1) "*vapors and fluids,*" (2) *preformation*, and (3) *particulate*. Such early Greek philosophers as Pythagoras (500 B.C.) proposed
that "vapors" derived from various organs unite to form a new individual.
Then Aristotle assigned a "vitalizing" effect to semen, which, he suggested,
was highly purified blood, a notion that was to influence thinking for almost
two thousand years.

By the seventeenth century sperm and egg had been discovered, and the
Dutch scientist Swammerdam theorized that sex cells contained miniatures
of the adult. Literature of that time contains drawings of models or manikins
within sperm heads which imaginative workers reported seeing (Fig. 1-3).
Such theories of preformation persisted well into the eighteenth century,
by which time the German investigator Wolff offered experimental evidence
that no preformed embryo existed in the egg of the chicken.

But Maupertuis in France, recognizing that preformation could not easily account for transmission of traits to the offspring from both parents, had proposed in the early 1800s that minute particles, one from each body part, united in sexual reproduction to form a new individual. In some instances, he reasoned, particles from the male parent might dominate those from the female, and in other cases the reverse might be true. Thus the notion of particulate inheritance came into consideration. Maupertuis was actually closer to the truth, in general terms, than anyone realized for more than a century.

Charles Darwin suggested in the nineteenth century essentially the same basic mechanism in his theory of pangenesis, the central idea of which had first been put forward by Hippocrates (400 B.C.). Under this concept, each part of the body produced minute particles ("gemmules") which were contained in the blood of the entire body but eventually concentrated in the reproductive organs. Thus, an individual would represent a "blending" of both parents. Moreover, acquired characters would be inherited because, as parts of the body changed, so did the pangenes they produced. A champion weight lifter, therefore, should produce children with strong arm muscles; such transmission of acquired traits we know does not occur.

Pangenesis was disproved later in the same century by the German biologist Weismann. In a well-known experiment he cut off the tails of mice for twenty-two generations, yet each new lot of offspring consisted only of animals with tails. If the source of pangenes for tails was removed, how, he reasoned, could the next generation have tails? Yet, in spite of these early problems with the idea of particulate inheritance, its basic concept is the central core of our modern understanding.

Most attempts to explain observed breeding results failed because investigators generally tried to encompass simultaneously *all* variations, whether heritable or not. Nor was the progress of scientific thought or the development of suitable equipment and techniques ready to help point the way. It was the Augustinian monk Gregor Mendel who laid the groundwork for our modern concept of the particulate theory. He did so by attacking the problem in logical fashion, concentrating on one or a few observable, contrasting traits in a controlled breeding program. Both by his method and by his suggestion of causal "factors" (which we now call *genes*), Mendel came closer to a real understanding of heredity than had anyone in the preceding five thousand years or more, yet he only opened the door for others. An understanding of the cellular mechanisms was still to be developed.

## Characteristics of Useful Experimental Organisms

Even though Mendel's approach was probably more the result of luck than of thoughtful planning, it was elegant in its simplicity and logic. First, Mendel was fortunate to have in the garden pea (*Pisum sativum*) what we

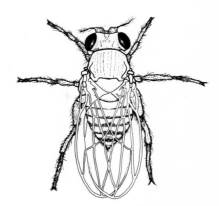

FIGURE 1-4. *The fruit fly,* Drosophila melanogaster, *an animal highly useful in genetic research.*

recognize today as a good subject for genetic study. There are six important considerations for choosing a plant or animal for genetic experiments:

*1. Variation.*   The organism chosen should show a number of detectable differences. Nothing could be learned of the inheritance of skin color in man, for example, if all human beings were alike in this respect. In general, the larger the number of discontinuous traits and the more clearly marked they are, the greater the usefulness of the species for genetic study.

*2. Recombination.*   Genetic analysis of a species is greatly expedited if it has some effective means of combining, in one individual, traits of two parents. Such *recombination* permits comparison of one expression of a character with another expression of the same trait (e.g., tall versus dwarf *size*, brown versus blue *eye color*) through several generations. In many organisms recombination occurs as the result of *sexual reproduction*, in which two sex cells (**gametes**), generally from two different parents, combine as a fertilized egg (**zygote**). The sexual process is characteristic of higher animals and plants, and occurs in many lower forms as well. In bacteria and viruses there occur such processes as conjugation and transduction which also bring about recombination. Life cycles of several genetically important organisms are reviewed in Appendix B.

On the other hand, many organisms reproduce *asexually* or *vegetatively* and cannot furnish recombinational information. Basically, asexual reproduction may involve specialized cells (often called **spores**), daughter cells (in unicellular forms), parts of a single parent (cuttings, grafts, fragmentation, etc.), or **parthenogenesis**, in which an individual develops from an unfertilized egg, as in the male honeybee. By and large, a means of recombination is required for genetic study.

*3. Controlled Matings.*   Systematic study of an organism's genetics is far easier if we can make controlled matings, choosing parental lines with particular purposes in mind, and keep careful records of offspring through several generations. The mouse, fruit fly (Fig. 1-4), corn, and the red bread mold (*Neurospora*), for instance, make better genetic subjects in this respect than does man. In human genetics we are dependent largely on pedigree analysis, or studies of traits as they have appeared in a given family line for several past generations. Although such analyses are certainly useful, the human geneticist must rely largely on lines of progeny that *have been* established and cannot devise desired crosses of his own.

*4. Short Life Cycle.* Acquisition of genetic knowledge is facilitated if the organism chosen requires only a short time between generations. Mice, which are sexually mature at 5 or 6 weeks of age and have a gestation period of about 19 to 31 days, are much more useful, for instance, than elephants, which mature in 8 to 16 years and have a gestation period of nearly 2 years. Likewise, the fruit fly, *Drosophila*, is much used in investigations because it may provide as many as five or six generations in a season. But first place for short life cycle goes to bacteria and to bacteriophages (or simply phages, viruses that infect bacteria), which, under optimum conditions, have a generation time of only 20 minutes! Both bacteria and phages also offer a number of other advantages for genetic study, as we shall subsequently see.

*5. Large Number of Offspring.* Genetic studies are greatly speeded if the organism chosen produces fairly sizeable lots of progeny per mating. Cattle, with generally one calf per breeding, do not provide nearly as much information in a given time as many lower forms of life where offspring may number many thousands.

*6. Convenience of Handling.* For practical reasons, an experimental species should be of a type that can be raised and maintained conveniently and relatively inexpensively. Whales are obviously less useful in this context than are bacteria!

## Methods of Genetic Study

Mendel's pea studies illustrate an approach useful both in classical, descriptive genetics and in modern molecular studies. This is the *planned breeding experiment*, in which parents exhibiting contrasting expressions of the same trait or traits are mated or crossed and careful records of results kept through several generations. We shall examine a number of such experiments in the next and succeeding chapters.

In addition to experimental breeding, we have already noted *pedigree analysis* in cases where controlled breeding programs are impossible. Pedigrees of three different conditions are shown in Figs. 1-5 to 1-7; Fig. 1-5 illustrates a pedigree of polydactyly, the occurrence of extra fingers, shaded symbols indicating this condition and unshaded ones representing individuals with the usual five fingers. As is customary in pedigree diagrams, squares represent males, circles females. Here we have a marriage between a polydactylous man and a "normal" woman (generation I). They have three

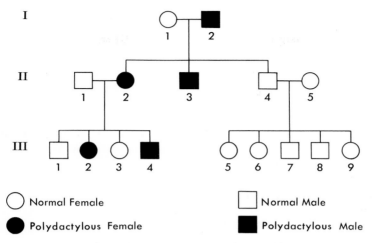

FIGURE 1-5. *Pedigree of polydactyly, occurrence of extra fingers, in human beings.*

children, a polydactylous girl, a polydactylous son, and a normal son (generation II). The first and third individuals of generation II each marry "normal" persons; their children are shown in generation III. Note in this case that affected individuals appear only when at least one parent is

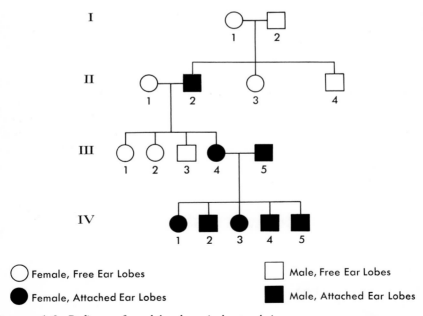

FIGURE 1-6. *Pedigree of ear-lobe shape in human beings.*

polydactylous; marriages between five-fingered persons appear to produce only "normal" offspring.

A different kind of situation is illustrated in Fig. 1-6. Here the condition with which we are concerned is the shape of the ear lobe, which may be either "free" or "attached" (Fig. 1-1). In this pedigree, the shaded symbols represent persons with attached ear lobes. Here we see that an individual may display this condition without its having appeared in either parent, whereas if both parents have attached ear lobes, all the children have the same condition. Does this mean that heredity is not operating in this case? Not at all. But certainly the genetic situation here is not the same as in the previous illustration of polydactyly.

As another example of pedigree, note the case shown in in Fig. 1-7. Here the shaded symbols represent hemophilia, in which an impairment of clotting mechanism causes severe bleeding from even minor skin breaks

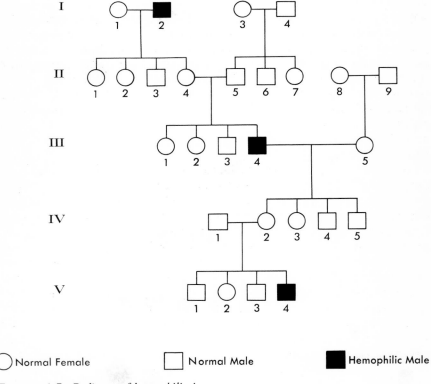

FIGURE 1-7. *Pedigree of hemophilia in man.*

with consequent danger to life. In this instance the trait appears to be confined to the males but transmitted from an affected male through his daughters to some of his grandsons. This pattern, repeated in many pedigrees of hemophilia, certainly suggests a genetic basis, but one that is quite different from either of the first two.

Finally, *statistical analyses* of several kinds are used (1) to predict the probability of certain results in untried crosses and (2) to provide degrees of confidence in a theory regarding the specific genetic mechanism operating in a given case. Geneticists employ primarily several statistics of probability which may be applied either to the results of an experimental breeding program or to a particular pedigree.

## Fields of Study Useful in Genetics

After an initial and appropriate preoccupation with descriptive genetics, scientists turned naturally to problems of the mechanics of the processes they observed. The "what" of the earliest twentieth century rapidly gave way to a concern with "how." Parallels between inheritance patterns and the structure and behavior of cells were noted by a number of pioneer investigators. Thus, *cytology* rapidly became an important adjunct to genetics. In fact, a pair of papers by Sutton as early as 1902 and 1903 clearly pointed the way to a physical basis for the burgeoning science of heredity. Sutton concluded his 1902 paper with a bold prediction: "I may finally call attention to the probability that (the behavior of chromosomes) may constitute the physical basis of the Mendelian law of heredity." Truly the door was thereby opened to an objective examination of the physical mechanisms of the genetic processes.

As the science of genetics developed rapidly during the first quarter of this century, a considerable body of knowledge was built up for such organisms as *Drosophila* (Fig. 1-8), corn (Fig. 1-9), the laboratory mouse, and tomato concerning *what* traits are inherited and how different expressions of these are related to each other. Genetic maps, based on breeding experiments, were constructed for these and other species showing relative distances between genes on their chromosomes (Fig. 1-9). Geneticists began to turn from concern with inheritance patterns of such traits as eye color in fruit flies to problems of *how* the observable trait is produced. Especially in the period since the beginning of World War II, a central question has been the *structure* of the gene and the mode of its operation. As the search for answers has proceeded ever more deeply into molecular levels, an increasingly important part in genetic study has been played by chemistry and physics. Contributions of these sciences have been such as to enable geneticists to gain a clear concept of the molecular nature of the gene and its operation.

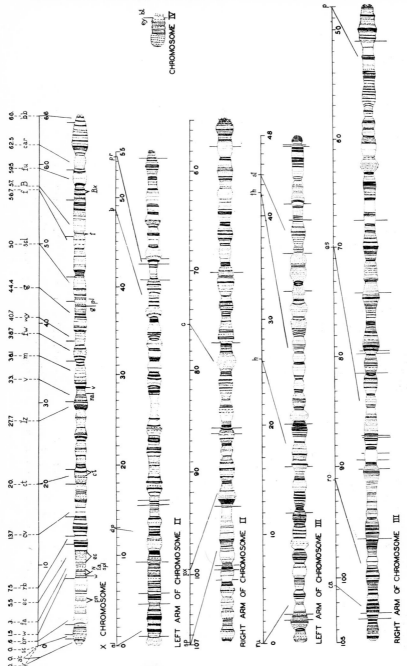

FIGURE 1-8. *Comparison of cytologic and genetic maps of the chromosomes of Drosophila melanogaster. For each chromosome, the genetic map is above the cytologic.* [From T. S. Painter, 1934, *Journal of Heredity,* **25:** 465–476. By permission.]

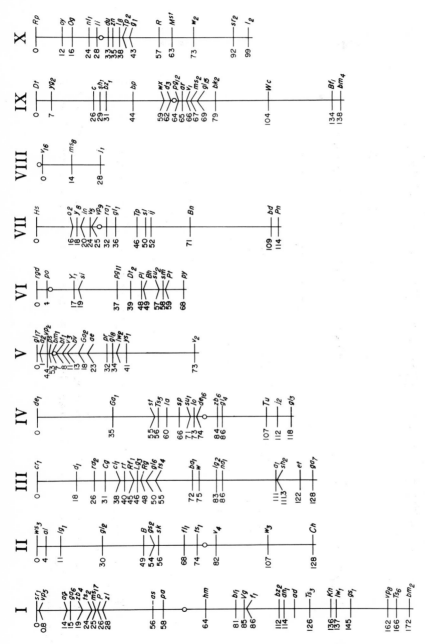

FIGURE 1-9. *Linkage map of the ten maize (corn) chromosomes, showing locations of various known genes (symbolized by letters). Distances between genes are obtained by breeding experiments described in Chapter 6.* [After Neuffer, 1965. Courtesy De Kalb Agricultural Association, Inc., De Kalb, Illinois. By permission.]

## Practical Applications of Genetics

Genetics appeals to many of us not only because we are parts of an ongoing genetic stream but also because it has had such an exciting history in which theory has evolved out of observation and led, in turn, to experimental proof of fundamental operating mechanisms, Of course, any science may make the same claim, but the history of man's knowledge and understanding of genetics is to other sciences as a time-lapse movie of a growth process is to a normal-speed film. A fraction of a century ago the scientific community at large knew nothing of genetic mechanisms. Now, however, we can, with considerable accuracy, even construct molecular models of genes, atom by atom. In fact, one relatively simple gene has recently been synthesized in the laboratory of Khorana and his associates (Agarwal et al., 1970). But besides being a fascinating intellectual discipline intimately related to ourselves, genetics has many important practical applications. Some of these are fairly familiar; others may be less so.

The history of improvement of food crops and domestic animals by selective breeding is too well known to warrant detailed description here (Figs. 1-10, 1-11). Increases in yield of crops like corn and rice, improvement in flavor and size, as well as the production of seedless varieties of fruits, and advances in meat production of cattle and swine have markedly benefited mankind. As the population of the world continues to increase, this practical utilization of genetics is likely to assume even greater significance. Appropriately, the 1970 Nobel Peace Prize was awarded to a scientist, Norman Borlaug, for more than a quarter century of successful work in breeding high-yield, stiff-stemmed varieties of Mexican wheat. These new varieties, incorporating genes from American, Japanese, Australian, and Colombian stocks, not only have much improved yield, but also wide geographic, photoperiodic, and climatic adaptability. They are successfully grown in such varied parts of the world as Mexico, Turkey, Afghanistan, Pakistan, and India. In the five year period ending in 1970, introduction of the new varieties into India resulted in raising the wheat crop from 12 to 21 million tons, a rate of increase greater than that of India's population, and this in a country that was saved from mass famine only three years earlier by importing 20 per cent of the American wheat crop, as well as by large imports from other countries. Borlaug's efforts will also buy precious time in the race to control population growth. Likewise, the problem of breeding disease-resistant plants is never ending. The 1970 epidemic of southern corn blight in the United States is a case in point.

Applications of genetics in the general field of medicine are numerous and growing. Many diseases and abnormalities are now known to have genetic bases. Hemophilia, some types of diabetes, an anemia known as hemolytic icterus, some forms of deafness and of blindness, several hemoglobin ab-normalities, and Rh incompatibility are a few conditions that fall into this

FIGURE 1-10. *Effects of breeding programs in cattle.* (*A*) *Texas Longhorn.* [USDA photo]. (*B*) *Hereford, bred for meat production.* [Photo courtesy National Hereford Association.]

FIGURE 1-11. *Effects of breeding programs in swine.* (*A*) *Wild boar.* [Photo courtesy of Tennessee Game and Fish Commission. By permission.] (*B*) *Modern Poland China barrow.* [Photo courtesy Poland China Record Association. By permission.]

category. Recognition of their inherited nature is important in anticipating their possible future occurrence in a given family, so that appropriate preventive steps may be taken.

Closely related is the whole field of genetic counseling. Some estimate of the likelihood of a particular desirable or undesirable trait appearing in the children of a given couple can be provided by one who has sound genetic training and some information on the ancestors of the prospective parents. Questions encountered might range from the probability of a couple's having any red-haired children to the chance of muscular dystrophy appearing in the offspring.

Genetics has its legal applications, too. Analysis of blood type, a genetically determined character, may be used to solve problems of disputed parentage. Questions of baby mixups in hospitals, illegitimate children, and estate claims can often be clarified by genetics.

So, in our study of genetics, we shall pursue somewhat the same general route followed by other scientists in their search for an understanding of the mechanisms of inheritance. Beginning with simple observations which could be made by anyone, in many cases without a laboratory or special equipment, we shall continually raise questions and explore possibilities concerning the causes of phenomena we observe. From these we shall attempt to arrive, by inductive reasoning, at the specific principles that form the groundwork of modern genetics. These we will then test deductively by application to still other cases. Our quest for the "why" and "how" of genetics will grow ever more specific until we are able to answer on the deepest molecular levels yet penetrated by science. In the process we should not only acquire some fundamental genetic knowledge about ourselves, but also sharpen our powers of critical, analytical, skeptical thinking.

## REFERENCES

AGARWAL, K. L., H. BÜCHI, M. H. CARUTHERS, N. GUPTA, H. G. KHORANA, K. KLEPPE, A. KUMAR, E. OHTSUKA, U. L. RAJBHANDARY, J. H. VAN DE SANDE, V. SGARAMELLA, H. WEBER, and T. YAMADA, 1970. Total Synthesis of the Gene for an Alanine Transfer Ribonucleic Acid from Yeast. *Nature*, **227**: 27–34.

ILTIS, H., 1932. *Life of Mendel*. New York, W. W. Norton.

MENDEL, G., 1865. *Experiments in Plant Hybridization*. Reprinted in J. A. Peters, ed., 1959. *Classic Papers in Genetics*. Englewood Cliffs, N.J., Prentice-Hall.

STURTEVANT, A. H., 1965. *A History of Genetics*. New York, Harper & Row.

## PROBLEMS

**1-1.** Suggest a number of ways in which bacteria make good genetic subjects.

**1-2.** Why are organisms that have only a single set of chromosomes (monoploid) often more favorable for genetic experiments than those having two sets (diploid)?

**1-3.** On the basis of the criteria of useful genetic organisms listed in this chapter, how do Mendel's peas measure up?

**1-4.** List as many reasons as possible why man is not a good experimental genetic organism.

**1-5.** Why is the inheritance of acquired characters no longer accepted as fact?

**1-6.** Devise an experiment of your own to test the question of inheritance of acquired characters.

**1-7.** How could you, at this stage of your study of genetics, justify Sutton's prediction (page 9) that the chromosomes may serve as a physical basis of inheritance?

**1-8.** Some races of corn produce red kernels, some white, and other have white kernels which turn red only if they are exposed to light during maturation. Does kernel color in corn appear to depend on heredity, environment, or both? Explain.

**1-9.** Poliomyelitis is a disease known to be caused by a specific virus. It has sometimes been observed to be more frequent in some families than in others, even where children appear to have the same degree of exposure to the disease. Suggest a possible explanation.

**1-10.** Blue-green algae are primitive plants which are known to reproduce only by cell division or fragmentation. They appear to have changed little over a very long period of geologic time. Moreover, all  individuals of a given species appear to be morphologically and physiologically alike. Suggest a rational explanation for these latter two observations.

**1-11.** Huntington's chorea (pages 32–35) is a genetically based disorder of the central nervous system leading to physical and mental deterioration and culminating in death. It most often begins to appear in middle age. Would this condition be easier or more difficult than ear lobes to study genetically? Why?

**1-12.** Considering variation in height in members of your family and in other families, would you say that height in human beings is determined by heredity, environment, or both? Why do you say so?

# CHAPTER 2
# *Monohybrid Inheritance*

I N the introduction we noted that early attempts to determine fundamental genetic mechanisms frequently failed because investigators tried to examine simultaneously all discernible traits. We saw that Mendel's success in preparing the groundwork of our modern understanding lay in (1) concentrating on one or a few characters at a time, (2) making controlled crosses and keeping careful records of the results, and (3) suggesting "factors" as the particulate causes of various genetic patterns. If we wished, for instance, to learn something of the inheritance of *vestigial* wing in the fruit fly, *Drosophila* (Fig. 2-1), we would cross an individual having normal, full-size wings with

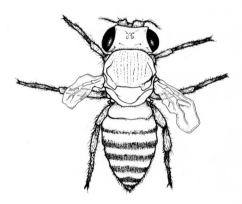

FIGURE 2-1. *Vestigial wing, due to the action of a recessive gene, in* Drosophila melanogaster.

one having vestigial wings, ignoring all other traits. The appearance of the offspring through several generations and the relative numbers of "normal" and "vestigial" individuals produced would be carefully recorded and evaluated.

Such a cross, involving contrasting expressions of the same trait, is referred to as a **monohybrid cross**. Although this term is restricted by some geneticists to cases in which the parents *differ* in one trait (as in our suggested cross of the preceding paragraph), it may also be used to refer to any cross in which only a single character is being considered, whether or not the parents differ *detectably*. We shall use it in this latter, wider sense.

Let us begin our study of genetics along the general lines of Mendel, but using a different organism for the sake of variety.

FIGURE 2-2. *The common house plant,* Coleus, *showing shallow lobed leaves.*

## The Standard Monohybrid Cross

### COMPLETE DOMINANCE

The common house plant, variegated coleus (*Coleus blumei,* of the mint family), is a frequently encountered angiosperm which lends itself readily to simple genetic experimentation. It has many of the desirable characteristics, listed in Chapter 1, of an organism useful for genetic experimentation. Its reproductive cycle is relatively short, crosses between different individuals are easily made, yet self-pollination is also possible, and many of its genetically determined characteristics are vegetative, appearing even in the seedling stage.

One such character is seen in the shape of the leaf margins. Some plants have shallowly crenate edges; others have rather deeply incised leaves (Figs. 2-2 and 2-3). Plants displaying one or the other of these two traits may be referred to as "shallow" and "deep" respectively. Imagine two such plants, each the product of a long series of generations obtained by self-pollination, in which the same individual serves as both maternal and paternal parent.[1] If, in such repeated breeding, deep always gave rise to deep offspring only, and shallow to shallow only, each such line of descent would be established as "pure-breeding" for this trait. The geneticist customarily uses the term **homozygous** in such cases. The precise genetic implication of this latter term will be seen shortly.

[1] See Appendix B for a review of life cycles which demonstrates how this can occur in many plants.

FIGURE 2-3. *Deep-lobed leaves in* Coleus. *Compare with Figure 2-2.*

Suppose now a cross were to be made between two such homozygous individuals, one deep and the other shallow. In theory, the outcome might be any one of the following: (1) all the offspring may resemble one or the other parent only; (2) some of the progeny may resemble one parent, whereas the remainder may look like the other parent; (3) all the offspring, though like each other, may be intermediate in appearance between the two parents; (4) the offspring may look like neither parent and yet not be clearly intermediate between them; or (5) there may be a considerable range of types in the progeny, some being about as deeply lobed as one parent, some about as shallowly cut as the other, with the remainder forming a continuum of variation between the two parental types. When the offspring of this cross are examined, however, all of them are seen to be *deep*, like one parent. The *shallow* trait does not appear at all. Since the days of Mendel, such a characteristic that thus expresses itself in all the offspring (as *deep* does in this case) has been termed **dominant**, and the trait that fails to be expressed (here, *shallow*) has been referred to as **recessive**.

If we now either cross various individuals of this progeny or allow them to self-pollinate, what will be the results? From similar work of Mendel (Table 2-1) we can predict that about three fourths of the second generation should

TABLE 2-1. Mendel's Earliest Experiments on Peas

| Parents | First Generation | Second Generation | | Ratio |
|---|---|---|---|---|
| Round × wrinkled seed | round | 5,474 round | 1,850 wrinkled | 2.96:1 |
| Yellow × green cotyledons | yellow | 6,022 yellow | 2,001 green | 3.01:1 |
| Gray-brown × white seed coats | gray-brown | 705 gray-brown | 224 white | 3.15:1 |
| Inflated × constricted pods | inflated | 882 inflated | 299 constricted | 2.95:1 |
| Green × yellow pods | green | 428 green | 152 yellow | 2.82:1 |
| Axial × terminal flowers | axial | 651 axial | 207 terminal | 3.14:1 |
| Long × short stems | long | 787 long | 277 short | 2.84:1 |
| TOTALS | | 14,949 | 5,010 | Av. 2.98:1 |

be deep, and about one fourth shallow. This is what we actually observe. (It should be pointed out that only in cases of quite large samples would one expect to approach a $3:1$ ratio closely.)

According to standard genetic terminology, our results in *Coleus* may be summarized as follows:

$$\text{(\textit{Parental Generation}) \quad P \quad deep × shallow}$$
$$\text{(\textit{First Filial Generation}) \quad } F_1 \quad \text{all deep}$$
$$\text{(\textit{Second Filial Generation}) \quad } F_2 \quad \tfrac{3}{4} \text{ deep} + \tfrac{1}{4} \text{ shallow}$$

$F_2$ progeny are obtained either by "selfing" or by interbreeding members of the preceding $F_1$.

## MECHANISM OF THE MONOHYBRID CROSS

*Genes and Their Location.*   It now becomes our task to determine what mechanism might exist that will account for these results. Obviously something is transmitted from parent to offspring; just as obviously it must not be the trait itself, but rather something that *determines* the later development of that trait at an appropriate time and place in a particular environment. These determiners are called *genes*; we shall leave for later discussions their actual structure and behavior.

Since the sex cells or gametes constitute the only link in sexually reproducing organisms between parent and offspring, it is clear that genes must be transmitted from generation to generation via this gametic bridge. Where, then, are the genes located in the gametes? Cytological examination of the gametes of a great many sexually reproducing organisms, both plant and animal, discloses that, although the egg cell has a large amount of cytoplasm, the sperm is largely nucleus, having relatively little cytoplasm. This relationship breaks down, of course, in such isogamous forms as some of the algae where no size difference exists between fusing gametes. Though this observation does not furnish conclusive *proof* of the location of the genes within the

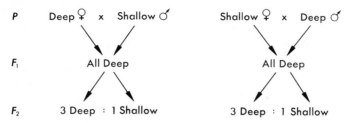

FIGURE 2-4. *Diagram of reciprocal cross in* Coleus. *Note that, in this case, results in the* $F_1$ *and* $F_2$ *are the same regardless of which plant is used as the pistillate parent.*

nuclei of the sex cells, it does offer a *probability* that the genes with which we are dealing here are more likely to be nuclear than cytoplasmic in location. The possibility of other genes being located in the cytoplasm is discussed in Chapter 19. For the present, until and unless contrary evidence becomes available, we shall therefore pursue the thesis that these genes are nuclear in location.

That sperm and egg in this particular kind of cross do make equal genetic contribution to the next generation is strongly indicated by the fact that, whether *deep* serves as the pistillate (egg contributing) parent or as the staminate (sperm contributing) parent, the result is the same: all the $F_1$ are deep lobed (Fig. 2-4). It should be emphasized, however, that such **reciprocal crosses** do not, in every case, produce identical results. In fact, whether reciprocal crosses give the same or different results provides certain important additional information concerning the genes involved. (See Chapter 11.)

If these genes are situated in the nucleus, it would be helpful to be able to fix their location within the nucleus more exactly. We shall have to look, therefore, for something that is (1) quantitatively distributed with complete exactness during nuclear division and (2) contributed equally by sperm and egg at gametic union, or syngamy. Although we shall look more closely in the next chapter at the cellular process involved, previous work that you as a student have had in the life sciences surely suggests, on these two bases, implication of the chromosomes as the vehicles of gene transmission in the kind of case under consideration. Pending a test of that hypothesis, this is the assumption on which we shall base our present attempts to explain our observations in *Coleus*. Regardless of the attractiveness of a theory, however, our acceptance of it must rest on testing, and we must always be ready to revise our theory in the light of new experimental evidence.

For the present, then, we shall assume genes to be situated on the chromosomes in the cell nuclei, transmitted via the gametes from one generation to the next, and contributed equally by both parents. If we designate the dominant gene for deep lobes as $D$, and the recessive as $d$, we can represent the gametic contribution of the P generation as

$$\textcircled{D} \text{ and } \textcircled{d}$$

where the two genes, one for deep (*D*) and one for shallow (*d*), are said to be **alleles** of each other, or to form an allelic pair.

Based on (1) the observation that chromosomes of both fusing gametes become incorporated within the nucleus of the zygote, maintaining their separate identities, and (2) the assumption that chromosomes serve as likely candidates for gene location, it then follows that the zygotes (which will become $F_1$ individuals) can be represented as *Dd*. So, also, the P individuals must be represented as *DD* and *dd*, respectively. Thus, either of the P individuals possesses two identical genes in each of its somatic (body, or vegetative) cells—that is, they are **homozygous**. In the same way, the $F_1$ plants must have in each of their somatic cells one gene for deep (*D*) *and* one for shallow (*d*); they are thus **heterozygous** with respect to this pair of alleles. Because, in the heterozygous $F_1$, the effect of the dominant gene appears to mask completely the presence of the recessive allele, this case illustrates **complete dominance**.

The assumption is, therefore, that there are two genes for a given trait in the somatic cells and only one in the gametes. Some sort of nuclear division, prior to sex cell formation, which will reduce the gene number from two per trait to one—i.e., separate the alleles—is thus required. The next chapter explores this possibility further. Our original *Coleus* cross may now be written as follows:

$$
\begin{array}{ccc}
\text{P} & \text{deep} & \times & \text{shallow} \\
 & DD & & dd \\[4pt]
\textit{P gametes} & \textcircled{D} & \times & \textcircled{d} \\[4pt]
\text{F}_1 & & \text{deep} \\
 & & Dd \\[4pt]
\textit{F}_1 \textit{ gametes} & \textcircled{D} & + & \textcircled{d}
\end{array}
$$

***Phenotype and Genotype.***   The *appearance* of the organism, with regard to the character or characters under consideration, constitutes its **phenotype**, which is generally designated by a descriptive word or phrase. On the other hand, an individual's *genetic makeup* is its **genotype**, and is customarily given by letters of the alphabet or other convenient symbol. In this case, *deep* and *shallow* represent *phenotypes*, whereas *DD*, *Dd*, *dd*, *D*, and *d* represent *genotypes* (somatic and gametic).

An individual's phenotype is not always a rigidly expressed, "either-or" condition but is often modified by environmental influences. For example, such a quantitative character as height is genetically determined in many plants (and in man), yet even in those cases in plants where only a single pair of genes can be shown to be operating, height variation in both the tall and short individuals often occurs. These latter variations, usually clustering

FIGURE 2-5. *"Sun-red" corn. Action of the sun-red gene is to produce red kernels when these are exposed to light; in the absence of light, kernels remain white. In this instance, the husks had been replaced by the black mask shown below.* [Courtesy Department of Plant Breeding, Cornell University.]

fairly closely about a mean, can be shown, in suitable, controlled experiments, to be due to environment. In other words, genotype determines the phenotypic *range* within which an individual will fall; environment determines where in that range the individual will occur. In certain environments, too, it is conceivable that a particular genotype will not express itself at all. In corn, for example, one gene ("sun-red") produces red grains if the ear is exposed to light (Fig. 2-5), but as long as the husks are intact the grains remain white, so that both sun-red and white genotypes remain phenotypically indistinguishable. Furthermore, as we shall soon see, phenotype may often be physiological and therefore "observable" only in the biochemical sense.

*Probability Method of Calculating Ratios.* If a nuclear division, which segregates the alleles $D$ and $d$, occurs in the $F_1$ prior to gamete formation, then *one half* of the $F_1$ gametes should carry the dominant $D$ and *one half* the recessive $d$. If, furthermore, syngamy is random, so that a $D$ egg has an equal chance to be fertilized by either a $D$ or a $d$ sperm, for example, we can represent mating of the $F_1$ to produce the $F_2$ in this way:

$$\textit{eggs from } ♀\ F_1 \quad \tfrac{1}{2}\ \textcircled{D}\ +\ \tfrac{1}{2}\ \textcircled{d}$$
$$\textit{sperms from } ♂\ F_1 \quad \tfrac{1}{2}\ \textcircled{D}\ +\ \tfrac{1}{2}\ \textcircled{d}$$
$$F_2 \quad \tfrac{1}{4}\ DD\ +\ \tfrac{1}{4}\ Dd\ +\ \tfrac{1}{4}\ dD\ +\ \tfrac{1}{4}\ dd$$

or $\tfrac{1}{4}\ DD\ +\ \tfrac{2}{4}\ Dd\ +\ \tfrac{1}{4}\ dd$ for a **1:2:1 $F_2$ monohybrid genotypic ratio.**

The basis for this kind of calculation is the "product law of probability." Briefly stated, this law holds that the probability of the simultaneous occurrence of two independent events equals the product of the probabilities of their separate occurrences. Thus, if one half the eggs are of genotype $D$ and one half of the sperms have the same genotype, and if fertilization is a completely random event, then the probability of getting a $DD$ zygote is $\frac{1}{2} \times \frac{1}{2} = \frac{1}{4}$.

As to phenotypes, we see that $DD$ and $Dd$ organisms appear indistinguishable on visual bases, giving our observed **3:1 $F_2$ monohybrid phenotypic ratio**. A 3:1 ratio is shown in Fig. 2-6. (As we shall see, these ratios may occur in the $F_1$, given certain P individuals, and are, of course, not the only possible monohybrid ratios.) Thus our assumptions have led to an explanation completely compatible with our earlier observations. These assumptions remain to be tested further, both by cytological examination and by additional breeding experiments. It should be noted that we have not used the so-called checkerboard or Punnett Square method but rather a probability method of calculating genotypic and phenotypic ratios. This latter system becomes extremely advantageous when calculating ratios involving several pairs of genes.

### THE TESTCROSS

As we have indicated, $DD$ and $Dd$ individuals in *Coleus* cannot be distinguished visually from each other. This raises two questions. First, can homozygous dominant and heterozygous individuals be distinguished in *any* manner? The answer is "yes," and the **testcross** can supply the answer. In the testcross the individual having the dominant phenotype (which can be represented here as $D$–) is crossed with one having a recessive phenotype which is, of course, homozygous. In our *Coleus* case the testcross of a homozygous dominant is as follows:

$$
\begin{array}{llll}
\text{P} & \text{deep} & \times & \text{shallow} \\
 & DD & & dd \\
\textit{P gametes} & \textit{eggs} & (1) & \textcircled{D} \\
 & \textit{sperms} & (1) & \textcircled{d} \\
\text{F}_1 & \text{all} & & \overline{Dd \text{ (deep)}}
\end{array}
$$

If the P dominant phenotype had been heterozygous, the result would be the classic **1:1 monohybrid testcross ratio**:

$$
\begin{array}{lll}
\text{P} & \text{deep} \times & \text{shallow} \\
 & Dd & dd \\
\textit{P gametes} & \textit{eggs} & \frac{1}{2}\textcircled{D} + \frac{1}{2}\textcircled{d} \\
 & \textit{sperms} & (1)\,\textcircled{d} \\
\text{F}_1 & & \overline{\frac{1}{2}\,Dd + \frac{1}{2}\,dd} \\
 & & \text{deep} \quad \text{shallow}
\end{array}
$$

FIGURE 2-6. *A 3 : 1 purple : white ratio in corn. This is the* F₂ *of homozygous purple* × *white.*

Note that *DD* × *dd* produces an F₁ all of the dominant phenotype, whereas *Dd* × *dd* gives rise to a 1 : 1 ratio in the progeny. A 1 : 1 testcross ratio in corn is shown in Fig. 2-7.

At this point it is important to emphasize our usage of the expression "F₁." We shall use it to designate the first generation resulting from *any* given mating, regardless of the parental genotypes. Therefore, the term F₁ does not necessarily imply heterozygosity. In the two testcrosses just outlined, note that the F₁ genotype depends on the P genotypes and may, of course, be either heterozygous (as in the first instance) or homozygous (as in the *dd* individuals of the second case).

The second question suggested by the visual similarity of homozygous dominants and heterozygotes is the matter of how genes operate to exert their phenotypic effect. Although a complete answer must be deferred to later considerations of the molecular nature of the gene and the chemistry of its action, a genetic trait in Mendel's peas offers a tempting suggestion. It also furnishes an introduction to a variation in the classic 3 : 1 phenotypic ratio which we have seen in *Coleus*. We shall examine this case in the following section.

## Modifications of the 3:1 Phenotypic Ratio
### INCOMPLETE DOMINANCE

***Peas.*** The data of Table 2-1 were first reported by Mendel in a pair of originally widely ignored papers read before the Natural History Society at Brünn on February 8 and March 8, 1865. Mendel's results led him to designate round seeds as (completely) dominant to wrinkled seeds; indeed, homozygous and heterozygous round seeds cannot be differentiated macroscopically. However, when cells of the cotyledon of the three genotypes (*WW, Ww* round, and *ww* wrinkled) are examined *microscopically*, an abundance of well-formed starch grains is seen in the *WW* plants, and very few in *ww* individuals. Heterozygotes show an intermediate number of grains, many of them being imperfect or eroded. Moreover, *ww* embryos test higher in reducing sugars (the raw material from which starch molecules are constructed) than do those of $Ww$ genotype. $WW$ embryos test lowest of all for sugar. In plant cells starch is synthesized from glucose-1-phosphate under the influence of an enzyme system. Although a discussion of the chemistry of the sugar $\rightleftharpoons$ starch interconversion is outside the scope of a beginning course in genetics, it appears plausible that gene $W$ is responsible for the production of one of the enzymes required for the reaction glucose-1-phosphate $\rightarrow$ starch. Likewise, it may be surmised that gene $w$ produces either a smaller quantity of this enzyme or, perhaps, a molecule differing sufficiently in structure so that it functions only imperfectly, producing a less efficient enzyme molecule. The larger amount of starch in $WW$ plants is associated with higher water retention (starch is a hydrophilic colloid) and, therefore, with plump, distended, spherical seeds. Homozygous recessive embryos, on the other hand, retain considerably less water upon reaching maturity and hence appear shriveled. The starch content of heterozygotes, however, is apparently sufficient to produce embryos visually indistinguishable from those of $WW$ genotype. Consistent with these differences in starch content, it is found that heterozygotes have an intermediate amount of functional enzyme. The relationship between genes and enzymes suggested here is a fundamental concern of modern genetics and offers considerable help in elucidating the nature and action of the gene. It will receive considerable attention in later chapters of this book.

For our present purposes, however, it is clear that on the gross, macroscopic level, we have a case of complete dominance, yielding the familiar 3:1 phenotypic and 1:2:1 genotypic ratios. But on the microscopic, chemical, or molecular level we are faced with the realization that gene $W$ must be considered only **incompletely dominant** to its allele. Therefore, at the *physiological* level the cross $Ww \times Ww$ yields identical phenotypic and genotypic ratios of 1:2:1.

*Other Organisms.* Examples of incomplete dominance at the macroscopic level occur in both plants and animals. For example, radishes may be long, oval, or round in shape. Crosses of long $\times$ round produce an $F_1$ of wholly oval phenotype:

$$\begin{array}{ccc} \text{P} & \text{long} \quad \times & \text{round} \\ & l_1 l_1 & l_2 l_2 \end{array}$$

$$\begin{array}{cc} F_1 & \text{all oval} \\ & l_1 l_2 \end{array}$$

$$\begin{array}{llc} F_1 \text{ gametes} & \textit{eggs} & \tfrac{1}{2}\, \textcircled{$l_1$} + \tfrac{1}{2}\, \textcircled{$l_2$} \\ & \textit{sperms} & \tfrac{1}{2}\, \textcircled{$l_1$} + \tfrac{1}{2}\, \textcircled{$l_2$} \end{array}$$

$$\begin{array}{lc} F_2 & \tfrac{1}{4}\, l_1 l_1 + \tfrac{2}{4}\, l_1 l_2 + \tfrac{1}{4}\, l_2 l_2 \\ & \quad\text{long} \qquad \text{oval} \qquad \text{round} \end{array}$$

FIGURE 2-7. *A 1:1 testcross ratio in corn. This ear resulted from the cross white ×
heterozygous purple.*

It will be our practice to use lower case letters with numeral subscripts to
designate incompletely dominant alleles.

Another well-known case occurs in shorthorn cattle. Genes for red and for
white occur in this breed. If we designate the genotype of the red parent $r_1r_1$
and of the white parent $r_2r_2$, a cross of two such animals will produce progeny
all of which are $r_1r_2$ and whose phenotype is reddish gray, or "roan." A
similar case occurs in snapdragon (Fig. 2-8).

In human beings one of the blood types involves action of a pair of alleles
for certain antigenic substances, known as M and N, in the blood. Although
the genetics of blood antigens is described more fully in Chapter 7, it is interesting to note here that genes for these two substances are both active in
heterozygotes. Accumulation of data on families where both parents are of
type MN (i.e., produce both M and N antigens) show a close approximation
to the 1:2:1 phenotypic ratio of incomplete dominance, as would be expected.

### CODOMINANCE

From the facts we have looked at here, the case cited for radishes appears
to be a clear example of incomplete dominance—that is, one in which the
heterozygote is distinctly intermediate in phenotype between the two homozygotes. From a superficial standpoint, roan in cattle and the MN blood type
in man also seem to be examples of intermediate phenotypes in the heterozygote. However, if one examines closely the coat of roan cattle, it is seen that
the individual hairs are not intermediate in color between red and white, but
rather the roan phenotype is characterized by a *mixture of red hairs and white
hairs*. Likewise, in man the MN genotype produces *both antigens* M and N,
rather than a single intermediate substance. Cases such as these for cattle and
man are sometimes termed **codominance**. Of course, ratios are identical in
incomplete dominance and codominance, and the distinction is of only
minor importance at this stage of our discussion. Note that incomplete
dominance and codominance necessarily produce an *increase* of phenotypic
classes from two to three and therefore identical genotypic and phenotypic
ratios of 1:2:1.

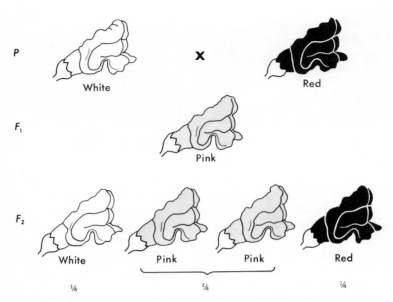

FIGURE 2-8. *A case of incomplete dominance in snapdragon. The pink* $F_1$ *hybrid is truly intermediate between the red and white parents, and the* $F_2$ *segregates in a characteristic 1:2:1 phenotypic ratio.*

### LETHAL GENES

A second major modification of the classic monohybrid ratios is produced by genes whose effect is sufficiently drastic to kill the bearers of certain genotypes. Here both the effect itself and the developmental stage at which the lethal effect is exerted are important.

Most plants with which a nonbotanist is familiar are characteristically autotrophic, being able to manufacture their own food from carbon dioxide and water in the process of photosynthesis. For this process, in all but the few autotrophic bacteria, the presence of a green, light-absorbing pigment, chlorophyll, is required. In corn (*Zea mays*) several pairs of genes affecting chlorophyll production have been described in the literature. One such gene, which we shall designate $G$, for normal chlorophyll production, is completely dominant to its allele $g$, so that $G-$ plants contain chlorophyll and are photosynthetic. On the other hand, $gg$ plants produce no chlorophyll and are yellowish white in appearance (because they still produce the yellow carotenoid pigments). (See Fig. 2-9.)

On the average, about one fourth of the progeny of two heterozygous parents are thus without chlorophyll, and seedlings show the classic 3:1 ratio. In corn, germination and early seedling development take place at the expense of a food storage tissue, the endosperm, in the grain. In normal

FIGURE 2-9. *A lethal gene in corn. The chlorophyll-less plants are unable to manufacture their own food and will die as soon as food stored in the grain has been con-
sumed. Photo shows progeny plants of the cross heterozygous green × heterozygous
green; there are 36 green and 12 "albino" seedlings in the flat, a perfect 3:1 ratio.*

green plants, by the time this food reserve has been exhausted (in about 10–14
days' time), the seedling has developed a sufficient root system and amount of
green tissue to be physiologically independent. Therefore, in the cross of two
heterozygotes the initial 3 : 1 phenotypic ratio becomes what might be termed
a 3 : 0 or a " 1 : 0 " ratio after some two weeks:

$$
\begin{array}{cccc}
\text{P} & \text{green} & \times & \text{green} \\
 & Gg & & Gg \\
\end{array}
$$

$$
\text{F}_1 \quad \tfrac{1}{4}\text{ green} + \tfrac{2}{4}\text{ green} + \tfrac{1}{4}\text{ nongreen (die)}
$$

$$
\begin{array}{ccc}
GG & Gg & gg \\
\end{array}
$$

Note that, after the lethal gene $g$ has exerted its effect, the genotypic ratio has been converted from the usual $1:2:1$ to $2:1$. So, whereas homozygous green plants, for example, initially make up one fourth of the $F_1$, they later come to comprise *one third* of the surviving progeny because of the death of the $gg$ individuals. This $2:1$ genotypic ratio, or the occurrence of only one phenotypic class where two would be expected in $3:1$ ratio, is a clear indication of a (recessive) lethal gene.

In the instance just described, the occurrence and action of the lethal gene is easily discerned because the death of the homozygous recessives takes place only after nearly two weeks of growth following germination. Yet other lethals might conceivably produce their effect at almost any time between syngamy (i.e., in the zygote stage) on through embryogeny to a very late point in life. Obviously, lethals killing very late in life might well be hard to separate from other causes of death.

A classic case of a recessive lethal that kills early in embryo development, and one of the first to be reported in the literature, was "yellow" in mice. Early in this century Cuénot (1904, 1905) noted that black × black always produced black offspring, but that yellow × black produced yellow and black in a $1:1$ ratio. He correctly concluded that yellow is heterozygous. Yet crosses of yellow × yellow always produced yellow and black in a ratio of $2:1$, with litters of such matings being about one-fourth smaller than those from other crosses. Letting $A^Y$ represent a gene for yellow and $a$ one for black, we have:

Testcross:

$$
\begin{array}{ccc}
P & \text{yellow} \times & \text{black} \\
& A^Ya & aa \\
F_1 & \tfrac{1}{2}\,\text{yellow} + & \tfrac{1}{2}\,\text{black} \\
& A^Ya & aa
\end{array}
$$

or,

simple monohybrid:

$$
\begin{array}{ccc}
P & \text{yellow} \times & \text{yellow} \\
& A^Ya & A^Ya \\
F_1 & \tfrac{1}{4}\,A^YA^Y + \tfrac{2}{4}\,A^Ya & + \tfrac{1}{4}\,aa \\
& \text{die} \quad \text{yellow} & \text{black}
\end{array}
$$

Thus gene $A^Y$ appears to be dominant with respect to coat color, but recessive as to lethality. For some time the nature of the action of $A^YA^Y$ was unknown. Although selective fertilization was considered a possible factor, Castle and Little (1910) suggested that $A^YA^Y$ animals are conceived but die soon after. Robertson (1942) and later Eaton and Green (1962) were able to demonstrate that about one fourth of the embryos of pregnant yellow ($A^Y a$) females that had been mated to yellow males did die soon after conception. In this case death usually occurs at gastrulation.

The well-known "creeper" condition in fowl falls into this same category. Creeper birds have much shortened and deformed legs and wings, giving them a squatty appearance and creeping gait. Creeper × creeper always produces 2 creeper to 1 normal, the homozygous creepers having such gross deformities (greater than in heterozygotes) that they die during incubation, generally about the fourth day:

$$\text{P} \quad \underset{c_1 c_1}{\text{creeper}} \quad \times \quad \underset{c_1 c_2}{\text{creeper}}$$

$$\text{F}_1 \quad \underset{c_1 c_1}{\tfrac{1}{4}\text{ normal}} + \underset{c_1 c_2}{\tfrac{2}{4}\text{ creeper}} + \underset{c_2 c_2}{\tfrac{1}{4}\text{ (die)}}$$

Landauer has shown that the creeper gene produces general retardation of embryo growth, the effect being greatest at the stage of limb bud formation.

In man there occurs a significant hemoglobin effect, to which we shall devote considerable attention in a discussion of how genes act (Chapter 17). Particularly among certain African tribes, a gene, $Hb_1{}^S$, when homozygous, produces a syndrome termed sickle-cell anemia that leads to death, generally at least by late adolescence. The condition is characterized by a collection of symptoms, chiefly a chronic hemolytic anemia. In the blood of such persons the erythrocytes become distorted, many being essentially sickle-shaped (Figs. 2-10, 2-11). Such cells not only impede circulation by blocking capillaries, but also cannot properly perform their function of carrying oxygen and carbon dioxide to and from the tissues.

Under normal conditions, heterozygotes ($Hb_1{}^A Hb_1{}^S$) manifest none of these symptoms, being outwardly indistinguishable from the normal homozygotes ($Hb_1{}^A Hb_1{}^A$). But some erythrocytes of heterozygotes will sickle under low oxygen concentrations, and such persons may develop anemia if they remain at high altitudes. Thus we have two gross phenotypes, normal and sickle-cell, as might be expected in a monohybrid situation. At the microscopic level, however, we can distinguish the homozygous normal individual from the heterozygote under conditions of low oxygen tension, giving what appears to be the 1:2:1 phenotypic ratio associated with incomplete dominance, although $Hb_1{}^S$ still behaves as a recessive with regard to its lethality under normal conditions. Generally now three phenotypes are recognized because of the probability of marriages of heterozygotes producing sickle-cell offspring:

$Hb_1{}^A Hb_1{}^A$ normal (no sickling of red cells)
$Hb_1{}^A Hb_1{}^S$ sickle-cell trait (sickling under reduced $O_2$ tension)
$Hb_1{}^S Hb_1{}^S$ sickle-cell anemia (sickling under normal $O_2$ tension)

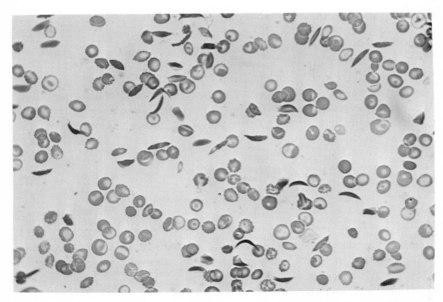

FIGURE 2-10. *Blood smear showing normal and sickle erythrocytes.* [Courtesy Carolina Biological Supply Co.]

Experimental evidence, outlined in Chapter 17, however, indicates that the relation between the two alleles of this pair is best described as one of codominance, since two kinds of hemoglobin (A and S) are involved, and both kinds are produced by heterozygotes.

Thus far we have examined only cases where the lethality of the lethal gene is recessive. Reasoning *a priori*, there is no cause not to expect genes whose lethal effect is dominant, provided death of the affected individual occurs somewhat after reproduction has taken place. Huntington's chorea, a disease in man characterized by involuntary jerking of the body and a progressive degeneration of the nervous system, accompanied by gradual mental and physical deterioration, illustrates just such a situation. The mean age of onset of these symptoms is between forty and forty-five (though it is reported to occur as early as the first decade of life and as late as sixty or seventy), by which time, of course, many afflicted persons have produced

FIGURE 2-11. (*A*) *Normal red blood cell and* (*B*) *sickled red blood cells.* [Samples courtesy Dr. Patricia Farnsworth, Barnard College.] *The photomicrographs were taken at magnifications of* (*A*) *10,000 × and* (*B*) *5,000 × by Irene Piscopo of Philips Electronic Instruments on a Philips EM 300 Electron Microscope with Scanning Attachment.* [Photos courtesy Philips Electronic Instruments.]

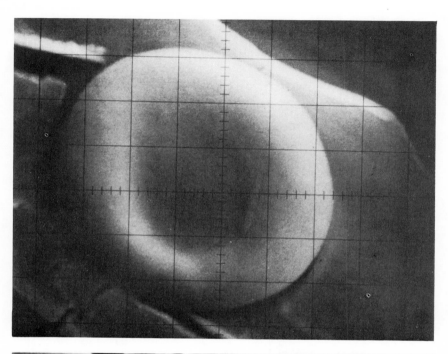

TABLE 2-2. Comparison of Certain Lethal Genes

| Organism | Phenotype | Dominance | | F₁ Phenotypic Ratio of Heterozygote × Heterozygote | | Age at Death |
|---|---|---|---|---|---|---|
| | | Phenotype | Lethality | Before Lethality Occurs | After Lethality Occurs | |
| Corn | Albinism | Recessive | Recessive | 3 green:1 albino | All green ("3:0") | 10–14 days |
| Mouse | Yellow | Dominant? | Recessive | Unknown | 2 yellow:1 black | Postzygote |
| Fowl | Creeper | Inc. dom. | Recessive | Unknown | 2 creeper:1 normal | Early embryo |
| Man | Sickle-cell | Codom. | Recessive | 1 normal:2 sickle-cell trait:1 sickle-cell anemia | 1 normal:2 sickle-cell trait | Adolescence |
| Man | Huntington's Chorea | Dominant | Dominant | 3 choreic:1 normal | All normal ("0:1") | Middle age |

(The 1:2:1 ratio listed under F₁ phenotype for sickle cell anemia is based on microscopic examination of blood samples.)

children. Affected offspring always have at least one parent who, sooner or later, is also choreic, though the variability of the age of onset (which may be due to the action of still other genes) makes this difficult to demonstrate in some cases, and impossible where parents and grandparents die at early ages from other causes. Clearly, then, on available evidence, this disease is due to a dominant gene, both as to lethality and as to its abnormal phenotype.

The lethals discussed in this chapter are summarized in Table 2-2.

Many morphological and physiological traits in a wide variety of animals and plants give evidence of being the result of action of a single pair of genes, and new ones are continually being reported. Thus, Parks and Fowler (1970) suggest that resistance to blister rust in the sugar pine is due to a dominant gene, Abbott et al. (1970) describe a recessive lethal in fowl causing coloboma (with "profound effects on all body parts through its effects on cartilage formation"), Bouwkamp and Honma (1970) report early seed stalk development ("bolting") in celery to result from action of a dominant gene, and Hennault and Craig (1970) show that height in the cultivated geranium (*Pelargonium*) results from the action of a pair of incompletely dominant genes.

## REFERENCES

ABBOTT, U. K., R. M. CRAIG, and E. B. BENNETT, 1970. Sex-Linked Coloboma in the Chicken, *Jour. Hered.*, **61**: 95–102.

BOUWKAMP, J. C., and S. HONMA, 1970. Vernalization Response, Pinnae Number, and Leaf Shape in Celery. *Jour. Hered.*, **61**: 115–118.

CUÉNOT, L., 1904. L'Hérédité de la Pigmentation chez les Souris, (3me Note). *Arch. Zool. Exp. et Gén.*, 3me Série, 10, Notes et Revues, 27–30.

CUÉNOT, L., 1905. Les Races Pures et Leur Combinaisons chez les Souris. *Arch. Zool. Exp. et Gén.*, **3**: 123–132.

EATON, G. J., and M. M. GREEN, 1962. Implantation and Lethality of the Yellow Mouse. *Genetica*, **33**: 106–112.

GREEN, E. L., 1967. Shambling, a Neurological Mutant of the Mouse. *Jour. Hered.*, **58**: 65–67.

HENAULT, R. E., and R. CRAIG, 1970. Inheritance of Plant Height in the Geranium. *Jour. Hered.*, **61**: 75–78.

PARKS, G. K., and C. W. FOWLER, 1970. White Pine Blister Rust: Inherited Resistance in Sugar Pine. *Science*, **167**: 193–195.

ROBERTSON, G. G., 1942. An Analysis of the Development of Homozygous Yellow Mouse Embryos. *Jour. Exp. Zool.*, **89**: 197–231.

STERN, C., 1960, 2nd ed. *Principles of Human Genetics*. San Francisco, W. H. Freeman.

## PROBLEMS

**2-1.** Make a list of several phenotypic characters in your family for as many generations and individuals as possible. Considering traits singly, try to determine the kind of inheritance involved. Save any that seem not to fit patterns developed in this chapter until somewhat later on.

**2-2.** In human beings, ability to curl the tongue into a U-shaped trough is a heritable trait. "Curlers" always have at least one curler parent, but "noncurlers" may occur in families where one or both parents are curlers. Using $C$ and $c$ to symbolize this trait, what is the genotype of a noncurler?

**2-3.** Some individuals have one whorl of hair on the back of the head whereas others have two. In the following pedigree, solid symbols represent one whorl, open symbols two:

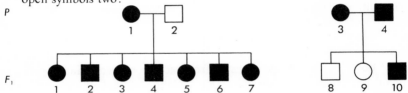

(a) Using the first letter of the alphabet, give the probable genotype of (1) P #2; (2) P #3; (3) F₁ #8; (4) F₁ #10.

(b) What should be the phenotypic ratio of an F₂ produced by the marriage of F₁ #5 × F₁ #8, assuming a large family?

**2-4.** Albinism, the total lack of pigment, is due to a recessive gene. A man and woman plan to marry and wish to know the probability of their having any albino children. What could you tell them if (a) both are normally pigmented, but each has one albino parent; (b) the man is an albino, the girl is normal, but her father is an albino; (c) the man is an albino and the girl's family includes no albinos for at least three generations?

**2-5.** Cystic fibrosis of the pancreas is an inherited condition characterized by faulty metabolism of fats. Affected individuals are homozygous for the gene responsible and ordinarily die in childhood. Such individuals also produce a much higher concentration of chlorides in their sweat than homozygous normals, whereas heterozygotes, who live a normal life-span, have an intermediate chloride concentration. In terms of the types of genes discussed in this chapter, how would you designate (a) this pair of alleles as to dominance; (b) the gene for cystic fibrosis?

**2-6.** One study estimates the number of persons heterozygous for the cystic gene at about 8 million. A couple planning marriage decide to have a sweat test because a brother of the man died in infancy from the disease. The tests disclose the man to be heterozygous and the woman homozygous normal. (a) How many of their children will have cystic fibrosis? (b) Could any of their grandchildren have it?

**2-7.** In a certain plant the cross purple × blue yields purple and blue flowered progeny in equal proportions, but blue × blue gives rise only to blue. (a) What does this tell you about the genotypes of blue and purple flowered plants? (b) Which phenotype is dominant?

2-8. In cattle, the cross horned × hornless sometimes produces only hornless offspring, and, in other crosses, horned and hornless appear in equal numbers. A cattleman has a large herd of hornless cattle in which horned progeny occasionally appear. He has red, roan, and white animals and wishes to establish a pure-breeding line of red hornless animals. How should he proceed?

2-9. In corn, resistance to a certain fungus is conferred by gene $h$, which is completely recessive to its allele, $H$, for susceptibility. If a resistant plant (♀) is pollinated by a homozygous susceptible plant (♂), give the genotypes for (a) pistillate parent; (b) the staminate parent; (c) sperm; (d) egg; (e) polar nucleus; (f) $F_1$ embryo; (g) endosperm surrounding the $F_1$ embryo; (h) epidermis of kernels which contain the $F_1$ embryos.

2-10. Two curly-winged fruit flies (*Drosophila*) are mated; the $F_1$ consists of 341 curly and 162 normal. Explain.

2-11. Using the sixth letter of the alphabet, give the genotype for each of the following persons from Fig. 1-5: I-1, I-2, II-4, III-2, III-3.

2-12. The marriage between II-1 and II-2 in Fig. 1-5 represents what sort of genetic cross?

2-13. Using the first letter of the alphabet, give the genotype of each of the following persons from Fig. 1-6: I-1, II-1, III-4.

2-14. No ancestry information is given for II-1 in Fig. 1-6; how do you justify your designation of her genotype?

2-15. In hemophilia, homozygous normal females may be designated as $HH$, heterozygous females as $Hh$, homozygous hemophilic females as $hh$, normal males as $HY$, and hemophilic males as $hY$. Using these symbols, give the genotype of each of the following persons in Fig. 1-7: II-4, II-5, IV-2.

2-16. If V-2 (Fig. 1-7) planned to marry a normal male but asked you whether they might have any hemophilic children, what could you tell her?

2-17. In families where both parents have sickle-cell trait, what is the probability of their having (a) a child also with sickle-cell trait; (b) a normal child?

2-18. A normal individual, $Hb_1{}^A Hb_1{}^A$, receives a transfusion of blood from a person who has sickle-cell trait. Would this transfusion transmit sickle-cell trait to the recipient? Explain.

2-19. Phenylketonuria (PKU) is an inherited metabolic defect in human beings involving failure to produce the enzyme parahydroxylase. Such individuals are unable to metabolize the essential amino acid phenylalanine; as a result they exhibit such serious mental retardation that they almost never reproduce. The defect itself does not materially shorten life. PKU may occur in families where both parents are completely normal. Would you describe the gene responsible for PKU as dominant, recessive, codominant, or lethal from this information?

2-20. The normal brother of a PKU seeks the advice of a genetic counselor before a contemplated marriage. (a) What is the probability that he is heterozygous? (b) If PKU occurs once in 10,000 live births and he contemplates marrying a normal woman in whose family no cases of PKU occurred since her ancestors came over on the *Mayflower*, what is the probability of their having a PKU child?

2-21. In juvenile amaurotic idiocy children are normal until about age 6. Subsequently there is a progressive decline in mental development, an impairment of vision leading to blindness, and muscular degeneration, culminating in death, usually before age 20. The trait may appear in families where both parents are completely normal. A couple, age 25, planning marriage, are first cousins; siblings of both parties have died of the disorder. (a) What is the probability that both man and woman *might* be heterozygous? (b) If they *might* both be heterozygous, what could you tell them about the chance of their having an affected child? (c) Heterozygotes can be detected by an increase in vacuolization of lymphocytes (a type of white blood cell). If such a test should disclose that both persons are actually heterozygotes, what then could you say about the probability of their having an affected child?

# CHAPTER 3
# *Cytological Bases of Inheritance*

I N Chapter 2 we assumed that the genes with which we were dealing might well be located in the nucleus. If this assumption is true, we should be able to find some confirming, objective evidence. Such evidence does exist and can be conveniently designated as of two kinds, cytological and chemical. In the history of the development of the science of genetics the former preceded the latter by many years. Let us now examine the cytological evidence, deferring the chemical to a later and more logical point in the development of our concepts of genetic mechanisms.

## The Interphase Nucleus

As your previous experience in the life sciences has shown you, living cells of most organisms ("eukaryotes") are characterized by the presence of a discrete, often spherical body, the **nucleus** (Fig. 3-1). Notable exceptions are such "prokaryotes" as the blue-green algae and the bacteria in which, although "nuclear material" can be shown to occur, the visible, structural organization so typical of the cells of most higher organisms is lacking. Prokaryotes, of course, lack the conventional mitotic and meiotic nuclear divisions which characterize eukaryotes. In addition to these two types of genetic systems, we can recognize still a third in the viruses. The structure of an important type of virus, the bacteriophages, is described more fully in Chapter 14.

The interphase (nondividing) nucleus is bounded by an interface, the **nuclear membrane**, which is not clearly visible with the light microscope. Electron micrographs, however, reveal this membrane to be a double layer, provided with pores of the order of 40 nm in diameter.[1] It is continuous with a cytoplasmic double membrane system, the **endoplasmic reticulum**, to which dense granules called **ibosomes** can usually be seen attached (Fig. 3-2). These ribosomes are rich in **ribonucleic acid** (RNA) and play an important role in protein synthesis (see Chapter 15).

Within the interphase nucleus three parts can be distinguished. The first of these is nuclear sap or **karyolymph**, a clear, generally nonstaining, fluid material. The second intranuclear structure is a generally spherical, densely

---

[1] Forty nanometers (nm); a nanometer is $1 \times 10^{-9}$ meter. In older usage a nanometer was called a millimicron (m$\mu$).

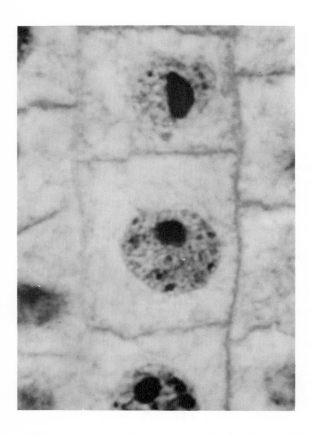

FIGURE 3-1. *Interphase nucleus of onion root tip, as seen with the light microscope. Compare with Fig. 3-2. Note the prominent nucleolus.* [Courtesy Carolina Biological Supply Co.]

staining body, the **nucleolus**. Many nuclei contain two or more nucleoli. The nucleolus contains both RNA and protein. The remainder of the nucleus consists of separate, fine, threadlike strands, the **chromatin**, which may be considered the substance of the **chromosomes**. Chromosomes contain both protein and deoxyribonucleic acid (DNA) the role of which is discussed in Chapter 15.

The number and morphology of the chromosomes are specific, distinct, and constant for each species, although, especially in plants, subspecific taxonomic categories with multiple sets (polyploids) are not infrequent (Table 3-1; see also Chapter 12).

## Cell Division

Growth and development of every organism depends in large part upon multiplication and enlargement of its cells. In multicellular individuals attainment of adult form depends on a coordinated sequence of increase

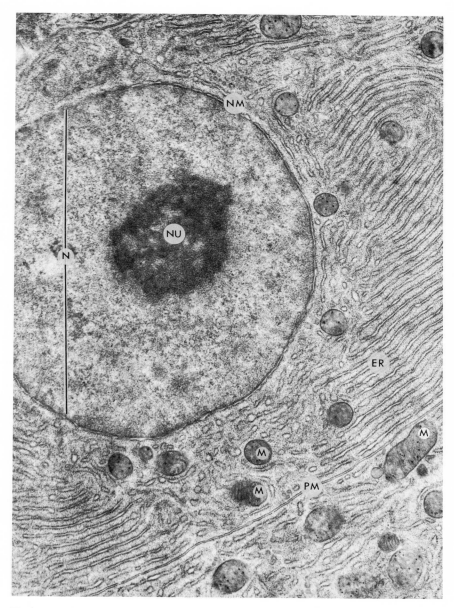

FIGURE 3-2. *Electron micrograph of interphase cell from bat pancreas. N, nucleus; NU, nucleolus; NM, nuclear membrane; ER, endoplasmic reticulum with ribosomes attached; M, mitochondria; PM, plasma membrane delimiting the cell. Note doubleness of the membrane systems.* [From *Cell Ultrastructure* by William Jensen and Roderic Park. © 1967 by Wadsworth Publishing Co., Inc., Belmont, California. Reproduced by permission.]

TABLE 3-1. Chromosome Numbers in Some Plants and Animals*

| | Common Name | Scientific Name | Chromosome Number Monoploid† | Diploid† |
|---|---|---|---|---|
| | | **PLANTS** | | |
| I Algae | Chlamydomonas | *Chlamydomonas reinhardtii* | 8 | |
| II Mycota | Bread mold | *Mucor hiemalis* | 2 | |
| | Red bread mold | *Neurospora crassa* | 7 | |
| | Penicillium | *Penicillium* sp. | 2 | |
| III Bryophyta | Liverwort | *Sphaerocarpos donnellii* | ♂7 + Y ♀7 + X | |
| IV Pterophyta Gymnospermae | Spruce | *Picea abies* | | 24‡ |
| | White pine | *Pinus strobus* | | 24 |
| Angiospermae Dicotyledonae | Watermelon | *Citrullus vulgaris* | | 22§ |
| | Coleus | *Coleus blumei* | | 24 |
| | Jimson weed | *Datura stramonium* | | 24 |
| | Tomato | *Lycopersicon esculentum* | | 24 |
| | Evening primrose | *Oenothera* spp. | | 14‡§ |
| | Pea | *Pisum sativum* | | 14 |
| | African violet | *Saintpaulia ionantha* | | 28 |
| | Swamp saxifrage | *Saxifraga pensylvanica* | | 56‡§ |
| | Alsike clover | *Trifolium hybridum* | | 16 |
| | Red clover | *T. pratense* | | 14 |
| | White clover | *T. repense* | | 32§ |
| Mono-cotyledonae | Onion | *Allium cepa* | | 16‡ |
| | Slender oat | *Avena barbata* | | 28 |
| | Wild oat | *A. brevis* | | 14 |
| | Cultivated oat | *A. sativa* | | 42 |
| | Asiatic tree cotton | *Gossypium arboreum* | | 26 |
| | Upland cotton | *G. hirsutum* | | 52 |
| | Regal lily | *Lilium regale* | | 24 |
| | Rice | *Oryza sativa* | | 24 |
| | Rye | *Secale cereale* | | 14 |
| | Smooth cordgrass | *Spartina alterniflora* | | 70 |
| | Cordgrass | *S. stricta* | | 56 |
| | Cordgrass | *S. townsendii* | | 126 |
| | Emmer wheat | *Triticum dicoccum* | | 28 |
| | Wild emmer | *T. dicoccoides* | | 28 |
| | Durum wheat | *T. durum* | | 28 |
| | Einkorn | *T. monococcum* | | 14 |
| | Spelt | *T. spelta* | | 42 |
| | Common wheat | *T. vulgare* | | 42 |
| | Corn | *Zea mays* | | 20 |
| | | **ANIMALS** | | |
| I Protozoa | Paramecium | *Paramecium aurelia* (micronucleus) | | 30–40 |

TABLE 3.1—[*continued*]

| | Common Name | Scientific Name | Chromosome Number | |
| | | | Monoploid† | Diploid† |
|---|---|---|---|---|
| II Aschelminthes | Roundworm | *Ascaris megalocephala* | | 2 |
| III Arthropoda | Honeybee | *Apis mellifica* | ♂16 | ♀32 |
| | Crayfish | *Cambarus clarkii* | | 200 |
| | Fruit fly | *Drosophila affinis* | | 10 |
| | | *D. hydei* | | 12 |
| | | *D. melanogaster* | | 8 |
| | | *D. prosaltans* | | 6 |
| | | *D. pseudoobscura* | | 10 |
| | | *D. virilis* | | 12 |
| | | *D. willistoni* | | 6 |
| | Grasshopper | *Melanoplus differentialis* | | ♀24, ♂23 |
| | Habrobracon | *Habrobracon juglandis* | ♂10 | ♀20 |
| | Housefly | *Musca domestica* | | 12 |
| IV Chordata | Cattle | *Bos taurus* | | 60 |
| | Cat | *Felis domesticus* | | 38 |
| | Fowl | *Gallus domesticus* | | 78 |
| | Man | *Homo sapiens* | | 46 |
| | Rhesus monkey | *Macaca mullatta* | | 42 |
| | Mouse | *Mus musculus* | | 40 |
| | Chimpanzee | *Pan troglodytes* | | 48 |
| | Rat | *Rattus norvegicus* | | 42 |
| | Rabbit | *Sylvilagus floridanus* | | 44 |

\* An extensive list of chromosome numbers is given in P. L. Altman and D. S. Ditmer, 1962. *Growth Including Reproduction and Morphological Development.* Federation of American Societies for Experimental Biology, Washington. In each plant example, the chromosome number of the *dominant* generation (gametophyte or sporophyte) is cited. See also Appendix B.

† *Diploid,* from the Greek *di* (as a prefix), two, and *ploid* (unit), refers to any nucleus, cell or organism which has two "units" or sets of chromosomes which, in sexually reproducing organisms, are normally composed of one paternal and one maternal set. The often used but anomalous "haploid" (literally half unit or set) for structures having but one set of chromosomes is here replaced by the more logical *monoploid* (Greek *monos*, only or alone, hence one, and *ploid*).

‡ Tetraploid (4*n*) forms also known.

§ Triploid (3*n*) forms also known.

in cell number, size, and differentiation from zygote to maturity. In unicellular organisms cell division serves also as a form of reproduction, often the only one. Sexually reproducing forms also depend in most instances directly on cell division for the formation of sex cells or gametes.

Division of nucleate cells consists of two distinct but integrated activities, nuclear division (**karyokinesis**) and cytoplasmic division (**cytokinesis**). In general, cytokinesis begins after nuclear division is well inder way, but in many instances may be deferred or, indeed, entirely lacking. For example, in the development of the female gametophyte of pine (see Appendix B), about eleven nuclear divisions occur before cytokinesis begins, and in

FIGURE 3-3. *Various stages of mitosis in onion root tip cells.* [Courtesy General Biological Supply House, Inc., Chicago.]

some algae and fungi the plant body is a coenocyte, without any walls separating nuclei except for the reproductive cells.

Two types of nuclear division, **mitosis** and **meiosis**, are characteristic of most plant and animal cells. The first of these is regularly associated with nuclear division of vegatative or somatic cells; the latter occurs in conjunction with formation of reproductive cells (either gametes or meiospores) in sexually reproducing species.

### MITOSIS

As a process, mitosis is remarkably similar in all but relatively small details in both plants and animals, from the least specialized to the most highly evolved forms. Although mitosis is a smoothly continuous process, it is divided arbitrarily into several stages or phases for convenient reference. The following description of the mitotic process in plant cells will adequately serve our purpose of determining whether the mechanism provides a reasonable basis for our genetic assumptions developed in Chapter 2 (Fig. 3-3).

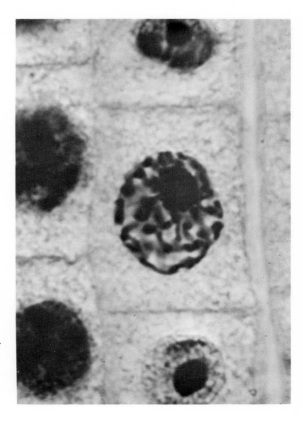

FIGURE 3-4. *Mitosis in onion root tip cell; early prophase. Longitudinal doubleness is evident in a few areas (e.g., lower left portion of the nucleus); the nuclear membrane is becoming indistinct.* (Courtesy Carolina Biological Supply Co.]

*Prophase.* As interphase gives way to prophase, the long slender chromatin threads shorten and thicken to form individually recognizable chromosomes (Fig. 3-4). As they do, it soon becomes apparent that each chromosome consists of two or more delicate, helically coiled, parallel filaments often more or less entwined about each other, called **chromonemata**. Electron microscope studies (DuPraw, 1970) suggest that an unreplicated chromosome is a single supercoiled double helix of DNA (see Chapters 14 and 15), folded in a complex, still undetermined fashion. As we learn more of chromosome structure through electron microscopy, such terminology as chromonema is becoming less meaningful. However, in relation to studies with the light microscope, the term retains some usefulness. Each chromosome at this stage appears in the light microscope to consist of at least two chromonemata. In well-prepared stained material, each of the chromonemata of a given chromosome may be seen to share a common, small, relatively clear, spherical zone, the **centromere**. The centromere (or kinetochore) has also been termed a spindle-attachment region (see later). That it is an essential part is indicated

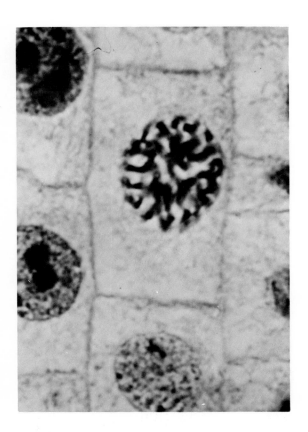

FIGURE 3-5. *Mitosis in onion root tip cell; late prophase. Chromosomes are shorter and thicker than in early prophase; note the chromatids.* [Courtesy Carolina Biological Supply Co.]

by the fact that chromosome fragments, such as may result from x-ray induced breakage, which lack it fail to move normally during nuclear division and are generally, therefore, lost from reorganizing nuclei. The centromere becomes progressively more accentuated as the chromosome further shortens and thickens by coiling changes of the chromonemata. Cytologists recognize several kinds of coiling, including **minor coils** which persist throughout interphase and mitosis, and **major cells** which appear in the chromonemata during early prophase. The tightening of these coils contributes in part to the shortening and thickening of chromosomes during nuclear division.

Thus, in earliest prophase, chromosomes appear longitudinally double. Each such half-chromosome (which initially consists only of a chromonema or chromonemata and a portion of the centromere) is called a **chromatid**. Later on in prophase, a matrix appears to be deposited around each chromonema or chromonemal group, so that thickening is further accentuated. Not all cytologists today agree on the existence of such a matrix, but it does appear to occur in at least one plant, *Luzula campestris,* a wood rush of the family Juncaceae. **A chromatid is, therefore, a longitudinal half-chromosome, sharing a common centromere with its sister chromatid** (Fig. 3-5).

As prophase continues, the nucleolus gradually disappears. Some cytologists have attributed the accumulation of a matrix to this event. During the closing stages of prophase the nuclear membrane loses its identity and a football-shaped **spindle** begins to take form. The "fibers" or strands, of the spindle may be formed by rearrangement of both nucleoplasmic and cytoplasmic materials, and are probably composed of protein chains, lipoproteins, and a small amount of RNA in the form of a highly elastic gel. Some of these fibers are continuous from pole to pole (i.e., from end to end) of the completed spindle ("**continuous fibers**"); others appear to run from pole to chromosomal centromeres to which they are attached ("**chromosomal fibers**"); and a few (**interzonal fibers**) connect the centromeres of the separating daughter chromosomes later on in anaphase.

FIGURE 3-6. *Chromosomes nearing equatorial plane of developing spindle; prometaphase.* [Courtesy Carolina Biological Supply Co.)

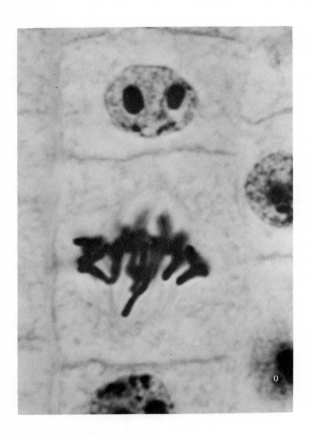

FIGURE 3-7. *Mitosis in onion root tip cell; metaphase. Note the spindle.* [Courtesy Carolina Biological Supply Co.]

As prophase draws to a close, the chromosomes move or are moved in the direction of the midplane ("equator") of the forming spindle, a period often designated as prometaphase (Fig. 3-6).

*Metaphase.*   Metaphase (Fig. 3-7) is that period of time in which the centromeres of the longitudinally double chromosomes occupy the plane of the equator of the spindle, although the arms of the chromosomes may extend in any direction. During metaphase the centromere of each chromosome is divided, but only one functions as an attachment point for the chromosomal fibers. It is at this period that chromosomes are shortest and thickest. Polar views furnish good material for chromosome counts.

*Anaphase.*   Anaphase is characterized by the separation of the metaphase sister chromatids and the movement of these bodies to the spindle poles. It begins at the moment when the centromeres of each pair of sister chromatids become *functionally* double and ends with the arrival of chromosomes at the poles. Thus, as soon as anaphase begins, our definition of chromatid is no longer applicable and the bodies that move and/or are moved poleward are best referred to as daughter chromosomes. Thus, whereas a

FIGURE 3-8. *Mitosis in onion root tip cell; anaphase. The daughter chromosomes are nearing the spindle poles which are clearly evident.* [Courtesy Carolina Biological Supply Co.]

metaphase cell contains a number of sister chromatids equal to twice the number of chromosomes, the anaphase cell, by definition, contains no sister chromatids. Anaphase therefore accomplishes the *quantitively* equal distribution of chromosomal material into two developing daughter nuclei.

The mechanism of the anaphasic movement of chromosomes is not understood. Contraction of the chromosomal fibers would certainly draw the sister chromosomes poleward, and it is true that the centromere "leads the way" in the anaphase movement. At the same time, an expansion of the interzonal fibers between the daughter chromosomes could likewise push them toward the poles. Expenditure of energy also appears to be involved, but its precise utilization is not yet known (Fig. 3-8).

*Telophase.* The arrival of daughter chromosomes at the spindle poles marks the beginning of this phase; its conclusion occurs with the reorganization of two interphase nuclei. In general terms, the events of prophase occur in reverse sequence. New nuclear membranes are constructed, the spindle and matrix disappear, the nucleolus or nucleoli reappear, and the chromosomes resume their long slender, extended form (Fig. 3-9).

Cytokinesis, if it is to occur, usually takes place during telophase, though it may be initiated in anaphase. In the cells of higher plants cytokinesis is typically accomplished by the formation of a cell plate across the equatorial region of the spindle (which now becomes somewhat barrel-shaped,

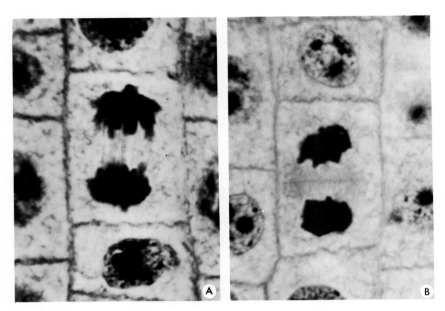

FIGURE 3-9. *Mitosis in onion root tip; telophase. (A) Early telophase; chromosomes have just arrived at the poles. The cell plate has begun to form. (B) Later telophase. The cell plate is prominent, and will later extend from side wall to side wall.* [Courtesy Carolina Biological Supply Co.]

contacting the side walls of the original cell) with subsequent wall formation on both sides of the cell plate. In animal cells, furrowing gradually separates two newly constructed cells.

Note that each daughter chromosome in telophase must consist of a *single* visible chromonema, or group of chromonemata, whereas in early prophase chromosomes are longitudinally double. This implies that replication of chromosomal material, in preparation for the next mitosis, must occur during interphase. This implication is confirmed by chemical analyses described in Chapter 14. If this interphase replication of chromosomal material was *qualitatively equal* (and we shall examine this possibility in Chapter 14), then the chromosomes will serve quite adequately as physical bearers of genes. This will be a matter of critical importance in the development of our concepts. The process of mitosis is summarized in a series of diagrams in Fig. 3-10.

### SIGNIFICANCE OF MITOSIS

The process of mitosis as we have seen it has the inevitable result, if the cell " makes no mistakes," of creating from one cell two new ones which are chromosomally identical, both quantitatively and qualitatively (Fig. 3-11).

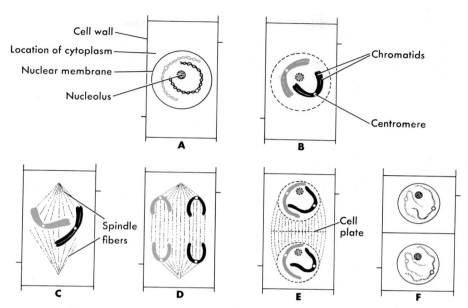

FIGURE 3-10. *Diagrammatic summary of mitosis in onion root tip cell. Only two of the total complement of sixteen chromosomes are shown; the black and gray represent a "paternal" and a "maternal" chromosome, respectively, of one of the eight pairs. (A)* **Prophase,** *showing chromonemata; nuclear membrane and nucleolus still evident. (B)* **Late prophase;** *chromosomes becoming shorter and thicker, nucleolus and nuclear membrane disappearing. Note that each chromosome consists of two chromatids. (C)* **Metaphase;** *centromeres aligned on the midplane of the spindle, chromatids still present. (D)* **Anaphase;** *daughter chromosomes moving poleward. (E)* **Telophase;** *chromosomes have reached poles, nucleoli and nuclear membranes reappearing, cytokinesis by cell plate underway. (F)* **Interphase.** *See text for details.*

(Actually, "mistakes" do occur now and then; these, however, shed considerable light on the nature of the gene, as detailed in Chapter 17). The Mendelian pattern of inheritance which we followed for *Coleus* in Chapter 2 requires that genes be transmitted in cell division from the zygote to every cell of the mature organism. In mitosis there exists a process that inevitably results in the precise, equal distribution of structures called chromosomes from a parent nucleus to daughter nuclei. Our assumptions in Chapter 2 regarding genes are well served if the genes are indeed located on the chromosomes; certainly the behavior of these bodies makes them ideal vehicles for genes in terms of our earlier speculations. Before we can be certain of the chromosomal location of genes, however, we shall need to note additional parallels between the behavior of genes as deduced from breeding experiments and the behavior of chromosomes as seen under the

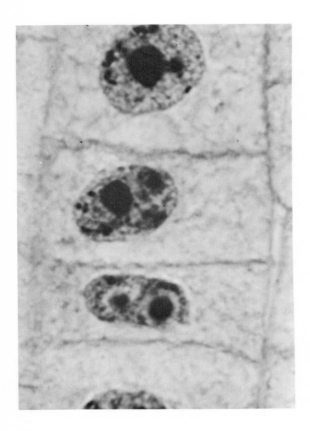

FIGURE 3-11. *After completion of mitosis in an onion root tip cell, two new interphase nuclei have been formed. In plant cells these are typically separated by a wall as a result of cytokinesis begun during telophase.* [Courtesy Carolina Biological Supply Co.]

microscope. In the mechanism of mitosis we have begun to accumulate good presumptive evidence that many of our theories regarding gene location are sound. We shall still require physical and chemical *proof*, but our theory looks sufficiently promising to retain for the present.

### DURATION OF MITOSIS

Although not directly germane to our purposes at this point, it is interesting to note that the rather complicated physical and chemical changes in mitotic nuclei often occur in a surprisingly short time. Table 3-2 summarizes a few studies from the literature.

### CHROMOSOME MORPHOLOGY

As noted earlier, chromosomes undergo progressive changes in length and width from interphase through mitosis to the next interphase. During metaphase and anaphase they appear as more or less cylindrical objects, as

TABLE 3-2. Duration of Mitosis in Living Cells

| Name of Organism | | | | Duration, minutes | | | | |
|---|---|---|---|---|---|---|---|---|
| Common | Scientific | Tissue | Temp. °C | P | M | A | T | Total |
| PLANTS (ANGIOSPERMS) | | | | | | | | |
| Onion | *Allium cepa* | Root tip | 20 | 71 | 6.5 | 2.4 | 3.8 | 83 |
| Oatgrass | *Arrhenatherum sp.* | Stigma | 19 | 36–45 | 7–10 | 15–20 | 20–35 | 78–110 |
| Pea | *Pisum sativum* | Endosperm | — | 40 | 20 | 12 | 110 | 182 |
| Pea | *Pisum sativum* | Root tip | 20 | 78 | 14.4 | 4.2 | 13.2 | 110 |
| Spiderwort | *Tradescantia sp.* | Stamen hair | 20 | 181 | 14 | 15 | 130 | 340 |
| Broad bean | *Vicia faba* | Root tip | 19 | 90 | 31 | 34 | 34 | 155 |
| ANIMALS | | | | | | | | |
| Fowl | *Gallus* sp. | Fibroblast culture | — | 19–25 | 4–7 | 3.5–6 | 7.5–14 | 34–52 |
| Mouse | *Mus musculus* | Spleen mesenchyme | 38 | 21 | 13 | 5 | 20 | 59 |
| Salamander | *Salamandra maculosa* | Embryo kidney | 20 | 59 | 55 | 6 | 75 | 195 |

short as a fraction of a micrometer[2] to as long as perhaps 400 micrometers or more, depending upon the species, and between about 0.2 and 2 micrometers in diameter (Fig. 3-12). Each chromosome of a somatic cell has its own characteristic length (within narrow limits) and centromere location, but in organisms with large numbers of chromosomes there is often considerable size similarity in some of the members of a set. In somatic cells of higher plants and animals, careful examination of metaphase smears reveals that chromosomes occur in matching pairs (except for one heteromorphic pair or a single odd chromosome associated with the sexes, especially in many animals; refer to Chapter 10). Photographs of such smears (Fig. 3-13) may be cut apart and the chromosomes arranged by matching pairs in many organisms to form an **idiogram** (Fig. 3-14).

Although no such thing as a "typical" chromosome exists, a composite chromosome is diagrammed in Fig. 3-15. Many chromosomes, however, show a distressing lack of morphological landmarks such as satellites and secondary constrictions. Every normal one does possess a centromere; its position and therefore the lengths of the "arms" are relatively constant. Often small chromatic thickenings, the **chromomeres**, occur along the chromosome. Although chromomere number and, to some extent, their size are constant, no general agreement has been reached as to their genetic

[2] A micrometer ($\mu$m) is $1 \times 10^{-6}$ meter; in older usage, a micron ($\mu$).

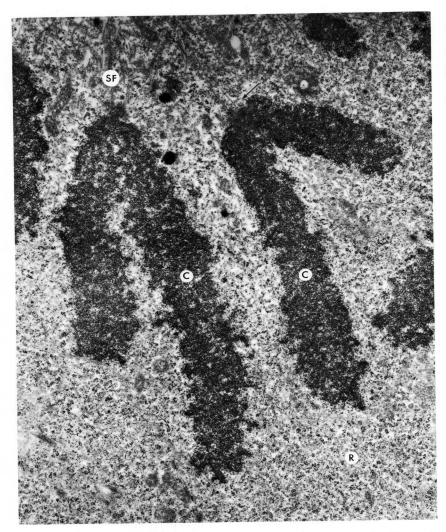

FIGURE 3-12. *Electron micrograph of anaphase chromosomes of the Tasmanian Wallaby. C, chromosome; SF, spindle fibers; R, ribosomes. Note attachment of spindle fibers at centromere (arrow).* [From *Cell Ultrastructure* by William Jensen and Roderic Park. © 1967 by Wadsworth Publishing Co., Inc., Belmont, California. Reproduced by permission.]

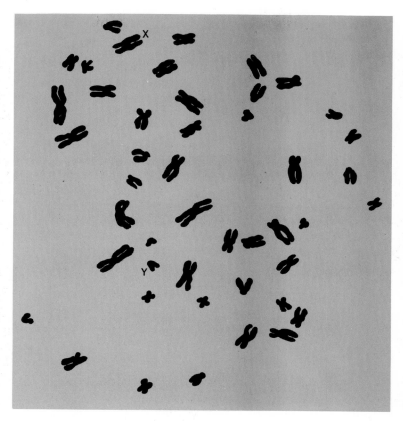

FIGURE 3-13. *Drawing of the chromosomes of a normal human male, from a photograph. Chromosomes marked X and Y are the sex chromosomes.* [After J. H. Tjïo and T. T. Puck, *Proceedings of the National Academy of Sciences,* **44**: 1229–1237, 1958.]

significance. Recent work indicates that they represent regions of tighter coiling. Figure 3-16 shows chromonemata clearly.

In summary, morphological individuality of chromosomes is seen in the position of the centromere, the length of the "arms" thus delimited, the average overall length, the occurrence of satellites and secondary constrictions (if any), and, to a lesser extent, the arrangement of chromomeres.

## MEIOSIS

One of two fundamental cytological and genetic events in the life cycle of sexually reproducing plants and animals is the union of gametes or sex cells to form a zygote, a process to which the term **syngamy** is applied. Studies

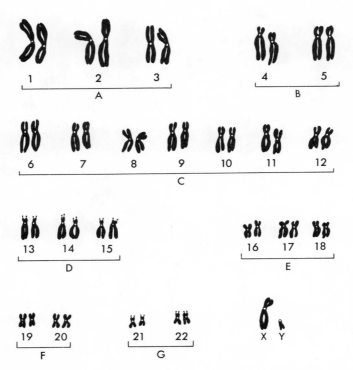

FIGURE 3-14. *The chromosomes of a normal human male arranged as a karyotype. Note the knobs or satellites on several pairs. Because of morphological similarities among several of the human chromosomes, groups are assigned letter designations as shown here.*

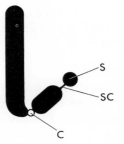

FIGURE 3-15. *Diagram of a composite chromosome as it might appear at high magnification with a light microscope. For simplicity chromatids are not represented, and the matrix obscures internal structure. C, centromere; S, satellite or knob; SC, secondary constriction.*

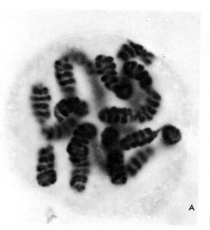
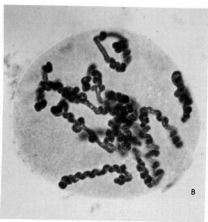

FIGURE 3-16. *Chromonemata can be made visible by treatment with nitric acid vapor. These are meiotic metaphase-I chromosomes in the spiderwort plant,* Tradescantia virginiana. *(A)* × 2400; *(B)* × 1800. [Courtesy Dr. L. F. Lacour, John Innes Institute.]

from as long ago as the last century clearly indicate that in gametic union the chromosomes contributed by each gamete retain their separate identities in the zygote nucleus. The zygote thus contains twice as many chromosomes as does a gamete or, more accurately, all the chromosomes of each of the two gametes whose union created it.

This fact, of course, is responsible for the occurence in diploid or *2n* cells of matching pairs of chromosomes; each member of a given pair is the **homolog** of the other. In each diploid nucleus, then, there occurs the monoploid number of homologous *pairs* of chromosomes, one member of each pair having been contributed by the paternal parent, the other by the maternal parent. Thus, if among the chromosomes of the sperm, there is a metacentric chromosome (Fig. 3-17) of, for example, an average metaphase length of 5 μm, there will be in the chromosomal complement of the egg an identical chromosome. This statement applies to all of the **autosomes** (those chromosomes not associated with the sex of the bearer). In the zygote, and all cells derived from it by mitosis, *two* metacentric autosomes having an average metaphase length of 5 μm will be found. As we shall see later, these statements will have to be modified for the so-called sex chromosomes where these occur.

The result of syngamy is the incorporation into a zygote nucleus of all the chromosomes of each gamete. Such facts would seem to require a counterbalancing event whereby the doubling of chromosome quantity at syngamy is offset by a nuclear division which halves the amount of chromatin per

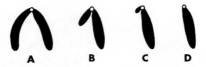

FIGURE 3-17. *Four major morphological chromosome types are recognized on the basis of centromere position and consequent relative arm length, (A) metacentric; (B) submetacentric; (C) acrocentric; (D) telocentric.*

nucleus at some point prior to gamete formation. Such a "reduction division" does occur in all sexually reproducing organisms that have discrete nuclei. This is **meiosis**, the second of the two fundamental cytological and genetic events in the sexual cycle.

Meiosis as a form of nuclear division differs greatly from mitosis. It consists of two successive divisions, each with its own prophase, metaphase, anaphase, and telophase; it thereby results in *four* daughter nuclei instead of two as in mitosis (although in many species not all of the cellular products are functional). Furthermore, because of fundamental "procedural" differences between mitosis and meiosis, not only do the nuclear products of a meiotic division have one set of chromosomes each (monoploid or "haploid") as opposed to the two sets (diploid) of the parent nucleus, but the nuclear products are, if genes and chromosomes have any relationship, also genetically unlike the original diploid nucleus and often genetically unlike each other.

The term **meiocyte** is a convenient general one to designate any diploid cell whose next act will be to undergo meiosis. In seed plants and other heterosporous forms, for example, meiocytes are represented by the megasporocytes and microsporocytes ("spore mother cells"), in homosporous plants (those producing only one kind of spore by meiosis) by sporocytes or "spore mother cells," and in higher animals by primary spermatocytes and primary oocytes. The position of the meiocyte in the life cycle varies greatly from one major group to another. For instance, in the vascular plants, the meiocytes give rise directly to megaspores and microspores (i.e., the **meiospores**), which, by mitosis, produce gamete-bearing plants. In the seed plants these gamete-bearing plants (the gametophytes) are much reduced; refer to Appendix B. In man, on the other hand, meiocytes give rise directly to gametes. In many algae and fungi the zygote nucleus itself functions as a meiocyte, giving rise to monoploid cells which ultimately, by mitosis, produce monoploid, gamete-bearing plants. In summary, meiosis may be sporic (vascular plants and others) or gametic (man and many other animals), and may be performed by (1) sporocytes ("spore mother cells," Fig. 3-18), (2) primary spermatocytes and oocytes, or even, (3) by the zygote itself.

FIGURE 3-18. *Meiocytes (microsporocytes, microspore mother cells, or pollen mother cells) in anther of lily stamen. These cells are diploid (2n) and are about to undergo meiosis.* [Courtesy Carolina Biological Supply Co.]

***First Division: Prophase-I.*** Although most cytologists recognize and name at least five stages of prophase-I because of its complexities of chromosome behavior, it will suffice for our purposes merely to describe these events in sequence. In very early prophase-I, the diploid number of chromosomes gradually becomes recognizable under the light microscope as long, slender, longitudinally single, threadlike structures. This apparent longitudinal singleness of the chromosomes in early prophase-I is the first noticeable difference from a mitotic cell. Recalling the meaning of the term, by definition no " chromatid " exists at this time in a meiocyte. The centromere and chromomeres are recognizable in well-prepared material. The chromosomes shorten and thicken during this stage, presumably by the same mechanism as for mitosis.

While this contraction is under way, a second event that characterizes meiosis (as opposed to mitosis) takes place. Recall that each diploid nucleus (including meiocytes) contains *pairs* of homologous chromosomes. In early prophase-I these homologs begin to pair, or **synapse**. This **synapsis** is remarkably exact and specific, taking place point for point, with the two homologs usually somewhat twined about each other (relational coiling). Although synapsing homologous chromosomes at this stage appear longitudinally single (no chromatids), there is mounting chemical evidence that replication of deoxyribonucleic acid (DNA), which is almost uniquely characteristic of chromosomes, has occurred at some time prior to prophase-I, although the visual evidence appears somewhat afterward, later in prophase-I. The mechanism of synapsis has not been satisfactorily explained.

As the synapsed chromosomes still further shorten and thicken, their longitudinally double nature does become visible with light microscopy, each chromosome of the synapsed pair then clearly consisting of two sister chromatids at the visual level. A meiocyte nucleus at this stage of prophase-I, then, contains the reduced or monoploid number of **bivalents** (pairs of synapsed homologous chromosomes) or **tetrads**[3] (groups of four chromatids, two sister chromatids per synapsed chromosome). Each longitudinally double chromosome in a synapsed pair has its own individual centromere.

During synapsis, and while in the so-called tetrad stage, another important difference in chromosome behavior which further sets meiosis apart from mitosis becomes visually evident. Chromatids are ordinarily very intimately intertwined. Either during this time or prior to prophase-I an exchange of material between nonsister chromatids occurs in most meiocytes. Though we shall examine the possible mechanism later when we consider the genetic material at the molecular level, it is as though each of two nonsister chromatids breaks at an identical point during this intimate association, subsequent repair joining to a given chromatid the area of the other (nonsister) chromatid beyond the break. There is some evidence of DNA synthesis in meiocytes at this stage, very possibly related to the repair of such breaks. The visible evidence of this exchange between chromatids is a characteristic and more or less X-shaped configuration called a **chiasma** (plural, *chiasmata*), as seen in Fig. 3-19. The longer the chromosome pair, the greater the likelihood of more than one chiasma, although one chiasma appears to **interfere** with the formation of another in a closely adjacent region of the chromosomes on the same side of the centromere. The basis for this **interference** is not clear. Chiasmata have been observed in all but a few plant and animal meiocytes. We shall examine the genetic implications (referred to as crossing-over) in Chapter 6.

As prophase-I progresses, coiling and consequent shortening of the chromosomes increases with the result that chiasmata appear to move toward the ends of the synapsed chromosomes in the process of terminalization. By this time the nucleolus is well on the way to disappearance, the nuclear membrane becomes disrupted, and spindle formation is well under

---

[3] Use of the term "tetrad" at this point should not be confused with the frequent use of the same term to refer to the four nuclear or cellular products of meiosis.

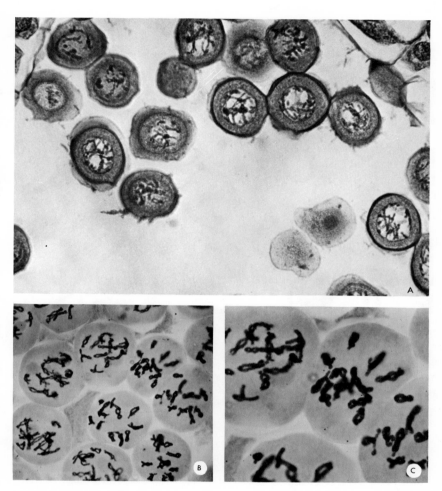

FIGURE 3-19. *Meiosis in microsporocytes in plants of the lily family; prophase-I.*
*(A) Lily; synapsis is underway but chromatids cannot easily be distinguished at this*
*magnification.* [Courtesy Carolina Biological Supply Co.); *(B) and (C) Synapsis*
*in fritillary* (Fritillaria); *chiasmata show clearly.* [Courtesy Dr. L. F. LaCour,
John Innes Institute.]

way. The arrival of synapsed homologous chromosome pairs at the equator
of the complete spindle ends prophase-I and begins the next phase.

*Metaphase-I.* This phase differs from mitotic metaphase in (1) the
arrangement of the monoploid number of chromosome *pairs* on the equatorial plane and (2) the tendency for the centromere of each homolog to be
directed somewhat toward one of the poles (Fig. 3-20). An important point
to be noted here is the randomness of arrangement of the paired homologs;

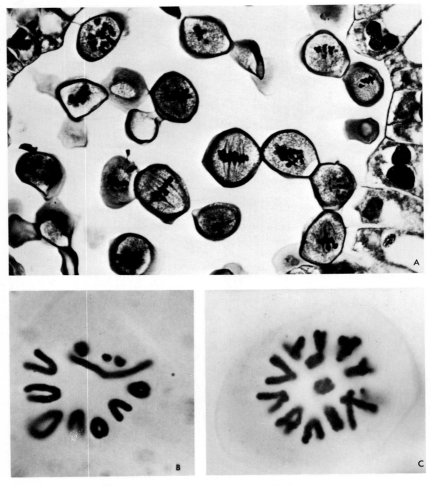

FIGURE 3-20. *Meiosis metaphase-I.* (*A*) *In lily microsporocytes. Cell in the upper left of the anther cavity is seen in polar view, most of the remainder are seen in side view with spindles clearly evident.* (Courtesy Carolina Biological Co.] (*B*) *Polar view in spermatocytes of the orthopeteran* Mecostethus grossus. (*C*) *Microsporocytes of* Fritillaria, *a plant of the lily family.* [B and C courtesy Dr. L. F. LaCour, John Innes Institute.]

that is, for a given pair, it is just as likely that the paternal member will be directed toward the "north" pole as it is for the maternal member to be so oriented. This will be well worth recalling in considering later the gamete genotypes a polyhybrid individual produces.

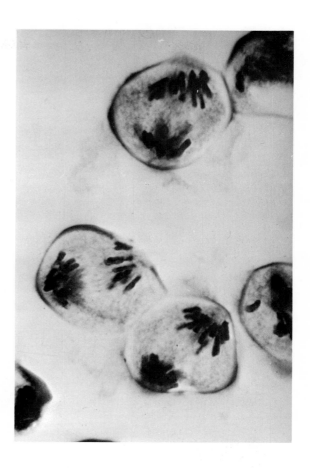

FIGURE 3-21. *Anaphase-I in lily microsporocytes.* [Courtesy General Biological Supply House, Inc., Chicago.]

*Anaphase-I.* In anaphase-I actual **disjunction** of synapsed homologs occurs, one longitudinally double chromosome of each pair moving to each pole, thereby completing the process of terminalization. Here is an additional difference from mitosis, mitotic anaphase being marked by separation of sister chromatids which then move poleward as longitudinally single daughter chromosomes. Thus, in mitosis, one of each of the chromosomes present (i.e., of the entire chromosomal complement) travels to each pole, with the result that each new nucleus has just as many chromosomes as had the parent nucleus, whether monoploid or diploid. In meiosis, however, whole chromosomes of each homologous pair (as modified by any crossing-over that has occurred in prophase-I) separate, so that each pole receives either a paternal or a maternal, longitudinally double chromosome of each pair. This insures a change in chromosome number from diploid to monoploid in the resultant reorganized daughter nuclei. In short, whereas mitotic

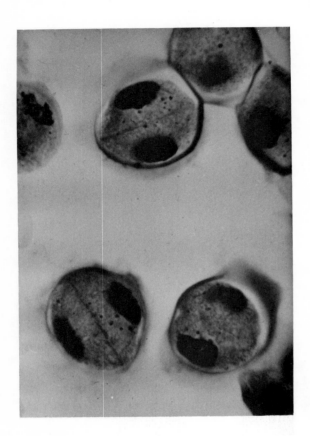

FIGURE 3-22. *Telophase-I in lily microsporocytes. Note the prominent cell plate.* [Courtesy General Biological Supply House, Inc., Chicago.]

anaphase was marked by the separation of sister chromatids, anaphase-I of meiosis is characterized by separation of homologous entire chromosomes (Fig. 3-21). This is so because in mitosis division of the centromere occurs in anaphase, whereas in meiosis centromere division is delayed until anaphase-II.

*Telophase-I.* The arrival of chromosomes at the poles of the spindle signals the end of anaphase-I and the beginning of telophase-I. During this phase the chromosomes may persist for a time in the condensed state, the nucleolus and nuclear membranes may be reconstituted, and cytokinesis may also occur (Fig. 3-22). In some cases, as in the liliaceous genus *Trillium*, meiocytes are reported to progress virtually directly from anaphase-I to prophase-II; in other organisms there may be either a short or fairly long interphase between the first and second meiotic divisions. In any event, the first division has thus accomplished the separation of the chromosomal complement into two monoploid nuclei.

*Prophase-II.* This phase is generally short, and superficially resembles

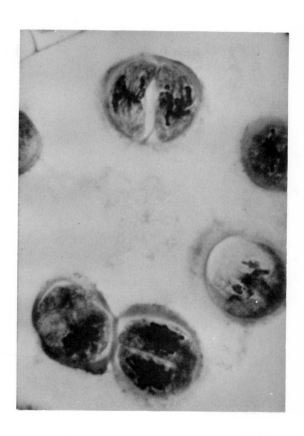

FIGURE 3-23. *Metaphase-II in lily microsporocytes.* [Courtesy General Biological Supply House, Inc., Chicago.]

mitotic prophase except that sister chromatids of each chromosome are often widely divergent (i.e., no relational coiling).

*Metaphase-II.* On two spindles, generally oriented at right angles to the first division spindle, and often separated by a membrane or wall, the monoploid numbers of chromosomes, each consisting of two chromatids joined by a common centromere, are arranged in the equatorial plane. This stage is generally brief (Fig. 3-23).

*Anaphase-II.* Centromeres now separate and the sister chromatids of metaphase-II now move poleward as daughter chromosomes, much as in mitosis. Their arrival at the poles marks the close of this phase.

*Telophase-II.* Following the arrival of the monoploid number of daughter chromosomes at the poles, the chromosomes return to their long, attenuate, reticulate conformation, nuclear membranes are reconstituted, nucleoli reform, and cytokinesis generally separates each nucleus from the others (Fig. 3-24).

The process of meiosis is summarized diagrammatically in Fig. 3-25.

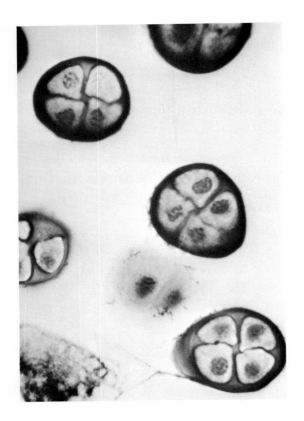

FIGURE 3-24. *Tetrads of lily microspores within the old microsporocyte wall. In some of the nuclei the chromosomes retain the telophase-II morphology, not yet having assumed the long, attenuate form of interphase.* [Courtesy General Biological Supply House, Inc., Chicago.]

## SIGNIFICANCE OF MEIOSIS

Cytologically, the basic significance of meiosis is the formation of four monoploid nuclei from a single diploid one in two successive divisions, thus balancing off, as it were, the doubling of chromosome number that

FIGURE 3-25. *Diagrammatic representation of meiosis in a meiocyte having one pair of homologous chromosomes (2n = 2). (A) prophase-I, chromosomes long and slender, appearing longitudinally single; (B) prophase-I, homologs synapsing; (C) prophase-I chromatids now evident, with one chiasma; (D) prophase-I, disjunction underway, chiasma still evident; (E) metaphase-I, chromosomes on midplane of spindle with centromeres divergent; (F) anaphase-I, poleward separation of previously synapsed homologs; note that each chromosome is still composed of two chromatids but some of these have been modified by crossing over; (G) telophase-I, each reorganizing nucleus now contains the monoploid number of chromosomes which are still composed of two chromatids each; (H) prophase-II; (I) metaphase-II; (J) anaphase-II; (K) a postmeiotic tetrad of monoploid cells; note that each in this case contains a genetically unique chromosome because of crossing over.*

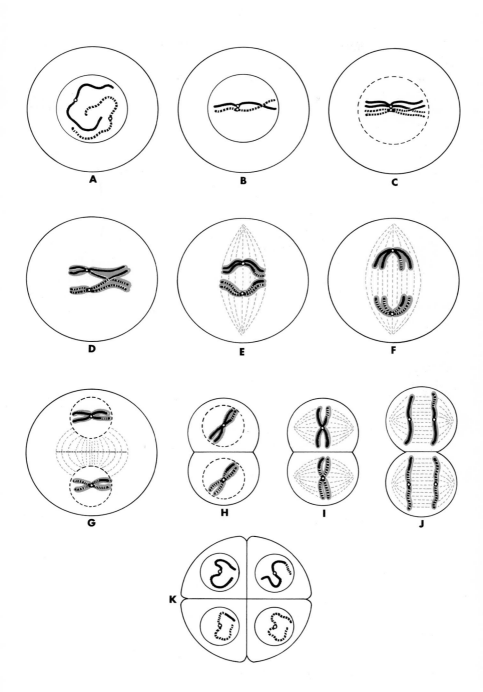

results from syngamy. Note that the first meiotic division accomplishes the reduction in chromosome number from diploid to monoploid, whereas the second is equational in distributing equal numbers of daughter chromosomes to developing new nuclei. In higher animals the cellular products of meiosis directly become gametes and/or polar bodies (Appendix B-8), but in vascular plants they are meiospores which give rise to reduced gamete bearing plants (Appendix B-6).

But how does meiosis relate to the hypotheses we raised concerning probable gene distribution in somatic and gametic cells in the preceding chapter? If genes are located on chromosomes, the process of meiosis generates genetic variability in two important ways: (1) random assortment of paternal and maternal chromosomes and (2) crossing-over. Assume, for example, an organism heterozygous for three pairs of genes (a trihybrid), *AaBbCc* in which *ABC* was derived from its paternal parent and *abc* from its maternal parent. If these three pairs of genes are located on three *different* chromosome pairs (which we might designate as pair 1, pair 2, and pair 3), then in prophase-I the paternal and maternal number 1 chromosomes (bearing genes *A* and *a*, respectively) will synapse, as will the number 2's (bearing genes *B* and *b*) and the number 3's (with genes *C* and *c*). Arrangement of each pair of synapsed homologs on the metaphase-I spindle is random; i.e., the paternal member of each pair has an equal chance of being oriented toward either pole, as does the maternal member. In anaphase-I each (longitudinally double) chromosome moves toward the nearer pole as it separates from its homolog. Therefore, each telophase-I nucleus has an equal chance of receiving a paternal or a maternal chromosome. The same chance exists for each remaining chromosome pair. Hence, for three pairs of genes on three different pairs of chromosomes, eight possible telophase-I genotypic combinations are possible:

| Daughter Nucleus No. 1 | Daughter Nucleus No. 2 |
|:---:|:---:|
| *ABC* | *abc* |
| *ABc* | *abC* |
| *AbC* | *aBc* |
| *Abc* | *aBC* |
| *aBC* | *Abc* |
| *aBc* | *AbC* |
| *abC* | *ABc* |
| *abc* | *ABC* |

The second division will simply increase the number of each genotype from one to two. The number of possible gamete genotypes occurring after the second meiotic division is here $2^3$ or 8. That is, a given gamete in this example has $(1/2)^3$ chance of receiving any particular arrangement of paternal and/or maternal chromosomes and genes. Furthermore, in a sample of several hundred gametes from such an individual, each of the eight genotypes would be expected to occur in approximately equal numbers. For organisms with many chromosomes the number of possible combinations becomes very large. In man, for instance, with 23 pairs of chromosomes, the probability that any particular gamete will have a specific combination of chromosomes (excluding crossing-over) is $(1/2)^{23}$, or about one in eight million. Possible zygote genotypes resulting from random fusions of these gametes rise to about sixty-four million (see pages 77–78). A good deal of the variation in natural populations is due to this kind of **independent segregation** of genes normally occurring in the breeding population.

What would be the situation if these three gene pairs are, instead, located on a single pair of homologous chromosomes (i.e., linked)? Assume, for the purpose of illustration, that one member of the pair of homologs bears genes $A$, $B$, $C$ on a given arm, and that the other homolog bears genes $a$, $b$, and $c$. If no chiasmata are formed, then only two kinds of gametes ($ABC$ and $abc$) will be produced, and these will occur in equal number. If, on the other hand, as is more often the case, chiasmata do form between genes $A$ and $B$ and between genes $B$ and $C$ in at least some meiocytes, then eight gamete genotypes will again be produced. However, in this case, the fraction of each type produced will depend upon the frequency with which crossing-over occurs between $A$ and $B$ and between $B$ and $C$. This will have considerable importance in the mapping of genes which will be considered in detail in Chapter 6.

In this examination of two types of nuclear division so nearly universal in a wide variety of plant and animal forms, in fact always occurring in all organisms having discrete nuclei and sexual reproduction, we have met some impressive similarities between visually observable chromosome behavior and our postulated gene behavior of Chapter 2. Of course, this could conceivably be an unusual case of multiple coincidences, but, on the other hand, the very multiplicity of these parallels furnishes a strong presumptive basis for the **chromosomal theory** of genetics. We shall, however, demand not only further parallels but also, more importantly, some positive experimental *proof*. This proof we shall seek not only from the science of genetics itself but also from cytology, physics, and chemistry. Much of the remainder of this book is devoted, then, to the quest for a sound understanding of what a gene is, even at the molecular level, how it operates, and where in the cell it is located.

### REFERENCES

BRACHET, J., and A. E. MIRSKY, eds., 1961. *The Cell*, vol. III. New York, Academic Press.

COHN, N. S., 1969, 2nd ed. *Elements of Cytology*. New York, Harcourt Brace Jovanovich.

DE ROBERTIS, E. D. P., W. W. NOWINSKI, and F. A. SAEZ, 1970, 5th ed. *Cell Biology*. Philadelphia, W. B. Saunders.

DU PRAW, E. J., 1970. *DNA and Chromosomes*. New York, Holt, Rinehart and Winston.

SWANSON, C. P., 1969, 3rd ed. *The Cell*. Englewood Cliffs, N.J., Prentice-Hall.

WILSON, G. B., and J. H. MORRISON, 1966, 2nd ed. *Cytology*. New York, Reinhold.

### PROBLEMS

**3-1.** In *Coleus* the somatic cells are diploid, having 24 chromosomes. How many of each of the following are present in each cell at the stage of mitosis or meiosis indicated? (Assume cytokinesis to occur in mid telophase.) (a) centromeres at anaphase; (b) centromeres at anaphase-I; (c) chromatids at metaphase-I; (d) chromatids at anaphase; (e) chromosomes at anaphase; (f) chromosomes at metaphase-I; (g) chromosomes at the close of telophase I; (h) chromosomes at telophase II.

**3-2.** Based on your present knowledge or after consulting Appendix B, how many human eggs will be formed from (a) 40 primary oocytes; (b) 40 secondary oocytes; (c) 40 ootids?

**3-3.** From your present knowledge or from Appendix B, 20 microsporocytes of a flowering plant would be expected to produce how many (a) microspores; (b) sperms?

**3-4.** Corn is a flowering plant whose somatic chromosome number is 20. Either from information you already have or based on facts in Appendix B, how many chromosomes are present in each of the following: (a) leaf epidermal cell; (b) antipodal nucleus; (c) endosperm cell; (d) generative nucleus; (e) egg; (f) megaspore; (g) microspore mother cell.

**3-5.** How many different gamete genotypes will be produced by the following parental genotypes if all genes shown are unlinked: (a) *AA*; (b) *Aa*; (c) *AaBB*; (d) *AaBb*; (e) *AAbbCc*; (f) *AaBbCcDdEe*?

**3-6.** Consult Table 3-1 in answering the following questions. (a) What is the probability in cattle that a particular egg cell will contain only chromosomes derived from the maternal parent of the cow producing the egg? (b) If this cow is mated to its brother, what is the probability that their calf will receive only chromosomes originally contributed by the calf's grandmother?

**3-7.** Triploid watermelons have the advantage of being seedless. (a) What is the somatic chromosome number of such plants? (b) What explanation can you offer for their lack of seeds?

**3-8.** A student examining a number of onion root tips counted 1,000 cells in some phase of mitosis. He noted 692 cells in prophase, 105 in metaphase, 35 in anaphase, and 168 in telophase. From these data what can be concluded about relative duration of the different stages of the process?

**3-9.** Garden peas have 14 chromosomes in their somatic cells. How many groups of linked genes occur in this plant?

**3-10.** What is the probability that any ascospore of the red bread mold (*Neurospora crassa*) will have all its chromosomes derived from the + parent? (You may wish to consult Table 3-1 and Appendix B before trying to answer.)

**3-11.** The red bread mold, *Neurospora crassa*, is an ascomycete fungus much used in genetic research. As pointed out more fully in Appendix B, sexual reproduction occurs when the tubular filaments of plants of opposite mating strain come into contact. The fusion nucleus (zygote) that results is the only diploid nucleus in *Neurospora*'s life history. It quickly undergoes meiosis into meiospores within a developing saclike structure (the ascus) which is relatively long and narrow, so that the meiospores cannot slip past each other. They are arranged serially and may be removed in sequence for separate germination and study with full knowledge of which spore, with reference to position in the ascus, produces which phenotype. One mitosis follows meiosis, so that 8 ascospores occur in each ascus. Prior to sexual reproduction, large numbers of asexual reproductive bodies, called conidia, are produced. These are pink to red (wild type), or yellow in another strain.

In the case of asci resulting from the cross pink (+) × yellow (*y*), where + and *y* are alleles, it is observed that in some cases the ascospores, in order from tip of ascus to bottom, were arranged + + + + *y y y y*, whereas less often they were + + *y y* + + *y y*. In terms of chromosome behavior, account for each of these arrangements.

**3-12.** Refer back to the linkage map of corn, Fig. 1-9. Recessive gene *hm* at locus 64 on chromosome 1 determines susceptibility to the fungus *Helminthosporium* which produces lesions on leaves and in kernels, reducing vigor, yield, and market value of the crop. Its dominant allele determines resistance to the fungus. Another recessive gene, $br_1$, at locus 81 on this same chromosome produces shortened internodes (segments of stem between successive leaves) and stiff, erect leaves (brachytic plants). The dominant allele is responsible for normal plant form. If a resistant, normal plant, heterozygous for both pairs of genes (with dominants of each pair on one homologous chromosome) is pollinated by a susceptible, brachytic plant, (a) would you expect any resistant, brachytic and susceptible, normal individuals in the progeny? (b) Explain the cytological basis of your answer.

**3-13.** Assume an individual heterozygous for three genes, *A*, *B*, and *C*. Assume further that these three dominant genes are linked in that order on one chromosome and *a*, *b*, and *c* linked (in that sequence) on the homologous chromosome. If crossing-over occurs between *A* and *B* with a frequency of 0.05, and between *B* and *C* with a frequency of 0.10, what should be the frequency of *aBc* and *AbC* gametes produced by that individual if there is no interference?

# CHAPTER 4
# Dihybrid Inheritance

**W**E have seen in Chapter 2 the genetic results of the action of a single pair of genes through several generations. In Chapter 3 we examined both mitotic and meiotic nuclear divisions, noting an extensive array of parallels between observable chromosome behavior and our postulates on gene behavior. It will be interesting now to determine whether the ideas developed thus far apply equally well to crosses involving two pairs of genes.

## Classic Two-Pair Ratios

### COMPLETE DOMINANCE IN TWO PAIRS

In addition to the leaf margin trait of *Coleus* which we considered in Chapter 2, another vegetative character involves the venation pattern of leaves. This is easily observed on their lower surfaces. A commonly encountered vein arrangement is the typically regular one shown in Fig. 4-1. Here a single midvein branches in a rather standard pinnate fashion. An alternative expression is the highly irregular arrangement seen in Fig. 4-2. For convenience we may attach the terms "regular" and "irregular," respectively, to these two phenotypes, By a simple monohybrid cross involving these two characters, it can easily be determined that *irregular* is completely *dominant* to *regular*.

Therefore a cross of a doubly homozygous *deep irregular* with a *shallow regular* individual (using *D* and *d* again to represent the deep and shallow genotypes, and *I* and *i* to denote irregular and regular) may be represented as follows:

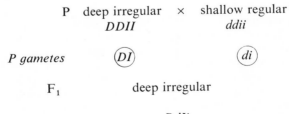

P   deep irregular   ×   shallow regular
        *DDII*                     *ddii*

P gametes        $\widehat{DI}$                    $\widehat{di}$

F$_1$                    deep irregular

                        *DdIi*

The F$_1$ individuals in this instance are referred to as **dihybrid** individuals because they are heterozygous for each of the two pairs of genes.

What will be the result of crossing two members of this F$_1$ to produce

FIGURE 4-1. *Regular venation pattern, a trait caused by a recessive gene, in* Coleus.

an $F_2$? Let us try to predict the outcome of this cross on the basis of the theses so far developed. Recalling our assumptions and the experimental evidence therefor, it is clear that, *considering one pair of genes at a time*, the phenotypic result will be the usual 3:1 ratio:

$$Dd \times Dd$$

$$eggs \quad \tfrac{1}{2}\,\widehat{D} + \tfrac{1}{2}\,\widehat{d}$$
$$sperms \quad \tfrac{1}{2}\,\widehat{D} + \tfrac{1}{2}\,\widehat{d}$$
$$\underbrace{\tfrac{1}{4}\,DD + \tfrac{2}{4}\,Dd} + \tfrac{1}{4}\,dd$$
$$\tfrac{3}{4}\ \text{deep} \qquad + \tfrac{1}{4}\ \text{shallow}$$

Likewise, $Ii \times Ii$ will produce the same $\tfrac{3}{4}$ irregular $(I-)$: $\tfrac{1}{4}$ regular $(ii)$ progeny. To determine the *phenotypic ratio* of the dihybrid cross $DdIi \times DdIi$, it should appeal to you as logical and as the *simplest* (though not necessarily therefore correct) expectation, that either the deep or shallow phenotype may be associated *at random* with either the irregular or regular phenotype if the two pairs of genes involved are on different pairs of chromosomes (recall the behavior of chromosomes from Chapter 3). That is, utilizing the

FIGURE 4-2. *Irregular venation pattern, produced by the dominant allele of the gene for regular venation in* Coleus.

product law of probability noted in Chapter 2, we expect the phenotypic ratio here to be the *product* of its two component monohybrid ratios, thus:

$$Dd \times Dd \text{ yields: } \tfrac{3}{4} \text{ deep } + \tfrac{1}{4} \text{ shallow}$$
$$Ii \times Ii \text{  yields: } \tfrac{3}{4} \text{ irregular } + \tfrac{1}{4} \text{ regular}$$

F₂ result, based on random combination of phenotypic classes:
$\tfrac{9}{16}$ deep irregular + $\tfrac{3}{16}$ shallow irregular + $\tfrac{3}{16}$ deep regular + $\tfrac{1}{16}$ shallow regular.

This is what we will actually observe as soon as F₂ seedlings have developed from this cross. It is also the same ratio that Mendel observed in his work with peas, and is one of the classic phenotypic ratios. On this basis, it

FIGURE 4-3. *A 9:3:3:1 purple-starchy:purple-sweet:white-starchy:white-sweet $F_2$ phenotypic ratio in corn. Sweet kernels are shriveled, starchy are plump.*

should also be possible to calculate readily the genotypic ratio of this cross:

$$Dd \times Dd \text{ yields:} \quad \tfrac{1}{4} DD + \tfrac{2}{4} Dd + \tfrac{1}{4} dd$$
$$Ii \times Ii \text{ yields:} \quad \tfrac{1}{4} II + \tfrac{2}{4} Ii + \tfrac{1}{4} ii$$
$$F_2 \text{ genotypes:} \quad \tfrac{1}{16} DDII + \tfrac{2}{16} DdII + \tfrac{1}{16} ddII$$
$$+ \tfrac{2}{16} DDIi + \tfrac{4}{16} DdIi + \tfrac{2}{16} ddIi$$
$$+ \tfrac{1}{16} DDii + \tfrac{2}{16} Ddii + \tfrac{1}{16} ddii$$

Closer examination of this $1:2:1:2:4:2:1:2:1$ genotypic ratio reveals the $9:3:3:1$ phenotypic ratio:

$$
\begin{array}{llll}
\tfrac{1}{16} DDII & \tfrac{1}{16} ddII & \tfrac{1}{16} DDii & \tfrac{1}{16} ddii \\
\tfrac{2}{16} DdII & \tfrac{2}{16} ddIi & \tfrac{2}{16} Ddii & \\
\tfrac{2}{16} DDIi & & & \\
\tfrac{4}{16} DdIi & & & \\
\hline
\tfrac{9}{16} D{-}I{-} + & \tfrac{3}{16} ddI{-} + & \tfrac{3}{16} D{-}ii + & \tfrac{1}{16} ddii \\
\text{deep} & \text{shallow} & \text{deep} & \text{shallow} \\
\text{irregular} & \text{irregular} & \text{regular} & \text{regular}
\end{array}
$$

Alternatively, we could have calculated this $9:3:3:1$ ratio more quickly in this fashion:

$$Dd \times Dd \text{ yields} \quad \tfrac{3}{4} D{-} + \tfrac{1}{4} dd$$
$$Ii \times Ii \quad \text{yields} \quad \tfrac{3}{4} I{-} + \tfrac{1}{4} ii$$

to get the same result as we obtained by collecting and summing the nine genotypes immediately above. It will be useful later on to recall this ratio:

$$
\begin{array}{l}
9 \ D{-}I{-} \\
3 \ ddI{-} \\
3 \ D{-}ii \\
1 \ ddii
\end{array}
$$

A $9:3:3:1$ $F_2$ phenotypic ratio in corn is shown in Fig. 4-3.

Note that, in calculating our expected two-pair results, we once more followed the probability method, avoiding the more cumberosme "checkerboard." This approach reflects the random association of different pairs of genes which is operating here and is more direct, especially in cases where one wishes to know what fraction of the progeny in a particular cross will be of a given genotype or phenotype. For instance, in this example with *Coleus*, the probability method permits an almost instant answer to such questions as what fraction of the offspring of the cross *DdIi* × *DdIi* will be (1) shallow irregular or (2) of the genotype *ddII*? In the first case, if we note that both parents are doubly heterozygous and that we seek just those offspring which combine the recessive phenotype of one trait with the dominant expression of the other character, it is clear that the cross *DdIi* × *DdIi* will produce $\frac{1}{4}$ shallow × $\frac{3}{4}$ irregular, or $\frac{3}{16}$. The second question is calculated in the same manner, the P individuals given producing $\frac{1}{4}$ of their progeny having *each* of the genotypes *dd* and *II*, or $\frac{1}{4} \times \frac{1}{4} = \frac{1}{16}$. Compare these calculations, which, with a little practice and remembering the classic 3 : 1 and 1 : 2 : 1 ratios, can be determined mentally, with the results previously arrived at on page 75. The same approach can be used to great advantage with trihybrid and other polyhybrid crosses where, as in the sample just given, only the specific information sought is obtained with no need for culling out those facts from a mass of unneeded information about the entire range of progeny types.

It is most important to recognize one tacit assumption involved in our method of calculating these particular dihybrid ratios. Recall particularly the behavior of chromosomes at meiosis and the subsequent gamete genotypes. If genes are indeed located on chromosomes, it is clear that our calculation (page 75) is based on the expectation that, in gametes, association of *D* with *I* or *i*, and of *d* with *I* or *i*, is random. Therefore we are implying *equal* numbers of four possible gamete genotypes: *DI*, *dI*, *Di*, and *di* from a *DdIi* individual. We could calculate the results of the cross *DdIi* × *DdIi* either as we did on page 75 or by expected gamete genotypes:

$$DdIi \ eggs: \quad \tfrac{1}{4} \ \textcircled{DI} \ + \ \tfrac{1}{4} \ \textcircled{dI} \ + \ \tfrac{1}{4} \ \textcircled{Di} \ + \ \tfrac{1}{4} \ \textcircled{di}$$

$$DdIi \ sperms: \quad \tfrac{1}{4} \ \textcircled{DI} \ + \ \tfrac{1}{4} \ \textcircled{dI} \ + \ \tfrac{1}{4} \ \textcircled{Di} \ + \ \tfrac{1}{4} \ \textcircled{di}$$

Satisfy yourself that, if gamete union is also random, the phenotypic and genotypic ratios arrived at in this way will be identical with those calculated on page 75. Production of four kinds of gametes in equal number by a doubly heterozygous individual will occur, of course, if each pair of genes is on a different pair of chromosomes. That is, each pair of genes here behaves exactly as it would in a one-pair cross. Therefore, *each pair of genes located on a different pair of chromosomes segregates independently of all other such pairs at meiosis*. Recall the behavior of chromosomes in meiosis, especially their metaphase-I arrangement and anaphase-I movement.

## GAMETE AND ZYGOTE COMBINATIONS

As seen earlier, a monohybrid such as *Dd* produces two kinds of gametes (*D* and *d*) in equal numbers which can combine by syngamy to form three different zygote genotypes (*DD, Dd, dd*), from which two phenotypes (deep and shallow) will be discernible in the progeny. Likewise, a doubly heterozygous individual (*DdIi*) produces four kinds of gametes (*DI, Di, dI, di*), again in equal numbers if the two pairs of genes are located on different chromosome pairs. With random syngamy, nine different zygote genotypes are produced:

$$\begin{array}{ll} DDII & Ddii \\ DDIi & ddII \\ DdII & ddIi \\ DdIi & ddii \\ DDii & \end{array}$$

from which four phenotypes (deep irregular, deep regular, shallow irregular, shallow regular) will be apparent in the young seedlings.

A third pair of genes in *Coleus* can be symbolized as follows:

*W* no white area at the base of the leaf blade
*w* white area at the base of the leaf blade

What gamete combinations can be produced by the trihybrid *DdIiWw*? If each of the three pairs of genes is on a different chromosome pair, then either allele of any pair can combine with either allele of any other pair. A simple application of the probability method indicates eight possible gamete genotypes. We have just seen that the dihybrid *DdIi* produces four gamete genotypes, $\frac{1}{4} DI + \frac{1}{4} Di + \frac{1}{4} dI + \frac{1}{4} di$. With the addition of the *W, w* pair, two additional gamete genotypes, *W* and *w*, become possible. These, of course, may combine with any of the dihybrid gamete genotypes:

$$\frac{1}{4} \; \boxed{DI} + \frac{1}{4} \; \boxed{Di} + \frac{1}{4} \; \boxed{dI} + \frac{1}{4} \; \boxed{di}$$
$$\frac{1}{2} \; \boxed{W} + \frac{1}{2} \; \boxed{w}$$

$\frac{1}{8}$ each of *DIW, DiW, dIW, diW, DIw, Diw, dIw, diw*

If we apply again the same probability method used for monohybrid and dihybrid cases, these 8 gamete genotypes may be expected to combine randomly into 27 zygote genotypes producing 8 phenotypic classes in the progeny.

Thus, considering the number of possible gamete genotypes per pair of heterozygous alleles in which dominance is complete and which are located on different chromosome pairs, we can detect the emergence of these mathematical relationships (where *n* = number of pairs of chromosomes with single gene differences):

**number of gamete genotypes produced by parents** $= 2^n$
**number of zygote genotypes of the progeny**          $= 3^n$
**number of progeny phenotypic classes**               $= 2^n$

These relationships are summarized and extended in Table 4-1.

TABLE 4-1. Gamete and Zygote Combinations Produced by Heterozygous
Parents (Dominance Complete in All Pairs)

| Number of Pairs of Heterozygous Genes | Number of Gamete Genotypes | Number of Zygote Genotypes | Number of Zygote Combinations | Number of Progeny Phenotypes |
|---|---|---|---|---|
| 1 | 2 | 3 | 4 | 2 |
| 2 | 4 | 9 | 16 | 4 |
| 3 | 8 | 27 | 64 | 8 |
| 4 | 16 | 81 | 256 | 16 |
| $n$ | $2^n$ | $3^n$ | $4^n$ | $2^n$ |

**TESTCROSS**

Just as the testcross is a useful way of determining homozygosity or heterozygosity of a dominant phenotype in one-pair cases, it is equally valuable in determining genotypes in situations with two or more pairs of genes. In a two-pair cross, where each pair of genes is on a different chromosome pair (i.e., the genes are not linked), the resulting progeny ratio can be seen to be the product of two one-pair ratios. Thus, as we have seen, a monohybrid testcross ratio is $1:1$, and a dihybrid testcross produces a $1:1:1:1$ ratio when one parent is heterozygous for both gene pairs:

P                              $DdIi \times ddii$
P gametes    $\frac{1}{4}$ (DI) $+ \frac{1}{4}$ (dI) $+ \frac{1}{4}$ (Di) $+ \frac{1}{4}$ (di)
                           1 (di)

---

F$_1$        $\frac{1}{4}$ DdIi    $+ \frac{1}{4}$ ddIi    $+ \frac{1}{4}$ Ddii    $+ \frac{1}{4}$ ddii
            deep        shallow      deep        shallow
            irregular   irregular    regular     regular

Such a testcross is a very useful technique in mapping of gene locations on chromosomes, as we shall see in Chapter 6.

With the information you now have, you might also find it useful to determine testcross ratios in (1) cases where only one of two pairs is heterozygous and (2) trihybrids or other polyhybrids. Problems at the end of this chapter explore cases such as these.

## Modifications of the 9:3:3:1 Ratio

### INCOMPLETE DOMINANCE

We have seen the breeding results in dihybrids where dominance is complete. What effect on ratios and on numbers of phenotypic classes does incomplete dominance in one or both pairs produce?

In tomato, two pairs of genes, located on different pairs of chromosomes, are

$D-$    tall plant     $h_1h_1$    hairless stems
$dd$    dwarf plant    $h_1h_2$    scattered short hairs
                        $h_2h_2$    very hairy stems

Crossing two individuals of the genotype $Ddh_1h_2$ produces progeny as follows:

$\frac{3}{16}$ tall, hairless
$\frac{6}{16}$ tall, scattered hairs
$\frac{3}{16}$ tall, very hairy
$\frac{1}{16}$ dwarf, hairless
$\frac{2}{16}$ dwarf, scattered hairs
$\frac{1}{16}$ dwarf, very hairy

Note that this is precisely what one would expect. Tall and dwarf segregate in a 3:1 ratio, and hairless, scattered hairs, and very hairy segregate in a 1:2:1 ratio, producing a 3:6:3:1:2:1 ratio here. In such a case as this, because $Dd \times Dd$ produces two phenotypic classes in the offspring, and $h_1h_2 \times h_1h_2$ is responsible for three phenotypic classes, the cross $Ddh_1h_2 \times Ddh_1h_2$ produces offspring of $2 \times 3 = 6$ phenotypic classes. Adding to our mathematical expressions developed on page 78, we see that, if dominance is *in*complete, the number of phenotypic classes is $3^n$ (where again $n =$ the number of chromosome pairs with a single gene difference). In a dihybrid situation where one pair of genes exhibits complete dominance and the other incomplete dominance, as in this example from tomato, the number of $F_1$ phenotypic classes from two doubly heterozygous P is $2^n \times 3^n$.

Thus, again, incomplete dominance increases the number of phenotypic classes. Further possibilities of this sort are suggested in some of the problems at the end of this chapter.

### EPISTASIS

*Mouse.* The laboratory mouse occurs in a number of colors and patterns. The wild type,[1] or "agouti," is characterized by color-banded hairs in which

---

[1] That is, the customary or most frequently encountered phenotype in natural populations, often used as a standard of comparison.

the part nearest the skin is gray, then a yellow band, and finally the distal part is either black or brown. The wild type has rather obvious selection value in natural surroundings where it enhances concealment of the individual. Two other colors are albino and solid black. In albinos there is a total lack of pigment, producing white hair and pink eyes (the latter results when blood vessel color shows through unpigmented irises).

The cross *black* × *albino* produces a uniform $F_1$ of agouti which, in certain instances, when inbred, results in an $F_2$ of 9 *agouti* : 3 *black* : 4 *albino*. The segregation of the $F_2$ into sixteenths immediately suggests two pairs of genes, and this particular ratio implies a $9:3:3:1$ ratio in which the $\frac{1}{16}$ class and one of the $\frac{3}{16}$ classes are indistinguishable.[2] These results would then indicate further that the $F_1$ individuals in this case are heterozygous for both pairs of genes. We could assume one of the two pairs of genes to include one allele for color production and another allele for color inhibition (the latter perhaps responsible for either a defective enzyme or the absence of a particular enzyme required for a specific intermediate biochemical step in pigment production). We might further assume the other pair of genes to include one allele for agouti and one for black. Let us try genotypes as follows:

$$A \quad \text{agouti} \qquad C \quad \text{color}$$
$$a \quad \text{black} \qquad\; c \quad \text{color inhibition}$$

Note that dominance of agouti over black is suggested by the $\frac{9}{16}$ agouti class versus the $\frac{3}{16}$ black in the $F_2$ (this is tantamount to a $3:1$ segregation). On these assumptions, the cross in mouse may be diagrammed in this way:

$$P \quad \text{black} \times \text{albino}$$
$$\quad\; aaCC \quad AAcc$$

$$F_1 \qquad \text{agouti}$$
$$\qquad\; AaCc$$

$$F_2 \quad \tfrac{9}{16}\; A-C-\text{agouti}$$
$$\qquad \tfrac{3}{16}\; aaC-\quad \text{black}$$
$$\qquad \left.\begin{array}{l}\tfrac{3}{16}\; A-cc\\[2pt]\tfrac{1}{16}\; aacc\end{array}\right\} \text{albino}$$

In this particular example, gene *c* (which is recessive to its own allele *C*) actually masked the effect of either $A-$ or $aa$ so that any $-cc$ individual is albino. Such a gene which masks the effect of one or both members of a *different* pair of genes is said to be *epistatic*; the masked gene or genes may be termed hypostatic. Here, *c* is epistatic to *a* and *A*, and we may refer to this case as one of recessive epistasis, since it is the recessive of one pair that is epistatic to another pair. Note that epistasis is quite different from dominance.

---

[2] How could you determine that this is *not* an approximation of a $1:2:1$ ratio?

FIGURE 4-4. *A 9:7 purple:yellow epistatic ratio in corn.*

*Clover.* An interesting example in white clover (*Trifolium repens*, the clover so frequently seen in lawns), reported in 1943 by Atwood and Sullivan, furnishes presumptive evidence that epistasis depends on a gene-enzyme relationship in a series of sequential biochemical steps.

Some strains of white clover test high in hydrocyanic acid (HCN), whereas others test negatively for this substance. HCN content is associated with more vigorous growth; it does not harm cattle eating such varieties. Often the cross *positive × negative* results in an $F_1$ testing uniformly positive for HCN and an $F_2$ segregating 3 positive : 1 negative, clearly suggesting a single pair of genes with positive dominant.

One series of crosses reported by Atwood and Sullivan, however, produced unexpected totals:

P       positive × negative
$F_1$            positive
$F_2$      351 positive + 256 negative

A 3:1 expectancy in the $F_2$ would be approximately 455 positive : 152 negative; the actual results differ sufficiently from a 3:1 ratio to cast doubt on its relevance here. (Statistical tests, described in Chapter 5, give objective support to the hypothesis that, although a ratio of 351:256 *could* occur by chance alone in a 3:1 expectancy, this result is unlikely enough to cause one to look for a better explanation.) Note that these results are very close to a 9:7 ratio, which would be 342 positive : 265 negative. A 9:7 ratio immediately suggests an epistatic expression of the 9:3:3:1 which, in turn, indicates two pairs of genes. One such 9:7 ratio (purple : yellow) in corn is illustrated in Fig. 4-4.

It is known that HCN formation follows a path which may be represented thus:

$$\longrightarrow \text{(precursor)} \xrightarrow{\text{enzyme } ``\alpha\,"} \text{cyanogenic glucoside} \xrightarrow{\text{enzyme } ``\beta\,"} \text{HCN}$$

Each of the conversions indicated by the arrows is enzymatically controlled. Tests of $F_2$ individuals of the cross just described for (1) HCN, (2) enzyme "$\beta$," and (3) cyanogenic glucoside revealed four classes of individuals:

| Class | HCN | Enzyme "$\beta$" | Glucoside |
|-------|-----|------------------|-----------|
| 1 | + | + | + |
| 2 | 0 | + | 0 |
| 3 | 0 | 0 | + |
| 4 | 0 | 0 | 0 |

Each of these four classes was then tested for HCN after adding either enzyme "$\beta$" or glucoside to their leaf extracts, with the following results:

| Class | Control Test for HCN | HCN Test After Adding Enzyme "$\beta$" | HCN Test After Adding Glucoside |
|-------|----------------------|----------------------------------------|---------------------------------|
| 1 | + | + | + |
| 2 | 0 | 0 | + |
| 3 | 0 | + | 0 |
| 4 | 0 | 0 | 0 |

Thus it appears that class 1 plants produce both glucoside and enzyme "$\beta$" (and, by inference, also enzyme "$\alpha$"); class 2 plants produce enzyme "$\beta$" but no glucoside (hence, by inference, no enzyme "$\alpha$"); class 3 plants produce glucoside (and, therefore, enzyme "$\alpha$") but no enzyme "$\beta$"; class 4 plants produce neither enzyme "$\beta$" nor glucoside (therefore, by inference, no enzyme "$\alpha$"). We can summarize our conclusions in tabular form:

| | Production | | | Substance Accumulating |
|-------|------------|-----------|-----------|------------------------|
| Class | Enzyme "$\alpha$" | Glucoside | Enzyme "$\beta$" | |
| 1 | + | + | + | HCN |
| 2 | 0 | 0 | + | precursor |
| 3 | + | + | 0 | glucoside |
| 4 | 0 | 0 | 0 | precursor |

It therefore seems highly likely that production of enzyme "$\alpha$" and "$\beta$" is determined by two different pairs of genes:

$$\longrightarrow \text{(precursor)} \xrightarrow[\text{enzyme "}\alpha\text{"}]{\textit{Gene A}} \text{cyanogenic glucoside} \xrightarrow[\text{enzyme "}\beta\text{"}]{\textit{Gene B}} \text{HCN}$$

So an individual must have at least one dominant of each of two pairs of genes, *A* and *B*, in order to carry the process from precursor to HCN. We may now add genotypes to the cross developed on page 81 as follows:

P      positive × negative
    *AABB*    *aabb*

$F_1$       positive
       *AaBb*

$F_2$  $\frac{9}{16}$ HCN positive $A-B-$ ("class 1")    (9)
    $\frac{3}{16}$ HCN negative *aaB−*   ("class 2")
    $\frac{3}{16}$ HCN negative $A-bb$ ("class 3")    (7)
    $\frac{1}{16}$ HCN negative *aabb* ("class 4")

A little reflection will serve to indicate that this situation may be considered in any of the following ways:

    9 : 7   HCN : no HCN
   12 : 4   glucoside : no glucoside
   9 : 3 : 4   HCN : glucoside : precursor
9 : 3 : 3 : 1   enzymes "$\alpha$" and "$\beta$" : enzyme "$\beta$" only:
            enzyme "$\alpha$" only : neither enzyme

The ratio we choose depends, of course, on the level of chemical analysis to which consideration is carried. Thus, we are talking about phenotype in terms of chemical reaction and content or of enzyme production. Because enzymes are proteins in whole or in part, this, in turn, suggests again a relationship between gene and enzyme and, therefore, between protein synthesis and phenotype. This will be a promising avenue to explore later in this book.

Incidentally, an explanation for the occurrence of all positive cyanide content progeny from crosses of negative × negative (which is also reported) works out on these bases quite readily:

P      negative × negative
    *aaBB*    *AAbb*

$F_1$      positive
       *AaBb*

The cross (P) positive × negative which produces an $F_2$ of 3 positive : 1 negative, referred to on page 81, genotypically would look like this:

P      positive × negative
    *AABB*    *aaBB*

$F_1$     positive
      *AaBB*

$F_2$  3 positive : 1 negative
    $A-BB$    *aaBB*

We can recognize epistasis (which can operate in any cross involving two or more pairs of genes) *by the reduction in number of expected phenotypic classes*

TABLE 4-2. Summary of Dihybrid Ratios in F$_2$ of the Cross $AABB \times aabb$

| | | AABB | AABb | AaBB | AaBb | AAbb | Aabb | aaBB | aaBb | aabb |
|---|---|---|---|---|---|---|---|---|---|---|
| More than 4 phenotypic classes | A and B both incompletely dominant | 1 | 2 | 2 | 4 | 1 | 2 | 1 | 2 | 1 |
| | A incompletely dominant; B completely dominant | | 3 | | 6 | 1 | 2 | | 3 | 1 |
| 4 phenotypic classes | A and B both completely dominant (classic ratio) | | | | 9 | | 3 | | 3 | 1 |
| Fewer than 4 phenotypic classes | aa epistatic to B and b  Recessive epistasis | | | | 9 | | 3 | | | 4 |
| | A epistatic to B and b  Dominant epistasis | | | | 12 | | | | 3 | 1 |
| | A epistatic to B and b; bb epistatic to A and a  Dominant and recessive epistasis | | | | 13* | | | | 3 | |
| | aa epistatic to B and b; bb epistatic to A and a  Duplicate recessive epistasis | | | | 9 | | | 7 | | |
| | A epistatic to B and b; B epistatic to A and a  Duplicate dominant epistasis | | | | | 15 | | | | 1 |
| | Duplicate interaction | | | | 9 | | | 6 | | 1 |

* The 13 is composed of the 12 classes immediately above, plus the 1 *aabb* from the last column.

in which two or more of the classes become indistinguishable from each other.

Many other ratios are, of course, possible and have been reported in the literature. Additional examples are included in the problems at the end of this chapter, as well as in Table 4-2. One of these, however, requires additional explanation. In certain breeds of domestic fowl (e.g., White Leghorn), individuals are white because of a dominant color-inhibiting gene *I*. Even though birds may carry genes for color, such genes cannot be expressed in the presence of *I*−. On the other hand, such breeds as the White Silkie, are white because they are homozygous for the recessive gene *c*, which blocks synthesis of a necessary pigment precursor.

Crosses of White Leghorn (*IICC*) × White Silkie (*iicc*) produce an $F_2$ ratio of 13:3 as follows:

9 *I*−*C*− white (because of color-inhibitor *I*)
3 *iiC*− colored
3 *I*−*cc* white (because of both *I* and *cc*)
1 *iicc* white (because of *cc*)

The actual color of the *iiC*− individuals depends on the presence of additional genes for particular colors. These are not shown here.

## LETHAL GENES

It no doubt occurs to you that lethal genes also reduce the number of expected phenotypic classes in a two-pair cross, but the change is somewhat different from that caused by epistasis. For example, consider the case of corn where tall (*D*−) and dwarf (*dd*) phenotypes are known in addition to the green and "albino" condition described in Chapter 2. Note that the cross *DdGg* × *DdGg* will produce the classic 9:3:3:1 phenotypic ratio of seedlings, but because of the lethal effect of *gg*, this becomes 9 tall green : 3 dwarf green (that is, 3 tall : 1 dwarf) after *gg* has exerted its lethal effect. In man, for example, consider the dominant lethal for Huntington's chorea (Chapter 2) together with another pair of genes, free ear lobes (*A*−) versus attached ear lobes (*aa*) (Fig. 1-1). A marriage involving two double heterozygotes, *HhAa* (where *H* represents the dominant lethal for chorea, and *h* its recessive allele for "normal"), would, statistically (or actually in collections of family data), produce a 9:3:3:1 ratio initially, which would ultimately become 3 free (normal) : 1 attached (normal) after the choreic individuals had died.

## REFERENCES

ATWOOD, S. S., and J. T. SULLIVAN, 1943. Inheritance of a Cyanogenetic Glucoside and Its Hydrolyzing Enzyme in *Trifolium repens*. *Jour. Hered.*, **34**: 311–320.

STEWART, R. N., and T. ARISUMI, 1966. Genetic and Histogenic Determination of Pink Bract Color in Poinsettia. *Jour Hered.*, **57**: 217–220.

## PROBLEMS

**4-1.** If two *DdIi Coleus* plants are crossed, what fraction of the offspring will be (a) shallow irregular; (b) deep regular; (c) *DDIi*; (d) *ddII*?

**4-2.** How many progeny phenotypic classes result if two *Coleus* plants (a) of genotype *DdIiWw* are crossed; (b) heterozygous for one pair of genes (showing complete dominance) on each of its pairs of chromosomes?

**4-3.** What is the phenotypic ratio of the testcross (a) *DdII* x *ddii* in Coleus? (b) *DdIiWw* x *ddiiww* in *Coleus*?

**4-4.** How many phenotypic classes are produced by a testcross where one parent is heterozygous for (a) 2 pairs of genes; (b) 3 pairs of genes; (c) 4 pairs of genes; (d) *n* pairs of genes?

**4-5.** How many different progeny phenotypic classes result from self-pollinating a plant of genotype *AaBbCcDdEe*?

**4-6.** How many different progeny genotypic classes result from the cross given in problem 4-5?

**4-7.** You raise 100 tomato plants from seed received from a friend and find 37 red-fruited plants with scattered short hairs on stems and leaves, 19 red hairless, 18 red very hairy, 13 yellow fruited with scattered short hairs, 7 yellow very hairy and 6 yellow hairless. Suggest genotypes and phenotypes for the unknown parent plants from which the 100 seeds were obtained.

**4-8.** Coat in guinea pigs may be either long or short; matings of short × short may produce long haired progeny, but long × long gives rise only to long. Additionally, coat color may be yellow, cream, or white. The mating cream × cream produces progeny of each of the three colors. Given the following incomplete pedigree:

$$P \quad \text{long yellow} \times \text{short white}$$
$$F_1 \qquad\qquad \text{all short} \text{——}$$

(a) What is the coat color in the $F_1$? (b) If members of the $F_1$ were interbred, what fraction of their progeny would be long cream?

**4-9.** Normal hearing depends upon the presence of at least one dominant of each of two pairs of genes, *D* and *E*. If you examined the collective progeny of a large number of *DdEe* x *DdEe* marriages, what phenotypic ratio would you expect to find?

**4-10.** In sweet pea the cross white flowers × white flowers produced an $F_1$ of all purple flowers. An $F_2$ of 350 white and 450 purple was then obtained. (a) What is the phenotypic ratio in the $F_2$? Using the first letter of the alphabet and as many more in sequence as needed, give (b) the genotype of the purple $F_2$; (c) the genotype of the $F_1$; (d) the genotypes of the two P individuals.

**4-11.** The fruit of the weed shepherd's purse (*Capsella bursa-pastoris*) is ordinarily heart-shaped in outline and somewhat flattened, but occasionally individuals with ovoid fruits occur. Crosses between pure-breeding heart and ovoid yield all heart in the $F_1$. Selfing this $F_1$ produces an $F_2$ in which 6 per cent of the individuals are ovoid. Starting with the first letter of the alphabet, and using as many more as necessary, give the genotypes of (a) ovoid; (b) $F_1$ heart; (c) $F_2$ heart.

**4-12.** In the mouse, $C-$ animals are pigmented, $cc$ individuals are albino. Another pair of genes determines the difference between black ($B-$) and brown ($bb$). What $F_2$ will be produced as a result of the cross $CCBB \times ccbb$?

**4-13.** In some plants cyanidin, a red pigment, is synthesized enzymatically from a colorless precursor; delphinidin, a purple pigment may be made from cyanidin by the enzymatic addition of one —OH group to the cyanidin molecule. In one cross where these pigments were involved, purple × purple produced $F_1$ progeny as follows: 81 purple, 27 red, and 36 white. (a) How many pairs of genes are involved? (b) What is the genotype of the purple parents? (c) What is the genotype of each of the three $F_1$ phenotypic classes? (Use as many letters of the alphabet as needed, starting with $A$.)

**4-14.** In terms of *enzyme production*, instead of flower color, as a phenotypic character in the data of problem 4-13, what is the $F_1$ phenotypic ratio? The enzyme catalyzing conversion of percursor to cyanidin may be designated enzyme #1, and that controlling the production of delphinidin from cyanidin may be designated enzyme #2.

**4-15.** In the plants of problem 4-13, one cross of white × red produced all purple progeny, whereas another white × red cross gave rise to 1 purple:2 white:1 red. What were the parental genotypes in each of these two crosses?

**4-16.** In addition to the round, oval, and long radishes mentioned in Chapter 2, radishes may be red, purple, or white in color. Red × white produces progeny all of which are purple. If purple oval were crossed with purple oval, how many pure-breeding types occur in the progeny?

**4-17.** In cattle, "short spine" is lethal shortly after birth; it is caused by the homozygous recessive genotype, $ss$. Heterozygotes are normal. A series of matings between roan animals heterozygous for the short spine gene produces what phenotypic ratio (a) at birth and (b) after several days?

**4-18.** In the summer squash, fruits may be white, yellow, or green. In one case, the cross of yellow × white produced an $F_1$ of all white-fruited plants which, when selfed, gave an $F_2$ segregating 12 white : 3 yellow : 1 green. (a) Suggest genotypes for the white, yellow, and green phenotypes. (b) Give genotypes of the P, $F_1$, and $F_2$ of this cross. Use genotype symbols starting with the first letter of the alphabet.

**4-19.** Summer squash fruit shape may be disk, sphere, or elongate. The cross of sphere × sphere produced an $F_1$ with all disk-shaped fruits. Selfing the $F_1$ gave 9 disk : 6 sphere: 1 elongate. (a) Suggest genotypes for disk, sphere, and elongate. (b) Give genotypes of the P, $F_1$, and $F_2$ of this cross. Use genotype symbols beginning with the first letter of the alphabet *after* those used for problem 4-18.

**4-20.** Considering the facts suggested by problems 4-18 and 4-19, how many different genotypes are responsible for the (a) yellow sphere; (b) elongate green; (c) disk white phenotypes?

**4-21.** A tetrahybrid white disk plant is selfed; (a) how many phenotypic classes could occur in its $F_1$? (b) What fraction of the $F_1$ will be white disk?

**4-22.** In Duroc Jersey pigs, two pairs of interacting genes, $R$ and $S$, are known.

(a) The cross of red × red sometimes produces an $F_1$ phenotypic ratio of 9 red:6 sandy:1 white; what is the genotype of each of these $F_1$ phenotypes? (b) For each of the crosses that follow, give the parental genotypes:

| P | $F_1$ | $F_2$ |
|---|---|---|
| Case 1.  Red × red | All red | All red |
| Case 2.  Red × red | 3 red : 1 sandy | Not reported |
| Case 3.  Red × white | All red | 9 red : 6 sandy : 1 white |
| Case 4.  Sandy × sandy | All red | 9 red : 6 sandy : 1 white |
| Case 5.  Sandy × sandy | 1 red : 2 sandy : 1 white | Not reported. |

**4-23.** Determine the genotypic and phenotypic ratios resulting from each of the following dihybrid crosses (assume lethals to exert their effect during early embryo development):

| Parental Genotypes | Gene Characteristics | | Progeny Ratios | |
|---|---|---|---|---|
| | First Pair | Second Pair | Genotypic | Phenotypic |
| (a)  $AaBb \times AaBb$ | Complete Dominance | Complete Dominance | | |
| (b)  $Aab_1b_2 \times Aab_1b_2$ | Complete Dominance | Incomplete Dominance | | |
| (c)  $a_1a_2b_1b_2 \times a_1a_2b_1b_2$ | Incomplete Dominance | Incomplete Dominance | | |
| (d)  $AaBb \times AaBb$ | Complete Dominance | Recessive Lethal | | |
| (e)  $a_1a_2Bb \times a_1a_2Bb$ | Incomplete Dominance | Recessive Lethal | | |
| (f)  $AaBb \times AaBb$ | Recessive Lethal | Recessive Lethal | | |

**4-24.** In a hypothetical flowering plant assume petal color to be due to a pair of codominant genes, $a_1$ and $a_2$, heterozygotes being purple, and homozygotes either red ($a_1a_1$) or blue ($a_2a_2$). Assume also another pair of genes, completely dominant $B$ for color, and recessive $b$ for color inhibition. This pair is not linked to the $a_1$, $a_2$ pair. Two doubly heterozygous purple plants, $a_1a_2Bb$, are crossed. What phenotypic ratio results in the progeny?

# CHAPTER 5
# *Probability and Goodness of Fit*

**A**N understanding of the laws of probability is of fundamental importance in (1) appreciating the operation of genetic mechanisms, (2) predicting the likelihood of certain results from a given cross, and (3) assessing how well an $F_1$ phenotypic ratio fits a particular postulated genetic mechanism. We have already been applying one of the fundamental laws of probability in our study of dihybrid ratios in the preceding chapter, based on transmission of two pairs of genes which are assumed to be on separate chromosome pairs. That law is the law of the probability of coincident independent events, and states, in essence, that **the chance (or probability) of the simultaneous occurrence of two or more independent events is equal to the product of the probabilities that each will occur separately.** Application of this " product law of probability " to genetics permits elucidation of the three points referred to.

## Two Independent, Nongenetic Events
### SINGLE-COIN TOSSES

The laws of probability can be applied to *any* chance or random event. For example, a coin tossed into the air and allowed to come to rest is likely to land either " heads " or " tails," if we neglect the highly improbable chance of its landing on edge. We would, therefore, predict (on the basis of certain implicit assumptions to be detailed) that, in the total array of possibilities (heads plus tails), the probability of a " head " is one in two, or $\frac{1}{2}$, and the same for a " tail." But if we toss one coin four successive times, we would surely not be surprised to get some ratio other than 2 heads : 2 tails. In addition to that possibility, one should expect, on occasion, to get such a combination as 4 heads, or 3 heads and 1 tail, or 1 head and 3 tails, or even 4 tails. If, however, a very large number of tosses were to be made, we would expect to come quite close to a 1 : 1 ratio. Note that we are assuming successive tosses to be independent of each other; that is, the result of one toss has no effect on any succeeding toss.

### TWO-COIN TOSSES

What can we expect if we toss two coins simultaneously for, say, 50 tosses? Let us approach this problem through some actual situations. Two students were each asked to toss two coins simultaneously 50 times by shaking the coins in closed, cupped hands and letting them fall lightly on a table. Ignoring the possibility of a coin landing " on edge," only two results can occur: each coin will come to rest flat on the table, with either one side (which we elect to call "heads") up or the other side (which we elect to call "tails") up. With two coins, then, the outcome of any single toss will be: HH, HT, or TT. The result of the series of tosses by student "A" was

$$
\begin{array}{ll}
\text{HH} & 12 \\
\text{HT} & 27 \\
\text{TT} & 11
\end{array}
$$

Now, one has to ask himself, "Are these the results I could have expected, based on the theory that each coin has an equal chance of landing either 'heads' or 'tails'?" Or, in a genetic experiment, having made a given cross and gotten certain results, "What possible mechanism could be operating in order to produce these results?" In either a coin toss or a genetic breeding experiment, one of the first necessary steps is to formulate certain hypotheses to predict or explain results, then ask oneself whether, *in terms of those hypotheses, deviation from the predicted result is within limits set by chance alone?* If so, sufficient credence can be placed in the hypothesis to use it in predicting outcomes of untried cases; if not, we will have to alter our hypotheses.

In order to make a judgment on this question, one must make several simplifying assumptions about the coins and the general conditions surrounding the experiment itself. We would have to ask ourselves: *were the coins themselves unbiased*; that is, were they so constructed physically that each coin had an equal chance of landing "heads" or "tails"? Since we have no real evidence to the contrary, let us assume, at least for the time being, that our coins are indeed unbiased. If this assumption should turn out not to be true, then our ultimate evaluation of the results will have to be changed.

We must also examine the question of whether the "headness" or "tailness" of the fall of one of the two coins will have any effect on the fall of the second coin. That is to say, if two coins are tossed simultaneously, does *each* one of them have an *equal* chance of coming to rest heads or tails? Certainly in this experiment there should be no more than a remote chance that the ultimate fall of one coin affects the other. Therefore, our *second assumption* will be that *the coins themselves are independent of each other.*

A *third assumption* we will have to make, at least at the outset, is that *successive tosses (events) are also independent of each other.* This would imply, for example, that having gotten two heads the first toss does not in any way affect the outcome of the second or any other toss.

If, then, we assume for the present that the coins are (1) unbiased and (2) independent of each other and also that (3) the several trials or tosses are likewise independent of each other, what kind of results would we *expect* to get? Obviously, each coin has one chance in two, or a probability of $\frac{1}{2}$, of coming to rest heads and a probability of $\frac{1}{2}$ of landing tails. By the product law of probability, the chance of *both* coins showing heads in the same toss is $\frac{1}{2} \times \frac{1}{2}$ or $\frac{1}{4}$. We see our student did, indeed, get two heads in almost exactly one fourth of his tosses.

Likewise, the probability of having two tails simultaneously is also $\frac{1}{2} \times \frac{1}{2} = \frac{1}{4}$. This result was not quite obtained in the example under consideration.

What should we expect with regard to one head and one tail? The chance of coin 1 landing heads is $\frac{1}{2}$; the chance of coin 2 coming to rest tails is also $\frac{1}{2}$. Now $\frac{1}{2} \times \frac{1}{2} = \frac{1}{4}$, but the total array of possibilities thus arrived at ($\frac{1}{4}$ HH + $\frac{1}{4}$ TT + $\frac{1}{4}$ HT) equals only three fourths, leaving one fourth of the possibilities unaccounted for. Note that the chance of one head plus one tail is really the sum of the probability of coin 1 being heads and coin 2 being tails, *plus* the probability of coin 1 being tails and coin 2 being heads; i.e., our HT category is really HT + TH, or 2 HT. Therefore, the probability of one head and one tail is $2(\frac{1}{2} \times \frac{1}{2})$, or $\frac{1}{2}$.

The general statement for two independent events of known probability may be stated as $a^2 + 2ab + b^2$, where $a$ represents the probability of a head and $b$ the probability of a tail. If, as in this instance, $a$ and $b$ each equal $\frac{1}{2}$, then the value of this expression upon substitution becomes $(\frac{1}{2})^2 + 2(\frac{1}{2} \times \frac{1}{2}) + (\frac{1}{2})^2$ or $\frac{1}{4} + \frac{2}{4} + \frac{1}{4} = 1$. Notice that the total array of probabilities here is one, and also that $a^2 + 2ab + b^2$ is the expansion of the binomial $(a + b)^2$.

Our observations and expectations for a two-coin toss can therefore be summarized as follows:

| Class | Observed | Expected |
|-------|----------|----------|
| HH | 12 | 12.5 |
| HT | 27 | 25.0 |
| TT | 11 | 12.5 |
|  | 50 | 50.0 |

Student B's results, however, were a little different:

| Class | Observed | Expected |
|-------|----------|----------|
| HH | 10 | 12.5 |
| HT | 33 | 25.0 |
| TT | 7 | 12.5 |
|  | 50 | 50.0 |

Obviously the first set of data is closer to the results expected with our assumptions, yet the second set of results *was*, nevertheless, actually obtained. We shall shortly examine each of these sets of data to see if the departure from the expected results is too great for *chance alone* to have operated.

### FOUR-COIN TOSSES

But let us first examine an experiment involving four coins tossed together 100 times. The possible combinations of heads and tails, and the results actually obtained in a particular trial, are as follows:

| Class | Observed |
|-------|----------|
| HHHH  | 9        |
| HHHT  | 32       |
| HHTT  | 29       |
| HTTT  | 25       |
| TTTT  | 5        |

Having found that the expansion of $(a + b)^2$ enables us to determine a set of (ideal) expected results in a two-coin toss, let us try, for the four-coin toss, expanding $(a + b)^4$ to determine the expectancy. Again, let

$$a = \text{probability of a head for any coin} = \tfrac{1}{2}$$

and

$$b = \text{probability of a tail for any coin} = \tfrac{1}{2}$$

Expanding $(a + b)^4$, we get

$$a^4 + 4a^3b + 6a^2b^2 + 4ab^3 + b^4$$

Substituting the numerical values of $a$ and $b$, we arrive at

$$(\tfrac{1}{2})^4 + 4[(\tfrac{1}{2})^3 \cdot \tfrac{1}{2}] + 6[(\tfrac{1}{2})^2 \cdot (\tfrac{1}{2})^2] + 4[(\tfrac{1}{2}) \cdot (\tfrac{1}{2})^3] + (\tfrac{1}{2})^4 = 1$$

or

$$\tfrac{1}{16} + \tfrac{4}{16} + \tfrac{6}{16} + \tfrac{4}{16} + \tfrac{1}{16} = 1$$

The first term of the expression, $(\tfrac{1}{2})^4$, gives us the probability of all four coins coming up heads simultaneously; the second term the probability of 3 heads $(a^3)$ plus 1 tail $(b)$, and so on. We can now compare our observed results with these calculated results for expectancy in a 4-coin toss:

| Class | Observed | Calculated | |
|-------|----------|------------|---|
| HHHH  | 9        | 6.25       | $(= \tfrac{1}{16} \text{ of } 100)$ |
| HHHT  | 32       | 25.00      | $(= \tfrac{4}{16} \text{ of } 100)$ |
| HHTT  | 29       | 37.50      | $(= \tfrac{6}{16} \text{ of } 100)$ |
| HTTT  | 25       | 25.00      | $(= \tfrac{4}{16} \text{ of } 100)$ |
| TTTT  | 5        | 6.25       | $(= \tfrac{1}{16} \text{ of } 100)$ |
|       | 100      | 100.00     | |

Again we are faced with the problem of determining *how well* our observations compare with the results expected on the basis of our three assumptions with only chance deviations—that is, whether we should accept our results as chance expressions of two- and four-coin tosses wherein the coins are unbiased and independent of each other, as are successive tosses. We shall probe this question very shortly.

## The Binomial Expression

Answers to many genetic problems involving "either-or" situations, including those with which members of the medical or legal profession must deal from time to time, are easily provided by the binomial approach. Therefore, we should be certain we understand the method of binomial expansion before going on. Rather than multiplying out algebraically, one can remember the following simple rules for expansion of $(a + b)^n$:

1. *The power of the binomial chosen, that is, the value of* n, *is determined by the number of coins, individuals, etc.* Thus, for two coins the expression $(a + b)^2$ is used, even if the coins are tossed 20 times; for a four-coin toss, $(a + b)^4$, etc. The same principle applies to families of $n$ children displaying one or the other of two phenotypic expressions.
2. *The number of terms in the expansion is* n + 1. Thus $(a + b)^2$ expands to $a^2 + 2ab + b^2$, having three terms, $(a + b)^4$ expanded contains five terms, etc.
3. *Every term of the expansion contains both* a *and* b. The power of $a$ in the first term equals $n$, the power of the binomial, and descends in units of one to zero in the last term (and $a^0$, which equals 1, is not written in); likewise, $b$ increases from $b^0$ (not written) in the first term to $b^n$ in the last. Furthermore, the sum of the powers *in each term* equals $n$. Check this against the expansion of $(a + b)^4$ just used.
4. *The coefficient of the first term is* 1 (not written); the coefficient of the second term is found by multiplying the coefficient of the preceding term by the exponent of $a$ and dividing by the number indicating the position of that preceding term in the series:

coefficient of next term =

$$\frac{\text{coefficient of preceding term} \times \text{exponent of preceding term}}{\text{ordinal number of preceding term}}$$

The same principle may be represented graphically in the form of Pascal's triangle, where each coefficient is shown as the sum of two numbers immediately above:

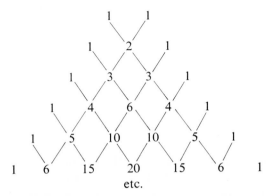

etc.

Note that the second coefficient in each horizontal like also represents the power of the binomial. Thus, the second number of the last line is 6, so that this line represents the series of coefficients in the expansion of $(a + b)^6$.

Thus, in expanding $(a + b)^4$, the first term is $a^4$ (for $1a^4b^0$). The second is $4a^3b$; i.e., from the preceding term, $a^4$,

$$\frac{4 \times 1}{1} = 4$$

which is the coefficient of the second term. The third term, which from rule 3 we know contains $a^2b^2$, becomes $6a^2b^2$ in the same way:

$$\frac{4 \times 3}{2} = 6$$

and so on.

In this way we obtain the binomial expansions listed in Table 5-1.

TABLE 5-1. Expansions of Binomials

| | |
|---|---|
| $(a + b)^1$ | $a + b$ |
| $(a + b)^2$ | $a^2 + 2ab + b^2$ |
| $(a + b)^3$ | $a^3 + 3a^2b + 3ab^2 + b^3$ |
| $(a + b)^4$ | $a^4 + 4a^3b + 6a^2b^2 + 4ab^3 + b^4$ |
| $(a + b)^5$ | $a^5 + 5a^4b + 10a^3b^2 + 10a^2b^3 + 5ab^4 + b^5$ |
| $(a + b)^6$ | $a^6 + 6a^5b + 15a^4b^2 + 20a^3b^3 + 15a^2b^4 + 6ab^5 + b^6$ |

If $a$ and $b$ are each equal to $\frac{1}{2}$, this yields symmetrical *probability curves* as shown in Fig. 5-1. On the other hand, if $a = \frac{3}{4}$ and $b = \frac{1}{4}$, a skewed curve is obtained as indicated in Fig. 5-2.

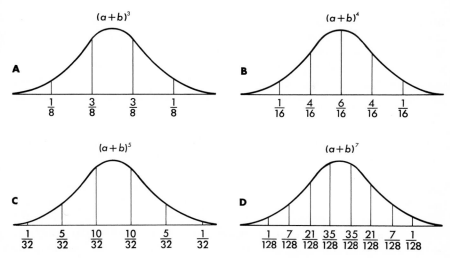

FIGURE 5-1. *Probability curves for binomial expansions where* $a = b = \frac{1}{2}$. *(A)* $(a + b)^3$; *(B)* $(a + b)^4$; *(C)* $(a + b)^5$; *(D)* $(a + b)^7$.

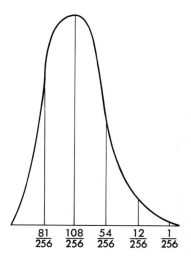

FIGURE 5-2. *Skewed curve for expansion of the binomial* $(a + b)^4$ *where* $a = \frac{3}{4}$ *and* $b = \frac{1}{4}$.

## GENETIC APPLICATIONS OF THE BINOMIAL

Just as we have utilized the binomial to ascertain expectancies in coin tosses, we can also employ the same method to determine the probability of children showing a given heritable trait in a particular family.

For instance, ptosis (drooping eyelids) is an inherited trait in which affected persons are unable to raise the eyelids, so that only a relatively small space between upper and lower lids is available for vision, giving them a "sleepy" appearance. Most pedigrees indicate ptosis to be due to an autosomal dominant. Suppose a young man with ptosis, whose father also displayed the trait, but whose mother did not, wishes to marry a woman with normal eyelids. They consult a physician to determine the likelihood of the occurrence of the defect in their children. If, for example, they plan to have three children, what is the probability of two of those being normal and one having ptosis?

From the known facts, it is evident that the young man is heterozygous because he has ptosis (letting $P$ represent the trait, his phenotype alone tells us he is $P-$) although his mother was normal and, therefore, $pp$. So having the trait and having necessarily received a recessive gene from his mother, he must be $Pp$. The woman, on the other hand, is $pp$, as determined by her normal phenotype. So, we are faced with the cross $Pp \times pp$. This is recognized as a testcross, so that the probability of normal children is $\frac{1}{2}$. But what is the chance of a family of *two normal children and one affected child* if they have three? The expansion of the binomial $(a + b)^3$ will provide the answer. If we let

$$a = \text{probability of a normal child} = \tfrac{1}{2}$$
$$b = \text{probability of ptosis} = \tfrac{1}{2}$$

we see that the second term, $3a^2b$, of the expansion will, upon substitution, yield the information:

$$3a^2b = 3[(\tfrac{1}{2})^2 \times \tfrac{1}{2}] = \tfrac{3}{8}$$

We choose the second term, $3a^2b$, in this expansion because it contains $a^2$ (for two children of the phenotype represented by $a$) and $b$ (for one child of the phenotype represented by $b$). Therefore, there is a probability of three in eight, or a 37.5 per cent chance, that *if they have three children*, two will be normal and one will have ptosis. Likewise, there is one chance in eight ($a^3$), or 12.5 per cent, that all three will be normal or ($b^3$) that all three will have ptosis. Or it can be said that of all families of three children born of parents with these genotypes, it is to be expected that three out of eight will consist of two normal children and one who is affected.

On the other hand, consider a young man and woman, each with ptosis, and whose pedigrees indicate that each is heterozygous. If such a couple should marry and have three children, what is the probability of two of the children being normal and one having ptosis? We can represent the potential parents as $Pp \times Pp$. From previous experience with monohybrid crosses of two heterozygous individuals, we know that, in cases of complete dominance, the phenotypic ratio in the offspring is $3:1$. That is, we should expect the probability here of an affected child to be $\frac{3}{4}$, and of a normal one to be $\frac{1}{4}$. As in the preceding example, let

$$a = \text{probability of a normal child} = \tfrac{1}{4}$$

and

$$b = \text{probability of an affected child} = \tfrac{3}{4}$$

Because we are again concerned with a family of three, we once more use the binomial $(a + b)^3$. Referring back to the expansion of this expression on page 94, and remembering the meaning of $a$ and $b$ that we have set up, we see that the term $3a^2b$ will have to be substituted and solved:

$$3a^2b = 3[(\tfrac{1}{4})^2 \times \tfrac{3}{4}] = \tfrac{9}{64}$$

This is quite different from the $\tfrac{3}{8}$ probability for the preceding case.

## PROBABILITY OF SEPARATE OCCURRENCE OF INDEPENDENT EVENTS

Just as the probability of the simultaneous occurrence of two independent events is the product of their separate probabilities, **the probability of the separate occurrence of either of two independent events equals the square root of their simultaneous occurrence**, provided, of course, the two events are of equal probability. In the preceding section we saw that the probability of tossing two heads simultaneously is $\tfrac{1}{4}$. The probability of tossing a head in one toss is $\sqrt{\tfrac{1}{4}}$ or $\tfrac{1}{2}$.

This same approach can be applied in genetics. Suppose we wish to determine the frequency of the gene for albinism in a particular human population. In western European countries about 1 in every 20,000 babies is an albino, a condition generally ascribed to a recessive autosomal gene. If we consider the population as a whole, each albino child, therefore, represents the simultaneous occurrence of independent events of equal frequency, the union of two gametes each carrying the recessive gene. The probability that any given gamate of the population will carry the gene for albinism is equal to $\sqrt{\tfrac{1}{20,000}}$ or about $\tfrac{1}{141}$.

# Determining "Goodness of Fit"

## NONGENETIC EVENTS

In our discussion of calculating expected results of coin tosses, we raised one as yet unanswered question: *In terms of our hypotheses, are the results obtained valid by chance alone?* This question implies that we do not expect to achieve results *exactly* equal to our calculations very often, and raises the problem of how much deviation from our expectations we can accept as likely being due purely to chance. Reference to Table 2-1 shows that even Mendel's results, involving hundreds or thousands of individuals, did not reflect *exactly* the expected ratios (although they are surprisingly close!). In other words, we need a mathematical tool to determine "goodness of fit." We have such a tool in the chi-square ($\chi^2$) test.

To understand how to use this important statistical test, let us reexamine our earlier coin tosses. Recall our two sets of two-coin tosses made by students A and B:

| | A's Tosses | | | B's Tosses | |
|---|---|---|---|---|---|
| Class | Observed | Calculated | Class | Observed | Calculated |
| HH | 12 | 12.5 | HH | 10 | 12.5 |
| HT | 27 | 25.0 | HT | 33 | 25.0 |
| TT | 11 | 12.5 | TT | 7 | 12.5 |

Obviously, A's tosses are closer to our expected results, but they do not correspond exactly. Do we accept both sets of results, or just A's, or neither, as valid reflections of our assumptions regarding the coins and tosses (page 90)? That is, are the deviations shown in each case to be expected when our assumptions are correct and complete, and only chance is operating? How much deviation from results expected under a given set of assumptions can we tolerate as representing merely chance departures from our calculated expectancy? The chi-square test will enable us to make a judgment in this question.

The formula for calculating chi-square is

$$\chi^2 = \Sigma \left[ \frac{(o - c)^2}{c} \right]$$

where $o$ = observed frequencies, $c$ = calculated frequencies, and $\Sigma$ indicates that the bracketed quantity is to be summed for all classes. Both $o$ and $c$ must be calculated in actual numbers and not in percentages.

To calculate chi-square for student A's coin tosses (1:2:1 expectation), his data may conveniently be set up as follows:

| Class | Observed $o$ | Calculated $c$ | Deviation $o - c$ | Squared Deviation $(o - c)^2$ | $\frac{(o - c)^2}{c}$ |
|---|---|---|---|---|---|
| HH | 12 | 12.5 | − 0.5 | 0.25 | 0.02 |
| HT | 27 | 25.0 | + 2.0 | 4.00 | 0.16 |
| TT | 11 | 12.5 | − 1.5 | 2.25 | 0.18 |
| TOTALS | 50 | 50.0 | 0 | | $\chi^2 = 0.36$ |

With the value $\chi^2 = 0.36$, our question can now be stated as, " How often, *by chance alone*, will we find a deviation of this much or more when we expect a 1:2:1 ratio?" or, "How often, by chance, can we expect a value of $\chi^2 \geq 0.36$?" If this probability is quite high, then we shall be able to accept our original assumptions (page 90) as valid and also the thesis that the observed deviation was produced only by chance.

The answer to our question may be obtained by consulting a table of chi-square (Table 5-2).

Table 5-2. Table of Chi-Square

| Degrees of freedom | P = 0.99 | 0.95 | 0.80 | 0.70 | 0.50 | 0.30 | 0.20 | 0.05 | 0.01 |
|---|---|---|---|---|---|---|---|---|---|
| 1 | 0.00016 | 0.004 | 0.064 | 0.148 | 0.455 | 1.074 | 1.642 | 3.841 | 6.635 |
| 2 | 0.0201 | 0.103 | 0.446 | 0.713 | 1.386 | 2.408 | 3.219 | 5.991 | 9.210 |
| 3 | 0.115 | 0.352 | 1.005 | 1.424 | 2.366 | 3.665 | 4.642 | 7.815 | 11.341 |
| 4 | 0.297 | 0.711 | 1.649 | 2.195 | 3.357 | 4.878 | 5.989 | 9.488 | 13.277 |
| 5 | 0.554 | 1.145 | 2.343 | 3.000 | 4.351 | 6.064 | 7.289 | 11.070 | 15.086 |
| 6 | 0.872 | 1.635 | 3.070 | 3.828 | 5.348 | 7.231 | 8.558 | 12.592 | 16.812 |
| 7 | 1.239 | 2.167 | 3.822 | 4.671 | 6.346 | 8.383 | 9.803 | 14.067 | 18.475 |
| 8 | 1.646 | 2.733 | 4.594 | 5.527 | 7.344 | 9.524 | 11.030 | 15.507 | 20.090 |
| 9 | 2.088 | 3.325 | 5.380 | 6.393 | 8.343 | 10.656 | 12.242 | 16.919 | 21.666 |
| 10 | 2.558 | 3.940 | 6.179 | 7.267 | 9.342 | 11.781 | 13.442 | 18.307 | 23.209 |

Taken from Table 3 of Fisher, *Statistical Methods for Research Workers,* published by Oliver and Boyd, Ltd., Edinburgh, by permission.

To use the table it is necessary only to know the " degrees of freedom " operating in any particular case. This is here one less than the number of classes involved[1] and represents the number of *independent* classes which contribute to the calculated value of $\chi^2$. In A's coin tosses, two of the classes may have any value (between 0 and 50), but once we have values for these two, the third is automatically determined as the difference between the total of all classes and the total of all other classes. The values of P across the top in the table indicate the probability of obtaining a value of chi-square (and, therefore, a deviation) as large or larger, *purely by chance.*

In Table 5-2, then, with two degrees of freedom, we read across until we find either our value of $\chi^2$ or two which " bracket " it. In the case at hand, we find that our $\chi^2$ value of 0.36 does not appear in the table, but for two degrees of freedom we do find two values, 0.103 and 0.446, between which it lies. Reading up to values of P, we see that $\chi^2 = 0.36$ corresponds to a probability value of between 0.95 and 0.80. This means that, for an expectancy of 1:2:1, we can expect a deviation as large as or larger than we experienced in something between 80 and 95 per cent of repeated trials. Such a deviation could, therefore, readily be due to chance, and both our

[1] For an exception to this statement see page 252.

expectancy and the assumptions on which it was based appear good. That is, we have a good fit between observed results and our calculated expectancy.

In the same way, let us calculate $\chi^2$ for B's coin tosses ($1:2:1$ expectation):

| Class | Observed $o$ | Calculated $c$ | Deviation $o - c$ | Squared Deviation $(o - c)^2$ | $\dfrac{(o - c)^2}{c}$ |
|-------|----------|------------|-----------|-------------------|----------------|
| HH | 10 | 12.5 | $-2.5$ | 6.25 | 0.50 |
| HT | 33 | 25.0 | $+8.0$ | 64.00 | 2.56 |
| TT | 7 | 12.5 | $-5.5$ | 30.25 | 2.42 |
| TOTALS | 50 | 50.0 | 0 | | $\chi^2 = 5.48$ |

In Table 5-2, it is seen that we may expect, by chance, a value of $\chi^2 \geq 5.48$ in between 5 and 20 per cent of such trials. This is obviously not as good a fit between observed and calculated results as obtained by student A, but is it close enough to accept? In answer, statisticians usually choose the 5 per cent probability value as the significant level. In other words, wherever a $\chi^2$ value is equal to or greater than that for a probability value of 0.05, the deviation is considered significant and the likelihood of such a large discrepancy arising by chance too low for acceptance. At this level, only 1 in 20 such trials will produce this large a deviation by chance. In our two-coin tosses, then, values of $\chi^2$ up to (but not including) 5.991 indicate a sufficient probability of chance alone to accept, but larger values would require a careful review of the assumptions that led us to, in this case, a $1:2:1$ expectancy.

In the same way we calculate $\chi^2$ for the four-coin toss reported on page 92 to be 5.35. Table 5-2 shows that, for this value of $\chi^2$ and four degrees of freedom (remember, five different combinations are possible), $P = 0.30$ to 0.20, which shows our value of $\chi^2$ to be well below the level of significance.

Note that $\chi^2$ does not *tell* us that our results do or do not fit our theory, but this test does permit a judgmental answer regarding goodness of fit.

### GENETIC APPLICATIONS OF CHI-SQUARE

Recall the case of hydrocyanic acid in clover discussed in Chapter 4. A series of crosses (page 81) of two parental strains, one producing this substance in its leaves, the other not doing so, gave rise to an $F_2$ of 351 HCN:256 no HCN. Although the 607 $F_2$ individuals reported by Atwood and Sullivan resulted from some 23 different crosses, it will suffice for our purposes to treat them as though they were all sister progeny of the same cross. Chi-square calculation for a $3:1$ expectancy gives the value $\chi^2 = 95.48$:

| Class | $o$ | $c$ | $o - c$ | $(o - c)^2$ | $\dfrac{(o - c)^2}{c}$ |
|---|---|---|---|---|---|
| HCN positive | 351 | 455.25 | − 104.25 | 10868 | 23.87 |
| HCN negative | 256 | 151.75 | + 104.25 | 10868 | 71.61 |
| TOTALS | 607 | 607.00 | 0.0 | | $\chi^2 = 95.48$ |

Reference to Table 5-2 shows that, for one degree of freedom, such a value is highly significant, being likely to occur by chance in far fewer than one in a hundred trials. While the great deviation that produces this extremely high value of chi-square is not impossible when one expects a 3:1 ratio, it is so improbable that we prefer to reexamine our assumptions. For a 3:1 ratio, these would, of course, include the concept of a single pair of genes with one allele completely dominant, or (for a 12:4 ratio) two pairs in which, let us say, $A$ and $a$ are both epistatic to $B$ and $b$, though $A$ is dominant to $a$:

$$\left.\begin{array}{l} 9 \ A\text{--}B\text{--} \\ 3 \ A\text{--}bb \end{array}\right\} \quad \text{12 if } A \text{ is epistatic to } B \text{ and } b$$

$$\left.\begin{array}{l} 3 \ aaB\text{--} \\ 1 \ aabb \end{array}\right\} \quad \text{4 if } a \text{ is epistatic to } B \text{ and } b \text{ but recessive to } A$$

Since 351:256 is considerably closer to a 9:7 expectancy, it is worth determining $\chi^2$ for this ratio:

| Class | $o$ | $c$ | $o - c$ | $(o - c)^2$ | $\dfrac{(o - c)^2}{c}$ |
|---|---|---|---|---|---|
| HCN positive | 351 | 341.4 | + 9.6 | 92.16 | 0.27 |
| HCN negative | 256 | 265.6 | − 9.6 | 92.16 | 0.35 |
| TOTALS | 607 | 607.0 | 0.0 | | $\chi^2 = 0.62$ |

With one degree of freedom, Table 5-2 indicates, for this value of $\chi^2$, a probability of between 0.30 and 0.50. This value of $\chi^2$ is well below the level of significance, and interpolation in Table 5-2 indicates that such a value of $\chi^2$ will occur in slightly more than 44 per cent of similar trials when the assumptions underlying a 9:7 ratio are operating. Therefore, until conflicting data may be turned up, these assumptions are acceptable. As described in Chapter 4, these include the concept of two pairs of genes with "duplicate recessive epistasis" where only the $A-B-$ individuals are phenotypically distinguishable from other possible genotypes resulting from the crosses studied.

The chi-square test is a very useful one for obtaining an objective approximation of goodness of fit, but it is reliable only when the observed or expected frequency in any class is five or more. Its proper use in genetic situations can, as we have seen, shed considerable light on the mechanisms operating in particular crosses.

## PROBLEMS

**5-1.** In tossing three coins simultaneously, what is the probability, in one toss, of (a) three heads; (b) two heads and one tail?

**5-2.** A couple have two girls and are expecting their third child. They hope it will be a boy; what is the probability that their wish will be realized?

**5-3.** Another couple have eight children, all boys. What is the chance that their ninth child would be another boy?

**5-4.** What is the probability of getting (a) a five with a single die; (b) a five on each of two dice thrown simultaneously; (c) any combination totaling seven on two dice thrown simultaneously?

**5-5.** In crossing two heterozygous deep *Coleus* plants, what is the probability of the occurrence in the $F_1$ of (a) deep; (b) shallow?

**5-6.** In crossing two *Coleus* plants of genotype *DdIi*, what is the probability in the $F_1$ of (a) *DdIi;* (b) *ddII;* (c) deep irregular; (d) shallow irregular?

**5-7.** Astigmatism is a vision defect produced by unequal curvature of the cornea, causing objects in one plane to be in sharper focus. It results from a dominant gene. Wavy hair appears to be the heterozygous expression of a pair of alleles for straight ($h_1$) or curly hair ($h_2$). A wavy-haired woman who has astigmatism, but whose mother did not, marries a wavy-haired man who does not have astigmatism. What is the probability that their first child will be (a) curly-haired and nonastigmatic; (b) wavy-haired and astigmatic? (c) How many different phenotypes could appear in their children with respect to these hair and eye conditions?

**5-8.** Free ear lobes ($A-$) and clockwise whorl of hair on the back of the head ($C-$) are dominant to attached lobes and counterclockwise whorl, respectively. A husband and wife know their genotypes to be *AaCc* and *aaCc*. They expect to have five children; what is the probability that three will be "free-clockwise" and two "attached-counterclockwise"?

**5-9.** Red hair (*rr*) and left-handedness (*ll*) both appear to be inherited as recessive traits in most pedigrees. How many times in families of three children, where both parents are *RrLl* (nonred-haired and right-handed), will these consist of one left-handed red-haired boy and two right-handed girls whose hair is not red?

**5-10.** Multiple telangiectasia in man is the heterozygous expression of a gene that is lethal when homozygous. Heterozygotes have enlarged blood vessels of face, tongue, lips, nose, and/or fingers and are subject to unusually frequent, serious nose bleeding. Homozygotes for the trait have many fragile and abnormally dilated capillaries; because of severe, multiple hemorrhaging these individuals die within a few months after birth. Two heterozygotes married forty years ago and now have four grown children. What is the probability that two of these are normal and two have multiple telangiectasia?

**5-11.** It is estimated that, in the United States, 1 in 1,000 live births is an individual who has cystic fibrosis of the pancreas, an inherited recessive metabolic defect in digestion of fats, which is fatal in children homozygous for the gene. (a) What is the probability that any given gamete in the U.S. population carries this gene? (b) What fraction of the U.S. population is heterozygous for this gene?

**5-12.** A certain cross produces an $F_1$ ratio of 157:43. By means of the chi-square test, determine the probability of a chance deviation this large or larger on the basis of a 13:3 expectancy.

**5-13.** Another cross involving different genes gives rise to an $F_1$ of 110:90. By means of the chi-square test determine the probability of a chance deviation this large or larger on the basis of (a) a 1:1 expectancy and (b) a 9:7 expectancy. (c) Is the deviation to be considered significant in either case? (d) What do you do with these results?

**5-14.** Suppose, with the genes involved in problem 5-13, the $F_1$ ratio had been 1,100:900. Try a chi-square test with this sample to determine whether there is a significant deviation from (a) 1:1 and (b) 9:7 expectancy. (c) Is the deviation now significant in either case? (d) What is the effect of sample size on the usefulness of the chi-square test?

**5-15.** Following are listed some of Mendel's reported results in garden pea. Test each for goodness of fit to the given hypothesis:

| Cross | Progeny | Hypothesis |
|---|---|---|
| (a) yellow × green cotyledons | ($F_2$) 6,022:2,001 | 3:1 |
| (b) green × yellow pods | ($F_2$) 428:152 | 3:1 |
| (c) violet red × white flowers | ($F_1$) 47:40 | 1:1 |
| (d) round yellow × wrinkled green seeds | ($F_1$) 31:26:27:26 | 1:1:1:1 |

# CHAPTER 6

# Linkage, Crossing-Over, and Genetic Mapping of Chromosomes

I N our discussion of dihybrid inheritance (Chapter 4) we saw that the *Coleus* testcross *DdIi* (deep irregular) × *ddii* (shallow regular) produces four progeny phenotypic classes in a 1:1:1:1 ratio. We also noted that this result is to be expected on the basis of the behavior of chromosomes in meiosis, if each of the two pairs of genes is on a different pair of chromosomes. With this unlinked arrangement of genes, either member of one pair of genes can combine at random with either member of the other pair, resulting in the production of four kinds of gametes, *DI*, *Di*, *dI*, and *di*, in equal number, by the doubly heterozygous individual. Random fusion of these four gamete genotypes with the *di* gametes of the completely recessive parent results in the 1:1:1:1 progeny phenotypic ratio. But, as our knowledge of the genetics of various organisms increases, it becomes abundantly clear that the number of genes per species considerably exceeds its number of chromosomes pairs. For example, the fruit fly, *Drosophila melanogaster*, has only four pairs of chromosomes, yet experimental estimates place its number of genes at 10,000 or more. Therefore, each chromosome must bear many genes.

All the genes carried on a given chromosome constitute a **linkage group** and would be expected to be inherited as a block were it not for crossing-over (Chapter 3). Therefore, we should expect the number of linkage groups for any organism to equal its monoploid chromosome number.[1] Interestingly enough, linkage was anticipated before it was actually demonstrated. Just three years after the rediscovery of Mendel's pioneer papers, Sutton (1903) suggested that each chromosome must bear more than a single gene and that genes "represented by any one chromosome must be inherited together." However, Sutton was unable to support his hypothesis experimentally. Only a few years later, Bateson and Punnett (1905–1908) did have the data with which to do so, but failed to recognize that they were dealing with linked genes.

## Linkage and Cross-Over

### BATESON AND PUNNETT ON SWEET PEA

In the sweet pea, *Lathyrus odoratus*, two pairs of genes affecting flower color and pollen grain shape occur, each pair exhibiting complete dominance:

[1] This expectation will have to be amended when we consider the sex chromosomes (Chapter 10).

| | |
|---|---|
| *R* purple flowers | *Ro* long pollen grains |
| *r* red flowers | *ro* round pollen grains |

Bateson and Punnett crossed a completely homozygous purple long with a red round. The $F_1$ was, as expected, all purple long, and a $9:3:3:1$ phenotypic ratio was expected in the $F_2$. Results, however, were quite different:

| Phenotype | Observed | Expected ($9:3:3:1$) |
|---|---|---|
| purple long | 296 | 240 |
| purple round | 19 | 80 |
| red long | 27 | 80 |
| red round | 85 | 27 |
| | 427 | 427 |

Satisfy yourself that chi-square for a $9:3:3:1$ expectancy is 219.27. The basis for this expected ratio (independent segregation) is, therefore, not acceptable. Bateson and Punnett recognized that their results were "explicable on the assumption that . . . the gametes were produced in a series of 16, viz., 7 purple long, 1 purple round, 1 red long, and 7 red round." But they were unable to explain correctly why or how because they did not relate this $7:1:1:7$ gamete ratio to the behavior of chromosomes in meiosis.

We now know that genes for flower color and shape of pollen grains are linked.

## ARRANGEMENT OF LINKED GENES

When two pairs of genes are linked, the linkage may be of either of two types in an individual heterozygous for both pairs: (1) the two dominants, *R* and *Ro*, may be located on one member of the chromosome pair, with the two recessives, *r* and *ro* on the other, or (2) the dominant of one pair and the recessive of the other may be located on one chromosome of the pair, with the recessive of the first gene pair and the dominant of the second gene pair on the other chromosome. The first arrangement, with two dominants on the same chromosome, is referred to as the *cis* arrangement, the second, having one dominant and one recessive on the same chromosome, as the *trans* arrangement. Figure 6-1 illustrates these possibilities.

Thus the genotypes of the parental and first filial generations of the Bateson and Punnett cross may be written in standard fashion to reflect linkage:

P     *R Ro/R Ro* × *r ro/r ro*
$F_1$          *R Ro/r ro*

Without crossing-over, the $F_1$ would produce but two types of gametes, *R Ro* and *r ro*. Crossing-over, though, produces two additional gamete

FIGURE 6-1. Cis *and* trans *arrangements for two pairs of linked genes in a diploid cell.*

genotypes, *R ro* and *r Ro*. That these four genotypes are not produced in equal frequency could easily be seen from a testcross in which the double heterozygote carries these genes in the *cis* linkage:

$$\text{P} \female \text{ purple long} \times \text{red round } \male$$
$$R\ Ro/r\ ro \qquad r\ ro/r\ ro$$

Based on the 7:1:1:7 gamete frequency which Bateson and Punnett discerned, testcross progeny should occur in these frequencies:

| Phenotype | Genotype | Frequency | |
|---|---|---|---|
| 1. purple long | *R Ro/r ro* | 0.4375 | 0.875 |
| 2. red round | *r ro/r ro* | 0.4375 | |
| 3. purple round | *R ro/r ro* | 0.0625 | 0.125 |
| 4. red long | *r Ro/r ro* | 0.0625 | |

The first two phenotypic classes have received from the pistillate parent an unaltered chromosome carrying either *R Ro* or *r ro*. The latter two classes, however, have received a *crossover* chromosome, either *R ro* or *r Ro*. Gametes carrying each of these altered chromosomes must occur with a frequency of only 0.0625 ($= \frac{1}{16}$), rather than 0.25 as would be the case with unlinked genes. With genes *R* and *Ro*, the *crossover frequency* is 12.5 per cent. This frequency is remarkably constant, regardless of the type of cross or the kind of linkage (*cis* or *trans*).

To understand how this happens, recall the occurrence of chiasmata in prophase-I as described on page 60. If a chiasma occurs between these two pairs of genes, *crossing-over* will occur so that the original linkage, *R Ro/r ro*, becomes *R ro/r Ro*, as indicated in Fig. 6-2. For each meiocyte in which this happens, the result is four monoploid nuclei of genotypes *R Ro*, *R ro*, *r Ro*, and *r ro*. For each meiocyte in which a crossover *fails* to occur between these two pairs of genes, the result is four monoploid nuclei, two each of genotypes *R Ro* and *r ro*. If the meiocyte carries these genes in the *cis* configuration,

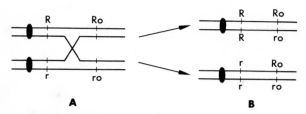

**A**          **B**

FIGURE 6-2. *Result of crossing-over. A chiasma occurring between linked genes* R *and* Ro, *and involving two nonsister chromatids as shown in* (A) *may result in "repair" such that the original* cis *linkage is converted to a* trans *linkage in two of the four chromatids, as depicted in* (B).

as in this case, *R ro* and *r Ro* gametes are referred to as *crossover gametes*, and *R Ro* and *r ro* sex cells as *noncrossover* types. Progeny such as classes 1 and 2, which receive one or the other *intact chromosome* from the heterozygous parent are referred to as **parental types**. Progeny making up classes 3 and 4 in this testcross incorporate new combinations of linked genes and are referred to as **recombinants**.

## Linkage, Linkage Groups, and Mapping

The chromosomal basis of heredity became clearly established in the second decade of this century, verifying Sutton's earlier hypothesis and supplying experimental data to explain and extend such cases as had puzzled Bateson and Punnett. Discovery followed discovery in rapid succession. In 1910 Thomas Hunt Morgan was able to provide evidence for the location of a particular gene of *Drosophila* on a specific chromosome (Morgan 1910a). Within a short time he was able to show clearly that linkage does exist and that linked genes are often inherited together, but may be separated by crossing over (Morgan 1910b, 1911a). Even more exciting than these proofs of earlier surmises was Morgan's conclusion that a definite relation exists between recombination frequency and the linear distance separating genes on their chromosome. As he wrote (Morgan 1911b), "In consequence, we find coupling in certain characters, and little or no evidence at all of coupling in other characters, the difference *depending on the linear distance apart of the chromosomal materials that represent the factors*." (Italics added.) Coupling is an older term for what is now recognized as linkage.

With these researches, it now became possible not only to identify certain genes with particular chromosomes, but also to begin construction of *chromosome maps* showing linkage groups and relative distances between successive genes. Linkage groups were developed rapidly for *Drosophila* and also for a variety of animals and plants. Perhaps the most remarkable aspect of this burgeoning genetic knowledge was that geneticists could now assign relative positions on chromosomes to genes whose nature and precise function were not to be clarified for another forty or fifty years and which could not be seen in the microscope.

As this kind of information accumulated, it became clear that the number of linkage groups in any species ultimately is found to equal its monoploid chromosome number. Thus, four linkage groups are known in *Drosophila melanogaster* where $n = 4$, and ten in corn (*Zea mays*) which has 10 pairs of chromosomes. In species whose genetics is less perfectly understood, of course, the number of *known* linkage groups is temporarily smaller than its monoploid chromosome number. In mice, for example, only 19 linkage groups are presently known although there are 20 chromosomes in a single set. In no event, however, does the number of linkage groups exceed the number of pairs of chromosomes in diploid species. Although a large number of genes in man have been assigned to the X chromosome (see Chapter 11), no more than three very incomplete linkage groups have yet been established for the autosomes. Progress and problems in mapping human chromosomes are described by McKusick (1971).

### CYTOLOGICAL EVIDENCE FOR CROSSING-OVER

Whenever a particular chromosome pair (bearing certain genes) can be clearly identified because of some structural characteristic, it can be shown that when there occurs an interchange of material between two homologs, there is likewise an interchange of genes (i.e., genetic crossing-over). The work to be described in this section also provides further evidence that genes are located on chromosomes. In an elegant analysis of such a situation in corn, Creighton and McClintock (1931) furnished such a convincing correlation between cytological evidence and genetic results that their work has rightly been called a landmark in experimental genetics.

In corn, chromosome 9 (the second shortest one in the complement of 10 pairs) ordinarily lacks a small knob (satellite). But in one particular strain investigated by these two workers, a single plant was found to have dissimilar ninth chromosomes. One of these possessed a satellite at the end of its short arm and also an added segment that had been translocated from chromosome 8. The other member of the pair was normal, lacking both the satellite and the added segment of number 8. Chromosome 9 bears, among other genes, the following:

| | |
|---|---|
| *C* colored aleurone | *Wx* starchy endosperm |
| *c* colorless aleurone | *wx* waxy endosperm |

Aleurone and endosperm are parts of the triploid food storage tissue in the grain. The plant having these dissimilar ninth chromosomes was heterozygous for both the aleurone and endosperm genes and, from earlier work, Creighton and McClintock knew which chromosome of the pair carried which gene. Thus, the two ninth chromosomes of this plant, which they used as the pistillate parent in their crosses, could be identified visually, and may be diagrammed thus:

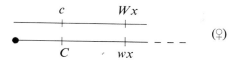

(♀)

The dashed portion indicates the translocated segment of chromosome 8. An individual possessing such a dissimilar ninth pair of chromosomes was crossed with a *c Wx/c wx* plant possessing two knobless ninth chromosomes which also did not have the added segment of chromosome 8 (i.e., "normal" ninth chromosomes):

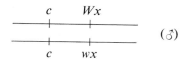

(♂)

Although only 28 grains resulted from this cross, cytological examination of microsporocytes from adults grown from these grains confirmed the predicted relation between cytology and genetics (except for one class which was not found).

This cross, with the ninth chromosome in each parent and progeny class, is diagrammed in Fig. 6-3.

The fact that endosperm and aleurone are triploid tissues need not complicate our understanding of this masterful research because, as indicated in Fig. 6-3, Creighton and McClintock used chromosomes of the *diploid* microsporocytes to demonstrate the correlation between cytological and genetic crossing-over.

A similar verification that genetic crossing-over is accompanied by a physical exchange between homologous chromosomes was also established in 1931 by Stern for *Drosophila*. He utilized a strain in which the females had a portion of the Y chromosome attached to one of their X chromosomes. Work by Stern and by Creighton and McClintock indicated a clear relationship between the interchange of material between homologs and genetic crossing-over.

We may summarize our progress thus far as follows:

1. (Chapter 4) Certain genes assort *at random.*
2. (Chapter 6) Other genes do not segregate randomly, but are *linked.* These *linkage groups* tend to be transmitted in unitary groups.
3. (Chapter 3) In diploid cells chromosomes also occur in pairs which tend to be transmitted as units to daughter nuclei.

4. (Chapter 6) Linked genes do not always "stay together" but are often exchanged reciprocally (genetic crossing-over).
5. (Chapters 3 and 6) Chromosomes may be seen to form chiasmata and exchange parts reciprocally. Such exchange is reflected in genetic crossing-over. Furthermore, chiasma formation and genetic crossing-over occur with closely similar frequencies.

Thus linkage is an exception to the pattern of random segregation of genes, and crossing-over results in an exception to the consequences of linkage.

## Mapping Chromosomes

As Morgan (1911b) predicted, frequency of crossing-over is governed largely by distances between genes. That is, the probability of its occurring between two *particular* genes increases as the distance between them becomes larger, so that crossover frequency appears to be directly proportional to distances between genes. As we shall see, this relationship is quite valid, though not equally so in all parts of a chromosome, for proximity of one crossover to another decreases probability of another very close by. The centromere has a similar interfering effect. But because of this general relationship between intergene distance and crossover frequency, and because we cannot yet measure such distances in customary units, geneticists use an arbitrary unit of measure, the **map unit**, to describe distances between linked genes. *A map unit is equal to one per cent of crossovers (recombinants);* i.e., it represents the linear distance for which one percent crossovers (recombinants) is observed. Thus, for sweet peas the distance from *R* to *Ro* would be described as 12.5 map units.

### THE THREE-POINT TESTCROSS

The most commonly employed method in genetic mapping of chromosomes is the trihybrid (or "three-point") testcross. Let us try such a cross in *Drosophila melanogaster*, the little fruit fly whose genetics is so well known. Using a plus sign to denote the so-called wild type, as is customary in mapping problems, we shall examine a three-point cross involving these known genes:

| Gene Symbol | Phenotype |
| --- | --- |
| + | normal wing (*dominant*) |
| cu | curled wing (*recessive*) |
| + | normal thorax (*dominant*) |
| sr | striped thorax (*recessive*) |
| + | normal bristles (*dominant*) |
| ss | spineless bristles (*recessive*) |

The actual numbers of each progeny class in the following illustration are hypothetical, but the percentages and the genes are real. For the moment we shall arbitrarily choose the gene sequence that follows, recognizing that the results may either confirm that order or dictate a different one. We shall see how to determine the correct sequence as soon as we have looked at the cross:

P  ♀ normal normal normal × curled spineless striped ♂
$+ + + /cu\ ss\ sr$         $cu\ ss\ sr/cu\ ss\ sr$

| $F_1$ Phenotype | Maternal Chromosome | # | % | Type |
|---|---|---|---|---|
| normal normal normal | $+ + +$ | 430 ⎫ | | ⎧ Parental or |
| curled spineless striped | $cu\ ss\ sr$ | 452 ⎭ 88.2 | | ⎩ noncrossover |
| normal spineless striped | $+ ss\ sr$ | 45 ⎫ | | ⎧ $cu$-$ss$ single |
| curled normal normal | $cu + +$ | 38 ⎭ 8.3 | | ⎩ crossovers |
| normal normal striped | $+ + sr$ | 16 ⎫ | | ⎧ $ss$-$sr$ single |
| curled spineless normal | $cu\ ss +$ | 17 ⎭ 3.3 | | ⎩ crossovers |
| normal spineless normal | $+ ss +$ | 1 ⎫ | | ⎧ double |
| curled normal striped | $cu + sr$ | 1 ⎭ 0.2 | | ⎩ crossovers |
| | | 1.000 | 100.0 | |

By grouping $F_1$ data as we have, several important considerations emerge:

1. **The maternal chromosome received by members of each of the two numerically largest classes** (noncrossover flies), determinable from the phenotypes, **discloses whether *cis* or *trans* linkage obtained in the maternal parent**. Here, for example, normal normal normal individuals must have received $+ + +$ from the maternal parent and $cu\ ss\ sr$ from the paternal. Because noncrossover gametes will be more frequent than crossover sex cells, $+ + +/cu\ ss\ sr$ and $cu\ ss\ sr/cu\ ss\ sr$ flies will occur in the majority if the linkage is in the *cis* configuration.[2]
2. **Double crossover individuals** (those that would not be noted in a two-pair cross involving only *cu* and *sr*) **show up**. These are individuals that as the term implies, result from the occurrence of two crossovers between the first and third genes in order on the maternal chromosome. *Even numbers of crossovers between two successive genes will not be picked up*:

[2] See also problem 6-24.

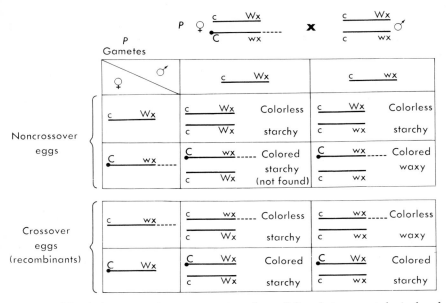

FIGURE 6-3. *A diagrammatic representation of parallelism between cytological and genetic crossing-over, showing the phenotypes of aleurone and endosperm of $F_1$ grains and the chromosome morphology and genotypes for microsporocytes produced by $F_1$ plants.* [Based on the work of Creighton and McClintock. See text for full explanation.]

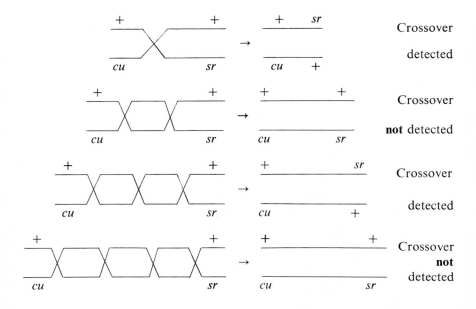

3. **The double crossovers are recognizable as the numerically smallest progeny groups and may be used to determine gene sequence**. Since + *ss* + and *cu* + *sr* are, therefore, here identifiable as double crossovers, there is only one sequence of genes in the *cis* configuration in the maternal parent which would yield these two gene combinations following a double crossover. This becomes clear if we think of the original *cis* arrangement and how the + *ss* + and *cu* + *sr* chromosomes can be derived therefrom. This will be only by two crossovers between the first and third genes in the sequence:

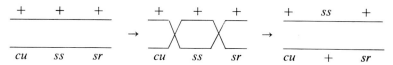

If, on the other hand, these genes were arranged in either of the other two possible sequences (*sr cu ss* or *ss sr cu*), the outcome of double crossing over would be incompatible with the results observed in our example:

$$
\begin{array}{ccc}
+ & + & + \\
\times & \times & \\
sr & cu & ss
\end{array}
\rightarrow
\begin{array}{ccc}
+ & cu & + \\
\hline
sr & + & ss
\end{array}
\left.\begin{array}{c} \\ \\ \end{array}\right\}
\begin{array}{l}\text{(These classes total} \\ \text{83 in our cross.)}\end{array}
$$

$$
\begin{array}{ccc}
+ & + & + \\
\times & \times & \\
ss & sr & cu
\end{array}
\rightarrow
\begin{array}{ccc}
+ & sr & + \\
\hline
ss & + & cu
\end{array}
\left.\begin{array}{c} \\ \\ \end{array}\right\}
\begin{array}{l}\text{(These classes total} \\ \text{33 in our cross.)}\end{array}
$$

Thus, the true sequence here can only be *cu ss sr*.

4. **The true distance** between *cu* and *ss* is, therefore, 8.3 + 0.2 = 8.5 (single crossovers + double crossovers).
5. **The true distance** between *ss* and *sr* is, therefore, 3.3 + 0.2 = 3.5 (single crossovers + double crossovers).
6. **The true distance** between *cu* and *sr* is 8.3 + 0.2 + 3.3 + 0.2 = 12.0 (*cu ss* single crossovers + *ss sr* single crossovers + *twice* the double crossovers). This is so because the double crossovers represent just what their name implies: *two* crossovers, one between *cu* and *ss*, plus a second one between *ss* and *sr*.

The genes here described constitute three members of a linkage group in *Drosophila*. With the cross outlined above, a beginning of genetically mapping one chromosome of *Drosophila* can be made. If these are thought of as the first three to be known in a new linkage group, they can be placed arbitrarily at particular *loci*:

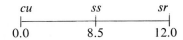

or, of course, *sr* may be placed at the "left" end and the sequence reversed. If later work shows another gene, *W* (dominant for wrinkled wing), to be located 4.0 map units to the "left" of *cu*, then the map is redrawn and each locus renumbered accordingly:

Figure 1-8 shows the locations of these and some other genes, as presently determined. Knowledge of which chromosome bears which genes in *Drosophila* and other dipterans is aided by a study of giant chromosomes (Chapter 12). The student is referred to the problems at the end of this chapter for further study in genetic mapping.

Interestingly enough, had we performed the reciprocal of this trihybrid testcross, namely,

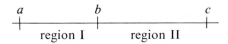

only the two parental phenotypes (normal-normal-normal and curled-spineless-striped) would have been recovered in the progeny! This is so because crossing-over does not occur in the male flies. Dipterans are unusual in this respect.

### INTERFERENCE AND COINCIDENCE

Our discussion of mapping techniques thus far would seem to imply that crossing-over in one part of a chromosome is independent of crossing-over elsewhere in that chromosome. That this is not so was demonstrated as long ago as 1916 by Nobel Prize winning geneticist H. J. Muller.

Consider for a moment a chromosome bearing three genes, *a*, *b*, and *c*:

```
    a              b                    c
    +              +                    +
       region I        region II
```

If we designate the *a-b* portion as region I and the *b-c* segment as region II, then, recalling the now familiar product law of probability (page 89), the frequency of double crossovers between genes *a* and *c* should equal the crossover frequency of region I times the crossover frequency of region II. Actually, this is seldom true.

For example, in our three-point mapping experiment in *Drosophila* we obtained the following crossover frequencies:

| "Region" | Genes | Percentage Crossovers | Map Distance (in map units) |
|---|---|---|---|
| I | *cu-ss* | 8.3 | 8.3 + 0.2 = 8.5 |
| II | *ss-sr* | 3.3 | 3.3 + 0.2 = 3.5 |
| Double Crossovers | *cu-ss-sr* | 0.2 | |

If crossing-over in regions I and II were independent, we should predict $0.085 \times 0.035$, or almost 0.3 per cent, double crossovers, whereas only 0.2 per cent was observed. A disparity of this kind, in which the number of actual double crossovers is less than the number calculated on the basis of independence, is very common. It clearly suggests that, once a crossover occurs, the probability of another crossover in an adjacent region is reduced. This phenomenon is called **interference**.

Interference appears to be unequal in different parts of a chromosome, as well as among the several chromosomes of a given complement. In general, interference appears to be greatest near the centromere and at the ends of a chromosome. Degrees of interference are commonly expressed as **coefficients of coincidence** or simply as **coincidence**:

$$\text{coincidence} = \frac{\text{actual frequency of double crossovers}}{\text{calculated frequency of double crossovers}}$$

In our *Drosophila* example coincidence is

$$\frac{0.002}{0.003} = 0.67$$

As interference decreases, coincidence increases. Coincidence values ordinarily vary between 0 and 1. Absence of interference gives a coincidence value of 1, whereas complete interference results in a coincidence of 0. Coincidence is generally quite small for short map distances. In *Drosophila*, coincidence is zero for distances of less than 10 map units, but gradualle increases to 1 as distances exceed 10 units. Furthermore, there seems to by no interference across the centromere from one arm of the chromosome to the other.

Similarly, interference is reported from a wide variety of organisms. For example, Hutchison (1922), who discovered the *c-sh* linkage in corn, reported map distances for three genes, *c* (colorless aleurone), *sh* (shrunken grains), and *wx* (waxy endosperm). His data indicated the following crossover frequencies:

| "Region" | Genes | Percentage Crossovers | Map Distance (in map units) |
|----------|-------|----------------------|----------------------------|
| I | c-sh | 3.4 | 3.4 + 0.1 = 3.5 |
| II | sh-wx | 18.3 | 18.3 + 0.1 = 18.4 |
| Double Crossovers | c-sh-wx | 0.1 | |

Again, if crossing-over in regions I and II were independent, we should predict $0.035 \times 0.184 = 0.6$ per cent double crossovers, whereas only 0.1 per cent was observed, giving a coefficient of coincidence of 0.167. On the other hand, especially in the bacterial chromosome and in bacteriophage genetics, double crossovers may be encountered in excess of random expectation, giving coincidence values $> 1$. This is referred to as *negative interference*.

## Linkage Studies in Bacteria

Present evidence indicates that such bacteria as the common colon bacillus, *Escherichia coli*, contain one to several *nucleoids*, rich in deoxyribonucleic acid (Chapter 14), that appear in electron micrographs as areas of lesser density. Internal organization is not clearly discernible, but studies strongly suggest that each nucleoid contains long, continuous fibrils of DNA having no free ends. Such a closed DNA structure of the nucleoid is functionally comparable to the chromosome of higher organisms. It is, however, *not* a chromosome in the structural sense of eukaryotic organisms. As described in Appendix B, during conjugation between donor and recipient ("male" and "female," respectively), this ring "chromosome" opens at a particular point and passes as a filament into the body of the recipient cell, the length of transferred segment depending upon the duration of the transfer process.

### EVIDENCE FROM CONJUGATION

In such monoploid organisms, the usual technique of determining linkage distances by means of recombinational frequencies cannot ordinarily be employed. Instead, donor cells of known genotypes are mixed with a large number of recipients of a different genotype, then separated at predetermined times by agitating with a Waring blender. After separation, progeny of the recipient cells are tested by inoculating them on different deficiency media in order to detect various physiologically deficient strains (**auxotrophs**). Genes are found to be located sequentially on the chromosome and are transferred in order to the recipient cell. For example, if we use donor cells with four known genes:

| | |
|---|---|
| *pan* | pantothenic acid |
| *arg D* | synthesis of the enzyme ornithine transcarbamylase |
| *lac Z* | synthesis of the enzyme $\beta$ galactosidase |
| *gal A* | synthesis of galactokinase |

and interrupt conjugation at different times, we find genes transferred in this time sequence:

| Duration of Conjugation (min.) | Genes Transferred |
|---|---|
| 1.5 | *pan* |
| 5.0 | *pan, arg D* |
| 10.0 | *pan, arg D, lac Z* |
| 16.0 | *pan, arg D, lac Z, gal A* |

Therefore, the order of these genes is as given in the 16-minute sequence.

A particular experiment might involve, for instance, these strains:

$$\text{(donor) } pan^- \; arg \; D^- \; lac \; Z^+ \; gal \; A^+ \; \ldots$$

$$\text{(recipient) } pan^+ \; arg \; D^+ \; lac \; Z^- \; gal \; A^- \; \ldots$$

Here a minus sign indicates inability to synthesize the substance listed in the previous paragraph (i.e., auxotrophic for that substance) and a plus sign indicates ability to produce the given substance (**prototrophic**). The two strains are mixed in a tube of liquid (complete) medium, then, after conjugation, plated out in an agar plate containing a complete medium. Here a large number of progeny colonies, both auxotrophs and prototrophs, develop. After incubation, colonies are transferred to a series of deficiency media to detect recombinations. This is done by pressing the master plate onto a sheet of velvet whose fibers pick up individuals of each colony. The velvet is then pressed to a series of replica plates of a deficiency medium.

Many such experiments, usually utilizing triple auxotrophs (e.g., $- - - + + + \times + + + - - -$) to reduce to a very low value the probability of mutation as a factor, have resulted in a fairly complete genetic map of *Escherichia coli*, as shown in Fig. 6-4. Note that a total time of 89 minutes is indicated for transfer of the complete chromosome during conjugation. Reference to Appendix B will show that the circular chromosome opens out at the point where the F ("fertility") factor is located. Although the fertility factor may be anywhere along the chromosome extent, opening of the chromosome is always on the same side of F. The F locus is the last to be transferred; hence the genes that enter the recipient first vary from strain to strain, although the *sequence* of genes is ordinarily identical.

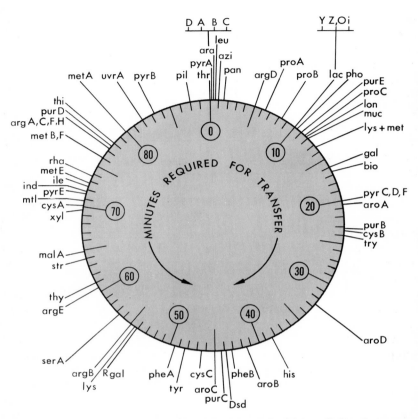

FIGURE 6-4. *Genetic map of the colon bacterium,* Escherichia coli, *based on recombination as determined by conjugation studies. The unit of map structure is the one-minute interval rather than the crossover frequency of higher organisms. A transfer time of 89 minutes for the entire chromosome is indicated. Symbols represent ability or inability to utilize or synthesize various substances.*

## Linkage Studies in Viruses

Bacteriophages or, more simply, phages are viruses that infect bacteria. Their structure and "life cycle" are described in Chapter 14. That they, like all viruses, have genetic systems is evident from the fact that they show, for instance, host and symptom specificities. Moreover, they can be shown to change in such genetically controlled properties as virulence toward a particular host, or in the kind of coat proteins produced, in short, to *mutate.* Although early thought ran more toward vague concepts of adaptation and induction, Luria and Delbrück (1943) opened the way to an understanding of mutation and selection in bacteria and their phages. These workers, and a host of others, in a flood of later papers demonstrated that both bacteria and viruses have genetic material just as do corn, mouse, fruit fly, and man.[3] Adaptation and induction have given way to the same processes of mutation and selection that operate in higher organisms.

Virulent phages destroy, or lyse, their hosts. One mutant in T2 and T4 phages (the T series infects the common colon bacterium, *Escherichia coli*) accomplishes this host destruction more rapidly than does the "wild-type" phage. These rapid lysing strains are designated as T2r, T4r, etc. If a culture of *E. coli* is infected by a mixture of T2 and T4r phages, *four* progeny types are recovered: the "parental" T2 and T4r, and also the recombinants T2r and T4!

Such recombination as this does not result from a sexual process, but rather by recombination and exchange of genetic material between the phages in conjunction with an involvement of the bacterial host's genetic material. We shall discuss the details of this process as soon as we know more about genetic material itself but, for our present purposes, it is important to note (1) that viruses can be "crossed," and (2) as a result, a map of the virus genome can be constructed. Rather early in these investigations, Hershey proposed three different linkage groups for T2, but more work has shown that the phage map, like that of bacteria, is "circular" in that each marker is linked to another on either side. One whole complex of T4r mutants, known as r-II (because they were originally assigned to linkage group II of Hershey), have thrown important light on the fine structure of the gene, and we shall examine them in more detail in Chapter 17.

## Mechanism of Recombination

The mechanism whereby the donated chromosomal segment and its genes become incorporated into the recipient's chromosome is not fully clear but two major theories have been proposed: (1) **copy-choice**, and (2) **break-and-exchange.** Both involve replication of DNA at the molecular level (see Chapter 14). For our purposes at this point, the essential outlines of the two possibilities may be described as follows:

*Copy-Choice.* By this method a daughter chromosome is formed by alternate use of recipient and donor chromosome material as a kind of model or template. The daughter chromosome is then like the recipient's except for portions "copied" from the donor chromosome segment. At the end of the process a recipient cell would contain (1) the original donor segment, (2) the original recipient whole chromosome, and (3) a "hybrid"

---

[3] Delbrück and Luria (along with Hershey, pages 274–277) shared the 1969 **Nobel Prize** for physiology and medicine for this work.

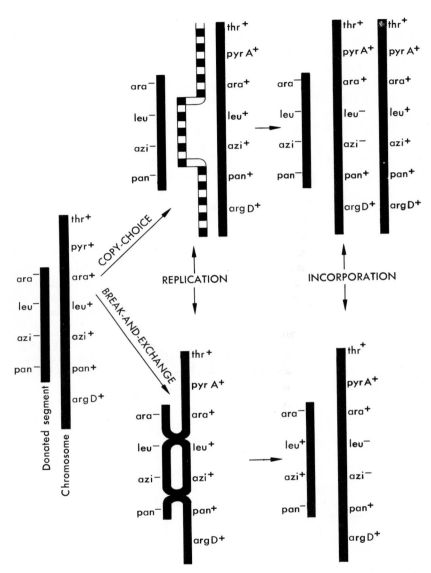

FIGURE 6-5. *Diagrammatic representation of comparison between copy-choice (upper bank) and break-and-exchange (lower bank) mechanisms of recombination.*

daughter chromosome. In succeeding divisions of the recipient cell, the donor segment is lost. (See Fig. 6-5.)

*Break-and-Exchange.* Under this theory breaks must occur on both sides of a block of genes in the donor segment as well as in the recipient's chromosome. This is followed by "repair" of the breaks such that a double crossover takes place (Fig. 6-5).

In one of the best summaries of the problem, Wollman, Jacob and Hayes (1962), conclude in this fashion: "In conjugation it is evident that a segment of donor chromosome . . . does not always participate in the formation of a recombinant chromosome and, when it does, that it is not necessarily incorporated as a whole. A mechanism analogous to crossing-over must therefore be assumed although its physical basis is likely to differ from one of simple breakage and reunion in view of the asymmetry of the parental components, one of which may be very small."

Neither theory alone is fully acceptable when applied to problems of the mechanics of crossing-over in the diploid organisms with which we opened this chapter. The break-and-exchange theory does not explicitly describe how two chromatids break at precisely the same points nor how the "repair" is effected. On the other hand, the copy-choice mechanism does not account for the fact that crossing-over often involves all four chromatids in prophase-I, rather than just the newly formed ones, as detailed in the next section.

*Tetrad Analysis.* The most suggestive evidence concerning the events of recombination is derived from certain plants that have a dominant monoploid phase—e.g., many algae, most true fungi, and all bryophytes (liverworts and mosses). In bryophytes, for example, meiosis results in a spherical tetrad of four *unordered* meiospores. But in such ascomycete fungi as *Neurospora*, the cells resulting from meiosis are *ordered*: that is, they are situated in line in the ascus (see life cycle, Appendix B). Such ordering reflects the pattern of chromosomal arrangement at each meiotic stage. Although meiosis in *Neurospora* produces the usual four meiospores, each of these divides once by mitosis to produce a total of eight ascospores, sequential pairs of which are genotypically identical. Each ascospore may be removed in order from the ascus and germinated to determine physiological phenotype, or examined visually for such morphological traits as color, etc. Such an analysis is termed **tetrad analysis**; it clearly indicates that recombination via crossing-over must occur at the four-chromatid stage, and thus supports the break-and-exchange hypothesis.

From a cross between an auxotroph (e.g., *prolineless*) and the wild-type prototroph, both + and *pro* ascospores are found in equal numbers in each ascus. However, the sequential arrangement of these spores may be either + + + + *pro pro pro pro*, or + + *pro pro* + + *pro pro*. The latter arrangement is possible only if recombination by crossing-over occurs during the four-strand stage (Fig. 6-6).

If a double auxotroph for the linked traits *prolineless/serineless*, *pro/ser*, and the wild-type +/+ are crossed, the reciprocal recombinants (+/*ser* and *pro*/+) are produced with equal frequency, along with the parental types.

Even more can be learned from studies of the segregation of blocks of three

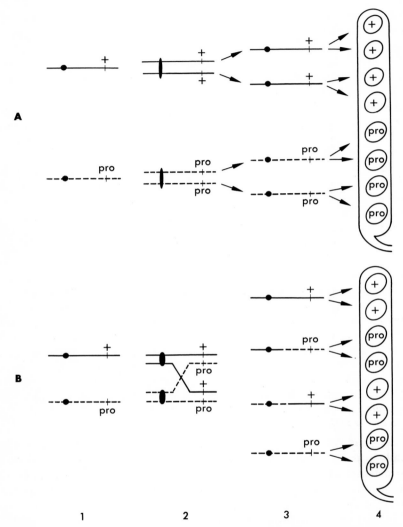

FIGURE 6-6. *Alternative arrangements of ascospores in ascus of* Neurospora. *In* (*A*) *crossing-over does not occur or does not involve genes* + *and pro; in* (*B*) *crossing-over occurs between the centromere and the* + *pro alleles* (*B 2*). *Only if crossing-over occurs in the 4-strand stage, involving nonsister chromatids, can the sequence of ascospores shown at* (*B 4*) *be attained. In 1 of both* (*A*) *and* (*B*), *the chromosomes contributed to the zygote by each parental strain are shown; in 2, replication has taken place and it is at this stage that synapsis and crossing-over* (*if any*) *occurs; in 3, the chromosomes of each of the meiospores resulting from meiosis are depicted; in 4, a mature ascus and the genotypes of each of its ascospores are shown. Meiosis is taking place between 1 and 3; mitosis occurs between 3 and 4.*

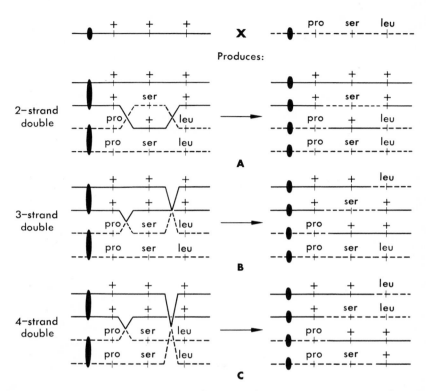

FIGURE 6-7. *Diagram showing possible types of double crossing-over involving (A) two chromatids only, (B) three chromatids, (C) all four chromatids, as inferred from tetrad analysis.*

linked markers. Tetrad analysis clearly shows that each crossover can involve either of the two chromatids of each homologous chromosome so that three different basic types of double crossover tetrads are possible:

1. *Two-strand doubles*, in which the same two chromatids are involved in both crossovers (Fig. 6-7A).
2. *Three-strand doubles*, in which three chromatids are involved, one of them participating twice (Fig. 6-7B).
3. *Four-strand doubles*, in which each of the crossovers involves a different pair of chromatids (Fig. 6-7C).

The observation of three- and four-strand doubles (Fig. 6-7 B and C) cannot be explained by a copy-choice mechanism alone, but requires break-and-exchange involving both sister and nonsister chromatids.

So tetrad analysis supports the cytological evidence that crossing-over occurs at the four-strand stage in cells with structurally organized chromosomes.

Since all four chromatids may be, and often are, involved in recombination by crossing-over, such an event cannot be limited to the newly synthesized strands as would be required under the copy-choice mechanism.

**Summary.**   Thus, as we should expect, we see that

1. The number of genes exceeds the number (of pairs) of chromosomes as our knowledge of the organism's genetics increases;
2. Therefore, certain blocks of genes are linked, and
3. The number of linkage groups is equal to the number (of pairs) of chromosomes, but
4. Linkage is not inviolable;
5. A reciprocal exchange of material between homologs in heterozygotes is reflected in crossing-over.
6. The frequency of crossing-over appears to be related to physical distance between genes on a chromosome and serves as a tool in constructing genetic maps of chromosomes, but
7. Although the actual *physical* mechanism of crossing-over remains unclear, the break-and-exchange hypothesis better fits observable facts than does the concept of copy-choice. Furthermore, an adequate theory must account for events at the molecular level, not only for bacteria and viruses, but for eukaryotes as well. At present our knowledge of the mechanics of recombination just does not extend to this level.

## REFERENCES

BATESON, W., and R. C. PUNNETT, 1905–1908. Experimental Studies in the Physiology of Heredity. Reports to the Evolution Committee of the Royal Society, 2, 3, and 4. Reprinted in J. A. Peters, ed., 1959. *Classic Papers in Genetics.* Englewood Cliff, N.J., Prentice-Hall.

CREIGHTON, H. S., and B. McCLINTOCK, 1931. A Correlation of Cytological and Genetical Crossing-Over in *Zea mays. Proc. Nat. Acad. Sci. (U.S.),* **17**:492–497. Reprinted in J. A. Peters, ed., 1959. *Classic Papers in Genetics.* Englewood Cliffs, N.J., Prentice-Hall.

HUTCHISON, C. B., 1922. The Linkage of Certain Aleurone and Endosperm Factors in Maize, and Their Relation to Other Linkage Groups. *Cornell Agr. Exp. Sta. Mem.,* **60**.

LURIA, S. E., and M. DELBRÜCK, 1943. Mutations of Bacteria from Virus Sensitivity to Virus Resistance. *Genetics,* **28**:491–511. Reprinted in E. A. Adelberg, ed., 1966, 2nd ed. *Papers on Bacterial Genetics.* Boston, Little, Brown.

McKUSICK, V. A., 1971. The Mapping of Human Chromosomes. *Sci. Amer.,* **224**:104–113.

MORGAN, T. H., 1910a. Sex-Limited Inheritance in *Drosophila. Science,* **32**:120–122.

MORGAN, T. H., 1910b. The Method of Inheritance of Two Sex-Limited Characters in the Same Animal. *Proc. Soc. Exp. Biol. Med.*, **8**:17.

MORGAN, T. H., 1911a. The Application of the Conception of Pure Lines to Sex-Limited Inheritance and to Sexual Dimorphism. *Amer. Nat.* **45**:65.

MORGAN, T. H., 1911b. Random Segregation Versus Coupling in Mendelian Inheritance. *Science*, **34**:384.

STERN, C., 1931. Zytologisch-genetische Untersuchungen als Beweise für die Morgansche Theorie des Faktorenaustauchs. *Biol. Zentralbl.*, **51**:547–587.

SUTTON, W. S., 1903. The Chromosomes in Heredity. *Biol. Bull.*, **4**:231–251. Reprinted in J. A. Peters, ed., *Classic Papers in Genetics.* Englewood Cliffs, N.J., Prentice-Hall.

WOLLMAN, E. L., F. JACOB, and W. HAYES, 1962. Conjugation and Genetic Recombination in *Escherichia coli* K-12. *Cold Spring Harbor Symp. Quant. Biol.*, **21**:141–162. Reprinted in E. A. Adelberg, ed., 1966, 2nd ed. *Papers on Bacterial Genetics.* Boston, Little, Brown.

## PROBLEMS

**6-1.** The following four pairs of genes are linked on chromosome 2 of tomato:

> *Aw, aw* purple, green stems
> *Dil, dil* normal green, light green leaves
> *O, o* oval, spherical fruit
> *Wo, wo* wooly, smooth leaves

Crossover frequencies in a series of two-pair testcrosses were found to be: *wo-o, 14 per cent*; *wo-dil, 9 per cent*; *wo-aw, 20 per cent*; *dil-o, 6 per cent*, *dil-aw*, 12 per cent; *o-aw*, 7 per cent (a) What is the sequence of these genes on chromosome 2; (b) why is not the *wo-aw* two-pair crossover frequency greater?

In the next four questions, the following facts will have to be used. In *Drosophila*, the following genes occur on chromosome III: *e*, ebony body; *fl*, fluted or creased wings; *jvl* ("javelin"), bristles cylindrical and crooked; *obt* ("obtuse"), wings short and blunt.

**6-2.** A series of dihybrid testcrosses shows the following crossover frequencies: *jvl-fl*, 3 per cent; *jvl-e*, 13 per cent; *fl-e*, 11 per cent. (a) What is the gene sequence? (b) How do you account for the fact that the sum of the *fl-e* and *fl-jvl* frequencies exceeds the *jvl-e* frequency?

**6-3.** Another cross discloses a crossover frequency of 19 per cent between *jvl* and *obt*. How well can you locate *obt* in the sequence established in problem 6-2?

**6-4.** If the *e-obt* crossover frequency is next found to be 7 per cent, where should gene *obt* be located in the sequence?

**6-5.** The *fl-obt* crossover frequency is determined by the cross + +/*fl obt* (♀) × *fl obt/fl obt* (♂) to be 17.5 per cent.
(a) Does this confirm your answer to 6-4? (b) What should be the frequency of double crossovers in a trihybrid testcross involving genes *fl, e*, and *obt* if there is no interference?

**6-6.** As pointed out in the explanatory note preceding problem 6-2, genes *e*, *fl*, *jvl*, and *obt* are located on chromosome III, along with many other known genes, thus constituting part of one linkage group. How many linkage groups are there altogether in *Drosophila melanogaster* females?

**6-7.** Mendel studied seven pairs of contrasting characters in the garden pea. Why did he not discover the principle of linkage?

**6-8.** How many linkage groups are there in the (a) female grasshopper; (b) male grasshopper; (c) human female; (d) human male?

**6-9.** Referring back to problems 6-2 through 6-5, how many different gamete genotypes are produced by (a) the female in the cross $+ + /jvl\,fl$ ($♀$) × *jvl fl*/ *jvl fl* ($♂$); (b) the male in the cross $+ + /jvl\,fl$ ($♀$) × $+ +/jvl\,fl$ ($♂$)?

**6-10.** How many different gamete genotypes are produced by (a) the female in the cross $+ + +/jvl\,fl\,e$ ($♀$) × *jvl fl e*/*jvl fl e* ($♂$); (b) the male in the cross $+ + +/jvl\,fl\,e$ ($♀$) × $+ + +/jvl\,fl\,e$ ($♂$)?

**6-11.** The cross $+ + +/abc$ ($♀$) × *abc*/*abc* ($♂$) in the fruit fly gives the following crossover results:

| | | |
|---|---|---|
| *a-b* | single crossovers | 5.75 per cent |
| *b-c* | single crossovers | 8.08 per cent |
| *a-c* | double crossovers | 0.25 per cent |

What is the coincidence?

**6-12.** Two of the pairs of alleles known in tomato are:

*Cu*,  "curl" (leaves curled)

*cu*,  normal leaves

*Bk*,  "beakless" fruits

*bk*,  "beaked" fruits, having sharp-pointed protuberance on blossom end of mature fruit

The cross of two doubly heterozygous "curl beakless" plants yields four phenotypic classes in the offspring, of which 23.04 per cent are "normal beaked." Are these two pairs of genes linked? How do you know?

**6-13.** From the data of problem 6-12 can you deduce (a) whether, in the parents, *cu* and *bk* were in the *cis* or *trans* configuration; (b) the distance between them in map units (assuming no interference)?

In the next four problems, use this information. Two of the many known pairs of genes in corn are:

*Pl*  purple plant

*pl*  green plant

*Py*  tall plant (normal height)

*py*  pigmy (very dwarf)

These genes are 20 map units apart on chromosome 6. The cross *Pl Py*/*pl py* ⁄ *Pl Py*/*pl py* is made. Now answer the following four questions.

**6-14.** What is the gamete genotypic ratio produced by each parent?

**6-15.** What percentage of the offspring has the genotype *pl py*/*pl py*?

**6-16.** What percentage of the progeny is purple pigmy?

**6-17.** What percentage of the offspring will be "true-breeding"?

**6-18.** In *Drosophila*, these genes occur on chromosome III:

+ wild    *h*   hairy (extra hairs on scutellars and head)
+ wild    *fz*   frizzled (thoracic hairs turn inward)
+ wild    *eg*   eagle (wings spread and raised)

The cross $+ + +/h\,fz\,eg \times h\,fz\,eg/h\,fz\,eg$ yielded this $F_1$:

| | | | | |
|---|---|---|---|---|
| wild wild wild | 393 | wild wild eagle | 28 |
| hairy frizzled eagle | 409 | hairy frizzled wild | 30 |
| wild frizzled eagle | 58 | wild frizzled wild | 1 |
| hairy wild wild | 80 | hairy wild eagle | 1 |

(a) Give the sequence of genes and the distances between them. (b) What is the coincidence?

**6-19.** In tomato the following genes are located on chromosome 2:

+ tall plant                *d*   dwarf plant
+ uniformly green leaves    *m*   mottled green leaves
+ smooth fruit             *p*   pubescent (hairy) fruit

Results of the cross $+ + +/d\,m\,p \times d\,m\,p/d\,m\,p$ were:

| | | | |
|---|---|---|---|
| + + + | 470 | + *m p* | 1 |
| + + *p* | 14 | *d* + *p* | 25 |
| *d* + + | 0 | *d m p* | 441 |
| + *m* + | 19 | *d m* + | 30 |

(a) Which groups represent double crossovers? (b) What is the correct gene sequence? (c) What are the distances in map units between the first and second, and between second and third genes? (d) Is there interference?

**6-20.** If, in sweet pea, the cross $R\,Ro/r\,ro \times R\,Ro/r\,ro$ is made, what would be the expected frequencies of (a) parental gametes of each of the possible genotypes; (b) $R\,Ro/R\,Ro$ progeny; (c) purple long progeny?

**6-21.** From the chromosome map for maize (corn), Fig. 1-9, note that genes $pg_{12}$, $gl_{15}$, and $bk_2$ are all on chromosome 9. The testcross $+ + +/pg_{12}\,gl_{15}\,bk_2 \times pg_{12}\,gl_{15}\,bk_2/pg_{12}\,gl_{15}\,bk_2$ is made. If there is complete interference, what is the frequency of (a) noncrossovers; (b) $pg_{12}\,gl_{15}$ single crossovers; (c) $gl_{15}\,bk_2$ single crossovers; (d) double crossovers in the progeny? (Assume all genotypes to be equally viable.)

**6-22.** With the cross of problem 6-21, what would be the frequencies of each of the eight progeny classes (a) if there is no interference; (b) if coincidence is 0.5? (Assume all genotypes to be equally viable, and crossover probabilities to be equal in all parts of the chromosome.)

**6-23.** Although not much is yet known about autosomal linkage in man, studies indicate linkage between the genes for the Rh blood factor and elliptocytosis (a rare but harmless dominant condition in which erythrocytes are ellipsoidal instead of the more common disc shape). These studies suggest a distance of 3 map units between these genes. For the sake of simplification, consider the

Rh + phenotype (production of the rhesus antigen) to be due to a single gene that is dominant to its allele for the Rh- phenotype (nonproduction of the rhesus antigen). If a doubly heterozygous man, known to have these two genes linked in the *cis* configuration, marries an Rh- woman who has normal, disc-shaped red blood cells and if coincidence is assumed to be 1, what is the probability of each of the following phenotypes among their children: (a) Rh +, elliptocytosis; (b) Rh +, without elliptocytosis?

**6-24.** Look again at the trihybrid testcross on page 111. If the cross + *ss* +/*cu* + *sr* × *cu ss sr*/*cu ss sr* had been made instead, what would be the percentage of (a) + *ss* + and *cu* + *sr*; (b) + + + and *cu ss sr* flies in the progeny, assuming the same crossover frequencies and the same interference?

# CHAPTER 7

# Multiple Alleles, Pseudoalleles, and Blood Group Inheritance

I N our discussions thus far, we have assumed that a particular chromosomal position, or **locus**, is occupied by either of two alleles. Many instances are now known, however, in which a given locus may bear any one of a series of several alleles, so that a diploid individual possesses any two genes of the series. When any of three or more genes may occupy the same locus in a given pair of homologous chromosomes they are said to constitute a series of **multiple alleles**.

## The Concept of Multiple Alleles

### COAT COLOR IN RABBITS

The coat of the ordinary (wild type) rabbit is referred to as "agouti" or full color, in which individuals have banded hairs, the portion nearest the skin being gray, succeeded by a yellow band, and finally a black or brown tip (Fig. 7-1). Albino rabbits, totally lacking in pigmentation, have also long been known (Fig. 7-2). Crosses of homozygous agouti and albino individuals produce a uniform agouti $F_1$; interbreeding of the $F_1$ produces an $F_2$ ratio of 3 agouti : 1 albino. Two thirds of these latter agouti individuals can be shown by testcrosses to be heterozygous. Clearly then, this is a case of monohybrid inheritance, with agouti completely dominant to albino.

Other individuals, lacking yellow pigment in the coat, have a silvery-gray appearance because of the optical effect of their black and gray hairs. This phenotype is referred to as chinchilla (Fig. 7-3). Crosses between chinchilla and agouti produce all agouti individuals in the $F_1$ and a 3 agouti : 1 chinchilla ratio in the $F_2$. Thus genes determining chinchilla and agouti appear to be alleles, with agouti again dominant. If, however, the cross chinchilla × albino is made, the $F_1$ are all chinchilla, and the $F_2$ shows 3 chinchilla : 1 albino. Therefore, genes for chinchilla and albino are also alleles, and agouti, chinchilla, albino are said to form a multiple allele series.

Still another phenotype is often encountered in pet shops. This is Himalayan (Fig. 7-4), in which the coat is white except for black extremities (nose, ears, feet, and tail). Eyes are pigmented, unlike albino. By appropriate crosses it can be shown that the gene for Himalayan is dominant to that for albino, but recessive to those determining agouti and chinchilla. Some of the possible

FIGURE 7-1.  *Wild type agouti rabbit.* [Photo courtesy American Genetic Association.]

FIGURE 7-2. *Albino rabbit. Albino animals are totally lacking in pigment.* [Photo courtesy American Genetic Association.]

FIGURE 7-3. *Chinchilla rabbit.* [Photo courtesy American Genetic Association.]

crosses, with $F_1$ and $F_2$ progeny, are shown in Fig. 7-5. Gene symbols often assigned are $c^+$ (agouti), $c^{ch}$ (chinchilla), $c^h$ (Himalayan), and $c$ (albino). From these crosses, we see the following dominance interrelationships:

$$c^+ > c^{ch} > c^h > c$$

It is easy, of course, to predict $F_1$ and $F_2$ progeny for two crosses not shown in Fig. 7-5; agouti × Himalayan, and chinchilla × albino.

Phenotypes and their associated genotypes, therefore, for this series in rabbit are as follows:

| Phenotype | Genotype |
|-----------|----------|
| agouti | $c^+c^+$, $c^+c^{ch}$, $c^+c^h$, $c^+c$ |
| chinchilla | $c^{ch}c^{ch}$, $c^{ch}c^h$, $c^{ch}c$ |
| Himalayan | $c^hc^h$, $c^hc$ |
| albino | $cc$ |

Note that ten different genotypes occur in this series. Earlier (Chapter 2), we saw that a single pair of alleles at a given locus produces three genotypes where dominance is complete. By the same token, a series of three multiple

FIGURE 7-4. *Himalayan rabbit*. [Photo courtesy American Genetic Association.]

alleles produces six genotypes. Note that as the number of genes in a series of multiple alleles increases, the variety of genotypes rises still more rapidly:

| # Alleles in Series | # Genotypes |
|:---:|:---:|
| 2 | 3 |
| 3 | 6 |
| 4 | 10 |
| 5 | 15 |
| $n$ | $\frac{n}{2}(n+1)$ |

With the number of possible genotypes increasing more rapidly than the number of alleles, a considerable increase in genetic variability ensues. Consider, for example, a hypothetical organism having only 100 loci, with a series of exactly 4 multiple alleles at each locus. Ten genotypes are possible at the first locus; these 10 can be combined with any of the 10 at the second locus, and so on. The total number of possible genotypes becomes $10^{100}$, or 1 followed by 100 zeroes! 

Available evidence indicates that a given locus may mutate in several directions many times in the history of a species. The various members of the series in rabbit undoubtedly arose at different times and places as mutations of an ancestral gene, quite possibly $c^+$. Small wonder, then, that many apparent cases of one pair differences ultimately turn out to involve series of

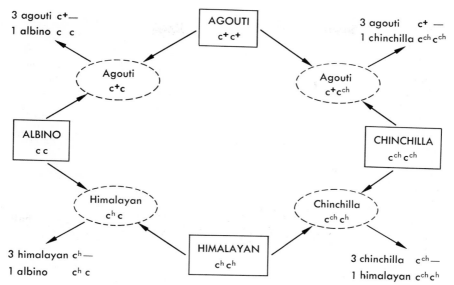

FIGURE 7-5. *Diagram representing several crosses in the multiple allele coat series in the rabbit. Parental generations in solid rectangles. $F_1$ generations within dashed ovals, $F_2$ generations not enclosed.*

multiple alleles! Other instances in animals and plants are referred to in the problems at the close of this chapter, though some interesting series in man are described in the following sections.

## The Blood Groups in Man

### THE ANTIGEN-ANTIBODY REACTION

Blood consists of two principal components: cells (red, white, and platelets) and liquid (plasma). Plasma, minus the clotting protein fibrinogen, is referred to as serum. In early attempts at transfusion, in fact as long ago as the eighteenth century, death of the recipient sometimes ensued for no determinable reason. But around 1900, Dr. Karl Landsteiner, working in a laboratory in Vienna, observed that red blood cells (erythrocytes) of certain individuals would clump together into macroscopically visible groups when mixed with the serum of some, but not all, other persons.

The basis for this clumping is the **antigen-antibody reaction**, an understanding of which is helpful at this point. Injection of a foreign substance **(antigen)** into the bloodstream of an animal brings about the production by some component of the blood of a characteristic **antibody** which reacts with the antigen. The antigen is ordinarily a protein, at least in part, and may be some plant or animal protein, a bacterial toxin, or even derived from pollen.

The antibody is highly specific for a particular antigen (though cross-reactions of varying degree may occur between one antibody and other closely similar antigen molecules). Such antibodies are termed *acquired*, because their production depends upon the entry of the foreign antigen; they are not otherwise produced. These form the basis of immunization practices as well as of allergic reactions. On the other hand, in a few cases, antibodies are produced naturally and normally by the blood, even in the absence of the appropriate antigen. These *natural antibodies* include several of those involved in human blood groups, particularly the important A-B-AB-O groups, which we shall discuss shortly.

Depending on the nature of the antigen and of its antibody, numerous sorts of each can be differentiated, each producing its own typical antigen-antibody reaction. If, for example, the antigen is a *toxin* (such as produced by typhoid, cholera, staphylococcus, whooping cough, and many other bacteria, or such substances as snake venom), neutralizing antibodies are called *antitoxins*. If the antigen is cellular in nature, the antibody may be a *lysin*, which lyses or disintegrates the invading cells, or an *agglutinin*, which causes clumping or agglutination of the cells. These are but a few of the recognized antibody types.

Following Landsteiner's discovery of agglutination of red blood cells and an understanding of the antigen-antibody reaction, further study by a number of investigators disclosed the occurrence of two natural antibodies in blood serum and two antigens on the surface of the erythrocytes. With regard to antigens, an individual may produce either, both, or neither; he may produce either, neither, or both antibodies. After some early and confusing multiplicity of nomenclature for these substances, the system in most general use today designates the antigens as A and B, and the corresponding antibodies as anti-A (or α) and anti-B (or β). Chemically, the A and B antigens are mucopolysaccharides, consisting of a protein and a sugar. The protein portion is identical in both antigens; it is the sugar that is the basis for the antigen-antibody specificity. An individual's blood group is denoted by the type of antigen he produces, as indicated in Table 7-1; blood tests for each of the four major groups are shown in Fig. 7-6.

TABLE 7-1. Antigens and Antibodies of the Human
Blood Groups

| Blood Group | Antigen on Erythrocytes | Antibody in Serum |
|---|---|---|
| A | A | anti-B |
| B | B | anti-A |
| AB | A and B | none |
| O | neither | anti-A and anti-B |

Anti-A     Anti-B     Blood Group

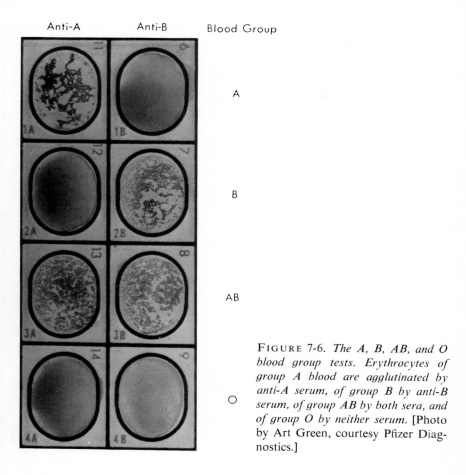

A

B

AB

O

FIGURE 7-6. *The A, B, AB, and O blood group tests. Erythrocytes of group A blood are agglutinated by anti-A serum, of group B by anti-B serum, of group AB by both sera, and of group O by neither serum.* [Photo by Art Green, courtesy Pfizer Diagnostics.]

A rather uncommon subgroup of A was discovered in 1911 so that group A was subdivided into $A_1$ and $A_2$. More recently, a still rarer subgroup, $A_3$, has been found, and even a still less common $A_4$ is known. Three slightly different variants of B are also reported. Although the A, B, AB, and O groups are important in transfusions, such subgroups as those of A are relevant to certain legal problems. We shall, therefore, direct our attention first to the genetics of the A, B, AB, and O blood groups.

## INHERITANCE OF A, B, AB, AND O BLOOD GROUPS

Studies of large numbers of human pedigrees have shown that children produce the A antigen only if at least one parent also produces it. Similarly, the B antigen is found only in individuals where at least one parent likewise has it. However, group O individuals may occur in the progeny of A and/or

TABLE 7-2. Inheritance of Blood Group Phenotypes in Man (Group A is arbitrarily shown as consisting of three subtypes. Phenotypes of parents are listed across the top and at the left; phenotypes of possible children are shown in the body of the table.)

| Parental Groups | $A_1$ | $A_2$ | $A_3$ | $B$ | $O$ | $A_1B$ | $A_2B$ | $A_3B$ |
|---|---|---|---|---|---|---|---|---|
| $A_1$ | $A_1$ $A_2$ $A_3$ $O$ | $A_1$ $A_2$ $A_3$ $O$ | $A_1$ $A_2$ $A_3$ $O$ | $A_1B$ $A_2B$ $A_3B$ $B$ $O$ $A_1$ $A_2$ $A_3$ | $A_1$ $A_2$ $A_3$ $O$ | $A_1$ $A_1B$ $A_2B$ $A_3B$ $B$ | $A_1$ $A_1B$ $A_2B$ $A_3B$ $B$ | $A_1$ $A_2$ $A_1B$ $A_2B$ $A_3B$ $B$ |
| $A_2$ | | $A_2$ $A_3$ $O$ | $A_2$ $A_3$ $O$ | $A_2B$ $A_3B$ $B$ $A_2$ $A_3$ $O$ | $A_2$ $A_3$ $O$ | $A_1$ $A_2B$ $A_3B$ $B$ | $A_2$ $A_2B$ $A_3B$ $B$ | $A_2$ $A_3$ $A_2B$ $A_3B$ $B$ |
| $A_3$ | | | $A_3$ $O$ | $A_3B$ $B$ $A_3$ $O$ | $A_3$ $O$ | $A_1$ $A_3B$ $B$ | $A_2$ $A_3B$ $B$ | $A_3$ $A_3B$ $B$ |
| $B$ | | | | $B$ $O$ | $B$ $O$ | $A_1$ $A_1B$ $B$ | $A_2$ $A_2B$ $B$ | $A_3$ $A_3B$ $B$ |
| $O$ | | | | | $O$ | $A_1$ $B$ | $A_2$ $B$ | $A_3$ $B$ |
| $A_1B$ | | | | | | $A_1$ $A_1B$ $B$ | $A_1$ $A_2$ $A_1B$ $A_2B$ $B$ | $A_1$ $A_3$ $A_1B$ $A_3B$ $B$ |
| $A_2B$ | | | | | | | $A_2$ $A_2B$ $B$ | $A_2$ $A_3$ $A_2B$ $A_3B$ $B$ |
| $A_3B$ | | | | | | | | $A_3$ $A_3B$ $B$ |

B parents, but O parents have only O children, suggesting recessiveness of the gene for group O. Yet marriages of A and B parents produce, in some cases, children having both A and B antigens, indicative of *codominance* of the genes for these latter antigens. Table 7-2 presents a summary of progeny phenotypes.

Pedigree analysis clearly shows that an individual possesses, in either the homozygous or heterozygous state, any two of a series of *multiple alleles*. Because the antigens involved are of the type known as isoagglutinogens (or isohemagglutinogens) these genes are designated as $I^A$, $I^B$, and $i$. Neglecting for the moment the subgroups of A, dominance relationships of these three alleles would be represented thus: $I^A = I^B > i$. Additional studies which take into account the subgroups of the A antigen indicate that gene $I^A$ may occur in at least three allelic forms, $I^{A_1}$, $I^{A_2}$, and $I^{A_3}$, with $I^{A_1}$ dominant over both $I^{A_2}$ and $I^{A_3}$, and $I^{A_2}$ dominant over $I^{A_3}$. Considering, then the three forms of $I^A$, and one of $I^B$, and one of $i$, dominance within the complete series may be designated in this way:

$$[(I^{A_1} > I^{A_2} > I^{A_3}) = I^B] > i$$

Thus, this series of multiple alleles produces 15 genotypes and 8 phenotypes:

| Genotype | Phenotype | Genotype | Phenotype |
|---|---|---|---|
| $I^{A_1} I^{A_1}$ | | $I^{A_1} I^B$ | $A_1B$ |
| $I^{A_1} I^{A_2}$ | | | |
| $I^{A_1} I^{A_3}$ | $A_1$ | $I^{A_2} I^B$ | $A_2B$ |
| $I^{A_1} i$ | | | |
| | | $I^{A_3} I^B$ | $A_3B$ |
| $I^{A_2} I^{A_2}$ | | | |
| $I^{A_2} I^{A_3}$ | $A_2$ | $I^B I^B$ | B |
| $I^{A_2} i$ | | $I^B i$ | |
| $I^{A_3} I^{A_3}$ | $A_3$ | $i\,i$ | O |
| $I^{A_3} i$ | | | |

Response to anti-A, anti-B, and other antisera, however, may be weakened or even eliminated by leukemia in persons whose red blood cells had previously given normal reactions with the appropriate antisera. This is especially well documented in the case of anti-A serum; in a few instances a diminished response to anti-A serum is reported to be accompanied by a weak reaction with anti-B in leukemic persons of group A. Except for such unusual situations one's blood antigen/antibody traits are constant and accurate reflections of his genotype.

## MEDICOLEGAL ASPECTS OF THE A-B-O-SERIES

From Table 7-2 and a knowledge of the dominance relationships of the multiple allele series involved, from which the data of the table are derived, applications to cases of disputed parentage can readily be seen. Although mixups are rare today in hospitals, situations have occurred in the past where one or more sets of parents have believed they were given someone else's child upon discharge of mother and new baby from the hospital. For example, a court case of some years ago involved just such a situation. Two sets of parents had taken babies home from a particular hospital at about the same time; in the process, the identification bracelet of the infant taken by family #1 had become detached. Family #2 soon discovered family #1's name on the child they had received, but the latter family would not agree to an exchange. Fortunately, blood tests quickly demonstrated that neither child could have belonged to the family that had taken it home, but each *could* belong to the other parents:

|  | Parental<br>Blood Groups | Blood Group of<br>Child Taken Home |
|---|---|---|
| Family # 1 | A × AB | O |
| Family # 2 | O × O | B |

An exchange thereupon satisfied both families. Obviously, the tests in this case did not *prove* that the child received by family #1 belonged to family #2, but only that it *could*. Suppose the two families had been A × B and O × B, and that the children given to each had been found to be O and B respectively. With no additional information from other tests (some of which are described later in this chapter) it would be manifestly impossible to make a valid decision, since either family could have produced either child.

Quite clearly, too, blood tests are of considerable value in cases of illegitimacy. Again, tests cannot *prove* a man to be the father, but they can, in some instances show that he could *not* be.[1] Unfortunately, though, the courts do not all accord this kind of evidence the same weight. One of the most celebrated cases of this kind occurred late in 1944 in California. A widely known movie star was accused by a former starlet-protégé of being the father of her young daughter. The plaintiff's case rested on a remarkable memory for dates and details, a memory so precise that all other potential fathers were

[1] According to Race and Sanger (1968), tests for ABO, MNSs, Rh, Kell, Lutheran, Duffy, and Kidd groups (see later sections of this chapter) can exonerate about 62 per cent of western Europeans incorrectly charged with paternity. The percentage would be expected to be about the same in the United States.

eliminated. Three physicians made blood tests of the alleged father, the mother, and the baby with these results:

|                | Blood Group |
|----------------|-------------|
| Alleged father | O           |
| Mother         | A           |
| Daughter       | B           |

A moment's reflection on the genetics of these phenotypes, or reference to Table 7-2, shows clearly that the defendant could not possibly have been the father (barring a highly improbable mutation). Rather, the real father must have belonged either to group B or AB. In spite of such scientific evidence, the jury in a second trial (the first ended in a "hung jury") found the plaintiff *guilty*! So far as can be determined, he was required to contribute for twenty-one years to the support of a child not his own.

Laws of various states differ considerably with regard to the weight to be attached to blood test results in paternity cases; frequently the importance of such evidence is up to the court! In a few states (e.g., New York) results of such tests are definitive or conclusive evidence if they establish nonpaternity; in many, blood tests constitute admissible or introduced evidence, to be accorded no greater weight than any other; in some, such evidence may not even be introduced. A brief and partial survey of several states makes interesting if, in some instances, appalling reading:

*California*: blood tests may be used as introduced evidence; not conclusive (Berry v. Chaplin).

*Colorado*: (1963) defendant entitled to have blood test results received in evidence when exclusion is indicated (Beck v. Beck).

*Maine*: (1956) admissible evidence when nonpaternity is indicated (Jordan v. Davis).

*Massachusetts*: (1960) admissible evidence (Comm. v. D'Avulla).

*New York*: (1959) blood tests that demonstrate nonpaternity constitute conclusive evidence (statute).

*Ohio*: (1945) blood test results may be used as evidence with "whatever weight it may have" (State of Ohio ex. rel. Walker v. Clark).

*Pennsylvannia*: (1959) blood tests may be used "not [as] conclusive [evidence] but are entitled to the same evidentiary weight as other evidence" (Comm. v. Cline).

*Wisconsin*: (1957) blood test evidence admissible but given consideration with other evidence.

It should be emphasized that, in staes in which blood test evidence is not "conclusive," considerable weight is given to the current or most recent decision. For example, in one recent opinion in Ohio, the judge wrote, "In accordance with the enlightened judicial acceptance of the high value of blood grouping tests properly conducted, I hold that, in the absence of any competent proof that blood grouping tests were not properly made, the results of such tests . . . should be given such great weight by the Court that the exclusion of the defendant as the father of the child follows irresistably." In the juvenile court of one Ohio county, in a fourteen-year period, some 12,000 paternity suits were handled. Blood tests were made in 734 of these; in 104 exclusions were demonstrated. In 102 of these latter, the defendant won the decision or the case was dropped; of the remaining two, one won a second trial and the other (surprisingly) settled out of court.

Blood tests involving the A-B-O series, as well as others to be described, may, of course, also be used to a good advantage in cases of claimants to estates or in certain kinds of criminal proceedings, particularly since blood group may usually be determined from corpses. In fact, blood type can often be determined from mummies, and this has become an important anthropological tool in some investigations. Problems at the end of this chapter explore some hypothetical possibilities.

### PSEUDOALLELES

*Drosophila.*   By the early 1900s a large number of sex-linked genes affecting eye color in *Drosophila* was known, among them red (wild type), coral, cherry, apricot, eosin, ivory, and white. All of these were considered, on the basis of $F_2$ ratios, to form a multiple allele series, wild being dominant to all others, and white recessive to all. All are located at about 1.5 on the X chromosome map. However, in crosses that ordinarily produced only apricot and white progeny, about 1 in 10,000 individuals had wild-type red eyes. By using the "marker genes," *y* (yellow body color), at locus 1.0 and *spl* (split bristles) at locus 3.0, it was possible to show that apricot and white occupied separate, but extremely close, loci with a crossover frequency of approximately 0.01.

Surprisingly, the two possible kinds of heterozygous females have different phenotypes. Thus, *w* +/+ *apr* is pale apricot and + +/*w apr* is wild type. If the wild-type alleles are in the *cis* position, red eyes occur, if they are in the *trans* configuration, the phenotype is pale apricot (mutant). This is the **cis-trans effect**. Genes *w* and *apr* are *functionally allelic* in that they produce different expressions of the same phenotypic trait, but *structurally nonallelic* in that (1) they are separable by a very low order of crossing-over and (2) they exhibit the *cis-trans* effect. Such functionally related and closely linked genes as these are referred to as **pseudoalleles** which, because of their extremely close linkage, are most often inherited together.

Pseudoallelism is now widely known in many organisms; an important instance in man is described in the next section and others are taken up in the problems at the end of this chapter. But now how does one define a gene? Certainly it cannot be defined as a unit of *both* structure and function, but can be considered in either of two ways. Lewis (1955) and Green (1963) proposed that pseudoalleles be regarded as distinct and separate genes, with their own particular functions which must be carried out in sequence at the same intracellular (chromosomal) location. *Cis* heterozygotes would thus be able to carry out the total function but *trans* heterozygotes would not. The *cis-trans* position effect would, therefore, be the result of the product of one gene (which serves as the substrate for the other gene) not being able to diffuse from one chromosome to its homolog for action of the other gene. Another interpretation, championed by Pontecorvo (1958), regards pseudoalleles as different mutational and recombinational sites *within the same gene*—that is, **the gene must be regarded as subdivisible** and defined by functional properties. The gene then functions only when all its subunits occur in one sequential group; its function is interfered with by change (mutation) at any of several internal points. Recombination, by crossing-over, may also occur *within* such a gene rather than only *between* genes. Such a functional gene, as defined by the *cis-trans* test, has been termed a **cistron** (Benzer, 1957). Its more precise structure and operation is discussed in Chapter 17.

The Pontecorvo concept, as we shall see, appears to be more widely applicable. At this point the importance of pseudoallelism for our purpose is twofold: (1) the classical gene now appears to be separable into structural and functional units, and (2) intragenic units of recombination and of mutation may be recognizable.

*The Rh Factor in Man.* The now well-known Rh factor was discovered in 1940 by Landsteiner and Wiener, who reported that if a rabbit was injected with blood of the *Macaca rhesus* monkey, antibodies were formed which would agglutinate the red blood cells of all rhesus monkeys. Thus, the erythrocytes of this species of monkey contain a specific antigen, designated as "Rh." Tests of human beings show that most persons also produce the same antigen; in fact, some 85 per cent of white Americans do. They are designated Rh positive (Rh+); the much smaller percentage who do not produce the rhesus antigen are designated Rh negative (Rh−). Interestingly enough, no cases are known of persons whose blood naturally contains anti-Rh antibodies, though Rh− individuals can and do develop them if exposed to the Rh antigen. Such exposure can occur by transfusion, and this is the reason the Rh type is now routinely determined for blood donors and recipients.

But anti-Rh antibody development can occur also in certain pregnancies, often resulting in a fetal condition known as erythroblastosis. This is a hemolytic anemia in the fetus, often accompanied by jaundice as liver capillaries become clogged with red blood cell remains and bile is absorbed by the blood. The damaged erythrocytes are imperfect oxygen carriers and resemble the immature cells of the marrow, where they are normally formed. Death may take place shortly before birth or soon after unless appropriate corrective measures are taken in time.

The disease occurs only when a number of coincident conditions are met. The mother must be Rh−, the fetus Rh+ (therefore only marriages of Rh− women and Rh+ men are involved); see next paragraph. There must also be a placental defect whereby blood, carrying the Rh antigen from the Rh+ embryo, passes into the maternal circulation. As a consequence Rh antibody concentration is gradually built up in the mother. These antibodies return to the fetus, where they destroy the antigen-carrying red blood cells. There is some thought that the placental defect itself may have a genetic basis as indicated from pedigree studies; by no means all marriages between Rh− women and Rh+ men result in erythroblastosis. Buildup of antibodies in the mother's blood is slow, so that the first pregnancy does not ordinarily result in trouble unless she has previously received a tranfusion of Rh+ blood. However, subsequent pregnancies may result in erythroblastosis. Although fetal erythroblastosis is a severe and tragic condition, it is, fortunately, relatively infrequent. One study in Chicago showed only 91 affected children in 22,742 births in a six-year period. This is approximately 0.4 per cent. Compare this observed frequency with calculations by the Hardy-Weinberg law (Chapter 13).

Evidence almost immediately indicated a genetic basis to the Rh+ and Rh− phenotypes, with the former dominant. A single pair of genes, $R$ and $r$, was postulated for Rh+ and Rh− blood, respectively. A number of subtypes of the Rh antigen was rapidly discovered, and the genetics of the system has turned out to be fairly complicated, with about 30 antigens and antibodies recognized at present. Race and Sanger (1968) present a detailed summary of the complexities of the Rh blood groups. Two major explanatory hypotheses were developed, one by the American investigator Wiener, and a second, chiefly in England, by Fisher and others. The Wiener theory postulates a number (at least eight) of multiple alleles at a single locus, whereas Fisher

TABLE 7-3. Comparision of Wiener and
Fisher Theories

| Gene Symbols | | Antigens Produced | Phenotype |
|---|---|---|---|
| Wiener | Fisher | | |
| $r$ | $cde$ | none | Rh − |
| $R_o$ | $cDe$ | $R_o$ | Rh + |
| $R'$ | $Cde$ | $R'$ | Rh + |
| $R''$ | $cdE$ | $R''$ | Rh + |
| $R_1$ | $CDe$ | $R_o$ and $R'$ | Rh + |
| $R_2$ | $cDE$ | $R_o$ and $R''$ | Rh + |
| $R_x$ or $R_z$ | $CDE$ | $R_o$, $R'$, and $R''$ | Rh + |
| $R_y$ | $CdE$ | $R'$ and $R''$ | Rh + |

TABLE 7-4. Rh Phenotypes and Genotypes (Fisher) and
Per Cent Frequencies in the American Population

| Phenotype | Genotype | $n = 135$ Black | $n = 105$ Oklahoma Indian | $n = 766$ White |
|---|---|---|---|---|
| Rh + | cDe/cde | 45.9 | 2.9 | 2.2 |
| Rh + | CDe/CDe | 0.9 | 34.3 | 20.9 |
| Rh + | CDe/cde | 22.8 | 5.7 | 33.8 |
| Rh + | cDE/cDE | 16.3 | 17.1 | 14.9 |
| Rh + | CDe/cDE | 4.4 | 36.2 | 13.9 |
| Rh + | CDe/CDE | 0.0 | 2.9 | 0.1 |
| Rh − | cde/cde | 9.6 | 0.9 | 13.9 |

proposes a series of at least three pairs of pseudoalleles so closely linked that they are usually inherited as a block. Present evidence tends to favor the Fisher hypothesis, in part because of occasional crossing-over between the "Fisher pseudoalleles," and in part because of the difficulty involved in the postulated relationships between genes and antigen production under the Wiener system. In the table of comparison (Table 7-3), note that the Wiener theory dictates production of antigen $R_o$ by gene $R_o$, antigen R' by gene R', but production of both antigens together by a different gene $R_1$. Some of the more common genotypes are listed in Table 7-4, together with their approximate frequencies in the American population.

TABLE 7-5. Rh Phenotypes, Genotypes, and Per Cent Frequencies in 8,297 Swedish Children (Based on Work of Heiken and Rasmuson, 1966).*

| Phenotype | Representative Probable Genotype | Per Cent of Sample | Phenotype | Representative Probable Genotype | Per Cent of Sample |
|---|---|---|---|---|---|
| Rh + | cDe/cde | 1.48 | Rh − | cde/cde | 14.90 |
| Rh + | cDE/cDE | 3.08 | Rh − | cdE/cde | 0.22 |
| Rh + | cDE/cde | 12.50 | Rh − | $C^w$de/cde | 0.02 |
| Rh + | CDe/cde | 32.72 | Rh − | Cde/cde | 0.39 |
| Rh + | $C^w$De/cde | 1.45 | | | |
| Rh + | CDe/cDE | 14.46 | | | |
| Rh + | CDE/cDE | 0.05 | | | |
| Rh + | $C^w$De/cDE | 0.66 | | | |
| Rh + | CDe/CDe | 16.16 | | | |
| Rh + | $C^w$De/CDE | 1.86 | | | |
| Rh + | CDE/CDe | 0.05 | | | |
| | Total | 84.47 | | Total | 15.53 |

* In this work a positive reaction with anti-D serum is used to designate an Rh+ phenotype; a negative reaction with anti-D designates an Rh− phenotype.

Many other less common rhesus antigens have also been listed since 1940. One of these is $C^W$, originally described by Callender and Race (1946), and since found on numerous occasions. It is assumed to be due to gene $C^W$, an allele of $C$. Heiken and Rasmuson (1966) have published an extensive list of Rh frequencies on a large sample of Swedish children (Table 7-5).

The sequence of these three genes appears to be $D$-$C$-$E$, as suggested by Fisher (1947). He based this conclusion on the observation that $D$-$E$ crossovers, infrequent though they are, exceed those occurring between $C$ and $E$, which is less likely to be the case if the order is $C$-$D$-$E$. Moreover, antisera that react with compound antigens such as Ce and ce suggest a possible *cis-trans* effect which, in turn, clearly indicates pseudoallelism. For example, genotype $CDe/cDE$ shows a reaction with anti-Ce antiserum but not to anti-ce, but genotype $CDE/cDe$ gives the opposite result, reacting with anti-ce but not anti-Ce. That is, only when genes $c$ and $e$ are in the *cis* configuration can they produce the compound antigen ce. So it would appear that the $c$ and $e$ genes, at least, are part of the same cistron which would then be expected to contain several different mutational and recombinational sites. Present evidence does not indicate whether gene $d$ is or is not part of the same cistron. Thus the concept of three pseudoallelic loci, in the sequence $D$-$C$-$E$, seems to be valid at this time.

## OTHER BLOOD PHENOTYPES

*The H Antigen.*   With genotypes $HH$ or $Hh$ a so-called H-substance is present on the erythrocytes and may be demonstrated by agglutination by anti-H serum. The H antigen is believed to be an intermediate between a precursor mucopolysaccharide and antigens A and B to which it is partly converted in the presence of genotypes $I^A-$ or $I^B-$. So long as they are of genotype $H-$, group A individuals produce antigens A and H, group B persons test positively for antigens B and H, and group AB persons produce antigens A, B, and H. Individuals of group O produce only antigen H if their genotype is $iiH-$, but none of these antigens if the genotype is $iihh$. Persons whose blood gives no reaction with anti-A, anti-B, or anti-H belong to the very rare Bombay phenotype, so named because it was first described in a small group from that city. Figure 7-7 shows these relationships.

*The Secretor Trait.*   As study of the A, B, AB, and O blood groups continued, it was noted that with some, but not all, persons whose erythrocytes contain A, B, and/or H antigens, these antigens could also be detected in such aqueous secretions as those from eyes, nose, and salivary glands. Persons with this trait are referred to as *secretors*; they produce water-soluble antigens. Several reports in the literature indicate that about 77 to 78 per cent of all persons tested are secretors. Individuals lacking this trait are termed *non-secretors*, and their antigens are only alcohol soluble. Note that the secretor/nonsecretor phenotype can be determined only for $HH$ or $Hh$ genotypes. The

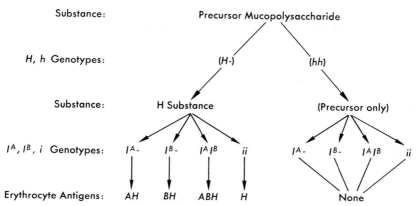

FIGURE 7-7. *Pathways leading to production of antigens on the red blood cells. The precursor mucopolysaccharide is converted into H substance in the presence of genotype H- and is, itself, partly converted into A and/or B antigens in the presence of genes $I^A$ and/or $I^B$, with $I^{A1}$ more effective than $I^{A2}$, and $I^{A3}$ least effective. The very rare gene h (for lack of H substance) is epistatic to the multiple alleles at the A-B-O locus. Cells of persons of --hh genotype give no reaction with anti-A or anti-B sera (even though they possess genes $I^A$ or $I^B$; this is the rare Bombay phenotype).*

blood group of $H-$ secretors can be determined even from dried saliva.

Pedigree studies indicate a single pair of genes, *Se* and *se*, to be responsible. The secretor trait is completely dominant. This pair of genes markedly increases the number of blood phenotypes.

**The M-N Series.** In the course of their investigations of human blood antigens, Landsteiner and Levine in 1927 discovered two, M and N, which, when injected into rabbits or guinea pigs, stimulated antibody production in the serum of the experimental animal. Apparently, human beings do not produce their own antibodies for these antigens, so they are of no importance in transfusion. They are, however, of some interest in genetics, since inheritance of the trait depends upon a pair of codominant genes sometimes referred to as $L^M$ and $L^N$ (for Landsteiner), but more frequently now simply as *M* and *N*, producing phenotypes as follows:

| Phenotype | Antigen Produced |
|-----------|------------------|
| M | antigen M only |
| MN | antigens M *and* N |
| N | antigen N only |

No allele for the absence of either antigen is known. Statistical analysis reflects the 1:2:1 phenotypic ratio to be expected in instances of codominance.

One study of 6,129 individuals in this country included 29.2 per cent M, 49.6 per cent MN, and 21.2 per cent N type persons. It should be noted, however, that the *frequencies* of genes *M* and *N* must have been close to 0.5 each in the parents of these 6,129 individuals in order for this progeny ratio to be produced. Frequencies of the members of a pair of alleles, of course, need not necessarily be close to equality in a randomly mating group, and progeny ratios depend in large part on the frequencies with which the alleles occur. This topic is explored and extended in Chapter 13.

Another pair of antigens, S and s, with intimate genetic relation to the M-N series, was discovered in 1947. Unfortunately, the designation of antigens has developed rather randomly, so that we have here two sets of antigens, one denoted by two different capital letters (M and N), the other by the same letter in upper and lower case (S and s). Studies show that all human beings produce either antigen S, antigen s, or both; therefore, another pair of codominant genes (now generally designated as *S* and *s*) is involved.

As indicated, there is a close genetic relationship between the *M-N* and *S-s* pairs of genes. For example, in families where the parents are phenotypically MNSs and NS, the children, with very rare exceptions, fall into either of two categories: (1) MNS and NSs, or (2) MNSs and NS. Clearly in the first of these two cases, children received genes for either MS or Ns from the heterozygous parent, whereas in the second they received either genes for Ms or NS. Earlier explanations favored a series of four multiple alleles at a single locus: $M^S$, $M^s$, $N^S$, and $N^s$ and, indeed, such results as those just cited could rest on a multiple allele mechanism. However, Race and Sanger (1968), in their extensive studies on human blood groups, prefer an alternate explanation, i.e., two pairs of very closely linked codominant genes, *M-N*, and *S-s*. This conclusion is based on rare instances of recombination between the two suggested loci. On the basis of the latter assumption, the two cases described in this paragraph may be diagrammed as follows:

$$\text{Case 1:} \quad \text{P} \quad MS/Ns \times NS/NS$$
$$\text{F}_1 \quad \tfrac{1}{2}\,MS/NS + \tfrac{1}{2}\,Ns/NS$$
$$\text{Case 2:} \quad \text{P} \quad Ms/NS \times NS/NS$$
$$\text{F}_1 \quad \tfrac{1}{2}\,Ms/NS + \tfrac{1}{2}\,NS/NS$$

Upward of a dozen and a half other antigens, most of them quite uncommon, have been shown to be related to the M-N and S-s substances. The explanation probably lies in a sequential series of gene-mediated reactions on one or a few precursor substances.

*Other Antigens.*   Many other blood antigens have been described in the literature, some quite rare. These are usually designated by the family name of the individual in whom the antigen or antibody was first demonstrated. Thus, we have the Kidd factor (about 77 per cent of the tested United States population is reported to be Kidd-positive), the Cellano, Duffy, Kell, Lervis, and Lutheran factors, to list but a few.

These and a large number of additional antigens and/or antibodies produce a great diversity of human blood groups. In one test of 475 persons in London for $A_1$-$A_2$-B antigens, the M-N-S-s series, Rh, Kell, Lutheran, and Lervis groups, 269 types were reported, of which 211 included only a single person each. Considering the presently known groups and the fact that additional ones continue to be reported, the already large number of blood phenotypes may someday rise to the point where an individual's blood group may identify him as certainly as do his fingerprints. Only identical twins, etc., who have identical genotypes, would then be indistinguishable by appropriate tests.

## REFERENCES

BENZER, S., 1957. The Elementary Units of Heredity. In W. D. McElroy and B. Glass, *The Chemical Basis of Heredity*. Baltimore, John Hopkins Press.

CALLENDER, S. T., and R. R. RACE, 1946. A Serological and Genetical Study of Multiple Antibodies Formed in Response to Blood Transfusion by a Patient with Lupus Erythematosus Diffusus. *Ann. Eugen.*, **13**:103–117.

FISHER, R. A., 1947. The Rhesus Factor: A Study in Scientific Method. *Am. Scien.*, **35**:95–103.

GREEN, M. M., 1963. Pseudoalleles and Recombination in *Drosophila*. In W. J. Burdette, ed., *Methodology in Basic Genetics*. San Francisco, Holden Day.

HEIKEN, A., and M. RASMUSON, 1966. Genetical Studies on the Rh Blood Group System. *Hereditas Lund*, **55**:192–212.

LEWIS, E. B., 1952. The Pseudoallelism of White and Apricot in *Drosophila melanogaster*. *Proc. Nat. Acad. Sci. (U.S.)*, **38**:953–961.

LEWIS, E. B., 1955. Some Aspects of Pseudoalleles. *Amer. Natur.* **89**:73.

PONTECORVO, G., 1958. *Trends in Genetic Analysis*. New York, Columbia University Press.

RACE, R. R., and R. SANGER, 1968, 5th ed. *Blood Groups in Man*. Philadelphia, F. A. Davis.

WIENER, A. S., and I. B. WEXLER, 1958. *Heredity of the Blood Groups*. New York, Grune & Stratton.

## PROBLEMS

**7-1.** Is it possible to cross two agouti rabbits and produce both chinchilla and Himalayan progeny?

**7-2.** A series of rabbit matings, chinchilla $\times$ Himalayan, produced a progeny ratio of 1 Himalayan:2 chinchilla:1 albino. What were the parental genotypes?

**7-3.** In the ornamental flowering plant nasturtium, flowers may be either single, double, or superdouble. These differ in number of petals, superdouble having the largest number. Crosses of superdouble $\times$ double sometimes yield 1 superdouble:1 double, and sometimes all superdouble. Superdouble $\times$ superdouble produces all superdouble, or 3 superdouble:1 double, or 3 superdouble:1 single. Single $\times$ single produces only single. (a) How many multiple alleles occur in this series? (b) Arrange the phenotypes in order of relative dominance. (c) Another cross of superdouble $\times$ double produces progeny in the ratio of 1 double:2 superdouble:1 single. What do you know about the parental genotypes?

Use the following information in answering the next four problems. In the Chinese primrose the flower has a center, or "eye," of a color different from the remainder of the petals. Normally this eye is of medium size and yellow in color. These variants also occur: very large yellow eye ("Primrose Queen" variety), white eye ("Alexandra"), and blue eye ("Blue Moon"). Results of certain crosses are:

| P | $F_1$ | $F_2$ |
|---|---|---|
| Normal $\times$ Alexandra | Alexandra | 3 Alexandra:1 Normal |
| Alexandra $\times$ Primrose Queen | Alexandra | (not reported) |
| Blue Moon $\times$ Normal | Normal | 3 Normal:1 Blue Moon |
| Primrose Queen $\times$ Blue Moon | Blue Moon | (not reported) |

**7-4.** Arrange these phenotypes in order of relative dominance.

**7-5.** How many genotypes can produce the "Alexandra" phenotype?

**7-6.** How many genotypes can produce the "Primrose Queen" phenotype?

**7-7.** How many different combinations of parental genotypes will produce a progeny ratio of 3 Alexandra:1 normal?

Use the following information in the next four problems: A series of multiple alleles for coat color is reported in the mouse. One series of breeding results was:

| P | $F_1$ |
|---|---|
| plain black $\times$ white-bellied | white-bellied |
| plain black $\times$ dark-bellied | dark-bellied |
| white-bellied $\times$ dark-bellied | white-bellied |

**7-8.** What should be the $F_1$ of the cross plain black $\times$ plain black?

**7-9.** The cross of two heterozygous dark-bellied animals will produce what $F_1$ phenotypic ratio?

**7-10.** A cross between two white-bellied animals produced an $F_1$ ratio of 3 white-bellied:1 dark-bellied. What were the parental genotypes?

**7-11.** Later, an additional allele in this series, producing black-and-tan coat, was discovered. Crosses of black-and-tan with white-bellied produce all white-bellied in the $F_1$; black-and-tan $\times$ dark-bellied produce all dark-bellied in the $F_1$. Crossing a different black-and-tan with plain black produced 3 black-and-tan:1 plain black. What is the order of relative dominance among these four phenotypes?

**7-12.** A hypothetical series of 20 multiple alleles is known for a certain locus. How many phenotypic classes are possible?

**7-13.** How many different genotypic classes are possible for the locus referred to in problem 7-12?

**7-14.** Considering human blood group A to include 3 subtypes, and groups B and O to include 1 each, how many phenotypes are included in the A-B-O series?

**7-15.** How many phenotypes are possible if two Rh classes are included?

**7-16.** How many phenotypes are possible if A-B-O, Rh, and MN classes are all considered?

**7-17.** How many phenotypic classes are possible if the A-B-O, Rh, MN, Ss, and Hh phenotypes are considered together?

**7-18.** A woman of group $A_2$ charges a man of group $A_2$ as the father of her group $A_3$Rh+ child. Could he be?

**7-19.** Both the man and woman of problem 7-18 are Rh—; does this change the situation?

**7-20.** A couple believe they have brought the wrong baby home from the hospital. The wife is group O; her husband is group B, and the child is group O. Could the baby be theirs?

**7-21.** Both the husband and wife of problem 7-20 are Rh+, whereas the baby is Rh—. Does this change the situation?

**7-22.** Both the husband and wife of problems 7-20 and 7-21 are of blood type M; the child is MN. Does this change the situation?

**7-23.** An elderly couple are killed in an accident; no survivors are known. Their estate has been willed to charity. Later, a man claims the estate on the grounds that he is their son who left home at an early age. It is known by friends that this couple had had a son, but he was thought to have died while quite young. Unfortunately, birth records for the period involved have been destroyed in a courthouse fire. Their child was born at home, the attending physician has been dead for some time, and his records are no longer available. From various hospital and medical records, it is determined that the dead man was of blood type A, MS/Ns, Rh+; his wife was B, MS/NS, Rh—. The claimant's blood tests as O, MS/Ns, Rh+. Does it appear that his claim is valid? Justify your conclusion.

**7-24.** In a court action a man claims that some of the six children purportedly belonging to him and his wife are not his children. Blood tests of husband, wife and the six children gave the following information:

husband:  O, cDe/cDE, MS/Ms
wife:     $A_1$, cDE/cde, MS/Ns
child 1:  $A_1$, cDE/cDE, MS/MS
child 2:  O, cDe/cde MS/Ns
child 3:  O, cDE/cde, Ms/Ns
child 4:  $A_1$, cDE/cde, NS/Ns
child 5:  O, cde/cde, MS/NS
child 6:  $A_1$B, CDe/cDE, MS/NS

Assuming all were, in fact, born to the wife, could all these children belong to the husband? Explain.

# CHAPTER 8
# *Polygenic Inheritance*

I F you think back over the heritable traits we have examined thus far in text and problems, you will note that phenotypic classes have always been distinct and easily separable from each other; that is, they have been sharply *discontinuous*. The traits themselves may be termed *qualitative* ones. Thus, *Coleus* leaves have either regular or irregular venation; cattle have horns or they do not, and may be red, roan, or white; rabbits may be distinguished by coat color; people belong to one blood group or another, and so on. This has been the case whether we are dealing with form and structure, pigments, antigens and antibodies, etc., and whether the genes involved show complete dominance, incomplete dominance, or codominance.

Not all inherited traits are expressed in this discontinuous fashion, however. For example, in man height is a genetically determined trait. But if you were to attempt to classify a random sample of students on your campus according to height you would quickly find that you were dealing with a trait showing essentially *continuous* phenotypic variation. Many other traits are expressed in a similar fashion, including intelligence and skin color in man, color and food yield in various plants, size in many plants and animals, as well as degree of coat spotting in animals or of seed coat mottling in some plants. The essential difference between continuous and discontinuous inheritance is illustrated with generalized data from crosses of each type compared graphically in Fig. 8-1. Clearly, our concepts of simple Mendelian inheritance, with the reappearance of the parental phenotypes as distinct and separate classes in the $F_1$ and $F_2$ generations, must be modified in order to explain continuous variation in *quantitative* characters such as height, weight, intelligence, or color.

We are concerned not with just tall *versus* dwarf, but with *how* tall, that is, with *continuous characters of degree rather than discontinuous characters of kind*. Moreover, quantitative inheritance more often deals with a population in which all possible matings occur, and less often with individual matings.

## Kernel Color in Wheat

Among the earliest investigations that gave a significant clue to the mechanism of quantitative inheritance was the work of Nilsson-Ehle (1909) with wheat. One of his crosses consisted of a red-kerneled variety × a white-kerneled strain. Grain from the $F_1$ was uniformly red, but of a shade intermediate between the red and white of the parental generation. This might

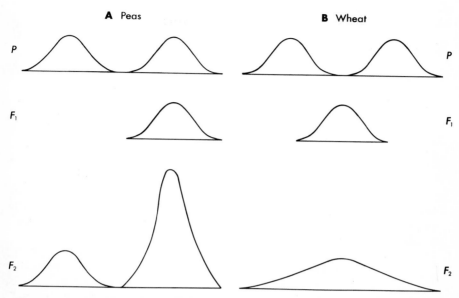

FIGURE 8-1. *Curves comparing results of crosses involving (A) height, a discontinuous trait in peas and (B) kernel color, a continuous trait in wheat, followed for three generations. Ordinates represent the number of individuals, abscissas the particular quantitative trait.*

suggest incomplete dominance, but by crossing members of the $F_1$ among themselves, Nilsson-Ehle produced an $F_2$ in which he was able to discern five phenotypic classes in a $1:4:6:4:1$ ratio. Noting that $\frac{1}{16}$ of the $F_2$ was as extreme in color as either of the parental plants (i.e., as red or as white as the P individuals), he theorized that two pairs of genes controlling production of red pigment were operating in this cross. If we symbolize the genes for red with the capital letters "$A$" and "$B$" and their alleles resulting in lack of pigment production by "$a$" and "$b$," we can diagram this cross as follows

$$P \quad AABB \quad \times \quad aabb$$
$$\text{dark red} \qquad \text{white}$$
$$F_1 \quad AaBb \quad (\times AaBb)$$
$$\text{intermediate red}$$
$$F_2 \quad \tfrac{1}{16} AABB + \tfrac{2}{16} AaBB + \tfrac{1}{16} aaBB$$
$$+ \tfrac{2}{16} AABb + \tfrac{4}{16} AaBb + \tfrac{2}{16} aaBb$$
$$+ \tfrac{1}{16} AAbb + \tfrac{2}{16} Aabb + \tfrac{1}{16} aabb$$

Assuming each "dose" of a gene for pigment production increases the depth of color, we can sort this $F_2$ out phenotypically according to the number of genes for red in the following way:

| Genotype | Number of Genes for Red | Phenotype | Fraction of $F_2$ |
|---|---|---|---|
| AABB | 4 | dark red | $\frac{1}{16}$ |
| AABb, AaBB | 3 | medium red | $\frac{4}{16}$ |
| AAbb, aaBB, AaBb | 2 | intermediate red | $\frac{6}{16}$ |
| aaBb, Aabb | 1 | light red | $\frac{4}{16}$ |
| aabb | 0 | white | $\frac{1}{16}$ |

Genes symbolized by capital letters, those "*contributing*" to red color in this case, are termed **contributing alleles**. Those that do not "contribute" to red color (here symbolized by lower case letters) may be designated **noncontributing alleles**. Some geneticists refer to these as "effective" and "noneffective" alleles, respectively. Here, then, we have a polygene series of as many as four contributing alleles. The term "polygene" was introduced by Mather (1954), who has summarized the modern interpretation of quantitative inheritance. This term has since found wide usage, and is supplanting the older term multiple gene.

In an effort to determine whether the mechanism of polygene inheritance is the same as that which we have seen operating in instances of qualitative characters, several simplifying assumptions must be made. We will *assume* that

1. Each contributing gene in the series produces an equal effect.
2. Effects of each contributing allele are cumulative or additive.
3. There is no dominance.
4. There is no epistasis among genes at different loci.
5. There is no linkage involved.
6. Environmental effects are absent or may be ignored.

Certainly, as the number of pairs of genes increases, the probability of linkage rises, and the effect of environment can be ignored only in the most closely controlled experiments. Furthermore, some geneticists have disagreed with the first two of these assumptions. But many polygene effects do appear to operate in a manner consistent with the first four points, and our task is eased considerably if we can make all six as *simplifying assumptions*.

## Calculating the Number of Polygenes

In another cross in wheat reported by Nilsson-Ehle, a different red variety was used with the result that $\frac{1}{64}$ of the $F_2$ was as extreme as either parent with seven classes in a $1:6:15:20:15:6:1$ ratio. A little reflection will serve to suggest the operation here of *three* pairs of genes. From earlier chapters on monohybrid inheritance, we can see that, if only one pair of genes were involved, one fourth of the $F_2$ should be as extreme as either parent. If information for one, two, and three pairs of polygenes is tabulated, we can see a pattern emerging:

| Number of Pairs of Polygenes in Which Two Parents Differ | Fraction of $F_2$ Like Either Parent | Number of Genotypic Classes in $F_2$ | Number of Phenotypic Classes in $F_2$ |
|:---:|:---:|:---:|:---:|
| 1 | $\frac{1}{4}$ | 3 | 3 |
| 2 | $\frac{1}{16}$ | 9 | 5 |
| 3 | $\frac{1}{64}$ | 27 | 7 |
| $n$ | $(\frac{1}{4})^n$ | $3^n$ | $2n + 1$ |

Thus, with 4 pairs of polygenes, $\frac{1}{256}$ of the $F_2$ is as extreme as either parent, with 5 only $\frac{1}{1,024}$, with 10 the fraction drops to $\frac{1}{1,648,570}$, and with 20 pairs, only 1 in 1,099,511,637,776 of the $F_2$ will have measurements like one parent or the other! The number of genotypic classes increases, of course, with startling rapidity as the number of pairs of polygenes becomes larger: for 4 pairs of genes there are 81 $F_2$ classes, 5 pairs of genes produce 243 $F_2$ genotypes, 10 pairs 59,049, and 20 pairs 3,486,784,401! Thus, as the number of polygenes governing a particular trait goes up, the progeny very quickly form a continuum of variation in which class distinctions become virtually impossible to make.

If we wished to calculate the number of contributing alleles instead of the number of pairs of polygenes, we would use the expression $(\frac{1}{2})^n$. Dividing the total quantitative difference by the number of contributing alleles, of course, indicates the amount contributed by each effective allele. For example, in the following hypothetical case, in pumpkin, how many contributing alleles are operating and how much does each contribute?

> P      5 lb. fruits $\times$ 21 lb. fruits
> $F_1$          13 lb. fruits
> $F_2$   $\frac{3}{750}$   5 lb. fruits . . . $\frac{3}{750}$   21 lb. fruits

Note that $\frac{3}{750}$, the fraction of the $F_2$ that has fruits as light or as heavy as the P generation, simplifies to $\frac{1}{250}$. Considering the formula $(\frac{1}{4})^n$, we see that $(\frac{1}{4})^n = \frac{1}{256}$ if $n = 4$ (*pairs* of genes), and $\frac{1}{250}$ is close only to this fraction $(\frac{1}{256})$ in the series. Therefore, we must be dealing with a case of 4 pairs of genes, where the plants producing the heaviest fruits have all *8* contributing alleles. Since the total weight difference is 16 pounds ($21 - 5$), $\frac{16}{8} = 2$ pounds contributed by each effective allele. Alternatively, we could solve by using $(\frac{1}{2})^n$ to determine directly the number of contributing alleles (instead of the number of *pairs*). In this case $(\frac{1}{2})^n = \frac{1}{256}$ only if $n = 8$. In our illustration with weight of pumpkin fruits, a weight of 5 pounds is termed the *base weight*, suggesting that of all the polygenes which may be involved in fruit weight in this species, the two parental strains were homozygous and alike for all but the four pairs our calculations showed.

## Calculating Phenotypic Classes and Ratios

It is also apparent that the number of $F_2$ phenotypic classes follows a pattern, but one which produces a less dramatic increase as the number of pairs of polygenes becomes larger. Thus, with one pair, the $F_2$ of the cross $AA \times aa$ includes three phenotypic classes, which corresponds to the number of genotypic classes ($AA$, $Aa$, and $aa$). The two examples from Nilsson-Ehle's work on wheat indicate that the number of $F_2$ *phenotypic classes* is one more than twice the number of pairs of polygenes, or $2n + 1$.

Note that the phenotypic *ratio* also follows a pattern. One pair gives rise to a $1:2:1$ $F_2$ ratio, two pairs to $1:4:6:4:1$, and three to $1:6:15:20:15:6:1$. You will recognize that these ratios are the same as the sequence of *coefficients* in binomial expansions of a power equal to twice the number of pairs of multiple genes. Thus, expansion of $(a + b)^2$ gives a coefficient sequence of $1:2:1$, which is the same as the $F_2$ phenotypic ratio for one pair of polygenes; expanding $(a + b)^4$ produces the coefficient series $1:4:6:4:1$; and so on. So we can determine an $F_2$ phenotypic ratio for any number of pairs of polygenes by thinking of the sequence of coefficients given by expanding a binomial raised to the power $2n$ where, again, $n$ represents the number of pairs of polygenes.

## Transgressive Variation

Not infrequently some progeny are more extreme than either parent or grandparent. You are probably familiar with examples among your own acquaintances where, say, some children are shorter or taller than either parent or any of their more remote ancestors. The same phenomenon sometimes occurs, too, with respect to intelligence. Such examples illustrate **transgressive variation**.

One of the earliest instances of transgressive variation to be reported in the literature was one described in 1914 and 1923 by Punnett and Bailey. They crossed the large Golden Hamburg chicken with the smaller Sebright Bantam. The $F_1$ was intermediate in weight between the parents and fairly uniform, but a few of the $F_2$ birds were heavier or lighter than either of the parental individuals. Their results suggested to Punnett and Bailey four pairs of genes, with the Golden Hamburg being of, say, genotype $AABBCCdd$ and the

FIGURE 8-2. *Variation in degree of spotting in a herd of cattle. Amount of spotting depends upon a series of multiple genes, but these are hypostatic to* S (*solid color*). [Photo courtesy Ayrshire Breeders' Association.]

Sebright Bantam then *aabbccDD*. Some of the problems at the end of this chapter deal with some interesting variations of transgressive variation.

## Other Organisms

Instances of polygene inheritance are known from many other plant and animal species. One of the more suggestive was discovered in tomato by Lindstrom (1924 and 1926). Crosses between the larger-fruited Golden Beauty (average fruit weight 166.5 grams) and the smaller-fruited Red Cherry (average fruit weight 7.3 grams) varieties produced an $F_1$ having fruits intermediate in size between the parental types, but distinctly closer to the smaller-fruited variety (average weight 23.9). Such results could be explained by assuming dominance or unequal effect among at least some of the noncontributing alleles.

In cattle both solid color and spotting occur. Solid color is due to a dominant gene, *S*, spotting to its recessive allele, *s*. Studies indicate that the degree of spotting in *ss* individuals depends on a rather large series of poly-genes (Fig. 8-2). Those cattle which are *S*— will, of course, not be spotted, regardless of the remainder of their genotype.

Chai (1970) has shown clearly that the difference between high and low leukocyte count in the mouse is a polygenic trait. He suggests dominance, however, for low count and goes on to make the interesting point that "the evidence is accumulating . . . that a quantitative trait is an aggregate of effects from different biological systems, each of which contributes specific effects that differ in magnitude and biological effect under the control of individual genes. The present results, although not considered as definitive, further indicate this to be the case."

Skin color in man depends upon relative amounts of the pigment melanin. Studies by Davenport and by others, which relate observed sample frequencies to models based on different numbers of pairs of polygenes, show best agreement between observation and theoretical expectation for four, five, or six pairs rather than for fewer or for more. As might be expected, some Caucasians in the samples were darker than some blacks, and vice versa. Although polygene inheritance is clearly suggested in man for many quantita-tive traits such as height, intelligence, and pigmentation, no complete hypothesis setting forth the exact number of pairs of genes and their individual and collective effect has yet been developed for any of these traits.

Nevertheless, we see that the basic mechanisms operative in quantitative inheritance appear to be the same as those for qualitative characters. Such studies as are reported here also further emphasize the fact that many traits are the result of *interaction* of one kind or another among several pairs of genes.

It should be emphasized in your thinking about such *quantitative characters* as we have dealt with here that the possible effect of environment must be considered and carefully regulated in any controlled experiment. For example, height in many plants (e.g., corn, tomato, pea, marigold) is a genetically controlled character, but we also know that such environmental factors as soil fertility, texture, and water, the temperature, the duration and wavelength of incident light, the occurrence of parasites, to name just a few, also affect height. Or, with identical twins (who have identical genotypes) growing up in different kinds of environments, many classical studies indicate intelligence quotients sufficiently different that environment surely played a significant role. In summary, *genotype* determines the range an individual will occupy with regard to a given quantitative character; environment determines the *point* within the genetically determined range at which an individual's mea-surement will fall.

Study and evaluation of polygene inheritance requires certain statistical treatments, particularly those which describe populations. These we shall examine in the next chapter.

**REFERENCES**

CHAI, C. K., 1970. Genetic Basis of Leukocyte Production in Mice. *Jour. Hered.*, **61**:67–71.

DAVENPORT, G. C., and C. B. DAVENPORT, 1910. Heredity of Skin Pigmentation in Man. *Amer. Natur.*, **44**:641–672.

LINDSTROM, E. W., 1924. A Genetic Linkage Between Size and Color Factors in the Tomato. *Science*, **60**:182–183.

LINDSTROM, E. W., 1926. Hereditary Correlation of Size and Color Characters in Tomatoes. *Iowa Agr. Exper. Sta. Research Bull.*, **93**.

LINDSTROM, E. W., 1929. Linkage of Qualitative and Quantitative Genes in Maize. *Amer. Natur.*, **63**:317–327.

MATHER, K., 1954. The Genetical Units of Continuous Variation. *Proc. IX International Cong. Genet.*, **Part I**:106–123.

NILSSON-EHLE, H., 1909. *Lunds Univ. Arsskrift N.F. Avd.*, **2**:Bd. 5.

PUNNETT, R. C., 1923. *Heredity in Poultry*. New York, Macmillan (pp. 44 ff.).

**PROBLEMS**

**8-1.** Which of the following human phenotypes would appear to be based on polygene inheritance: intelligence, absence of incisors, height, phenylketonuria (inability to metabolize the amino acid phenylalanine), ability to taste phenylthiocarbamide, skin color, cryptophthalmos (failure of eyelids to separate in embryonic development), eye color?

**8-2.** Show, by means of appropriate genotypes, how parents may have children taller than themselves.

**8-3.** Suppose another race of wheat is discovered in which kernel color is determined to depend on the action of six pairs of polygenes. From the cross *AABBCCDDEEFF* × *aabbccddeeff*, (a) what fraction of the $F_2$ would be expected to be like either parent? (b) How many $F_2$ phenotypic classes result? (c) What fraction of the $F_2$ will possess any six contributing alleles?

**8-4.** Two races of corn, averaging 48 and 72 inches in height, respectively, are crossed. The $F_1$ is quite uniform, averaging 60 inches tall. Of 500 $F_2$ plants, 2 are as short as 48 inches and 2 as tall as 72 inches. What is the number of polygenes involved, and how much does each contribute to height?

**8-5.** Two other varieties of corn, averaging 48 and 72 inches in height, respectively, are crossed. The $F_1$ is again quite uniform at an average height of 60 inches. Out of 3,100 $F_2$ plants, 4 are as short as 36 inches, and 2 as tall as 84 inches. How many polygenes are involved, and how many inches of height are contributed by each effective allele?

**8-6.** In problems 6-14 to 6-17 it was pointed out that *Pl–* corn plants are purple, whereas *pl pl* individuals are green. Assume now that the parents in problem 8-5 are also *Pl pl*. A breeder wishes to recover a pure-breeding green, 84-inch variety from the cross given in problem 8-5. What fraction of the $F_2$ will satisfy his requirement?

**8-7.** Two 30-inch individuals of a hypothetical species of plant are crossed, producing progeny in, the following ratio: one 22-inch, eight 24-inch twenty-eight 26-inch, fifty-six 28-inch, seventy 30-inch, fifty-six 32-inch, twenty-eight 34-inch, eight 36-inch, and one 38-inch. What are the genotypes of the parents? (Start with the first letter of the alphabet and use as many more letters as needed.)

**8-8.** Two different 30-inch plants of the same species are crossed and produce all 30-inch progeny. What parental genotypes are possible?

**8-9.** As noted in the text, spotting in certain breeds of cattle is dependent on interaction of $S-$ (solid color) or $ss$ (spotted) and a number of polygenes for degree of spotting. Assume four pairs of the latter (which is almost certainly too low), designated as $A, a; B, b; C, c; D, d$. If data are accumulated from enough $SsAaBbCcDd \times SsAaBbCcDd$ crosses to give a total of, say, 1,024 calves from such matings, how many of these should be unspotted?

**8-10.** Among $ss$ animals how many different degrees of spotting could be found, using information from problem 8-9?

**8-11.** Assume height in a particular plant to be determined by two pairs of unlinked polygenes, each effective allele contributing 5 centimeters to a base height of 5 centimeters. The cross $AABB \times aabb$ is made. (a) What are the heights of each parent? (b) What height is to be expected in the $F_1$ if there are no environmental effects? (c) What is the expected phenotypic ratio in the $F_2$?

**8-12.** If each pair of alleles in problem 8-11 exhibited complete dominance instead of an additive effect, (a) what are the heights of each parent? (b) What height would be expected in the $F_1$? (c) What is the expected phenotypic ratio in the $F_2$?

# CHAPTER 9
# *Statistical Concepts and Tools*

IN the preceding chapter we saw that polygenes govern continuously variable, quantitative traits. Analysis of this kind of inheritance requires application of certain techniques from the branch of mathematics called statistics. Statistics are useful in two fundamental problems commonly encountered in scientific research: (1) what can be learned about a population from measurements of a sample of it and (2) how much confidence can be placed in judgments about that population.

There is a clear difference between **population** and **sample**. A population is a series of numbers that represent some variable, quantitative character being treated as a whole. Thus, figures showing gains in weight of all adult laboratory rats that have been fed a specific diet for a certain number of days represent a biological population, as do height measurements of all adult males or weights of all ripe pumpkin fruits. The population is not the rats, the people, or the pumpkins themselves, but *figures* representing a particular quantitative character they possess. A population thereby is usually infinite in size. As populations, height measurements of men or pumpkin fruit weights include all individuals who have been or will be alive. The rat population really consists of an infinite number of measurements obtained from an infinite number of experimental rats. Such populations, of course, never actually exist. Even a more discrete problem dealing with a population of an endemic species on an isolated small island includes *all* the individuals of the species on that island. For obvious reasons, it is either impractical or impossible to accumulate measurements for such a group; rarely is the population sufficiently finite for *all* individuals to be measured.

So descriptions of the population must generally be formulated from *samples* of it. To be useful in making estimates of a population, the sample must have been drawn as randomly as possible. In dealing with heights or weights, for example, sample measurements must not be selected more from the taller, or shorter, or heavier, or lighter individuals, but should reflect the same kind and degree of variability as does the population. This it will do if it is large and chosen at random.

Actual values for populations are constants called **parameters**; estimates of populations based on samples are **statistics**. The statistics are, of course, subject to some degree of chance error due to sampling practices, but once a statistic is determined, it is possible to state the range of the corresponding parameter with a particular degree of confidence. The geneticist needs to be able not only to estimate the parameters with which he is concerned, but also to determine how likely it is that he is dealing with individuals from either the same or different populations.

In the genetic context, then, the uses of statistics listed in the first paragraph of this chapter may be rephrased to state that statistics provide

1. A concise description of the quantitative characteristics of the sample;
2. An estimate of
   (a) the quantitative characteristics of the population from which the sample was drawn, and
   (b) how well the sample represents that population;
3. An expression of the probability that two samples differ significantly (or, conversely, only within limits set by chance alone) in terms of a particular theory as to the reason for observed differences.

## Basic Statistics

Four principal statistics will provide the estimates and descriptions just referred to.

### 1. THE MEAN

A very elementary statistic, and one with which you are undoubtedly familiar, is the average or **mean**. Calculation of the mean, symbolized by $\bar{x}$ ("x-bar"), may be represented by the formula

$$\bar{x} = \frac{\sum x}{n} \tag{1}$$

where $\Sigma$, the upper case Greek letter sigma, directs us to sum all following terms, $x$ the individual measurements, and $n$ the number of individuals in the sample. Often, when $n$ is quite large, it becomes convenient to *group* data by *classes*. Thus, in computing the average grade on a quiz in a large class it might be more practical to tally the number or *frequency* of individuals scoring between 96 and 100 in one class or group, those between 91 and 95 in another, and so on. A "class value" midway between the extremes of each class range is also entered. The tabulated data would then be arranged as follows:

| Class Range | Class Value $x$ | Frequency $f$ | $fx$ |
|---|---|---|---|
| 96–100 | 98 | 1 | 98 |
| 91–95 | 93 | 4 | 372 |
| 86–90 | 88 | 8 | 704 |
| 81–85 | 83 | 12 | 996 |
| 76–80 | 78 | 18 | 1,404 |
| 71–75 | 73 | 25 | 1,825 |
| 66–70 | 68 | 17 | 1,156 |
| 61–65 | 63 | 10 | 630 |
| etc. | etc. | etc. | etc. |

If the data are grouped in this way, the mean will, of course, be given by

$$\bar{x} = \frac{\sum fx}{n} \tag{2}$$

Formula (2) loses a little in accuracy over formula (1), but the much simpler arithmetic of its method more than offsets this.

Although the mean is a necessary statistic, it is a rather uninformative one in that a comparison of means of different samples reflects nothing of their spread, or variability. Consider as an example three students, the first having grades of 75, 75, 75, the second 65, 75, 85, and the third 50, 75 and 100. Obviously the mean for each is 75, but the distributions reflect quite different spreads. There is no variability in the first student's record and quite a bit in the last. Furthermore, the mean is greatly affected by a few extreme values.

## 2. STANDARD DEVIATION

A statistic measuring the spread or variability of the sample is the **standard deviation**, $s$, which is given by the formula

$$s = \sqrt{\frac{\sum f(x - \bar{x})^2}{n - 1}} \tag{3}$$

In effect, the standard deviation reflects the extent to which the mean represents the entire sample. If all individuals had exactly the same value, there would be no variability and the mean would represent the sample perfectly. Examination of formula (3) indicates that the standard deviation would then be *zero*. But as the sample becomes more variable, the mean serves progressively less well as an index of the entire sample. The standard deviation not only measures that variability but is also useful in determining other sample statistics.

Formula (3) requires extraction of the square root of the summed frequencies ($f$) times the squared deviations from the mean $(x - \bar{x})^2$, divided by one less than the number of individuals in the sample. Therefore, as the departures from the mean, class by class, increase, so does the standard deviation.

To see how this statistic may be calculated and what it discloses regarding the sample, consider some length measurements of 200 hypothetical $F_1$ plants resulting from a particular cross. Calculation will be facilitated if data are grouped by classes and tabulated as follows:

| 1 | 2 | 3 | 4 | 5 | 6 |
|---|---|---|---|---|---|
| Class Value cm. $x$ | Fre- quency $f$ | $fx$ | Deviation from Mean $(x - \bar{x})$ | Squared Deviation $(x - \bar{x})^2$ | $f(x - \bar{x})^2$ |
| 48 | 8 | 384 | −4.75 | 22.56 | 180.48 |
| 50 | 32 | 1,600 | −2.75 | 7.56 | 241.92 |
| 52 | 75 | 3,900 | −0.75 | 0.56 | 42.00 |
| 54 | 52 | 2,808 | +1.25 | 1.56 | 81.12 |
| 56 | 28 | 1,568 | +3.25 | 10.56 | 295.68 |
| 58 | 5 | 290 | +5.25 | 27.56 | 137.80 |
| | $n = 200$ | $\sum fx = 10{,}550$ | | | $\sum f(x - \bar{x})^2 = 979.00$ |

$$\bar{x} = \frac{\sum fx}{n} = \frac{10{,}550}{200} = 52.75 \text{ cm.}$$

$$s = \sqrt{\frac{\sum f(x - \bar{x})^2}{n - 1}} = \sqrt{\frac{979}{199}} = \sqrt{4.92} = 2.213$$

This calculation provides a mean, plus or minus a standard deviation; that is, $\bar{x} = 52.75 \pm 2.22$. To understand the meaning of this expression and the information it conveys, "curves of distribution" must be examined.

As data for large samples are plotted with a quantitative measurement, such as length, along the abscissa and numbers of individuals (frequency) along the ordinate, the resulting curve is frequently bell-shaped; the variation is rather symmetrical about the largest class (or mode), as indicated in Fig. 9-1. Such a curve is a **normal curve** or a curve of normal distribution. If data are carefully plotted and a perpendicular erected from the abscissa at a value equal to the mean, it will intersect such a curve at the latter's highest point and will divide the area under the curve into two equal parts (Fig. 9-1) and, therefore, the sample into two groups of equal size. Now, if perpendiculars to the abscissa are erected on it at points having values equal to $\bar{x} + s$ and $\bar{x} - s$, the area under the curve between $\bar{x} - s$ and $\bar{x} + s$ is 68.26 per cent of the area under the curve (Fig. 9-2).

Similarly, the area under the curve between $\bar{x} - 2s$ and $\bar{x} + 2s$ is 95.44 per cent of the total area; for $\bar{x} \pm 3s$, the area included is 99.74 per cent of the total (Fig. 9-3). This means that, *in a normal distribution*, about 68 per cent (or roughly two thirds) of the individuals will have values between $\bar{x} - s$ and $\bar{x} + s$, about 95 per cent between $\bar{x} - 2s$ and $\bar{x} + 2s$, and so on. Therefore, if an individual is chosen *at random* from a normally distributed population, the chances are about 68 per cent that it will belong to that part of the population lying in the range $\bar{x} \pm s$. Similarly there is a 95 per cent

FIGURE 9-1. *The curve of normal distribution. A perpendicular erected from the abscissa at a value equal to the mean intersects the curve at its highest point and divides the area under the curve into areas of equal size.*

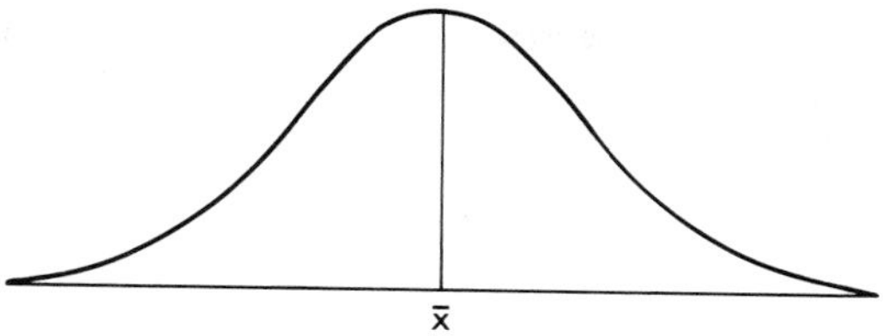

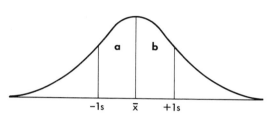

FIGURE 9-2. *The curve of normal distribution with perpendiculars to the abscissa erected at points having values of $\bar{x} + s$ and $\bar{x} - s$. Areas* a *and* b *each comprise 34.13 per cent of the area under the curve.*

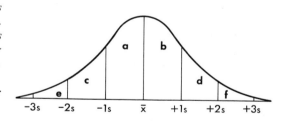

FIGURE 9-3. *Curve of normal distribution with perpendiculars to the abscissa erected at values $\bar{x} \pm 1s$, $\bar{x} \pm 2s$, and $\bar{x} \pm 3s$. Areas under the curve are as follows:* a + b = 68.26 *per cent;* (a + b) + (c + d) = 95.44 *per cent;* (a + b) + (c + d) + (e + f) = 99.74 *per cent.*

chance that the individual selected will lie within the limits $\bar{x} \pm 2s$ or, to phrase it another way, only a 5 per cent chance that the randomly chosen individual will lie outside those limits. The percentages of the sample determined by the mean plus or minus different multiples of the standard deviation are shown more fully in Table 9-1. Thus the standard deviation is a useful description of the variability of the sample and, if the sample is large and randomly chosen, a good indicator of the variability of the population. As variability of the sample increases, so does its standard deviation.

## 3. THE STANDARD ERROR OF THE SAMPLE MEAN

If a series of samples were to be drawn from the same population, their means and standard deviations would probably not be the same. Page 162 carried measurements for a sample of hypothetical plants having a mean of 52.75 cm. Another group of 200 $F_1$ plants from the same population would be expected, by chance, to have a somewhat different mean. Yet, if a series

TABLE 9-1. Percentages of the Sample Falling Within Given
Multiples of the Standard Deviation from the Mean

| Mean ± Values of $s$ | Per Cent of Sample Included | Mean ± Values of $s$ | Per Cent of Sample Included |
|---|---|---|---|
| 0.1 | 7.96 | 2.0 | 95.44 |
| 0.2 | 15.86 | 2.1 | 96.42 |
| 0.3 | 23.58 | 2.2 | 97.22 |
| 0.4 | 31.08 | 2.3 | 97.86 |
| 0.5 | 38.30 | 2.4 | 98.36 |
| 0.6 | 45.14 | 2.5 | 98.76 |
| 0.675 | 50.00 | 2.58 | 99.00 |
| 0.7 | 51.60 | 2.6 | 99.06 |
| 0.8 | 57.62 | 2.7 | 99.30 |
| 0.9 | 63.18 | 2.8 | 99.48 |
| 1.0 | 68.26 | 2.9 | 99.62 |
| 1.1 | 72.86 | 3.0 | 99.74 |
| 1.2 | 76.98 | 3.1 | 99.80 |
| 1.3 | 80.64 | 3.2 | 99.86 |
| 1.4 | 83.84 | 3.3 | 99.90 |
| 1.5 | 86.64 | 3.4 | 99.94 |
| 1.6 | 89.04 | 3.5 | 99.96 |
| 1.645 | 90.00 | 3.6 | 99.96 |
| 1.7 | 91.08 | 3.7 | 99.98 |
| 1.8 | 92.82 | 3.8 | 99.98 |
| 1.9 | 94.26 | 3.9 | 99.99 |
| 1.96 | 95.00 | 4.0 | 99.99 |

of samples of 200 individuals each were to be drawn at random, it is fair to assume from our knowledge of the laws of probability that only a few samples would have relatively low means and a few relatively high, but that most would be intermediate. In fact, if a large number of these successive sample means were plotted, they would be found to form a normal curve, giving a fairly clear picture of the population distribution. The population mean and standard deviation could then be calculated. Practical limitations preclude doing exactly this, but the standard deviation of means, or the **standard error of the sample mean**, can be calculated from one good-sized sample. This will give a good picture of the population.

The standard error of the sample mean, $s_{\bar{x}}$, represents an estimate of the standard deviation of the means of many samples which might be taken, and is a measure of the closeness with which the sample mean, $\bar{x}$, represents the population mean, $\mu$. The size of the sample used and the variability of the population affect the reliability of $\bar{x}$ as an estimate of $\mu$. The greater the variation in the population, the larger the sample needed to provide an adequate representation of the population. Both these factors are taken into account in the formula for calculating the standard error of the sample mean:

$$s_{\bar{x}} = \frac{s}{\sqrt{n}} \tag{4}$$

where $s$ is the standard deviation of the sample and $n$, of course, the number of individuals composing the sample.

In the hypothetical sample of 200 $F_1$ plants (page 162), where $\bar{x} = 52.75$ cm. and $s = 2.22$, the standard error of the sample mean becomes

$$s_{\bar{x}} = \frac{2.22}{\sqrt{200}} = \frac{2.22}{14.14} = 0.1564, \text{ or about } 0.16$$

Because $s_{\bar{x}}$ represents the standard deviation of a *series* of sample means, and recalling the areal relationships of a normal curve (page 163) where $\bar{x} \pm s$ includes 68.26 per cent of the sample, etc., the value $s_{\bar{x}} = 0.16$ indicates that there is about a 68 per cent probability that $\mu$ lies in the range 52.75 cm. $\pm$ 0.16, i.e., between 52.59 cm. and 52.91 cm. Likewise, the probability that $\mu$ is in the range $\bar{x} \pm 2s_{\bar{x}}$, or between 52.43 and 53.07, is about 95 per cent. Thus, $\bar{x} = \mu \pm s_{\bar{x}}$ 68.26 per cent of the time by *chance alone*, $\bar{x} = \mu \pm 2s_{\bar{x}}$ in 95.44 per cent of the cases, and $\bar{x} = \mu \pm 3s_{\bar{x}}$ 99.74 per cent of the time. If the sample is large ($> 100$), other confidence levels may be determined from Table 9-1. For example, there is a 90 per cent probability that $\mu$ lies in the range $52.75 \pm 1.645\ s_{\bar{x}}$, or $52.75 \pm 0.263$ cm., and a 50 per cent probability that it is within the range $52.75 \pm 0.675$, and so on. Obviously, the smaller the standard error, the more reliable the estimate of the population mean. As sample size, $n$, increases, the magnitude of the standard error decreases. Therefore, it is desirable to use samples as large as possible in order to determine characteristics of the population.

In cases involving polygene inheritance, the standard error of the sample mean will give a measure of the population mean. It will also help to fix, for example, a parental mean to which a given fraction of the $F_2$ may be compared. In other words, in the example of pumpkin fruits (page 153), the question could be raised as to what value between 4 and 6 or 19 and 23 is acceptable as representative of the parental strains so that certain $F_2$ individuals can be designated as being as extreme as either parent. If the standard error of the mean is calculated for each parental sample, a range is arrived at within which there is 68, 95, or 99 per cent confidence that the population mean lies and, therefore, a value representative of the parental populations against which we can compare the $F_2$.

## 4. STANDARD ERROR OF THE DIFFERENCE IN MEANS

It is often necessary to determine whether the difference in the means of two samples is statistically significant—that is, to determine the likelihood that two sample means represent genetically different populations rather than chance differences in two samples from the same population. A judgmental answer to this problem is provided by a statistic known as the **standard error of the difference in means** $(S_d)$:

$$S_d = \sqrt{(s_{\bar{x}_1})^2 + (s_{\bar{x}_2})^2} \tag{5}$$

For example, consider the statistics developed for the hypothetical group of 200 plants ("sample 1") as compared with like statistics for a second hypothetical sample:

|  *Sample* 1 |  *Sample* 2 |
|---|---|
| $n_1 = 200$ | $n_2 = 200$ |
| $\bar{x}_1 = 52.75$ | $\bar{x}_2 = 55.87$ |
| $s_1 = 2.213$ | $s_2 = 3.150$ |
| $s_{\bar{x}1} = 0.16$ | $s_{\bar{x}2} = 0.22$ |

Substituting in formula (5) to determine $S_d$ for these two samples gives

$$
\begin{aligned}
S_d &= \sqrt{(0.16)^2 + (0.22)^2} \\
&= \sqrt{0.026 + 0.048} \\
&= \sqrt{0.074} \\
&= 0.272
\end{aligned}
$$

The meaning of a value of $S_d = 0.272$ can be seen by comparing the difference in sample means, here $\bar{x}_2 - \bar{x}_1$, with the standard error of the difference in means, $S_d$:

$$\frac{\bar{x}_2 - \bar{x}_1}{S_d} \tag{6}$$

Substituting values, formula (6) becomes

$$\frac{3.12}{0.27} = 11.6$$

The difference in sample means is thus about 11.6 times the standard error of the difference in means.

What, then, does the value of $S_d$ and its relation to the difference in sample means signify? Remember that, in a normal curve, the area under the curve equal to $\bar{x} \pm 2s$ comprises about 95 per cent of the total area, which is to say that 95 per cent of the individuals will have a quantitative value between

$\bar{x} - 2s$ and $\bar{x} + 2s$. Now, a standard error represents the standard deviation of a series of means, so in a standard error of the difference in sample means, we are still dealing with this same relationship between $\pm 1s$, $\pm 2s$, etc., assuming, of course, a normal curve. So, *if the difference in sample means is greater than twice the standard error of the difference of the sample means, then the difference in sample means is considered significant.* Significance begins whenever $\bar{x}_1 - \bar{x}_2 > 2S_d$. Here, significance means two different populations.

Would a difference in means of, say, *exactly* twice the value of $S_d$ mean that two different populations are not represented by the two samples? No! But the values of $\bar{x}_1 - \bar{x}_2 = 2S_d$ would give us 95 *per cent confidence* that two populations are involved. Or, to state this another way, there would then be only a 5 per cent probability that the two samples happened to have been drawn from the same population. *When the probability that two samples have come from the same population falls BELOW 5 per cent ($P < 0.05$), the difference in means is considered significant.* So, to be significant, $\bar{x}_1 - \bar{x}_2$ must *exceed* $2S_d$. In the example here, $\bar{x}_1 - \bar{x}_2 = 11.6\ S_d$, hence $\bar{x}_1 - \bar{x}_2$ is considered highly significant. The probability that only one population is represented is so very small that we reject it.

Note, incidentally, that a significant difference between two sample means is inherently neither "good" nor "bad." In some situations we may be pleased to find significance; in others we may be just as happy to find a lack of significance.

These four statistics are summarized in Appendix D.

## Applications of Statistics to Genetic Problems

Two illustrations of the application of statistics to genetic problems will serve to point up the usefulness of such analyses.

In the first instance, assume a commercial producer of hybrid seed corn wishes to market grains that will produce plants having ears of very uniform length. He has two varieties, A and B, both of which produce ears of just under 8 inches, which is a satisfactory length for his marketing purposes. Although variety A averages closer to 8 inches than does B, it appears to be more variable. He grows several acres of each variety in as uniform an environment as possible, then analyzes 100 ears from each. Variety A has the following statistics:

$$\bar{x} = 7.95 \text{ inches}$$
$$s = 0.52$$
$$s_{\bar{x}} = 0.05$$

Although the sample mean is very close to the desired length, the standard deviation indicates that two thirds of the ears of this variety may be expected to vary up to 0.52 inches from the mean of 7.95 inches. Of course, one third will deviate more than this.

This is more variability than the grower would prefer, so, for comparison, 100 ears of variety B are similarly analyzed. This variety has these statistics:

$$\bar{x} = 7.88 \text{ inches}$$
$$s = 0.23$$
$$s_{\bar{x}} = 0.02$$

Although the ears average slightly shorter than those of variety A, B has a much narrower range of variation. Two thirds of the ears of the latter may be expected to fall within the range 7.65 to 8.11 inches, as compared with 7.43 to 8.47 for A. Therefore, the breeder elects to use B.

The standard errors of the two samples are useful in indicating to the grower just how much the mean length of his samples might be expected to vary from the mean lengths of *all* plants of the two varieties. His samples are sufficiently large, and the standard errors are quite small, showing that the samples do reflect reliably the magnitude of variability in the two varieties.

Another example will show an application of statistics to a more theoretical type of problem (Table 9-2). Data were accumulated on days to maturity for two varieties of tomato (Burpeeana Early Hybrid, $P_1$, and Burpee Big Boy, $P_2$) and their hybrids ($F_1$ and $F_2$). Maturation time is dependent on both heredity and environment, so environmental differences must be minimized. This is often done in randomized plots, whereby different varieties are distributed randomly in the field. The time elapsing between setting the plants in the field and the ripening of the first fruit was recorded as "days to maturation" and data recorded for samples of 100 plants of each of the four varieties, all grown in the same season in randomized plots.

Inspection of the data in Table 9-2 clearly suggests that $P_1$ and $P_2$ represent different populations, and this is amply confirmed by the standard deviation and standard error of each, as well as by the standard error of the difference in sample means. In fact, the difference in sample means is 19.54 days, which is about 108 times the standard error of the difference in means! Remembering that a difference in sample means of more than $2S_d$ is considered significant, the difference here is highly significant.

The same statistics for the $F_1$ and $F_2$ generations also show that although differences in maturation times are considerably less than for the parental strains, they are significantly different. One therefore has more than 95 per cent confidence that they represent two genetically different populations. The difference in means for these two samples is only 0.92 day, but this is about 2.5 times the standard error of the difference in the sample means.

These data clearly suggest polygenes. The $F_1$ is intermediate between the parents, as is the $F_2$, but the $F_2$ has a wider range than the $F_1$. If $P_1$ and

TABLE 9-2. Data for Two Parental and Two Progeny Strains of Tomato Based on Days Required to Reach Maturity

| Days | $P_1$ | $P_2$ | $F_1$ | $F_2$ |
|------|-------|-------|-------|-------|
| 55 | 1 | | | |
| 56 | 6 | | | |
| 57 | 9 | | | 1 |
| 58 | 40 | | | 1 |
| 59 | 28 | | | 2 |
| 60 | 14 | | | 3 |
| 61 | 2 | | 3 | 4 |
| 62 | | | 8 | 9 |
| 63 | | | 20 | 10 |
| 64 | | | 31 | 12 |
| 65 | | | 19 | 14 |
| 66 | | | 10 | 20 |
| 67 | | | 8 | 7 |
| 68 | | | 1 | 4 |
| 69 | | | | 3 |
| 70 | | | | 3 |
| 71 | | | | 1 |
| 72 | | | | 2 |
| 73 | | | | 1 |
| 74 | | | | 1 |
| 75 | | 4 | | 1 |
| 76 | | 12 | | 1 |
| 77 | | 20 | | |
| 78 | | 35 | | |
| 79 | | 15 | | |
| 80 | | 10 | | |
| 81 | | 3 | | |
| 82 | | 1 | | |
| $\bar{x}$ | 58.38 | 77.92 | 64.22 | 65.14 |
| $s$ | 1.14 | 1.42 | 1.49 | 3.41 |
| $s_{\bar{x}}$ | 0.114 | 0.142 | 0.149 | 0.341 |
| $S_d$ | 0.181 | | 0.372 | |

$P_2$ are assumed to be completely homozygous, then the variability each shows must be wholly environmental. The $F_1$ would then be completely and uniformly heterozygous, and its variability again environmental. The $F_2$ would be expected to segregate so that genetic variation is superimposed on environmental.

The $F_2$ data may be used to furnish a very rough estimate of the number of contributing alleles. Eleven of the 100 $F_2$ were as extreme as $P_1$, and 2 as extreme as $P_2$. Now $\frac{11}{100}$ simplifies to about $\frac{1}{9}$, and $\frac{2}{100}$ to $\frac{1}{50}$. Recalling the formula for computing numbers of effective alleles from the $F_2$ data (page 153), it is seen that $\frac{1}{16}$, which indicates four contributing alleles, is between the two extremes of $\frac{1}{9}$ and $\frac{1}{50}$. This approach is really too simple and probably gives too low an estimate, for it would take many hundreds or thousands of $F_2$ individuals to provide a reasonable chance of recovering the maximum extremes possible.

Sewall Wright has shown that the number of *pairs* of polygenes ($n$) can be calculated from the formula

$$n = \frac{R^2}{8(s^2{}_{F_2} - s^2{}_{F_1})}$$

where $R$ is the range (difference) between the mean values of extreme phenotypes (whether found in the parental generations or elsewhere), $s^2{}_{F_2}$ is the *variance*[1] of the $F_2$, and $s^2{}_{F_1}$ the variance of the $F_1$. Applying this formula to the data of Table 9-2 and substituting, we obtain

$$n = \frac{(77.92 - 58.38)^2}{8(11.63 - 2.22)} = \frac{(19.54)^2}{8(9.41)} = 5.07$$

or about five pairs of polygenes.

In using this formula we have tacitly assumed (1) no environmental effects, (2) no dominance, (3) no epistasis, (4) equal, additive contributions by all loci, (5) no linkage, and (6) complete homozygosity in each parent, with complete heterozygosity in the $F_1$. With these assumptions, the $F_1$ mean would be expected to fall midway between the parental means. That it does not suggests that not all of our assumptions may be completely valid in this case and/or that the sample is too small. Moreover, the fact that a crude estimate of the number of pairs of genes from the fraction of the $F_2$ as extreme as either parent is lower than the value given by the Wright formula also points up the need for a considerably larger sample.

These are practical contributions of statistical analyses to genetic problems. But application of statistics provides additional, more subtle benefits. In many cases it has been possible to separate genetic mechanisms from sampling errors, and in others to differentiate between genetic and environmental variation. Above all, critical attitudes toward design of experiments and treatment of data have been sharpened.

### PROBLEMS

The following data were obtained on the weight in pounds of a given sample of pumpkin fruits:

| | | | | |
|---|---|---|---|---|
| 30 | 26 | 22 | 16 | 24 |
| 24 | 24 | 30 | 22 | 14 |
| 28 | 22 | 16 | 26 | 22 |
| 24 | 20 | 28 | 14 | 28 |
| 22 | 24 | 22 | 22 | 26 |

---

[1] The variance ($s^2$) is the square of the standard deviation.

**9-1.** What is the mean to the nearest tenth of a pound?

**9-2.** What is the standard deviation?

**9-3.** If an individual is selected at random from this sample, what is the chance that it will weigh more than 18 but less than 28 pounds?

**9-4.** What is the standard error of the sample mean?

**9-5.** What is the probability that the population mean lies between about 21 and 25 pounds?

Data on a second sample were collected and the following statistics arrived at:

mean of sample #2                      = 21.8 pounds
standard deviation of sample #2   =   2.0
standard error of sample mean     =   0.8

**9-6.** What is the standard error of the difference of the means?

**9-7.** What is the approximate probability that samples 1 and 2 represent two different populations?

**9-8.** Is the difference in sample means, therefore, to be considered significant? Why?

**9-9.** Two parental strains, having mean heights of 64.29 cm. and 135.0 cm., respectively, were crossed. The $F_1$ and $F_2$ that resulted had the following statistics:

|       | $\bar{x}$ | $s$ |
|-------|-----------|--------|
| $F_1$ | 99.64     | 10.000 |
| $F_2$ | 102.11    | 13.346 |

If we neglect any possible environmental effects, dominance, linkage, or epistasis, and assume each effective allele to make the same additive contribution, how many pairs of polygenes are involved? (Let the difference in parental means represent the range between extreme phenotypes.)

# CHAPTER 10
# Sex Determination

Two types of sexually reproducing animals and plants may be recognized: (1) **monoecious** (from the Greek *monos*, only, and *oikos*, house) in which each individual produces two kinds of gametes, sperm and egg, and (2) **dioecious** (Greek prefix *di-*, two, and *oikos*) in which a given individual produces only sperms or eggs. In dioecious organisms, the **primary sex difference** concerns the kind of gamete and the primary sex organs by which these are produced. Each sex also exhibits many **secondary sex characters**. In humans, these include voice, distribution of body fat and hair, and details of musculature and skeletal structure; in *Drosophila*, the number of abdominal segments, presence (♂) or absence (♀) of sex combs, etc. (Fig. 10-1). Our immediate

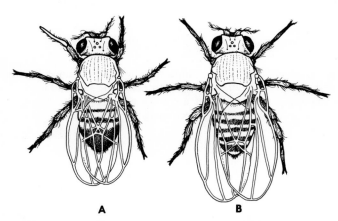

**A**                    **B**

FIGURE 10-1. Drosophila melanogaster, *(A)* male; *(B)* female.

problem is that of examining mechanisms whereby the sex of an individual is determined. We shall discuss two basic types, chromosomal and genic, though the distinction is not always a sharp one.

## Sex Chromosomes

### DIPLOID ORGANISMS

*XX-XO System.* Chromosomal differences between the sexes of several dioecious species were found early in the course of cytological investigations. Henking, a German biologist, in 1891 noted that half the sperms of certain insects contained an extra nuclear structure, which he called the "X body." The significance of this structure was not immediately understood, but in 1902 an American, McClung, reported the somatic cells of the female grasshopper contained 24 chromosomes, whereas those of the male had only 23. Three years later, Wilson and Stevens succeeded in following both oogenesis and spermatogenesis in several insects, and it was realized that the X body was a chromosome, so the X body became known as an X chromosome. Thus, in many insects there is a chromosomal difference between the sexes, females being referred to as XX (having two X chromosomes) and males as XO ("X-oh," having one X chromosome). As a result of meiosis, all the eggs of such species carry an X chromosome, whereas only half the sperms have one, the other half having none.

*XX-XY System.* In the same year, 1905, Wilson and Stevens found a different arrangement in other insects. In these cases females were again XX, but males had, in addition to one X chromosome, an odd one of a different size which was called the Y chromosome, males thus being XY. Half the sperms carry an X, and half a Y. The so-called XY type occurs in a wide variety of animals, including *Drosophila* and mammals, as well as in at least some plants (e.g., the angiosperm genus *Lychnis*) (Fig. 10-2).

A distinction can thus be made between the X and Y chromosomes associated with sex, and those that are alike in both sexes. The X and Y chromosomes are called **sex chromosomes**; the remaining ones of a given complement, which are the same in both sexes, are **autosomes**. In both the XX-XO and XX-XY types described thus far, all the eggs have one X chromosome, whereas the sperms are of two kinds, X and O, or X and Y. In each case, the male is the **heterogametic** sex (producing two kinds of sperms), while the female is the **homogametic** sex (producing but one kind of egg).

*ZZ-ZW System.* A final major type of chromosomal difference between the sexes is that in which the female is heterogametic and the male homogametic. The sex chromosomes in this case are often designated as Z and W to avoid confusion with instances in which the female is homogametic. Females are thus ZW and males ZZ. Birds (including the domestic fowl), butterflies, and some fishes belong to this group.

## MONOPLOID ORGANISMS

*Liverworts.* Like all sexually reproducing plants, liverworts (phylum *Bryophyta*) are characterized by a well-marked alternation of generations (see Appendix B), in which a monoploid, sexually reproducing phase or generation (the gametophyte) alternates in the life history with a diploid, asexually reproducing individual (the sporophyte). Allen (1919) reported the chromosome complement of the sporophyte of the liverwort *Sphaerocarpos* to consist of seven matching pairs, plus an eighth pair in which one

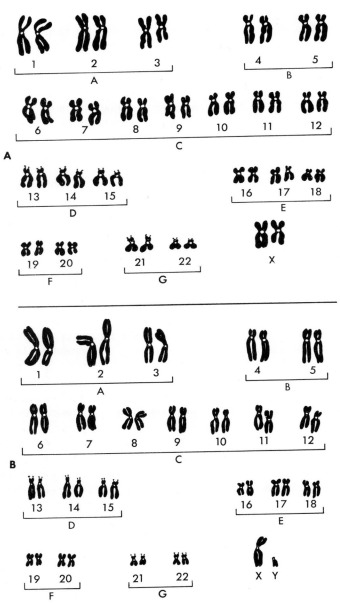

FIGURE 10-2. *Karyotypes of human beings showing sex differences. (A) female; (B) male. Chromosome pairs 1–22 are autosomes, customarily designated by letter groups. The X and Y are sex chromosomes; structurally, X is similar to group C, and Y to group G.*

of the two chromosomes was much larger than the other. The larger member of this eighth pair has been designated the X chromosome, its smaller partner the Y chromosome. At meiosis, which terminates the diploid sporophyte generation, X and Y chromosomes are segregated, so that of the four meiospores produced from each meiocyte, two receive an X chromosome and two a Y chromosome. Meiospores containing an X chromosome develop into female gametophytes, those with a Y into males. Thus females are X, males Y, and asexual sporophytes XY.

## SUMMARY OF SEX CHROMOSOME TYPES

The various types of chromosomal differences between the sexes may be summarized as follows:

| ♀ | ♂ | Examples |
|---|---|---|
| XX | XY | *Drosophila*, man and other mammals, some dioecious angiosperm plants |
| XX | XO | Grasshopper; many Orthoptera and Hemiptera |
| ZW | ZZ | Birds, butterflies, and moths |
| X | Y | Liverworts |

# Determination of Sex Under the Chromosomal System

Such chromosomal differences as these raise certain fundamental questions. For example, is a *Drosophila* individual a male because he has a Y or because he has only one X chromosome? Is an individual female because of the absence of the Y or because of the presence of two X chromosomes? Do the autosomes have anything to do with sex determination? Is the system identical in *Drosophila* and man, both of which have the XX-XY sex difference? What do genes have to do with the situation? What causes sex reversal, in which an individual of one sex becomes one of the other sex? Or, what operates to produce individuals that are part male and part female in species where the sexes are ordinarily separate and distinct? At least partial answers are available for all these questions.

## DROSOPHILA

***Primary Nondisjunction of X Chromosomes.*** Work on *Drosophila* genetics showed that sex determination, at least in that animal (where $2n = 8$), was far less simple than the mere XX-XY difference would suggest. From some unusual breeding results in Bridges' laboratory, he was able, in a masterpiece of inductive reasoning, to lay the groundwork for a complete understanding of sex determination in *Drosophila* (Bridges, 1916a, 1916b, and 1925).

The gene for wild type red eyes (+) is carried on the X chromosome; a recessive allele (*v*) produces vermilion eyes in homozygous females and in all males (which, of course, have only one X chromosome). Ordinarily, vermilion-eyed females mated to red-eyed males produce only red-eyed daughters and vermilion-eyed sons:

$$P \quad vv \times +Y$$

$$P \; gametes: \quad \begin{array}{c} \female \quad v \\ \male \; \frac{1}{2}+ \quad + \quad \frac{1}{2} \; Y \\ \hline F_1 \quad \frac{1}{2}+v \quad + \quad \frac{1}{2} vY \\ (\text{red} \; \female) \quad (\text{vermilion} \; \male) \end{array}$$

However, in rare instances, crosses of this type produced unexpected vermilion-eyed daughters and red-eyed sons with a frequency of one per 2,000 to 3,000 offspring. Bridges surmised that these unusual progeny were due to a failure of the X chromosomes in an XX female to disjoin during oogenesis. Such *primary nondisjunction* (Bridges, 1916a) then, he reasoned, would produce three kinds of eggs, the majority containing the normal single X chromosome, and a small number bearing either two X chromosomes or no X at all. Symbolizing each X chromosome as either $X^+$ (carrying the dominant gene for red eyes) or $X^v$ (bearing the recessive gene for vermilion eyes), and each *set of three* autosomes as $A$, Bridges' cross may be represented in this way:

$$P \quad AAX^vX^v \times AAX^+Y$$
$$(\text{vermilion} \; \female) \quad (\text{red} \; \male)$$

$$P \; gametes: \; \female \quad AX^v \; (\text{numerous}) + AX^vX^v \; (\text{rare}) + AO \; (\text{rare})$$
$$\male \quad AX^+ + AY$$

| $F_1$ | $AAX^+X^v$ | red $\female$ (numerous; normal) |
|---|---|---|
| | $AAX^+X^vX^v$ | " metafemale " (rare; die) |
| | $AAX^+O$ | sterile red $\male$ (rare) |
| | $AAX^vY$ | vermilion $\male$ (numerous; normal) |
| | $AAX^vX^vY$ | vermilion $\female$ (rare) |
| | $AAOY$ | die (rare) |

The metafemales ($AAXXX$) are weak, seldom living beyond the pupal stage; $AAOY$ individuals die in the egg stage. Note that the presence of a Y chromosome does not determine maleness itself, though males lacking it are sterile.

**Secondary Nondisjunction.**   Bridges next mated the exceptional vermilion-eyed females ($AAX^vX^vY$) which arose as a result of primary nondisjunction to normal red-eyed males ($AAX^+Y$), obtaining progeny in these frequencies:

0.46  red ♀
0.02  vermilion ♀
0.02  red ♂
0.46  vermilion ♂
0.02  metafemales ⎫
0.02  *OYY*        ⎬ die
                  ⎭

Occurrence of the vermilion-eyed females and red-eyed males is due to *secondary nondisjunction*. Meiosis in XXY females would be expected to be somewhat irregular because of pairing problems and, indeed, Bridges' results indicate that it is. In oogenesis, synapsis may involve either the two X chromosomes (XX type) with the Y chromosome remaining unsynapsed, or one X and the Y (XY type) with the other X remaining free. Bridges found XY synapsis to occur in about 16 per cent of the cases, and XX synapsis in about 84 per cent. After XY synapsis, disjunction segregates the X and Y synaptic partners to opposite poles. The unsynapsed X may go to *either* pole so that XY synapsis produces four kinds of eggs with a frequency of 0.04 each: XX, Y, X, and XY (Fig. 10-3). On the other hand, XX synapsis is followed by disjunction of the two previously synapsed X chromosomes and their movement to opposite poles. The free Y may, of course, go to either pole, but the result is only two kinds of eggs, X and XY, with a frequency of 0.42 each. The overall result of secondary nondisjunction is four kinds of eggs, in these frequencies:

$$0.46 \ X^vY + 0.46 \ X^v + 0.04 \ X^vX^v + 0.04 \ Y$$

Fertilization by sperm from a cytologically normal, red-eyed male $(X^+Y)$ produces eight types of zygotes which may be grouped in six classes:

| Frequency | Zygote | Phenotype |
|-----------|--------|-----------|
| 0.23 | $X^+X^vY$ ⎫ | red ♀ |
| 0.23 | $X^+X^v$ ⎬ | |
| 0.02 | $X^+X^vX^v$ | metafemale (die) |
| 0.02 | $X^+Y$ | red ♂ |
| 0.23 | $X^vYY$ ⎫ | vermilion ♂ |
| 0.23 | $X^vY$ ⎬ | |
| 0.02 | $X^vX^vY$ | vermilion ♀ |
| 0.02 | $YY$ | die |

The chromosomal constitution of each of the six viable genotypes was verified by Bridges.

As Bridges used the terms, *primary nondisjunction* may occur in either XX females or XY males. In the former it leads to the producton of XX and O

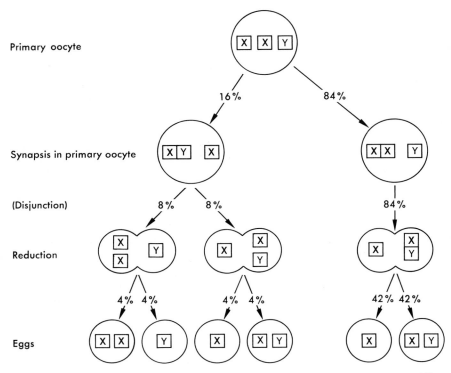

FIGURE 10-3. *Diagram of secondary nondisjunction in XXY female* Drosophila, *resulting in 46 per cent X, 46 per cent XY, 4 per cent XX, and 4 per cent Y eggs. If the egg is, for example, XX, then the polar bodies are XX (1) and Y (2); if the egg is Y, then polar bodies are Y (1) and XX (2), and so forth. For full explanation see text.* [Based on work of Bridges, 1916a.]

eggs. If it occurs in the first meiotic division of males, XY and O sperm are produced. Should it take place during the second division, XX, YY and O sperms result. *Secondary nondisjunction*, on the other hand, occurs in XXY females where it gives rise to XX, XY, X, and Y eggs. As the term nondisjunction implies, production of these aberrant gametes results only from a failure of the sex chromosomes to disjoin after synapsis; they are not physically attached.

*Attached-X Flies.* Another strain of flies in which nondisjunction of the X chromosomes occurred in *all* females was discovered by L. V. Morgan (1922). When such females were mated to cytologically normal males carrying a recessive gene on the X chromosome, all viable male progeny were phenotypically like the father (but sterile), whereas all viable female offspring were like the mother. In addition, one fourth of the total progeny were metafemales and another fourth ($AAOY$) died in the egg stage. Morgan reasoned that in these attached-X females ($\hat{X}X$) the two X chromosomes were physically attached so that only two kinds of eggs, $A\widehat{XX}$ and $AO$ were produced. This explanation was soon confirmed cytologically.

*Polyploid Flies.* Experimentally produced triploid (3 whole sets of chromosomes, or 3*n*) and tetraploid (4*n*) flies were next incorporated into Bridges' work, so that many kinds of flies with respect to chromosome complements were ultimately produced. As this work was carried forward, it became increasingly clear that, in *Drosophila* at least, the important key to the sex of the individual was provided by the *ratio of X chromosomes to sets of autosomes.* The *Y,* then, has nothing to do with sex determination but does govern male fertility. These results are summarized in Table 10-1.

TABLE 10-1. Summary of Chromosomal Sex Determination
in Drosophila (After Bridges)

| Number of X Chromosomes | Number of Sets of Autosomes | X/A Ratio | Sex Designation |
|---|---|---|---|
| 3 | 2 | 1.50 | Metafemale |
| 4 | 3 | 1.33 | Triploid metafemale |
| 4 | 4 | 1.00 | Tetraploid female |
| 2 | 2 | 1.00 | Female |
| 3 | 4 | 0.75 | Tetraploid intersex |
| 2 | 3 | 0.67 | Triploid intersex |
| 1 | 2 | 0.50 | Male |
| 1 | 3 | 0.33 | Triploid metamale |
| 1 | 4 | 0.25 | Tetraploid metamale |

Metamales (or supermales) are to the male sex as metafemales (or super-females) are to the female sex. That is, they are weak, sterile, underdeveloped, and die early. Intersexes are sterile individuals displaying secondary sex characters between those of the male and female (Fig. 10-4).

From all these results the mechanism of sex determination in *Drosophila* may be summarized:

1. Sex is governed by the ratio of the number of X chromosomes to sets of autosomes. Thus, from Table 10-1, females have an X/A ratio = 1.0, males = 0.5. This relationship applies even to polyploid flies so long as the appropriate X/A ratio is maintained.
2. Genes for maleness *per se* are apparently carried on the autosomes, those for femaleness on the X chromosome.
3. The Y chromosome governs male *fertility,* rather than sex itself, since AAXY and AAXO flies are both male as to secondary sex characters but only the former produce sperm; it has no effect in AAXXY flies which have an X/A ratio of 1.0 and are female.

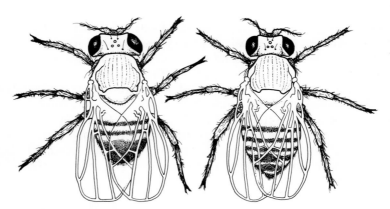

FIGURE 10-4. *Triploid intersexes* (*X/A ratio 0.67*) *in* Drosophila.

4. An X/A ratio $>1.0$ or $<0.5$ results in certain characteristic malformations (*metafemales* and *metamales*).
5. An X/A ratio $< 1.0$ but $> 0.5$ produces individuals intermediate between females and males (*intersexes*). The degree of femaleness is greater where the X/A ratio is closer to 1.0, and the degree of maleness is greater where that ratio is closer to 0.5.

Other workers have confirmed and extended these observations on intersexes in *Drosophila*. By using x-rays to fragment chromosomes, it is possible to develop lines of flies having extra fragments of the X chromosome. Thus, an individual with, say, about two and two-thirds X chromosomes and three sets of autosomes (X/A ratio $= 2.67/3 = 0.89$), although an intersex, displayed secondary sex characters more female in nature than did one with two and a third X and three sets of autosomes (X/A ratio $= 2.33/3 = 0.78$), and so on.

The same system where the X/A ratio is critical is reported for the angiosperm weed, dock (*Rumex acetosa*), by Warmke (1946).

***Temperature and Intersexes.*** As we have noted, intersexes vary from a strong resemblance (in secondary sex characters) to males through degrees of intermediacy to a condition closely approximating femaleness. Yet in a given series of crosses where this difference occurred, the chromosomal situation could be shown to be identical in all pedigrees. That is, in some crosses AAAXX intersex flies closely approximated males, in others females, but often they were somewhat intermediate. Temperature was found to be the critical factor, higher temperatures shifting the balance toward femaleness, lower toward maleness.

***The Transformer Gene.*** One additional complicating factor in sex determination in *Drosophila* is worth examining briefly. A recessive gene, *tra* on the third chromosome (an autosome), when homozygous, "transforms" normal diploid females (AAXX) into sterile males. The XX *tra tra* flies have many sex characters of males (external genitalia, sex combs, and male type abdomen) but, as noted, are sterile.

**Gynandromorphs.** Concepts of sex determination as developed for *Drosophila* are verified by the occasional occurrence of **gynandromorphs** (or gynanders). These are individuals in which part of the body expresses male characters whereas other parts express female characters. A bilateral gynandromorph, for example, is male on one side (right or left) and female on the other. The male portions of such flies would be expected to have a male chromosomal composition. By ingenious experiments using known "marker" genes on the X chromosome, it has been shown indeed that this is so. In *Drosophila*, right and left body halves are determined at the first cleavage of the zygote. Lagging of the X chromosome at this first mitosis can result in two daughter cells of the chromosomal complement AAXX and AAXO when the laggard X fails to be incorporated in a daughter nucleus. The portion of the body developing from the former cell will be normal female, that from the latter (sterile) male. Gynandromorphs represent one kind of *mosaic*, or organisms part of which are composed of cells genetically different from the remaining part.

**Sex As a Continuum.** So we see that sex in *Drosophila* is far from the simple, either-or, male or female, XX or XY condition it was initially thought to be. Instead, sex may be viewed as a continuum, ranging from supermaleness through maleness, intersexes of varying degree, to femaleness and on to superfemaleness. Where an individual places in such a continuum is seen to be related to the ratio of X chromosomes to autosomes. But this is something of an understatement, for it must be genes on the chromosomes that are the deciding factors, rather than chromosomes as gross structures. Thus, genes for maleness are associated with the autosomes, those for femaleness with the X chromosomes. Yet this entire sex-determining arrangement may, in some cases, be upset by a single pair of recessive autosomal genes (*tra*)!

## MAN

In normal human beings males are XY and females are XX, just as in *Drosophila*. But is sex here likewise determined by the X/A ratio? With regard to sex, does the Y chromosome bear genes for male fertility as in *Drosophila* or for male sex *per se*? Answers to these questions have come largely through studies of a relatively small number of sex anomalies and their chromosomal makeup.

A clue to the chromosomal complement of an individual may be gotten quite simply by examining squamous epithelial cells from scrapings of the lining of the cheek. Normal females show a characteristic structure, the Barr body, so named after its discoverer, Murray Barr, who first described it in 1949 (Fig. 10-5). Females are said to be sex chromatin positive. Normal males

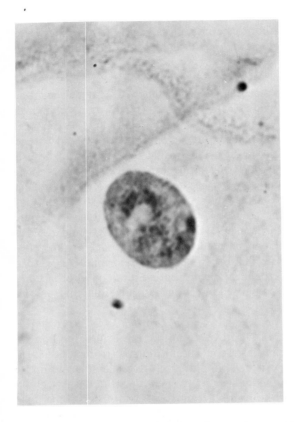

FIGURE 10-5. *Nucleus of normal human female squamous epithelial cell showing prominent, dark Barr body against the nuclear membrane* [Courtesy Carolina Biological Supply Co.]

do not show a Barr body (sex chromatin negative). Lyon (1962) suggested that one X chromosome in females becomes genetically inactive and more deeply staining; this is the Barr body. A number of investigations have supported this explanation and extended it to other mammals.

*The Klinefelter Syndrome.* One in about 500 "male" births produces an individual with a particular set of abnormalities known collectively as the Klinefelter syndrome (Fig. 10-6). These persons are phenotypically male, though genitalia are underdeveloped, and body hair is sparse. Most cases have some degree of breast development and tend to have longer than normal legs and arms. Intelligence is generally subnormal. Although appearing to be male, Klinefelter individuals are sterile and sex chromatin positive. Cytological examination discloses them to be AAXXY, with a somatic chromosome number of 47 instead of the usual 46.

*The Turner Syndrome.* A second major sex anomaly is represented by the Turner syndrome in which the individual is phenotypically female, but with poorly developed ovaries, and sterile. Characteristically such persons exhibit "webbing" of the neck, low-set ears, broad chest, underdeveloped breasts, and

usually below average intelligence (Fig. 10-7). They are sex chromatin negative, which suggests a single X chromosome instead of the expected pair. This
is confirmed by cytological studies which show the somatic chromosome
number to be 45. Arrangement of chromosomes from leukocyte cultures into
an idiogram indicates the missing chromosome to be the X; that is, these
unfortunates are AAXO.

**Other Sex Chromosome Anomalies in Man.** Infrequently other aberrations
of the sex chromosomes in man are reported. For example, Jacobs and others
(1959) described a female of reduced intelligence who was AAXXX. Other
such *triplo-X* individuals have been discovered; some are of normal intelligence and some are fertile, while others are apparently infertile.

Fortunately, such sex chromosome aberrations are not frequent. Lubs and
Ruddle (1970), in a study of 4,366 consecutive newborns over a one year
period at Yale-New Haven Hospital, found the following frequencies:

| Type | Frequency/1,000 Births |
|------|------------------------|
| XYY  | 0.69 |
| XXY  | 0.92 |
| XXX  | 0.69 |
| XO   | 0.23 |

Still higher frequencies have been found for certain of these types of aberrations in other samples. For example, German (1970) has reported XYY
births to occur with a frequency of 1 to 3 per 1,000 male births and XXY in
2.5 per 1,000 male births in groups he studied. No clear relationship between
sex chromosome anomalies in children and any particular parental characteristics, except for a tentative suggestion of a higher risk in mothers with
thyroid disorder (hyperthyroid and hypothyroid), could be discerned.

Known sex chromosome anomalies are summarized in Table 10-2 along
with normal individuals.

**The XYY Male.** Particular interest has recently focused on behavior
patterns in XYY men. These individuals are unusually tall, averaging well
over six feet, and are often described as being more aggressive than the normal
XY male. Some, but not all, are somewhat retarded mentally. However,
other XYY men are of average intelligence and able to make a normal
social adjustment, and some investigators do not agree that XYYs are
aggressive psychopaths.

Incidence of the XYY condition in the general population, based on
relatively few data, appears to be of the order of one in 570 male births. They
do appear to be more frequent in penal and/or mental institutions. Jacobs
et al. (1965) report nine XYY men among a group of 315 mentally retarded
inmates housed in the maximum security section of one mental institution.

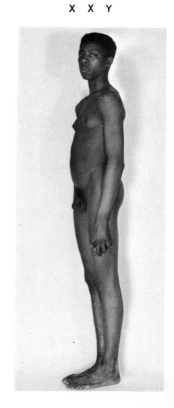

FIGURE 10-6. *The Klinefelter syndrome in man. Such persons are AAXXY, with 47 chromosomes as shown in the karyotype. External genitalia are male-type, but there is usually some female-like breast development as in this case.* [Photo courtesy Dr. Victor A. McKusick; karyotype redrawn from V. A. McKusick, Medical Genetics, *Journal of Chronic Diseases*, **12**: 1–202, 1960 by permission of The C. V. Mosby Co.]

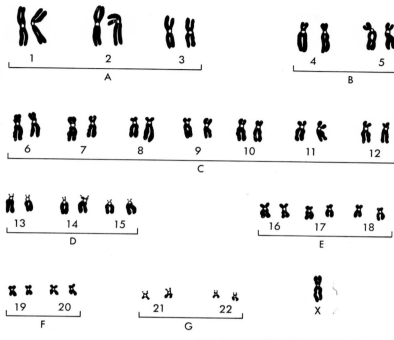

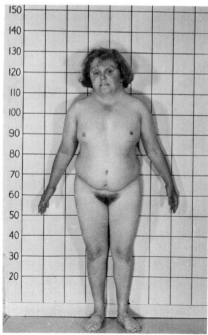

FIGURE 10-7. *The Turner syndrome in man. Such persons are AAXO, with only 45 chromosomes as shown in the karyotype. Note external female genitalia, webbed neck, broad chest, underdeveloped breasts, and short stature. Turner individuals have a small uterus and vestigial ovaries.* [Photo courtesy Dr. Victor A. McKusick; photo and karyotype reproduced from V. A. McKusick, Medical Genetics, *Journal of Chronic Diseases*, **12**: 1–202, 1960, by permission of The C. V. Mosby Co.]

TABLE 10-2. Known Sex Chromosome Anomalies in Man

| Designation | Chromosome Constitution | Somatic Chromosome Number | Sex Phenotype | Fertility |
|---|---|---|---|---|
| Normal ♂ | AAXY | 46 | ♂ | + |
| Normal ♀ | AAXX | 46 | ♀ | + |
| Klinefelter syndrome | AAXXY | 47 | ♂ | — |
| Turner syndrome | AAXO | 45 | ♀ | — |
| Triplo-X | AAXXX | 47 | ♀ | ± |
| Tetra-X | AAXXXX | 48 | ♀ | unknown |
| Triplo-X-Y | AAXXXY | 48 | ♂ | — |
| Tetra-X-Y | AAXXXXY | 49 | ♂ | — |
| Penta-X | AAXXXXX | 49 | ♀ | unknown |
| XYY | AAXYY | 47 | ♂ | ± |
| Klinefelter XXYY | AAXXYY | 48 | ♂ | not reported |
| Klinefelter XXXYY | AAXXXYY | 49 | ♂ | not reported |

All exhibited violent and aggressive behavior. In another study Price et al. (1966) report that, of nine institutionalized XYY males, eight were retarded and one was schizophrenic; six were more than six feet tall. But Lubs and Ruddle (1970) point out that none of the infants with XYY (or other sex chromosome aberrations) in their study had any detectable developmental retardation or consistent phenotype by the age of one year.

The XYY individual is receiving increased attention because of certain legal implications. In several especially vicious murder cases (in France, Australia, and the United States) pleas of not guilty by reason of insanity (based on an XYY finding) have been entered for the accused. Court decisions have not been consistent, some resulting in "guilty" and others in "not guilty" verdicts. The preponderance of present evidence does suggest that XYY males may be more likely to exhibit over-aggressive behavior, to make poor social adjustment, and to have a higher risk of committing crimes of violence. Borgaonkar (1969) has compiled an extensive bibliography on the XYY syndrome.

Some of the problems of characterizing behavior patterns in men with 47 chromosomes may well revolve around the difficulty of distinguishing clearly between Y and the morphologically similar G-group of autosomes. Comparing replication patterns by the technique of labeling cultured cells with tritiated thymidine offers some assistance in this regard (Borgaonkar et al., 1970), because the Y chromosome appears to replicate later than autosomes 21 and 22 (German, 1967).

*Mechanism of Sex Determination in Man.* Table 10-2 clearly indicates that individuals having at least one Y chromosome are male, at least as to external genitalia, though they may be sterile. Contrariwise, persons with one or more X chromosomes are phenotypically female as long as no Y is present, though, again, sometimes infertile. So it would seem that genes for maleness are carried on the Y chromosome in man, those for femaleness on the X. One Y chromosome offsets several X's, so that even XXXXY persons are male, though sterile. Thus sex in man appears to be determined by presence of X and Y chromosomes.

The question of whether or not autosomes play any part is seen in individuals with exceptional numbers of autosomes. Although these will be dealt with more fully under chromosomal aberrations (Chapter 12), suffice it to say here that most variations in number of autosomes involve persons all of whose somatic cells contain one extra of a particular autosome, not additional whole sets. No complete living polyploids are known in man, though an interesting **mosaic** was reported some years ago in Sweden. This was a young male, at first reported to be triploid (69 chromosomes). It was later determined that he was a mosaic for 2*n* and 3*n* tissues. Phenotypically, this individual was male. In both autosomal trisomics (individuals with 47 chromosomes, in which the 47th is a specific autosome) and in the Swedish mosaic, sex appears to be determined only by the X and Y chromosomes.

On the other hand, several cases are reported in the literature of spontaneously aborted, completely triploid fetuses. With regard to the sex chromosomes, some of these were XXX, some XXY, and a few XYY. A very small number of completely tetraploid, aborted fetuses is also known. From available evidence, it would appear that the genic imbalance produced by extra whole genomes in man is lethal.

We can then summarize the situation in man in this way:

1. Autosomes play no part in determining sex.
2. The Y chromosome determines maleness, even a single one outweighing any number of Xs.
3. The X chromosome determines femaleness *in the absence of any Ys.*

Sex determination in man, then, although related to the X-Y chromosome makeup, operates differently than in *Drosophila*. Mammals, generally, appear to follow the mechanism outlined for human beings.

### PLANTS

One flowering plant, the wild campion, *Lychnis dioica* (formerly *Melandrium*) of the pink family (Caryophyllaceae), has been extensively investigated. It is worth reporting here because it illustrates still another variation of the XX-XY system. In angiosperms, the plant we recognize by name is the asexual, diploid sporophyte generation. The sexual phase is microscopic and contained largely within the tissues of the sporophyte, on which it is parasitic. Flowers contain either or both of two essential organs, stamens and/or pistils. The former produce microspores which develop into male-gamete-bearing plants (at one stage these are the well-known pollen grains). Pistils produce and contain the egg-bearing sexual plant. Many plants have so-called perfect flowers which contain both stamens and one or more pistils. *Lychnis* has "imperfect" flowers which bear either stamens *or* pistils. The species is, moreover, dioecious, so that there are staminate (male-producing) individuals and pistillate (female-producing) ones. Though not accurate, staminate plants are often referred to as male plants and pistillate as female.

In *Lychnis*, staminate plants are XY, pistillate plants XX. Warmke (1946) found the X/A ratio to bear no relation to "sex" but, through studies of polyploid strains, determined the X/Y ratio to be critical. X/Y ratios of 0.5, 1.0, and 1.5 were found in plants having only staminate flowers; in plants whose X/Y ratio was 2.0 or 3.0, occasional perfect flowers occurred among otherwise staminate flowers. In plants having 4 sets of autosomes, 4 X chromosomes and a Y, flowers were perfect but with an occasional staminate one. These results are summarized in Table 10-3, and illustrated in Fig. 10-8.

TABLE 10-3. "Sex" and X/Y Ratios in *Lychnis* (After Warmke.) Each A = one set of 11 autosomes, each X = an X chromosome, each Y = a Y chromosome.

| Chromosome Constitution | X/Y ratio | "Sex" |
|---|---|---|
| 2 AXYY | 0.5 | ♂ |
| 2 AXY | | |
| 3 AXY | 1.0 | ♂ |
| 4 AXY | | |
| 4 AXXXYY | 1.5 | ♂ |
| 2 AXXY | | |
| 3 AXXY | | |
| 4 AXXY | 2.0 | ♂ with occasional ⚥ flower |
| 4 AXXXXYY | | |
| 3 AXXXY | | |
| 4 AXXXY | 3.0 | ♂ with occasional ⚥ flower |
| 4 AXXXXY | 4.0 | ⚥ with occasional ♂ flower |

♂ = staminate; ♀ = pistillate; ⚥ = perfect.

Westergaard (1948) extensively investigated the cytology of *Lychnis* and, from studies of plants from which portions of the X or Y chromosome were deleted, arrived at a comparison of the X and Y chromosomes, as shown in Fig. 10-9. The sex chromosomes are quite dissimilar in size, the Y being larger than the X, and each larger than any autosome. Only a small portion of the X is homologous with a similar small bit of the Y, as suggested by their synaptic figures in meiosis. When region I is deleted, perfect flowered plants are produced, whereas loss of region II produces pistillate plants (that is, whereas AAXY plants are staminate, $AAXY^{-II}$ plants are pistillate), and deletion of region III produces sterile staminate plants with aborted stamens.

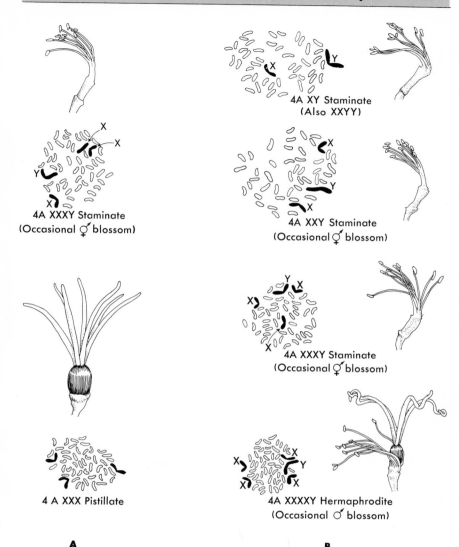

FIGURE 10-8. (*A*) *Reproductive parts and camera lucida drawings of the somatic chromosomes from 4A XXXY and 4A XXX plants of* Lychnis (Melandrium). *Note that a single Y chromosome produces a staminate plant having occasional perfect flowers; in the absence of the Y chromosomes, plants are pistillate.* (*B*) *Reproductive parts and camera lucida drawings of the somatic chromosomes of* Lychnis *in a series showing pistillate-determining tendency of the X chromosome. All plants shown are tetraploid with respect to autosomes, but differ in the number of X chromosomes present. Tendency to produce pistillate flowers increases as the number of X chromosomes rises.* [Redrawn from H. W. Warmke, 1946, Sex Determination and Sex Balance in *Melandrium. American Journal of Botany*, **33:** 648–660, by permission of the author and the Botanical Society of America, Inc., Washington.]

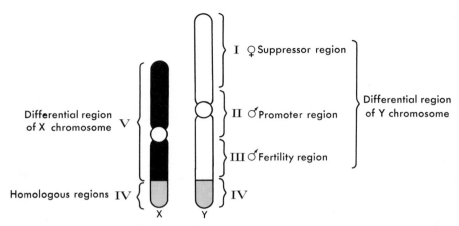

FIGURE 10-9. *Comparison of X and Y chromosomes of the plant,* Lychnis. *Regions I, II, and III bear holandric genes, and region V sex-linked genes. Genes in region IV are termed incompletely sex linked.* Lychnis *is unusual in that its Y chromosome is the larger of the two sex chromosomes.*

## Genic Determination of Sex

Sex does not appear to be controlled in all dioecious organisms by numerous genes on two or more chromosomes, however. Several examples will serve to illustrate some variations on the so-called chromosomal method.

*Asparagus.* Rick and Hanna (1943) presented evidence to show that sex in asparagus is determined by a single pair of genes, with "maleness" (i.e., formation of staminate flowers) the dominant character. Asparagus is normally dioecious, some plants producing only staminate flowers, others only pistillate. Rudimentary pistils occur in staminate flowers, and abortive stamens in pistillate blossoms. These rudimentary organs are ordinarily nonfunctional. However, the pistils in staminate flowers do very rarely function to produce viable seeds. Flower structure in this species is such that these seeds most likely result from self-pollination. In effect, this is a "male × male" cross from the genetic standpoint. The basis for the occasional functional pistils in staminate plants is not known, but both genetic and environmental factors have been suggested.

Rick and Hanna germinated 198 seeds from these uncommon functional pistils produced on staminate plants, finding a progeny ratio of 155 staminate to 43 pistillate. This is a close approximation to a 3:1 ratio, as a chi-square test will indicate. One-third of the staminate progeny, when crossed with normal pistillate plants, yielded only staminate offspring. The rest proved to be heterozygous, producing staminate and pistillate offspring in a ratio close to 1:1.

If "maleness" is represented as $A-$ and "femaleness" as $aa$, the original "male × male" cross would be

$$P \quad Aa \times Aa$$
$$F_1 \quad \tfrac{3}{4} A- + \tfrac{1}{4} aa$$

On the basis of monohybrid inheritance examined in Chapter 2, one third of the $A-$ (staminate) plants should be $AA$ and two thirds $Aa$. Crosses between these genotypes and normal pistillate ($aa$) individuals would produce the results reported by Rick and Hanna.

**Honeybee.** Worker and queen bees are diploid females, with 32 chromosomes. Drones, on the other hand, are males having but 16 chromosomes and develop from unfertilized eggs. Whiting (1945), through extensive studies on the parasitic wasp *Habrobracon*, postulated that femaleness in such hymenopterans as these is determined by heterozygosity of a number of different chromosome segments. The situation is analogous to a series of multiple alleles but is based on chromosomal segments containing several genes each. Monoploid individuals, hatching from unfertilized eggs, cannot be heterozygous, hence are male. As you might suspect, Whiting was able to produce diploid males by developing individuals homozygous in a sufficient number of chromosomal segments.

**Corn.** Unlike the organisms so far described, corn (*Zea mays*) is monoecious. The "tassel" consists of staminate flowers, and the ear of pistillate flowers. Among several controls over "sex" in this plant are two interesting pairs of genes. The genotype *bs bs* ("barren stalk") results in plants having no ears at all, though a normal tassel is present (Fig. 10-10). Such individuals are staminate ("male"). Gene *ts* ("tassel seed"), when homozygous, converts the tassel to pistillate flowers, so that ears develop at the top of the plant (Fig. 10-11). Therefore, *ts ts* individuals are pistillate ("female"). If we let ♂ represent staminate flowers, and ♀ pistillate ones, the various genotypes and phenotypes are as follows:

| Genotype | Phenotype | |
|---|---|---|
| *Bs — Ts —* | Normal monoecious | ♂ ♀⌐♀ |
| *bs bs Ts —* | Staminate | ♂ ♀ |
| *Bs — ts ts* | Pistillate; ears terminal *and* lateral | ♀ ♀⌐♀ ♀ |
| *bs bs ts ts* | Pistillate; ears terminal only | ♀ |

FIGURE 10-10. *Barren stalk corn*, bsbs. *Note the absence of ears.* [From *The Ten Chromosomes of Maize*, DeKalb Agricultural Association, DeKalb Illinois. Reproduced by permission.]

Plants of genotype *bs bs Ts* — plus either *Bs* — *ts ts* or *bs bs ts ts* comprise a dioecious race of corn. Such a race may easily be produced by making the cross *bs bs ts ts* × *bs bs Ts ts* which will segregate pistillate and staminate in a 1:1 ratio. Perhaps some sort of development like this has occurred in the evolution of dioecism. The practical advantage of the dioecious state to the breeder is obvious.

   *Bacteria.*   Until relatively recently, bacteria were believed to reproduce only asexually. The discovery by Lederberg and Tatum (1946) of conjugation in the colon bacillus, *Escherichia coli*, opened the way to a whole new area of understanding in genetics. We shall consider some of its implications later, but as a variant in sex determination, it should be noted here.

   Conjugation in bacteria involves a process in which two cells become joined by a bridge (Fig. 10-12) through which one cell "donates," to the other, part or all of its single chromosome (Appendix B). Conjugation results in a temporary diploid of the recipient cell. This diploidy is complete for all

FIGURE 10-11. *Tassel seed corn*, ts ts. *Note silks of developing ear at top of stem in place of tassel.* [From *The Ten Chromosomes of Maize*, DeKalb Agricultural Association, DeKalb, Illinois. Reproduced by permission.]

genes only if the entire chromosome of the donor passes into the recipient; otherwise it is partial for only certain genes. The usual monoploid condition is restored at the next cell division (Appendix B).

The donor cell may be thought of as analogous to a male, the recipient cell to a female. "Maleness," in this sense, is determined by possession of an **episome** or fertility factor, F, femaleness by its absence. The F factor may be located in the cytoplasm, extrachromosomally, or it may be integrated into the bacterial chromosome. If the F factor is transferred during conjugation, the recipient cell is converted from "female" to "male." Much has been learned about the nature of the genetic material itself from studies of recombination resulting from conjugation in bacteria, and we shall explore this matter in Chapter 14.

*Chlamydomonas.* The common, microscopic, unicellular green alga *Chlamydomonas* (Fig. 10-13) reproduces sexually by isogametes. These are gametes in which no morphological differences can be observed. Vegetative cells and gametes are monoploid. But syngamy is selective in that the gametes of all individuals are not equally capable of fusing. Mating strains, designated as + and −, rather than male and female, are recognized. Plus strains

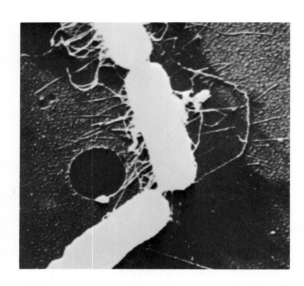

FIGURE 10-12. *Electron micrograph of conjugating* E. coli *cells. The bridge connecting the two conjugants may be seen at the angle between upper and lower partners. It happens that the conjugating cells are both in late stages of fission as well, and one of them is coincidentally being attacked by bacteriophages.* [Photo courtesy Dr. Thomas F. Anderson, Institute for Cancer Research, Philadelphia.]

conjugate only with minus. Mating type appears to be related to physiological differences within the cell and is, in turn, known to be genetically determined. Thus, zygotes produce 4 cells by meiosis, 2 becoming plus adults and 2 minus. Ebersold (1967) was able to develop diploid adults from zygotes by mitosis. All of these unusual $2n$ individuals were of the minus mating strain, indicating dominance of this trait. Progeny ratios resulting from crosses involving diploids confirm this. So, in this simple alga where evolution of sex has not progressed very far, sex appears to be controlled by a single pair of genes responsible for physiological rather than morphological differences.

### CONCLUSION

Sex represents something of a continuum in many organisms, but is basically gene-determined. Species differ with respect to (1) the number of genes that appear to play a part and (2) the locations of those genes (X chromosome, Y chromosome, autosomes, cytoplasmic). The genes an individual receives at the moment of syngamy determine which kind of gonads, and therefore of gametes, will be formed. Later processes of sex differentiation are quite distinct from the initial event of sex determination. In insects the critical factors in sex differentiation appear to be intracellular. In man and other mammals, however, sex differentiation is hormonal. Sex hormones, produced by the gonads, interact with endocrine glands elsewhere in the body to affect the multiplicity of secondary sex characters. These latter may be markedly affected by hormone injections, suggesting that each individual has some potentialities for either sex.

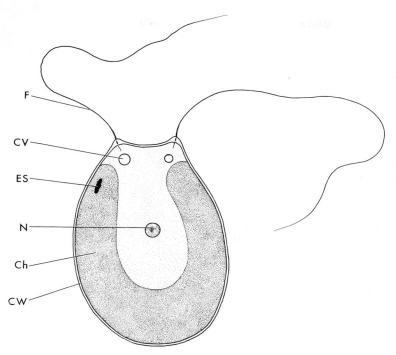

FIGURE 10-13. *Diagram of vegetative cell of the green alga,* Chlamydomonas: *F, flagellum; CW, cell wall; CV, contractile vacuole; ES, eye spot; Ch, chloroplast; N, nucleus.*

## REFERENCES

ALLEN, C. E., 1919. The Basis of Sex Determination in *Sphaerocarpos. Proc. Amer. Phil. Soc.,* **58**.

ALLEN, C. E., 1935. The Genetics of Bryophytes. *Bot. Rev.,* **1**:269–291.

BORGAONKAR, D. S., 1969. 47, XYY Bibliography. *Ann. Genet.,* **12**:67–70.

BORGAONKAR, D. S., H. M. HERR, and J. NISSIM, 1970. DNA Replication Pattern of the Y Chromosome in XYY and XXYY Males. *Jour. Hered.,* **61**:35–36.

BRIDGES, C. B., 1916a. Nondisjunction as Proof of the Chromosome Theory of Heredity. *Genetics,* **1**:1–52.

BRIDGES, C. B., 1916b. Nondisjunction as Proof of the Chromosome Theory of Heredity (concluded). *Genetics,* **1**:107–163.

BRIDGES, C. B., 1925. Sex in Relation to Chromosomes and Genes. *Amer. Natur.,* **59**:127–137.

EBERSOLD, W. T., 1967. *Chlamydomonas reinhardii*: Heterozygous Diploid Strains. *Science*, **157**:447–449.

GERMAN, J., 1967. Autoradiographic Studies of Human Chromosomes. In J. F. Crow and J. V. Neel, eds., 1967. *Proc. Third Int. Cong. Human Genetics.* Baltimore, The Johns Hopkins Press.

GERMAN, J., 1970. Studying Human Chromosomes Today. *Amer. Scientist*, **58**: 182–201.

JACOBS, P. A., A. G. BAIKIE, W. M. COURT BROWN, T. N. MACGREGOR, N. MACLEAN, and D. G. HARNDEN, 1959. Evidence for the Existence of the Human "Superfemale." *Lancet*, **2**:423.

JACOBS, P. A., M. BRUNTON, M. M. MELVILLE, R. P. BRITTAIN, and W. F. MCCLERMONT, 1965. Aggressive Behavior, Mental Subnormality and the XYY Male. *Nature*, **208**:1351–1352.

LEDERBERG, J., and E. L. TATUM, 1946. Gene Recombination in *Escherichia coli. Nature*, **158**:558.

LUBS, H. A., and F. H. RUDDLE, 1970. Chromosomal Abnormalities in the Human Population: Estimation of Rates Based on New Haven Newborn Study. *Science*, **169**:495–497.

LYON, M. F., 1962. Sex Chromatin and Gene Action in Mammalian X-Chromosomes. *Amer. Jour. Human Genetics*, **14**:135–148.

MORGAN, L. V., 1922. Non-Criss-Cross Inheritance in *Drosophila melanogaster. Biol. Bull.*, **42**:267–274.

PRICE, W. H., J. A. STRONG, P. B. WHATMORE, and W. F. MCCLERMONT, 1966. Criminal Patients with XYY Sex-Chromosome Complement. *Lancet*, **1**:565–566.

RICK, C. M., and G. C. HANNA, 1943. Determination of Sex in *Asparagus officinalis L. Amer. Jour. Bot.*, **33**:711–714.

WARMKE, H. E., 1946. Sex Determination and Sex Balance in *Melandrium. Amer. Jour. Bot.*, **33**:648–660.

WESTERGAARD, M., 1948. The Relation Between Chromosome Constitution and Sex in the Offspring of Triploid *Melandrium. Hereditas*, **34**:257–279.

WHITING, P. W., 1954. The Evolution of Male Haploidy. *Quart. Rev. Biol.*, **20**:231–260.

## PROBLEMS

**10-1.** What is the sex designation for each of the following fruit flies (each A = one set of autosomes, each X = one X chromosome): (a) AAXXXX; (b) AAAAAXX; (c) AAXXXXXX; (d) AAAAAXXX; (e) AAAAXXXX?

**10-2.** What is the sex designation for the following human beings: (a) AAXXX; (b) AAXXXYYY; (c) AAXO; (d) AAXXXXXY; (e) AAXYYY?

**10-3.** What phenotypic ratio results in corn from selfing *Bs bs Ts ts* plants?

**10-4.** In *Drosophila*, what fraction of the progeny of the cross *Tra tra* XX × *tra tra* XY are "transformed"?

**10-5.** What is the sex ratio in the progeny of the cross given in problem 10-4?

**10-6.** In poultry, the dominant gene, *B*, for barred feather pattern is located on the Z chromosome. Its recessive allele, *b*, produces nonbarred feathers. What is the genotype of a (a) nonbarred female; (b) barred male; (c) barred female; (d) nonbarred male?

**10-7.** An XXY *Drosophila* female is mated to a normal male. The progeny include 5 per cent metafemales. If secondary nondisjunction occurred, what was the frequency of XX eggs?

**10-8.** From your answer to 10-7, and further assuming Y eggs to occur with a frequency of 0.1, what percentage of the progeny of the cross of problem 10-7 will be phenotypically normal females?

**10-9.** An attached-X female *Drosophila* is mated to a normal male. (a) What fraction of the zygotes become viable females? (b) What fraction of the zygotes are metafemales in chromosomal constitution? (c) What fraction of the viable, mature progeny are sterile males?

**10-10.** If the female parent of problem 10-9 is $AAX^+X^w$ and the male $AAX^wY$, what will be the eye color of (a) viable, mature male progeny and (b) viable, mature female progeny?

**10-11.** In poultry, removal of the ovary results in the development of the testes. Thus a female can become converted to a male, producing sperm and developing male secondary sex characters. If such a "male" is mated to a normal female, what sex ratio occurs in the progeny?

**10-12.** If you assume parents to be $AAXX$ and $AAXY$, how could you account in man for children of each of the following types: (a) $AAXYY$; (b) $AAXXY$; (c) $AAXO$?

**10-13.** In the literature numerous cases of human mosaics are reported. How could you account cytologically for an $AAXX$-$AAXO$ mosaic?

**10-14.** From the standpoint of survival of the species, which system of sex determination, that of *Asparagus* or of man, seems to offer the greater advantage? Why?

## CHAPTER 11
# Inheritance Related to Sex

THE fact that males in *Drosophila* and in man have an X and a Y chromosome, whereas females have two Xs and no Y, raises some interesting genetic possibilities. This is especially so when it is realized that the sex chromosomes do not bear genes affecting the same traits throughout their entire lengths and do carry some genes other than sex determiners. Therefore, we should expect to find inheritance patterns related to the sex of the individual and somewhat different from those examined previously. For example, genes occurring only on the X chromosome will be represented twice in females, once in males; recessives of this type might be expected to show up phenotypically more often in males. Genes located exclusively on the X chromosome are called **sex-linked genes**. On the other hand, genes occurring only on the Y chromosome can produce their effects only in males; these are **holandric genes** (Greek, *holos*, whole, and *andros*, man). Still other mechanisms are known whereby a given trait is limited to one sex (**sex-limited genes**), or even in which dominance of a given allele depends on the sex of the bearer (**sex-influenced genes**). Genes occurring on homologous portions of the X and Y chromosomes are called **incompletely sex-linked**. We shall examine the first four of these types of sex-related inheritance in this chapter.

## Sex Linkage

*Drosophila.* From 1904 to 1928, T. H. Morgan taught at Columbia University, attracting many students who were later to become brilliant geneticists. Most of these men worked in what became known fondly as "the fly-room." This must have been a remarkable and stimulating group; as one of them (Sturtevant, 1965) describes it, "There was an atmosphere of excitement in the laboratory, and a great deal of discussion and argument about each new result as the work rapidly developed."

For example, in a long line of wild-type, red-eyed flies, an exceptional white-eyed male was discovered. To the Columbia group this was a new character, apparently arising through mutation or change of the gene for red eyes (Fig. 11-1). Morgan and his students crossed this new male to his wild-type sisters; all the offspring had red eyes, indicating that white was recessive. An $F_2$ of 4,252 individuals was obtained: 3,470 were red-eyed and 782 white-eyed. This is not a good representation of the expected 3:1 ratio, but it is now known that white-eyed flies do not survive as well as their wild-type sibs and are therefore less likely to be counted. However, the important

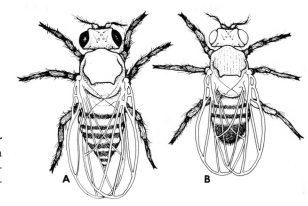

FIGURE 11-1. *Eye color mutation in* Drosophila melanogaster. *(A) Red-eyed female; (B) white-eyed male.*

point here is that all 782 white-eyed F$_2$ flies were males! About an equal number of males had red eyes.

From Chapter 10 you will recall that these genes for eye color are on the X chromosome. Again using $Y$ to represent the Y chromosome (which does not carry a gene for eye color), $+$ for red eyes, and $w$ for white eyes (alleles on the X chromosome), Morgan's crosses may be represented thus:

$$P \quad ++ \quad \times \quad wY$$
$$\text{red } \female \qquad \text{white } \male$$
$$F_1 \quad \tfrac{1}{2} + w \quad \text{and} \quad \tfrac{1}{2} + Y$$
$$\text{red } \female \qquad \text{red } \male$$
$$F_2 \quad \underbrace{\tfrac{1}{4} ++, \tfrac{1}{4} + w,}_{\text{red } \female} \quad \underbrace{\tfrac{1}{4} + Y,}_{\text{red } \male} \quad \underbrace{\tfrac{1}{4} wY}_{\text{white } \male}$$

*[handwritten marginal note: Hemizygous / Red ♀ : Red ♂ : White ♂ / 2 : 1 : 1]*

Morgan correctly predicted that white-eyed females would be produced by the cross $+w \times wY$. A perpetual stock of white-eyed flies of both sexes was then established by mating white-eyed males and females.

An important characteristic of sex-linked inheritance emerges from an examination of the original Morgan cross. Note that the F$_2$ white-eyed males have received their recessive gene from their F$_1$ mothers, and these, in turn, have received gene $w$ from their own white-eyed fathers. This "crisscross" pattern from father to heterozygous daughter (often termed a "carrier") to son is typical for a recessive sex-linked gene. Moreover, in this particular pedigree, about half the sons in the F$_2$ show the trait, whereas none of the daughters do. Of course, in the cross $+w \times wY$ half the daughters as well as half the sons have the recessive phenotype. Notice that normal females ($AAXX$) carry two of these genes and thus may be either homozygous ($++$ or $ww$) or heterozygous ($+w$), but normal males ($AAXY$) can only be **hemizygous** ($+Y$ or $wY$).

***Sex Linkage in Man.*** More than fifty sex-linked traits have been described in man. Most of these appear to be due to recessive genes. Red-green color blindness was the first such to be described, and also appears to be the most commonly encountered such trait. It is reported that about 2 out of every 25 white males are red-green color blind, but only about 1 in 150 women is so affected.

Hemophilia, a well known disorder in which blood clotting is deficient due to a lack of the necessary substrate thromboplastin, is likewise a sex-linked recessive condition. Two types of sex-linked hemophilia are recognized:

1. *Hemophilia A*, characterized by lack of anti-hemophilic globulin (Factor VIII). About four fifths of the cases of hemophilia are of this type.
2. *Hemophilia B*, or " Christmas disease," due to a defect in plasma thromboplastin component (Factor IX). This is a milder form of the condition.

From an unusual family in which both types of hemophilia were segregating, Woodliff and Jackson (1966) concluded that the two loci involved were far apart on the X chromosome. Incomplete evidence suggests a distance of more than forty map units. Hemophilia is well known in the royal families of Europe, where it is traceable to Queen Victoria who must have been heterozygous (Fig. 11-2). No hemophilia is known in her ancestry, hence it is often surmised that she arose from a mutant gamete.

Male hemophiles occur with a frequency of about 1 in 10,000 male births, and heterozygous females may be expected in about twice that frequency. The method of calculating this is explored on pages 255 and 256. Under a system of random mating, hemophilic females would be expected to occur once in $10,000^2$ or 100,000,000 births. But this probability is reduced by the likelihood of male hemophiles dying before reaching reproductive age. Moreover, a hemophilic girl would almost certain die by adolescence. Consequently, few cases of female hemophiles are known, though they have been reported in pedigrees of frequent first-cousin marriages. Because clotting time in different hemophiles varies somewhat, it has been suggested that the condition is affected by various modifying genes, perhaps even a series of multiple alleles (rather than a single pair). At present heterozygous women can be detected by a small increase in clotting time.

Some of the other sex-linked traits in man include two forms of diabetes insipidus, nonfunctional sweat glands (anhidrotic ectodermal dysplasia), absence of central incisors, certain forms of deafness, spastic paraplegia, uncontrollable rolling of the eyeballs (nystagmus), a form of cataract, night blindness, optic atrophy, juvenile glaucoma, juvenile muscular dystrophy, and white forelock (a patch of light frontal hair on the head). Most of these are fairly clearly due to recessive genes. On the other hand, defective tooth enamel, which results in early wearing of the teeth down to the gums, is due to a dominant sex-linked gene. Women, with their two X chromosomes,

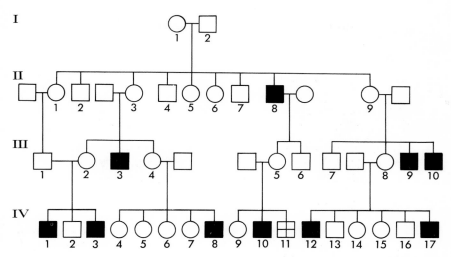

FIGURE 11-2. *Pedigree of some of the descendants of Queen Victoria showing incidence of hemophilia (shaded symbols). (I-1) Queen Victoria; (II-8) Leopold, Duke of Albany; (III-3) Frederick of Hesse; (III-8) Victoria Eugenie, who married Alfonso XIII of Spain; (III-9) Lord Leopold of Battenberg; (III-10) Prince Maurice of Battenberg; (IV-1) Waldemar of Prussia; (IV-3) Henry of Prussia; (IV-8) Tsarevitch Alexis of Russia; (IV-10) Rupert, Viscount Trematon; (IV-12) Alfonso of Spain; (IV-17) Gonzolo of Spain. (IV-11) died in childhood; (II-2) represents Edward VII of England, great-grandfather of Elizabeth II.*

have twice as great a probability of receiving this gene as men in the same family.

**Sex Linkage in Other Organisms.** Sex linkage in XX-XO species is, of course, just as it is in *Drosophila* and man, because sex-linked genes are, by definition, those on the X chromosome. Here again only females can be heterozygous.

In birds, where the female is the heterogametic sex, the situation is reversed, although the mechanism is unchanged. Sex-linked genes follow the "crisscross" pattern, but from mother through heterozygous sons to granddaughters.

Although the barred feather pattern, due to a dominant sex-linked gene in Plymouth Rock chickens (Fig. 11-3), is a frequently cited illustration, a pair of alleles governing speed of feather growth is a more interesting one. Both traits have been used for identifying chick sex, but feather color patterns are sometimes modified by other genes. Gene $k$, for slow feather growth, eliminates such complications and can be detected within hours after hatching. For example, remembering males to be homogametic, the cross $+W(♀) \times kk (♂)$ results in two kinds of progeny, $+k$ (males with normal feather growth) and

FIGURE 11-3. *Barred feather pattern, due to a dominant sex-linked gene, in Plymouth Rock female (left) and male (right).*

$kW$ (females with slower feather growth). Gene $k$ has no effect on other characters of commercial value.

**Sex-Linked Lethals.** It might occur to you that the gene for hemophilia is actually a recessive, sex-linked *lethal*, for it may often cause death. Slight scratches or accidental injuries, which would not be serious in normal persons, often result in fatal bleeding for the hemophile. Sex-linked lethals, then, may alter the sex ratio in a progeny as soon as they bring about death.

Duchenne (or pseudohypertrophic) muscular dystrophy is a rare disease in which the affected individual, though apparently normal in early childhood, exhibits progressive wasting away of the muscles, which results in death in the teen years (Fig. 11-4). Like hemophilia, it is due to a recessive sex-linked gene. At present, no means of arresting or preventing the disease is known; a given genotype dooms the bearer at conception to death in adolescence. The gene responsible is, then, to be considered a lethal, and will change the sex ratio in a given group of offspring over time. Letting $+$ represent the normal (dominant) gene and $d$ the gene for muscular dystrophy, consider children of many marriages between heterozygous women and normal men, $+d \times +Y$. The offspring would be expected in a ratio of $\frac{1}{4} + +$, $\frac{1}{4} + d$, $\frac{1}{4} + Y$, and $\frac{1}{4} dY$ at birth, but individuals of the last genotype die off before age 20. So, an initial approximately 1:1 female:male ratio will later become 2:1 female:male. If a recessive sex-linked lethal kills before birth, the ratio of female to male live births is changed from nearly 1:1 to 2:1. A 2:1 female:male ratio is always a strong indication of a sex-linked recessive lethal.

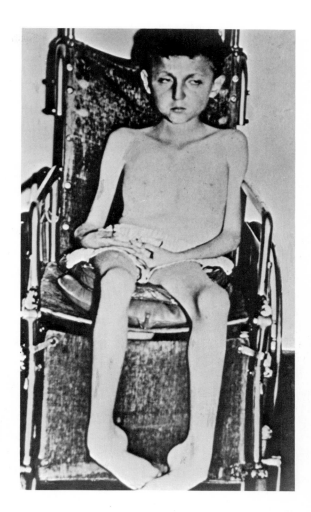

FIGURE 11-4. *Duchenne pseudohypertrophic) muscular dystrophy, due to a recessive sex-linked gene. This case will terminate in death.* [Courtesy Muscular Dystrophy Association of America, Inc., New York.]

## Holandric Genes

Not many genes are clearly established as having loci on the rather small Y chromosome in human beings. Traits due to such genes can occur only in men and, moreover, must appear in all the sons of an affected father. It should, therefore, be relatively easy to detect such **holandric** genes in man, but partly because of the relative genetic inertness of Y and partly because of the difficulty of distinguishing them from sex-limited genes (see next section), no unequivocal case has been established in man. The best candidate for the holandric pattern in man is one causing excessive hair development on the ears (hypertrichosis). This trait is seen rather frequently in India (Fig. 11-5).

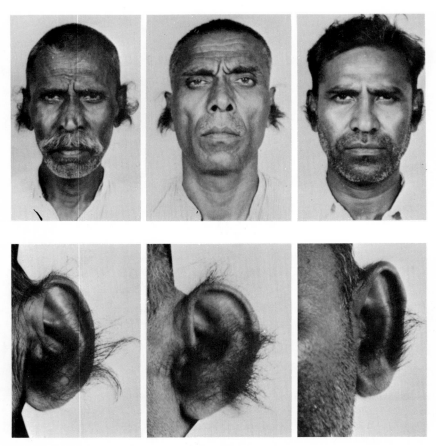

FIGURE 11-5. *"Hairy ears," a trait common in certain parts of the world. It may be caused by a holandric gene.* [From C. Stern, W. R. Centerwall, and S. S. Sarker, New Data on the Problem of Y-Linkage of Hairy Pinnae, *American Journal of Human Genetics*, **16:** 455–471, 1964. By permission Grune and Stratton, Inc. Photo courtesy Dr. Curt Stern.]

## Sex-Limited Genes

Sex-limited genes are those whose phenotypic expression is determined by the presence or absence of one of the sex hormones. Their phenotypic effect is thus *limited* to one sex or the other.

Perhaps the most familiar example occurs in the domestic fowl where, as in many species of birds, males and females may exhibit pronounced differences in plumage. In the Leghorn breed, males have long, pointed, curved,

FIGURE 11-6. *Hen-feathering (left) and cock-feathering (right) in domestic fowl. Cock-feathering is characterized by long, pointed, curving neck and tail feathers.*

fringed feathers on tail and neck, but feathers of females are shorter, rounded, straighter, and without the fringe (Fig. 11-6). Thus, males are cock-feathered and females hen-feathered. In such breeds as the Sebright bantam, birds of both sexes are hen-feathered. However, in others (Hamburg or Wyandotte) both hen- and cock-feathered males occur, but all females are hen-feathered. Leghorn females are hen-feathered, males all cock-feathered.

It has been shown that hen-feathering results from a single gene, $H$, and cock-feathering from its allele, $h$:

| Genotype | ♀ | ♂ |
|----------|-----|-----|
| $HH$ | hen-feathered | hen-feathered |
| $Hh$ | hen-feathered | hen-feathered |
| $hh$ | hen-feathered | cock-feathered |

Thus, Sebright bantams are all $HH$, Hamburgs and Wyandottes may be $H-$ or $hh$, but Leghorns are all $hh$. Cock-feathering, where it occurs, is *limited* to the male sex.

The basis for the differential behavior of gene $h$ is seen in chickens from which the ovaries or testes have been removed. These gonadectomized birds all become cock-feathered at the next molt following surgery, regardless of genotype! The particular kind of plumage thus appears to depend upon a specific combination of genotype and sex hormone. The action of the two alleles may be summarized thus:

$H$ produces hen-feathering in the presence of either sex hormone, and cock-feathering in the absence of any hormone; dominant to

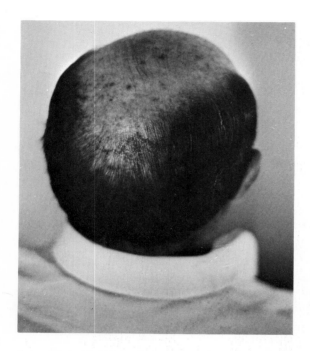

FIGURE 11-7. *Pattern baldness in man, a sex-influenced trait dominant in males and recessive in females.*

*h* produces cock-feathering if female hormone is absent, hen-feathering if it is present.

Sex-limited inheritance patterns are quite different from those of sex-linked genes. The latter may be expressed in either sex, though with differential frequency. Sex-limited genes express their effects in only one sex or the other, and their action is clearly related to sex hormones. They are principally responsible for secondary sex characters. Beard development in human beings is such a sex-limited character, men normally having beards, women normally not. Yet studies indicate no significant difference between the sexes in number of hairs per unit area of skin surface, only in their development. This appears to depend on sex hormone production, changes in which may result in a genuine bearded lady.

## Sex-Influenced Genes

In contrast to sex-limited genes where one expression of a trait is limited to one sex, sex-influenced genes are those whose dominance is *influenced* by the sex of the bearer.

Although baldness may arise through any of several causes (e.g., disease, radiation, thyroid defects), "pattern" baldness exhibits a definite genetic

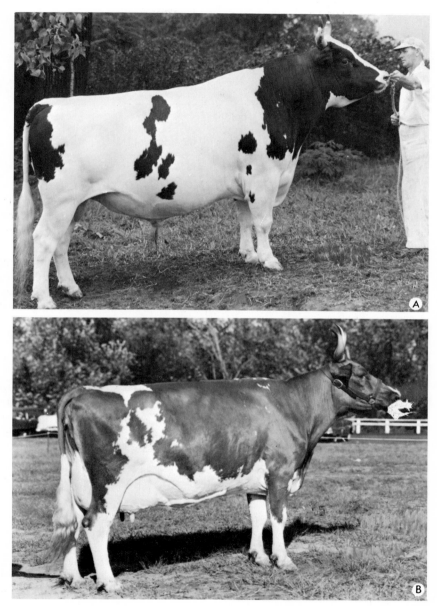

FIGURE 11-8. *A sex-influenced trait in cattle. (A) Mahogany and white, dominant in males, recessive in females; (B) red and white, dominant in females, recessive in males.* [Courtesy Ayrshire Breeders' Association, Brandon, Vermont.]

pattern. In this condition, hair gradually thins on top, leaving ultimately a fringe of hair low on the head (Fig. 11-7). Pattern baldness is more prevalent in males, but may occur in females. Indications are that a single pair of autosomal genes operates in this fashion:

| Genotype | ♂ | ♀ |
|----------|-----|-----|
| *BB* | bald | bald |
| *Bb* | bald | not bald |
| *bb* | not bald | not bald |

Gene *B* behaves as a dominant in males and as a recessive in females, appearing to exert its effect in the heterozygous state only in the presence of male hormone. A number of reports in the literature dealing with abnormalities leading to hormone imbalance or with administration of hormone support this view.

A few well-known cases occur in lower animals—e.g., horns in sheep (dominant in males) and spotting in cattle (mahogany and white dominant in males, red and white dominant in females, Fig. 11-8). Some hypothetical crosses involving these characters are explored in problems at the end of this chapter.

## REFERENCES

MORGAN, T. H., 1910. Sex Limited Inheritance in *Drosophila. Science*, **32**:120–122. Reprinted in J. A. Peters, ed., 1959. *Classic Papers in Genetics.* Englewood Cliffs, N.J., Prentice-Hall.

STURTEVANT, A. H., 1965. *A History of Genetics.* New York, Harper & Row.

WOODLIFF, H. J., and J. M. JACKSON, 1966. Combined Haemophilia and Christmas Disease. A Genetic Study of a Patient and his Relatives. *Med. Jour. Aust.*, **53**:658–661.

## PROBLEMS

**11-1.** "Bent," a dominant sex-linked gene (*B*) in the mouse, results in a short, crooked tail; its recessive allele (*b*) produces normal tails. If a normal-tailed female is mated to a bent-tail male, what phenotypic ratio should occur in the $F_1$?

**11-2.** Nystagmus is a condition in man characterized by involuntary rolling of the eyeballs. The gene for this condition is incompletely dominant and sex-linked. Three phenotypes are possible: normal, slight rolling, severe rolling. A woman who exhibits slight nystagmus and a normal man are considering marriage and ask a geneticist what the chance is that their children will be affected. What will he tell them?

11-3. "Deranged" is a phenotype in *Drosophila* in which the thoracic bristles are disarranged and the wings vertically upheld, producing a characteristic appearance. Crosses between deranged females and normal males results in a 1:1 ratio of normal females to deranged males in the progeny. What is the mode of inheritance and how would you describe the dominance of this gene?

11-4. In poultry, sex-linked gene *B*, producing barred feather pattern, is completely dominant to its allele, *b*, for nonbarred pattern. Autosomal gene *R* produces rose-comb; its recessive allele, *r*, produces single comb in the homozygous state. A barred female, homozygous for rose-comb is mated to a nonbarred, single comb male. What is the $F_1$ phenotypic ratio?

11-5. Members of the $F_1$ from problem 11-4 are then crossed with each other. What fraction of the $F_2$ is barred rose, and are these male or female?

11-6. In what ratio does (a) barred, nonbarred and (b) rose, single segregate in the $F_2$ of problem 11-5?

11-7. A family has five children, three girls and two boys. One of the latter died of muscular dystrophy at age 15. The others graduate from college and are concerned over the probability that their children may develop the disease. What would you tell them?

11-8. "Jimpy" is a trait in the mouse characterized by muscular incoordination which results in death at an age of three to four weeks. Crosses between heterozygous females and normal males produce litters in which half the males are jimpy. What type of gene is jimpy?

11-9. At locus 0.3 on the X chromosome of *Drosophila* there occurs a recessive gene, *l*, which is lethal in the larval stage. A heterozygous female is crossed to a normal male; what $F_1$ adult sex phenotypic ratio results?

11-10. A woman with defective tooth enamel and normal red-green color vision, who had a red-green blind father with normal tooth enamel and a mother who had defective tooth enamel and normal red-green vision, marries a red-green blind first cousin with normal tooth enamel. What is the probability of their having a child with normal tooth enamel and red-green color blindness if crossing-over does not occur?

11-11. What is the probability, if they have three children, that these will be two red-green blind girls with normal teeth and one boy with defective teeth but normal red-green color vision?

11-12. The bald phenotype can sometimes be distinguished at a relatively early age. A nonbald, red-green blind man marries a nonbald, normal-visioned woman whose mother was bald and whose father was red-green blind. What is the probability of their having each of the following children: (a) bald girls; (b) bald normal-visioned boys; (c) nonbald boys; (d) red-green blind children of either sex?

11-13. In addition to the allelic pair determining pattern baldness (*B,b*) described in this chapter, consider early baldness to be due to another autosomal gene (*E*) on a different pair of chromosomes, and also dominant in males. The phenotype for *ee* may be either late baldness or nonbaldness, depending on sex and the genotype for the *B,b* alleles. Two doubly heterozygous persons (*BbEe*) marry. (a) What is or will be the phenotype of the male parent? (b) What is or will be the phenotype of the female parent? (c) What is the phenotypic ratio among *male* children of couples such as this one? (d) What is the phenotypic ratio among *female* children of couples such as this one?

**11-14.** A mahogany-and-white cow has a red-and-white calf. What is the sex of the calf?

**11-15.** The cross of a horned female ewe and a hornless ram produces a horned offspring. What is the sex of the $F_1$ individual?

**11-16.** In the clover butterfly, males are always yellow, but females may be either yellow or white. What kind of inheritance is operating?

**11-17.** In the clover butterfly, white is dominant in females. Crossing of two heterozygotes produces what $F_1$ phenotypic ratio?

**11-18.** How could you differentiate between a sex-linked recessive trait and a holandric one?

**11-19.** Why is nothing known regarding dominance of holandric genes?

**11-20.** How could you differentiate between a sex-linked dominant gene and a holandric one?

**11-21.** If hairy ears (hypertrichosis) is a holandric trait, what kind of children can be produced by a hairy-eared man?

**11-22.** In poultry, a particular cross produced an $F_1$ ratio of 3 hen feathering: 1 cock feathering. One third of the hen-feathered progeny were males. What were the parental genotypes?

**11-23.** Which of the individuals in Fig. 11-2 of the text was heterozygous for hemophilia?

**11-24.** What is the probability that any woman shown in generation IV of Fig. 11-2 was heterozygous?

**11-25.** King Edward VII (Fig. 11-2) married Princess Alexandra of Denmark; their son was George V, who married Princess Mary of Teck. George VI, son of George V, married Lady Elizabeth Bowes-Lyon; one of their children is the present Queen Elizabeth II, whose husband is Prince Philip. None of these men were hemophilic, and the disease did not occur in the families of their wives. Would it be possible for Queen Elizabeth II to have any hemophilic children?

# CHAPTER 12
# Chromosomal Aberrations

I N earlier chapters it was pointed out that each species of plant and animal is characterized by a particular chromosome complement or set, represented once in monoploid cells (e.g., gametes and spores) and twice in diploid cells. Possession of such sets of chromosomes, or **genomes**, gives to each species a specific chromosome number (see Table 3-1). But irregularities sometimes occur in nuclear division, or "accidents" (as from radiation) may befall interphase chromosomes so that cells or entire organisms with aberrant genomes may be formed. Such chromosomal aberrations may include whole genomes, entire single chromosomes, or just parts of chromosomes. Thus cytologists recognize (1) **changes in number of whole chromosomes (hetero-ploidy)** and (2) **structural modifications**. Heteroploidy may involve either entire extra sets of chromosomes (**euploidy**), or loss or addition of single chromosomes (**aneuploidy**). Each of these may produce phenotypic changes, modifications of phenotypic ratios, or alteration of linkage groups. Many are of some evolutionary significance.

## Changes in Chromosome Number
### EUPLOIDY

*Monoploids.* Euploids are characterized by possession of entire sets of chromosomes, monoploids carrying one genome ($n$), diploid, two ($2n$), and so on. Monoploidy is rare in animal adults (the male honeybee is an outstanding exception), but common in plants. In most sexually reproducing algae and fungi and in all bryophytes (liverworts and mosses), the monoploid phase represents the dominant part of the life cycle and is the plant we recognize by species name. In vascular plants (*Tracheophyta*), this stage is short-lived and microscopic, though occasionally adult monoploid vascular plants may be recognized in natural populations. These are ordinarily weak, small, and highly sterile. Blakeslee and Belling appear to have reported the first such case in 1924, in the Jimson weed; there is good evidence that these have developed from unfertilized eggs. Sterility in monoploids is due to extreme irregularity of meiosis because of the impossibility of chromosomal pairing and the very low probability of their distribution in complete sets to daughter nuclei. Thus, viable gametes are rarely formed; their occurrence depends on the chance movement of the whole monoploid set to one pole at meiosis. This is a highly improbable event.

*Polyploidy.* Euploids with three or more genomes are called **polyploids**.

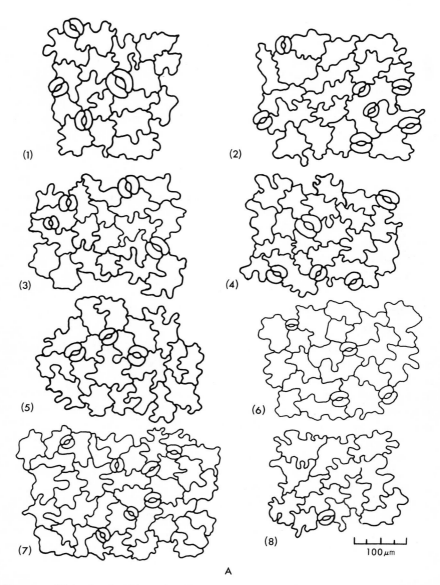

(1)

(2)

(3)

(4)

(5)

(6)

(7)

(8)

100 μm

A

FIGURE 12-1. *Leaf epidermal cells of saxifrage* (Saxifraga pensylvanica). *(A) Diploids; mean cell area ranges from 1147 μm² to 1897 μm².*

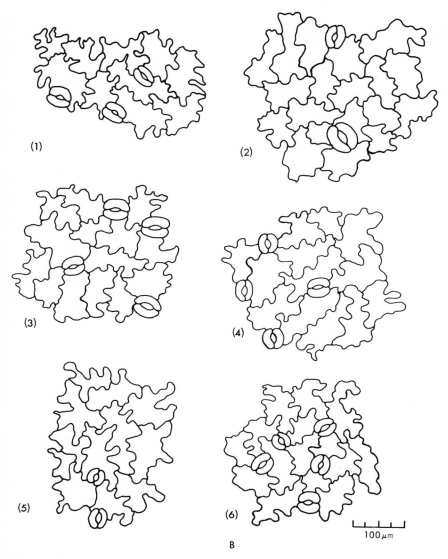

(1)

(2)

(3)

(4)

(5)

(6)

100 μm

B

FIGURE 12-1 [continued]. (B) Tetraploids; mean cell area ranges from 2378 μm²
to 3408 μm².

This condition is rather common in the plant kingdom but rare in animals Whereas one 4$n$ plant, for example, would produce 2$n$ gametes and could, in many species, be self-fertilized to produce more 4$n$ progeny, the probability of *two* such *animals* (one of each sex) mating is extremely low. Furthermore, the imbalance of sex-determining mechanisms that would result from polyploidy would be expected to result in sterility because of aberrant meiosis or to produce individuals which, for many morphological reasons, might be at a considerable disadvantage in mating.

By contrast, many plant genera consist of species whose chromosome numbers constitute a euploid series. The rose genus, *Rosa*, includes species with the somatic numbers 14, 21, 28, 35, 42, and 56. Notice that each of these numbers is a multiple of 7. Thus, this is a euploid series of the basic number, 7, giving diploid, triploid, tetraploid, pentaploid, hexaploid, and octoploid species. All but the diploids may be collectively referred to as polyploids. One authority has estimated that at least two thirds of all grass species are polyploids.

In many instances, morphological differences between diploids and their related polyploids are not great enough for taxonomists to give the latter forms species rank, although the polyploids can usually be distinguished visually. Thus, Burns (1942) found that a large amount of morphological variation within a single species of swamp saxifrage (*Saxifraga pensylvanica*) was associated with polyploidy and that diploids, triploids, and tetraploids differed consistently in several respects. The larger chromosome number of polyploids was found to be reflected in larger cell size (Fig. 12-1). Measurement of lower leaf epidermal cell size, for example, of randomly selected diploids and tetraploids showed mean cell area of diploids to be 1,608 square micrometers and, for tetraploids, 2,739 square micrometers. Burns found the greater cell size of the tetraploids to be associated with larger size of plant and plant parts, and a lower length : width ratio of leaves, giving 2$n$ and 4$n$ plants distinctly different appearances in the field. Leaves of tetraploids are noticeably wider for their length than those of the 2$n$ plants (Fig. 12-2). Such differences between diploid and tetraploid were found to be significant; statistical tests provided a very high degree of confidence in the premise that two different populations exist, as seen in the following comparison of length: width ratios of leaves:

|  | Diploids | Tetraploids |
|---|---|---|
| $\bar{x}$ = | 4.67 $\mu$m$^2$ | 3.44 $\mu$m$^2$ |
| $s$ = | 1.109 | 0.837 |
| $s_{\bar{x}}$ = | 0.158 | 0.119 |
| $S_d$ = | 0.194 | |

FIGURE 12-2. *Herbarium specimens of* Saxifraga pensylvanica. *(A) Diploid; (B) tetraploid. Note differences in leaf length-width ratio. Other characteristic dissimilarities occur in shapes and sizes of flower parts, fruits, and seeds.*

The difference in sample means is 4.67 − 3.44 = 1.23, which is 6.34 times greater than the standard error of the difference in sample means. Chromosomes of the various members of the series are illustrated in Fig. 12-3.

In general, tetraploids are often hardier, more vigorous in growth, able to occupy less favorable habitats, and/or have larger flowers and fruits. Burns (1942) reported tetraploid swamp saxifrage to extend a little farther west into drier habitats in Minnesota, and Dean (1959) found the tetraploids of the spiderwort plant (*Tradescantia ohioensis*) to occupy drier and more disturbed areas than their diploid relatives.

In many cultivated plants tetraploid varieties are commercially more desirable than their diploid counterparts and are commonly available from seed or plant suppliers (Fig. 12-4). As might be expected, polyploid varieties with an even number of genomes (e.g., tetraploids) are often fully fertile,

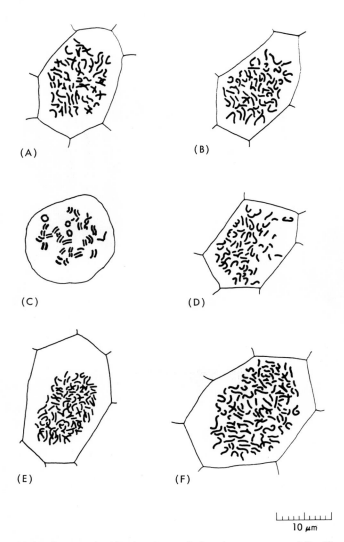

(A)

(B)

(C)

(D)

(E)

(F)

|⌊⌊⌊⌊⌊⌊⌊⌊⌊⌋|
10 μm

FIGURE 12-3. *Camera lucida drawings of the chromosomes of* Saxifraga pensylvanica. *(A), (B), and (D) diploids, 2n = 56; (C) microsporocyte at synapsis, n = 28;
(E) triploid, 3n = 84; (F) tetraploid, 4n = 112. All but (C) show polar views of
mitotic metaphase chromosomes in root tip cells.*

whereas those with an odd number of genomes (e.g., triploids) are highly
sterile. This latter fact is made use of in marketing of seeds containing triploid
embryos. Triploid watermelons, for example, are nearly seedless and are
listed in a number of seed catalogs (Fig. 12-5). Triploids are commonly

FIGURE 12-4. (*A*) *Diploid and* (*B*) *tetraploid snapdragons. Note larger and more numerous flowers in the tetraploid* (*the somewhat open character of the diploid flowers is not related to chromosome number*). [Courtesy Burpee Seeds.]

created by crossing the normal diploid, whose gametes are *n*, with a tetraploid, gametes of which are 2*n*.

**Production of Polyploids.**   Polyploids may arise naturally or be artificially induced. In plants it appears that diploidy is more primitive, and that polyploids have evolved from diploid ancestors. In natural populations this may arise as the result of interference with cytokinesis once chromosome replication has occurred, and may occur either (1) in somatic tissue, giving tetraploid branches, or (2) during meiosis, producing unreduced gametes. It has been found that chilling may accomplish this in natural populations (Belling, 1925).

Application of the alkaloid colchicine, derived from the autumn crocus (*Colchicum autumnale*), either as a liquid or in lanolin paste, induces polyploidy. Although chromosome replication is not interfered with, normal spindle formation is prevented and the double number of chromosomes becomes incorporated within a common nuclear membrane. Subsequent nuclear divisions are normal, so that the polyploid cell line, once initiated, is

FIGURE 12-6. *Synapsis in an autotetraploid. Pairing is in twos, but all four chromosomes are included in each synaptic figure. An actual case would be far more complicated in appearance because of the intertwining of chromatids, omitted here for simplicity.*

maintained. Polyploidy may also be induced by other chemicals (acenaphthene and veratrine) or by exposure to heat or cold.

*Autopolyploidy and Allopolyploidy.* If a tetraploid is developed by the colchicine treatment, for example, its cells contain four genomes, all of the same species. Such a polyploid is an **autotetraploid**. Autopolyploids may, of course, exist with any number of genomes. The same situation results if an individual is formed from the fusion of two diploid gametes; the four sets of its chromosomes all belong to the same species.

Synapsis in autotetraploids usually involves groups of four homologs, though these ordinarily associate only in pairs for given segments. The result is a characteristic quadrivalent configuration in prophase-I (Fig. 12-6). Subsequent disjunction and passage of chromosomes to spindle poles may be highly irregular, so that very few functional gametes are formed. Such sterility is not universal in autotetraploids, however, synapsis apparently occurring normally in some so that only bivalent chromosomes are seen. Fertility then is unimpaired.

On the other hand, polyploids may develop (and be developed) from hybrids between different species. These are **allopolyploids**; the most commonly encountered type is the allotetraploid, having two genomes from each of the two ancestral species. The Russian cytologist Karpechenko (1928) synthesized a new genus from crosses between vegetables belonging to different genera, the radish (*Raphanus*) and the cabbage (*Brassica*). These plants are fairly closely related and belong to the mustard family (*Cruciferae*). Each has a somatic chromosome number of 18; but those of radish have many genes not

FIGURE 12-5. *(A) Diploid watermelon with numerous seeds; (B) Triploid variety with few and imperfect seeds.* [Courtesy Burpee Seeds.]

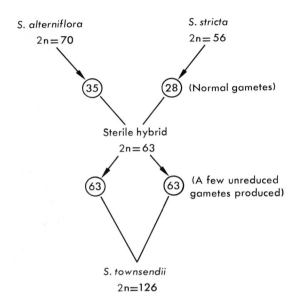

FIGURE 12-7. *Development of* Spartina townsendii, *an allotetraploid (amphidiploid). The cross* S. alterniflora × S. stricta *produced a sterile hybrid having one complete genome from each of its quite different parents. Production of infrequent gametes having all 63 chromosomes, followed by their fusion, results in the completely fertile hybrid* S. townsendii.

occurring in cabbage chromosomes, and vice versa. Karpechenko's hybrid had in each of its cells 18 chromosomes, 9 from radish and 9 from cabbage. The very unlike genomes failed to pair, and the hybrid was largely sterile. A few 18-chromosome gametes were formed, however, and a few allotetraploids were thereby produced as an $F_2$. These were completely fertile, since two sets each of radish and cabbage chromosomes were present and pairing between homologs occurred normally. The allotetraploid was named *Raphanobrassica*. Unfortunately it has the root of cabbage and leaves of radish and is of no direct economic importance. The method does, however, offer a means of producing fertile interspecific or intergeneric hybrids.

*Polyploidy in Man.*   Complete polyploid human beings are, as might be expected, quite rare and the few cases known are either born dead or live for but a matter of hours. Gross and multiple malformations, reflecting the extreme genic imbalance of these individuals, occur in all cases. Schindler and Mikamo (1970) have reported a triploid male (69, XXY), born after 39 weeks' gestation, with extreme malformations. The chromosome count was verified as consistent in various tissues, including blood, skin, and muscle. A live-born 69, XXX premature female who survived less than 24 hours was found by Butler et al. (1970) who also have tabulated the malformations of other complete and mosaic triploids.

*Evolution Through Polyploidy.*   Interspecific hybridization combined with polyploidy offers a mechanism whereby new species may arise suddenly in natural populations. Cytogenetic investigations of such instances of

speciation in many cases have involved real "detective work" and even cul-
minated in the artificial production of the new species.

An excellent example of this is furnished by the work of Huskins (1930) on
the marsh grass, *Spartina*. In the latter part of the eighteenth century *S.
townsendii* was first collected along the shores of England and France on both
sides of the English Channel. By the early 1900s it had spread over considerable areas of both countries. Townsend's grass combines many characters of
*S. stricta*, a European species, and the American *S. alterniflora* and was
thought perhaps to represent a hybrid between the Old and New World
species, seed of the latter apparently having been accidentally introduced into
Europe in ship cargoes. It is fully fertile and has a diploid chromosome number
of 126. Diploid numbers for its suspected parents were found to be 56
(*S. stricta*) and 70 (*S. alterniflora*). It therefore appeared probable that
Townsend's grass was an allotetraploid of the cross *S. stricta* × *S. alterniflora*.
This did prove to be the case, for *S. townsendii* has actually been created (or
recreated) in experimental plots. As suspected, the diploid hybrid ($2n = 63$)
was sterile, since its somatic cells contained 28 "*stricta* chromosomes" and
35 of *S. alterniflora*. Doubling the chromosome number of this sterile hybrid
resulted in the synthesizing of *S. townsendii*, surely a triumph of cytological
research (Fig. 12-7).

Similarly, other workers investigated the origin of New World cotton
(*Gossypium*). Briefly, Old World cotton has 26 rather large chromosomes,
whereas a Central and South American species has 26 much smaller ones.
The cultivated cotton has 52, of which 26 are large and 26 smaller, and was
suspected of being an allotetraploid of a cross between Old and New World
species. Beaseley was able to reconstitute the cultivated species by crossing
the two putative parents and using colchicine to double its chromosome
number.

But in considering polyploidy as a mechanism of evolution, a note of
caution must be inserted. Basically, polyploidy adds no new genes to a
gene pool but, rather, results in new combinations, especially in allopolyploids. Phenotypic effects of autopolyploidy generally represent merely
exaggerations of existing characters of the species. Possession of multiple
genomes reduces the likelihood that a recessive mutation will express itself
until and unless its frequency becomes quite high in the population. Polyploidy, therefore, has the potential for actually decreasing genetic variation.
So, although entities that we recognize as new species do arise through
allopolyploidy, and although vigor and often geographic range may be
increased by autopolyploidy, it is nevertheless wise to view polyploidy in its
proper perspective as both a positive and negative force in evolution.

### ANEUPLOIDY

***Trisomy.*** The Jimson weed, *Datura stramonium*, shows a considerable

Normal
DIPLOID

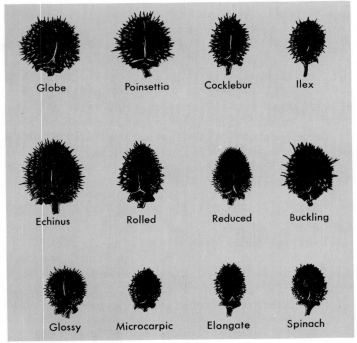

FIGURE 12-8. *Fruits of normal diploid Jimson weed (top) and its twelve possible trisomics below. Each of the latter was produced experimentally by Blakeslee and Belling.* [Redrawn from A. B. Blakeslee and J. Belling. Chromosomal Mutations in the Jimson Weed, *Datura stramonium. Journal of Heredity*, **15**: 195–206, 1924, by permission of the American Genetic Association, Washington, D.C.]

amount of morphological variation in many traits but particularly in fruit characters. The normal chromosome number for this plant is $2n = 24$, but in a now classical study, Blakeslee and Belling (1924) showed that each of several specific morphological variants had 25 chromosomes. One of the 12 kinds of chromosomes was found to be present in triplicate; that is, the somatic cells were $2n + 1$. Such a **trisomic** plant has three of each of the genes of the extra chromosome. Since the Jimson weed has 12 pairs of chromosomes, 12 recognizable trisomics should be possible, and Blakeslee and his colleagues succeeded in producing all of them (Fig. 12-8). Trisomics usually arise through nondisjunction so that some gametes contain two of a given chromosome.

When trisomics are crossed, ordinary Mendelian ratios do not result. For example, the trisomic "poinsettia" (Fig. 12-8) has an extra ninth chromosome (i.e., it is triplo-9), which carries gene $P$ (purple flowers) or its allele $p$ (white flowers). One possible genotype, therefore, for a purple-flowering "poinsettia" is $PPp$. Crossing two such plants produces a 17:1 $F_1$ phenotypic ratio. Pollen (and hence sperms) carrying either more or less than 12 chromosomes is nonfunctional. Megaspores (and eggs that develop from them), however, are not so affected. Meiosis in trisomics ordinarily results in two of the three homologs going to one pole, and one to the other, giving rise to some gametes carrying various combinations of two homologs and others carrying but one. With this in mind we can represent the cross $PPp \times PPp$ as follows:

$$PPp\,♀ \qquad \times \qquad PPp\,♂$$
$$\text{"purple poinsettia"} \qquad \text{"purple poinsettia"}$$

*P gametes:*

$$♀ \quad \tfrac{1}{6} \text{ ea.}: P + P + Pp + Pp + PP + p$$
$$♂ \quad \tfrac{1}{3} \text{ ea.}: P + P + p$$

$F_1$  $\tfrac{4}{18}$ $PP$  homozygous purple diploid
$\tfrac{4}{18}$ $Pp$  heterozygous purple diploid
$\tfrac{5}{18}$ $PPp$  heterozygous purple trisomic ("poinsettia")
$\tfrac{2}{18}$ $Ppp$  heterozygous purple trisomic ("poinsettia")
$\tfrac{2}{18}$ $PPP$  homozygous purple trisomic ("poinsettia")
$\tfrac{1}{18}$ $pp$  homozygous white diploid

Purple and white thus segregate in a 17:1 ratio. Other ratios are, of course, possible with different parental genotypes; some of these are taken up in problems at the end of this chapter.

*Trisomy and Mongolism.* An important and tragic instance of trisomy in man involves mongoloid idiocy or Down's syndrome (Fig. 12-9). Afflicted persons are mentally retarded, have a specific peculiarity of the upper eyelid which suggests Oriental eyes, are relatively short in stature, exhibit characteristic abnormalities of palm prints, and certain other malformations, especially of heart, hands, and feet. Sexual maturity and fertility are only rarely attained. These unfortunate persons are trisomic for chromosome 21, one of the smaller autosomes (Fig. 12-10). Various studies give an overall incidence of trisomy-21, where mothers were under 40, ranging from 0.45 to 3.6 per 1,000 births, with a mean of about 1.6/1,000.

Actually, from the cytological viewpoint, two types of mongolism may be recognized: (1) *triplo-21*, in which the affected individual has 47 somatic

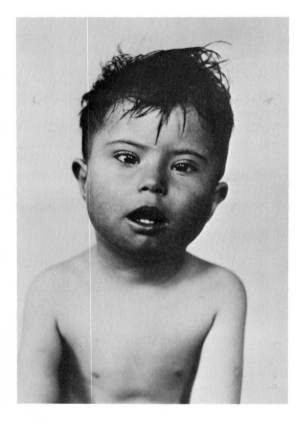

FIGURE 12-9. *Down's syndrome (Mongoloid idiocy) in a child.* [Courtesy National Foundation, New York.]

chromosomes, and (2) *translocation mongolism*, in which the extra twenty-first chromosome has become attached to one of the other autosomes, generally thought to be number 15 (Fig. 12-11), giving a somatic chromosome number of 46. Translocations will be discussed more fully in the next section, but suffice it to point out here that both types involve an extra number 21; in one case it is a separate entity, in the other it has become attached to another chromosome. Phenotypes of triplo-21 and translocation-21 are identical. Triplo-21s appear to arise through nondisjunction in the ovum during meiosis, whereby some eggs receive 24 chromosomes (including two 21s) and others only 22 (no 21). Thus, upon fertilization by normal sperms, two kinds of zygotes are possible: triplo-21s and haplo-21s. No children having just one 21 have ever been reported, so it is presumed that haplo-21 fetuses are aborted. The probability of mongoloid children increases rapidly with age of the mother, as shown in Table 12-1. Age of the father appears to have no direct bearing on the occurrence of mongolism in the children.

Pantelakis et al. (1970) also report a higher incidence of maternal history of infectious hepatitis, a viral disease, in 22 trisomy-21 cases among 10,412 live

FIGURE 12-10. *Karyotype of trisomic mongoloid idiot having 47 chromosomes (triplo-21).* [Courtesy National Foundation, New York.]

TABLE 12-1. Frequency of Mongoloid Children in Relation to Maternal Age (Based on work of Carter and Evans, 1961)

| Maternal Age | Risk of Mongoloid Child per 1,000 Births |
|---|---|
| <30 | 0.6 |
| 30–34 | 1.3 |
| 35–39 | 3.6 |
| 40–44 | 11.0 |
| 45–49 | 19.0 |

births over a two year period. Doxiadis and others (1970) report the risk of having a child with Down's syndrome to be about three times greater, age group for age group, in mothers who have had clinically infectious hepatitis

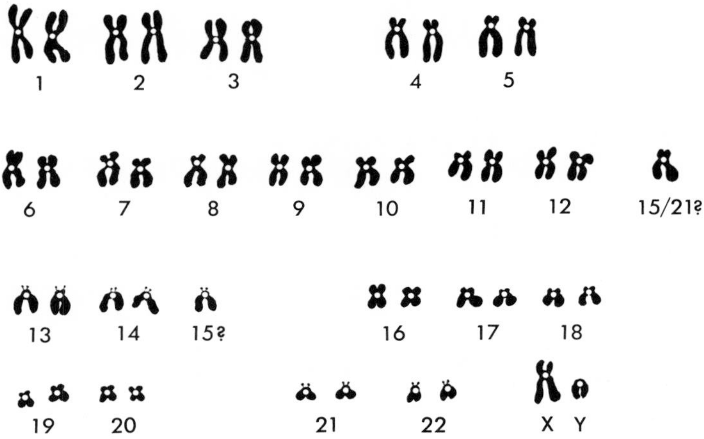

FIGURE 12-11. *Karyotype of translocation mongoloid. This individual has 46 chromosomes, but only one normal 15 and a large one formed by union of a 21 and the other 15. Two normal 21s are also present, giving the individual three "doses" of chromosome 21.*

prior to pregnancy. Fialkow et. al. (1971) report a statistically significant increase in the frequency of thyroid disease (thyroiditis, hypothyroidism, hyperthyroidism, and nontoxic goiter) in mothers, but not in fathers, of subjects with Down's syndrome. Some form of clinical thyroid disorder was determined in only 11 of 177 control mothers (i.e., those without mongoloid children) as compared with 30 of 177 mothers of affected children in matched families.

Examination of parents of translocation mongoloids usually discloses one of them to have only 45 chromosomes, including one 21, one 15, and a fused 15-21. Such individuals are phenotypically normal, since the genetic material is present in proper amount. If the centromere of the translocation chromosome is that of number 15, these individuals can produce four kinds of gametes:

| Gamete | | Zygote Produced |
|---|---|---|
| 15, 21 | Normal | Normal |
| 15 | $n - 1$ | Presumably lethal |
| 15 + 21, 21 | $n + 1$ | Translocation mongoloid |
| 15 + 21 | Translocation | Translocation carrier |

That Down's syndrome may also occur in other animals is clear from the work of McClure et al. (1969) who have described a trisomic young female chimpanzee. This animal displayed clinical and behavioral features similar to those of human mongolism, scoring below normal in a variety of behavioral and postural tests. Chimpanzees have a diploid chromosome number of 48 (Table 3-1) but in the animal in question most of the blood cells examined had 49, with an extra small acrocentric chromosome which matched pair 22 (the second smallest of the autosomal pairs). This same chromosome was identifiable in triplicate even in the few cells where only a total of 46, 47, or 48 chromosomes could be counted. Both parents were cytologically and behaviorally normal. McClure and his colleagues note that "... a comparable condition has not been reported in nonhuman primates. The occurrence of this condition in a lower primate again emphasizes the close phylogenetic relation between man and the great apes and may provide a model for studying this relatively frequent human syndrome."

***Other Human Trisomics.*** Trisomy for other human autosomes has been reported, though less often than trisomy-21. Edwards' syndrome, which includes mental retardation, slow growth, and a variety of skeletal and internal organ deformities, is believed to be due to trisomy-18. Few affected individuals live beyond the age of one year, but one fifteen year old mentally defective female has been detected. Incidence of this disorder appears to be about 0.3/1,000 births. As in trisomy-21, maternal age is again an important factor; more than half the mothers of known children of this type were over 35. The defect seems to occur about three times more frequently in females, though the reason is not clear.

Trisomy D13-15, characterized by mental retardation and varied and variable deformities as well as defects of the central nervous system and both internal and external organs, has been known for some time, although it is

TABLE 12-2. Summary of Variations in Chromosome Number (Heteroploidy)

| Type | Designation | Chromosome Complement (where one set consists of four chromosomes, numbered 1, 2, 3, and 4) |
|---|---|---|
| **Euploids** | | |
| Monoploid | $n$ | 1-2-3-4 |
| Diploid | $2n$ | 1-2-3-4 1-2-3-4 |
| Triploid | $3n$ | 1-2-3-4 1-2-3-4 1-2-3-4 |
| Autotetraploid | $4n$ | 1-2-3-4 1-2-3-4 1-2-3-4 1-2-3-4 |
| Allotetraploid etc. | $4n$ | 1-2-3-4 1-2-3-4 1′-2′-3′-4′ 1′-2′-3′-4′ |
| **Aneuploids** | | |
| Trisomic | $2n + 1$ | 1-2-3-4 1-2-3-4 1 |
| Triploid tetrasome | $3n + 1$ | 1-2-3-4 1-2-3-4 1-2-3-4 1 |
| Tetrasomic | $2n + 2$ | 1-2-3-4 1-2-3-4 1-1 |
| Double trisomic | $2n + 1 + 1$ | 1-2-3-4 1-2-3-4 1-2 |
| Monosomic | $2n - 1$ | 1-2-3-4 2-3-4 |
| Nullisomic | $2n - 2$ | 2-3-4 2-3-4 |

not common. Several reports indicate an incidence of about 0.2/1,000 births. Fewer than a third of these trisomics live more than three months. Because of similarities among members of the D group of chromosomes, it is not possible to determine with certainty which one of the three members is present in excess. In fact, there may well be more than one type of D trisomy. As in other kinds of trisomy, risk increases sharply with maternal age. Smith (1964), for example, reports 40 per cent of the D13-15 trisomics in his study were born to mothers over 35, whereas this age group accounted for only about 12 per cent of all births.

*Other Aneuploids.* Aneuploids other than trisomics are reported in the literature, but the best known ones occur in the Jimson weed because of the extensive work of Blakeslee and his associates and because most of them are lethal in many organisms. They are summarized in Table 12-2, along with the other modifications of chromosome number already considered.

## Structural Changes in Chromosomes

### DETECTION OF STRUCTURAL CHANGES

For all their complexities of structural organization, chromosomes are far from indestructible. Through such agents as radiation and chemicals they can suffer breakage which may result in genetic damage to subsequent generations. Suitable precautions, of course, must be taken in X-ray diagnoses, and nuclear weaponry constitutes a definite hazard. Lisco and Conard (1967), for example, report chromosomal aberrations associated with breaks in 23 of 43 Marshall Islanders ten years after accidental exposure to radioactive fallout following testing of a high yield nuclear device at Bikini in the Pacific. A wide variety of chemical substances, some formerly or presently in common use by man, have been implicated or suspected in inducing chromosomal damage. The once widely used artificial sweetener sodium cyclamate for example, is reported to produce chromosomal breaks and gaps in cultured human lymphocytes (Stoltz et al., 1970). Breaks may also occur "naturally," for no assignable cause. They may produce any of several cytological and genetic consequences; they may be detected in almost any dividing cell (though certain kinds offer particular advantage), and their genetic effects are observable in unexpected phenotypes or altered linkage relationships.

*LSD and Chromosome Damage.* Because of therapeutic use of LSD (lysergic acid diethylamide) in treatment of some mental disorders and its frequent illicit use, many investigators have recently turned their attention to the question of whether this drug produces chromosomal and genetic damage. Studies have been carried on in vivo and in vitro with man, other animals, and plants. Conclusions are contradictory, but results certainly indicate that in at least some individuals of some species an increased frequency of breaks is found. Cohen and others (1967) report that addition of LSD to cultured human leukocytes resulted in a considerable increase in chromosomal abnormalities, the principal result being a significantly larger number of breaks, most of then involving number 1, the largest autosome. This team also observed a similar increase in a paranoid schizophrenic who had been extensively treated for four years with the drug. Irwin and Egozcue (1967) found a significant increase in frequency of breaks in a large group of illicit users of LSD and other drugs. They concluded that LSD was the probable principal cause.

Singh and his colleagues (1970) report a high incidence of breaks in the chromosomes of root tip cells of barley, about half of them in the vicinity of the centromere. Likewise, meiotic chromosomes of mice injected with heavy doses of LSD showed a considerable increase in breaks and fragments over control animals (Skakkebaek et al., 1968).

On the other hand, Bender and Sankar (1968), commenting on the great concern of psychiatrists with this problem because of medical use of LSD in treatment of certain disorders, particularly schizophrenia, object to the conclusions of Irwin and Egozcue, in part on the grounds that users could not be examined for possible breaks prior to their use of the drug. In studies on schizophrenic children under their care, they report no difference in break frequencies between the treated children and other subjects who had not received the drug. However, LSD treatment had been discontinued in their treated group twenty to forty-eight months before leukocyte screening was done. But Irwin and Egozcue (1968), in response to Bender and Sankar, point out the lack of data to rule out LSD as a causative agent in chromosome damage.

Loughman and others (1967) also found no significant difference in incidence of chromosome aberrations in leukocytes of admitted drug users who reported their dosages from memory. But they do point out that "other tissues of the body must be examined before ruling out the possibility of chromosome damage to cells actively dividing in vivo." Sparkes and his colleagues (1968) report inability to detect significant chromosomal damage in small samples of users, but suggest that some of the disagreement among various studies may arise because of the possibility that some persons may be more susceptible than others to chromosomal damage by LSD. They note that data before and after LSD use in the same individuals would be far more informative than comparisons of different individuals with different physiologies, some of whom had used or been treated with the drug for short or long periods and others of whom had never been exposed to it.

Birth of a child with several congenital abnormalities to parents who had both used LSD prior to conception (but not during pregnancy) has been reported by Hsu and others (1970). Although the infant was found to have 46 chromosomes, she was trisomic for autosome 13, and exhibited a translocation (see page 235) involving members of the D group. Hsu and his colleagues suspect drug-induced damage (including breaks) to maternal germ cells, with the child resulting from fertilization of an egg having an unbalanced chromosome complement.

Many of the studies in the literature are not, and cannot be, based on standardized doses because they involve illicit users of probably quite variable drug concentration and purity. Furthermore, some of the subjects admit to use of other drugs as well. Much remains to be learned from in vivo studies of various kinds of cells, especially gametes, under rigidly controlled experimental conditions, and more data are needed on children born to persons using or receiving LSD. In such a controlled experiment, Hungerford et al. (1968) first established aberration frequencies in cultured leukocytes from a control group, and also from an experimental group whose members were later to receive LSD therapy. Aberrations scored included acentric fragments, dicentrics, deletions, breaks, and gaps. These researchers report that administration of three intravenous doses (usually of 200 $\mu$g each) was followed by some increase in aberration frequency, as well as the appearance of new abnormalities in the experimental group. However, they found a return to the lower control levels ensued within one to six months after the last dose.

At the present time risk of chromosomal aberrations in users and, therefore, of genetic damage to their descendants cannot be ruled out, although the period of time involved may be limited. Sanders (1969a, 1969b) has summarized evidence to that time concerning chromosomal damage believed to be due to LSD and other chemicals. But Dishotsky et al. (1971), after surveying the literature to that date, conclude that "pure LSD in moderate doses does not damage chromosomes in vivo (and) does not cause detectable genetic damage."

*Salivary Gland Chromosomes.* Structural changes in chromosomes resulting from breakage are most profitably studied in (1) salivary gland chromosomes of dipteran insects (such as *Drosophila*) and (2) meiocytes during the process of meiosis. Because of their large size and banded structure, salivary gland chromosomes offer particularly favorable material for such studies. So, before discussing the several kinds of structural modifications, let us examine these unusual chromosomes more closely.

Nuclei of the salivary gland chromosomes of the larvae of dipterans like *Drosophila* have unusually long and wide chromosomes, 100 or 200 times the size of the chromosomes in meiosis or mitosis of the same species (Fig. 12-12). This is particularly surprising, since the salivary gland cells do not divide after the glands are formed, yet their chromosomes replicate several times and become unusually long as well. Moreover, these chromosomes are marked by numerous cross bands which are apparent even in unstained nuclei. These bands are widely assumed to represent chromomeres, side by

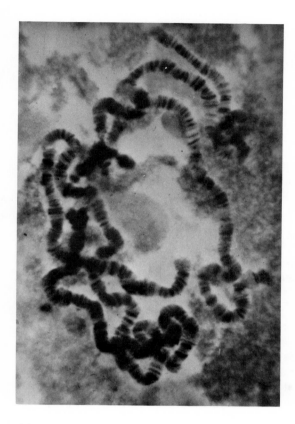

FIGURE 12-12. *Salivary gland chromosomes of* Drosophila. *The banding permits rather accurate cytological mapping. By appropriate studies, each band is usually found to include several genes.* [Courtesy General Biological Supply House, Inc., Chicago.]

side, of the replicated chromonemata; they are quite constant in size and spacing for a given normal chromosome. The multiple chromosomes appear to be in a perpetual prophase and are synapsed. Thus any differences in banding between homologs can be easily compared.

### TYPES OF STRUCTURAL CHANGES

A chromosomal break may or may not be followed by a "repair." If segments are rejoined as they were, the break ordinarily passes undetected. Should such normal repair not be effected, one or more of the aberrations in Table 12-3 occur. Note that a deficiency in one chromosome may be accompanied by a duplication or a translocation in another. Reciprocal translocations, in which two nonhomologs *exchange* segments, often unequal in length, may also occur.

### DEFICIENCIES

*Deficiencies and Cytological Mapping.* Perhaps the simplest result of breakage is the loss of a part of a chromosome. Portions of chromosomes without a centromere lag in anaphasic movement and are lost from re-organizing nuclei. Such loss of a portion of a chromosome is called a **deficiency** or a deletion.

TABLE 12-3. Types of Aberrations Produced by Chromosomal Breaks

| Type | Description | Gene Changes |
|------|-------------|--------------|
| Normal | (*ABCDEFGH*) | None |
| Deficiency | No rejoining, chromosomal segment lost | *ABFGH, CDEFGH*, etc. |
| Inversion | Broken segment reattached to original chromosome in reverse order | *ABFEDCGH*, etc. |
| Duplication | Broken segment becomes attached to homolog that has experienced a break; homolog then bears one block of genes in duplicate | *ABCDEFGEFGH* |
| Translocation | Broken segment becomes attached to a non-homolog resulting in new linkage relations | *LMNOPQRCDEFGH*, etc. |

Deficiencies often make possible *cytological mapping* of chromosomes. For example, if large numbers of flies of the autosomal genotype *ABCDEF* ...*/ABCDEF*... (i.e., homozygous dominant for several traits) are subjected to x-irradiation, a few of the individuals may suffer a break and deletion in one of the chromosomes bearing these genes. If such deficiency for genes *C* and *D* occurs in one primary spermatocyte, then two of the four sperms produced from it would have an intercalary deficiency in this particular autosome:

Primary Spermatocyte (irradiated)

$$\frac{AB--EF...}{ABCDEF...}$$

Secondary sperm-
   atocytes       *ABEF...*, *ABCDEF...*

Spermatids and
   sperms       *ABEF...*, *ABEF...*, *ABCDEF...*, *ABCDEF...*

Mating such males to recessive females, *abcdef.../abcdef...*, will produce offspring, some of which will have the genotype *abcdef.../ABEF*. Therefore these flies will express the recessive phenotype for genes *c* and *d*, whereas those receiving an *ABCDEF...* sperm from the male parent will express the dominant phenotype for all six genes. The expression of genes *c* and *d* where they would have been obscured by genes *C* and *D* had these been present is called **pseudodominance**. This is really not a good term, but it is a useful one and is firmly established in the literature.

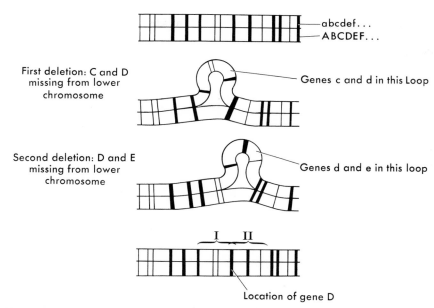

FIGURE 12-13. *Determining which band of salivary gland chromosomes bears a given gene is done by a series of overlapping deficiencies. See text for details.*

Next, flies showing pseudodominance are mated with normal *abcdef.../ abcdef...* individuals. Half the offspring will now exhibit pseudodominance for the same genes. Examination of the salivary gland chromosomes of larvae of this cross will quickly disclose the *abcdef.../ABEF* individuals. Remember, these chromosomes are banded and pair exactly, band for band. The segment that includes genes *C* and *D* will also include some of the bands, and the giant chromosomes of *abcdef.../ABEF...* would appear somewhat as shown in Fig. 12-13, the normal, unaltered chromosome showing a characteristic **deficiency loop**.

Now, another strain of flies with an *overlapping deficiency* such as *ABC − −F.../ABCDEF...* might be developed and mated as in the preceding case. Giant chromosomes of *abcdef.../ABCF...* individuals will again display the characteristic deficiency loop. Comparison with the loops produced by the *abcdef.../ABEF...* individuals permits easy detection of the precise chromosomal region which bears gene *D*; its locus can be seen to be associated with a particular band (Fig. 12-13).

Detailed *cytological maps* of *Drosophila* have been prepared in just this way. The geneticist now has visible bands within which genes appear to be located, and he can measure their distances in ordinary units. Comparison of cytological and genetic maps confirms the linear sequence given by the latter.

Cytological maps, however, show known genes to be more uniformly distributed over the chromosome than is suggested by the genetic map. This results from the greater degree of interference near the centromere and termini of the chromosome. For example, in chromosome II of *Drosophila* the centromere is at locus 55.0. Painter's map (Fig. 1-8, page 10) shows gene *pr* (purple eyes) to be at locus 54.5, just 0.5 unit to the left of the centromere. This is about 1 per cent of the 55 map units between the centromere and the end of the left arm. Yet on the salivary gland map gene *pr* is about 12 genetic map units to the left of the centromere, or nearly 22 per cent of the total distance involved. Fig. 12-14 compares genetic and cytological map locations for several genes of chromosome II.

*Deficiencies in Man.* Probably the best known disorder to be associated definitely with a chromosomal deficiency in man is the "cri du chat" or cat-cry syndrome described by Le Jeune (1963). Symptoms include severe mental retardation, a round "moon face," and a characteristic, plaintive cry similar to that of a cat. More than twenty cases have been studied; in each, a large portion of the shorter arm of an autosome, believed to be number 5, is deleted (Fig. 12-15). Several other deficiencies are known and new instances are being reported in the literature from time to time. German (1970) described an infant male having a deletion of the short arm of a number 4 autosome (Fig. 12-16). This child was "unusually small, (with) severe psychomotor retardation, convulsions, a wide, flat nasal bridge, a prominent forehead, cleft palate, and congenital heart disease" (German, 1970). Some mentally defective patients have been found to have other chromosomal deficiencies; de Grouchy and others, for example, reported one such individual in 1963 who lacked the short arm of chromosome 18.

Increasing use is being made of cultured amniotic fluid cells obtained by amniocentesis[1] to determine fetal karyotypes. Amniotic cells appear to show a rather high frequency of tetraploidy, unaccompanied by any cytological abnormality of the fetus, but structural aberrations, trisomy, and the like are fairly easy to detect from these cells around the sixteenth week of gestation. This information can, of course, be extremely useful to parents and physician in considering a possible termination of the pregnancy.

## INVERSIONS

Numerous **inversions** have been described in *Drosophila*. These probably arise when breaks occur at a place where a chromosome forms a tight loop during synapsis. An inversion heterozygote, in which only one of two homologs has a particular inversion, forms a characteristic "**inversion**

---

[1] Amniocentesis involves the withdrawal of fluid, containing sloughed fetal epithelial cells, from the amniotic cavity. Chromosomal analysis can then be made from subcultured cells.

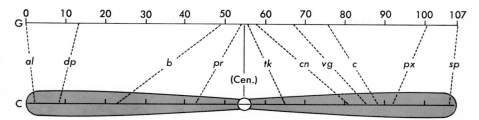

FIGURE 12-14. *Diagrammatic comparison of genetic map* (*G*) *and cytological map* (*C*) *of chromosome II of* Drosophila melanogaster. *Note particularly the much closer spacing of genes near the centromere on the genetic map, as opposed to the distances between them on the cytological map. This reflects the interference effect of the centromere.* (Cen = *centromere.*)

loop " in prophase-I of meiosis (Fig. 12-17). With a little care these can be distinguished easily from deficiency loops.

An inversion requires two breaks in a chromosome, followed by reinsertion of the segment in the opposite direction. A particular block of genes thus occurs in reverse sequence (Table 12-3). Inversions may either include the centromere (pericentric inversions) or not include the centromere (paracentric inversions). Homologous chromosomes, with identical inversions in each member, pair and undergo normal distribution in meiosis. On the other hand, should only one member of the chromosome pair experience a given inversion, synapsis produces a characteristic inversion loop (Fig. 12-18). If a chiasma forms within a paracentric inversion, for example, a dicentric bridge is produced at anaphase-I, resulting in the loss of an acentric fragment (Fig. 12-18). The bridge itself breaks as anaphase-I progresses, resulting in additional aberrations such as deficiencies or duplications. Although inversions have been referred to as " crossover suppressors," it is the *products* of crossing-over that are eliminated. Crossing-over itself is not actually suppressed.

### TRANSLOCATIONS

As indicated on page 231, **translocations** involve the shift of a part of one chromosome to another, nonhomologous chromosome. We can recognize two principal types of translocation:

1. *simple*, in which, following breaks, a segment of one chromosome is transferred to another, nonhomologous chromosome where it occupies an intercalary location, and
2. *reciprocal* (interchange) in which segments, which need not be of the same size, are exchanged between nonhomologous chromosomes.

Reciprocal translocations are well known in animals and plants that have

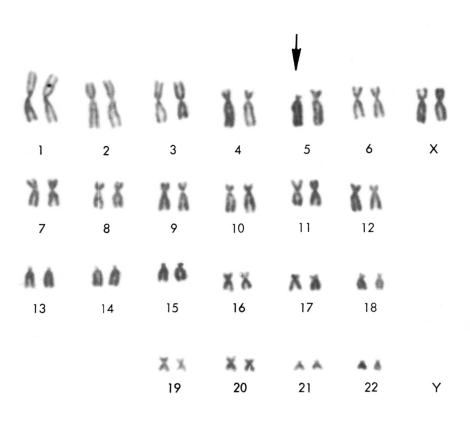

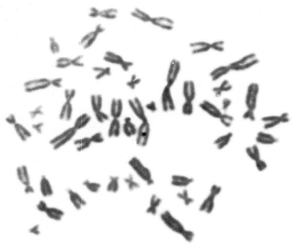

been studied extensively. They have been produced frequently by radiation in *Drosophila* (as well as in other organisms) and have occurred widely in natural populations of the evening primrose (*Oenothera*), the plant whose resulting phenotypic variability led De Vries to formulate his mutation theory. Simple translocations have been found in man where they often lead to gross phenotypic deviations.

Two reciprocal translocation types may be recognized: homozygotes and heterozygotes (Fig. 12-19). The former may have normal meiosis and, in fact, be difficult to detect cytologically unless morphologically distinctive chromosome segments are involved. Genetically they are marked by altered linkage groups and by the fact that a gene with "new neighbors" may produce a somewhat different effect in its new location. We shall examine this **position effect** shortly.

Translocation heterozygotes, however, are marked by a considerable degree of meiotic irregularity. Peculiar and characteristic formations occur at synapsis because of the difficulty of attaining pairing of homologous parts. Typically, a cross-shaped formation is seen in prophase-I; this often opens out into a ring as chiasmata terminalize (Figs. 12-20, 12-21).

In addition to altered linkage groups, translocation heterozygotes are frequently partially sterile because between half and two thirds of gametes (in animals) or meiospores (in plants) fail to receive the full complement of genes required for normal development. Semisterility resulting from reciprocal translocations is easily observed in such plants as corn. Ears lack about half the kernels, and these are arranged irregularly (Fig. 12-22). Abortive pollen is seen to be reduced in size.

***Translocations in Man.*** Translocations in addition to the 15/21 associated with mongolism, have been reported in a few instances for human beings. Those most likely to receive attention involve chromosomal segments present in triplicate. Among others, D/D, G/G, B/D, and C/E have been detected. Because it is not easy to differentiate between members of the several groups of autosomes, translocations in man are often designated by two letters separated by a slash, the first letter indicating the chromosome group supplying the translocated segment and the second the group to which it has been transferred.

In most cases there are numerous phenotypic abnormalities, and spontaneous abortion or death within a few months after birth usually ensues. Those who do live longer frequently exhibit mental retardation. Bray and Josephine (1964) reported a probable unbalanced translocation in which a large part of one of the D-group chromosomes was present in triplicate

FIGURE 12-15. *Karyotype of child with "cri du chat" syndrome. Note deletion of the short arm of one of the number 5 autosomes.* [Photo courtesy Dr. James German, New York Blood Center.]

and a small part of one of the B chromosomes was lacking. There were numerous anatomical abnormalities and death of the subject occurred at 7 months. Forty-six chromosomes were present, including an unusually long one believed to be a B + D. Both parents were cytologically normal.

A C/E translocation with effects resembling mongolism was apparently first detected in 1969 at a Boston hospital. The child had one extra long chromosome in its complement of 46, interpreted as an E with added material from a C-group member which material was thus present in triplicate. This diagnosis was made on the basis of the mother's karyotype which showed one shortened member of group C (believed to be number 8) and a longer than normal E chromosome (probably number 18). The mother was pheno-typically normal, as would be expected because she had the normal amount of chromosomal material.

### DUPLICATIONS AND THE POSITION EFFECT

Duplications occur when a portion of a chromosome is represented more than twice in a normally diploid cell. The extra segment may be attached to the chromosome whose loci are repeated, or to a different linkage group,

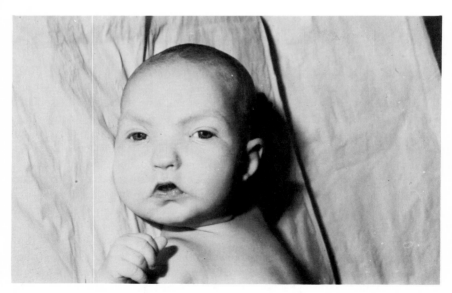

FIGURE 12-16. (A) *Infant with a deletion of the short arm of one of the number 4 autosomes. The syndrome is described in the text. (B) Karyotype of the child in Fig. 12-16(A). Note missing segment of the short arm of one of the number 4 autosomes (arrow).* [Photos courtesy Dr. James German, New York Blood Center. Copyright 1970 by The Society of the Sigma Xi. Used by permission.]

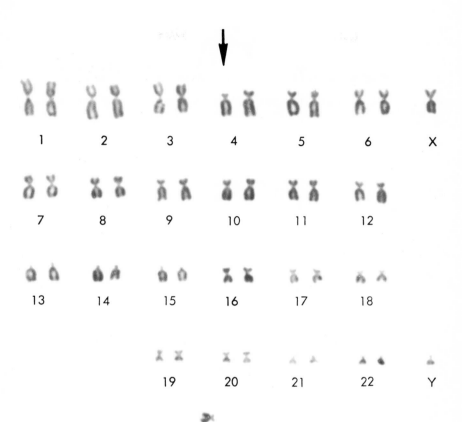

FIGURE 12-17. *Diagrammatic representation of synapsis of a pair of homologous chromosomes, the lower of which has sustained an inversion.*

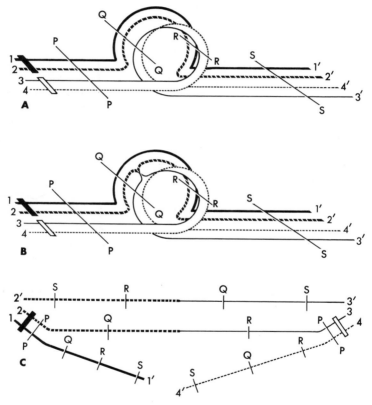

FIGURE 12-18. *Crossing-over within the inversion loop decreases the probability of functional, chromosomally normal gametes. (A) Synapsis of homologous chromosomes; the lower chromosome has sustained the inversion. (B) Crossing-over within the inversion loop between chromatids 2-2′ and 3-3′. (C) The resulting production of one acentric chromosome (2′-3′) and a dicentric complex. The former is quickly lost from reorganizing nuclei, the latter either breaks (losing some genes from the re-organizing nuclei) or behaves in some other irregular fashion, disturbing the normal gene balance in the nuclei that result from meiosis.*

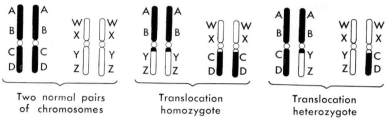

| Two normal pairs of chromosomes | Translocation homozygote | Translocation heterozygote |

FIGURE 12-19. *Translocation homozygotes and heterozygotes compared.*

or even be present as a separate fragment. Duplications are useful in studying the quantitative effects of genes normally present only in pairs in diploid cells.

The first duplication to receive critical study was the *bar eye* variant in *Drosophila*. The wild-type eye is essentially oval in shape; the bar eye phenotype is characterized by a narrower, oblong, bar-shaped eye with fewer facets. The now classical studies of Bridges (1936) showed this trait to be associated with the duplication of a segment of the X chromosome called section 16A, as observed in salivary gland chromosomes. Each added section 16A intensifies the bar phenotype. However, the narrowing effect is greater if the duplicated segments are on the same chromosome. Letting $A$ represent one section 16A in a given X chromosome, we can recognize the genotypes and phenotypes listed in Table 12-4. Other arrangements are of course also possible, but these show clearly that the bar effect of a given number of duplicated 16A sections is intensified if the duplications occur in one X chromosome rather than being divided between the two of the female. Compare heterozygous ultrabar and homozygous bar eyes, for example.

Such a change in the effect of the gene or genes in a chromosomal segment is known as the **position effect**. In bar eye, each added segment narrows

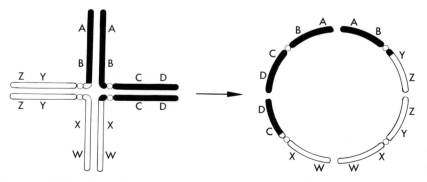

FIGURE 12-20. *Cross-shaped figure occurring in late prophase-I because of translocation heterozygosity. Such a figure often opens out into a ring.*

TABLE 12-4. Comparison of Genotypes and Phenotypes for Bar Eye in *Drosophila*
Females
(*A* = One section 16A of the X chromosome).

| X Chromosome | Phenotype | | Mean Number of Facets |
|---|---|---|---|
| *A/A* | Normal | | 779 |
| *AA/A* | Heterozygous bar eye | | 358 |
| *AA/AA* | Homozygous bar eye | | 68 |
| *AAA/A* | Heterozygous Ultrabar | | 45 |
| *AAA/AAA* | Homozygous Ultrabar | | 25 |

the eye still farther, and this effect is enhanced as more duplications occur
in one chromosome. Other duplications are known which produce the
opposite effect, counteracting the effect of mutant genes. Moreover, duplications need not always be immediately adjacent to exert this position effect.

## Chromosomal Aberrations and Evolution

Speciation, the evolutionary divergence of segments of a population to
the point where they are no longer able to combine their genes through

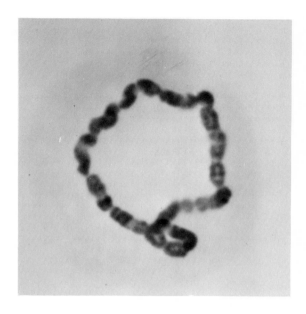

FIGURE 12-21. *Ring of 12 chromosomes in the tropical plant* Rhoeo discolor, *resulting from translocation.* [Courtesy Dr. L. F. LaCour, John Innes Institute.]

sexual reproduction, is a complex process with no single causative mechanism. The diversification on which evolution is built does, in every case, however, require alterations in the genetic material itself (mutation, Chapter 17), and/or changes in its arrangement (chromosomal aberrations), both leading to reproductive incompatibility. The effectiveness of both of these factors is increased if the population is broken into two or more geographically isolated groups. In this way, frequency of mutant genes may often be spread more rapidly, probability of *different* mutations arising in separated groups is increased, and differing groups are often prevented by geographic barriers from crossing.

Each of the chromosomal aberrations here is related to the evolutionary development of new species, though each rarely acts alone over time. Thus, trisomy in the Jimson weed leads to morphological differences that are recognizable and forms a basis for an aneuploid series. Certainly aneuploid series, which may arise in a variety of ways, do exist in many plant families and genera, and are associated with interspecific morphological differences. The role of polyploidy, especially allopolyploidy, in what one writer has called "cataclysmic evolution," has already been described.

But structural changes, too, are important in a gradual, step-by-step change. Many inversions are known to differentiate the several species of *Drosophila*. Thus, *Drosophila pseudoobscura* and *D. persimilis*, morphologically very similar, produce sterile male but fertile female hybrids and differ

FIGURE 12-22. *Partial sterility results from a reduction in functional gametes caused by multiple translocations.* [Courtesy DeKalb Agricultural Association, Inc., DeKalb, Illinois.]

in four major inversions. On the other hand, *D. pseudoobscura* and *D. miranda* produce completely sterile offspring when crossed. The very complex pairing arrangements assumed by giant chromosomes in hybrid larvae of this interspecific cross indicate repeated and extensive inversions. Translocations in the evening primrose, *Oenothera*, were largely responsible for the differences on which DeVries based his mutation theory. A series of many reciprocal translocations in isolated populations may lead to complete reproductive incompatibility, as well as definitive morphological differences, so that speciation may be said to have occurred. Comparison of the chromosome complements of several species of *Drosophila* (Fig. 12-23) suggests all manner of chromosomal aberrations, including translocations (even unions of whole chromosomes) and deficiencies, at least. Note the aneuploid series 3, 4, 5, 6.

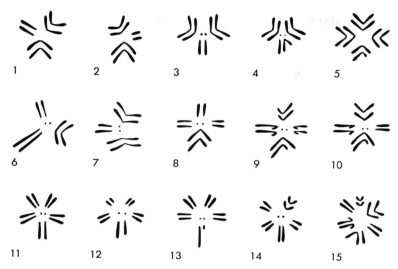

FIGURE 12-23. *Male karyotypes in several species of* Drosophila. *The X and Y chromosomes are at the bottom of each drawing.* (*1*) D. willistoni; (*2*) D. prosaltans; (*3*) D. putrida; (*4*) D. melanogaster; (*5*) D. ananassae; (*6*) D. spinofemora; (*7*) D. americana; (*8*) D. pseudoobscura; (*9*) D. azteca; (*10*) D. affinis; (*11*) D. virilis; (*12*) D. funebris; (*13*) D. repleta; (*14*) D. montana; (*15*) D. colorata.

## REFERENCES

BELLING, J., 1925. Production of Triploid and Tetraploid Plants. *Jour. Hered.*, **16**:463–464.

BENDER, L., and D. V. SIVA SANKAR, 1968. Chromosome Damage not Found in Leukocytes of Children Treated with LSD-25. *Science*, **159**:749.

BLAKESLEE, A. F., and J. BELLING, 1924. Chromosomal Mutations in the Jimson Weed, *Datura stramonium. Jour. Hered.*, **15**:195–206.

BRAY, P. E., and SISTER A. JOSEPHINE, 1964. Partial Autosomal Trisomy and Translocation. Report of an Infant with Multiple Congenital Anomalies. *Jour. Amer. Med. Assn.*, **187**:566.

BRIDGES, C. B., 1936. The Bar "Gene," a Duplication. *Science*, **83**:210–211. Reprinted in J. A. Peters, ed., 1959. *Classic Papers in Genetics.* Englewood Cliffs, N.J., Prentice-Hall.

BURNS, G. W., 1942. The Taxonomy and Cytology of *Saxifraga pensylvanica L.* and Related Forms. *Amer. Midl. Nat.*, **28**:127–160.

BUTLER, L. J., C. CHANTLER, N. E. FRANCE, and C. G. KEITH, 1970. A Liveborn Infant with Complete Triploidy (69, XXX). *Jour. Med. Genet.*, **6**:413–421.

CARTER, C. O., and K. A. EVANS, 1961. Risk of Parents Who Have Had One

Child with Down's Syndrome (Mongolism) Having Another Child Similarly Affected. *Lancet*, **2**:785–787.

COHEN, M. M., M. J. MARINELLO, and N. BACK, 1967. Chromosomal Damage in Human Leukocytes Induced by Lysergic Acid Diethylamide. *Science*, **155**:1417–1419.

DEAN, D. S., 1959. Distribution of Tetraploid and Diploid *Tradescantia ohioensis* in Michigan and Adjoining Areas. *Amer. Midl. Nat.*, **61**:204–209.

DE GROUCHY, J., M. LAMY, S. THIEFFRY, M. ARTHUIS, and C. SALMON, 1963. Dysmorphie Complexe avec Oligophrénie: Délétion des Bras Courts d'un Chromosome 17–18. *Compt. Rendus Acad. Sci. Paris*, **256**:1028–1029.

DISHOTSKY, N. I., W. D. LOUGHMAN, R. E. MOGAR, and W. R. LIPSCOMB, 1971. LSD and Genetic Damage. *Science* **172**:431–440.

DOXIADIS, S., S. PANTELAKIS, and T. VALAES, 1970. Down's Syndrome and Infectious Hepatitis. *Lancet*, **1**:897.

FIALKOW, P. J., H. C. THULINE, F. HECHT, and J. BRYANT, 1971. Familial Predisposition to Thyroid Disease in Down's Syndrome: Controlled Immunologic Studies. *Amer. Jour. Hum. Gen.*, **23**:67–86.

HSU, L. Y., L. STRAUSS, and K. HIRSCHORN, 1970. Chromosome Abnormality in Offspring of LSD User. *Jour. Amer. Med. Assn.*, **211**:987–990.

HUNGERFORD, D. A., K. M. TAYLOR, C. SHAGASS, G. U. LaBADIE, G. B. BALABAN, and G. R. PATON, 1968. Cytogenetic Effects of LSD 25 Therapy in Man. *Jour. Amer. Med. Assn.*, **206**:2287–2291.

HUSKINS, C. L., 1930. The Origin of *Spartina townsendii*. *Genetica*, **12**:531–538.

IRWIN, S., and J. EGOZCUE, 1967. Chromosomal Abnormalities in Leukocytes from LSD-25 Users. *Science*, **157**:313–314.

IRWIN, S., and J. EGOZCUE, 1968. (Untitled reply to Bender and Sankar, 1968). *Science*, **159**:749.

KARPECHENKO, G. D., 1928. Polyploid Hybrids of *Raphanus sativus L.* X *Brassica oleracea L. Ztschr. ind. Abst. Vererb.*, **48**:1–83.

LeJEUNE, J., 1963. Trois Cas de Délétion du Bras Court d'un Chromosome 5. *Compt. Rendus Acad. Sci. Paris*, **257**:3098–3102.

LISCO, H., and R. A. CONARD, 1967. Chromosome Studies on Marshall Islanders Exposed to Fallout Radiation. *Science*, **157**:445–447.

LOUGHMAN, W. D., T. W. SARGENT, and D. M. ISRAELSTAM, 1967. Leukocytes of Humans Exposed to Lysergic Acid Diethylamide: Lack of Chromosomal Damage. *Science*, **158**:508–510.

McCLURE, H. M., K. H. BELDEN, W. A. PIEPER, and C. B. JACOBSON, 1969. Autosomal Trisomy in a Chimpanzee: Resemblance to Down's Syndrome. *Science*, **165**:1010–1011.

PANTELAKIS, S. N., O. M. CHRYSSOSTOMIDOU, D. ALEXIOU, T. VALAES, and S. A. DOXIADIS, 1970. Sex Chromatin and Chromosome Abnormalities Among 10,412 Liveborn Babies. *Arch. Dis. Childhood*, **45**:87–92.

REGAN, J. D., and J. B. SMITH, 1965. Triploidy in a Human Cell Line. *Science*, **149**:1516–1517.

SANDERS, H. J., 1969a. Chemical Mutagens, the Road to Genetic Disaster. *Chem. and Eng. News*, **47** (#1):50–65, 71.

SANDERS, H. J., 1969b. Chemical Mutagens, an Expanding Roster of Suspects. *Chem. and Eng. News*, **47** (#3):54–68.

SCHINDLER, A.-M., and K. MIKAMO, 1970. Triploidy in Man: Report of a Case and a Discussion on Etiology. *Cytogenetics*, **9**:116–130.

SINGH, M. P., C. S. KALIA, and H. K. JAIN, 1970. Chromosomal Aberrations Induced in Barley by LSD. *Science*, **169**:491–492.

SKAKKEBAEK, N. E., J. PHILIP, and O. J. RAFAELSON, 1968. LSD in Mice: Abnormalities in Meiotic Chromosomes. *Science*, **168**:1246–1248.

SMITH, D. W., 1964. Autosomal Abnormalities. *Amer. Jour. Obstet. Gynec.*, **90**:1055.

SPARKES, R. S., J. MELNYK, and L. P. BOZZETTI, 1968. Chromosomal Effect in vivo of Exposure to Lysergic Acid Diethylamide. *Science*, **160**:1343–1344.

STOLTZ, D. R., K. S. KHERA, R. BENDALL, and S. W. GUNNER, 1970. Cytogenetic Studies with Cyclamate and Related Compounds. *Science*, **167**:1501–1502.

## PROBLEMS

**12-1.** Application of colchicine to a vegetative bud of a homozygous tall diploid tomato plant (*DD*) causes development of a tetraploid branch. What is the genotype of the somatic cells of this branch?

**12-2.** Flowers are produced on the tetraploid branch of the plant in problem 12-1. What is the genotype of the gametes?

**12-3.** If the plant in problem 12-1 had been heterozygous tall, (*Dd*), what would be the genotype of the somatic cells of the tetraploid branch?

**12-4.** Give the gamete genotypes produced by flowers on the tetraploid branch of problem 12-3; in what ratio are they produced?

**12-5.** Self-pollinating flowers on one of these tetraploid branches would produce embryos with what kind of chromosomal complement?

**12-6.** Pollinating one of the flowers of problem 12-2 with pollen from a diploid dwarf plant produces embryos of what genotype?

**12-7.** A number of species of the birch tree have a somatic chromosome number of 28. The paper birch, *Betula papyrifera*, is reported as occurring with several different chromosome numbers, individuals with the somatic numbers 56, 70, and 84 being known. With regard to chromosome number, how should the 28, 56, 70, and 84 chromosome individuals be designated?

**12-8.** The sugar maple (*Acer saccharum*) and the box elder (*Acer negundo*) each have diploid chromosome numbers of 26. Note that they are different species of the same genus. However, hybrids between the two are sterile. What explanation can you offer?

**12-9.** Should it be possible to secure a fertile hybrid of the cross sugar maple × box elder? How?

**12-10.** Different species of rhododendron have somatic chromosome numbers of

26, 39, 52, 78, 104, and 156. By what means does evolution appear to be taking place in this genus?

**12-11.** What appears to be the basic chromosome number in rhododendrons?

**12-12.** How many sets are represented in the species having 156 chromosomes?

**12-13.** In the jimson weed, what gamete ratios are produced by (a) $Ppp$♀; (b) $Ppp$♂; (c) $PPP$♀; (d) $PPP$♂; (e) $PPp$♂?

**12-14.** What is the $F_1$ phenotypic ratio produced in jimson weed by crossing (a) purple $Ppp$♀ × purple $PPp$♂; (b) $PPp$♀ × $Pp$♂; (c) $Ppp$♀ × $Ppp$♂?

**12-15.** Eyeless (eyes small or absent) is a recessive character whose gene is located on the small chromosome IV of *Drosophila*. Both triplo-IV eggs and triplo-IV sperms are functional. The dominant gene for normal eyes is designated +, the recessive for eyeless *ey*. What is the $F_1$ phenotypic ratio produced by each of the following crosses: (a) $+ ey\ ey$ × $+ ey\ ey$; (b) $+ + ey$ × $+ ey\ ey$; (c) $+ + ey$ × $+ + ey$?

**12-16.** Suggest a meiotic configuration at synapsis for a situation where six chromosomes have undergone reciprocal translocations of about the same length.

**12-17.** In relation to the information in Table 12-4, where would $AAA/AA$ and $AAAA/AAA$ be properly placed? Note that progressively narrower eyes are shown from the top to the bottom of Table 12-4.

**12-18.** In *Drosophila*, *e* is a gene at locus 70.7 on chromosome III; *ee* flies have ebony bodies, much darker than wild-type flies of genotype $+ +$ or $+ e$. If the cross $+ +$ × *ee* yields a small percentage of ebony flies, but greater than could be accounted for by the known mutation frequency of this gene, (a) what would you suspect as the cause; (b) what would you look for as confirmation?

**12-19.** Could use of LSD have any effect on progeny of users? Explain.

**12-20.** What explanation could you offer for the fact that, although human trisomics are known for a number of different autosomes, no autosomal monosomics are reported among live births?

**12-21.** The jimson weed (*Datura*) has twelve pairs of chromosomes, and twelve different trisomics are known. How would you explain the fact that the only trisomics known in living human beings are those for chromosomes 13, 18, 21, X, and Y?

**12-22.** In a hypothetical organism, gene *a* maps genetically three map units from the centromere. Would a cytological map be expected to show this gene farther from, closer to, or the same distance from the centromere? Why?

# CHAPTER 13

# *Population Genetics*

U P to this point we have been largely concerned with the results of experimental breeding programs from which we have seen certain now familiar genotypic and phenotypic patterns emerge. In producing $1:2:1$ and $3:1$ $F_2$ ratios, however, note that we began with two homozygous parental strains, such as $AA$ and $aa$; that is, we introduced the alleles $A$ and $a$ *in equal frequency*. Similarly, in all of the other experiments with which we have dealt, gene frequency was intentionally included among the controlled factors. But in natural populations, frequencies of alleles may vary considerably. We have noted, for example, that the gene for polydactyly is dominant, yet the polydactylous phenotype is fairly infrequent among newborn infants even though it is not known to play any part in survival. Apparently the *frequency* of the dominant gene here is lower than that of its recessive allele; they evidently do not exist in the population in the $1:1$ ratio so commonly encountered in the laboratory. But the frequencies of these and other genes might well be expected not to be equal in different populations, and even to differ in the same population at different times. Population genetics deals with the analysis of changes in gene frequencies in a population over time.

Just as gene frequency is controlled in the genetics laboratory, so is the mating pattern, generation after generation. But outside the laboratory, mating is a chance or random affair. In natural populations, as a result, an ultimate **equilibrium frequency** is attained by alleles, governed by such factors as

1. **Breakdown of isolating mechanisms** whereby additional numbers of one allele or the other are introduced from outside the group.
2. **Frequency of mutation** (change in the nature of the gene).
3. **Selection** (environmental and reproductive).
4. **Random genetic drift**.

The ultimate equilibrium frequency, which approximates the binomial distribution, is then maintained, subject only to random genetic drift, until and unless admixture from outside the population occurs, mutation frequency changes, and/or selection forces change.

In 1908, G. H. Hardy, a British mathematician, and the German physician W. Weinberg independently developed a relatively simple mathematical concept, now referred to as the Hardy-Weinberg theorem, to describe this genetic equilibrium. This principle is the foundation of population genetics.

**249**

It is used to determine the frequency of each allele of a pair or a series, and of homozygotes and heterozygotes in the population. In this chapter we shall examine the applications of this theorem and the forces that affect genetic equilibrium.

## Calculating Gene Frequency

*Codominance.* The M-N blood type furnishes a useful example of a series of phenotypes due to a pair of codominant genes. None of the three possible phenotypes, M, MN, and N, appears to have any selection value and in fact, most persons do not know their M-N type. We shall calculate frequencies of the two alleles involved for samples from two different groups.

On page 146 a study of M-N types for 6,129 white Americans living in New York City, Boston, and Columbus, Ohio was cited. Since the closely related alleles $S$ and $s$ (see page 146) were not included in the data, we can group these individuals according to genotypes on the M-N system alone:

| Genotype | Number |
|:--------:|:------:|
| *MM* | 1,787 |
| *MN* | 3,039 |
| *NN* | 1,303 |
|      | 6,129 |

To calculate frequencies of the two alleles, $M$ and $N$, remember that these 6,129 persons possess a total of $6,129 \times 2 = 12,258$ alleles. The number of $M$ alleles, for example, is $1,787 + 1,787 + 3,039$. Thus, calculation of the frequencies for $M$ and $N$ may be worked out in this way:

$$(1) \quad M = \frac{1,787 + 1,787 + 3,039}{12,258} = \frac{6,613}{12,258} = 0.5395$$

$$(2) \quad N = \frac{1,303 + 1,303 + 3,039}{12,258} = \frac{5,645}{12,258} = 0.4605$$

So frequencies of the two alleles in this sample are almost equal, and this is reflected in the close approximation to a $1:2:1$ ratio we so often see in laboratory results.

Gene frequencies expressed as decimals may be used directly to state probabilities. If we can assume this sample to be representative of the population, then there is a probability of 0.5395 that of the chromosomes bearing this pair of alleles, any one selected randomly will bear gene $M$, and 0.4605 that it will bear $N$. Thus the frequencies of the three phenotypes to be expected in the population are as follows:

| Genotype | Phenotype | Phenotypic Frequency |
|---|---|---|
| $MM$ | M | $0.5395 \times 0.5395 = 0.2911$ |
| $MN$ <br> $NM$ | MN | $2(0.5395 \times 0.4605) = 0.4968$ |
| $NN$ | N | $0.4605 \times 0.4605 = 0.2121$ |
|  |  | $1.0000$ |

Notice that these genotypic frequencies follow a binomial distribution. If we let $p$ represent the frequency of $M$, and $q$ that of $N$, then the total array of probabilities of the three genotypes ($MM$, $MN$, and $NN$) is

$$p^2 + 2pq + q^2$$

which is the expansion of $(p + q)^2$. Note also that $p + q = 1$ and, of course, so does $(p + q)^2$. Thus the probability of a type M individual, for example, under a system of random mating is given by the expression $p^2$, where we have already calculated the value of $p$ to be 0.5395.

Alternatively, we could calculate the frequencies of $M$ and $N$ by another approach. Recall that an individual of genotype $NN$, for example, represents the simultaneous occurrence of two events of equal probability, namely the fusion of two gametes, each with the genotype $N$. Thus, $q^2$ has the value $1,303/6,129 = 0.2126$, and $q = \sqrt{0.2126}$, or 0.46. Because $p + q = 1$, $p = 1 - q$, or $1 - 0.46 = 0.54$.

For comparison let us look briefly at a sample of 361 Navaho Indians from New Mexico:

| Phenotype | Number |
|---|---|
| M | 305 |
| MN | 52 |
| N | 4 |
|  | 361 |

This sample is far from a laboratory type $1:2:1$ ratio; does it mean that the Navahos do not conform to the same genetic laws as the previous sample? The answer is "no" as soon as it is recalled that the $1:2:1$ proportion is based on an equal frequency of the alleles in the population. The raw data clearly suggest that $M$ is considerably more frequent in Navaho Indians than is its allele. Let us, then, calculate gene frequencies by the same method as was used for the earlier sample:

$$\text{let } p = \text{frequency of } M = \frac{305 + 305 + 52}{722} = 0.9169$$

$$\text{let } q = \text{frequency of } N = \frac{52 + 4 + 4}{722} = \frac{0.0831}{1.0000}$$

Applying these gene frequencies to the sample, we have:

| Genotype | Gene Frequencies | Genotype Probability | Genotypes in Sample | |
|---|---|---|---|---|
| | | | Expected | Observed |
| $MM$ | $p^2 = (0.9169)^2$ | 0.8407 | 303.5 | 305 |
| $MN$ | $2pq = 2(0.9169 \times 0.0831)$ | 0.1524 | 55.0 | 52 |
| $NN$ | $q^2 = (0.0831)^2$ | 0.0069 | 2.5 | 4 |
| | | 1.0000 | 361.0 | 361 |

A chi-square test of the data for the Navaho sample shows $\chi^2 = 1.071$; for the earlier sample of 6,129 persons, $\chi^2 = 0.0237$. So deviation from expectancies based on the calculated gene frequencies is well below the level of significance in each case. Remember that although there are three phenotypic classes there is but *one* degree of freedom, since only one class can be set at random. For example, in a sample of 400 persons having just 200 $M$ alleles and, therefore, 600 $N$ alleles, any number of individuals *up to* 100 may be of genotype $MM$. If there are, say, 60 persons of type M, the other two classes are thereby automatically determined:

| Phenotype | Number of Persons | Number of Alleles | |
|---|---|---|---|
| | | $M$ | $N$ |
| M | 60 | 120 | — |
| MN | 80 | 80 | 80 |
| N | 260 | — | 520 |
| Totals | 400 | 200 | 600 |

*Complete Dominance.* An interesting phenotypic trait having no known selection value is the ability or inability to taste the chemical phenylthio-carbamide ("PTC," $C_7H_8N_2S$), also called phenylthiourea. This was reported by Fox in 1932, who found a similar situation for several other thiocarbamides. The test is a simple one which can easily be performed by any genetics class. The usual procedure is to impregnate filter paper with a dilute aqueous solution of PTC (about 0.5 to 1 gram per liter), allow it to dry, then place a bit of the treated paper on the tip of the tongue. About 70 per cent of the white American population can taste this substance, generally as very bitter, rarely as sweetish. Although the physiological basis is unknown, tasting ability does depend on a completely dominant gene, which we will designate as $T$. Thus tasters are $T - $ (i.e., $TT$ or $Tt$); non-tasters are $tt$.[1]

From 146 genetics students who tested themselves for tasting ability, 105 were tasters and 41 were nontasters. From such results as these the frequencies of genes $T$ and $t$ in the sample may be readily calculated. The 41 (28 per cent of the sample) nontasters are persons of genotype $tt$, and in the Hardy-Weinberg theorem may be represented by $q^2$. Therefore,

$$q^2 = 0.28 \text{ and}$$

$$q = \sqrt{0.28} = 0.53 \text{ (frequency of } t)$$

Since $p + q = 1$, $p = 1 - q$; $p = 1 - 0.53 = 0.47$ (frequency of $T$). The frequency of homozygous and heterozygous tasters may now be computed. Using the expression $p^2 + 2pq + q^2 = 1$, we obtain

$$
\begin{aligned}
p^2 = TT &= (0.47)^2 &= 0.2209 \\
2pq = Tt &= 2(0.47 \times 0.53) &= 0.4982 \\
q^2 = tt &= (0.53)^2 &= 0.2809 \\
\hline
& & 1.0000
\end{aligned}
$$

By testing representative samples of different populations, the frequencies of $T$ and $t$ in those groups may similarly be calculated. We shall examine the significance of different frequencies of the same alleles in different populations in the concluding section of this chapter.

*Multiple Alleles.* The binomial $(p + q)^2 = 1$ can be used only when two alleles occur at a particular locus. For cases of multiple alleles we simply add more terms to the expression. Recall that the A-B-O blood groups are determined by a series of three multiple alleles, $I^A$, $I^B$, and $i$,

---

[1] Blakeslee and Salmon (1935) report the lowest concentration detectable by tasters to vary from 1:500,000 to 1:5,000, with a mean around 1:80,000. Sensitivity among tasters decreases with age, and females are slightly more sensitive than males.

if we neglect the various subtypes. Hence, in a gene frequency analysis, we can here let

$$p = \text{frequency of } I^A$$
$$q = \text{frequency of } I^B$$
$$r = \text{frequency of } i$$
$$\text{and } p + q + r = 1$$

Thus, genotypes in a population under random mating will be given by $(p + q + r)^2$.

To see how this trinomial is applied, consider the following sample of 23,787 persons from Rochester, New York:

| Phenotype | Number | Frequency |
|---|---|---|
| A | 9,943 | 0.418 |
| B | 2,379 | 0.100 |
| AB | 904 | 0.038 |
| O | 10,561 | 0.444 |
| | 23,787 | 1.000 |

The frequency of each allele may now be calculated from these data, remembering that we have let $p$, $q$ and $r$ represent the frequencies of genes $I^A$, $I^B$, and $i$, respectively. The value of $r$, that is, the frequency of gene $i$, is immediately evident from the figures given:

$$r^2 = 0.444, \text{ hence}$$
$$r = \sqrt{0.444} = 0.6663 \ (= \text{frequency of } i)$$

The sum of A and O phenotypes is given by $(p + r)^2 = 0.418 + 0.444 = 0.862$; therefore,

$$p + r = \sqrt{0.862} = 0.9284$$

so $p = (p + r) - r = 0.9284 - 0.6663 = 0.2621$ (= frequency of $I^A$). Because $p + q + r = 1$, $q = 1 - (p + r) = 1 - 0.9284 = 0.0716$ (=frequency of $I^B$); we can now calculate genotypic frequencies as shown in Table 13-1. The probability figures arrived at for this large sample check quite closely with those arrived at for other samples of the general United States population.

Samples taken from other races and/or nationalities, however, may show quite different frequencies for these alleles. In a sample of Navaho Indians, the following gene frequencies were obtained in one study:

$$I^A = 0.1448$$
$$I^B = 0.0020$$
$$i = 0.8532$$

TABLE 13-1. Calculation of Genotypic Frequencies for a Sample of 23,787 Persons Living in Rochester, New York

| Phenotypes | Genotypes | Genotypic Frequencies | Population Probability Based on Sample | |
|------------|-----------|----------------------|--------------------------|---|
| O | $ii$ | $r^2$ | | 0.4440 |
| A | $I^A I^A$ | $p^2$ | 0.0687 | |
| | $I^A i$ | $2pr$ | 0.3493 | 0.4130 |
| B | $I^B I^B$ | $q^2$ | 0.0051 | |
| | $I^B i$ | $2qr$ | 0.0954 | 0.1005 |
| AB | $I^A I^B$ | $2pq$ | | 0.0375 |
| | | | | 1.0000 |

If this sample is representative of the Navaho population, the percentage of individuals of each genotype and phenotype may be calculated from these frequencies as shown in Table 13-2. Thus, we may either calculate gene frequencies from numbers of each phenotype, or compute percentages of the population having each phenotype if we know gene frequencies.

TABLE 13-2. Probabilities of Genotypes and Phenotypes for a Sample of Navaho Indians

| Phenotypes | Genotypes | Genotypic Frequencies | Population Probability Based on Sample | |
|------------|-----------|----------------------|--------------------------|---|
| O | $ii$ | $r^2$ | $(0.8532)^2 =$ | 0.7280 |
| A | $I^A I^A$ | $p^2$ | $(0.1448)^2 = 0.020967$ | |
| | $I^A i$ | $2pr$ | $2(0.1448 \times 0.8532) = 0.247087$ | 0.2680 |
| B | $I^B I^B$ | $q^2$ | $(0.002)^2 = 0.000004$ | |
| | $I^B i$ | $2qr$ | $2(0.002 \times 0.8532) = 0.003413$ | 0.0034 |
| AB | $I^A I^B$ | $2pq$ | $2(0.1448 \times 0.002) =$ | 0.0006 |
| | | | | 1.0000 |

***Sex Linkage.*** Thus far, in considering gene frequencies, we have dealt exclusively with autosomal genes. The same techniques, with one small modification, may be used in treating sex-linked genes, however. Since human males have only one X chromosome, they cannot reflect a binomial distribution for random combination of pairs of sex-linked genes as do females. Equilibrium distribution of genotypes for a sex-linked trait, where $p + q = 1$, is given by

$$(\male)\, p + q$$
$$(\female)\, p^2 + 2pq + q^2$$

Consider, for example, red-green color blindness. This trait is due to a sex-linked recessive, which we may designate $r$. About 8 per cent of males are color blind. This tells us at once that $q$, the frequency of gene $r$, is 0.08 and $p$, the frequency of its normal allele, $R$, 0.92. Thus, the frequency of color blind females is expected to be $q^2 = 0.0064$. This is about what is found. Sex-linked dominants may be handled in the same way; in the case of normal color vision, with the value of $p = 0.92$, the incidence of normal women is $p^2 + 2pq = 0.9936$.

## Factors Affecting Gene Frequency

***Breakdown of Isolating Mechanisms.*** In the first part of this chapter we saw that about 30 per cent of the white American population is unable to taste PTC, being homozygous recessive $tt$. By the Hardy-Weinberg equation we can calculate the frequency of $t$ in this population to be about 0.548 and, therefore, of its dominant allele as 0.452. It should not surprise you to know that groups in other parts of the world show considerably different gene frequencies for this pair. Table 13-3 summarizes phenotype percentage for various populations; from it, gene frequencies may be readily determined.

TABLE 13-3. Percentage of PTC Tasters in Various Human Populations

| Population | Place | Sample Size | Per Cent Tasters | Gene Frequencies | |
|---|---|---|---|---|---|
| | | | | $T$ | $t$ |
| Welsh | Five towns | 237 | 58.7 | 0.36 | 0.64 |
| Eskimo (unmixed) | Labrador and Baffin | 130 | 59.2 | 0.36 | 0.64 |
| Arab | Syria | 400 | 63.5 | 0.40 | 0.60 |
| American white | Montana | 291 | 64.6 | 0.41 | 0.59 |
| Eskimo (mixed) | Labrador and Baffin | 49 | 69.4 | 0.45 | 0.55 |
| American white | Columbus, Ohio | 3,643 | 70.2 | 0.45 | 0.55 |
| American black | Alabama | 533 | 76.5 | 0.52 | 0.48 |
| Flathead Indians (mixed) | Montana | 442 | 82.6 | 0.58 | 0.42 |
| Flathead Indians (unmixed) | Montana | 30 | 90.0 | 0.68 | 0.32 |
| American black | Ohio | 3,156 | 90.8 | 0.70 | 0.30 |
| African black | Kenya | 110 | 91.9 | 0.72 | 0.28 |
| African black | Sudan | 805 | 95.8 | 0.80 | 0.20 |
| Navaho Indians | New Mexico | 269 | 98.2 | 0.87 | 0.13 |

Comparison of frequencies for mixed and unmixed Eskimo and Flathead Indian samples shows that gene frequencies in a population may be changed by admixture of genes from other populations. Presumably the "mixing" in these cases is from the western European–American complex where percentage of tasters averages roughly 62–72 per cent with corresponding frequencies of $T$ of 0.384 to 0.471. Note how the frequency of this gene has been increased by admixture in the Eskimo. The same sort of change, though in the opposite direction, has occurred by outbreeding of Flathead Indians where the frequency of $T$ is high (0.683) in the unmixed group and somewhat lower (0.583) in the mixed population. The lower frequency of $T$ in the American black as compared to African blacks has undoubtedly come about in similar fashion. Data for the multiple allele series $I^A$, $I^B$, and $i$, for the Rh alleles $D$ and $d$, and for the $M - N$ pair show similar population differences (Table 13-4).

TABLE 13-4. Gene Frequencies for Three Blood Group Loci for Selected Populations

| Population | $I^A$ | $I^B$ | $i$ | $D$ | $d$ | $M$ | $N$ |
|---|---|---|---|---|---|---|---|
| U.S. white | 0.28 | 0.08 | 0.64 | 0.61 | 0.39 | 0.54 | 0.46 |
| U.S. black | 0.17 | 0.14 | 0.69 | 0.71 | 0.29 | 0.48 | 0.52 |
| West African | 0.18 | 0.16 | 0.66 | 0.74 | 0.26 | 0.51 | 0.49 |
| American Indian | 0.10 | 0.00 | 0.90 | 1.00 | 0.00 | 0.76 | 0.24 |

In summary, different populations are often characterized by particular gene frequencies, producing phenotypic frequencies which may be expected to fluctuate narrowly around a mean until something occurs to alter gene frequencies. Figure 13-1 indicates how frequencies of homozygotes and heterozygotes are changed by shift in gene frequencies.

On page 249 we noted that, in large populations, changes in gene frequency may come about not only through alteration of isolating mechanisms but also through mutation and selection. But in populations of finite size, an additional factor comes into play. This is random fluctuation in gene frequency, or **genetic drift**. We should now briefly examine each of these latter three forces as mechanisms of change in gene frequency.

*Mutation.* Basically, a mutation is a sudden, random alteration in the genotype of an individual. Strictly speaking, it is a change in the genetic material itself, but the term is often loosely extended to include chromosomal aberrations of the sorts already considered (Chapter 12). Its importance in the genetics of populations is to provide new material on which selection can operate as well as to alter gene frequencies.

If, for example, gene $T$ mutates to $t$, the relative frequencies of the two alleles are changed. If the mutation $T \rightarrow t$ recurs consistently, $T$ could disappear from the population. But not only is mutation recurrent, it is also reversible, with a known frequency in many cases. These *back mutations* will at least slow the otherwise inexorable shift of $T$ to $t$ and perhaps

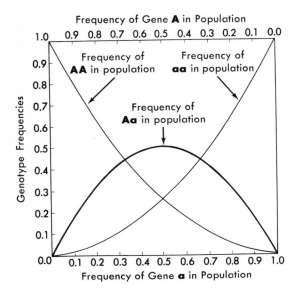

Frequency of Gene **A** in Population

FIGURE 13-1. *The effect of changes in gene frequencies on frequencies of genotypes in a population.*

prevent the total disappearance of $T$. But notice that the mutation $T \rightarrow t$ inevitably would shift gene frequencies over time (1) unless the rate of back mutation ($T \leftarrow t$) equals the rate of forward mutation ($T \rightarrow t$), and (2) only if possession of gene $t$ either gives its bearer an advantage or confers no disadvantage. Thus mutation as a force in altering gene frequencies can scarcely be considered apart from the factor of selection.

Equilibrium due to mutation is easily derived algebraically. Since the rate of mutation $T \rightarrow t$ generally does not equal the rate of change $t \rightarrow T$, we can show this relationship as

$$T \underset{v}{\overset{u}{\underset{\longleftarrow}{\longrightarrow}}} t$$

where $u$ is the rate of mutation $T \rightarrow t$, and the back mutation $t \rightarrow T$ occurs at rate $v$, with $u \neq v$.

Letting $q$ represent the frequency of mutating gene $t$ in any one generation and $1 - q$ the frequency of its mutating allele, $T$, the change in frequency of $T$ *due to mutation* for the succeeding generation will be caused by

1. the addition of $T$, to the limit set by $vq$ and
2. the loss of $T$, to the limit set by $u(1 - q)$.

Frequencies of $T$ and $t$ will be in equilibrium under mutation when additions and losses balance, or $vq = u(1 - q)$.

Thus $\hat{q}$, the equilibrium frequency of $t$ under mutation, will equal the rate $T \rightarrow t$, divided by the sum of the rates $T \rightarrow t$ and $t \rightarrow T$:

$$\hat{q} = \frac{u}{u + v}$$

If, for example, $T$ mutates to $t$ three times as often as $t$ mutates to $T$,

$$u = 3v$$

and

$$\hat{q} = \frac{3v}{3v + v} = \tfrac{3}{4}$$

So the population will reach equilibrium with regard to the frequencies of the mutating alleles $T$ and $t$ when $q$, the frequency of $t$, is 0.75, and $1 - q$, the frequency of $T$, is 0.25.

**Selection.** The common colon bacillus, *Escherichia coli*, is usually killed by the antibiotic streptomycin; the normal, wild-type phenotype is thus "streptomycin-sensitive." The alleles for this trait are designated $str^+$ (streptomycin-sensitive) and $str$ (streptomycin-resistant). Because vegetative cells of *E. coli* are monoploid, any given cell has the genotype $str^+$ or $str$. In a freely growing culture of this organism, about one in ten million cells can be shown by appropriate culture techniques to be streptomycin-resistant. Gene $str^+$ mutates to $str$ with a frequency of about $10^{-7}$. Now, in its normal streptomycin-free environment, neither $str^+$ nor $str$ confers any advantage or disadvantage. Hence, the frequency of $str$ would reach equilibrium after a number of generations. However, let streptomycin be introduced into the environment, and possession of $str$ becomes a distinct advantage; without it, an individual does not survive. So, with a specific environmental change, $str$ individuals survive, $str^+$ cells do not. One might say an ordinarily inconsequential gene ($str$) has thus suddenly assumed a very high positive selection value and, at the same time, $str^+$ has acquired a strong negative selection value.

Sickle-cell anemia affords an interesting and simple case of selection as a force in maintaining, in certain human populations, a surprisingly high frequency of an otherwise deleterious gene, $Hb^S$. Briefly, this gene is most frequent in almost precisely those regions where falciparum malaria is prevalent. These areas include principally the Mediterranean basin, central Africa from roughly 10° north latitude to 25° south latitude, the valley of the Nile, Madagascar, and portions of the Arabian peninsula. There is evidence to indicate that S-hemoglobin produces conditions unfavorable to the growth of the malarial parasite in the blood. Hence, an environment that includes this disease confers some selective advantage on individuals having S-hemoglobin. Homozygous "normal" persons, $Hb^A Hb^A$, do not suffer sickle-cell anemia, of course, but are more susceptible to malaria; $Hb^S Hb^S$ individuals are resistant to malaria but develop the anemia and die before reaching reproductive maturity. Heterozygotes, $Hb^A Hb^S$, have some advantage in respect to both malaria and sickle-cell anemia.

The impact of selection may also be seen in an extreme example from tomato. In this plant several linkage groups contain dominant genes which confer resistance to different strains of the leaf mold fungus, *Cladosporium*. The disease is not ordinarily a problem in outdoor culture, but frequently becomes severe in commercial greenhouses where temperature and humidity may be consistently high enough to cause severe infestation of susceptible plants. In such cases, homozygous recessives, which are susceptible, are quickly killed and may not live to reproductive age. For simplicity, let us consider this situation as due to a single pair of alleles, $C$ and $c$, with $cc$ plants being susceptible to the fungus. As noted, the outdoor environment is generally not conducive to fatal infections in northern parts of the country. We shall assume a population of plants in which the frequencies of $C$ and $c$ are each 0.5; we shall further imagine continuous greenhouse culture in which seed for new plantings is obtained from the crop being grown.

Initially, then, we can represent the parental generation as follows:

$$\text{Frequency of } C = p = 0.5; \text{ frequency of } c = q = 0.5$$

P    Genotypes:            $CC$     $Cc$     $cc$

Genotypic frequencies:     $p^2 + 2pq + q^2$

$$= 0.25 + 0.50 + 0.25$$

If $cc$ individuals are unable to reproduce in this environment, the breeding population is reduced to $CC$ and $Cc$ plants now occurring in the ratio of $1:2$.

$$CC: \quad \frac{0.25}{0.25 + 0.50} = 0.33 \text{ (new genotypic frequency)}$$

$$Cc: \quad \frac{0.50}{0.25 + 0.50} = 0.67 \text{ (new genotypic frequency)}$$

This leaves only $C- \times C-$ crosses possible, with consequent changes in phenotypic and genotypic frequencies in the next generation (Table 13-5). The frequency of $c$ has declined in a single generation from 0.5 to 0.33 $(= \sqrt{0.11})$, and C's frequency has risen from 0.5 to 0.67.

In effect, we have been considering complete selection against a recessive lethal. We can represent the frequency of such a gene after any given number of generations as

$$q_n = \frac{q_0}{1 + nq_0}$$

TABLE 13-5

| Crosses | Frequencies | F₁ Genotypic Frequencies | | |
|---|---|---|---|---|
| | | $CC$ | $Cc$ | $cc$ |
| $CC \times CC$ | $(0.33)^2 \quad = 0.11$ | 0.11 | | |
| $CC \times Cc$ | $2(0.33 \times 0.67) = 0.44$ | 0.22 | 0.22 | |
| $Cc \times Cc$ | $(0.67)^2 \quad = 0.45$ | 0.11 | 0.23 | 0.11 |
| | | 0.44 | 0.45 | 0.11 |

where $q_n$ = the frequency of the recessive lethal after $n$ additional generations, and $q_0$ = the initial frequency of that gene. Thus, in our tomato example where $q_0 = 0.5$ and $n = 1$,

$$q_1 = \frac{0.5}{1 + (1 \times 0.5)} = \frac{0.5}{1.5} = 0.33$$

In a closed population, with no admixture from other groups, only mutation can prevent the frequency of a gene so radically selected against from dropping quickly toward zero. The curve for complete selection against a recessive gene, however, is hyperbolic, with the final slope being determined less by mutation than by the fact that the deleterious gene persists in rare heterozygotes which more frequently mate with homozygous dominant individuals. The number of additional generations ($n$) required to reduce $q$ from a value of $q_0$ to some desired value, $q_n$, is given by the equation

$$n = \frac{1}{q_n} - \frac{1}{q_0}$$

Thus, to reduce $q$ from 0.5 ($=q_0$) to 0.33 ($=q_n$), one additional generation is required:

$$n = \frac{1}{0.33} - \frac{1}{0.5} = 3 - 2 = 1$$

With this equation, the frequency of a recessive lethal for any number of generations can be calculated readily, as shown in Table 13-6.

Note that the frequency of the lethal is reduced by half in three generations, but four more are required to reduce it by half again, and so on. Furthermore, the number of generations required to halve the frequency of such a gene is very large when the initial frequency is quite low. On the other hand, had the lethal been a dominant instead of a recessive, it would have been eliminated in one generation in the absence of complicating influences.

More often the genotypes involved differ much less in their relative advantage and disadvantage, and the homozygous recessive, for example,

TABLE 13-6. Reduction in Frequency ($q$) of a Recessive Lethal by Generations

| Generation | $q$ |
|---|---|
| 1 | 0.500 |
| 2 | 0.333 |
| 3 | 0.250 |
| 4 | 0.200 |
| 5 | 0.167 |
| 6 | 0.143 |
| 7 | 0.125 |
| 8 | 0.111 |
| 9 | 0.100 |
| 10 | 0.091 |
| 50 | 0.020 |
| 100 | 0.010 |
| 1,000 | 0.001 |

will be eliminated much more slowly than in the illustration from tomato. For instance, assume genotype $A-$ produces 100 offspring, all of which reach reproductive maturity in a given environment, whereas genotype $aa$ produces only 80 that do so. We may designate the proportion of the progeny of one genotype surviving to maturity (relative to that of another genotype) as its fitness or *adaptive value*, $W$. Thus, in this case, $W_{A-}$ may be set arbitrarily at 1; $W_{aa}$ is then 0.8. The measure of reduced fitness of a given genotype is referred to as its **selection coefficient**, $s$. We can express the relationship between adaptive value ($W$) and the selection coefficient ($s$) as

$$W = 1 - s, \quad \text{or} \quad s = 1 - W$$

In the example we are considering, $s = 0$ for genotype $A-$, and $1 - 0.8 = 0.2$ for $aa$.

If we let $p$ = the frequency of gene $A$ and $q$ = the frequency of its recessive allele $a$, selection against the latter is as shown in Table 13-7.

TABLE 13-7. Selection Against a Recessive Allele

| | $AA$ | $Aa$ | $aa$ | Total |
|---|---|---|---|---|
| Initial frequency | $p^2$ | $2pq$ | $q^2$ | 1 |
| Adaptive value ($W$) | 1 | 1 | $1 - s$ | |
| Frequency after selection | $p^2$ | $2pq$ | $q^2(1-s)$ | $p^2 + 2pq + q^2 - sq^2 = 1 - sq^2$ |

By the same method we have used to calculate frequencies of genes $T$ and $t$, for example, in the Hardy-Weinberg equilibrium (page 253), the information in Table 13-7 gives us an equation for determining the frequency of gene *a* when we know the value of $W_{aa}$:

$$q_1 = \frac{q_0 - sq_0^2}{1 - sq_0^2}$$

where $q_0$ again is the frequency of *a* in a given generation, $q_1$ its frequency one generation later under selection, and *s* the selection coefficient.

If, for instance, $q_0 = 0.5$, then substituting in this equation, $q_1 = 0.4737$. So, with *partial selection* against a fully recessive gene, the decrease in its frequency is much less per generation than for complete selection against a recessive lethal. We can represent the change in frequency of *a* under partial selection ($\Delta q$, or $q_1 - q_0$) by the equation

$$q_1 - q_0 = \frac{-sq_0^2(1 - q_0)}{1 - sq_0^2}$$

Upon substituting here, $q_1 - q_0 = -0.0263$. If $q_0$ were very small, as it would ordinarily be in the case of deleterious mutations, the quantity $q_1 - q_0$ becomes almost equal to $-sq_0^2$.

In time, a large population attains a genetic equilibrium which is the resultant between selection forces and rate of mutation. This is apparent in many different species of animals and plants, as well as in man. Recall, for example, the frequencies of genes governing such diverse traits as PTC-tasting ability, blood antigens, and skin pigmentation. But note also the suggestive evidence in such data as those of Tables 13-3 and 13-4 that, once a population ceases to be isolated, gene frequencies begin to change as genetic material is contributed by members of other populations.

*Random Genetic Drift.* From generation to generation the number of individuals carrying a particular allele, in either the homozygous or heterozygous state, may be expected to vary somewhat so that, in any one generation, gene frequencies will fluctuate about a mean. This *random genetic drift* is due to the vagaries of chance mating and to the fact that, even in cases where $p = q = 0.5$, theoretical ratios (e.g., 3:1, 1:1, 1:2:1) are certainly not always produced. If a population is large, drift is of small magnitude and may be expected to vary within rather narrow limits above and below the mean. But in small breeding populations, all of the progeny might, by chance alone, be of the same genotype with respect to a particular pair of alleles. If this should happen, *fixation* would have occurred at that locus; that is, either $p = 1.00$ or $q = 1.00$. Fixation, if it does occur, may do so in one or any number of generations, but the important fact is that, in moving toward fixation, gene frequencies drift.

The formation of a new population by migration of a sample of individuals may likewise lead to different gene frequencies. Imagine a large population in which $p = 0.4$ and $q = 0.6$. The most probable values of $p$ and $q$, therefore, in a *sample* from this population are also 0.4 and 0.6, respectively. Expected deviation from these values is, of course, provided by the standard deviation. The standard deviation for a simple proportionality, such as heads versus tails, is given by

$$s = \sqrt{\frac{pq}{n}}$$

where $n$ is the number of observations. But when gene frequencies are calculated from the frequency of homozygous recessive phenotypes, as we have been doing, the formula for standard deviation becomes

$$s = \sqrt{\frac{pq}{2N}}$$

where $N$ is the number of (diploid) individuals in the sample.

If, in the large population under consideration, we take a sample of 50,000 persons,

$$s = \sqrt{\frac{0.24}{100,000}} = 0.00155$$

That is, in any sample of 50,000 individuals from this population with $p = 0.4$ and $q = 0.6$, 68 per cent of the time $p$ will lie between 0.39845 and 0.40155, and 95 per cent of the time it will fall within the range 0.3969 to 0.4031. But if the sample were to consist of only 50 persons,

$$s = \sqrt{\frac{0.24}{100}} = 0.049$$

In 68 per cent of samples of this size, $p$ would be expected to fall between 0.351 and 0.449. Similarly, in 95 per cent of the cases of samples of 50, $p$ would be within the range of 0.302 to 0.498. Formation of a new population by emigration of a sample as small as 50 would be expected to lead purely by chance to a different gene frequency in the next generation.

A presumed example of just such a case of genetic drift has been reported for the Dunkers of Pennsylvania. These are members of a religious sect who migrated from Germany in the early eighteenth century and have remained relatively isolated. The frequency of group A in this small group is almost 0.6 whereas it is between 0.40 and 0.45 in German and American populations, and the $I^B$ allele is nearly absent in the Dunkers, whereas group B persons comprise 10 to 15 per cent of German and American populations.

# The Mechanism of Evolution

The principles we have been examining, especially in this and the preceding chapter, constitute the basic mechanism whereby new species evolve, sometimes slowly, sometimes suddenly, from preexisting ones. A species is more a taxonomic concept than a concrete entity, and its parameters necessarily differ somewhat among various groups of animals and plants. Thus, a species in bacteria is quite a different concept from one in birds. Species " boundaries " in viruses and vertebrates have different emphases, as they do even in more closely related units like freely hybridizing, genetically plastic willows versus the more stable maples. However, in very general terms, speciation, or the origin of new species, depends largely on such cytological and genetic mechanisms as these which have been described:

1. Chromosomal aberrations, especially translocations and allopolyploidy (in plants).
2. Addition of new genetic material by mutation (although most are either neutral or disadvantageous in an existing environment).
3. Changes in gene frequencies:
    (a) By mutation
    (b) Through random drift
    (c) By migration or the breaking down of isolating barriers
    (d) By environmental selection

These agencies may sooner or later break up larger populations into smaller units which (1) develop genetically determined, distinctive morphological and/or physiological characters differing from those of other such units, and (2) become reproductively isolated from related groups, developing thereby into " Mendelian populations " having their own gene pools. How, in what direction(s) and to what extent, evolution thus directed will develop depends on an intricate interaction among a variety of influences. But basically only those changes in the genetic material that can be passed on to succeeding generations and do not disappear from the gene pool can serve as agents of evolution in living organisms.

**REFERENCES**

BLAKESLEE, A. F., and T. N. SALMON, 1935. Genetics of Sensory Thresholds: Individual Taste Reactions for Different Substances. *Proc. Nat. Acad. Sci. (U.S.)*, **21**:84–90.

FOX, A. L., 1932. The Relationship Between Chemical Composition and Taste. *Proc. Nat. Acad. Sci. (U.S.)*, **18**:115–120.

**PROBLEMS**

**13-1.** A sample of 1,000 persons tested for M-N blood antigens was found to be distributed: M, 200; MN, 600; N, 200. What is the frequency of genes *M* and *N*?

**13-2.** A sample of 1,522 persons living in London disclosed 464 of type M, 733 of type MN, and 325 of type N. Calculate gene frequencies of *M* and *N*.

**13-3.** A sample of 200 persons from Papua (southeast New Guinea) showed 14 M, 48 MN, and 138 N. Calculate gene frequencies for *M* and *N*.

**13-4.** A sample of 100 persons disclosed 84 PTC tasters. Calculate gene frequencies for *T* and for *t*.

**13-5.** How many (a) heterozygotes should there be in the sample of problem 13-4; (b) *TT* persons?

**13-6.** Albinism is the phenotypic expression of a homozygous recessive genotype. One source estimates the frequency of albinos in the American population as 1 in 20,000. What percentage of the population is heterozygous for this gene if albinos born of homozygous parents are ignored?

**13-7.** Alcaptonuria, due to the homozygous expression of a recessive autosomal gene, occurs in about 1 in 1,000,000 persons. What is the proportion of heterozygous "carriers" in the population?

**13-8.** A sample of 1,000 hypothetical persons in the United States showed the following distribution of blood groups; A, 450; B, 130; AB, 60; O, 360. Calculate the frequencies of genes $I^A$, $I^B$, and $i$.

**13-9.** Another sample of 1,000 hypothetical persons had these blood groups; A, 320; B, 150; AB, 40; O, 490. What is the frequency in this sample of each of the following genotypes: $I^A I^A$, $I^A i$, $I^B I^B$, $I^B i$, $I^A I^B$, $ii$?

**13-10.** Assume the data of Table 13-1 to represent accurately the distribution of A, B, AB, and O blood groups in the United States population. Using the $x^2$ test, determine whether the sample of problem 13-8 represents a significant deviation. (Round the frequencies of Table 13-1 to the whole numbers 440, 420, 100, and 40, respectively, to obtain calculated values for computing chi-square.)

**13-11.** A sample of 429 Puerto Ricans showed the following gene frequencies: $I^A$, 0.24; $I^B$, 0.06; $i$, 0.70. Calculate the percentage of persons in this sample with A, B, AB, and O blood.

**13-12.** What percentage of the sample is (a) homozygous A; (b) heterozygous B?

**13-13.** If 1 man in 25,000 is a hemophile, what is the frequency of gene *h* in the population?

**13-14.** One man in a hundred exhibits a trait due to a certain sex-linked recessive gene. What is the frequency of (a) heterozygous women; (b) homozygous recessive women?

**13-15.** Data presented in Table 13-4 show a frequency of 0.64 for gene *i*, and 0.61 for the Rh allele *D*. Considering only these two genes, what would be the frequency of O+ persons in the population?

**13-16.** Considerable progress is being made in the eradication of malaria. If malaria is eventually eliminated, what effect will this be likely to have on the frequency of gene $Hb^s$?

**13-17.** Great effort is being made to eliminate the muscular dystrophy caused by gene $d$. If we are someday successful in eliminating the *effect* of this gene in *treated* individuals, will this result in genetic improvement or deterioration in the world population?

**13-18.** Considering the tabulated data (text) concerning frequency of gene $c$ in tomato, what would the frequency of this gene be after one more generation of inbreeding?

**13-19.** Considering the tabulated data (text) concerning frequency of gene $c$ in tomato, (a) what would be the frequency of this gene in the 20th generation of inbreeding? (b) Considering the parental generation as generation $\#1$, in what generation would the frequency of $c$ be reduced to exactly 0.005?

**13-20.** Gene $f$ is an autosomal recessive lethal which kills $ff$ individuals before they reach reproductive age. If, in an isolated population, this gene had a frequency of 0.4 in the P generation, what would be its frequency in the $F_2$?

**13-21.** For a certain pair of alleles, completely dominant gene $A$ has an initial frequency of 0.7 and an adaptive value of 1. Its recessive allele has a frequency of 0.3 and an adaptive value of 0.5. What is the frequency of $a$ in the next generation?

**13-22.** Gene $A$ mutates to its recessive allele $a$ four times more frequently than $a$ mutates to $A$. What will be the equilibrium frequency of $a$ under mutation?

**13-23.** In a given population gene $C$ has a frequency of 0.2. If 50 individuals from that population are sampled, there is a 0.68 probability that the frequency of $C$ will be no more than how much above or below 0.2 in the sample?

**13-24.** The autosomal recessive lethal gene for cystic fibrosis of the pancreas is estimated by one authority to have a frequency of 0.02 in the United States population. (a) If a human generation is regarded as being 30 years, how many years would be required to reduce this frequency to 0.01? (b) Is this likely to occur? Why?

**13-25.** Let $p$ represent the frequency of dominant autosomal gene $A$ and $q$ the frequency of its recessive allele $a$. For a randomly mating population, give a mathematical expression for (a) the frequency of an $AA$ individual; (b) the probability of an $AA \times AA$ mating; (c) the frequency of an $Aa$ individual; (d) the probability of an $Aa \times Aa$ mating; (e) the probability of an $Aa \times aa$ mating; (f) the total of all possible matings.

**13-26.** Give a mathematical expression for the frequency of (a) dominant and (b) recessive progeny phenotypes from a *single $Aa \times Aa$* mating.

**13-27.** Considering the *entire* randomly mating population, with all possible matings equally free to occur, give (a) a mathematical expression for the frequency of recessive progeny in the population resulting from such random matings and (b) the numerical value of this expression if $p = q = 0.5$.

# CHAPTER 14
# The Identification of the Genetic Material

U P to this point we have made a variety of genetic observations in a wide assortment of organisms. We have seen that all of these observations can be explained by theorizing that genes occur at specific loci, in linear order, on chromosomes. But there remains an important body of questions to which we must now seek answers:

1. What is *the* genetic material?
2. How does this genetic material operate to produce observable phenotypic traits?
3. In terms of *the* genetic material, what actually is a gene? Can its molecular configuration be determined?
4. In terms of the nature of the genetic material and of the gene, what really is a mutation? That is, when a gene changes and produces a different effect, what happens to it at the level of its molecular structure?
5. Differentiation in multicellular organisms suggests that not all genes function all the time. If this is so, how are genes regulated?
6. Is this genetic material, are these genes, all located in chromosomes, or does the cytoplasm play any part in inheritance?

These questions we shall pursue in the remaining chapters; in this one we shall turn our attention to the problem of identifying the genetic material itself. Basically, there are three avenues of approach, dealing primarily with microorganisms. It is much easier to find answers to these questions in bacteria and viruses than it is in rather complex individuals like ourselves. Interestingly enough, knowledge gained from studies on these simpler forms is found to be perfectly applicable to all of the more highly evolved ones. These three approaches are **transformation**, **transduction**, and **conjugation**.

## Bacterial Transformation

*The "Griffith Effect."* In 1928, Frederick Griffith published a paper in which he cited a number of what were, at that time, remarkable results for which he had no explanation. His observations involved a particular bacterium, *Diplococcus pneumoniae*, which is associated with certain types of pneumonia. This organism occurs in two major forms: (1) *smooth* (S), whose cells secrete a covering capsule of polysaccharide materials, causing its colonies on agar to be smooth and rather shiny, and which is virulent in that it produces bacterial pneumonia in suitable experimental animals, and (2) *rough* (R), cells of which lack a capsule, whose agar colonies have a rough, rather dull surface, and which is nonvirulent. Smooth and rough characters are directly related to the presence or absence of the capsule, and this trait is known to be genetically determined.

The smooth types (S) can be distinguished by their possession of different capsular polysaccharides (designated as I, II, III, IV); the specific polysaccharide is antigenic and genetically controlled. Mutations from smooth to rough occur spontaneously with a frequency of about one cell in $10^7$, though the reverse is much less frequent. Mutation of, say, an S-II to rough may occur, and these may rarely revert to smooth. When that happens the smooth revertants are again S-II.

In the course of his work Griffith injected laboratory mice with live R pneumococci derived from an S-II culture; the mice suffered no ill effects. Injection of mice with a living S-III culture (or smooth cultures of any other antigenic type) was fatal, but logically enough, use of heat-killed suspensions of either S or R bacteria did not produce pneumonia. Inoculating the animals with live R-II bacteria (i.e., a rough form derived from S-II) *plus* dead S-III, however, resulted in a high mortality. This surely was an unexpected turn of events. The heat-killed S-III were checked; all indeed were dead. Yet both living R-II and S-III organisms were subcultured following autopsy of the dead mice!

An explanation was not immediately forthcoming. It was as though the killed S-III individuals were somehow restored to life, but this was patently absurd. The then rather recently understood phenomenon of mutation might be implicated, but the frequency of occurrence in the Griffith experiments was far too high to be compatible with known mutation rates. Scientists were left only with the idea that, in some way, the heat-killed cells conferred virulence on the previously nonvirulent strain; in short, the living cells were somehow *transformed*. So the Griffith effect gradually became known as *transformation* and turned out to be the first major step in the identification of *the* genetic material.

***Identification of the " Transforming Substance."*** Sixteen years after Griffith's work, Avery, MacLeod, and McCarty (1944) reported successful repetition of the earlier work, but in vitro, and were able to identify the "transforming substance." They tested fractions of heat-killed cells for transforming ability. Completely negative results were obtained with fractions containing only the polysaccharide capsule, various cell proteins, or ribonucleic acid (RNA); only extracts containing deoxyribonucleic acid (DNA) were effective. Even highly purified fractions containing DNA and less than two parts protein per ten thousand, for example, retained the transforming ability. DNA, plus even minute amounts of protein, plus proteolytic

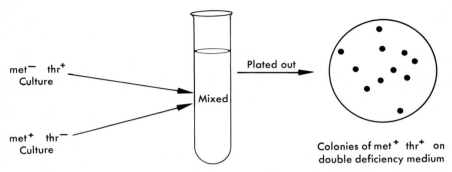

FIGURE 14-1. *Schematic diagram of the first of the Zinder and Lederberg experiments. Two strains, each auxotrophic for a different trait, are grown separately, mixed, then plated out on double deficiency medium. Colonies developing there are prototrophs.*

enzymes, was fully effective. But DNA, plus DNAase, an enzyme that destroys DNA, lost its transforming capability.

Therefore, it began to appear that, *beyond any reasonable doubt, DNA must be the genetic material.* Moreover, this landmark of genetic research indicated also that *the genetic material, DNA, differs from the end product it determines.* Evidence has been since accumulated to show that transformation is of fairly wide occurrence in bacteria at least. We shall examine the intracellular mechanism of this process later in this chapter.

## Transduction

The clear implication of DNA as the genetic material that was furnished by transformation experiments was extended and confirmed by a series of elegant experiments begun by Zinder and Lederberg (1952) on the mouse typhoid bacterium, *Salmonella typhimurium.* Several auxotrophic strains were used. One of these (*met⁻ thr⁺*) was unable to synthesize the necessary amino acid methionine from simple raw materials, and required it in the medium in order to grow. Another was prototrophic for methionine, but auxotrophic for a second amino acid, threonine (*met⁺ thr⁻*).

Several of the experiments of Zinder and Lederberg were of critical importance in confirming that DNA is the genetic material and in disclosing a modified method by which it converts a cell from one genotype to another. In each of these experiments, *met⁻ thr⁺* and *met⁺ thr⁻* auxotrophic cultures were first grown separately. In the first experiment, the two cultures were simply mixed and plated out on double deficiency medium (i.e., lacking both methionine and threonine); many colonies subsequently appeared (Fig. 14-1). Any colony on such double deficiency agar must be able to produce its own

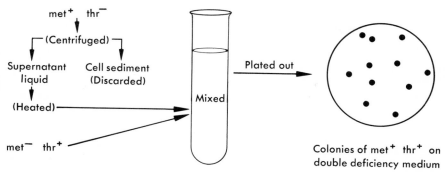

FIGURE 14-2. *Modification of the original Zinder and Lederberg experiment in which only cell-free extract of one auxotroph is added to a culture of the other auxotroph. Again, prototroph colonies develop on double deficiency medium, indicating that their occurrence is not based on conjugation.*

amino acids of both types. The number of such prototrophic colonies was far too great to be accounted for by mutation. But could it be due to conjugation (Appendix B)? Or were these results perhaps to be explained by transformation? Two more experiments answered each of these questions.

Zinder and Lederberg next treated the *met⁺ thr⁻* culture differently before adding it to the *met⁻ thr⁺* cells. The *met⁺ thr⁻* culture was (1) centrifuged to throw down living cells, then (2) the supernatant culture fluid, presumably now cell-free, was heated to kill any cells that might possibly have failed to be sedimented. Upon adding this cell-free, heat-treated supernate to the culture of *met⁻ thr⁺* strain and plating on double deficiency medium, again a very large number of *met⁺ thr⁺* colonies was obtained. Thus, since living cells were not required, the origin of the prototrophic colonies is clearly not the result of conjugation (Fig. 14-2).

As a modification of this latter procedure, Zinder and Lederberg added DNAase to the supernate, and again many prototrophs were recovered. Therefore, this was not the result of transformation as we saw it in the work of Griffith and of Avery and his colleagues. It was found that the "*met⁺* factor" could pass through filters that hold back bacteria but allow viruses to pass. On the other hand, the reciprocal of this experiment, using filtrate of *met⁻ thr⁺* to convert *met⁺ thr⁻* cells, did not produce prototrophs (Fig. 14-3).

The particular *met⁺ thr⁻* "donor" was found to harbor a virus, identified as P22, in a commensal relationship. Viruses that infect bacteria, you will recall, are termed phages. It was known that the genetic material of *Salmonella* is DNA, so it was considered probable that the "*met⁺* factor" was also composed of this substance. Their use of DNAase convinced Zinder and Lederberg that the "*met⁺* factor" was located inside the virus whose genetic material is also DNA.

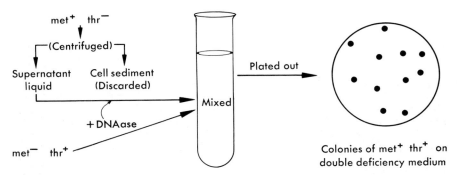

FIGURE 14-3. *Modification of the original Zinder and Lederberg experiment in which DNAase is added to the cell-free extract of one auxotroph. The appearance of prototroph colonies on double deficiency medium suggests that transformation is not occurring.*

The name **transduction** has been given to the process just described. The genetic material of the transducing phage includes a small portion of DNA from its previous bacterial host which it injects into the next host cell. Transduction is, then, essentially a transformation of one bacterial strain by another, but the introduction of the "foreign" DNA occurs via a phage. Before we can understand the mechanism of the process, or that of trans-formation as described earlier, we must look at the structure and "life cycle" of phages, and also at the structure and properties of deoxyribonucleic acid.

## Phage Structure and Life Cycle

*Structure of T Phages.*   There is no "typical" virus structure, but there are several modifications of a basic structure. In general terms, viruses consist of an outer, inert, nongenetic protein "shell" and an inner core of genetic material. In many cases the genetic material is DNA, but in some it is RNA. The T series of phages are perhaps the best known structurally; one is shown in electron micrograph view and in diagrammatic sectional view in Figs. 14-4, 14-5.

The T phages are of a general "tadpole" shape, outwardly differentiated into a "head" and a "tail" region. The former is hexagonal in outline, bearing numerous facets, and contains genetic material, in this case DNA. The "tail" is a hollow cylinder and can contract longitudinally. Six tail fibers arise from a plate at the far end of the so-called tail. Other phages are quite different in structure. Phage $\phi$X174, for example, appears in electron micrographs as a cluster of twelve identical, adherent but morphologically distinct, spherical subparticles. Two general types of phage replication cycles can be recognized: (1) *virulent* phages, in which infection is followed by *lysis*

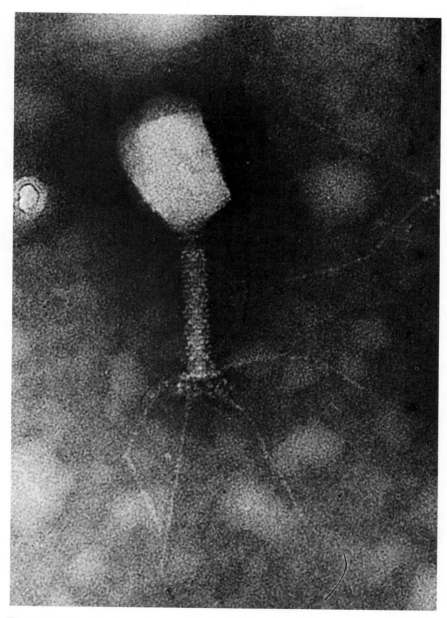

FIGURE 14-4. *Electron micrograph of a T4 bacteriophage,* ×630,000. [Courtesy Dr. Thomas F. Anderson, Institute for Cancer Research, Philadelphia.]

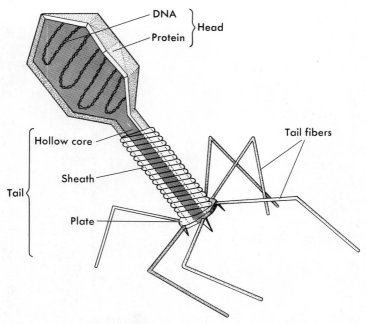

FIGURE 14-5. *Diagrammatic longitudinal section of a T4 bacteriophage. Only a small portion of the total DNA content is shown.*

(bursting) of the host cell and release of new, infective phages and (2) *temperate* phages, in which infection only rarely causes lysis.

   ***Life Cycle of a Virulent Phage.***   The life cycle of the T series of phages begins with the attachment of the viral particles by their tail fibers to the host cell (Fig. 14-6). An opening is produced in the bacterial cell at the point of attachment, probably enzymatically. Determination of immediately subsequent events is made easy by the fact that the protein outer shell contains sulfur but no phosphorous, whereas DNA contains phosphorous but no sulfur. Use of two samples of phage, one containing radioactive $S^{35}$ and the other radioactive $P^{32}$, enabled Hershey and Chase (1952) to ascertain that all the DNA of the T phages enters the host cell following attachment; most of the protein shell remains outside. Within a short time (e.g., 13 minutes for phage T1, and 22 minutes for phage T2), the host cell lyses and releases several hundred new viral particles, which can then repeat the process (Fig. 14-7). During the period between attachment and lysis, evidence indicates that host DNA is broken down and resynthesized, along with material from the outside medium, as new phage particles under the direction of the invading viral DNA. Evidence indicates that the bacterial DNA disintegrates quickly after infection

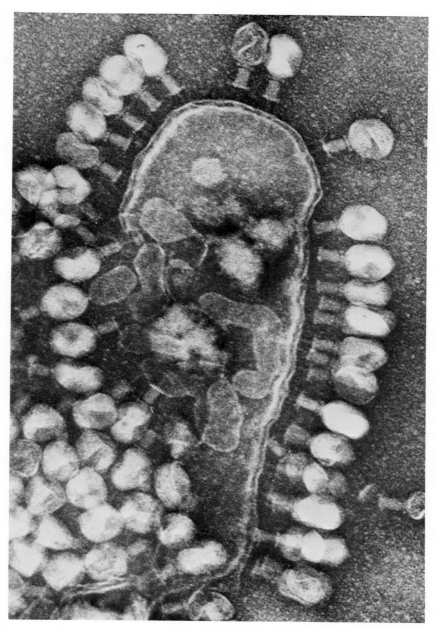

FIGURE 14-6. *Electron micrograph of T4 phage attacking* Escherichia coli. *Not only can phage particles be seen attached by their tail fibers to the cell wall of the bacterium* (top and right), *but new phage particles are shown being released from the lysed bacterial cell* (left). [Photo by Dr. L. D. Simon, courtesy Dr. Thomas F. Anderson, Institute for Cancer Research, Philadelphia.]

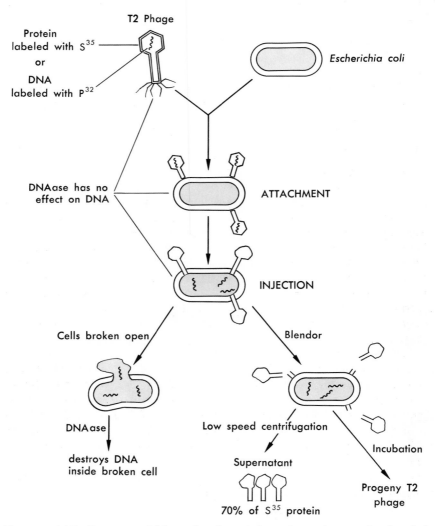

FIGURE 14-7. *Diagram of life cycle of a virulent phage showing details of the Hershey-Chase experiment. Phage particles and bacterial cells are not to scale.* [From Fraser, *Viruses and Molecular Biology*, Macmillan, 1967. By permission.]

and that phage DNA then begins to accumulate. Materials for the protein shell are derived from the external medium, and assembly of a mature phage begins with the enclosure of newly formed phage DNA by protein within a few minutes. Because, in this case, the phage destroys its host this is a **virulent phage**. We can recognize the following steps in the process:

1. *Attachment* of phage tail to specific receptor sites on the bacterial cell wall;
2. *Injection* of phage DNA;
3. *Eclipse period*, in which no infective phage is recoverable if the bacterial cell is artificially lysed and during which synthesis of new phage DNA and protein shells is taking place;
4. *Assembly* of phage DNA into new protein shells;
5. *Lysis* of host cell and release of several hundred infective phage particles.

*Life Cycle of a Temperate Phage.* Temperate phages ordinarily do not lyse their hosts, but their genomes persist in association with that of the host cell as *prophage*. Such prophages replicate more or less synchronously with the bacterial DNA, and both maturation of phage as well as infection by a virulent phage are prevented. Infrequently, however, phage maturation, lysis of host cell, and release of infective phage do occur spontaneously, or maturation may be induced in high frequency by ultraviolet radiation or such chemicals as nitrogen mustard. Because such hosts are potentially subject to lysis, they are termed **lysogenic**. The P22 phage of the Zinder and Lederberg experiments was such a temperate phage and the $met^+$ $thr^-$ strain of *Salmonella* was lysogenic, whereas their $met^-$ $thr^+$ strain was nonlysogenic (or sensitive).

When we recognize that the chromosomal material transferred during bacterial conjugation (pages 116 and 117 and Appendix B) is also DNA, we see that the three processes—conjugation, transformation, and transduction—all implicate DNA as *the* genetic material. Experimental evidence is rapidly accumulating to show that in all but the RNA-containing viruses,[1] DNA has this important property, as it also does in all eukaryotes such as man. The essential feature of heredity, then, is the transmission of this "information tape" unchanged from one generation to the next. If we are to identify genes, then we must understand the structure of this all important molecule which has been appropriately called the "thread of life."

## Deoxyribonucleic Acid

*Structure.* In 1953, Watson and Crick proposed a molecular model for DNA, based on X-ray diffraction pictures by Wilkins (Fig. 14-8). So completely was their model substantiated by subsequent investigations that this team shared a Nobel Prize in 1962. The basic structure they deduced was that

---

[1] For example, influenza, poliomyelitis, and tobacco mosaic viruses.

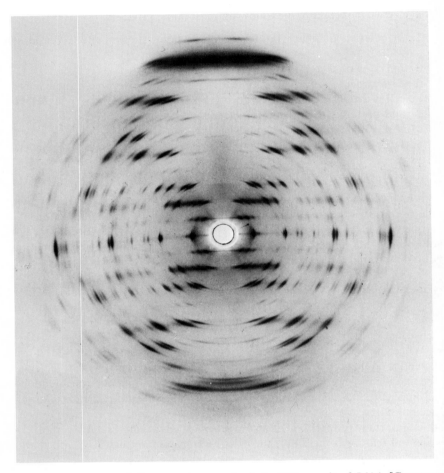

FIGURE 14-8. *X-ray diffraction photograph of the lithium salt of DNA.* [Courtesy Dr. M. H. F. Wilkins and Dr. W. Fuller, Medical Research Council, Biophysics Research Unit, King's College, London.]

of a very long molecule, of high molecular weight, composed of two sugar-phosphate strands, oriented in opposite directions and together forming a double helix making a complete turn every 34 angstrom units (i.e., 3.4 nm). These sugar-phosphate "backbones" are cross-connected by nitrogen-containing bases, two of them of the class of chemicals known as **purines**, and two **pyrimidines**. The whole, then, may be likened to a rope ladder which is helically twisted as suggested in Fig. 14-9.

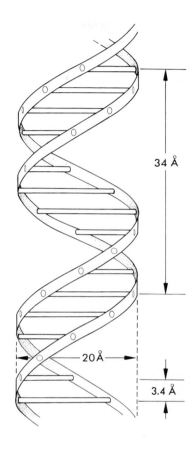

FIGURE 14-9. *The general structure of double-stranded deoxyribonucleic acid. (1Å = 0.0001 μm or 0.1 nm)*

The sugar is the 5-carbon **deoxyribose** whose molecular structure is shown by Fig. 14-10; these are linked together by **phosphoric acid** so that sugar and phosphate alternate along the length of the strand. The purine and pyrimidine bases are spaced 3.4 angstrom units, (0.34 nm) apart, with the result that there are 10 base pairs per complete turn of the sugar-phosphate strands.

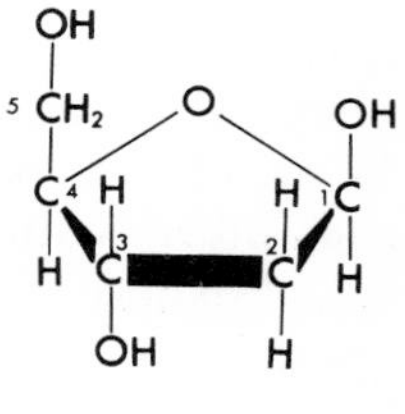

FIGURE 14-10. *Molecular structure of deoxyribose, the sugar of DNA.*

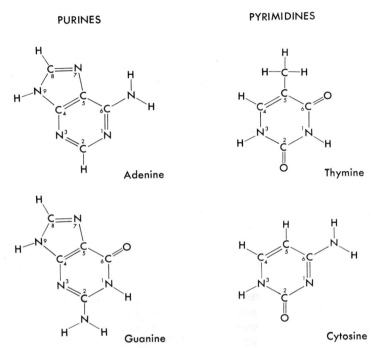

FIGURE 14-11. *Molecular structure of the four nitrogenous bases of DNA.*

Typically, only four different nitrogenous bases occur; the purines **adenine** and **guanine,** and the pyrimidines **thymine** and **cytosine**. Their molecular structure, shown in Fig. 14-11, is such that adenine is connected by two hydrogen bonds only to thymine, and cytosine by three hydrogen bonds only to guanine:

| Purines | | Pyrimidines |
|---------|---|-------------|
| Adenine | = | Thymine |
| Guanine | ≡ | Cytosine |

Since pairing occurs in this way, the amounts of adenine and thymine should be equal, and quantities of cytosine and guanine should likewise be equal to each other. Within the limits of experimental error, this is what is actually found. Notice in Table 14-1 that, for all sources listed (except phage $\phi$X174) the ratios A/T and G/C are near 1.

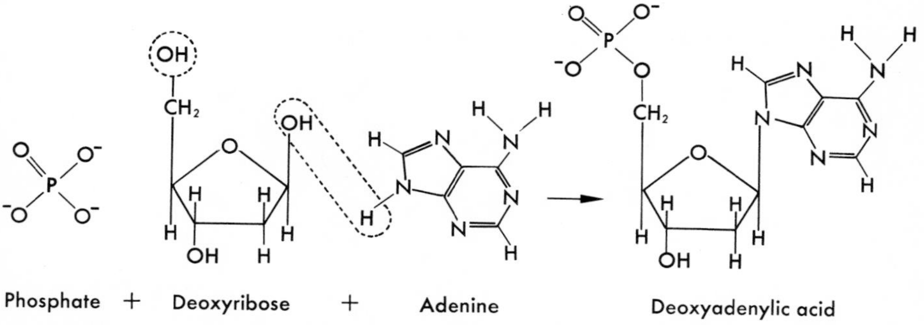

Phosphate + Deoxyribose + Adenine → Deoxyadenylic acid

FIGURE 14-12. *The formation of the deoxyribonucleotide deoxyadenylic acid.*

TABLE 14-1. Comparison of Nucleotide Composition of DNA

| Source | A | T | G | C | $\dfrac{A}{T}$ | $\dfrac{G}{C}$ | $\dfrac{A+T}{G+C}$ |
|---|---|---|---|---|---|---|---|
| Human sperm | 31.0 | 31.5 | 19.1 | 18.4 | 0.98 | 1.03 | 1.67 |
| Salmon sperm | 29.7 | 29.1 | 20.8 | 20.4 | 1.02 | 1.02 | 1.43 |
| *Euglena* nucleus | 22.6 | 24.4 | 27.7 | 25.8 | 0.93 | 1.07 | 0.88 |
| *Euglena* chloroplast | 38.2 | 38.1 | 12.3 | 11.3 | 1.00 | 1.09 | 3.23 |
| *Escherichia coli* | 26.1 | 23.9 | 24.9 | 25.1 | 1.09 | 0.99 | 1.00 |
| *Mycobacterium tuberculosis* | 15.1 | 14.6 | 34.9 | 35.4 | 1.03 | 0.98 | 0.42 |
| Phage T2 | 32.6 | 32.6 | 18.2 | 16.6* | 1.00 | 1.09 | 1.87 |
| Phage $\phi$X174 | 24.7 | 32.7 | 24.1 | 18.5 | 0.75 | 1.30 | 1.35 |

* 5-hydroxymethyl cytosine.

The DNA of phage $\phi$X174 is *single stranded*, hence values for A/T and G/C depart considerably from unity. In fact, whenever this kind of deviation is found it is indicative of single strandedness. Note also that values for A + T/G + C vary widely from well below to well above 1; that is, although the relationships A = T and C = G are valid, it is also true that A + T $\neq$ C + G in most cases. Certainly the structure of DNA does not require equality in that relationship. In fact, *DNA of different species is distinguished by the relative numbers of AT and CG pairs, their sequence, whether these occur as AT or TA and as CG or GC, and the number of such base pairs* (and, therefore, the length of the DNA molecules).

Certain useful terms are applied to parts of the DNA molecule. One phosphate and one attached sugar are collectively called **deoxyribose phosphate**, one deoxyribose molecule plus its attached purine or pyrimidine is a **nucleoside**, and a purine or a pyrimidine plus one deoxyribose phosphate unit constitutes a **nucleotide**. The purines and pyrimidines are attached to the

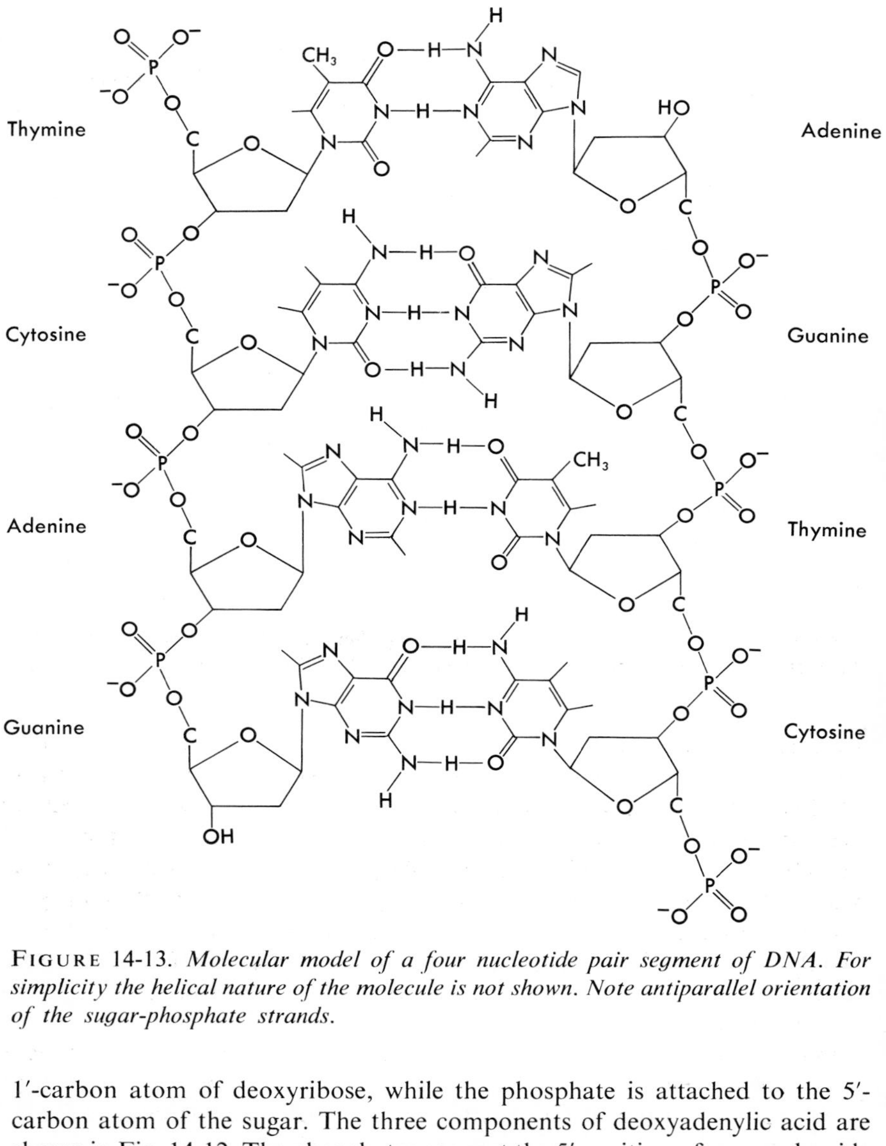

FIGURE 14-13. *Molecular model of a four nucleotide pair segment of DNA. For simplicity the helical nature of the molecule is not shown. Note antiparallel orientation of the sugar-phosphate strands.*

1'-carbon atom of deoxyribose, while the phosphate is attached to the 5'-carbon atom of the sugar. The three components of deoxyadenylic acid are shown in Fig. 14-12. The phosphates connect the 5' position of one nucleoside to the 3' position of the next. A molecular model of a segment of DNA consisting of just a few nucleotide pairs is shown in Fig. 14-13. Note that the two " backbones " are oriented in different directions; the 5' to 3' direction is oriented from "top to bottom " in the strand at the left, whereas in the other it is oriented from " bottom to top." That is, it runs antiparallel. By convention,

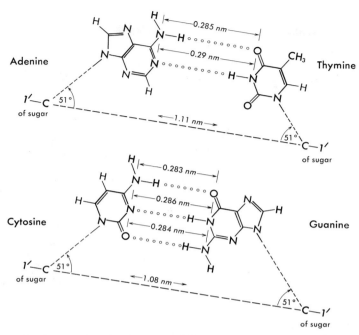

FIGURE 14-14. *Details of hydrogen bonding between deoxyribonucleotide pairs. Note the close similarity of measurements of AT and GC pairs. (0.1 nm = 1 Å.)*

geneticists "read" the molecule in the 5′ to 3′ direction. There is a definite reason for this as we shall see in subsequent chapters on the function of DNA. Hydrogen bonding between nucleotide pairs was deduced by Watson to be such as to give closely similar measurements to AT and GC pairs (Fig. 14-14). In a molecule such as this, with only four bases, the possible kind and number of sequences are virtually infinite, and we might anticipate that the DNA of different species is further distinguished by differences in length. As we shall see in the next chapter, the DNA of different species is distinctive through just such qualitative and quantitative differences in nucleotide pairs.

On the other hand, not all DNA is built exactly according to the pattern just described. The DNA of some phages (e.g., $\phi$X174) is only single stranded as we have noted previously. It does, however, become temporarily double stranded after infection of a host cell as a prelude to replication (see pages 285–287). In some DNA, other rarer bases regularly replace some of the four common bases. Phage T2, for instance, contains 5-hydroxymethyl cytosine instead of cytosine, but in an amount equal to the guanine content, thus indicating its pairing qualities. Other similar substitutions are known, but the exact role of these rare bases is only partly understood.

*Location of DNA in Cells.*   A cytochemical test known as the Feulgen technique is specific for DNA; any cellular structure containing this substance retains a purple color. Not only is this process specific for DNA, but the intensity of staining is directly proportional to the amount of deoxyribonucleic acid present. Measurements of light absorption by structures colored by the Feulgen process can be used to determine the relative amounts of this nucleic acid present. Such techniques, applied to many different kinds of eukaryotic cells, show DNA to be almost entirely restricted to the chromosomes.[2] Such microspectrophotometric techniques also employ ultraviolet light, the peak absorption being near 260 nm. It is significant that, although ultraviolet radiation is a relatively weak mutagenic agent, its most effective wavelengths as such are also near 260 nm.

The physical arrangement of DNA in the chromosomes of eukaryotes is still an unsettled matter of some conjecture. Various experimental techniques of recent development disclosed what clearly seem to be extremely long but intricately folded DNA molecules in the chromosome. The total length of the DNA of *Drosophila*, for example, is calculated to exceed by far the length of the entire metaphase chromosome complement. Yet chromosomes replicate, exhibit crossing-over, and mediate the transmission of heritable traits as though they are each composed of a single DNA molecule running the length of the chromosome. The "packaging problem" has simply not yet been solved.

On the other hand, the bacterial "chromosome" clearly appears to be a single long DNA molecule in the form of a "naked," continuous, closed, no-end structure. Even here, though, there are some packaging problems because it can be shown that the length of such a "chromosome" in *Escherichia coli*, for instance, is about 1 mm ($= 1,000$ $\mu$m) or a little more, whereas the average length of a mature *E. coli* cell is of the order of 1 or 2 $\mu$m! Moreover, such a cell may temporarily have more than one of these "chromosomes," depending on its stage in the life cycle.

*Cyclic Quantitative Changes in DNA Content.*   By appropriate quantitative measurements of DNA content of cells, a number of striking parallels with chromosome behavior and our earlier postulates regarding genes can be seen:

1. The quantity of DNA detected in gametes is, within limits of experimental error, half that of diploid meiocytes.
2. Zygotes contain twice the amount of DNA in gametes.
3. The amount of DNA increases during interphase by a factor of two. Telophase nuclei have half the DNA content of late interphase or early prophase nuclei.

---

[2] The fact that minute amounts of DNA are also found in such cytoplasmic organelles as chloroplasts and mitochondria does not weaken the cytological, chemical, and genetic evidence that DNA is genetic material. See also Chapter 19.

4. DNA content of polyploid nuclei is proportional to the number of sets of chromosomes present; i.e., tetraploid nuclei can be shown to have twice as much DNA as diploid cells, and so on.

***Replication of DNA.*** Because DNA is the genetic material, its mode of increase should be such as to *replicate* exactly. Much of what we know about DNA replication comes from the work of Kornberg and his colleagues. In 1960, Kornberg succeeded in synthesizing DNA in vitro using a small amount of DNA from *Escherichia coli* as a priming agent, plus the cellular enzyme DNA polymerase. However, this synthetic DNA was biologically inactive. Then, in 1967, several research teams independently discovered a "joining enzyme" which is required to close the bacterial or phage DNA into a circular pattern. Using DNA polymerase, the joining enzyme, and natural, single-stranded DNA from phage $\phi$X174, Kornberg and his associates (1967) electrified both scientists and nonscientists by reporting the synthesis of biologically active $\phi$X174 DNA of some 6,000 nucleotides. Infection of susceptible bacterial cells with this synthetic DNA resulted in replication of $\phi$X174 particles identical with natural phage and lysis of the host cells in the usual fashion.

Kornberg has suggested a model procedure for replication which leaves only a few questions unanswered. Under this *strand separation theory*, replication is *semiconservative*. The two nucleotide strands separate by breakage of the hydrogen bonding between purine-pyrimidine pairs so that the molecule begins "unzipping" into a Y-shaped figure. At the same time an enzymatic addition of complementary nucleotides (which must be available in the nucleus) by phosphodiester bonds takes place. The enzyme responsible has been discovered; it is *DNA polymerase*. It acts by adding a 5'-deoxyribonucleotide triphosphate to the 3'-hydroxyl end of the primer strand as suggested in Fig. 14-15. The base of the newly added triphosphate is then spontaneously hydrogen bonded to the complementary base of the primer strand. A phosphodiester bond is then made between the 3'-OH group of the newly added nucleotide and the 5'-OH of the next arriving one, with inorganic phosphate being split off as pyrophosphate. Thus, new and complementary nucleotides are added to the 5'-3' strand from the 3' toward the 5' end of the template strand.

We know that the result is two molecules of DNA, each exactly like the original in nucleotide pairs (if no "errors" have occurred) and each containing one "old" and one "new" sugar-phosphate strand. But there remains the problem of how, since the sugar-phosphate strands are antiparallel, the 3'-5' strand is added to as the DNA molecule unwinds and separates. As described in the preceding paragraph, only the 5'-3' strand can be replicated by the action of DNA polymerase. Either (1) the 3'-5' strand must await the complete unwinding of the molecule before synthesis can occur, (2) DNA polymerase

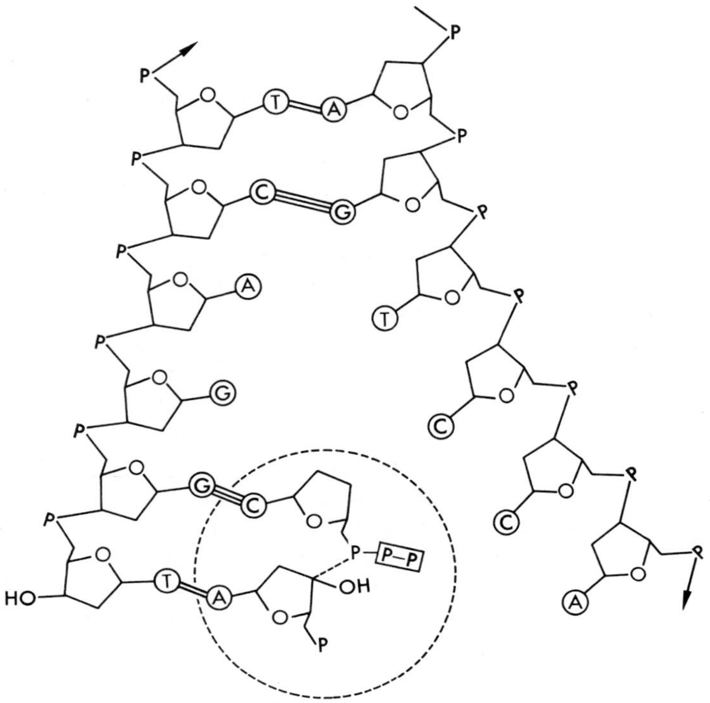

FIGURE 14-15. *Replication of DNA takes place by addition of complementary deoxyribonucleotides to the 5'-3' strand from the 3' end toward the 5' end of the template strand. For simplicity, such addition is shown for only one strand. See text for details.*

acts somewhat differently in vivo as compared to in vitro, (3) another enzyme, not presently identified, may bring about synthesis on the 3'-5' strand, or (4) whereas synthesis on the 5'-3' strand is smoothly continuous in the 3'-5' direction, synthesis in the other (3'-5') strand occurs in pulses, a few nucleotides at a time, in the 3'-5' direction. The problem is compounded by the requirement that the DNA molecule must, under the procedure described, make one complete rotation for every ten nucleotides synthesized. In the circular molecules of bacteria, for example, the entire closed molecule must then rotate once for every ten base replications. This would be no mean feat; the DNA of *Escherichia coli* is calculated to consist of about $4 \times 10^6$ nucleotide pairs! The mechanics would be simplified to a degree if, for instance, temporary breaks were to develop at intervals in the two strands, but there is no evidence that this occurs. At present we can only point out that the problem simply has not been solved at the molecular level.

Whatever the precise details of the operation of the copying mechanism, its speed and accuracy are quite high. The biologically active DNA of phage $\phi$X174 synthesized by Kornberg and his colleagues (page 285) behaved in all respects like native phage DNA, yet it consists of about 6,000 nucleotides. Speed in vitro has been reported as roughly 500 to 1,000 nucleotides per minute, but in vivo speeds as high as 100,000 per minute have been calculated.

Single-stranded viruses such as $\phi$X174 cannot, of course, follow exactly the procedure just outlined. The single strand present in the infective phage serves as a template in the host cell for synthesis of a complementary strand, forming a double-stranded molecule (the *replicative* form) which replicates many times. Finally, however, the replicative form begins to produce only single (infective) strands, which are then assembled within protein shells as mature phage and released (Sinsheimer et al., 1962).

However, in a pair of papers, Baltimore (1970) and Temin and Mizutani (1970) describe evidence that certain RNA tumor viruses (e.g., Rous sarcoma virus and Rauscher mouse leukemia virus) must either produce or induce an enzyme (RNA-dependent DNA polymerase) that catalyzes synthesis of DNA from an RNA template. Temin and Mizutani point out that " if the present results and Baltimore's results with Rauscher leukemia virus are upheld, they will constitute strong evidence that the DNA provirus hypothesis is correct and that RNA tumour viruses have a DNA genome when they are in cells and an RNA genome when they are in (virus particles)." Thus, replication of at least these RNA viruses would take place through a DNA intermediate rather than through an RNA intermediate as described for other RNA viruses. Furthermore, this discovery may be expected to throw considerable light on carcinogenesis by RNA viruses, as well as eventually to elucidate the process of transcription in general.

Under the strand separation hypothesis, each newly replicated double helix must consist of one " old " strand and one " new " one. By a series of ingenious experiments, Meselson and Stahl (1958) showed that this does, indeed, occur. Bacteria were cultured for some time in a medium containing only the heavy isotope of nitrogen, $N^{15}$, until all the DNA should be labeled with heavy nitrogen. These cells were next removed from the $N^{15}$ medium, washed, and transferred to a medium all of whose nitrogen was the usual isotope, $N^{14}$. After one bacterial generation, a sample of cells was removed, and the DNA extracted. All DNA which replicated once in $N^{14}$ medium should be " hybrid "—that is, consist of one strand whose nitrogen is all $N^{15}$ (" old ") and one in which the nitrogen should be all $N^{14}$ (" new "), as suggested in Fig. 14-16.

Differentiation between $N^{14}$-DNA and $N^{15}$-DNA is readily made by *density gradient centrifugation*. The now generally employed technique was developed by Meselson, Stahl, and Vinograd. In it, particles of different densities (like $N^{14}$-DNA and $N^{15}$-DNA) are suspended in a concentrated solution of the salt of a highly soluble heavy metal like cesium chloride and subjected to intense centrifugation in an ultracentrifuge. The centrifugal field produces a density gradient in the tube of both the salt and the suspended

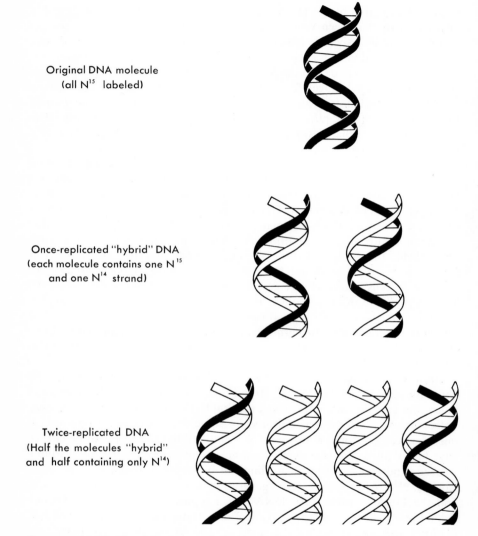

Original DNA molecule
(all $N^{15}$ labeled)

Once-replicated "hybrid" DNA
(each molecule contains one $N^{15}$
and one $N^{14}$ strand)

Twice-replicated DNA
(Half the molecules "hybrid"
and half containing only $N^{14}$)

FIGURE 14-16. *The Meselson and Stahl experiment demonstrating the semiconservative replication of DNA. See text for details. Strands labeled with $N^{15}$ are shaded; $N^{14}$-labeled strands are unshaded.*

particles. After several hours, the gradient reaches an equilibrium in which densities of the solution and the suspended material match at a level in the tube where all of the suspended particles of like density collect in a narrow band (Fig. 14-17). Here the particles will remain, subject only to their

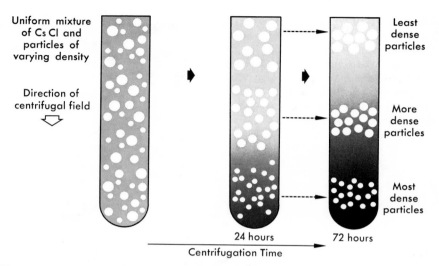

Uniform mixture
of Cs Cl and
particles of
varying density

Direction of
centrifugal field

Least
dense
particles

More
dense
particles

Most
dense
particles

24 hours          72 hours

Centrifugation Time

FIGURE 14-17. *The mechanics of density gradient centrifugation in a cesium chloride solution.* [Adapted from D. Fraser, *Viruses and Molecular Biology*, Macmillan, 1967. By permission.]

diffusibility. It is possible to separate particles differing in density by extremely small amounts with this technique.

When the "hybrid" DNA of Meselson and Stahl was ultracentrifuged in a cesium chloride solution, after some 20 to 50 hours all of this DNA was found by ultraviolet absorption (260 nm) to have taken a position exactly intermediate between that previously established for DNA ($N^{15}$ only) and DNA ($N^{14}$ only). After two cell generations, in which DNA has replicated a second time, half would be expected to contain only $N^{14}$, and half should be "hybrid." Therefore, there should be two bands of DNA in the ultracentrifuge tube, one at the intermediate position, and one at the "all $N^{14}$" position, and this was precisely what was observed.

The results of these elegant experiments are entirely consistent with the strand separation theory (Fig. 14-18), although they do not eliminate such other possibilities as lengthwise extension of the unseparated double strand. But there is good experimental evidence from other sources that this latter type of behavior does not occur. In fact, autoradiographs of DNA from *E. coli* which had been allowed to replicate in radioactive thymidine show that replicating DNA does have a kind of Y-shaped orientation. Cairns (1963, 1966) was able to verify this configuration in *E. coli* by autoradiography which revealed two such Y-shaped regions in the replicating circular DNA molecule (Fig. 14-19). One of these is the "growing point" at which synthesis of new complementary strands is occurring, and the other is the "initiating" or

FIGURE 14-18. *DNA replication by the strand separation theory where "old" and "new" duplexes are assumed to unwind and wind simultaneously as nucleotides are assimilated into newly developing strands.* [Redrawn from D. Fraser, *Viruses and Molecular Biology*, Macmillan, 1967. By permission.]

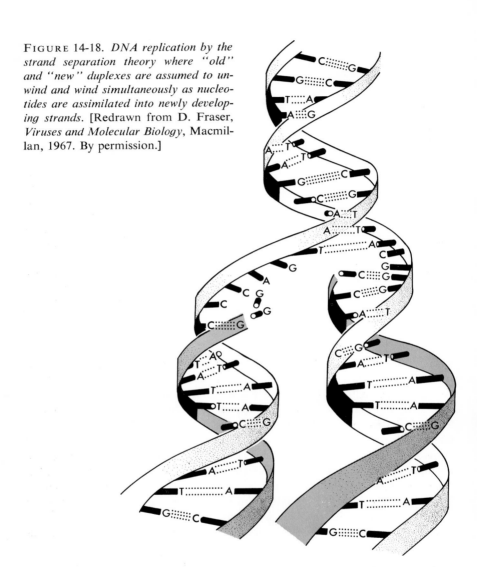

"swivel" point which allows for an untwisting of the original or parent helix.

However, the question of how the strands "unwind" to permit this type of replication is unanswered, and the nature of the triggering mechanism that starts it is unknown. Nevertheless, available evidence is good, if not quite complete; furthermore, you may be able to discern, in the possibility of an occasional error in the replication process, a mechanism for mutation. This we shall explore in Chapter 17.

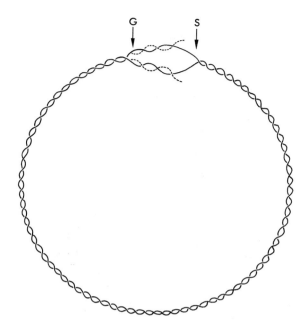

FIGURE 14-19. *Model for replication of circular DNA molecule of* Escherichia coli, *based on work of Cairns (1963, 1966).* S, *swivel or initiating point at which the template molecule untwists;* G, *growing point at which synthesis of new complementary strands takes place. Parent (template) strands are represented by solid lines, the newly synthesized daughter strands by dashed lines.*

**Behavior of DNA in Transformation and Transduction.** We are now in a position to understand what occurs in a bacterial cell that is about to undergo either transformation or transduction. In both, DNA from another bacterial cell enters the cell that is about to be converted. In the first process, naked DNA derived from dead cells, and probably a good bit less than their complete DNA complement, penetrates the living cell. In transduction the process is modified in that the entering DNA is "injected" from a virus. The events occurring in the living cell are undoubtedly similar, but the entering DNA differs in one important respect. Transforming DNA is strictly bacterial DNA, whereas transducing DNA is phage material which includes some genetic material from the previous bacterial host! To understand this, let us look briefly at each process again, as events take place within the living bacterial cell.

If transforming DNA is to bring about transformation, it must be "integrated" into the host DNA. Chilton (1967) has found that each of the two complementary strands of *Bacillus subtilis* DNA has identical transforming capability. She suggests, however, that it is probable that only one is physically integrated into the recipient genome. As was indicated in Chapter 6, two possible mechanisms have been proposed, copy-choice and break-and-exchange. In the former, host DNA, at the time of its replication and during synapsis with the "foreign" DNA, uses itself as a model or template for part of its length, then switches to the transforming DNA for a part of the latter's length, and finally back to itself as suggested in Fig. 6-5. The result would be (1) the original DNA strand, (2) a new DNA strand which is like the original except at those loci where the transforming segment has been copied, and (3) the original transforming segment. At cell division the two complete helices of DNA, the original and the "hybrid," are each apportioned to one of the daughter cells, and the transforming segment is lost. Under this theory recombination would have to take place *during synthesis*, and the recombinant chromosome would contain all the newly synthesized DNA.

In the break-and-exchange method, both original and transforming chromosomes replicate synchronously. Double breaks occur, followed by rejoining so that a double crossover is formed (Fig. 6-5). Early explanations suggested that physical stresses and strains incident to pairing and disjunction produced the breaks, but it appears much more likely that breakage is an enzymatically controlled process, though the cause of such enzyme action is still unknown. There is, for example, no observable twisting of bacterial "chromosomes" or parts thereof around each other in transformation, transduction, or conjugation. Repair of the broken sugar-phosphate strands by reforming the necessary covalent bonds is likewise certainly enzymatically controlled.

In a pair of important papers (Meselson and Weigle, 1961, and Kellenberger et al., 1961) it was clearly shown by appropriate labeling techniques that the break-and-exchange mechanism is substantially correct for bacteriophage. There is no reason to believe that DNA from any other source behaves differently, and the present evidence has been well elaborated by Simon (1965). The sequence of events that follows entry of "foreign" DNA in both transformation and transduction now appears to be:

1. association or pairing of transforming or transducing DNA with corresponding lengths of the recipient's DNA,
2. synchronous replication of both "foreign" (exogenous) and recipient's (endogenous) DNA,
3. enzymatic breaking of both exogenous and endogenous DNA,
4. exchange between exogenous and endogenous DNA by enzymatic repair, resulting in
5. formation of a recombinant DNA molecule which "breeds true" for the traits introduced by transformation or transduction.

Creation of recombinants by conjugation operates intracellularly in the same manner.

In transduction, the DNA of the temperate phage associates with or attaches to that of the host cell as a prophage (Fig. 14-20A) and replicates synchronously with the host DNA. Very occasionally, however, an apparently faulty attachment between prophage and endogenous DNA may occur (Fig. 14-20C) with the result that an exchange of DNA between the two molecules takes place. Later infection of another host bacterium may then introduce

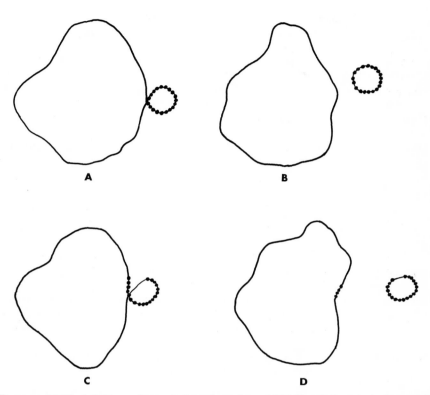

FIGURE 14-20. (A) *Normal association of prophage DNA (beaded) with the bacterial chromosome, and (B) its separation. (C) "Faulty" attachment between prophage and bacterial DNA, resulting in (D) an exchange of DNA between prophage and bacterium. As a consequence of this latter, aberrant association, the phage DNA includes a bit of bacterial DNA and vice versa.* [Redrawn from Werner Braun, *Bacterial Genetics*, W. B. Saunders and Company, 2nd ed., 1965. By permission of author and publisher.]

such a bit of exogenous bacterial DNA into the new host with the result that recombinant progeny are formed. In the previously cited work of Zinder and Lederberg, the *met*⁺ gene from the *met*⁺ *thr*⁻ host is accepted by the phage and later, in the process of transduction, integrated into the DNA of a *met*⁻ *thr*⁺ strain, some of whose progeny are then recombinants of the genotype *met*⁺ *thr*⁺.

Transformation, in particular, provides the identification of the genetic material as a complex molecule, deoxyribonucleic acid. Our next concern will be to relate the gene to this remarkable substance.

### REFERENCES

AVERY, O. T., C. M. MACLEOD, and M. MCCARTY, 1944. Studies on the Chemical Nature of the Substance Inducing Transformation of Pneumococcal Types. *Jour. Exp. Med.*, **79**:137–158. Reprinted in J. A. Peters, ed., 1959. *Classic Papers in Genetics.* Englewood Cliffs, N.J., Prentice-Hall.

BALTIMORE, D., 1970. Viral RNA-Dependent DNA Polymerase. *Nature*, **226**: 1209–1211.

CAIRNS, J., 1963. The Bacterial Chromosome and Its Manner of Replication as Seen by Autoradiography. *Jour. Molec. Biol.*, **6**:208–213.

CAIRNS, J., 1966. The Bacterial Chromosome. *Sci. Amer. Offprints* (1030). San Francisco, W. H. Freeman.

CHILTON, M. F., 1967. Transforming Activity in Both Complementary Strands of *Bacillus subtilis* DNA. *Science*, **157**:817–819.

GOULIAN, M., A. KORNBERG, and R. L. SINSHEIMER, 1967. Enzymatic Synthesis of DNA, XXIV. Synthesis of Infectious Phage $\phi$X-174 DNA. *Proc. Nat. Acad. Sci. (U.S.)*, **58**(6):2321–2328.

GRIFFITH, F., 1928. The Significance of Pneumococcal Types. *Jour. Hygiene*, **27**:113–156.

GROSS, J. D., and L. CARO, 1965. Genetic Transfer in Bacterial Mating. *Science*, **150**:1679–1684.

HERSHEY, A. D., and M. CHASE, 1952. Independent Functions of Viral Protein and Nucleic Acid in Growth of Bacteriophage. *Jour. Gen. Physiol.*, **36**:39–56. Reprinted in G. S. Stent, ed., 1965, 2nd ed., *Papers on Bacterial Viruses.* Boston, Little, Brown.

KELLENBERGER, G., J. L. ZICHICHI, and J. J. WEIGLE, 1961. Exchange of DNA in the Recombination of Bacteriophage. *Proc. Natl. Acad. Sci. (U.S.)*, **47**:869–878.

KORNBERG, A., 1960. Biologic Synthesis of Deoxyribonucleic Acid. *Science*, **131**: 1503–1508.

MESELSON, M. S., and F. W. STAHL, 1958. The Replication of DNA in *Escherichia coli. Proc. Nat. Acad. Sci. (U.S.)*, **44**:671–682.

MESELSON, M., and J. J. WEIGLE, 1961. Chromosome Breakage Accompanying Genetic Recombination in Bacteriophage. *Proc. Natl. Acad. Sci. (U.S.)*, **47**:857–868. Reprinted in G. S. Stent, ed., 1965, 2nd ed., *Papers on Bacterial Viruses.* Boston, Little, Brown.

OZEKI, H., and H. IKEDA, 1968. Transduction Mechanisms. In H. L. Roman, ed., 1968. *Annual Review of Genetics*, volume 2. Palo Alto, California, Annual Reviews, Inc.

SIMON, E., 1965. Recombination in Bacteriophage T-4: A Mechanism. *Science*, **150**:760–763.

SINSHEIMER, R. L., B. STARMAN, C. NAGLER, and S. GUTHRIE, 1962. The Process of Infection with Bacteriophage $\phi$X174, I. Evidence for a Replicative Form. *Jour. Molec. Biol.*, **4**:142–160.

TEMIN, H. M., and S. MIZUTANI, 1970. RNA-Dependent DNA Polymerase in Virions of Rous Sarcoma Virus. *Nature*, **226**:1211–1213.

Tomaz, A., 1969. Some Aspects of the Competent State in Genetic Transformation. In H. L. Roman, ed., 1969. *Annual Review of Genetics*, volume 3. Palo Alto, California, Annual Reviews, Inc.

Watson, J. D., and F. H. C. Crick, 1953. Molecular Structure of Nucleic Acids. A Structure for Deoxyribonucleic Acid. *Nature*, **171**: 737–738. Reprinted in J. H. Taylor, ed., 1965, *Selected Papers on Molecular Genetics*. New York, Academic Press.

Zinder, N. D., and J. Lederberg, 1952. Genetic Exchange in *Salmonella*. *Jour. Bact.*, **64**: 679–699.

## PROBLEMS

**14-1.** What are some of the genetic phenomena that can be investigated in corn, fruit flies, peas, and men which cannot ordinarily be studied in *Neurospora*, bacteria, and viruses?

**14-2.** If one strand of DNA is found to consist of bases A, A, C, G, T, A, C, T, G, C, in that order, what is the sequence on the other strand?

**14-3.** Phage T2 DNA is estimated to consist of about 200,000 base pairs. What is the length in micrometers of its DNA complement? (Note: 1 Å = 0.0001 $\mu$m.)

**14-4.** Determine the molecular weights of (a) adenine; (b) thymine; (c) cytosine; (d) guanine.

**14-5.** What is the molecular weight of the following nucleosides: (a) deoxyadenosine; (b) (deoxy)thymidine; (c) deoxycytidine; (d) deoxyguanosine?

**14-6.** Calculate the molecular weights of each of the following deoxyribonucleotides: (a) deoxyadenylic acid; (b) thymidylic acid; (c) deoxycytidylic acid; (d) deoxyguanylic acid.

**14-7.** Look again at problems 14-3 and 14-6. What is the molecular weight of T2 DNA, if we assume AT and GC pairs to occur with equal frequency?

**14-8.** In this chapter the generation time for virulent T2 phage was given as 22 minutes. It appears that there is no replication of DNA for about the first 6 minutes and that, thereafter, DNA replicates at an exponential rate for 5 minutes, after which the rate of replication declines to the end of the 22-minute period. In that 5-minute period, about 32 phage DNA molecules appear to be formed for each infecting phage particle. At what rate are phage DNA molecules being replicated during this exponential period?

**14-9.** At the rate calculated in problem 14-8, at what rate are nucleotide pairs being synthesized per minute for T2 phage?

**14-10.** Assume that you have just determined the adenine content of the DNA of *Bacillus hypotheticus* to be 20 per cent. What is the percentage of each of the other bases?

**14-11.** If you determined the adenine-guanine content of another species to total 25 per cent, should you believe it?

**14-12.** Note the nucleotide composition listed in Table 14-1 for phage $\phi$X174. Another report in the literature for this virus gives the following nucleotide percentages: A, 26.3; T, 26.4; G, 22.3; C, 22.3. (a) What are the A/T and G/C ratios? (b) What does your answer to part (a) suggest regarding the phage DNA whose composition is given in this problem? (c) How would you account for the considerable difference in these ratios from those given in Table 14-1?

**14-13.** What significance do you think might be attached to the fact that *Euglena* chloroplasts contain DNA and that this chloroplast DNA has a markedly different nucleotide composition from nuclear DNA reported for the same species as given in Table 14-1?

**14-14.** DNA of a species of the microscopic fungus yeast is reported to have a thymine content of 32.6 per cent. The A/T ratio is 0.97. What is the percentage composition for adenine?

**14-15.** If the molecular weight of *Escherichia coli* DNA is taken as $2.7 \times 10^9$ and the average molecular weight of any nucleotide pair is 650, (a) of how many nucleotide pairs would *E. coli* DNA consist, and (b) what would be its length in $\mu$m?

# CHAPTER 15
# Protein Synthesis

**W**ITH its precise replication and transmission, DNA serves to carry genetic information from cell to cell and from generation to generation. We need now to determine the way in which this information is translated into phenotype. Virtually all of the phenotypic effects with which we have been dealing are results of biochemical reactions occurring in the cell. All of these reactions require enzymes, and enzymes are proteins, either wholly or in part. Other phenotypic effects are due directly to the kinds and amounts of nonenzymatic proteins present, e.g., hemoglobin, myoglobin, gamma globulin, insulin, or cytochrome c. Proteins are built up from long-chain linear polymers of amino acid residues (polypeptide chains) and are synthesized almost exclusively in the cytoplasm. Since both polypeptide chains and DNA have linear structure, the problem reduces to the question of how DNA, located primarily in nuclear chromosomes, mediates the synthesis of proteins (on ribosomes) in the cytoplasm. In Chapter 4 we saw several cases that appeared to suggest a connection between genes and enzymes. Let us look briefly at a few additional instances which furnish clear proof of this gene-enzyme relationship before going on to an understanding of its operation.

## Genes and Enzymes

*Phenylalanine Metabolism.*  The groundwork for a functional relationship between genes and enzymes was laid in 1902 when Bateson reported that a rare human defect, *alcaptonuria*, was inherited as a recessive trait. Then in 1909, the English physician Garrod published a book, *Inborn Errors of Metabolism*, which was far ahead of its time in suggesting a relationship between genes and specific biochemical reactions.[1] Alcaptonuria was among the heritable diseases with which he dealt at length. This condition, manifested by a darkening of cartilaginous regions and a proneness to arthritis, results from a failure to break down alcapton (2,5-dihydroxyphenylacetic acid). Alcapton accumulates and is excreted in the urine which turns black upon exposure to the air. By the 1920s it was discovered that the blood of alcaptonurics is deficient in an enzyme which catalyzes the oxidation of alcapton.

[1] See also Knudson (1969).

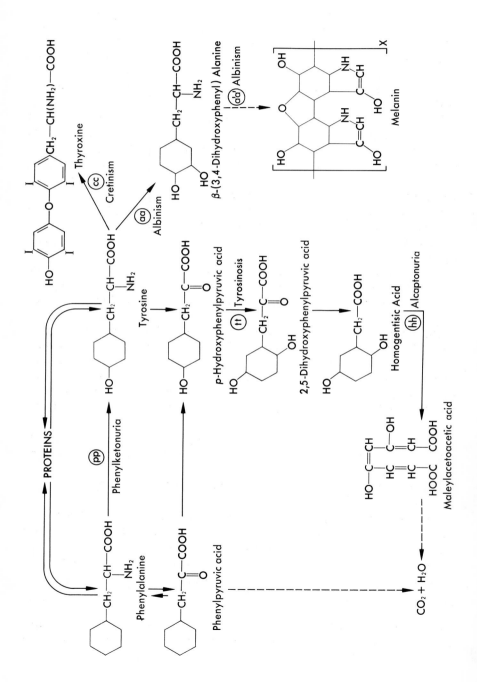

It is now known that this defect is but one of a group, all related to the body's ability to metabolize the essential amino acid phenylalanine. As diagrammed in Fig. 15-1, man receives his supply of this substance from ingested protein. Once in the body, phenylalanine may follow any of three paths. It may be (1) incorporated into cellular proteins, (2) converted to phenylpyruvic acid, or (3) converted to tyrosine, another amino acid.

Persons of genotype *pp* fail to produce the enzyme parahydroxylase, with the result that phenylalanine accumulates in the blood, excesses up to a gram a day being secreted in urine. Such persons are said to have *phenylketonuria* or PKU, which is accompanied by a serious mental and physical retardation. About two thirds of PKU's have an I.Q. below 20, hence are classed as idiots. However, if symptoms are diagnosed very early and the infant put on a diet low in phenylalanine (normal development requires some) for at least the first five years, brain development is more nearly normal.

Another apparently recessive gene, *t*, blocks the conversion of para-hydroxyphenylpyruvic acid to dihydroxyphenylpyruvic acid. This leads to the accumulation of tyrosine, excesses of which are excreted via the urine. This condition is called *tyrosinosis*; no serious symptoms appear to be associated with this defect, although it is known in but one human subject.

Other metabolic blocks indicated in Fig. 15-1, and all caused by recessive genes, lead to *albinism* or to *cretinism*. The latter condition is accompanied by a considerable degree of physical and mental retardation as well as certain thyroid defects. In each case, a particular gene appears to be associated with the production or nonproduction of a specific enzyme which catalyzes a specific reaction. Occurrence or nonoccurrence of the reaction then determines a related phenotypic trait.

Notice that all of these varied defects in the metabolism of phenylalanine are inherited as simple recessives, and all involve failure to produce a given functional enzyme. Heterozygotes do not display the disorder, one "dose" of the normal gene resulting in enough enzyme to permit the reaction to proceed. Because serious inherited metabolic defects such as PKU are (in the absence of highly uncommon mutation) the result of marriage between heterozygotes, it would be very desirable to be able to detect heterozygosity with certainty in phenotypically normal persons. Considerable progress is being made in this direction, and persons heterozygous for PKU can now be detected by the phenylalanine test. Levels of phenylalanine rise higher and

FIGURE 15-1. *Metabolic pathways of the amino acid phenylalanine in man. Different genotypes cause blocks at various points, producing such inherited metabolic disorders as phenylketonuria, tyrosinosis, cretinism, or albinism.*

are maintained longer in *Pp* individuals after administration of a standard dose of this amino acid.

*Tay-Sachs Disease.* Infants normally exhibit a "startle response," stiffening their arms and legs, upon hearing a sudden noise. Continuation of this response beyond the age of a few months may be symptomatic of Tay-Sachs disease which is due to a recessive gene. Homozygous recessives fail to produce the enzyme hexosaminidase A with the result that a lipid, ganglioside $GM_2$, accumulates in the brain. Mental and motor deterioration follow rapidly and death occurs by age four. Although heterozygotes have none of these symptoms, they can be shown to exhibit a reduced level of hexosaminidase A. O'Brien, et al. (1971) report success in diagnosing this defect by amniocentesis during the 16th to 28th week of pregnancy by testing the sloughed fetal cells present in the amniotic fluid for enzyme level. In this way they were able, in 15 different pregnancies, to detect normal homozygous embryos in 7 cases, 2 heterozygotes, and 6 with the Tay-Sachs condition. Five of the latter were therapeutically aborted; tests of various organs of these five showed hexosaminidase A to be absent. The remaining one was born and was developing marked symptoms of the Tay-Sachs disorder by the age of nine months.

The recessive gene responsible is reported to have a frequency of about 0.015 in the Jewish population of New York City, but no more than approximately 0.00015 in non-Jewish individuals.

*Neurospora.* Such studies of metabolic defects in man, important as they are to him, do not provide a set of experimental conditions for adequate testing of the gene-enzyme hypothesis. In fact, most other studies up to the 1940s had concerned themselves largely with morphological characters, many of them based on such complex biochemical reactions as to impede analysis, using genetically inefficient subjects like man. The real breakthrough was furnished by Beadle and Tatum in 1941 and in a series of later reports by them and their colleagues. It occurred to Beadle that an ascomycete fungus, the red bread mold (*Neurospora crassa*), was an ideal organism for this type of investigation. *Neurospora* is easily grown in the laboratory, has a simple life history (Appendix B), in which only the zygote is diploid (hence dominance is not a problem), and it has many easily detected physiological variants. Their aim was to induce metabolic deficiencies by x-irradiation, to identify them by comparing growing ability on minimal and various deficiency media, and so to determine the specific metabolic block. One mutant, for example, was found to be unable to synthesize vitamin $B_1$ (thiamine). Further tests showed this strain was able to synthesize the pyrimidine half of the thiamine molecule, but not the thiazole portion; the critical chemical difference was one of enzyme-producing ability. So the concept of a one gene–one enzyme–one phenotypic effect relationship developed.

## Protein Structure

As indicated earlier, all enzymes are protein, at least in part, and the catalytic property of an enzyme is conferred by its protein makeup, with or without added cofactors. Proteins are large, heavy, generally complex molecules of great variety and biological significance. Their basic structural unit is the amino acid, numbers of which are linked together to form polypeptide chains. Only 20 amino acids are biologically important, although others are necessary in specific instances. Each may be represented by the general structural formula

$$\begin{array}{ccc} H & H & O \\ | & | & \| \\ H\!-\!N\!-\!C\!-\!C\!-\!OH \\ & | \\ & \text{\textcircled{R}} \end{array}$$

where ⓇR represents a side chain. Differences in this side chain determine the specific kind of amino acid. Thus in glycine ⓇR is merely an H atom:

$$\begin{array}{ccc} H & H & O \\ | & | & \| \\ H\!-\!N\!-\!C\!-\!C\!-\!OH \\ & | \\ & H \end{array}$$

and in alanine ⓇR is only a little more complex:

$$\begin{array}{ccc} H & H & O \\ | & | & \| \\ H\!-\!N\!-\!C\!-\!C\!-\!OH \\ & | \\ & CH_3 \end{array}$$

while the addition of a benzene ring to the $CH_3$ side chain of alanine produces phenylalanine:

$$\begin{array}{ccc} H & H & O \\ | & | & \| \\ H\!-\!N\!-\!C\!-\!C\!-\!OH \\ & | \\ & CH_2 \\ & \text{(benzene ring)} \end{array}$$

and so on. The 20 biologically important amino acids are listed in Appendix C. Amino acids are linked by the **peptide bond** with the loss of the equivalent of a molecule of water. The formation of a dipeptide by condensation of two molecules of alanine may be represented thus:

$$
\begin{array}{c}
\text{H} \quad \text{H} \quad \text{O} \qquad\qquad\qquad \text{CH}_3 \\
| \quad\ | \quad\ \| \qquad\qquad\qquad | \\
\text{H}-\text{N}-\text{C}-\text{C}\!-\!(\text{OH} + \text{H})\!-\!\text{N}-\text{C}-\text{C}-\text{OH} \rightarrow \\
| \qquad\qquad\qquad\qquad | \quad\ | \quad\ \| \\
\text{CH}_3 \qquad\qquad\qquad\ \text{H} \quad \text{H} \quad \text{O}
\end{array}
$$

$$
\begin{array}{c}
\text{H} \quad \text{H} \quad \text{O} \qquad\quad \text{CH}_3 \\
| \quad\ | \quad\ \| \qquad\qquad | \\
\text{H}-\text{N}-\text{C}-\text{C}-\text{N}-\text{C}-\text{C}-\text{OH} + \text{H}_2\text{O} \\
| \qquad\quad | \quad\ | \quad\ \| \\
\text{CH}_3 \quad\ \ \text{H} \quad \text{H} \quad \text{O}
\end{array}
$$

in which CONH is the peptide bond. A polypetide is thus a series of **amino acid residues**, joined by peptide bonds, and having an amino end ($NH_2$) and a carboxyl end (COOH).

Protein structural characteristics, then, are based on the number and kind of amino acid residues and, therefore, can occur in infinite variety. In these residues, the side chains confer a number of properties. Some are large and complex, others are small and simple. Some carry a positive charge (lysine, arginine), others a negative charge (glutamic acid, aspartic acid), but most carry none. Differences in bulk and electrical charge along a polypeptide, plus an intricate folding of the protein molecule, impart much of the specificity of enzyme-substrate and antigen-antibody relations.

## Protein Synthesis

### THE NUCLEIC ACIDS

By its infinite variety of possible arrangements of groups of the four nucleotides, DNA is admirably suited for carrying the information needed to direct the synthesis of an almost unlimited number of different proteins. But DNA, except for small amounts in chloroplasts and mitochondria (the significance of which we shall examine in Chapter 19), is located in the eukaryote nucleus, whereas protein synthesis occurs almost entirely in the cytoplasm. Moreover, DNA is not degraded or "used up" in performing its function, and it differs from the end product for which it is responsible. It may be thought of as directing, through some intermediary substance or substances, protein synthesis out in the cytoplasm. In this sense we may refer to DNA as being *conserved*. The answer to the problem of how chromosomally located, conserved DNA, which carries the genetic information, mediates the synthesis of proteins in the cytoplasm is provided by a previously mentioned second nucleic acid, ribonucleic acid (RNA) of several kinds.

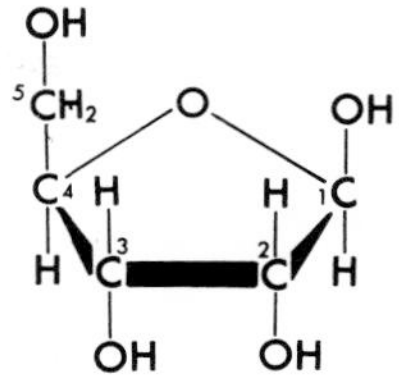

FIGURE 15-2. *Molecular structure of ribose, the sugar of ribonucleic acid. Compare the number 2 carbon with the number 2 carbon of deoxyribose (Fig. 14-10).*

### RIBONUCLEIC ACID

*RNA Structure.* Ribonucleic acid is single stranded, though certain types have a more complicated three-dimensional structure. The "backbone" strand consists of alternating phosphates and sugars, but the latter is ribose (Fig. 15-2) instead of deoxyribose. RNA is synthesized in the nucleus, using one of the strands of DNA as a template. Therefore, the sequence of **ribonucleotides** of RNA should be complementary to that of one of the DNA strands. This it is, except that uracil (Fig. 15-3) replaces thymine, so that RNA bases may be symbolized A, U, G, C. Thus, RNA, produced in the nucleus from DNA, carries the genetic message out into the cytoplasm. Three kinds of RNA, differing in structure and function, are recognized: ribosomal, messenger, and transfer.

*Ribosomes and Ribosomal RNA (rRNA).* The site of protein synthesis is the **ribosome**, a small cytoplasmic particle of some 20 nm (200 Å) in diameter, composed of protein and ribosomal RNA. Ribosomes of *E. coli* are composed of about 64 per cent RNA and 36 per cent protein but of about equal parts of each in animal cells. In eukaryotes the ribosomes are, in the main, attached to the endoplasmic reticulum, but in reticulocytes and in *E. coli* they are scattered through the cell.

Ribosomes are asymmetric aggregates of two subunits which are differentiated by the rates at which they sediment when centrifuged in an appropriate solvent. The rate of sedimentation per unit centrifugal field is referred to as the sedimentation coefficient $(s)$; for most proteins $s$ has a value of between $1 \times 10^{-13}$ and $2 \times 10^{-11}$ second. An $s$ value of $1 \times 10^{-13}$ is denoted as one **Svedberg unit** ($S$). The useful point here is that $s$ (and, therefore, $S$) for any molecule or small particle like a ribosome is determined, for any given temperature and solvent, by its shape, mass, and degree of hydration. The larger the $S$ value, the larger the particle, though the relation is not linear. Ribosomes of bacteria have a sedimentation coefficient of 70S and those of eukaryotes 80S. Each of these is composed of two unequal subunits: 50S and 30S in bacteria, and 60S and 40S in eukaryotes. Ribosomes active in protein synthesis occur in groups called **polysomes** (polyribosomes), held together by messenger RNA (see next section). The structure of ribosomes is not well understood yet, and they appear to be much more complex than heretofore believed, according to Kurland (1970).

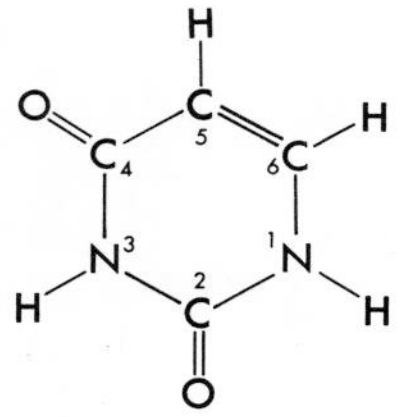

FIGURE 15-3. *Molecular structure of the pyrimidine uracil which replaces thymine in RNA.*

The major RNA content of a cell, often in the 80 to 90 per cent range, is within the ribosomes. This ribosomal RNA (rRNA) is single stranded and of fairly high molecular weight—between approximately $5.5 \times 10^5$ and $1.1 \times 10^6$ in *E. coli*. It is incorporated as ribonucleoprotein at the time of ribosome formation and appears to be synthesized from a small portion of the cell's DNA. Ritossa and Spiegelman (1965) report that rRNA in *Drosophila* is synthesized by the nucleolar organizing regions of the sex chromosomes. In general, it appears that the nucleolus of eukaryotes is the site of rRNA synthesis.

Ribosomal RNA is nonspecific for the amino acid sequence of proteins. Yčas (1969) summarizes three lines of evidence which indicate that rRNA is not specific for the amino acid sequences of polypeptide chains: (1) there is no correlation between the ribonucleotide sequence of rRNA and the type of protein synthesized—that is, although different proteins may be produced characteristically in different cells and in different organisms, there is no significant difference in the rRNA of these cells or organisms; (2) although phage infection results in synthesis of new kinds of protein, ribosomes and rRNA in the bacterial cell remain unchanged; (3) rRNA can be shown to be complementary to only very small sections of DNA (<1 per cent), strongly suggesting that rRNA is too limited in size and variety to carry the information needed for many different proteins.

*Messenger RNA (mRNA).* Specificity for an amino acid sequence is conferred by messenger RNA (mRNA), as shown, for example, by the fact that phage mRNA utilizes ribosomes made before infection to bring about synthesis of phage proteins. This ribonucleic acid directs assembly of various amino acids from the intracellular pool at the ribosome surface where enzymes effect the peptide linkage, forming polypeptide chains. We shall examine this process in detail in the next section.

The process by which mRNA is synthesized enzymatically from one strand of a length of DNA, to which it is complementary (except that, as we have noted, uracil replaces thymine) is referred to as **transcription**. The direction of synthesis has been shown to be from 5′ to 3′. Thus, if the template DNA strand begins with the deoxyribonucleotide sequence A T C G..., the mRNA which it transcribes will begin U A G C.... In transcription, DNA-dependent RNA polymerase attaches to DNA at a certain "start" point and proceeds to transcribe in the $5' \rightarrow 3'$ direction along one strand whose manner of selection is unclear. Successively bonded ribonucleoside triphosphates (ATP, adenosine triphosphate; GTP, guanosine triphosphate; UTP, uridine triphosphate; CTP, cytidine triphosphate) are joined enzymatically with the loss of two phosphates. The mRNA product is separated from the DNA template as transcription proceeds. Transcription ends when RNA polymerase reaches a deoxyribonucleotide "stop" sequence. ("Start" and "stop" signals are described in Chapter 16.) The mRNA then moves rapidly into the cytoplasm where it attaches to the smaller of the two ribosomal subunits, connecting the ribosomes into polysomes.

Messenger RNA in *E. coli* has an average molecular weight of about 500,000. Taking 337 as the average molecular weight of a ribonucleotide, this would mean an average of 500,000/337, or about 1,500 nucleotides if each of the four usual bases is equally represented. As we shall see from an examination of the process of protein synthesis (pages 309–314), the molecular weight, and hence the number of ribonucleotides, of any specific mRNA is closely related to the length of the particular polypeptide for whose synthesis it is responsible.

In those viruses whose genetic material is RNA instead of DNA, e.g., tobacco mosaic virus (TMV), there can be no copying of mRNA on DNA templates. In this case the infecting RNA can act directly as mRNA in a host cell or, through catalysis by the enzyme RNA replicase, produce an RNA whose nucleotide sequence is complementary. This latter molecule, in turn, then serves as the template for RNA that is just like the original infecting molecule.

Messenger RNA of *E. coli* is quite short-lived, functioning for only a few minutes. It appears to retain its stability only so long as it is attached to polysomes, with the result that bacterial cells do not become "cluttered" with large amounts of mRNA. For example, the antibiotic actinomycin-D blocks the synthesis of new mRNA in bacteria; studies using actinomycin-treated bacteria indicate that bacterial mRNA is usable only some ten to twenty times. Therefore, if different "species" of mRNA can be selectively produced (see pages 323–328), the cell is able to produce a variety of proteins at different times and under different conditions. On the other hand, mRNA that is associated with hemoglobin production in reticulocytes may persist for a much longer period, even after degeneration of the cell nucleus. In most cases, mRNA appears to be continuously produced, used, and degraded although the degradation mechanism is unknown.

*Transfer RNA (tRNA).* The structure of transfer RNA is much better understood than that of either rRNA or mRNA, and the literature on this molecule has become rather voluminous. Still, some questions remain to be answered.

The tRNA molecule has several unusual characteristics. Its low molecular weight indicates that it has no more than about 80 ribonucleotides. It is thus

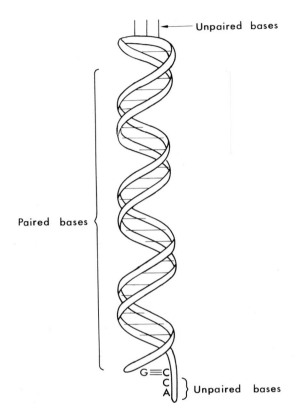

Unpaired bases

Paired bases

G≡C
C
A } Unpaired bases

FIGURE 15-4. *Early model of transfer RNA in which it was proposed that single stranded tRNA is helically arranged and doubled back through pairing of complementary bases, except for a terminal —C—A (which serves as an attachment point for an activated amino acid) and three others which "recognize" three complementary bases on mRNA.*

much smaller than either rRNA or mRNA. There are many "species" of tRNA (the significance of this fact is described later in this chapter), and nucleotide sequences for several different transfer RNA molecules are known (Holley and others, 1965; Madison, Everett, and Kung, 1966). Alanine tRNA of yeast consists of 77 nucleotides; yeast tyrosine tRNA has 78. Known tRNA molecules include a rather large variety of unusual bases, most of them methylated (Fig. 15-5). The majority of the usual bases are paired by hydrogen bonds, resulting in a particular three-dimensional shape. Early accounts suggested an *apparent* double helix produced by internal pairing of complementary bases, the whole being somewhat like a twisted hairpin (Fig. 15-4). More recent reports (Lake and Beeman, 1967; Dayhoff and Eck, 1968; Madison et al., 1966; Holley et al., 1965), some of them making use of x-ray scattering techniques, make it clear that tRNA molecules may have either three or four lobes depending on the sequence and number of nucleotides, giving them something of a cloverleaf shape. Madison's two-dimensional models are shown in Fig. 15-5 and a generalized diagram in Fig. 15-6.

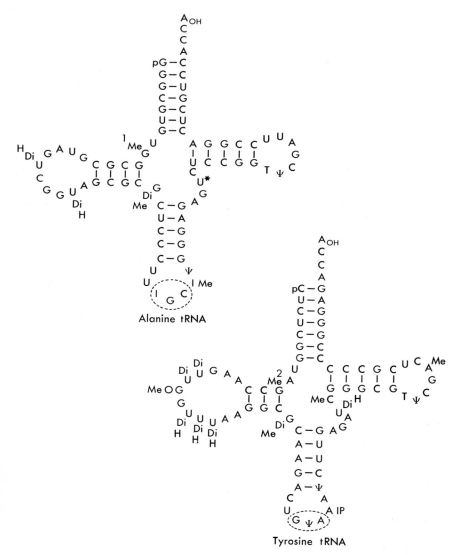

FIGURE 15-5. *"Cloverleaf"  model structure for yeast alanine tRNA and tyrosine tRNA. Note that internal pairing is far from complete, and a terminal —A—C—C—A occurs in each molecule. A large number of "unusual" bases, such as ψ, pseudouridine, occurs. The presumed anticodon (see text) is enclosed by the dashed oval.* [Courtesy Dr. J. T. Madison, USDA Agricultural Research Service, Ithaca, N.Y. Reprinted, with author's revisions, from *Science*, **153**: 531–534, by permission. Copyright 1966 by the American Association for the Advancement of Science.]

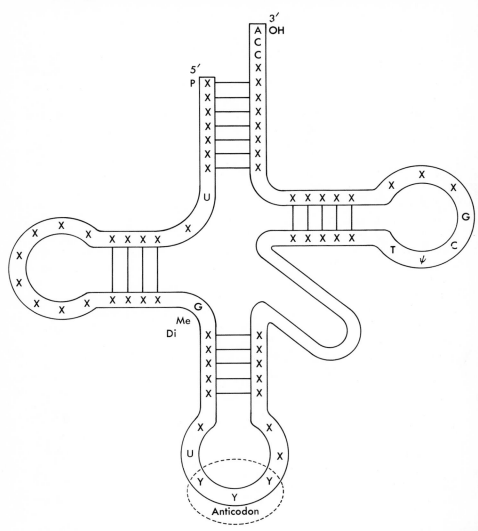

FIGURE 15-6. *Generalized two-dimensional cloverleaf model of tRNA, based on analyses of several yeast tRNA molecules by various investigators. The left lobe includes 8 to 12 unpaired bases, the lower lobe 7 (of which the 3 central ones are believed to be the anticodon), the upper right lobe also 7, and the lower right several unpaired bases that differ in number from one species of tRNA to another, or may even be entirely absent. Note the common 3' terminal -CCA, the TΨCG in the bottom of the upper right lobe, the "anticodon-U" (here YYYU) in the lower lobe, the DiMeG between the lower and left lobes, and the U as the first unpaired base on the 5' strand. As diagrammed here, the anticodon is read from right to left (3' to 5'). The number of paired bases in each lobe shown here appears to be constant for all tRNA species so far reported. (A = adenosine, C = cytidine, G = guanosine, T = ribothymidine, U = uridine, Ψ = pseudouridine, DiMeG = dimethylguanosine, Y = any base of the anticodon.)*

There are three common characteristics of this cloverleaf configuration: (1) the 3′ end carries a terminal −CCA sequence; (2) the "bottom" lobe includes a group of (three) unpaired bases (the *anticodon*) which is believed to permit complementary pairing of tRNA with mRNA during protein synthesis; (3) a TΨCG sequence in the "right" loop. Moreover, most of the tRNAs so far investigated carry a dimethylguanosine (DiMeG) in the "corner" between the "left" and lowermost lobes.

Transfer RNA is transcribed from a number of different sites on one strand of DNA. However, two kinds of enzymatic modifications occur after transcription: (1) the terminal −CCA is added, and (2) unusual and methylated nucleosides are incorporated. Transfer RNA occurs in both "active" and "inactive" forms, the latter lacking the 3′ terminal −CCA. Roles of the TΨCG sequence and the DiMeG are not yet established, but certain of the rare nucleosides, being unable to form hydrogen bonds with other nucleosides, are responsible for the formation of the lobes. Any other functions of the rare bases are not understood.

Present evidence favors the belief that all tRNA molecules terminate at one end with C-C-A (cytosine-cytosine-adenine), with adenine being the base at the extreme end. The other end of the ribose-phosphate strand appears usually to terminate in a guanine,[1] which may be hydrogen bonded to the fifth base from the other terminus.

## MINIMUM NECESSARY MATERIALS

The stage is now set for us to examine the role of each of these components in protein synthesis. Success in synthesizing proteins in cell-free systems, to be described, shows that the minimal necessary equipment is as follows:

1. Amino acids
2. Ribosomes (containing rRNA)
3. mRNA
4. tRNA
5. Enzymes
   (a) Amino acid activating system
   (b) Peptide polymerase system
6. Adenosine triphosphate (ATP) as an energy source
7. Guanosine triphosphate (GTP)

## POLYPEPTIDE SYNTHESIS

The first critical step in **translation**, i.e., the specification by mRNA of the sequence of amino acid residues in a polypeptide chain, involves the transport of amino acids from an intracellular pool to the ribosomes where

---

[1] Madison and his colleagues (1966) find cytosine at this end of tyrosine tRNA from yeast.

they are assembled into polypeptide chains which are then assembled into proteins elsewhere in the cytoplasm. Some of these amino acids are synthesized in human cells, but others (the *essential* amino acids, Appendix C) cannot be, and must be supplied by the diet. Transfer of amino acids to the ribosome surfaces is accomplished by tRNA and occurs in several stages.

*Amino Acid Activation.*    Each of the 20 kinds of amino acids must be *activated* before it can attach to its tRNA. In activation, an enzyme (amino acyl synthetase) catalyzes the reaction of a specific amino acid with adenosine triphosphate (ATP) to form amino acyl-adenosine monophosphate (amino acyl adenylate) and pyrophosphate:

$$AA + ATP \xrightarrow{\text{amino acyl synthetase}} AA \sim AMP + \text{pyrophosphate}$$

The amino acyl adenylate (AA $\sim$ AMP) is referred to as an activated amino acid.

As many as 20 different amino acids can be involved; hence each cell must have at least 20 different kinds of amino acyl synthetases. By its architecture, each kind of enzyme molecule must "recognize" and be able to fit with a particular amino acid. The specificity of the binding of synthetase to amino acid is dependent upon the structure of the latter's side group, though there is not a great size difference between side groups of, for example, glycine and alanine. In fact, one estimate is that the frequency of wrong insertions may be as high as 1 in 1,000.

The activated amino acid, however, is strongly attached to its enzyme and cannot, in this condition, be joined with another to begin formation of a polypeptide chain. This process requires transfer of the activated amino acid to the ribosomes.

*Transfer of Activated Amino Acid to tRNA.*    The same amino acyl synthetase that catalyzed the activation of the amino acid next attaches to a receptor site at the terminal adenine ribonucleotide of a particular tRNA molecule. Note that the enzyme must be able to bind specifically to both a particular amino acid and to a particular transfer RNA. Therefore, in addition to 20 different kinds of synthetases, each cell must have at least 20 different tRNA species. Evidence indicates that there are several instances in which at least two different tRNA molecules have some degree of specificity for the same amino acid; this will be elaborated in the next chapter on the genetic code.

The basis for specificity between the amino acyl synthetase and a particular tRNA is not yet understood. All active tRNA molecules have the same 3' terminal $-$CCA group. The activated amino acid is presumed to form an ester linkage with one of the hydroxyl groups in the ribose of the terminal adenylic acid. "Recognition" may reside in certain nonterminal nucleotides, and the specific structural configuration of tRNA and/or the particular amino acyl synthetase. In any event, there are at least 20 "species" of tRNA (and probably more), each recognizing in an undetermined way a particular activated amino acid. The 20 or more different kinds of amino acyl synthetases must, therefore, be capable of attaching to their own amino acids as well as to the proper tRNA.

*Assembly of Polypeptides.* Following amino acid activation and binding to transfer RNA, the tRNA-enzyme-amino acid complex diffuses to the ribosomes where actual assembly into polypeptide chains occurs. Experimental evidence indicates that mRNA of several hundred to several thousand ribonucleotides is reversibly bound to the smaller subunit of each ribosome and connects a number of ribosomes into a polysome. On the other hand, the larger ribosomal subunit serves as the brief attachment site for 2 or 3 molecules of tRNA. Distance between successive ribosomes along an mRNA strand is of the order of 5 to 15 nm (50 to 150 angstrom units). The ribosomes and mRNA then appear to move relative to each other, adding an amino acid each time the ribosome passes a new group of three mRNA nucleotides. Incorporation of additional molecules of amino acid is accomplished by the arrival of a succession of tRNA-enzyme-amino acid complexes at the mRNA-ribosome surface, a group of three unpaired bases of a tRNA molecule (its **anticodon**) pairing briefly with three complementary nucleotides of mRNA (the **codon**). Therefore, for example, only a tRNA with the anticodon UUU can insert its amino acid at the location of the mRNA codon AAA. However, this statement must be modified a bit for, as we will see shortly, pseudouridine also pairs complementarily with adenine. (Rationale for codons and anticodons of *three* nucleotides is developed in the next chapter.)

Thus, a tRNA molecule with its specific amino acid aligns on the mRNA molecule, its anticodon pairing briefly with the complementary codon of mRNA. A second tRNA then arrives to pair with the next codon as mRNA moves along the ribosomes. Immediately, the first amino acid is separated enzymatically from its tRNA and linked, also enzymatically, with the next incoming amino acid by means of a peptide bond. Momentarily, then, the growing polypeptide chain attaches to the incoming tRNA and is "passed along" to successively arriving tRNAs. The first tRNA is thereby released from mRNA and freed to function again in the same manner. The process continues in this way until a specific polypeptide chain, composed of a particular sequence of amino acid residues is formed. Upon its completion the polypeptide is released enzymatically from the polysome, though the exact mechanism is unknown. The then free ribosomes attach to a new starting point on mRNA. It should be noted that each ribosome has at least two sites for attachment of tRNA, one for the incoming molecule carrying an activated amino acid and another for binding the preceding tRNA which is carrying the developing polypeptide chain. The entire process is represented diagrammatically in Fig. 15-7.

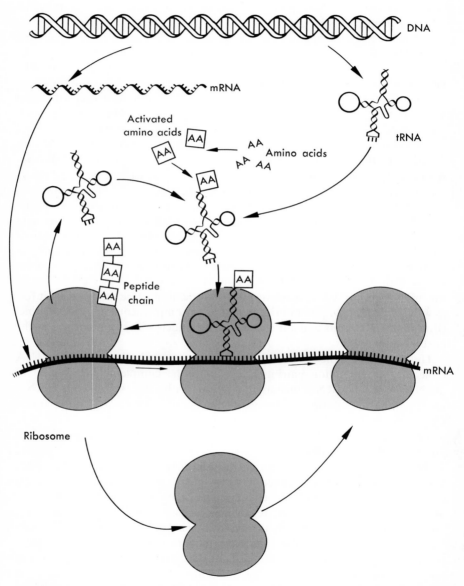

FIGURE 15-7. *A model schematic representation of protein synthesis in a living cell, based upon findings to date. AA = amino acid;* $\boxed{AA}$ = *activated amino acid. See text for details.*

The polypeptide chain grows by stepwise addition of individual amino acids, beginning at the 5′ terminal of mRNA, with the amino end of each succeeding amino acid linked enzymatically to the carboxyl end of the preceding one. Peptide chain growth stops when a particular group of (three) mRNA nucleotides is reached. The matter of chain-initiating and chain-terminating codons is discussed in the next chapter.

The presence of unusual bases in tRNA raises the question of their complementarity with the usual bases of mRNA. Reference to Fig. 15-5 indicates the anticodon of yeast alanine tRNA is likely to be CGI, and that of yeast tyrosine AΨG. Experimental work shows that inosine (I) pairs with cytosine, and pseudouridine (Ψ) with adenine (see also pages 324 and 325). The corresponding mRNA codons for these two yeast tRNA anticodons therefore are GCC and UAC, respectively.

***Summary of Polypeptide Synthesis.*** The process just described is represented diagramatically in Fig. 15-7. The following steps are involved:

1. Amino acid activation.
2. Coupling of the activated amino acid to its specific tRNA (charging of tRNA).
3. Diffusion of charged tRNAs to the mRNA-ribosome complex.
4. Transient binding of a charged tRNA to the mRNA site at which the tRNA anticodon is complementary to the appropriate codon of mRNA.
5. Insertion, by peptide bond formation, of the amino acid carried by this most recently arrived tRNA into the growing polypeptide chain (which is at that time temporarily bound to the preceding tRNA at the latter's binding site on mRNA).
6. Transfer of the entire growing chain (whose length has now been increased by one amino acid residue) to the just arrived tRNA and freeing of the preceding tRNA from the mRNA-ribosome surface.
7. Advance of mRNA by one codon relative to the ribosome, thus permitting the next amino acid to be added by the same repeating process.
8. Release of completed polypeptide from the mRNA-ribosome surface.

In vitro synthesis of phage φf2 protein coat begins with the sequence alanine-serine-asparagine-phenylalanine-, but is preceded by N-formylmethionine. This is methionine with a formyl group

attached to the amino group; it blocks the formation of a peptide bond with the carboxyl group of another amino acid. Present evidence indicates that polypeptide synthesis begins with N-formylmethionine which usually is later removed enzymatically.

Note that proteins are synthesized in one direction only (from amino to carboxyl end). Furthermore, regardless of the terminal codon for one chain, a second polypeptide encoded by the same mRNA could not become linked to the first because the initial amino acid of the second polypeptide contains a blocked amino group.

The entire process takes place with considerable rapidity. In hemoglobin production, for example, one polypeptide chain of some 150 amino acids required about 80 seconds for construction. This means addition of one amino acid in a little more than 0.5 second!

### IN VITRO PROTEIN SYNTHESIS

A superb confirmation of the general outline of protein synthesis is furnished by the work of Von Ehrenstein and Lipmann (1961), who succeeded in synthesizing hemoglobin in a cell-free system. Such a system included

1. Ribosomes in the form of polysomes from rabbit reticulocytes (immature red blood cells in which hemoglobin is almost the only protein synthesized) which included mRNA for rabbit hemoglobin.
2. An energy-yielding triphosphate.
3. tRNA from the bacterium *Escherichia coli*, previously charged with amino acids using *E. coli* activating enzymes.

The most exciting aspect of this work is that Von Ehrenstein and Lipmann were able to synthesize a protein of one species using its mRNA and the tRNA of a vastly different organism. Not only is universality of this general mechanism of protein synthesis strongly suggested, but the fundamental "kinship" of all living organisms through their DNA seems inescapable. It is abundantly clear that DNA is the genetic material of all living organisms (and many viruses, too) and that it is an information vocabulary of four "letters" (adenine, thymine, guanine, and cytosine). Differences among species thus reside in the sequences of the nucleotide "letters" to be formed into certain code "words" (amino acids), which will be combined sequentially into protein "sentences" and phenotypic "paragraphs."

But there is still another problem in translation that we must explore, namely just how the sequence of nucleotides in mRNA is responsible for the particular sequence of amino acid residues of a given polypeptide and just how synthesis of such chains starts and stops. In short, we are ready now to examine the nature of the *genetic code*. This we will do in the next chapter.

### REFERENCES

BEADLE, G. W., and E. L. TATUM, 1941. Genetic Control of Biochemical Reactions in *Neurospora. Proc. Nat. Acad. Sci. (U.S.)*, **27**:499–506. Reprinted in J. A. Peters, ed., 1959, *Classic Papers in Genetics*. Englewood Cliffs, N.J., Prentice-Hall.

DAYHOFF, M. O., and R. V. ECK, 1968. *Atlas of Protein Sequence and Structure*, 1967–1968. Silver Springs, Maryland, National Biochemical Research Foundation.

HOLLEY, R. W., J. APGAR, G. A. EVERETT, J. T. MADISON, M. MARQUISEE, S. H. MERRILL, J. R. PENSWICK, and A. ZAMIR, 1965. Structure of a Ribonucleic Acid. *Science*, **147**:1462–1465.

KNUDSON, A. G., JR., 1969. Inborn Errors of Metabolism. In H. L. Roman, ed., 1969. *Annual Reviews of Genetics*, volume 3. Palo Alto, California, Annual Reviews, Inc.

KURLAND, C. G., 1970. Ribosome Structure and Function Emergent. *Science*, **169**:1171–1177.

LAKE, J. A., and W. W. BEEMAN, 1967. Yeast Transfer RNA: A Small-Angle X-Ray Study. *Science*, **156**:1371–1373.

MADISON, J. T., G. A. EVERETT, and H. KUNG, 1966. Nucleotide Sequence of a Yeast Tyrosine Transfer RNA. *Science*, **153**:531–534.

O'BRIEN, J. S., S. OKADA, D. L. FILLERUP, M. L. VEATH, B. ADORNATO, P. H. BRENNER, and J. G. LEROY, 1971. Tay-Sachs Disease: Prenatal Diagnosis. *Science*, **172**:61–64.

RITOSSA, F. M., and S. SPIEGELMAN, 1965. Localization of DNA Complementary to Ribosomal RNA in the Nucleolus Organizer Region of *Drosophila melanogaster*. *Proc. Nat. Acad. Sci. (U.S.)*, **53**:737–745.

SILVESTRI, L., 1970. *RNA-Polymerase and Transcription*. New York, John Wiley & Sons (Interscience Division).

VON EHRENSTEIN, G., and F. LIPMANN, 1961. Experiments on Hemoglobin Biosynthesis. *Proc. Nat. Acad. Sci. (U.S.)*, **47**:941.

YČAS, M., 1969. *The Biological Code*. (Neuberger, A., and E. L. Tatum, eds., *Frontiers of Biology*, volume 12.) New York, American Elsevier.

## PROBLEMS

**15-1.** Could PKUs be helped by administration of parahydroxylase?

**15-2.** If alcaptonurics were given large quantities of parahydroxyphenylpyruvic acid would they excrete larger quantities of alcapton?

**15-3.** Would increased intake of maleylacetoacetic acid increase the excretion of alcapton?

Use the following information in answering the next four problems.

All microorganisms utilize thiamine (vitamin $B_1$) in their metabolism. Final steps in its synthesis involve enzymatic synthesis of a thiazole and of a pyrimidine, followed by the enzymatic combination of these two substances into thiamine. Consider the following mutant strains of *Neurospora*: strain 1 requires only simple inorganic raw materials in order to synthesize thiamine; strain 2 grows only if thiamine or thiazole is supplied; strain 3 requires thiamine or pyrimidine; strain 4 grows if thiamine or both thiazole and pyrimidine are supplied. Call the enzyme responsible for synthesis of thiazole from its precursor *enzyme "a,"* that catalyzing formation of pyrimidine *enzyme "b,"* and the enzyme catalyzing the combining of thiazole and pyrimidine into thiamine *enzyme "c."*

**15-4.** Which of the above strains is protrophic?

**15-5.** Which enzyme or enzymes is strain 2 incapable of producing?

**15-6.** Which enzyme or enzymes cannot be produced by strain 4?

**15-7.** If we assign gene symbol *a* to any strain incapable of producing enzyme "a," symbol *b* to strains not making enzyme "b," and symbol *c* to those not producing enzyme "c," with + signs denoting the ability to produce a given enzyme, each strain can be represented by 3 gene symbols, plus signs and/or letters in the appropriate grouping. Give the genotype, according to this plan, for each of the four strains listed above.

**15-8.** A short segment from a long DNA molecule has this sequence of nucleotide pairs (shown without the helical configuration):

$$\text{G T C T T T A C G C T A} \ldots$$

$$\text{C A G A A A T G C G A T} \ldots$$

If the "lower" DNA strand serves as the template for mRNA synthesis, what will be the sequence of nucleotides on the latter?

**15-9.** A sedimentation coefficient is calculated as $2 \times 10^{-11}$ second. Express this in Svedberg units.

**15-10.** Assume 102 nucleotide pairs of DNA to be responsible for transcription of a particular mRNA molecule. What is the length of that mRNA molecule in (a) Angstrom units; (b) micrometers (microns)?

**15-11.** Assume a certain tRNA molecule to consist only of the "usual" ribonucleotides cytidylic, uridylic, adenylic, and guanylic acids. You determine the molecular weight of that tRNA molecule to be about 27,000. (a) Of how many ribonucleotides does it consist? (b) How long would this molecule be in micrometers (microns) if it were laid out in a straight line?

**15-12.** A certain mRNA codon is determined to be AUG. (a) What is the tRNA anticodon if no "unusual" bases are involved? (b) What is the DNA sequence that is responsible for this mRNA codon?

**15-13.** Differentiate between transcription and translation.

# CHAPTER 16

# *The Genetic Code*

I N preceding chapters we have established that

1. DNA is *the* genetic material in all but some viruses (in which it is RNA);
2. DNA is responsible for phenotypic expression through transcription of mRNA from DNA templates; and
3. Specific nucleotide sequences on mRNA interact with complementary base groups of tRNA to translate mRNA base sequences into poly-peptides on ribosomal surfaces.

Studies of phenylalanine metabolism, the Tay-Sachs syndrome, and of nutritionally deficient strains of the fungus *Neurospora* (Chapter 15) make it clear that the occurrence of a particular biochemical reaction depends upon the presence of a specific enzyme which, in turn, is due to the action of a particular genetic locus. Originally described as " one gene—one enzyme," the problem quickly developed into one of determining the precise function of genes in enzyme (therefore, protein) synthesis. Exploration of hemoglobin variants in man (Chapter 17), for example, soon indicated that genes serve to specifiy the amino acid sequence of proteins (and therefore their precise structure), rather than to act merely as " switches " determining whether protein will or will not be produced.

Thus emerges the concept that the classical particulate gene is really a sequence of nucleotides with the relationship *gene → polypeptide → pheno-type*. But this concept raises two fundamental questions: (1) what sequence of how many mRNA nucleotides *codes* for a particular amino acid and for a given polypeptide, i.e., what is the **genetic code**, and (2) in these terms, then, just how many nucleotides equal one gene? The first of these questions we shall explore in this chapter, the second in Chapter 17.

## Problems of the Nature of the Code

Investigators of the genetic code faced many questions concerning its nature. Those which we shall examine in this chapter include:

1. How many nucleotides code for a given amino acid? That is, does a *codon* consist of one, two, three, or more nucleotides?

2. Are codons, whatever their nucleotide number, contiguous, or is there some sort of spacer "punctuation" separating the codons? In other words, is the code *commaless* or not?

3. If a codon is composed of two or more nucleotides, is the code *overlapping* or *nonoverlapping*? That is, in the mRNA nucleotide sequence beginning, for example, AUCGUA..., how many codons are there, AU, CG, UA (nonoverlapping doublet code), or AUC, GUA (triplet, nonoverlapping), or are the codons AU, UC, CG, GU, UA, A– (doublet, overlapping by one base), or AUC, UCG, CGU, GUA, UA–, A––(triplet, overlapping by two nucleotides), or some other arrangement?

4. What is the "*coding dictionary*," that is, precisely which codons code for which amino acids?

5. Is a given amino acid coded for by more than one codon; i.e., is the code *degenerate*?

6. Does, on the other hand, one codon code for more than one amino acid; is the code *ambiguous*?

7. Do the codons of mRNA and the corresponding amino acid residues of polypeptides occur in the same linear order; that is, is the code *colinear*?

8. Are there any codons which serve as "start" or "stop" signals; i.e., are there chain *initiating* and chain *terminating* codons?

9. Finally, is the code *universal* for all organisms? Does, in other words, the same codon signal for the same amino acid in phages, bacteria, corn, fruit flies, and man?

## THE BASIC PROBLEM

The basic problem of the genetic code is that there are 20 amino acids which must be coded for by some sequence of 4 nucleotides in DNA or their complements in mRNA. The nucleotide or nucleotide sequence that codes for a particular amino acid is called a **codon**. If a codon were to consist of only a single base, the genetic code would have to be quite *ambiguous*; that is, the same codon would have to code for different amino acids under different conditions. In other words, how would 4 bases code for 20 amino acids? Codons of 2 bases present the same kind of problem; this provides only $4 \times 4 = 16$ codons for the 20 amino acids. But 3-base groups provide 64 codons, *more* than enough for the number of amino acids involved. However, the system will work if the code is *degenerate* in that several codons code for the same amino acid. From the theoretical viewpoint, such a *triplet code* could include both *sense codons* (those that specify particular amino acids) and *nonsense codons* that do not specify any amino acid. Nonsense codons, might, of course, have some other function, such as signaling "start" or "stop" for polypeptide chain synthesis.

***Triplet Codons.*** The first key to the solution was provided in 1955 by Grunberg-Manago and Ochoa who isolated from bacteria an enzyme, polynucleotide phosphorylase, which catalyzes the polymerization of nucleoside triphosphates into a linear polyribonucleotide sequence, chemically and functionally similar to natural messenger RNA. No template is required by this enzyme and the sequence of ribonucleotides in the resulting polymer is random. Hence, polyribonucleotides containing one, two, three, or all four of the different bases can be tested in vitro for their protein synthesizing ability. To be incorporated into a polypeptide chain, some amino acids require a polyribonucleotide containing only one kind of ribonucleotide (e.g., uridylic acid); others require polyribonucleotides containing two or even three different ones. No amino acid, however, requires all four. This supplies evidence against a four-base code, but does not discriminate among one-, two-, three-, or even five- or six-base codes.

Two other lines of experimental evidence, both dating from 1961, (1) suggested that codons are triplets and (2) permitted the first specific codon assignment. Crick, Barnett, Brenner, and Watts-Tobin (1961) provided a significant clue not only as to the length of the codon but also, as we shall see, to the question of "punctuation" and overlap. To understand the relevance of their elegant experiments we need to digress for a moment to examine one of the important classes of substances that they employed.

***Frame Shifts.*** The acridine dyes (proflavin, acridine orange, and acridine yellow, among others) are substances that bind to DNA and, at least in phages, act as mutagens by causing additions or deletions in the nucleotide sequence during DNA replication. An acridine molecule may become inter-calated between previously adjacent nucleotides, doubling the distance between them. This may either allow later insertion of a new nucleotide during replication, or result in the deletion of a base, thus altering the sequence. Crick and his colleagues studied a number of acridine-induced mutants in the so-called rII region[1] of the DNA of phage T4. In brief, they found that mutant types arose through additions or deletions at any of a large number of sites within the rII region but these may revert to the wild type or a very similar one (pseudo-wild type) through deletions or additions elsewhere in the rII region. That is, in many cases, one mutation may be suppressed by another, particularly if the second change is located relatively close to the first. To illustrate, assume the code is triplet, nonoverlapping, and commaless, and has a repeating deoxyribonucleotide sequence

(transcription →)

$$\overline{\text{TAG}}\ \overline{\text{TAG}}\ \overline{\text{TAG}}\ \overline{\text{TAG}}\ \overline{\text{TAG}} \ldots \tag{1}$$

---

[1] The rII mutants are described more fully in another context in the next chapter.

Now, if the second T (the fourth base) in this hypothetical series is deleted, sequence (1) becomes

$$\overline{TAG}\ \overline{AGT}\ \overline{AGT}\ \overline{AGT}\ \overline{AG-}\ \ldots \qquad (2)$$

A deletion thus alters reading of all following groups; this is termed a *frame shift*. Transcription from the original DNA sequence (1) produces mRNA of repeating AUC codons, determining a peptide consisting only of the amino acid sequence coded for by AUC; and from (2) the codon sequence $\overline{AUC}\ \overline{UCA}\ \overline{UCA}\ \overline{UCA}\ \overline{UC-}$. This could well be expected to result in a change of amino acid composition of the peptide chain beyond the deletion, assuming, of course, that codons AUC and UCA code for different amino acids. We could represent the amino acid of the wild type (1) as aaX aaX aaX aaX ..., but after deletion the mutant type (2) might produce the amino acid sequence aaX aaY aaY aaY ... (a *missense* mutant). On the other hand, it might be possible a priori that UCA codes for *no* amino acid (a *nonsense* mutant).

Now, still carrying this deletion, assume a thymidylic acid (T) to be inserted at a different position in sequence (2), say between the sixth and seventh nucleotides. The DNA sequence then becomes

$$\overline{TAG}\ \overline{AGT}\ \overline{TAG}\ \overline{TAG}\ \overline{TAG}\ \ldots \qquad (3)$$

and the wild type reading is restored with the third triplet; only the second produces a misreading. Insertion of any of the other three nucleotides at the same point produces only a slightly longer faulty segment. Suppose deoxycytidylic acid (C) is inserted instead of thymidylic acid at the same point; the sequence then becomes

$$\overline{TAG}\ \overline{AGT}\ \overline{CAG}\ \overline{TAG}\ \overline{TAG}\ \ldots \qquad (4)$$

Wild type transcription in (4) is restored after two "wrong" triplets instead of one. Thus, an insertion farther down the reading sequence corrects for an earlier deletion, regardless of whether the inserted base is the same as the deleted one or not. A *single frame* shift, therefore, may be expected to result in a protein so altered in amino acid sequence that it is nonfunctional. On the other hand, if the altered reading between two opposing events (e.g., a deletion followed by an insertion) is of small enough magnitude that protein function is not disturbed, then the second event suppresses the first. The closer the points at which these opposing alterations occur, the higher the probability that this suppression will occur. In essence, this is precisely what the work of Crick and his group showed.

We may summarize the findings of Crick and his coworkers in this way (D = deletion; I = insertion):

| Pseudo-wild type | Mutant |
| --- | --- |
| D-I | D |
| I-D | I |
| D-D-D | D-D |
| I-I-I | I-I |
| D-D-D-D-D-D | D-D-D-D |
| | I-I-I-I |
| | D-D-D-D-D |
| | I-I-I-I-I |

*A Triplet, Commaless, Nonoverlapping Code.* Note that several aspects of the genetic code are made clear by these experiments. First, the code is likely to be *triplet* since a single frame shift results in missense, as do two, four or five frame shifts, but pairs of opposite kinds of frame shifts (if not too far apart) restore sense. Likewise, three deletions or three insertions restore sense. Although in a doublet code, for example, one deletion followed by one insertion will also restore sense, such will not always be the case with three (or multiples of three) deletions or insertions. Still other experimental data, to be described shortly, make it clear that the code is, indeed, triplet.

In addition, this kind of restoration of sense sequences clearly suggests that (1) there is no "punctuation" between the codons, that is, each codon is immediately adjacent to the next with no intervening "spacer" bases, and (2) it is *nonoverlapping*. We shall shortly examine some additional grounds against "punctuation." Another line of evidence for nonoverlap arises in the fact that amino acid residues appear to be arranged in completely random sequence when different polypeptide chains are analyzed; no one amino acid always, or even usually, has the same adjacent neighbors. This could be the case only if the code is *nonoverlapping*. If the code did overlap, a given amino acid would always have the same nearest neighbors. An mRNA sequence beginning, for example, A-A-C-C-G-A-G-C-A- . . . consists of three triplets, AAC, CGA, and GCA, which code for asparagine, and arginine, and alanine, respectively (Table 16-1). If the code overlapped by two bases, this sequence of nine letters would consist of the triplets AAC, ACC, CCG, CGA, GAG, AGC, and GCA, coding for asparagine, threonine, proline, arginine, glutamic acid, serine, and alanine. Thus, in that particular sequence of nucleotides, arginine would always be between proline and glutamic acid. This is not the case.

TABLE 16-1   The mRNA Code as Determined in Vitro for *E. coli.* (Degeneracies are shown; ambiguities are omitted.)

| | Codons | Amino acid | | Codons | Amino acid |
|---|---|---|---|---|---|
| AA- | AAU, AAC | Asparagine | UA- | UAU, UAC | Tyrosine |
| | AAA, AAG | Lysine | | UAA | "Ochre"* |
| | | | | UAG | "Amber" * |
| AC- | ACU, ACC, ACA, ACG | Threonine | UC- | UCU, UCC, UCA, UCG | Serine |
| AG- | AGU, AGC | Serine | UG- | UGU, UGC | Cysteine |
| | AGA, AGG | Arginine | | UGA | "Nonsense"* |
| | | | | UGG | Tryptophan |
| AU- | AUU, AUC, AUA | Isoleucine | UU- | UUU, UUC | Phenylalanine |
| | AUG | Methionine | | UUA, UUG | Leucine |
| CA- | CAU, CAC | Histidine | GA- | GAU, GAC | Aspartic acid |
| | CAA, CAG | Glutamine | | GAA, GAG | Glutamic acid |
| CC- | CCU, CCC, CCA, CCG | Proline | GC- | GCU, GCC, GCA, GCG | Alanine |
| CG- | CGU, CGC, CGA, CGG | Arginine | GG- | GGU, GGC, GGA, GGG | Glycine |
| CU- | CUU, CUC, CUA, CUG | Leucine | GU- | GUU, GUC, GUA, GUG | Valine |

* UAA, UAG, and UGA signal polypeptide chain termination.

Moreover, a replacement that involves a single base pair in DNA would, in an overlapping code, affect more than one amino acid. This does not occur; only single amino acids are changed by such "single site" mutations.

## THE CODING DICTIONARY

Once the genetic code was established as a commaless, nonoverlapping, triplet code, the question of which triplets code for which amino acids was pursued vigorously. Nirenberg and Matthaei, in the second of the important 1961 papers, pioneered in efforts to crack the code. It is possible to construct short synthetic polyribonucleotides and to test them in cell-free systems for ability to direct incorporation of specific amino acids into polypeptide chains. Using a mixture of amino acids, with a different one radioactively labeled in each run, in a cell-free suspension derived from *Escherichia coli* (tRNA, ribosomes, ATP, necessary enzymes and, interestingly enough, mRNA from tobacco mosaic virus), these men were able to bring about polypeptide synthesis in vitro. With polyribouridylic acid, for example, they were able to demonstrate the synthesis of a polypeptide consisting only of phenylalanine, even though other amino acids were present. So the mRNA codon for phenylalanine must be UUU.

Testing copolymers of only the ribonucleotides adenylic and cytidylic acids (poly-AC), Nirenberg and Matthaei showed that proline was coded by at least two triplets, one consisting only of cytidylic acid (CCC) and the other of both cytidylic and adenylic acids. Poly-A (AAA) was soon found to code for lysine. These determinations reinforce the concept of a commaless code for, in a code that includes punctuation, U and A would each have to serve both to code for their respective amino acids as well as to function as commas. From this time on the notion of a commaless code won general acceptance.

Testing random copolymers sheds some additional light on the code. When synthetic mRNA is constructed, it is found that the sequence of nucleotides is random, so that the relative frequency of incorporation of particular nucleotides is mathematically determined. Thus, a mixture containing 2 parts uracil to 1 part guanine is found to produce triplets in these combinations:

$$\text{UUU} \quad \tfrac{2}{3} \times \tfrac{2}{3} \times \tfrac{2}{3} = \tfrac{8}{27}$$
$$\text{GGG} \quad \tfrac{1}{3} \times \tfrac{1}{3} \times \tfrac{1}{3} = \tfrac{1}{27}$$
$$\text{UGU} \quad \tfrac{2}{3} \times \tfrac{1}{3} \times \tfrac{2}{3} = \tfrac{4}{27}$$
$$\text{UUG} \quad \tfrac{2}{3} \times \tfrac{2}{3} \times \tfrac{1}{3} = \tfrac{4}{27}$$
$$\text{GUU} \quad \tfrac{1}{3} \times \tfrac{2}{3} \times \tfrac{2}{3} = \tfrac{4}{27}$$
$$\text{GGU} \quad \tfrac{1}{3} \times \tfrac{1}{3} \times \tfrac{2}{3} = \tfrac{2}{27}$$
$$\text{UGG} \quad \tfrac{2}{3} \times \tfrac{1}{3} \times \tfrac{1}{3} = \tfrac{2}{27}$$
$$\text{GUG} \quad \tfrac{1}{3} \times \tfrac{2}{3} \times \tfrac{1}{3} = \tfrac{2}{27}$$

If each of the possible triplets were to code for a different amino acid, then various ones would be incorporated in the proportions shown. Except for the fact that *each* such 3-base group does not code a *different* amino acid, this is essentially what occurs. Use of a synthetic poly-UG, in the relative proportions just given, produced a mixture of polypeptides, of which $\frac{8}{27}$ of the amino acid residues were polyphenylalanine.

In this way it was known that poly-UG containing 2 U : 1 G codes for valine, but the sequence of bases, and therefore the exact codon(s) of those possible, cannot be determined from such random copolymers. Nirenberg and Leder (1965) devised a method by which short-chain polyribonucleotides of known sequence could be obtained. These were introduced into cell-free systems that included ribosomes and a variety of tRNA molecules charged with their amino acids. As in earlier work, one amino acid in each experimental run was labeled with $C^{14}$. Although the messengers used were too short for protein synthesis, two important considerations emerged: (1) little or no binding of tRNA took place in the presence of dinucleotide messengers, but occurred preferentially with trinucleotides, and (2) different sequences of the same three bases stimulated binding of different amino acids. Thus, the triplet nature of the code was again confirmed, and the way opened to develop a complete coding dictionary. The mRNA triplet code, as established principally in cell-free systems prepared from *E. coli*, is shown in Table 16-1. Kurland (1970) refers to the elucidation of the genetic code as "one of the principal triumphs of molecular biology," and Garen (1968) calls it "a notable milestone in biology," as, indeed, it is.

### DEGENERACY

Although the code is extensively degenerate (Table 16-1), a kind of order to this degeneracy can be seen. In many instances it is the first two bases which are the characteristic and critical parts of the codon for a given amino acid, whereas the third may be read only as a purine (e.g. glutamine, CAA and CAG), or only as a pyrimidine (e.g., histidine, CAU and CAC). In other cases, the third position is read merely as any base, for example, AC− for threonine, CC− for proline, and so forth.

Crick (1966) proposed a "*wobble hypothesis*" to describe this lack of specificity in the third base of the codon. If a variety of unusual bases occur at the corresponding position of the tRNA anticodon, pairing capabilities between codon and anticodon are increased by a "wobbly" third base in the codon. Crick has pointed out the pairing rules for the third position (Table 16-2). In addition, pseudouridine ($\Psi$), which occurs in the second position of the anticodon of yeast tyrosine tRNA, pairs with adenine (A).

But we also find some latitude in the first two positions. For example, arginine, leucine, and serine each have two different characteristic base pairs in the first two positions as seen in Table 16-1. Methionine (AUG) and tryptophan (UGG), having only one codon each, are exceptions to this general degeneracy.

TABLE 16-2. Pairing between Codon and Anticodon at the Third Position (Based on Work of Crick, 1966)

| Anticodon | Codon |
|---|---|
| A | U |
| C | G |
| G | U, C |
| I (inosine) | U, C, A |
| U | A, G |

## AMBIGUITY

Essentially, the code is nonambiguous in vivo under natural conditions. Ambiguity is encountered chiefly in cell-free systems under certain conditions. In such a system prepared from a streptomycin-sensitive strain of *E. coli* UUU (which ordinarily codes for phenylalanine) may also code for isoleucine, leucine, or serine in the presence of streptomycin. This ambiguity is enhanced at high magnesium-ion concentrations. Poly-U, in a cell-free system from thermophilic bacterial species, has been found to bind leucine at temperatures well below the optimum for growth of living cells of the same species (Friedman and Weinstein, 1964). Changes in pH or the addition of such substances as ethyl alcohol also result in ambiguity. However, ambiguities are seldom encountered in vivo under normal growing conditions for a given species.

## COLINEARITY

In a *colinear* code, the sequence of mRNA codons and the corresponding amino acid residues of a polypeptide chain are arranged in the same linear sequence. Now, both DNA and mRNA on the one hand, and polypeptides on the other, are linear, but this, in itself, does not require *colinearity*. That such colinearity does exist, however, is shown by studies of T4 mutants which produce incomplete head protein molecules. These mutants can be shown to map in linear sequence by using recombination techniques. Length of the incomplete head protein molecule made by each mutant is precisely proportional to the map distance involved. Thus, the code is determined to be *colinear*. The same conclusions are reached in the elegant work of Yanofsky and his colleagues (1964) on the tryptophan synthetase gene system of the colon bacillus. We shall refer again to Yanofsky's studies in the next chapter. Likewise, we shall examine in Chapter 17 similar evidence of colinearity in certain types of human hemoglobin.

## CHAIN INITIATION AND TERMINATION

All experimental data indicate that mRNA is synthesized sequentially in the 5′ → 3′ direction (Smith et al., 1965). The assembly of polypeptide chains is also sequential, from the amino to the carboxyl termini. The question, then, is what sort of signal (if any) directs the initiation and termination of polypeptide synthesis along a stretch of mRNA?

*Chain Initiation.*   It now appears clear that polypeptide chains in *Escherichia coli* are initiated with N-formylmethionine (Webster et al., 1966) which is then enzymatically removed before assembly into proteins. To illustrate, the coat protein of the RNA phage R17 begins with the N-terminal sequence alanine-serine-asparagine-phenylalanine-threonine . . . (Adams and Capecchi, 1966). In in vitro systems this sequence is preceded by N-formylmethionine; in these systems it is presumed that the necessary enzyme to remove the formylated methionine is lacking. In N-formylmethionine the amino group is blocked by a formyl group:

$$
\begin{array}{c}
\quad\ \ \overset{O}{\underset{\|}{}}\ \ \overset{H}{\underset{|}{}}\ \ \overset{H}{\underset{|}{}}\ \ \overset{O}{\underset{\|}{}} \\
H-C-N-C-C-OH \\
\quad\quad\quad\ \underset{|}{} \\
\quad\quad\quad CH_2 \\
\quad\quad\quad\ \underset{|}{} \\
\quad\quad\quad CH_2 \\
\quad\quad\quad\ \underset{|}{} \\
\quad\quad\quad S \\
\quad\quad\quad\ \underset{|}{} \\
\quad\quad\quad CH_3
\end{array}
$$

so that a peptide bond cannot be formed between it and a preceding amino acid.

Only one codon, AUG, exists for methionine (Table 16-1), so that the question arises as to how N-formylmethionine (chain initiating) and methionine (internally located) are distinguished in the biosynthesis of polypeptides. The answer in *E. coli* lies in the occurrence of two different tRNAs for methionine (Marcker and Sanger, 1964). The methionine bound to the initiating tRNA ($tRNA_f$) is formylated by enzymatic addition of the formyl group from a folic acid derivative. Methionine carried by the second type of met-tRNA ($tRNA_m$) cannot be formylated. However, the same amino acyl synthetase is responsible for charging both kinds of met-tRNA. The AUG codon rapidly initiates chain formation in vitro although, in the absence of AUG, initiation does occur but much more slowly and only at higher magnesium-ion levels. Moreover, in such circumstances initiation occurs randomly along the ribonucleotide. Yčas (1969) notes that N-formylmethionine may perhaps also be coded by GUG and GUA.

Hartman and Suskind (1969) point out that AUG determines the reading frames of mRNA. The synthetic ribonucleotide AUGGUUUUUUUU ... is translated only as N-formylmethionine-valine-phenylalanine-phenylalanine ... ; that is, the reading is AUG-GUU-UUU-UUU ... and GGU (glycine) is not read as such. Translation, once initiated, continues until a "stop" codon (see next section) is encountered. It would thus appear logical that a chain-initiating AUG should occur adjacent to, or at least fairly close to, a preceding chain-terminating codon. Otherwise, AUG would be read as an internal site by $tRNA_m$.

However, Steitz (1969) reports that RNA phage R17 has about 3,300 ribonucleotides, of which some 3,000 code for three proteins (phage coat, replicase enzyme, and a maturation protein involved in assembly of coat and RNA into a mature virus). She was able to isolate the beginning sections of each of the three genes with their initiator regions. Each initiator region began with AUG, but was *not immediately* preceded by any of the chain terminators that are described in the next section. Steitz believes that untranslated sequences intervene between the three structural genes of R17 and that chain termination and initiation codons may, therefore, be rather widely spaced. Various workers with different phages report that AUG codons do not occur until the 60th to 100th position from the 5' end, depending on the phage analyzed. The role of the untranslated bases has not been determined.

Recent evidence suggests that N-formylmethionine probably serves to initiate chain formation in all organisms, although various other blocked amino acids, such as N-acetylserine, have been detected in some higher plants and animals. In any event, the role of formylated amino acids in signaling "start chain" appears to rest on good experimental grounds.

*Chain Termination.* Three codons in Table 16–1, UAA, UAG, and UGA, are not assigned to any amino acids and hence are termed *nonsense codons*. Before their base sequences were determined, UAA was known as "ochre" and UAG as "amber"—terms that are still extensively employed for these two codons as a matter of convenience. Evidence from both in vitro and in vivo experiments demonstrates that all three nonsense codons cause both chain termination and chain release.

Last and others (1967), using short synthetic ribonucleotides (oligonucleotides) showed that UAA is responsible for both termination and release. Among their results, that from using the oligonucleotide AUG UUU UAA AAA ... AAA is highly significant in that formylmethionyl-phenylalanine *dipeptides* were isolated and recovered. Thus, the coding properties of AUG and UUU were verified, the ability of UAA to bring about both chain *termination* and *release* was demonstrated, and incidentally, the triplet nature of the code was given further proof.

Similarly, Zinder and colleagues (1966) showed that UAG ("amber") also serves in vitro in the same manner. Using natural RNA derived from the RNA phage f2, peptides terminating at the UAG site were recovered. Work of Sarabhai and Brenner (1967a, 1967b) indicates that UGA also serves as a chain terminator.

Stretton and Brenner (1965) used amber mutants of phage T4 (i.e., mutants in which the triplet UAG replaced another by single base substitution) to demonstrate that this codon functions as a chain terminator in vivo. In their work incomplete head proteins were formed, released from ribosomes, and recovered, the length of the protein being directly related to the position of amber. This also suggests that chain termination probably operates in translation rather than in transcription, though some interpretations suggest operation at the transcription level.

Chain release following termination appears to be enzymatically controlled. In highly purified cell-free systems no chain release takes place. However, although the process of release at the molecular level is not yet fully understood, it does not appear to depend solely on the mere occurrence of a nonsense codon.

### UNIVERSALITY

Significantly, the current evidence is that the code is universal for all living organisms and for viruses; the same triplets code similarly in a wide variety of organisms (Table 16-3). Compare codons for isoleucine, as an illustration, for the four very different species listed.

It should be expected that DNA from different species ought to exhibit degrees of similarity in nucleotide sequences in proportion to the closeness of evolutionary relationship of those species. Zoologists have long agreed that man and monkey are more closely related than is either to fish or bacteria, for example. Significant chemical proof was demonstrated in 1964 by Hoyer, McCarthy, and Bolton.

Their method was simple in concept but delicate in operation. DNA to be tested was first made to undergo strand separation by heating (denaturation), then cooled quickly to prevent recombining, and immobilized in agar. To this were added from another species short strands of denatured DNA which had previously been made radioactive by incorporation of carbon-14 or phosphorus-32. Pairing of homologous nucleotides from the two species occurred during several hours of incubation. The "hybrid" DNA was then recovered and assayed for radioactivity, yielding a measure of base-pair homology between the two species. Their results are summarized in Table 16-4.

The significance of these data lies in the similarity of probably fairly long sequences between man and monkey and between mouse and rat, and the evident dissimilarity of either with such taxonomically distant species as salmon or the colon bacillus. Hoyer and his colleagues conclude "This observation raises the question of whether there exists among the various animals a particular class of nucleotide sequences which have been retained during the diversification of the vertebrate forms. . . . It is clear . . . that there

TABLE 16-3. Comparison of mRNA Codons for Twenty Amino Acids in Different Organisms (After Groves and Kempner)

| Amino Acid | *Escherichia coli* (a bacterium) | Rat Liver | Wheat Embryo (flowering plant) | *Chlamy-domonas* (a green alga) |
|---|---|---|---|---|
| Alanine | GCU GCA GCC GCG | | | |
| Arginine | CGU CGA CGC CGG AGA AGG | | | |
| Asparagine | AAU AAC | | | |
| Aspartic acid | GAU GAC | | GAU | |
| Cysteine | UGU UGC AGU AGC | | | |
| Glutamine | CAA CAG | | | |
| Glutamic acid | GAA GAG | | GAU(?) | |
| Glycine | GGU GGA GGC GGG | GGU | GGU | |
| Histidine | CAU CAC | | | |
| Isoleucine | AUU AUC AUA | AUU | AUU | AUU |
| Leucine | CUU CUA CUC CUG UUA UUG | | CUU CUC | |
| Lysine | AAA AAG | AAA | AAU (?) | |
| Methionine | AUG | | AUG | |
| Phenylalanine | UUU UUC | UUU | UUU | UUU |
| Proline | CCU CCA CCC CCG | | CCU | |
| Serine | UCU UCA UCC UCG AGU AGC | UCU | UCC | UCU |
| Threonine | ACU ACA ACC ACG | | | |
| Tryptophan | UGG | UGG | UGG | |
| Tyrosine | UAU UAC | UAU | UAU | UAU |
| Valine | GUU GUA GUC GUG | GUU | GUU GUG | GUU |

exist homologies among polynucleotide sequences in the DNAs of such diverse forms as fish and man. These sequences represent genes which have been conserved with relatively little change throughout the long history of vertebrate evolution. Although we have no means yet of relating such genes to particular phenotypic expressions, it is conceivable that they are the determinants of the fundamental conservative characteristics of the vertebrate form." These latter would include such fundamental traits as skeletal structure and hemoglobin production. Man and mouse are mammals, having many traits in common, but within the primate group, man and monkey are phenotypically similar enough that rather long segments of their genetic codes are alike.

Certainly of equal significance in this regard is the fact that, as we noted in Chapter 15, in vitro protein synthesis is successful using rabbit reticulocyte mRNA and *E. coli* tRNA (plus other necessary components). The result was apparently normal rabbit hemoglobin, showing that bacterial tRNA can

TABLE 16-4. Percentage Recombining of $C^{14}$-Labeled Human DNA and $P^{32}$-Labeled Mouse DNA with Unlabeled DNA of Other Species
(Data from Hoyer, McCarthy, and Bolton, 1961)

| Unlabeled DNA Source | Percentage Labeled DNA Bound | |
|---|---|---|
| | $C^{14}$ Human | $P^{32}$ Mouse |
| Human | 18* | 5 |
| Rhesus monkey | 14 | 8 |
| Mouse | 6 | 22* |
| Cattle | 5 | 4 |
| Rat | 4 | 14 |
| Guinea pig | 4 | 3 |
| Hamster | 4 | 12 |
| Rabbit | 4 | 3 |
| Salmon | 1.5 | 1.5 |
| Colon bacillus | 0.4 | 0.4 |

* Human-human and mouse-mouse results serve as a base of comparison.

"recognize" mRNA and polysomes from a taxonomically very different organism. It is true, as has been reported frequently in the literature, that taxonomically divergent organisms do differ in the degree to which a given codon responds. For example, AAG codes readily for lysine in vertebrates, but rather weakly so in *E. coli*. But this is only a difference in degree, not in kind.

Furthermore, such proteins as cytochrome c show uniformity in several sequences of amino acids in such divergent groups as mammals, fishes, yeasts, and bacteria even though their evolutionary divergence must have taken place many hundreds of millions of years back in geologic time.

The question of *evolution* of the genetic code is, as you might guess, replete with problems. Its very universality complicates the question, as does the paradoxical situation wherein operation of the code requires precise functioning of many enzymes which, it would seem, could not be produced without the translation mechanism for which they are required. Woese (1970) discusses these problems in detail and suggests possible avenues of evolution.

In the next chapter we shall approach the concept of the ultimate structure of the gene through an examination of the process of mutation at the molecular level.

### SUMMARY OF CODE CHARACTERISTICS

In summary, the evidence is that the genetic code is *triplet, commaless, nonoverlapping, degenerate, essentially nonambiguous* under natural conditions, *colinear,* and *universal.* In addition, polypeptide chain *initiation* is signaled by certain codons (notably AUG in at least some bacteria) which bind tRNAs carrying blocked amino acids. Chain *termination* and release are governed by probably three nonsense codons (UAA, UAG, and UGA), although separation of the completed polypeptide from the polysome apparently requires more than just chain termination.

## REFERENCES

ADAMS, J. M., and M. R. CAPECCHI, 1965. N-formylmethionine-sRNA as the Initiator of Protein Synthesis. *Proc. Nat. Acad. Sci. (U.S.)*, **55**:147–155.

BRENNER, S., L. BARNETT, E. R. KATZ, and F. H. C. CRICK, 1967. UGA: A Third Nonsense Triplet in the Genetic Code. *Nature*, **213**:449–450.

BRENNER, S., A. O. W. STRETTON, and S. KAPLAN, 1965. Genetic Code: The "Nonsense" Triplets for Chain Termination and Their Suppression. *Nature*, **206**:994–998.

CRICK, F. H. C., 1963. On the Genetic Code. *Science*, **139**:461–464.

CRICK, F. H. C., 1966. Codon-Anticodon Pairing: the Wobble Hypothesis. *Jour. Molec. Biol.*, **19**:548–555.

CRICK, F. H. C., L. BARNETT, S. BRENNER, and R. J. WATTS-TOBIN, 1961. General Nature of the Genetic Code for Proteins. *Nature*, **192**:1227–1232.

FRIEDMAN, S. M., and I. B. WEINSTEIN, 1964. Lack of Fidelity in the Translation of Synthetic Polyribonucleotides. *Proc. Nat. Acad. Sci. (U.S.)*, **52**: 988–995.

FRISCH, L., ed., 1967. The Genetic Code. *Cold Spring Harbor Symposia Quant. Biol.*, **31** (1966). Cold Spring Harbor Laboratory of Quantitative Biology, Cold Spring Harbor, Long Island, New York.

GAREN, A., 1968. Sense and Nonsense in the Genetic Code. *Science*, **160**:149–159.

GOLDBERG, A. L., and R. E. WITTES, 1966. Genetic Code: Aspects of Organization. *Science*, **153**:420–424.

GROVES, W. E., and E. S. KEMPNER, 1967. Amino Acid Coding in *Sarcina lutea* and *Saccharomyces cerevisiae*. *Science*, **156**:387–390.

GRUNBERG-MANAGO, M., and S. OCHOA, 1955. Enzymatic Synthesis and Breakdown of Polynucleotides: Polynucleotide Phosphorylase, *Jour. Amer. Chem. Soc.*, **77**:3165–3166.

HARTMAN, P. E., and S. R. SUSKIND, 1969. *Gene Action*. Englewood Cliffs, N.J., Prentice-Hall.

HOYER, B. H., B. J. MCCARTHY, and E. T. BOLTON, 1964. A Molecular Approach in the Systematics of Higher Organisms. *Science*, **144**:959–967.

LAST, J. A., W. M. STANLEY, M. SALAS, M. B. HILLE, A. J. WAHBA, and S. OCHOA, 1967. Translation of the Genetic Message. IV. UAA as a Chain Terminating Codon. *Proc. Nat. Acad. Sci. (U.S.)*, **57**:1062–1067.

LEDER, P., and M. W. NIRENBERG, 1964. RNA Codewords and Protein Synthesis, III. On the Nucleotide Sequence of a Cysteine and a Leucine RNA Codeword. *Proc. Nat. Acad. Sci. (U.S.)*, **52**:1521–1529.

MARCKER, K., and F. SANGER, 1964. N-formylmethionyl-S-RNA. *Jour. Molec. Biol.*, **8**:835–840.

MARSHALL, R. E., C. T. CASKEY, and M. NIRENBERG, 1967. Fine Structure of RNA Codewords Recognized by Bacterial, Amphibian, and Mammalian Transfer RNA. *Science*, **155**:820–825.

NIRENBERG, M., and P. LEDER, 1964. RNA Codewords and Protein Synthesis. *Science*, **145**:1319–1407.

NIRENBERG, M. W., and J. H. MATTHAEI, 1961. The Dependence of Cell-Free Protein Synthesis in *E. coli* upon Naturally Occurring or Synthetic Polyribonucleotides. *Proc. Nat. Acad. Sci. (U.S.)*, **47**:1588–1602.

SARABHAI, A. S., and S. BRENNER, 1967a. Further Evidence that UGA Does Not Code for Tryptophan. *Jour. Molec, Biol.*, **26**:141–142.

SARABHAI, A. S., and S. BRENNER, 1967b. A Mutant which Reinitiates the Polypeptide Chain after Chain Termination. *Jour. Molec. Biol.*, **27**:145–162.

SARABHAI, A. S., A. O. W. STRETTON, and S. BRENNER, 1964. Co-linearity of the Gene with the Polypetide Chain. *Nature*, **201**:13–17.

SMITH, M. A., M. SALAS, W. M. STANLEY, JR., A. J. WAHBA, and S. OCHOA, 1966. Direction of Reading of the Genetic Message, II. *Proc. Nat. Acad. Sci. (U.S.)*, **55**:141–147.

STEITZ, J. A., 1969. Polypeptide Chain Initiation: Nucleotide Sequences of the Three Ribosomal Binding Sites in Bacteriophage R17 RNA. *Nature*, **224**: 957–964.

STRETTON, A. O. W., and S. BRENNER, 1965. Molecular Consequences of the *Amber* Mutation and its Suppression. *Jour. Molec. Biol.*, **12**:456–465.

WEBSTER, R. E., D. L. ENGLEHARDT, and N. D. ZINDER, 1966. In Vitro Protein Synthesis: Chain Initiation. *Proc. Nat. Acad. Sci. (U.S.)*, **55**:155–161.

WOESE, C. R., 1970. The Problem of Evolving a Genetic Code. *BioScience*, **20**: 471–485.

YANOFSKY, C., B. C. CARLTON, J. R. GUEST, D. R. HELINSKI, and U. HENNING, 1964. On the Colinearity of Gene Structure and Protein Structure. *Proc. Nat. Acad. Sci. (U.S.)*, **51**:266–272.

YČAS, M., 1969. *The Biological Code.* (Neuberger, A., and E. L. Tatum, eds., *Frontiers of Biology*, volume 12.) New York, American Elsevier.

ZINDER, N. D., D. L. ENGLEHARDT, and R. E. WEBSTER, 1966. Punctuation in the Genetic Code. *Cold Spring Harbor Symposia Quant. Biol.*, **31**:251–256.

ZUBAY, G. L., ed., 1968. *Papers in Biochemical Genetics.* New York, Holt, Rinehart and Winston. (A reprinting of some of the most important original papers in this field between 1953 and 1967.)

## PROBLEMS

**16-1.** Assume a length of single-stranded DNA with the deoxyribonucleotide sequence T A C C G G A A T T G C. (a) If the code is triplet, nonoverlapping, and commaless, of which amino acids (in sequence) will the polypeptide for which this stretch of DNA is responsible consist? (b) If the code is triplet, overlapping by two bases, and commaless, how would you answer the same question? (c) Of what significance could the TAC triplet in DNA be?

**16-2.** For the same DNA stretch (problem 16-1) assume the second C of DNA to be deleted. What now is the sequence of amino acids coded for if the code is assumed to be triplet, nonoverlapping, and commaless?

**16-3.** In the same DNA stretch (problem 16-1) assume the second C of DNA to be deleted and a T to be inserted after the G-C sequence so that the DNA now reads T A C G G T A A T T G C. How does the amino acid sequence now coded for compare with your answer to 16-1? (Assume the code still to be triplet, nonoverlapping, and commaless.)

**16-4.** Synthetic RNA is constructed from a mixture of nucleotides supplied to a cell-free system in this relative proportion: uracil, 3 parts; guanine, 2 parts; adenine, 1 part. What fraction of the resulting triplets will be (a) UGA; (b) UUU?

**16-5.** Assume an alanine tRNA charged with labeled alanine is isolated and the amino acid chemically treated so as to change it to labeled glycine. The treated amino acid-enzyme-tRNA complex is then introduced into a cell-free peptide synthesizing system. At which of two mRNA triplets, say GCU or GGU, would this tRNA now become bound? Why?

**16-6.** If single base changes occur in DNA (and therefore in mRNA), which amino acid, tryptophan or arginine, is most likely to be replaced by another in protein synthesis?

**16-7.** Wittmann-Liebold and Wittman studied a number of mutants in the coat protein of the RNA-containing tobacco mosaic virus. Two of their mutants were

| Mutant | Amino Acid Position | Replacement |
|--------|---------------------|-------------|
| A-14 | 129 | isoleucine → threonine |
| Ni-1055 | 21 | isoleucine → methionine |

By reference to Table 16-1, explain what has happened in each of these cases.

**16-8.** Yanofsky et al. studied a large number of mutants for the tryptophan synthetase A polypeptide chain of *Escherichia coli*. This polypeptide chain consists of approximately 267 amino acid residues. In the wild type enzyme a part of the amino acid sequence is: -tyrosine-leucine-threonine-glycine-glycine-glycine-glycine-glycine-serine-. In their mutant A446, cysteine replaces tyrosine; in mutant A187, the third glycine is replaced by valine. By reference to the genetic code, suggest a mechanism for each of these amino acid replacements.

**16-9.** How many different mRNA nucleotide codon combinations can exist for the internal pentapeptide threonine-proline-tryptophan-leucine-isoleucine?

**16-10.** From Table 16-1, note that (a) UUU and UUC code for phenylalanine; on the other hand, (b) So and Davie report that, with relatively high concentrations of ethyl alcohol, the incorporation of leucine, and isoleucine to a lesser degree, is sharply increased, while incorporation of phenylalanine is decreased, for these same codons. Which of the described situations, (a) or (b), represents ambiguity, and which degeneracy?

**16-11.** Assume a series of different one-base changes in the codon GGA, producing these several new codons: (a) UGA; (b) GAA; (c) GGC; (d) CGA. Which of these represent(s) degeneracy, which missense, and which nonsense?

# CHAPTER 17
# *Molecular Structure of the Gene*

I N our discussion of the genetic code we raised an important question: in terms of the operation of the genetic code, just how much of the nucleotide sequence comprises a gene? Even by raising this question, we have come a long way from the early, understandably vague concept of the gene as a "bead on a string" separated from adjacent genes by nongenetic material. To begin to solve this problem at the molecular level, let us first examine the process of mutation.

Mutations are sudden changes in genotype, involving **qualitative or quantitative alterations in the genetic material itself**. Under this concept, recombination is excluded, for this process merely redistributes existing genetic material among different individuals; it makes no *change* in it. Geneticists often distinguish between two kinds of mutation, chromosomal and "point." So-called chromosomal mutations, or, preferably, chromosomal aberrations, may result in alterations in the amount or position of genetic material. These have already been described in Chapter 12. "Point" mutations, however, are *changes within the DNA molecule*, and the term *mutation* is now generally employed by geneticists in this more restricted sense. We shall use the term in this narrower meaning.

Of course, mutations may occur in any living cell that contains genetic material, either a somatic or a reproductive cell, and at any stage in its life cycle. Somatic mutations are perpetuated only in the cells descended from the one in which the mutation originally took place. If the mutant trait is clearly detectable, a patch or sector of cells all having this new characteristic will result. For example, Fig. 17-1 shows the result of a somatic mutation from "peppermint" to solid color which occurred in a zinnia in the author's garden. Whether or not somatic mutations produce an immediate effect depends on the nature of the change, the dominance relations of the original and mutant genes, and the stage of development of the individual or part at which the mutation occurs. Unless mutation takes place in reproductive cells, or in tissues which will give rise to reproductive cells, and is maintained therein, the mutation will not be passed on to succeeding generations. Even so, whether it is detectable in a later generation depends on many factors, such as dominance, the environment, and so forth.

From our examination of protein synthesis and of the genetic code in the two preceding chapters, it might occur to you that it may well be both possible and useful to think of genes from more than just one viewpoint. Implicit in our discussion of protein synthesis and coding was the suggestion that we may

FIGURE 17-1. *Mutant flower heads (inflorescences) of* Zinnia. *The somatic mutation was from "peppermint" (splotched color) to solid color.*

identify a gene as a *functional unit*, having a definite cellular locus and consisting of many nucleotides. But you will recall that a single nucleotide change will, in many instances, code for a different amino acid. Thus, base changes of a certain kind and amount (an addition, a deletion, or a replacement) might be expected to result in one or several amino acid substitutions, or even a quite different protein and, therefore, a different (i.e., mutant) phenotype. As we saw in Chapter 16, a single insertion or deletion produces frame shifts which alter the reading of the remainder of the RNA message. This will often result in production of a very different protein, one which may be inactive, or even lethal if some vital function is interfered with or prevented. But a replacement of one base by another in certain positions in certain codons will affect the reading of only the codon in which it occurs, so that a protein with a single amino acid substitution may be produced, or (especially in the third position of a triplet) make no change in the amino acid coded for.

So, then, we may also be able to think of a gene as a *mutational unit* which we may, from what we have seen thus far, anticipate can be as small as a single deoxyribonucleotide pair. A functional gene might thus consist of several to very many mutational subunits. Very possibly, too, the genetic *recombinational unit* may be identifiable at the molecular level and, therefore, constitute a third view of the gene. It is also entirely to be expected that the

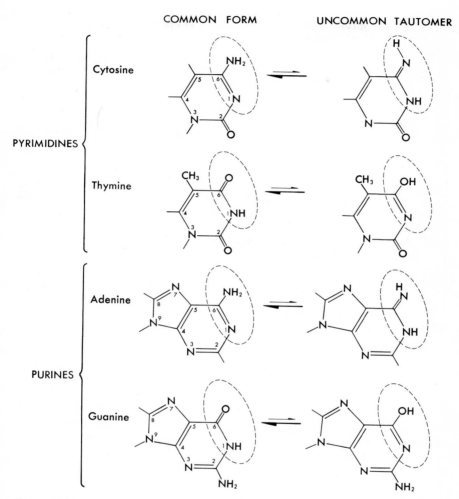

FIGURE 17-2. (A) *Comparison of common forms of DNA bases with their rare tautomers. Tautomers, which may occur in several forms, differ from each other by rearrangements of protons and electrons. This is symbolized in the structural formula by changes in positions of H atoms and double bonds within the dashed ovals. Only the tautomer thought to be important in each case as a mutagen is shown here; its occurrence is quite rare.*

gene, considered from these three points of view, may well show somewhat different characteristics.

Point mutations, what they consist of and how they come about, shed considerable light on the molecular nature of the gene.

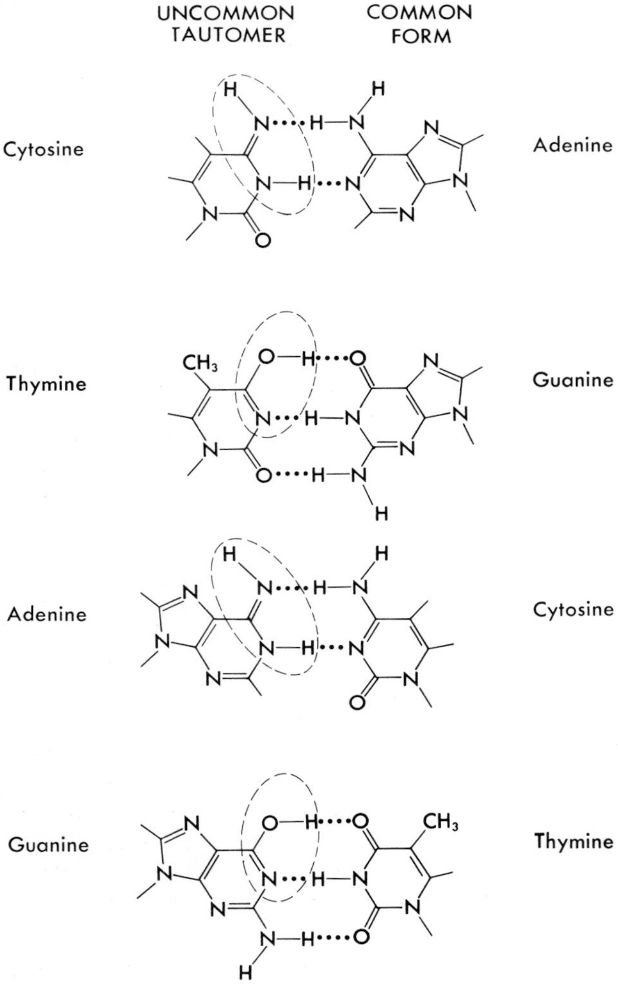

UNCOMMON   COMMON
TAUTOMER    FORM

Cytosine                    Adenine

Thymine                     Guanine

Adenine                     Cytosine

FIGURE 17-2. (B)
*Pairing qualities of
the rare tautomers
of the four bases.
Consequences of this
"erroneous pairing"
are discussed in the
text.*

Guanine                     Thymine

## Molecular Basis of Mutation

### SUBNUCLEOTIDE CHANGES

*Tautomerization.*  The purines and pyrimidines of DNA and RNA may
exist in several alternate forms, or **tautomers**. Tautomerism occurs
through rearrangements of electrons and protons in the molecule. Uncommon
tautomers of adenine, cytosine, guanine, and thymine, shown in Fig. 17-2(A),
differ from the common form in the position at which one H atom is attached.
As a result, some single bonds become double bonds, and vice versa.

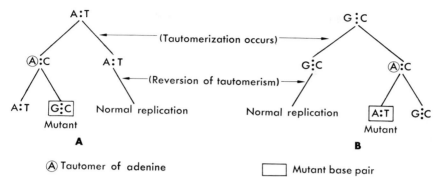

FIGURE 17-3. (*A*) *Conversion of an* A:T *pair to a* G:C *pair by tautomerization of an already incorporated adenine during the first replication of DNA. Reversion of the tautomerism in the second replication leads to the production of one mutant* G:C *strand.* (*B*) *Conversion of a* G:C *pair to an* A:T *pair by incorporation of a tautomer of adenine in the first replication of DNA. Assuming reversion of the tautomerism in the second replication, a mutant* A:T *pair is produced in place of the normal* G:C *pair. In both figures, the tautomer of adenine is indicated by the circled A; the mutant base pair is boxed.*

***Transitions.*** The significance of these tautomeric shifts lies in the changed pairing qualities they impart. The normal tautomer of adenine pairs with thymine in DNA; the rare (imino) form pairs with the normal tautomer of cytosine as depicted in Fig. 17-2(B). The rare tautomer is unstable and usually reverts to its common form by the next replication. If tautomerism occurs in an already incorporated adenine, the result is a conversion of an AT pair to GC (Fig. 17-3A). On the other hand, if tautomerism occurs in an adenine about to be incorporated, the result is a conversion of a GC pair to AT (Fig. 17-3B). Such substitution of one purine for another, or of one pyrimidine for another, is termed a **transition**. Transitions may come about in a number of other ways, as described in the following sections.

***Deamination.*** It is well known that various chemicals produce mutations; these are especially well documented in bacteria, yeasts, and phages. Nitrous acid ($HNO_2$) is one such *mutagenic* substance. It brings about changes in DNA bases by replacing the amino group ($-NH_2$) with an -OH (hydroxyl) group. Thus adenine, having an $-NH_2$ at the number 6 carbon (Fig. 17-2A), is deaminated by nitrous acid to hypoxanthine:

By a tautomeric shift, a more common (keto) tautomer is formed

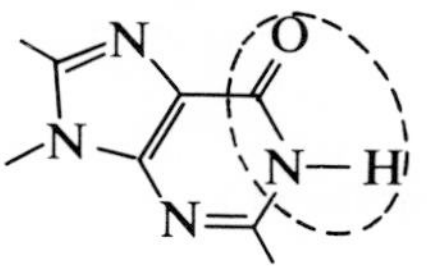

which pairs with cytosine. Thus an A:T pair can be converted to a G:C pair:

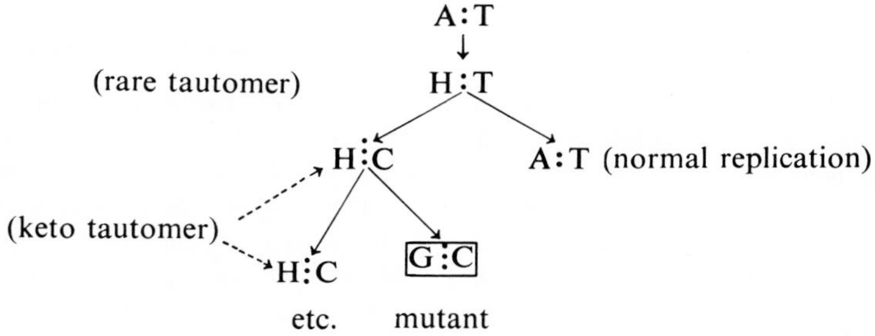

Similarly, deamination converts cytosine to uracil which pairs with adenine (thus C:G becomes T:A), and guanine to xanthine which pairs by *two* H bonds with cytosine.

**Base Analogs.** Certain substances have molecular structures so similar to the usual bases that, if they are available, such **analogs** may be incorporated into a replicating DNA strand. One example will suffice to indicate the process and consequence. For instance, 5-bromouracil in its usual (keto) form,

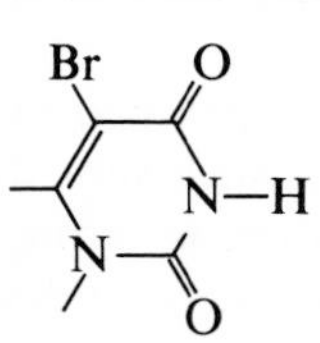

will substitute for thymine, which it closely resembles structurally (Fig. 17-2). Thus an AT pair becomes and remains ABu (Fig. 17-4). There is some in vitro evidence to indicate that Bu immediately adjacent to an adenine in one of the DNA strands causes the latter to pair with guanine. But, in its rarer (enol) state,

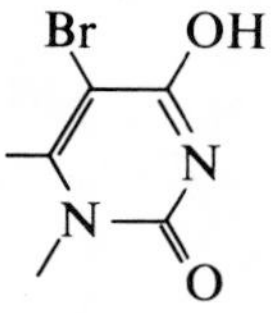

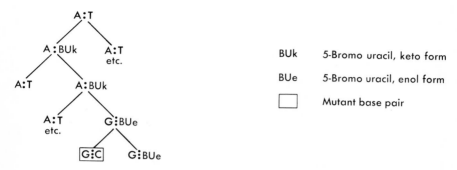

FIGURE 17-4. *Substitution of the common keto tautomer of 5-bromouracil for thymine; its subsequent tautomerization to the rarer enol form, if it occurs, converts an A:T pair to a G:C pair. Moreover, the presence of 5-BU itself in the DNA sequence may cause imperfections in RNA synthesis.*

5-Bu behaves similarly to the tautomer of thymine (Fig. 17-2) and pairs with guanine (Benzer and Freese, 1958). This converts AT to GC as shown in Fig. 17-4. Studies show that 5-Bu increases the mutation rate by a factor of $10^4$ in bacteria.

Nitrous acid and base analogs like 5-Bu can produce transitions as well as cause reversion of transition mutants in phages and bacteria to their original state, regardless of what the initial mutagen may have been. Some rII mutants of phage T4 (to be discussed shortly) are transitions and can be reversed in this fashion.

***Effect of Ultraviolet Light.*** Ultraviolet light is a fairly effective mutagenic agent. Its effect on the pyrimidines cytosine and thymine may produce (1) photoproducts which cause local strand separation in DNA, or (2) dimers which may prevent strand separation and replication or interfere with normal base-pairing.

Thus, ultraviolet may weaken the double bond between the fourth and fifth carbon of cytosine (Fig. 17-2), allowing water to be added at these points. The resulting photoproduct is unable to form hydrogen bonds properly with guanine, and this leads to strand separation. Ultraviolet radiation of about 2,800 Å likewise weakens the 4-5 C double bond, permitting two thymines to link as a dimer (Fig. 17-5). Such dimers may link thymine *between* strands, interfering with replication, or connect adjacent thymines of the same strand, disrupting normal T-A pairing.

Photoproducts and dimers, induced by ultraviolet irradiation, may be "repaired" (in *Escherichia coli* and phage) by (1) photoreactivation or (2) dark reactivation. In photoreactivation, an enzyme that has been bound to DNA during ultraviolet irradition is activated by intense visible light supplied following ultraviolet exposure. The enzyme then catalyzes the cleavage of

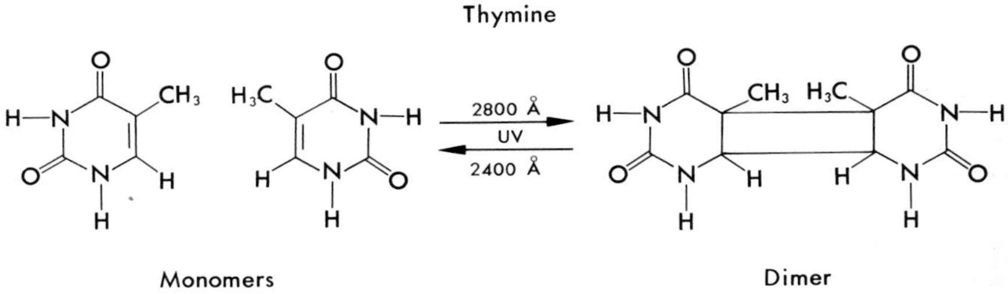

Thymine

Monomers                                                    Dimer

FIGURE 17-5. *The monomer ⇌ dimer conversion in thymine under ultraviolet light.*

pyrimidine dimers, restoring their normal structure. Dark reactivation involves instead the enzymatic removal of dimers from the DNA molecule and synthesis of normal replacement segments for those excised, at least in certain genetic strains of bacteria.

### WHOLE NUCLEOTIDE CHANGES

The acridine dyes are effective mutagens. As described in Chapter 16, they act by permitting base additions and/or deletions. If the intercalation of an acridine and consequent stretching of the DNA molecule occurs at the time of crossing-over between DNA molecules, the result can be unequal crossing-over. As a result, one strand may have one more nucleotide than its complement, producing one daughter helix with one base pair more than the other. In general, the acridines are mutagenic in bacteria only at the time of recombination.

### STRAND BREAKAGE

The fact that such ionizing radiation as x-rays produce mutations has been recognized since Nobel laureate Muller's pioneer paper in 1927. Although x-irradiation readily causes chromosome breakage, it may also act directly on DNA by breaking some of the bonds in the sugar-phosphate strand. Whereas single-strand breaks are repaired in at least some bacteria, those involving both strands appear not to be. Replication and normal base pairing are interfered with and may lead to losses of or alterations in one or more nucleotides.

## Genetics of Hemoglobin

Evidence for the foregoing mechanisms of change in nucleic acids has come from both in vitro studies and experimental work with bacteria and phages. It suggests that mutation can involve a single base change and therefore that, at least at the mutational level, a gene may be as little as one base or base pair. An elegant confirmation has been provided by Ingram (1957) and by

Hunt and Ingram (1958 and 1960) in studies on the chemical differences between normal and abnormal hemoglobins.

## STRUCTURE OF THE HEMOGLOBIN MOLECULE

Human hemoglobin is a protein with a molecular weight of about 67,000. The globin consists of four polypeptide chains, two alpha and two beta chains, each with iron-containing heme groups. The $\alpha$ chain includes 141 amino acid residues, the $\beta$ 146. In one molecule there are thus $(2 \times 141) + (2 \times 146)$ or 574 amino acid residues. Nineteen of the 20 biologically important amino acids are included.

## ANALYSIS OF THE HEMOGLOBIN MOLECULE

*Tryptic Digestion.*   Before biochemists had analyzed the complete sequence of amino acids in the $\alpha$ and $\beta$ chains of hemoglobin, Ingram (1956 and 1957) was able to report on chemical differences between hemoglobin of normal persons (hemoglobin A, or Hb-A) and that of individuals suffering sickle-cell anemia (hemoglobin S, or Hb-S). Because the molecule was too large and complex for total analysis at that time, Ingram digested it with trypsin. This enzyme breaks the peptide bonds between the carboxyl group of either arginine or lysine and the amino group of the next amino acid. Since there are about 60 of these amino acids in the hemoglobin molecule, approximately 30 shorter polypeptide segments (in duplicate) are produced in this way. Each of these was then analyzed by Ingram for amino acid content.

*" Fingerprinting " Peptides.*   Ingram placed small samples of the trypsin-digested hemoglobin (A or S) on one edge of a large square of filter paper, then subjected the peptide mixture to an electrical field in the process called electrophoresis. Under these conditions, differently charged portions will migrate characteristically. Next, the filter paper with its as yet invisible, spread-out " peptide spots " was dried, turned 90° and placed with one edge in a solvent (normal butyl alcohol, acetic acid, and water). Because of differences in solubility of the peptides in this solvent, additional migration and spreading ensued. The paper was finally sprayed with ninhydrin, which produces a blue color in reaction with amino acids. The resulting chromatogram was called a " fingerprint " by Ingram, an apt description because differences in charge and amino acid content can thereby be picked out (Fig. 17-6) readily and characteristically.

When Ingram fingerprinted the peptides produced from hemoglobin A and S by tryptic digestion, he discovered all " peptide spots," except one which he called " peptide #4," of each to be identical in their locations on filter paper. This means that the long $\alpha$ and $\beta$ chains of hemoglobins A and S are identical *except* for one peptide of the 30 kinds. This one carries a positive charge in Hb-S, and no charge in Hb-A, a difference which, by 1960, Hunt

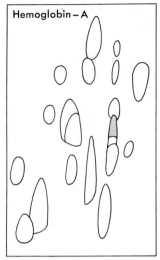 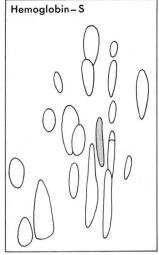

FIGURE 17-6. *Drawings of "fingerprint" chromatogram of the hemoglobins* A (*normal*) *and* S (*sickle cell*). *Each enclosed area represents the final location of a specific peptide; peptide 4 of Ingram is indicated by shading.*

and Ingram were able to relate directly to a *single amino acid* change in the sequence of 146 composing the β chain.

*Analyses of Several Hemoglobins.* With the development of the electrophoretic-chromatographic technique for peptide analysis, studies of many different hemoglobins progressed rapidly. In addition, the complete amino acid sequence for both polypeptide chains is now known. The amino acid sequence for the β chain of hemoglobin A begins with these eight, starting with the $NH_2$ end of the first: valine, histidine, leucine, threonine, proline, glutamic acid, glutamic acid, and lysine. Table 17-1 compares this

TABLE 17-1. Comparison of the First Eight Amino Acids of the β Chain
of Four Hemoglobins

| Hb-A | Hb-S | Hb-C | Hb-G |
|------|------|------|------|
| Valine | Valine | Valine | Valine |
| Histidine | Histidine | Histidine | Histidine |
| Leucine | Leucine | Leucine | Leucine |
| Threonine | Threonine | Threonine | Threonine |
| Proline | Proline | Proline | Proline |
| Glutamic acid | VALINE | LYSINE | Glutamic acid |
| Glutamic acid | Glutamic acid | Glutamic acid | GLYCINE |
| Lysine | Lysine | Lysine | Lysine |

| | | cistron ➤ | | | | | | | | |
|---|---|---|---|---|---|---|---|---|---|---|
| DNA | Hemoglobin A | GTA CAT | CAT GTA | CTT GAA | ACT TGA | CCT GGA | GAA CTT | GAA CTT | AAA TTT ... | ... |
| mRNA Codons | | GUA | CAU | CUU | ACU | CCU | GAA | GAA | AAA | |
| Amino Acids | | val | his | leu | thr | pro | glu | glu | lys | |
| DNA | Hemoglobin S | | | | | | G(T)A C(A)T | | | |
| mRNA Codons | | | | | | | G(U)A | | | |
| Amino Acid | | | | | | | val | | | |
| DNA | Hemoglobin C | | | | | | (A)AA (T)TT | | | |
| mRNA Codons | | | | | | | (A)AA | | | |
| Amino Acid | | | | | | | lys | | | |
| DNA | Hemoglobin G | | | | | | | G(G)A C(C)T | | |
| mRNA Codons | | | | | | | | G(G)A | | |
| Amino Acid | | | | | | | | gly | | |

FIGURE 17-7. *Suggested derivation of three mutant β-chain hemoglobins from hemoglobin A by single nucleotide changes. The codon for particular amino acids is arbitrarily chosen when several may code for the same amino acid. Altered nucleotides are enclosed by solid lines.*

series of the first eight amino acids for the β chains of four different hemoglobins.

The electrophoretic behavior of the peptides consisting of these eight amino acids is explainable by their electrical charge differences. Glutamic acid carries a negative charge, valine and glycine none, and lysine a positive charge.

Many other types of hemoglobin have been similarly analyzed. Each differs from Hb-A in the change of one amino acid; some of these are in the α chain, others in the β.

**Transversions.** Hemoglobin S differs from hemoglobin A, as we have seen (Table 17-1) by the substitution of valine for glutamic acid as the sixth amino acid in the $\beta$ chain. Now, the codons for glutamic acid (Table 16-1) are GAA and GAG, whereas valine is coded for by GUA, GUG, GUC, and GUU. If, say, a GAA (glutamic acid) codon undergoes a replacement to become GUA, valine will, of course, be coded for (Fig. 17-7). Such a replacement in mRNA will occur if the DNA trinucleotide CTT suffers a change to CAT; that is, the purine adenine replaces the pyrimidine thymine. The substitution of a purine for a pyrimidine (or vice versa) is called a **transversion**.

So the far-reaching and important phenotypic difference between hemoglobin A and that of persons with either sickle-cell trait or sickle-cell anemia is the result of transversion, the change of one nucleotide pair in DNA from AT to TA. A *single nucleotide* in mRNA thus may spell the difference between life and death.

### INHERITANCE OF HEMOGLOBIN TYPES

As described in Chapter 2, production of hemoglobin S is due to a single gene which is codominant with the gene for hemoglobin A. Present evidence is that genes for hemoglobins A, S, C, and G, all of which affect the $\beta$ chain, are multiple alleles, and that the $\alpha$ chain is specified by a different series of (probably multiple) alleles. Mutations producing changes in the $\alpha$ chain do not, themselves, cause changes in the $\beta$ chain, and vice versa.

## The Tryptophan Synthetase System

In a sense, Ingram's work really set the stage for the important work of Yanofsky on the tryptophan synthetase enzyme system of *Escherichia coli*. In this bacterium the complete enzyme molecule is a complex of two different subunits, A and B. The A component is a single polypeptide chain of 267 amino acid residues whose exact sequence is now known; the B component is a dimer of two identical polypeptide chains. The enzyme catalyzes three of the steps in tryptophan synthesis (Fig. 17-8). Both the A and B subunits are required for reaction $\overline{AB}$, whereas only the A component is necessary for indole production (reaction $\overline{A}$), and the B component alone is needed for reaction $\overline{B}$. Both the A and B components are required, then, for synthesis of tryptophan.

Some mutants that are incapable of forming functional tryptophan synthetase do, however, produce a protein that, although enzymatically inactive, does give an immunological reaction with tryptophan synthetase immune serum prepared from rabbit blood. This protein has been named *cross-reacting material* (CRM); both $CRM^+$ (producing cross-reacting material) and $CRM^-$ (not producing cross-reacting material) mutants have been detected. It is believed that the difference between $CRM^+$ and $CRM^-$ mutants lies in the

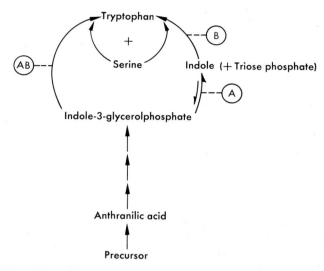

FIGURE 17-8. *Pathways of tryptophan synthesis involving tryptophan synthetase. The enzyme consists of two subunits, A and B, both of which are required for the reaction indole-3-glycerolphosphate + serine → tryptophan (reaction AB). The A subunit is required for production of indole and triose phosphate (reaction A), and the B subunit for the reaction indole + serine → tryptophan (reaction B). Thus, A-deficient mutants require indole or tryptophan for growth, and B-mutants must be supplied with tryptophan.*

fact that the latter produce either small fragments of the enzyme molecule or grossly abnormal molecules as a result of nonsense mutations.

Mutants defective in the A component occur, as do mutants defective in the B component. *Complementation tests* are used to check whether or not two mutations are in the same functional gene. Such tests involve the introduction of two different mutant genes into the same cell. If these are introduced in the *trans* configuration and if wild type activity is restored, the two mutations are determined to be in two different functional genes and to exhibit *complementarity*. Complementation tests require that the cell be diploid, or that it can be made diploid. In bacteria (in which the vegetative cells are monoploid) this requirement can be met through conjugation, transformation, or transduction whereby cells can be made temporarily diploid for the genes under study. In the tryptophan synthetase system it is found that every A mutant complements every B mutant, but that no complementation occurs between two A mutants or between two B mutants. It is clear, therefore, that a different functional gene (or cistron; see next section) is responsible for production of the A and the B polypeptide chains.

## Fine Structure of the Gene

The older concept of the gene as a single, indivisible entity can, as predicted in Chapter 7, no longer be valid. On the one hand, there is the series of nucleotides that specifies the sequence of amino acid residues of a polypeptide chain (such as those of the A and B chains of the tryptophan synthetase enzyme, or the $\alpha$ and $\beta$ chains of hemoglobin). But we have also seen that a change in as little as one nucleotide of the polypeptide-specifying gene may change (mutate) and produce a variant of the wild-type chain that differs in one amino acid residue. So the functional gene is not the same as the mutational gene, but appears to consist of many mutable sites. Then, too, the gene must be considered from the standpoint of the nature of the sites at which recombination may occur. The functional gene, therefore, appears to be composed of both mutational and recombinational subunits.

### THE CISTRON

The term **cistron** has been applied (by Seymour Benzer, 1961) to that segment of DNA which specifies one polypeptide chain. The term is derived from the *cis-trans* effect described in Chapter 7. Hemoglobin, therefore, would require two cistrons for its globin fraction, one each for the $\alpha$ and $\beta$ chains. If we accept the validity of the triplet code, then the cistron for the $\alpha$ chain is at least $141 \times 3 = 423$ nucleotides long, and the cistron for the $\beta$ chain $146 \times 3 = 438$ nucleotides in length. So a kind of multifaceted concept of the gene begins to emerge. At one extreme of size is the gene as a unit of function, the cistron, specifying a particular polypeptide chain, and presumably composed of a minimum of three times as many nucleotides as amino acids in the polypeptide.

### THE MUTON

But within the cistron there appear to exist a large number of mutable sites. So the gene as a unit of mutation is smaller—i.e., consists of fewer nucleotides —than a cistron. We may use Benzer's term **muton** for the smallest length of DNA capable of mutational change. From studies on hemoglobin, as well as extensive work on bacteria, it is seen that the muton may be as small as a single nucleotide pair in DNA.

We have already noted (pages 343–346 and Fig. 17-7) that mutant hemoglobins differ from normal hemoglobin A by single amino acid substitutions and that these may be accounted for by postulating single nucleotide changes (both transitions and transversions). By the same kind of reasoning, but with clear experimental evidence, Yanofsky (1963, 1967, and numerous other papers) has shown how each of the many tryptophan synthetase mutants may occur by nucleotide substitutions. Two ultraviolet-induced A-protein mutant strains, A23 and A46, have been especially revealing. In one of the A23

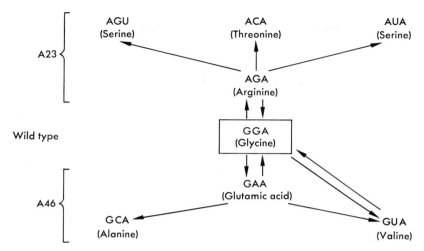

FIGURE 17-9. *Derivation of A23 and A46 tryptophan synthetase mutants in* E. coli *by single nucleotide substitutions. Based on the work of Yanofsky.*

mutants, glycine is replaced by arginine, whereas in one of the A46 mutants the *same* glycine is replaced by glutamic acid. The codon changes responsible may be designated, for example, as GGA (glycine, wild-type), *A*GA (arginine, A23), and G*A*A (glutamic acid, A46), as diagrammed in Fig. 17-9. These examples clearly indicate that the *muton can be as little as one nucleotide*, and that a cistron may be composed of many mutons. Nucleotide changes in these mutable sites may, of course, produce either sense, missense, or nonsense reading changes.

### THE RECON

***Tryptophan Synthetase System.*** You will recall that our discussion of pseudoalleles in Chapter 7 suggested that crossing-over may occur within a functional gene or, to use Benzer's terminology, a cistron. The A23 and A46 tryptophan synthetase mutants of *Escherichia coli* confirm this suggestion. These two mutants, involving the same glycine of the A protein (amino acid residue number 210), have been shown by recombinational studies *not* to map at precisely the same point, but to be 0.001 map unit apart (Yanofsky et al., 1967). In fact, Yanofsky (1967) comes to some interesting conclusions in comparing genetic map length with distances in the polypeptide chain. He finds the map length for 187 amino acid residues (positions 48 through 234) of the A protein in the *E. coli* tryptophan synthetase system to be about 3 map units, or $\frac{3}{187}$ = 0.016 map unit per amino acid residue and, thus, also for a group of three adjacent nucleotides. Distances between adjacent nucleotides are thus of the order of 0.001 to 0.005 map units.

It is therefore evident that, just as mutation may occur *within* a triplet codon, so may recombination. Furthermore, Yanofsky's studies of both mutation and recombination (by means of transduction) clearly show that in each protein with a different amino acid at a given position, the amino acids on either side remain unchanged. To quote Yanofsky (1963), "this is perhaps the most convincing evidence available that excludes overlapping codes." Thus, we are provided with still another subdivisional concept of the cistron, namely the **recon**. *A recon is the smallest unit of DNA capable of recombination* or (in bacteria) of being integrated by transformation or transduction.

***Complementation and Recombination in Phage.***   Phage T4 is a virus infecting the colon bacillus, *Escherichia coli*. Plaques, or clear areas on agar plates of the host, indicate areas of infection and lysis. Those formed by the wild type phage ($r^+$) are small and have rough edges. Many phage mutations that alter plaque morphology are known; the *r* (rapid lysis) mutants are easily recognizable because they produce large plaques with sharp edges. The *r* mutants have been shown to involve three major map regions in the phage DNA and are designated *rI*, *rII*, and *rIII*. Both *rI* and *rIII* lyse host strain K; *rII* mutants enter K-type cells but do not lyse them. But all three mutant classes, *rI*, *rII*, and *rIII*, lyse cells of host strain B.

The *rII* mutants fall into two groups, *rIIA* and *rIIB*. Each of these two groups has been found to have an internal linear arrangement and to be adjacent but nonoverlapping on the phage DNA molecule. The A region produces an "A" product, the B region a "B" product. Both substances are necessary for lysis of K-type host cells. The $r^+$ (wild type) phage forms both "A" and "B" products, having nonmutant A and B regions in the *cis* configuration. But an *rIIA* mutant produces only the "B" product and so cannot lyse K host cells but, as noted, does infect them. By the same token, *rIIB* mutants produce an "A" substance, but no "B," and also are unable to lyse K-type host cells. However, simultaneous infection of K host cells with an *rIIA* and an *rIIB* mutant (each with a single A or B mutation, respectively) does result in lysis. Here the "A" and "B" products are both being produced, but by two different phage DNA molecules (i.e., in the *trans* configuration). Thus, regions A and B are functionally different and exhibit *complementation* on the basis of a *cis-trans* test. From this fact Benzer derived the term *cistron* to denote a functional gene, that is, a segment of DNA responsible for formation of a particular polypeptide chain.

On the other hand, if two different A mutations or two different B mutations are located sufficiently far apart in their respective cistrons, *recombination* may occur between them. For example, infection of B-type hosts with two *different* A mutants results in lysis (rII mutants can lyse B cells) and release of progeny phage particles. These latter are then used to infect K-type hosts. Any lysis occurring in K cells must, therefore, result from recombination between two different A mutations to produce wild type phage ($r^+$) and their characteristic plaques. The same recombinational effect is observable within the B cistron. Careful study has made it possible to detect recombinants with frequencies as low as 0.00001 per cent ($1 \times 10^{-7}$). Some of the A × A and B × B "crosses" fail, however, to result in recombination; these have been found to be deletions.

In summary, it should be emphasized that complementation and recombination are entirely different. Complementation tests demonstrate whether two mutations are in the same cistron, that is, part of the same functional unit. On the other hand, recombination permits mapping the fine structure of a cistron.

From recombination experiments involving both "point mutations" and deletions, Benzer (1962) found over 3,000 mutants, having more than 300 sites identifiable by recombination in the entire *rII* region. Subsequent work has extended these findings to the point where at least 500 recombinational sites have been identified in the *rII*A region alone. From a variety of evidence, the T4 DNA molecule is calculated to have a molecular weight of about 130,000,000. With 650 as the average molecular weight of a deoxyribonucleotide *pair* (refer back to problems 14-6 and 14-15), the number of nucleotide pairs in the entire genome of T4 is $\frac{130,000,000}{650}$, or about 200,000. Estimates of the number of base pairs in the A cistron range up to 2,500, and generally between 1,000 and 1,500 for the B cistron. With an estimate of 2,000 nucleotide pairs for the rIIA region, the unit of recombination (the *recon*) in the A cistron can include no more than an average of $\frac{2,000}{500}$ or 4 nucleotide pairs. Evidence from the *E. coli* tryptophan synthetase system and the rII region of T4 phage indicates that, like the muton, the recon is very small and almost certainly *may consist of as little as one* deoxyribonucleotide pair. It is also quite probable that mutons and recons are structurally indistinguishable.

Incidentally, if some 1,000 to 2,500 nucleotide pairs are required to specify a particular polypeptide, this would indicate a polypeptide chain of some 300 to 800 amino acids and a total molecular weight of about 50,000 to 133,000. This is not an unreasonable estimate, for most proteins studied by biochemists range between about 20,000 and 70,000 in molecular weight.

### CONCLUSIONS

In the last four chapters we have reached some important conclusions regarding the gene:

1. The genetic material is DNA in all organisms except a few viruses where it is RNA.
2. A gene is a specific linear sequence of nucleotides and is usefully considered at more than one level of organization.

(a) The functional unit, the *cistron*, is responsible for specifying a particular polypeptide chain, and consists of three adjacent deoxyribonucleotide pairs for each amino acid residue in the chain, plus a chain initiating triplet and a chain terminating triplet.

(b) Each cistron is divisible into

    (i) *Mutons*, the smallest number of nucleotides independently capable of producing a mutant phenotype. This can be as little as one nucleotide.

    (ii) *Recons*, the smallest number of nucleotides capable of recombination. This likewise can be as small as one nucleotide. Recons and mutons appear to be structurally identical.

3. Specification of the amino acid sequence of a polypeptide chain by a cistron is made possible through the latter's particular nucleotide sequence.

(a) Mediation of protein synthesis operates through an intermediate, messenger RNA, which is ordinarily a single-stranded, base-for-base, complementary transcription of the nucleotide sequence on one DNA strand.

(b) Messenger RNA, in conjunction with polysomes, tRNA, energy sources, and a battery of enzymes, is directly responsible through its sequence of ribonucleotides (the genetic code) for protein biosynthesis at ribosomal surfaces, chiefly in the cytoplasm.

(c) The genetic code is

    (i) Triplet

    (ii) Commaless

    (iii) Nonoverlapping

    (iv) Degenerate

    (v) Essentially nonambiguous

    (vi) Colinear

    (vii) Universal

### REFERENCES

AUERBACH, C., and B. J. KILBEY, 1971. Gene Mutation. (In H. L. Roman, ed., 1971. *Annual Review of Genetics*, volume 5. Palo Alto, California, Annual Reviews, Inc.)

BENZER, S., 1961. On the Topography of the Genetic Fine Structure. *Proc. Nat. Acad. Sci (U.S.)*, 47:403–415.

BENZER, S., 1962. The Fine Structure of the Gene. *Sci. Amer.*, 206(1):70–84.

BENZER, S., and E. FREESE, 1958. Induction of Specific Mutations with 5-Bromouracil. *Proc. Nat. Acad. Sci. (U.S.)*, 44:112–119. Reprinted in G. S. Stent, ed., 1965, 2nd ed., *Papers on Bacterial Viruses*. Boston, Little, Brown.

BERNHARD, R., 1967. Methylation "Edits" the Genetic Code, May Be a Cancer Factor. *Sci. Res.*, **2**:46–50.

FISHBEIN, L., W. G. FLAMM, and H. L. FALK, 1970. *Chemical Mutagens.* New York, Academic Press.

HUNT, J. A., and V. M. INGRAM, 1958. Allelomorphism and the Chemical Differences of the Human Haemoglobins A, S, C. *Nature*, **181**:1062.

HUNT, J. A., and V. M. INGRAM, 1960. Abnormal Haemoglobins, IV. The Chemical Difference Beween Normal Human Haemoglobin and Haemoglobin C. *Biochim. Biophys. Acta*, **42**:409–421. Reprinted in J. H. Taylor, ed., 1965, *Selected Papers on Molecular Genetics*. New York, Academic Press.

INGRAM, V. M., 1956. A Specific Chemical Difference Between the Globins of Normal and Sickle-Cell Anaemia Haemoglobin. *Nature*, **178**:792–794.

INGRAM, V. M., 1957. Gene Mutations in Human Haemoglobin: the Chemical Difference Between Normal and Sickle-Cell Haemoglobin. *Nature*, **180**: 326–328. Reprinted in S. H. Boyer, ed., 1963, *Papers on Human Genetics*. Englewood Cliffs, N.J., Prentice-Hall.

INGRAM, V. M., 1965. *The Biosynthesis of Macromolecules*. New York, W. A. Benjamin.

MULLER, J. H., 1927. Artificial Transmutation of the Gene. *Science*, **66**:84–87.

WELSHONS, W. J., 1965. Analysis of a Gene in *Drosophila*. *Science*, **150**:1122–1129.

WOLSTENHOLME, G. E. W., and M. O'CONNOR, eds., 1969. *Mutation as Cellular Process.* London, J. & A. Churchill, Ltd.

YANOFSKY, C., 1963. Amino Acid Replacements Associated with Mutation and Recombination in the A Gene and their Relationship to in vitro Coding Data. *Cold Spring Harbor Symposia Quant. Biol.*, **28**:581–588.

YANOFSKY, C., 1967. Structural Relationships Between Gene and Protein. In H. L. Roman, ed., 1967. *Annual Review of Genetics*, volume 1. Palo Alto, California, Annual Reviews. Inc.

YANOFSKY. C., G. R. DRAPEAU, J. R. GUEST, and B. C. CARLTON, 1967. The Complete Amino Acid Sequence of the Tryptophan Synthetase A Protein ($\alpha$ Subunit) and its Colinear Relationship with the Genetic Map of the A Gene. *Proc. Nat. Acad. Sci.* (U.S.), **57**:296–298.

## PROBLEMS

**17-1.** A new and desirable character appears in a large herd of cattle. Suggest experimental procedures to determine whether the new trait is environmentally induced, a dominant mutation, or a recessive mutation.

**17-2.** By deamination, a $\frac{TTT}{AAA}$ segment of a DNA molecule is changed to a $\frac{TTG}{AAC}$ segment. What change in amino acid incorporation does this produce, assuming the "lower" strand serves as the template for mRNA?

**17-3.** Suppose a certain cistron is found to consist of 1,500 nucleotides in sequence. What is the maximum possible number of mutons of which this cistron could consist?

**17-4.** Work with phage T4 (among others) discloses many mutational "hot spots" —i.e., certain nucleotides or groups of nucleotides which are more likely to mutate under given conditions than are others. These "hot spots" are not the same for all chemical mutagens tested. Assume two kinds of micro-organisms, species *AT* in whose DNA adenine-thymine pairs constitute a large majority of the nucleotide pairs, and species *CG* having much more cytosine-guanine than adenine-thymine in its DNA. Cultures of each of these species are treated with a series of different mutagens. For each of the following indicate which species, *AT*, *CG*, or both, would be expected to show the higher mutation rate: (a) the enol form of 5-bromouracil; (b) the keto form of hypoxanthine; (c) uracil; (d) acridine orange; (e) ultraviolet radiation.

**17-5.** In the colon bacillus the enzyme system for the synthesis of tryptophan consists of an A protein and a B protein. The A protein chain has been found to be composed of 267 amino acid residues. The cistron for the A protein consists of how many codons?

**17-6.** How many nucleotides are there in the A protein cistron?

**17-7.** Why are not chemical and radiational mutagens used more widely in developing improved varieties of crop plants and domestic animals?

**17-8.** From this chapter and any other sources available to you, evaluate the short-term and long-term effects of mass irradiation of the human population.

**17-9.** In an imaginary flowering plant, petal color may be either red, white, or blue. White is due to the presence of a colorless precursor from which red and blue pigments may by synthesized in two consecutive, enzyme-controlled processes. The cross of two blue-flowered plants yields an $F_1$ ratio of 9 blue, 3 red, and 4 white. (a) How many pairs of genes are involved? (b) Suggest the correct sequence of enzyme controlled steps and products. (c) Starting with the first letter of the alphabet and using as many more in sequence as needed, give the genotype of (1) the P individuals; (2) the $F_1$ blue plants. (d) Give genotypes for (1) red and (2) white $F_1$ plants. (e) According to the system you have worked out, which pair of genes controls the first step of the process you have worked out in part (b) of this problem?

**17-10.** One calculation for the molecular weight of the DNA in a single (monoploid) set of human chromosomes is $1.625 \times 10^{12}$. (a) Assuming 650 as the average molecular weight of a pair of deoxyribonucleotides, how many nucleotide pairs comprise the DNA of one *diploid* somatic nucleus? (b) What, then, is the maximum number of mutons in each of your somatic cells? (c) What is the total length in micrometers (microns) of the DNA in the nucleus of one of your diploid somatic cells? (d) At these values, for how many mRNA codons is the DNA of *one* of your (monoploid) sets of chromosomes responsible? (e) Assuming an average of 300 amino acid residues per polypeptide chain, and neglecting start-stop signals, how many cistrons do you have in *one* of your sets of 23 chromosomes?

# CHAPTER 18
# Regulation of Gene Action

**M**ULTICELLULAR organisms normally develop by an orderly process of differentiation from a single cell, the zygote, to an adult form of many different kinds of cells, tissues, and organs. But because of the behavior of chromosomes in mitosis, all of the cells of a complex, multicellular soma may be presumed to have the same genotype. In short, between zygote and adult stages, cells of the organism *differentiate*, both physiologically and physically, yet the genome of all cells should be identical under normal conditions. The problem may be quite simply stated: how do genetically identical cells become functionally different?

Up to at least a certain point in development, the cells of a multicellular organism are *totipotent*; that is, they are capable of forming complete bodies if isolated after development has begun. For example, in carrot, excised, mature, differentiated cells from phloem (the food conducting vascular tissue) form an irregular mass of large, thin-walled, undifferentiated cells (called a callus) on a solid nutrient medium. Transfer of the callus to a liquid medium, which is kept gently shaken, separates the cells. Upon subsequent transfer to new cultures, these callus cells develop into embryo-like structures, or embryoids. Liquid media induce root formation by the embryoid; later transfer to a solid medium results in stem and flower production, in short, a fully differentiated, mature plant. A small section of the body of the flatworm *Planaria* or the mature leaf of a plant like the African violet (*Saintpaulia ionantha*) regenerates the entire organism under proper environmental conditions, though this is by no means true for all animals and plants. Many experiments with very young embryos of sea urchins and frogs indicate that even after the zygote has divided to produce two to eight cells, separation of cells or forcing them to divide in only one plane was followed by normal differentiation and embryo formation. Separation of the cells of two-celled rabbit embryos and then reimplantation into another female similarly produces normal embryos. In the tobacco plant Nitsch and Nitsch (1969) report in vitro development of microspores into monoploid plants that reach flowering stage, although seeds are not produced. Yet at later developmental stages, when differentiation has proceeded beyond a critical point, this totipotency is often lost, particularly in many animals.

The key to orderly structural and functional differentiation of multicellular organisms lies in the fact that their cells do not always produce the same proteins all of the time. Even unicellular forms like bacteria display a temporal shift in protein synthesis. Apparently, some mechanism exists in the

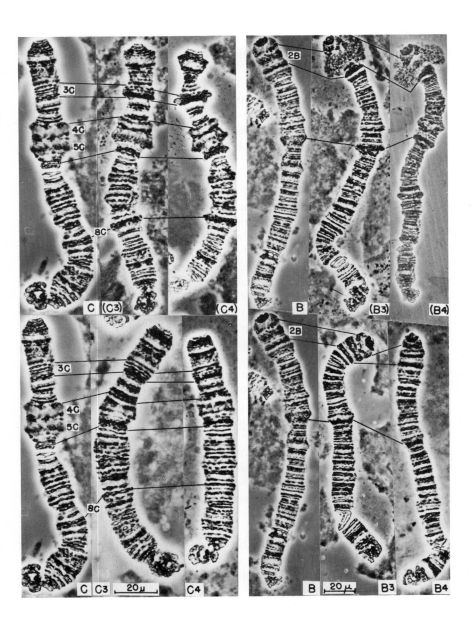

cell to turn genes "on" or "off" at different times and/or in different environments. In fact, it is now clear from considerable experimental evidence that differentiation is the consequence of orderly, temporal activation and repression of genetic material. This *regulation of gene action* is the problem we need now to examine.

## Evidence of Regulation of Gene Action

### CHROMOSOME PUFFS

*Giant Chromosomes.* In dipteran flies, the chromosomes of larval tissues such as the salivary glands regularly exhibit unusual behavior which has shed some light on gene regulation. Although the cells of these tissues do not divide, their chromosomes replicate repeatedly while permanently synapsed in homologous pairs, producing polytene or many-stranded giant chromosomes. If these chromosomes are examined at several stages of the individual's development, specific areas (sets of bands) are seen to enlarge into prominent "puffs" or Balbiani rings (Fig. 18-1). From electron micrographs Beerman and Bahr (1954) describe the puff as a loosening of the tightly coiled DNA into long, looped structures not unlike the lampbrush chromosomes described in the next section. These puffs appear and disappear in a given tissue at certain chromosomal locations as development proceeds, those at particular locations being correlated with specific developmental stages of the insect. The pattern of puffing varies in a regular and characteristic way with the tissue and its stage of maturation.

By means of differential staining techniques, biochemical tests, and use of radioactive isotopes, it has been demonstrated that each puff is an active site of RNA transcription. If we recall that genes (i.e., cistrons) are associated with particular sets of bands, this temporal puffing thus clearly indicates changes in gene activity over time. Tests show that the RNA synthesized in one puff is characteristic and differs from that produced by other puffs.

Injection of very small amounts of the hormone ecdysone, which is

---

FIGURE 18-1. *Chromosome puffs in polytene chromosomes of* Rhynchosciara, *at 4C and 5C. Top row, chromosomes* C *and* B *from controls* (*no ligation*) *and their appearance after 3* (C3 *and* B3) *and 4* (C4 *and* B4) *days. Note especially the development of puff* 2B (*upper right photograph*). *Bottom row, chromosomes* B *and* C *before ligation* (C *and* B)*; C3 and* B3*, chromosomes* C *and* B *3 days after ligation; C4 and* B4*, the same chromosomes 4 days after ligation. Note particularly the failure of puff 2B to develop in the experimental series.* [Courtesy Drs. J. M. Amabis and D. Cabral, Universidade de São Paulo, São Paulo, Brazil. Reprinted from *Science*, **169**: 692–694 (14 August 1970) by permission. Copyright 1970 by the American Association for the Advancement of Science.)

produced by the prothoracic glands and which induces molting, causes formation of the same puffs that occur normally prior to molting in untreated larvae.
The prothoracic glands are activated by the flow of brain hormone from
neurosecretory cells. This has been demonstrated in an ingenious experiment
reported by Amabis and Cabral (1970). Tying off the anterior part of the
larva of the dipteran *Rhynchosciara* just behind the brain, they found,
resulted both in failure of normal puffing and a decrease in size of puffs
already initiated at the time of ligation (Fig. 18-1). In other experiments,
injection of the antibiotic actinomycin D (which inhibits mRNA synthesis)
prevents puff formation for several hours, even when ecdysone is used simultaneously. Radioactive uridine, injected into larvae, accumulates only in the
puffs and nucleoli, but fails to do so if it is preceded by injection of actinomycin D.

All of these results clearly point to the puffs as sites of RNA synthesis
according to a pattern closely associated with the development of the individual. Evidently, then, genes (cistrons) undergo reversible changes in activity
(principally mRNA synthesis) that are related to the developmental stage of
the organism.

*Lampbrush Chromosomes.*   This "turning on and off" of genes is evident
also in the large chromosomes of amphibian oocytes (Fig. 18-2). Here the
DNA strands of the long axes form lateral loops. Ribonucleic acid is produced in the loops of these chromosomes in cyclic fashion, very much as in
the puffs of dipteran chromosomes. It seems likely that cyclic RNA production is a general phenomenon, though the morphological details of interphase
chromosomes of most cells cannot be studied adequately enough with present
techniques to provide visual evidence.

*Histones.*   X-ray diffraction and chemical studies indicate that the DNA
of all cells except bacteria and some sperm is intimately associated with a
fairly simple class of basic proteins called *histones.* There is some evidence
that the nucleolus is the most active site of histone synthesis (Flamm and
Birnstiel, 1964). The exact physical relationship between histones and the
helices of DNA is not settled, but it is considered likely that the histone
complexing of DNA either causes or enhances coiling which, in turn, is
related to gene repression. Zubay (1964) further suggests that the DNA
helices of eukaryote chromosomes are formed into supercoils whose adjacent
gyres are held together by histone bridges. Sluyser and Snellen-Jurgens (1970)
believe that histones rich in lysine readily form crosslinks between nucleic
acid molecules, whereas those rich in arginine do so less readily.

The degree of histone-DNA complexing appears, in at least some
organisms, to vary with the body part and with time. In developing pea
embryos, for example, the cotyledons (food storage organs of the embryo)
develop rather rapidly in embryogeny, then cease to grow further, even in

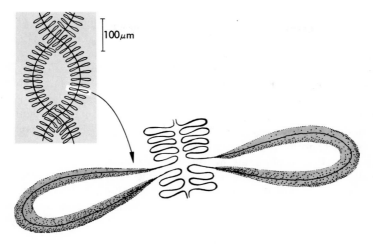

100μm

FIGURE 18-2. *Diagram of portion of a lampbrush chromosome as seen in an amphibian oöcyte.*

germination. Tests indicate that almost all of the DNA of mature cotyledons is histone-complexed, whereas the terminal meristems, active growth
regions which, at germination, produce all of the root and shoot of the
seedling, have more noncomplexed DNA.

This suggests an inverse relationship between histone complexing and
protein synthesis. Bonner and his colleagues (1963) have presented excellent
confirmation of this hypothesis. Pea cotyledons produce a protein, seed
reserve globulin, which is not produced in vegetative tissues. DNA from
cotyledons can be made to produce the mRNA necessary for in vitro synthesis of this protein. DNA from vegetative parts of the plant does not
yield mRNA for globulin unless the histone is chemically removed! Nezgovorova and Borisova (1970) have shown that maize embryos begin growth
and development into seedlings only when most of the DNA is not histone
complexed. They conclude that histone removal may therefore be involved
in the physiological mechanism that initiates germination of the grain. It
has been suggested by a number of researchers that histones inhibit DNA
strand separation by enhancing coiling; in that case, histone-complexed
DNA would be unable to serve as a template for either DNA or RNA
synthesis.

However, the role of histones in the regulation of gene activity must simply
be regarded at present as largely unsettled. It is known that at least certain
of the histones do very greatly inhibit DNA-dependent RNA synthesis
(transcription); in some way complexing of DNA by histones prevents action
of RNA polymerase. It has been suggested (Pogo et al., 1966; Allfrey et al.,

1968) that acetylation of histones precedes RNA synthesis by previously inactive cistrons. But Ellgaard (1967) and Clever and Ellgaard (1970) offer experimental evidence that, although this appears to be so, histone acetylation does not necessarily take place at loci being activated in heat-induced puffs in *Drosophila* chromosomes. Georgiev (1969) concludes that "the number of . . . facts is not enough to describe a general scheme of histone participation in the control of gene expression." Of many possibilities he concludes that (1) histones combine with and repress all DNA nonspecifically whereas other, nonhistone proteins recognize particular deoxyribonucleotide sequences, acting to eliminate histone repression, and/or (2) some histones, especially those rich in lysine, may be specific for certain DNA sequences. Perhaps the most concise statement of the present state of our information is that most histones appear to act as generalized repressors of mRNA transcription, and that various *inducers* (e.g., ecdysone) may bring about histone removal in some way at particular loci which, therefore, become de-repressed.

**Enzyme Regulation.** Inasmuch as the product of a cistron is a polypeptide chain, which is frequently an enzyme, a simple system of control would operate at the level of enzyme regulation. Evidence accumulated in recent years indicates two basic mechanisms, one controlling *activity* of enzymes whose production is not altered, the other regulating the *synthesis* of enzymes. The first of these is generally termed *end product inhibition*, the second involves the concept of the **operon**.

### END PRODUCT INHIBITION

In studies on isoleucine synthesis in *Escherichia coli*, Umbarger (1961) demonstrated that addition of isoleucine (the end product of a five-step conversion of threonine, Fig. 18-3) to a culture of the bacteria resulted in immediate blocking of the threonine → isoleucine pathway. In the presence of added isoleucine, the cells preferentially use this *exogenous* end product and cease their own isoleucine synthesis. Moreover, it has been shown that *production* of each of the five enzymes is *not* interfered with, but action of the enzyme responsible for the deamination of threonine to $\alpha$-ketobutyrate (Fig. 18-3) is *inhibited* by the end product, isoleucine.

Interestingly, this inhibition results from a binding of end product to the enzyme so that the inhibitor appears to compete with the substrate for a site on the enzyme molecule. But it is known that this competition is not for the same site, the enzyme apparently having two specific recognition sites, one for its substrate and another for the inhibiting end product. However, attachment at the inhibitor site affects the substrate site. The term *allosteric interaction* is now applied to such changes in enzyme activity produced by binding of a second substance at a different and nonoverlapping site.

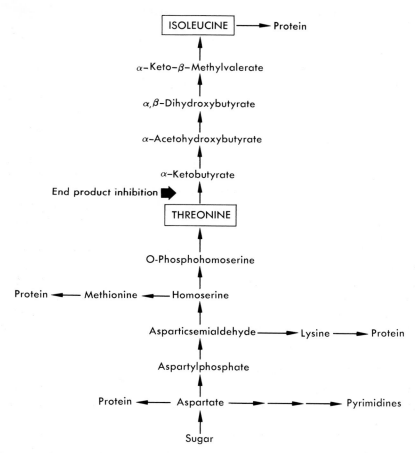

FIGURE 18-3. *Some steps in isoleucine synthesis. In end-product inhibition in* E. coli, *enzyme inhibition occurs in the deamination of threonine to α-ketobutyrate at the point indicated.*

### ENZYME REPRESSION AND INDUCTION

*Lactose Utilization in Escherichia coli.* Among the many strains of the colon bacillus, two in particular have shed considerable light on another system of gene regulation. Two enzymes are required for lactose metabolism in this organism: *β-galactoside permease*, responsible for transport of lactose into the cell and its concentration there, and *β-galactosidase*, which catalyzes the hydrolysis of lactose to galactose and glucose. The wild type E. coli produces these enzymes only in the presence of lactose; this is an *inductive* strain. Other strains, derived by mutation from the normal wild type, produce these enzymes continuously, whether lactose is present or not. These are *constitutive* strains. After some initial uncertainty over whether enzyme synthesis or enzyme activity was affected by lactose, it has become clear that the presence of lactose does indeed *induce* synthesis of enzymes in the inductive strain. Lactose, the substrate, is here acting as an enzyme inducer. Enzymes produced only when a substrate is present are designated as *inducible enzymes* Although inducers are quite specific, structural analogs may often function in the same way.

Just as some substances behave as enzyme inducers, others serve as *enzyme repressors*, a term originated by Vogel (1961). Whereas inducible enzymes increase in concentration in the presence of a suitable inducer, repressors decrease the rate of enzyme synthesis. In repression, the *synthesis* of enzymes is affected but, in end product inhibition, *activity* is altered. The lactose system (lac) in bacteria is the best understood example of enzyme induction and repression.

***The Lac System in Escherichia coli.***   The lac segment of the *E. coli* chromosome is known to include three cistrons, *z* for β-galactosidase, *y* for β-galactoside permease, and *a* for thiogalactoside transacetylase.[1] The three cistrons are closely linked and regulated coordinately. Jacob and Mon d and their associates (1959, 1960, 1961) developed a model of a genetic system that regulates lactose metabolism, to which they gave the name **operon**. With minor later refinements, this model appears to explain all observations in this bacterium, and several other similar regulatory systems have subsequently been described for this and other bacteria. Functioning of the lac operon is excellently summarized by Beckwith (1967), by Epstein and Beckwith (1968), and by Martin (1969) who describe its operation in the following way.

As already noted, genes *z*, *y*, and *a* are structural genes (cistrons) responsible for specific enzyme syntheses. All three map adjacent to each other; in the absence of any regulation, genetic information of these three cistrons is transcribed into mRNA which is then translated into the three enzyme (protein) products. Transcription is initiated at a **promoter site**, *p*, at which RNA polymerase binds. Jacob and Monod originally postulated the promoter site *p* to be adjacent to or even a part of the *z* cistron, a location now known to be incorrect. An **operator site**, *o*, lies to the "right" of *p* (i.e., in the direction of the three structural genes) and exercises a control over transcription that we shall examine shortly. Epstein and Beckwith (1968) identify another control site that serves as an initiation point for translation on the mRNA transcribed from DNA. The point on DNA responsible for transcription of this control site is symbolized in this account by an asterisk.

---

[1] The function of thiogalactoside transacetylase in vivo is unknown.

Recent mapping experiments show the sequence of these genetic elements of DNA to be

$$p \; o * z \; y \; a$$

*The three cistrons, together with the promoter and operator sites* (i.e., $p \; o * z \; y \; a$), *constitute the lac operon.* **An operon, then, consists of a system of cistrons, operator, and promoter sites.** Genes $z^+$, $y^+$, and $a^+$ produce their enzymes concurrently when lactose is available to inductive strains of the bacterium.

A regulator ($i$) is located near (but not immediately adjacent to) the promoter ($p$) and to the "left" of it. The complete map sequence, then, is

$$i \ldots p \; o * z \; y \; a$$

The wild-type regulator ($i^+$) constitutively specifies a protein (molecular weight 150,000) composed of four subunits. This regulator protein, or repressor, binds to the wild-type operator ($o^+$), thereby preventing progression of RNA polymerase (bound to $p$) so that transcription cannot proceed. In the absence of binding of the repressor, transcription is permitted to progress through all three cistrons. Subsequent translation then begins at the initiation site on mRNA near the beginning of the base sequence coded for by the $z$ cistron (Epstein and Beckwith, 1968).

In inductive strains of *E. coli*, the regulator gene, as usual, specifies a repressor protein which, in the absence of the inducer lactose, binds to the operator, preventing transcription. When lactose is supplied, however, it combines with the repressor so as to inactivate it. The repressor then cannot bind to the operator. RNA polymerase, binding first at the promoter site, is then able to progress past the unrepressed operator into the three cistrons. These then transcribe mRNA which, in turn, begins translation at the second control site (Fig. 18-4).

Constitutive strains of *E. coli* are characterized by either a defective regulator ($i^-$) or a mutant operator which is unable to bind the repressor. For example, $i^+ \ldots p^+ \; o^+ * z^+ \; y^+ \; a^+$ is an inductive strain, $i^+$ producing a repressor that binds to $o^+$, preventing transcription of $z^+$, $y^+$ and $a^+$ (Fig. 18-4). Presence of lactose, of course, inactivates the repressor so that $o^+$ permits transcription. On the other hand, $i^- \ldots p^+ \; o^+ * z^+ \; y^+ \; a^+$ is constitutive because a defective repressor, which will not bind to $o^+$, is produced, so transcription of the three cistrons is continuous. An $i^+ \ldots p^+ \; o^c * z^+ \; y^+ \; a^+$ mutant (an *operator-constitutive* strain) is also constitutive, producing enzymes continuously, but because the repressor binding site ($o$) rather than the repressor itself, is defective and cannot bind the repressor protein.

Interestingly enough, studies of merozygotes (partial diploids) produced through conjugation show $i^+$ to be dominant to $i^-$. In a cell of genotype $i^+ \ldots o^+ \; z^+ \ldots / i^- \ldots o^+ \; z^- \ldots$ one might expect normal $\beta$-galactosidase to be produced inductively and a modified form of the enzyme (i.e., lacking activity)

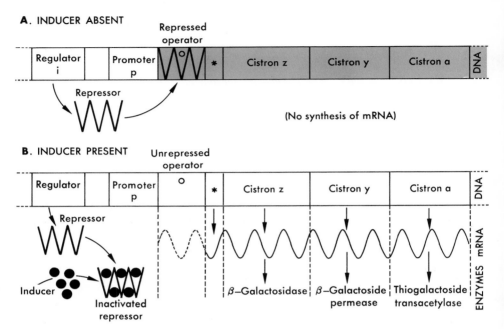

FIGURE 18-4. *Diagrammatic representation of the* lac *operon of* E. coli. *The promoter site* (p) *is the attachment point of RNA polymerase. If the operator* (o) *is repressed by binding of the repressor protein, no transcription of mRNA occurs but, if the operator is not repressed, RNA polymerase progresses in the 5′ → 3′ direction, transcribing cistrons z, y, and a into a single polycistronic mRNA molecule. It is possible that the unrepressed operator is also transcribed, as suggested by the dashed line representing mRNA in B. Another control site, proposed by Epstein and Beckwith (1968), symbolized by an asterisk, is presumed to transcribe the site of translation initiation. In inducible systems, the repressor binds to the operator, preventing mRNA transcription, but if the inducer (lactose) is supplied, it inactivates the repressor so that transcription proceeds and translation ensues. For further details see text.*

constitutively. Not so; both types of $\beta$-galactosidase are produced inductively. The repressor is able to diffuse from the $i^+ \ldots o^+ z^+$ chromosome to the other and to repress $z^-$ even though the latter is linked to $i^-$. The regulator gene thus functions in either the *cis* or *trans* position. On the other hand, the operator (*o*) functions only in the *cis* position; for example, the diploid $i^+ \ldots o^c z^+ \ldots / i^- \ldots o^+ z^- \ldots$ constitutively produces only normal $\beta$-galactosidase and no modified enzyme. This is to be expected if the operator is the place where mRNA transcription begins. Enzyme production by these several genotypes is summarized in Table 18-1.

The lac operon is an example of *negative* control, but there is evidence in other systems for *positive* control in which regulatory proteins serve to turn

TABLE 18-1. Production of Normal and Modified Beta-Galactosidase by Several Lac Genotypes in *E. coli*

| Genotype | Enzyme Production | | | |
| --- | --- | --- | --- | --- |
| | Constitutive | | Inductive | |
| | Normal | Modified | Normal | Modified |
| $i^+ o^+ z^+$ | | | + | |
| $i^- o^+ z^+$ | + | | | |
| $i^+ o^c z^+$ | + | | | |
| $i^+ o^+ z^+ / i^- o^+ z^-$ | | | + | + |

transcription on rather than off. Control at the level of translation is also possible, and there is increasing evidence that this may be relatively more important in eukaryotes.

## Summary of Gene Regulation

Genetic material has turned out to be fairly complicated in its regulation as well as in its action and structure. Yet it is an elegantly simple system for the production of an endless variety of phenotypes. Gene action appears to be related to certain proteins (histones) and/or to other genes or even to certain metabolites. So to our summary of gene function and fine structure (Chapter 17) we need to add the following points regarding the regulation of gene action:

1. The activity of many cistrons is regulated so that their polypeptide product is formed only under certain chemical conditions and/or at certain developmental stages.
2. Although the function of histones is not fully known, it has been suggested that they regulate gene activity in those cells in which they occur by affecting DNA coiling and RNA synthesis.
3. In other cells, notably bacteria, there is good evidence for a regulator-operon complex in which
   a. regulators produce repressor proteins which
   b. repress operator sites which otherwise
   c. allow cistrons to transcribe their information into mRNA, starting at the promoter site; however,
   d. repressors can be inactivated by inducers, and
   e. regulators, operators, and cistrons may be defective ($i^-$, $o^c$, $z^-$, etc.) in that their normal product or function is interfered with.
4. Control may be negative (lac operon) or positive, and may operate either at the level of transcription (lac operon) or at the level of translation.

In a superb piece of research, Beckwith and his colleagues (Shapiro et al., 1969), using two transducing phages, have been able to isolate and produce electron micrographs of a segment of the *E. coli* lac operon. This segment consists of only the promoter, operator, and $\beta$-galactosidase sites some 1.3 to 1.5 $\mu$m in length. Taking an average of 1.4 $\mu$m, their calculations show the promoter and operator sites to total approximately 0.14 $\mu$m in length (about 410 DNA base pairs) and the *z* cistron 1.26 $\mu$m (3,700 base pairs). It is to be expected that the techniques used will make it possible to answer hitherto unexplained problems of gene regulation, such as operation of the repressor, in this and in other operons, as well as to clarify the mechanism of RNA polymerase binding and the control of RNA synthesis. It is also conceivable that the methods used in this remarkable work will eventually have some application in " genetic surgery " (see Chapter 20).

### REFERENCES

ALLFREY, V. G., B. G. T. POGO, V. C. LITTAU, E. L. GERSHEY, and A. E. MIRSKY, 1968. Histone Acetylation in Insect Chromosomes. *Science*, **159**: 314–316.

AMABIS, J. M., and D. CABRAL, 1970. RNA and DNA Puffs in Polytene Chromosomes of *Rhynchosciara*: Inhibition by Extirpation of Prothorax. *Science*, **169**:692–694.

BECKWITH, J. R. 1967. Regulation of the Lac Operon. *Science*, **156**:597–604.

BECKWITH, J. R., and D. ZIPSER, eds., 1970. *The Lactose Operon*. Cold Spring Harbor, N.Y., Cold Spring Harbor Laboratory.

BEERMAN, W., and G. F. BAHR, 1954. The Submicroscopic Structure of the Balbiani Ring. *Exptl. Cell Res.*, **6**:195–201.

BONNER, J., R. C. HUANG, and R. V. GILDEN, 1963. Chromosomally Directed Protein Synthesis. *Proc. Nat. Acad. Sci. (U.S.)*, **50**:893–900.

BONNER, J., and P. T'SO, eds., 1964. *The Nucleohistones*. San Francisco, Holden-Day.

CLEVER, U., and E. G. ELLGAARD, 1970. Puffing and Histone Acetylation in Polytene Chromosomes. *Science*, **169**:373–374.

ELLGAARD, E. G., 1967. Gene Activation without Histone Acetylation in *Drosophila melanogaster*. *Science*, **157**:1070–1072.

EPSTEIN, W., and J. R. BECKWITH, 1968. Regulation of Gene Expression. *Ann. Rev. Biochem.*, **37**:411–436.

FLAMM, W. G., and M. L. BIRNSTIEL, 1964. *Studies on the Metabolism of Nuclear Basic Proteins*. In J. Bonner, and P. T'so, eds., *The Nucleohistones*. San Francisco, Holden Day.

GEORGIEV, G. P., 1969. *Histones and the Control of Gene Action*. In H. L. Roman, ed., 1969. *Annual Review of Genetics*, volume 3. Palo Alto, Calif., Annual Reviews, Inc.

JACOB, F., and J. MONOD, 1961. Genetic Regulatory Mechanisms in the Synthesis of Proteins. *Jour. Molec. Biol.*, **3**:318–356.

JACOB, F., D. PERRIN, C. SANCHEZ, and J. MONOD, 1960. The Operon: A Group of Genes Whose Expression Is Coordinated by an Operator. *Compt. Rend. Acad. Sci.*, **250**:1727–1729.

LOOMIS, W. F., ed., 1970. *Papers on Regulation of Gene Activity During Development.* New York, Harper & Row.

MARTIN, R. G., 1969. *Control of Gene Expression.* In H. L. Roman, ed., *Annual Review of Genetics*, volume 3. Palo Alto, Calif., Annual Reviews, Inc.

NEZGOVOROVA, L. A., and N. N. BORISOVA, 1970. On the Trigger Mechanism of Germinating Seeds. V. Histones, Their Relation to Nucleic Acids and Influence of Inhibitors. *Fiziol. Rast.*, **17**:322–329.

NITSCH, J. P., and C. NITSCH, 1969. Haploid Plants from Pollen Grains. *Science*, **163**:85–87.

PARDEE, A. B., F. JACOB, and J. MONOD, 1959. The Genetic Control and Cytoplasmic Expression of "Inducibility" in the Synthesis of $\beta$-galactosidase by *E. coli. Jour. Molec. Biol.*, **1**:165–178.

POGO, B. G. T., V. G. ALLFREY, and A. E. MIRSKY, 1966. RNA Synthesis and Histone Acetylation During the Course of Gene Activation in Lymphocytes. *Proc. Nat. Acad. Sci. (U.S.)*, **55**:805–812.

SHAPIRO, J., L. MACHATTIE, L. ERON, G. IHLER, K. IPPEN, and J. BECKWITH, 1969. Isolation of Pure *Lac* Operon DNA. *Nature*, **224**:768–774.

SLUYSER, M., and N. H. SNELLEN-JURGENS, 1970. Interaction of Histones and Nucleic Acids in vitro. *Biochim. Biophys. Acta*, **199**:490–499.

UMBARGER, H. E., 1961. Feedback Control by Endproduct Inhibition. *Cold Spring Harbor Symposia Quant. Biol.*, **26**:301–312.

VOGEL, H. J., 1961. Aspects of Repression in the Regulation of Enzyme Synthesis: Pathway-Wide Control and Enzyme-Specific Response. *Cold Spring Harbor Symposia Quant. Biol.*, **26**:163–172.

ZIPSER, D., 1967. Orientation of Nonsense Codons on the Genetic Map of the Lac Operon. *Science*, **157**:1176–1177.

ZUBAY, G. L., 1964. *Nucleohistone Structure and Function.* In J. Bonner, and P. T'so, eds., *The Nucleohistones.* San Francisco, Holden-Day.

## PROBLEMS

**18-1.** In what way or ways are operator and regulator loci similar? Dissimilar?

**18-2.** Differentiate between repressors and inducers.

**18-3.** Will production of *normal* beta-galactosidase be constitutive, inductive, or absent for each of the following genotypes:

(a) $i^+ p^+ o^+ * z^+ \ldots$; (b) $i^- p^+ o^+ * z^+ \ldots$;
(c) $i^+ p^+ o^c * z^+ \ldots$; (d) $i^+ p^+ o^+ * z^- \ldots$;
(e) $i^+ p^+ o^+ * z^- \ldots / i^+ p^+ o^c * z^+ \ldots$?

**18-4.** The second control site (designated as * in the text) has not been structurally identified. From its presumed function, could you suggest its possible nature?

**18-5.** State the present concept of the gene.

# CHAPTER 19

# *The Question of Cytoplasmic Genetic Systems*

T HE existence of genes as segments of nucleic acid molecules, located in chromosomes, and controlling phenotypes in known and predictable fashion has been amply demonstrated on sound, observable, verifiable bases. But the firm establishment of such a chromosomal mechanism of inheritance does not necessarily preclude a role by other cell parts. From time to time observations have been reported which suggest a cytoplasmic role in genetics. To evaluate these reports we need first to have a clear understanding of what cytoplasmic inheritance does or should mean.

## SUGGESTED CRITERIA FOR CYTOPLASMIC GENES

Before a particular genetic phenomenon is clearly acceptable as having a cytoplasmic basis, the following criteria should be applied:

1. *Is there evidence of genes physically and/or physiologically independent of any nuclear genetic material?*
2. *What is the chemical nature of the suspected cytoplasmic gene?*
   a. *Is it DNA? RNA? Something else?*
   b. *Is it operationally genetic, that is, is it a conserved structure whose activities govern the trait, or is it the trait itself which is being called a cytoplasmic gene?*
   c. *Is it a normal and usual part of the cell's cytoplasm (recognizing that " normal" may not be easy to define)?*
3. *What are its mutational properties and methods?*
4. *Do reciprocal crosses show clear evidence of a cytoplasmic role as opposed to sex (or other) chromosomes?*
5. *Does its pattern of inheritance bear no relation to chromosomal segregation?*
6. *Is it unequivocally not a part of any chromosomal linkage group?*
7. *Are there alternative phenotypic expressions and are they stable through syngamy and meiosis?*
8. *Is transmission of the trait unaffected by nuclear transplants?*

Although this list is neither exhaustive nor universally accepted, for our purposes cytoplasmic inheritance will be understood to be based on cytoplasmically located, independent, self-replicating nucleic acids, differing from chromosomal genes only in their location within the cell. Not many of the purported examples of cytoplasmic inheritance fit this concept, and few have been unequivocally established. We shall examine some of them in the following sections.

## MATERNAL EFFECTS

*Shell Coiling in the Snail, Limnaea.*   The direction of coiling of the shell in such snails as *Limnaea* illustrates the influence of nuclear genes acting through effects produced in the cytoplasm.

The shells of snails coil either to the right (dextral) or to the left (sinistral) as seen in Fig. 19-1. A shell held so that the opening through which the snail's body protrudes is on the right and facing the observer is termed dextral; if the opening is on the left, coiling is sinistral. Direction of coiling is determined by a pair of nuclear genes, dextral $(+)$ being dominant to sinistral $(s)$. But expression of the trait depends on the maternal genotype. Because snails may be self-fertilized, the following cross is possible:

$$P \quad + + \; (♀) \times ss \; (♂)$$

right      left

$$F_1 \qquad + s$$

right
(self-fertilized)

$$F_2 \quad \tfrac{1}{4} + + : \tfrac{2}{4} + s : \tfrac{1}{4} ss$$

right      right      right!

When each of the $F_2$ genotypes is again self-fertilized, progeny of the $+ +$ and $+ s$ animals are dextral, but those of the $ss$ individuals are sinistral.

Additional investigation has disclosed that direction of coiling depends upon the orientation of the spindle in the first mitosis of the zygote. Spindle orientation, in turn, is controlled by the genotype of the oocyte from which the egg develops and appears to be built into the egg before meiosis or syngamy occurs. The exact basis of this rather bizarre control is unknown.

*Water Fleas and Flour Moths.*   A closely similar situation occurs in at least two very different invertebrates, the water flea (*Gammarus*) and the flour moth (*Ephestia*). Pigment production in eyes of young individuals depends upon a pair of nuclear genes, $A$ and $a$. The dominant gene directs production of kynurenine, a diffusible substance which is involved in pigment synthesis. The cross $Aa$ (♀) $\times aa$ (♂), for example, produces progeny all of which have dark eyes while young. Upon reaching the adult stage, half the offspring (those of genotype $aa$) become light-eyed. The explanation,

Dextral          Sinistral

FIGURE 19-1. *Dextral and sinistral coiling of the shell in the snail,* Limnea.

of course, is that kynurenine diffuses from the *Aa* mother into all the young, enabling them to manufacture pigment regardless of their genotype. The *aa* progeny, however, have no means of continuing the supply of kynurenine, with the result that their eyes eventually become light. This is obviously a cytoplasmic effect, but wholly without a cytoplasmic genetic mechanism.

### INFECTIVE PARTICLES

***Carbon Dioxide Sensitivity in Drosophila.***   A certain strain of *Drosophila melanogaster* shows a high degree of sensitivity to carbon dioxide. Whereas the wild type can be exposed for long periods to pure $CO_2$ without permanent damage, the sensitive strain quickly becomes uncoordinated in even brief exposures to low concentrations. This trait is transmitted primarily, but not exclusively, through the maternal parent. Tests have disclosed that sensitivity is dependent upon an infective, viruslike particle, called sigma, in the cytoplasm. It is normally transmitted via the eggs' larger amount of cytoplasm but occasionally through the sperms as well. Sensitivity may even be induced by injection of a cell-free extract from sensitives. (See L'Heritier, 1951.)

Sigma contains DNA and is mutable, but is clearly an infective, "foreign" particle. Multiplication is independent of any nuclear gene, but the mechanism of its sensitizing action is unknown.

***Female Production in Drosophila.***   In another case in *Drosophila*, almost all male offspring die soon after zygote formation. This trait is transmitted by the female and is independent of nuclear genes. Studies have disclosed the trait to be dependent on a spirochete (one of the classes of bacteria) in the hemolymph of the female.

***Killer Trait in Paramecium.***   Some races ("killers") of the common ciliate, *Paramecium aurelia*, produce a substance called paramecin which is lethal to other individuals ("sensitives"). Paramecin is water-soluble, diffusible, and depends for its production upon particles called *kappa* in the cytoplasm. Kappa contains DNA and RNA and is mutable, but its presence is dependent on the nuclear gene *K*. Animals of nuclear genotype *kk* are unable to harbor kappa.

*K*− individuals do not possess kappa unless and until it is introduced through a cytoplasmic bridge during conjugation (Fig. 19-2). Nonkiller *K*− animals may also be derived from killers by decreasing the number of

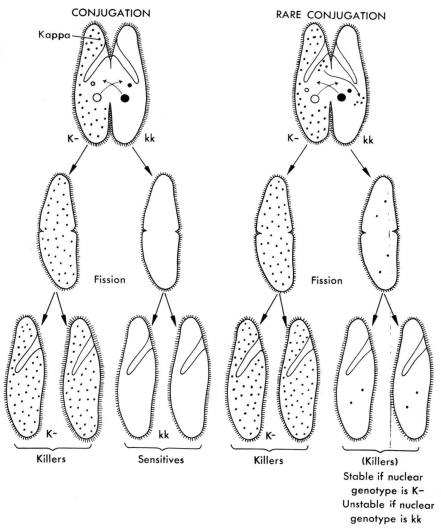

FIGURE 19-2. *Conjugation in* Paramecium *and the killer trait. Progeny of sensitives are killers only in rare situations where conjugation persists for a longer period so that kappa-containing cytoplasm is introduced into the conjugating sensitive. Kappa particles, however, are maintained only in the presence of a K– nuclear genotype.*

kappa particles. This may be accomplished either by near starvation of the culture or subjecting it to low temperatures or, on the other hand, by causing killers to multiply more rapidly than kappa.

Kappa particles can be seen with the microscope. Electron microscopy reveals them to have minute amounts of cytoplasm and to be bounded by a membrane. They can be transferred to other ciliates by feeding. Far from being the illustration of the cytoplasmic gene it was first surmised to be, kappa must be regarded as an infectious organism which has attained a high degree of symbiosis with its host.

Similarly, the mate-killer trait in *Paramecium* is imparted by a *mu* particle which, in turn, exists only in those cells whose micronucleus contains at least one dominant of either of two pairs of chromosomal genes. *Mu* particles, too, appear to be endosymbiotes.

***Milk Factor in Mice.***    The females of certain lines of mice are highly susceptible to mammary cancer. Results of reciprocal crosses between these and animals of a low-cancer-incidence strain depend on the characteristic of the female parent. Allowing young mice of a low-incidence strain to be nursed by susceptible foster mothers produces a high rate of cancer in these low-incidence young. Apparently this is a case of an infective agent being transmitted in the milk. This so-called milk factor meets many of the criteria of a virus and has been discovered to be transmissible also by saliva and semen. Its presence in body fluids, moreover, is again dependent upon certain nuclear genes.

Situations of the kind just described, often showing a maternal inheritance pattern, are certainly not examples of cytoplasmic inheritance as we have defined it. Rather than being components of the individual's genetic mechanism and due to independent, conserved, nucleic acids located in the cytoplasm, they are, in fact, simply acquired infective agents.

### NORMAL CELL COMPONENTS AND TRAITS

***Chloroplasts.***    Plastids are cytoplasmic organelles in the cells of many different kinds of plants. Those containing the green photosynthetic pigments, the chlorophylls, are called chloroplastids or simply *chloroplasts*. Plastids arise by differentiation from simpler structures, the proplastids. These are able to divide and so increase in number in a manner only in part under the control of nuclear DNA. Electron microscopy reveals chloroplasts as fairly complex structures (Fig. 19-3), and they do contain rather significant amounts

FIGURE 19-3. *Electron micrograph of a thin section of a chloroplast from corn leaf. The internal membrane system contains the chlorophylls and is the actual site of photosynthesis; DNA is contained within the stroma (S). GS, grana stacks; GL, grana lamellae; SL, stroma lamellae; S, stroma containing ribosomes and DNA. × 80,000.* [From *Cell Ultrastructure* by William Jensen and Roderic Park, © 1967 by Wadsworth Publishing Co., Inc., Belmont, California. Reproduced by permission.]

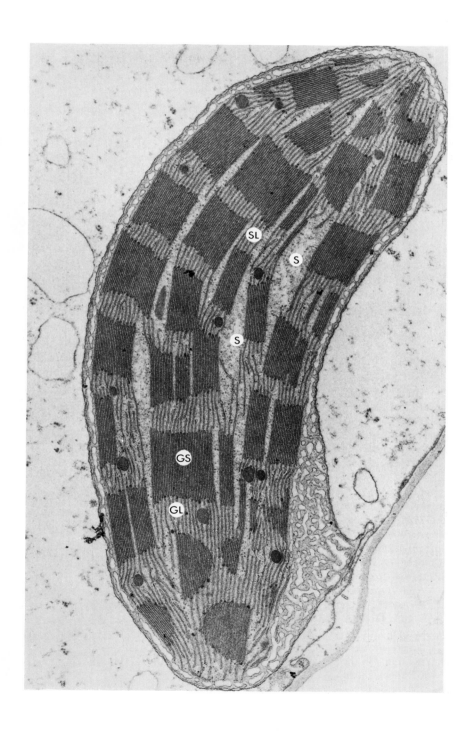

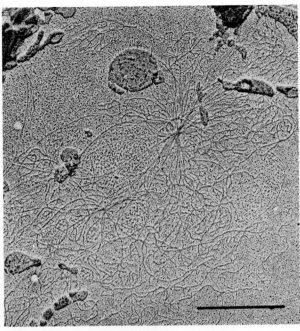

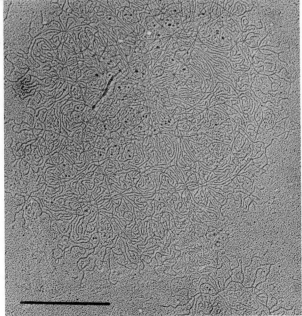

FIGURE 19-4. *Electron micrographs of chloroplast DNA from the green alga* Acetabularia mediterranea. *(A) Lysed chloroplast showing chloroplast DNA fibrils around a "center." (B) Large array of DNA released from a chloroplast. The bar represents 1 μm.* [Courtesy Dr. Beverley R. Green, University of British Columbia. Reprinted by permission of authors and publisher from Green, B. R., and H. Burton, *Acetabularia* Chloroplast DNA: Electron Microscope Visualization, *Science* (22 May 1970), **168**: 981–982. Copyright 1970 by The American Association for the Advancement of Science.]

of DNA. Green and Burton (1970) were able to release highly supercoiled plastid DNA by osmotic shock in the large unicellular green alga *Acetabularia* (Fig. 19-4). The largest intact segment sufficiently untwisted to permit measurement they report to be 419 $\mu$m in length, which would place intact plastid DNA in the general size range of bacterial DNA. But the supercoiling of chloroplast DNA, these authors indicate, does not imply circularity. In fact, Dr. Green points out (personal communication) that "it may well be linear, though quite long." Raven (1970), Margulis (1970), and other investigators have built a considerable case for the suggestion that chloroplasts and mitochondria have indeed originated as symbiotic prokaryotes.

Evidence is accumulating that plastid DNA differs, often greatly, in base composition from the nuclear DNA of the same species. Ultraviolet microbeam irradiation of the cytoplasm of the familiar one-celled *Euglena* results in plastid destruction whereas nuclear irradiation alone does not. This organism's chloroplasts do contain a unique DNA component of low guanine-cytosine content which is absent in plastid-less mutants. Plastids also contain a DNA polymerase and are able to synthesize their own DNA. Replication of plastid DNA has been shown to be semiconservative in *Chlamydomonas*, another unicellular green alga, with chloroplast DNA synthesis occurring (in synchronous cell cultures) at a time quite different from that of nuclear DNA. Sager and Ramanis (1970) have prepared linkage maps for *Chlamydomonas* of 8 cytoplasmic genes that they believe to be located in chloroplast DNA.

Chloroplasts also contain RNA and ribosomes. The latter, at least in higher plants, are smaller in mass than those in the cytoplasm of the same cell. They resemble much more closely bacterial ribosomes in size, as demonstrated by determinations of their sedimentation coefficients. They are also inactivated by chloramphenicol (as are bacterial ribosomes) which does not affect cytoplasmic ribosomes. Chloroplasts appear, then, to contain their own machinery for protein synthesis, and it is clear that their DNA does play a part in incorporating amino acids into the characteristic plastid proteins, though not always wholly independently of nuclear DNA.

So, here we have self-replicating structures, containing their own unique DNA and an array of protein synthesizing equipment, but, at the same time, under some control by nuclear DNA both as to their existence and as to their synthesis of proteins. Certainly plastids would appear to come closer to our concept of a cytoplasmic genetic system than the cases previously cited, lacking only independence from nuclear DNA. But chloroplasts themselves also constitute particular phenotypic traits (green color, ability to photosynthesize) of considerable complexity. Actually, we have something of a semantic problem to contend with; that is, we must distinguish between nuclear controlled presence or absence of plastids per se and their ability to play a part in the synthesis of their own proteins. From the former viewpoint plastids are just another aspect of phenotype, no different from those we have considered thus far; from the latter, they do demonstrate at least a degree of extranuclear genetic control by normally occurring organelles, whatever their ultimate origin and evolution.

Plastid inheritance in the four o'clock plant (*Mirabilis jalapa*, Fig. 19-5) is a classic illustration of purported cytoplasmic inheritance. This plant may exist in three forms: normal green, variegated (patches of green and of non-green tissue), and white (no chlorophyll). Now and then a plant with branches of two or three of these types occurs. Plastids in the white areas have no chlorophyll. Offspring of crosses are phenotypically like that of the pistillate (egg-producing) parent except where the pistillate parent is variegated, in which case the offspring are of all three types, in irregular ratio. Egg cells from green plants carry normal green plastids, those from white plants contain only white plastids, but eggs produced by variegated parents may have both plastid types. Pollen (which produces the sperm) has no effect on the progeny phenotype.

Note that all we are really dealing with here is the kind of plastid and proplastid present in the egg cytoplasm. If that plastid is defective as to chlorophyll synthesis, the $F_1$ plant will be nongreen; if not, it will be green. Eggs from variegated parents, containing normal and defective plastids, give rise to plants some of whose cells fortuitously receive a majority of green plastids, and some which receive larger numbers of white plastids resulting in variegated plants. Recall that division of the cytoplasm following mitosis is not a quantitatively exact process. Yet on the other hand, the situation here could be rationally explained on the basis of a nonchromosomal determinant which might or might not be located in the chloroplast. In fact, it could be located anywhere in the cytoplasm; but like others to be reported (pages 380 and 381), no site has ever been demonstrated. Most observational evidence, however, suggests that the chloroplast itself is *not* the actual genetic determiner.

The evening primrose, *Oenothera* spp., provides an interesting variant of plastid inheritance in which the nuclear material plays an important part. Many species of *Oenothera* are characterized by their own unique combinations of reciprocal translocations which result in only two types of viable gametes, those containing only a plant's maternal chromosomes or only its paternal chromosomes. Therefore, chromosomes in these species are transmitted as unitary groups.

Both *O. muricata* and *O. hookeri* are normal green plants. Crosses utilizing *O. muricata* as the pistillate parent produce normal green $F_1$ individuals. The reciprocal cross produces a nongreen $F_1$, all of which die. Thus, *muricata* plastids can develop in the presence of a *muricata-hookeri* nucleus, whereas *hookeri* plastids cannot. Again, *these* latter two illustrations do not appear to provide examples of an *independent* gene system in the cytoplasm.

FIGURE 19-5. *The four o'clock plant,* Mirabilis jalapa, *greenleaved variety.* [Photo courtesy Burpee Seeds.]

*Mitochondria.* All living cells except bacteria, blue-green algae, and mature erythrocytes contain *mitochondria,* small, self-replicating organelles of considerable internal structural complexity which are centers of aerobic respiration. A few are shown in sectional view in Fig. 3-2. Although the shape of a given mitochondrion is not constant, mitochondria often appear as elongate, slender rods of rather variable dimensions, averaging some 0.5 $\mu$m in diameter and 3 to 5 $\mu$m in length. Extremes of 0.2 to 7 $\mu$m in width and 0.3 to 40 $\mu$m in length have been reported. Their number per cell varies considerably, from one in the unicellular green alga *Micrasterias* to as many as about a half million in the giant amoeba *Chaos chaos.*

Like chloroplasts, mitochondria contain their own unique DNA (mDNA) whose base composition is known to differ from that of both nuclear and plastid DNA. Mitochondrial DNA is replicated independently of nuclear DNA through the action of a DNA polymerase whose chromatographic properties differ from those of the polymerase of the nucleus. In many multicellular animal tissues (e.g., rat liver and mouse fibroblast cells) mitochondrial DNA is present as a double-stranded, circular structure, strongly reminiscent of bacterial DNA, with a molecular weight of 9 to 10 $\times$ 10$^6$ (Margulis, 1970;

Raven, 1970). Satisfy yourself that this would indicate roughly 14,000 base pairs and a length of nearly 5 $\mu$m. Circular mitochondrial DNA has also been reported for man. Nass (1969) has described circular DNA molecules several times larger than 5 $\mu$m from mouse fibroblast cells (Fig. 19-6). On the other hand, mitochondrial DNA of the higher plants has not yet been shown to have this circular form.

Many of the mitochondrial proteins are synthesized within the organelle itself, utilizing mDNA as a template for unique mitochondrial RNA (Fan and Penman, 1970), but other proteins, notably cytochrome c, may be made elsewhere in the cell. Among the transfer RNAs identified in mitochondria is N-formylmethionyl tRNA (tRNA$_f$), known otherwise only from bacterial cells (Chapter 16). Mitochondrial ribosomes have also been identified (Bernhard, 1969), and Scragg et al. (1971) have obtained a cell-free protein synthesizing system from yeast mitochondria. So, as in the case of choroplasts, we have a semiindependent, DNA-containing organelle which is able to synthesize at least some of its own proteins.

The studies of Ephrussi (1953, 1955) on respiratory-deficient strains of baker's yeast (*Saccharomyces cerevesiae*) point up the genetic role of mito-chondria. Yeasts are unicellular ascomycete fungi. In the life cycle of some species (Appendix B) diploid and monoploid adults alternate, the former reproducing by meiospores called ascospores, the latter by isogametes. Respiratory-deficient strains are able to respire only anaerobically and, on agar, produce characteristically small colonies known as "petites." Ephrussi has shown that both nuclear and cytoplasmic controls affect this trait.

In one type of petite (segregational petite) respiratory deficiencies have been clearly shown to be caused by a recessive nuclear gene. Crosses between monoploid petite and normal result in all normal diploid $F_1$ progeny, but ascospores produced by the latter segregate 1:1 for petite and normal. On the other hand, another strain (neutral petite) has defective mitochondrial DNA. In these, the petite character fails to segregate and $F_1$ and $F_2$ of the cross petite × normal are all normal, the cytoplasm that contains normal mitochondria being incorporated into $F_1$ zygotes and vegetative cells and distributed to ascospores and monoploid vegetative cells of the next generation. In a third type of petite (suppressive petite), crosses with normals produce a highly variable fraction of petites in the progeny. Rank (1970) suggests that suppressives have rapidly replicating, abnormal mitochondrial DNA. So, petites may possess defective mitochondria because of either mutant nuclear DNA or mutant mitochondrial DNA, or both. Respiratory enzymes (except for cytochrome c) are thus under a double genetic control.

Carnevali, Morpurgo, and Tecce (1969) have shown that mutation of mitochondrial DNA probably involves a relative increase of adenine-thymine pairs and suggest that crossing-over may occur between molecules

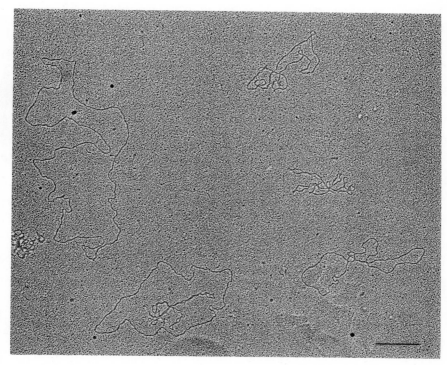

FIGURE 19-6. *Electron micrograph of DNA isolated from mitochondria of mouse fibroblast cells. Note the circularity of these molecules. A highly supercoiled molecule lies inside an open monomer (lower left), and three loosely twisted molecules are located at the right. The bar represents 1 μm.* [Courtesy Dr. Margit M. K. Nass, University of Pennsylvania. Reprinted by permission of author and publisher from Nass, M. M. K., Mitochondrial DNA: Advances, Problems, and Goals, *Science*, **165**: 25–35, 4 July 1970. Copyright 1970 by The American Association for the Advancement of Science.)

of cytoplasmic DNA. The action of various mutagens in producing the suppressive petite mutants, they believe, results from incomplete mDNA molecules produced by premature detachment of DNA polymerase. The defective, shorter DNA molecules are replicated more rapidly, resulting in the pseudodominant suppressive trait.

Here, as in the case of mediation of protein synthesis by plastid DNA, we certainly have a degree of cytoplasmic genetic control by DNA of unique and characteristic base sequence not, however, always and wholly independent of nuclear DNA. Whether or not mitochondria (and chloroplasts) have originated as independent, invading organisms that have now become normally occurring organelles in almost all living cells through progressively higher degrees of symbiosis by loss of some of their functions to the nucleus, as suggested by Raven (1970) and others, we do have in these two instances much more promising candidates for cytoplasmic genetic systems than, for example, female production in *Drosophila* or the milk factor in mice.

### NONCHROMOSOMAL INHERITANCE WITHOUT KNOWN CYTOPLASMIC STRUCTURES

A number of rather perplexing cases of apparent nonchromosomal inheritance which cannot at present be related to any identifiable structures or determinants has been reported from time to time. Examination of one of these will suffice to indicate the scope and nature of the problem.

*Chlamydomonas.* The ubiquitous unicellular green alga *Chlamydomonas* has a relatively simple life cycle (Appendix B). The motile vegetative cells are monoploid (haploid), the zygote being the only diploid structure. In germination the zygote undergoes meiosis to form four monoploid, fully functional vegetative cells. Sexual reproduction in most species represents morphological isogamy, although the gametes are, as we saw in Chapter 10, physiologically differentiated into plus and minus strains. Chemical attraction between individuals of opposite mating strains appears to be exerted through the flagella.

Wild-type cells are sensitive ($ss$) to the antibiotic streptomycin, but resistant ($sr$) mutants can be isolated. Somewhat confusingly, two kinds of $sr$ cells are known, those in which resistance segregates in the normal Mendelian manner, and those in which the trait does not. Consider, for example, the following series of matings ($sr$ = streptomycin-resistant, $ss$ = streptomycin-sensitive, + and − indicate mating strain):

(a) $\quad$ P $\qquad sr^+ \times ss^-$

$\quad\quad$ F$_1$ $\qquad \frac{1}{2} sr^+ + \frac{1}{2} sr^-$

(b) $\quad$ F$_1$ $sr^+ \times$ P $ss^- \longrightarrow \frac{1}{2} sr^+ + \frac{1}{2} sr^-$

$\quad\quad$ F$_1$ $sr^- \times ss^+ \longrightarrow \frac{1}{2} ss^+ + \frac{1}{2} ss^-$

Note that, in each case, mating strain is segregating in normal Mendelian fashion where + and − gametes unite to form a diploid ± zygote which later undergoes meiosis to produce two monoploid + and two monoploid − vegetative individuals. But streptomycin response as a trait is transmitted only by the + mating strain!

Much of this information on *Chlamydomonas* is the result of work by Sager (1963) and her colleagues at Columbia. Extensive tests with known mutagenic agents failed to produce any mutation of $sr$ to $ss$ cells over a period of years. Likewise, painstaking work has eliminated any possibility of polygene inheritance. A curious and apparently unexplained facet of the problem here lies in the anomaly of the apparent "maternal" inheritance of the streptomycin resistance-sensitivity trait and the fact that this occurs in an isogamous organism. Morphological isogamy means physical identity of fusing gametes; each carries relatively abundant amounts of cytoplasm. In fact, as seen in Appendix B, virtually the entire vegetative protoplast functions in sexual reproduction. There is no particular disparity in amount of cytoplasm as is usually the case with such unlike gametes as sperm and egg. Yet, resistance-sensitivity of progeny is clearly that of the plus parent. Furthermore, the detailed work of Sager and her associates has disclosed no identifiable cytoplasmic structure that appears to be functioning genetically.

To compound the complexity of the problem, other apparent nonchromosomal traits are known in *Chlamydonomas*, acetate requirement versus nonrequirement being one. In crosses involving both acetate requirement and the streptomycin character, it has been found that both traits segregate independently and do so *following* meiosis of the zygote nucleus (i.e., in the subsequent cytokinesis)! Neither character can be shown to have any association with the known linkage groups of this alga.

### EPISOMES

Perhaps the most unequivocal instance of a cytoplasmically located genetic determiner which comes closest to meeting the arbitrary criteria set up at the opening of this chapter is the bacterial episome F which we have already discussed (pages 192 and 193).

You will recall that this fertility factor, if present in a cell, may be either located in the cytoplasm or integrated into the single, circular bacterial chromosome. Cells lacking the F factor ($F^-$) are receptor ("female") cells at conjugation; those having F in the cytoplasm ($F^+$) are donors ("males"), and cells in which F is a part of the chromosome are high-frequency recombinant (Hfr) donors or, again, "males." Current interpretation is that there is but one fertility factor per $F^+$ cell (except just prior to fission), and one per chromosome in Hfr cells.

The chemical composition of the F factor, its mutability under the effect of acridine dyes, its ability to replicate autonomously, and its ability to be incorporated stably into the chromosome show F to be composed of genetic material. In fact, present evidence clearly indicates it to be composed of DNA. Density gradient centrifugation in cesium chloride shows the F episome to consist of about $10^5$ nucleotide pairs, as compared to about $4.5 \times 10^6$ for the chromosome of the colon bacillus. The fertility factor is thus about $\frac{1}{45}$ the size of the chromosome in *E. coli*. Whatever its evolutionary origin, it cannot now be regarded as an infective particle, but must be considered a normal component of those cells in which it occurs. Furthermore, it is replicated semiconservatively in cell division, autonomously in $F^+$ cells, and along with the chromosome, into which it has been integrated, in Hfr cells. In conjugation between $F^+$ and $F^-$ cells, a replicated F factor is the first, and most frequently the only, DNA element to be transferred to the $F^-$ conjugant (which is thereby converted to an $F^+$ individual). In mating of Hfr $\times$ $F^-$ cells, the fertility factor, integrated into the chromosome, is the last genetic material to be transferred, but generally conjugation is interrupted by natural forces so that F is, in these matings, usually not transferred at all. (See Appendix B-1.) Campbell (1962, 1969) and Falkow et al. (1967) describe the behavior and structure of episomes at length.

Multiple resistance to several drugs in a number of bacterial genera appears to depend upon a resistance transfer factor (RTF) which, though not yet well understood, has many of the properties of an episome. It is known chiefly in the genus *Shigella*, the causative agent of bacterial dysentery. It can be transferred intergenerically to the related *Salmonella* and *Escherichia* and can be modified by acridine dyes.

Some strains of *E. coli* produce highly specific antibiotic substances consisting of proteins (sometimes along with lipopolysaccharides) that kill other strains of the species. For this reason they have been named "colicins." An $F^- col^-$ cell may become $col^+$ by conjugation; in this case, all of its asexually derived progeny are also $col^+$. In this and other respects, colicins appear to be due to autonomous cytoplasmic particles, referred to as *col* factors. Although interpretations of experimental results are not all in agreement, there is no unambiguous evidence that either RTF or col factors may become chromosomally integrated.

Of all the cases we have examined in this chapter, the F factor appears to furnish the most nearly unequivocal illustration of a cytoplasmic genetic system, and there seems little reason at present not to consider resistance transfer, col factors, chloroplast DNA, and mitochondrial DNA in the same way.

### CONCLUDING VIEW

In this chapter we have examined the question of the existence of cytoplasmic genetic mechanisms by viewing some of the many purported illustrations in the literature against the backdrop of a working concept of what such mechanisms ought to entail. If we were to accept the broad notion of transmission of heritable traits themselves via the cytoplasm, then, from the examples cited, we would have to acknowledge that *cytoplasmic inheritance* does occur rather widely.

But application of our more rigorous criteria to a heterogeneous collection of cases eliminates most, *but not all*, of these as indications of the existence of *cytoplasmic genetic mechanisms*. Such instances as chloroplast inheritance and "petite" yeast are significant in that they reflect genetic mechanisms based on nucleic acids located in cytoplasmic organelles. Certainly the evidence implicates chloroplasts and mitochondria in their own heredity, but, as already noted, does not clearly suggest that they are wholly independent genetic determiners.

Drug resistance in *Chlamydomonas* is still an intriguing problem. Every bit of indirect evidence points to a cytoplasmic genetic mechanism, but its nature and identity elude us. Obviously, this is a cause-and-effect relationship, but, at present, we know only the effect; the cause has not yet been determined. On the other hand, such purely maternal effects as shell coiling in the snail or color in the young water flea can be dismissed rationally as the lingering effects of a parental genotype operating on Mendelian bases. They certainly give no indication of the existence of a genetic system in the cytoplasm even remotely resembling chromosomal DNA.

When we consider infective particles and episomes, it is necessary to distinguish carefully between fortuitous parasites, on the one hand, and "normal" cell components, on the other. At one end of the spectrum is the obvious, identifiable, dispensable parasite (such as the spirochete), on through the viruslike milk factor and sigma to asynchronously multiplying kappa, to apparently nonintegrable factors (such as RTF and col) and the fertility factor at the other. The very fact that we can arrange such a series opens a tempting ground for speculation regarding the possible evolution of such cytoplasmic genetic mechanisms as the F factor, a speculation that, we should clearly note, is as yet wholly without any tangible, experimental proof. Has there been a gradual evolution from virulent parasite through first dispensable then indispensable symbionts to a cytoplasmic genetic system which may even integrate into the chromosomal mechanism? Or has the episomic state derived from originally purely chromosomal genes? If there is a relationship, then why have not episome systems been discovered in any group outside the bacteria? Have virulent and temperate phages had anything to do with the development of extrachromosomal genetic systems? Where in this whole problem do transforming and transducing DNAs fit? At present we can only raise these questions; the answers are still being sought, but will surely one day be in hand.

## REFERENCES

BERNHARD, R., 1967. Chromosomes Are Not the Whole Story of Heredity. *Sci. Res.*, **2**:51–54.

BERNHARD, R., 1969. Mitochondrial "Genes": Some Gambles Pay Off. *Sci. Res.*, **4**:31–34.

CAMPBELL, A. M., 1962, Episomes. *Advances Genet.*, **11**:101–145.

CAMPBELL, A. M., 1969. *Episomes*. New York, Harper & Row.

CARNEVALI, F., G. MORPURGO, and G. TECCE, 1969. Cytoplasmic DNA from Petite Colonies of *Saccharomyces cerevesiae*: A Hypothesis on the Nature of the Mutation. *Science*, **163**:1331–1333.

EPHRUSSI, B., 1953. *Nucleo-Cytoplasmic Relations in Micro-Organisms.* Oxford, Oxford University Press.

EPHRUSSI, B., H. DE MARGERIE-HOTTINGUER, and H. ROMAN, 1955. Suppressiveness: A New Factor in the Genetic Determinism of the Synthesis of Respiratory Enzymes in Yeast. *Proc. Nat. Acad. Sci. (U.S.)*, **41**:1065–1070.

FALKOW, S., E. M. JOHNSON, and L. S. BARON, 1967. *Bacterial Conjugation and Extrachromosomal Elements.* In H. L. Roman, ed., 1967. *Annual Review of Genetics*, volume 1. Palo Alto, Annual Reviews, Inc.

FAN, H., and S. PENMAN, 1970. Mitochondrial RNA Synthesis during Mitosis. *Science*, **168**:135–138.

GREEN, B. R., and H. BURTON, 1970. *Acetabularia* Chloroplast DNA: Electron Microscopic Visualization. *Science*, **168**:981–982.

GREEN, B. R., and M. P. GORDON, 1966. Replication of Chloroplast DNA of Tobacco. *Science*, **152**:1071–1074.

JINKS, J. L., 1964. *Extrachromosomal Inheritance.* Englewood Cliffs, N.J., Prentice-Hall. (One of the *Foundations of Modern Genetics* series.)

L'HERITIER, P., 1951. The $CO_2$ Sensitivity Problem in *Drosophila. Cold Spring Harbor Symp. Quant. Biol.*, **16**:99–112.

MARGULIS, L., 1970. *Origin of Eucaryotic Cells.* New Haven, Yale University Press.

NANNEY, D. L., 1958. Epigenetic Control Systems. *Proc. Nat. Acad. Sci. (U.S.)*, **44**:712–717.

NASS, M. M. K., 1969. Mitochondrial DNA: Advances, Problems, and Goals. *Science*, **165**:25–35.

PREER, J. R., JR., 1971. *Extrachromosomal Inheritance.* In H. L. Roman, ed., *Annual Review of Genetics*, volume 5. Palo Alto, California, Annual Reviews, Inc.

RANK, G. H., 1970. Genetic Evidence for "Darwinian" Selection at the Molecular Level. I. The Effect of the Suppressive Factor on Cytoplasmically-Inherited Erythromycin-Resistance in *Saccharomyces cerevesiae. Can. Jour. Genet. Cytol.*, **12**:129–136.

RAVEN, P. H., 1970. A Multiple Origin for Plastids and Mitochondria. *Science*, **169**:641–646.

SAGER, R., and Z. RAMANIS, 1963. The Particulate Nature of Nonchromosomal Genes in *Chlamydomonas. Proc. Nat. Acad. Sci. (U.S.)*, **50**:260–268.

SAGER, R., and Z. RAMANIS, 1970. A Genetic Map of Non-Mendelian Genes in *Chlamydomonas. Proc. Nat. Acad. Sci. (U.S.)*, **65**:593–600.

SCRAGG, A. H., H. MORIMOTO, V. VILLA, J. NEKHOROCHEFF, and H. O. HALVORSON, 1971. Cell-Free Protein Synthesizing System from Yeast Mitochondria. *Science*, **171**:908–910.

## PROBLEMS

**19-1.** You have just discovered a new trait in *Drosophila* and find that reciprocal crosses give different results. How would you determine whether this trait was sex-linked, a purely maternal effect, or due to an extranuclear genetic system?

**19-2.** What phenotype would be exhibited by each of the following genotypes in the snail: $+s, s+, ss, + +$?

**19-3.** In yeast a neutral petite, although having defective mitochondrial DNA, may have a nuclear gene for normal mitochondrial function. As indicated in the text, a monoploid segregational petite carries a recessive nuclear gene for defective mitochondria, but it may possess normal mitochondrial DNA. If such a neutral is crossed with a segregational petite of the type described here, what is the phenotype of (a) the diploid $F_1$; (b) the monoploid generation developing from ascospores produced by these diploid cells?

**19-4.** Employing different substrains of *Escherichia coli* strain K-12 as *Hfr* conjugants produces different results (see linkage map, Fig. 6-4):

| | Chromosomal genes transferred in conjugation | |
|---|---|---|
| K-12 Substrain | First | Last |
| C | *lys* + *met* | *gal* |
| H | *pil* | *pyr-B* |

For each substrain, give (a) the location of F and (b) the second chromosomal gene that would be transferred.

**19-5.** Defend or oppose the thesis that chloroplast inheritance represents the action of a cytoplasmic genetic system.

**19-6.** Defend or oppose the thesis that the episome system represents an instance of a cytoplasmic genetic mechanism.

**19-7.** Defend or oppose the thesis that cytoplasmic genetic systems have not yet been adequately demonstrated.

**19-8.** Defend or oppose the thesis that mitochondria and/or chloroplasts originated as free-living prokaryotes. (You may wish to read some of the references before answering.)

# CHAPTER 20

# Genetics:
# Problems and Promise

THE exciting, breathtaking progress of the science of genetics following the rediscovery of Mendel's principles at the turn of the century has at no point been more apparent than in recent investigations at the molecular level of the nature and action of genetic material. Yet these studies, fruitful as they have been, have but lifted the veil slightly on many still unresolved problems. Both their solution and their application to the welfare of mankind constitute some of the fascinating challenges confronting this and the next generation of the world's scientists. In this concluding chapter we shall examine this prologue to the future.

## The Problems of the Present

### THE NUCLEIC ACIDS

*DNA Replication.* The molecular approach of the past two decades has paid rich dividends in the form of considerable knowledge about the nature of genetic material and its operation, as we have seen in the preceding pages. But many refinements of and additions to this new information remain ahead. For example, we need to know the nature of the signal for beginning replication of DNA, the way in which this signal acts, and just how, in terms of the molecular structure of deoxyribonucleic acid, the semiconservative replication process takes place.

*RNA Structure and Function.* A great deal remains to be learned about synthesis of RNA, as well as the structure of the different types of RNA— e.g. ribosomal, messenger, and transfer. Our knowledge of tRNA is tantalizingly limited, in spite of progress to date. The three-dimensional structure of tRNA is not known with certainty, nor is its internal base-pairing. Certainly the basis for uniqueness of different tRNAs and recognition of an amino acid by a given "species" of transfer RNA is not yet understood. Much also remains to be learned about the relative movements of tRNA, mRNA, and the developing polypeptide chains. The three-dimensional structure of the ribosome, and its precise relation to protein biosynthesis, is also yet to be worked out in detail.

*Complementation and Crossing-over.* Granted that a gene at a given functional level is so many sequential nucleotides, what is the basis of position effect? Closely related to this problem is the mechanism of complementation such as occurs in the rII mutants of phage T4 and in many other characters in a large number of other organisms. Our knowledge of the molecular nature of crossing-over and recombination in DNA is still quite incomplete. One wonders also whether this mechanism, when understood, will be able to account for visible chromosomal crossing-over. The mechanism and degree of genetic exchange between cells of higher organisms and between these cells and viruses is a largely unsolved problem and may well have significant implications for the future (see pages 390 and 402).

*Arrangement of DNA in Chromosomes.*  Closely related is the question of just how DNA is arranged on or in the chromosome of higher organisms. The simplest concept, of course, is that in which a chromosome consists of a single DNA molecule running the length of the chromosome. Certainly, chromosomes duplicate as if they were so constructed. But the probable untwisting of DNA chains in its replication is easier to understand if some kind of nongenetic links join different DNA molecules together. Although a number of hypothetical arrangements of this sort have been suggested, none is wholly satisfactory and none is supported by solid experimental proof.

Perhaps one of the greatest difficulties in reconciling DNA molecular structure with that of visible chromosomes is a purely physical one. For example, the total DNA complement of *Drosophila melanogaster* is estimated at some 16,000 $\mu$m (16 mm., or about $\frac{5}{8}$ inch); the total length of its diploid chromosome set is far less (Fig. 20-1). The disparity of length does not eliminate the end-to-end orientation of DNA, but it does pose some very real packaging problems.

The situation in phages and bacteria, where the chromosome appears to be a naked DNA molecule, is only a little simpler. Chemical determinations of the nucleotide content of a number of T phages (those infecting the colon bacillus) have indicated some 200,000 nucleotide pairs. From the dimensions of the Watson–Crick model, with 3.4 angstrom units between successive nucleotide pairs, the total length of the T phage DNA molecule can be calculated to be about 68 $\mu$m. This is packed into a phage " head " whose inside diameter is around 800 Å, or 0.08 $\mu$m. The circular chromosome of *Escherichia coli*, by the same kind of calculation, measures about 1,100 $\mu$m (Cairns, 1963), yet this bacterium is a cylinder some 2 $\times$ 0.5 $\mu$m. Granted a considerable degree of coiling of the DNA molecule, there is, nevertheless, a real problem in arranging relatively large DNA molecules into their containers, whether these latter are phage " heads," bacterial cells, or the chromosomes of higher organisms.

## THE GENETIC CODE

*Universality.*  Present evidence points to the universality of the genetic code for both viruses and living organisms. One wonders whether or not this code, as finally determined, has changed over time with evolution of different

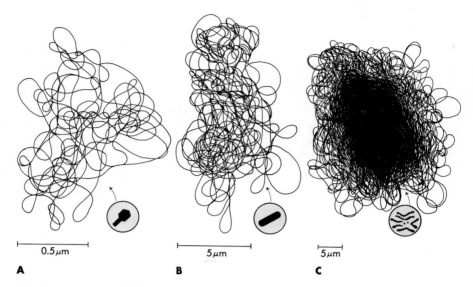

```
        0.5μm                        5μm                      5μm
A                            B                          C
```

FIGURE 20-1. *Total length of DNA of: (A) bacteriophage T-4 (about 68 μm); (B) the bacterium,* E. coli *(about 1,100 μm); (C) the fruit fly,* Drosophila melanogaster *(about 16,000μm). Compare these lengths to the size of the structures into which the DNA is packed.* [Redrawn from F. W. Stahl, *The Mechanics of Inheritance,* © 1964, Prentice-Hall, Inc., Englewood Cliffs, N.J., by permission of author and publisher.]

forms of life. Furthermore, the system seems so elegant in concept that the possibility of others, when the existence of life on other planets is verified, is an intriguing question.

*Operation.*    Much as is now known about the genetic code and its operation in protein synthesis, there are still gaps in our knowledge. In addition to problems having to do with replication of DNA and the synthesis and operation of the ribonucleic acids, the operation of the start-stop mechanism, the existence and operation of "gene-separators" (if any), and the implications of degeneracy in the code are still to be determined with certainty, as is also true of the significance of its ambiguity under special conditions.

## CHROMOSOMES OF HIGHER ORGANISMS

*Chromosome Breaks.*    Not only do we know little of the arrangement of DNA in the chromosome of organisms more advanced than bacteria, but the mechanism of chromosomal breaks, for example, is unknown. Chromosomes break "spontaneously"—i.e., as the result of causes not yet identified in specific cases. These lead to many of the chromosomal abberations discussed earlier. As in so many other instances, these are the *effects* in a cause-

and-effect relationship where the *causes* have not yet been determined. We can "induce" chromosome breaks by certain drugs and by ionizing radiation, but we cannot yet determine the mechanism thereof, nor can we direct a break at a preselected locus. In terms of the frequency of fetal death and defects that cripple, but may not kill, because of chromosomal abnormalities (see page 390), elucidation of their causes and prevention holds great importance for mankind.

*Chromosome Pairing.* The nature of synapsis is not understood. That it is precise, "gene" for "gene," is visually as well as experimentally evident, but the nature of the attraction between alleles has not been determined. Furthermore, genetic recombination may well precede synapsis. Thus, what we learn about recombination between different DNA molecules may tell us little about synapsis and segregation of homologous chromosomes.

## DIFFERENTIATION AND GENE REGULATION

Much has been discovered recently regarding the regulation of gene activity in bacteria. Yet we do not know the full extent to which the regulator gene concept operates in bacteria, nor is there any concrete evidence to suggest whether or not such a system operates in more complex organisms. Certainly the entire genetic capability of every cell in a multicellular body does not appear to be expressed all the time. Genes active in one group of cells may be inactive in other cells at the same time, and different genes may be active or inactive in the same cells at different times. This appears to be the immediate basis of differentiation in the multicellular organism, but what is the mechanism? Is it a system of regulator genes? Do histones play any part? If so, how? Chromosome "puffs" are clearly related to degree of RNA synthesis; what is the stimulus and what is the nature of the interaction between stimulus and gene activity? In some cases in *Drosophila*, certain regions of the chromosome may be made to "puff" upon administration of ecdysone, a molting hormone, but the interrelationship is still obscure. Is differential gene activity (hence, nucleic acid synthesis) the stimulus for, or the result of, developmental change?

The role of cytoplasm in differentiation, indeed in genetic transmission, is not clearly determined. How much of the information for phenotype and its development is located in cytoplasmic organelles, apart from lingering maternal effects? Nuclear transplant experiments, in which nuclei are transferred from either zygotes or mature cells to similar cells of different nuclear genotype, while not unequivocal in their implications, do suggest a cytoplasmic feedback of inducing or repressing influences on nuclear genes.

*Human Karyotyping and Mapping.* Because of the serious consequences of both chromosomal aberrations and gene mediated defects there is an urgent need for improvement in our ability (1) to identify *with certainty each member* of the human chromosome set, rather than just the seven autosomal groups,

(2) to detect subchromosomal abnormalities, and (3) to discover the causes of such cellular "mistakes" as trisomy (or of the nondisjunction which may lead to it), translocations, deletions, duplications, and so forth. Chromosome aberrations occur in much higher frequency in many kinds of malignancies; an understanding of the reasons would have obvious medical value.

Mapping of the human chromosomes is almost nonexistent, especially for the autosomes, and the role of various chromosome regions in development is largely unknown (see McKusick, 1971). Partly because of the nature of his society, in which laboratory study of his own species is burdened with social guidelines, and partly because he is simply not a facile genetic subject (see Chapter 1), man knows far less about his own genetics than that of many other organisms, even a number of viruses. Further study of man's genetics, especially his cytogenetics and molecular biochemical genetics, will certainly yield important as well as interesting information, some of it doubtless with a high survival value.

## The Problems of the Future

Man has made almost exponential progress, during his lifetime on this planet, in developing better varieties of plants and lower animals and in understanding the mechanisms of genetics and genetic change. In spite of the limitations cited earlier in this chapter, we know, for instance, a good deal about such processes as recombination, transformation, and mutation. Medical science is not only able to eradicate diseases which, a few years ago, were scourges annually decimating large segments of the world's population, but is also able to make up, to some extent, for deficiencies resulting from defective genes or chromosomes.

The lethal or disabling consequences of defective genotypes and karyotypes is fairly considerable. Roberts and his colleagues (1970), in a study of the causes of death of 1,041 children over a seven year period in the hospitals of Newcastle in Great Britain, found gene and chromosome defects to be responsible for 42 per cent of the deaths in their sample. Single gene defects accounted for 8.5 per cent of these childhood deaths, chromosome aberrations 2.5 per cent, and those probably due to complex genetic causes, 31 per cent. Heller (1969) estimates some type of chromosomal abnormality to be present in almost 0.5 per cent of live-born infants and to occur in nearly one fourth of all spontaneously aborted fetuses. Boué et al. (1967) found polyploidy or aneuploidy in almost two out of three such fetuses. You will recall from Chapter 10 that XYY and XXY chromosomal aberrations alone occur with frequencies of 0.2 per 1,000 live births to as much as the considerably greater frequency of up to 3 per 1,000 reported by German (1970).

It is only natural, therefore, to raise the question, "Can man control his own evolution?" In fact, this query is being raised with increasing frequency;

several symposia have addressed themselves solely to this question (Roslansky, 1966; Sonneborn, 1965). As you might well imagine, with the press of population becoming ever more acute, the problem of control of human evolution has engaged the serious thought of leaders from the natural sciences, the social sciences, philosophy, and religion. It is a problem to which you, as an educated, intelligent citizen, should be prepared to give some thought.

There are two broad facets to the question of man's control of his own evolution. Simply stated, they are "Can he?" and "Should he?" The second of these, raising as it does, profound moral, legal, and ethical considerations, lies beyond the immediate scope of an introductory course in genetics. But we can, and should, concern ourselves with the first.

## RATIONALE OF HUMAN EVOLUTION CONTROL[1]

Our bank of genetic material is undergoing a slow but inexorable decline in quality. Several dysgenic influences are contributing heavily to this qualitative dilution and, it is argued, must be counteracted by conscious efforts at quality control.

There is no doubt that the human population is increasing at a rate that no longer permits lack of concern (Table 20-1). The overall world average is

TABLE 20-1. Annual Rate of Increase in Population for Selected Countries

| Percentage Increase Per Year | Country |
|:---:|:---|
| 3.7 | South Vietnam |
| 3.4 | Venezuela |
| 3.3 | Malaysia |
| 3.2 | Ecuador |
| 3.0 | Brazil |
| 2.3 | India |
| 2.1 | China |
| 1.7 | U.S.S.R. |
| 1.6 | U.S.A. |
| 0.9 | Japan |
| 0.8 | Norway |
| 0.5 | Sweden |
| 0.4 | Hungary |

Based on World Population Data Sheet, Population Reference Bureau, Washington, 1964.

[1] Much of the remainder of this chapter follows closely the author's presidential address before the Ohio Academy of Science (Burns, 1970). See also Jaroff (1971).

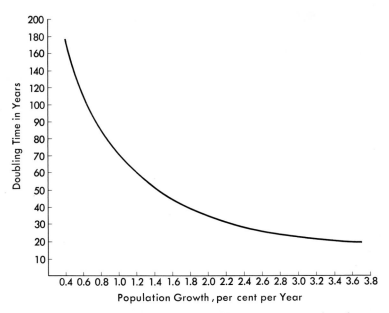

FIGURE 20-2. *Curve showing approximate doubling time in years plotted against rate of population growth in per cent per year. Compare with figures for actual annual growth for selected countries in Table 20-1.*

2 per cent annually. But when one considers the time required for doubling of populations at these rates (Fig. 20-2), the immediacy of the problem is obvious. The resulting competition for available resources is already strikingly evident in many countries of the world. Moreover, the doubling time for the world's population is decreasing alarmingly fast (Fig. 20-3). But population growth is perhaps more a function of decreased death rate than of increased birth rate. In India, for example, the birth rate has shown a gradual decline for much of this century, yet her population continues to grow. People are simply living longer. Life expectancy did not exceed 25 to 30 years well into the Middle Ages; since then it has risen sharply, especially in the "have" nations, to around 70. A great deal of this increase is due to medical and health advances. But every successful technique which lengthens the life span of persons with inherited defects increases the likelihood that such individuals will reproduce and pass on their defective genes to the genetic load of future generations. As Fleming (1969) puts it, " . . . conventional medicine is now seen by the biological revolutionaries as one of the greatest threats to the human race." Selection and survival of the genetically less fit does, indeed, slowly but relentlessly increase the frequencies of these genes and the probability that they will occur in their descendents.

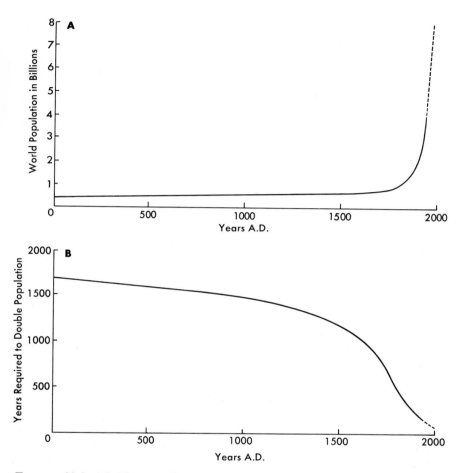

FIGURE 20-3. (*A*) *The rise of world population from the time of Christ projected to the year 2000, based on present rate of increase.* (*B*) *The diminishing time required to double the world's population from the beginning of the Christian era to the year 2000.*

Moreover, the nearly continuous warfare in which man chooses still to engage tends to siphon off the physically fittest and, often, the intellectually well endowed. In addition, the danger of accident or misuse of atomic energy is but a hand's motion away from wreaking nearly incalculable genetic damage on at least a share of the world's inhabitants. Again, Fleming (1969) sums up these concerns by pointing out that " . . . biologists deplore the aggressive instincts of the human animal, now armed with nuclear weapons, his lamentably low average intelligence for coping with increasingly complicated problems, and his terrible prolificity, no longer mitigated by a high enough death rate."

As we have noted, a significant percentage of all births carry some detectable, genetically based defect. Many of the bearers of these defect-producing genes die, some very early, others a little later, and a great many can look ahead only to a life of greater or lesser misery if, indeed, their deficiencies are not such as to impair their mental processes. An additional and apparently rather large number of fetuses, homozygous for recessive lethal genes or carrying some serious chromosome aberration, as we have seen, abort spontaneously. Quite aside from considerations of birth control and death control, those who *are* born ought to have a chance for life free from this type of defect. On the other hand, they should not serve as additional sources of input for deleterious genes.

### POSSIBLE SOLUTIONS

Three avenues of approach are available in meeting this kind of problem:

1. *Directed recombination*, involving selection of those genes which will be permitted to perpetuate themselves.
2. *Overriding the expression* of defect-producing genes without trying to control their frequencies.
3. *Genetic surgery*; that is, modifying or even replacing the defective genes themselves.

***Directed Recombination.***   In some ways, directed recombination, or gene selection, is mechanically the easiest, though not necessarily the most satisfactory, solution to the problem of quality control in the human gene pool. It requires no sophisticated equipment, no techniques which have not been available, even practiced in other species, for years. Basically, it involves only the selection of parental stocks, those whose genes are to be transmitted to future generations. The oldest technique would merely restrict child-bearing to those best fitted to perpetuate the species. But this raises significant problems. What are the standards? Who makes the decisions? Racially pernicious, politically unsound, such a solution is at best impractical, at worst dangerous.

Heterozygous "carriers" of defect-producing genes can now be identified by relatively simple tests in such varied inherited metabolic disorders as sickle-cell trait, cystic fibrosis, and galactosemia. Could we not limit or prevent reproduction by such persons? The problem of how that control might be accomplished becomes a very personal one when we recognize that each of us carries at least one, and probably several, such lethal, semi-lethal, or disabling genes. Should control be exercised through advice and counseling? On a distressingly small scale we are doing this now. Should it be by governmental restraint, by legislation, with penalties for breaking the law—or even by compulsory sterilization? Once again, the question of who should make these judgments is an exceedingly difficult one and may well have no acceptable answer. But, viewed coldly and impersonally, this approach does offer the advantage of being possible now in many instances, for it requires little more in the way of precise genetic knowledge than we already have.

If the concept of selective parenthood seems repugnant or impractical or dangerous, there is the additional problem of whether to allow fetuses that will express defective genes or which have been genetically damaged by such drugs as thalidomide or LSD to come to term. To permit them to do so is regarded by some as the deepest kind of cruelty, both to the new person and to his family. By others, *not* to do so is regarded as murder. It is time, as many have pointed out, to reexamine the philosophy underlying selective legalized abortion. Both Colorado and Hawaii have recently taken significant forward steps in this regard, and an even more liberal reform has been passed by the New York legislature. Whether prohibition of abortion is even a proper concern of the state is debatable.

On the other hand, still another avenue of directed recombination is, even now, open to us. Before long it may become much more practical as our knowledge of the human genotype and linkage groups increases. Rather than select certain *persons* who shall or shall not become parents, or which *embryos* will be allowed to mature, we may select the *reproductive cells* themselves. To a degree this is practiced now. Artificial insemination, so long applied with rather successful results in animal breeding, is currently used to a much more limited extent in mankind. But all too often no account is taken of the genetic constitution of the prospective mother and little more of the sperm donor. Ordinarily the goal is merely the *fact* of child production in families where it would not otherwise be possible and, incidentally, to produce children who could be mistaken for those of the nonbiological father.

The late Herman Muller (1965) proposed setting up sperm and egg banks, since sex cells can be kept alive and functional for considerable periods by freezing. Muller proposed such banks, with the most desirable male and female subjects serving as donors. By whatever standards that might be set up, the best sources could continue so to serve for a considerable period after their deaths and, with suitable precautions, even after a nuclear war. The question of determining genetic desirability here is, of course, no easier than in other systems of restrictive parenthood. But Muller, in his 1965 paper and in many addresses up until his death in 1967, expressed hope in these words: " With the coming of a better understanding of genetics and evolution, the individual's fixation on the attempted perpetuation of just *his* particular genes will be bound to fade. It will be superseded by a more rational view . . . he will condemn as childish conceit the notion that there is any reason for his unessential peculiarities, idiosyncrasies, and foibles to be expressed generation after generation." The background of Muller's philosophy is revealingly described by Sonneborn (1968), a long-time colleague, from a variety of sources that include Muller's unpublished autobiographical notes. Of course, society has not reached the stage of objectivity envisioned by Muller, and gamete banks still entail an element of chance in the recombination of disadvantageous genes, though the overall probability might well be lower than in a system of random mating.

The techniques are, again, relatively simple. Use of sperm requires no more elaborate methods than those currently used in the practice of artificial insemination. Implantation of selected eggs, fertilized or unfertilized, is already a fact in laboratory animals and involves little that is new for adaptation to humans. In fact, Edwards, Steptoe, and Purdy (1970) have already brought about fertilization of human eggs in vitro and have succeeded in carrying the resulting zygotes to the 16 cell stage of embryo development. Recently a team of British doctors disclosed that an egg, already fertilized in vitro by sperm from the husband, was to be implanted in the womb of a woman who could not conceive because of an obstruction in her fallopian tubes. The prospects of the birth of the first test tube conceived child appeared reasonable. Certainly there are difficulties ahead in such procedures, and many presently unanticipated problems will doubtless arise. But work in this direction *is* going on, and success *will* come.

Once the process of implantation is perfected, the prospects are virtually limitless. The possibility has been suggested of a system of volunteer "host" mothers who would bear other people's children for a fee where, perhaps, it may be physically unwise for a woman to undertake the risks and rigors of pregnancy, or even in case she simply does not wish to interrupt a career. Or, an infertile woman could bear children who are the product of her husband's sperm and an ovum from an unknown donor; such a fertilized egg might then easily be implanted in her body. Of course, the matter is more complicated than suggested here, but surely it will be feasible in the relatively near future.

Some writers, only partly with tongue in cheek, have compared human germinal choice to selection of a packet of desirable flower seeds in the supermarket. The container would carry a brief statement of the most probable traits, from intelligence to physical perfection and even sex[2]; selection could be made as simply as deciding on the kind of plants to grow. From the psychological standpoint, there is considerable doubt that man is ready for this, and our genetic knowledge of the human species is not yet up to our understanding of marigolds and petunias.

When it is—and some scientists have estimated that this will be before the end of the present century—perhaps rather than implant an egg in a human female, we could not only select sperm and egg and bring about fertilization in vitro, but even raise the embryo to term in a glass womb. In fact, although some scientists have expressed doubt, Petrucci in Italy is said to have raised human embryos in this way for as long as two months, and then deliberately

---

[2] However, predetermination of sex does not appear imminent; for a statement of the problem see Etzioni (1968).

terminated the experiment. The moral question "Is it murder?" is reported to have deeply disturbed him as a Catholic. Others have worked and are working along these lines and someday, somewhere, someone is going to be successful in producing such a person. Think of the cognate problems: who is he? who is or are his parents? what are his legal rights? will we mass produce a new race of slaves? One day these questions, and more, are going to have to be answered.

Further afield, but interesting speculatively, is the possibility of vegetative multiplication or cloning. It has long been possible to maintain cultures of human cells; will it eventually be possible to induce differentiation and thereby create unlimited numbers of custom-made, identical individuals to certain specific genetic designs? Already we can do this with lower forms of life, and some scientists feel it is more a question of "when" than "if."

*Overriding Gene Expression.*    As another approach, consider the modification of the expression of the genes with which one was born. Diabetes, for example, is a genetic disorder which affects several million persons in this country, many of whom are kept alive only by injection of the hormone, insulin. This is one of the simpler proteins synthesized by the human body. Its structure is well known, consisting of two polypeptide chains, one of 21 amino acid residues, the other of 30 (Fig. 20-4). It is formed only in certain cells of the pancreas from its percursor protein, proinsulin. Proinsulin is manufactured in the usual biological way, in which the appropriate sequence of deoxyribonucleotides is transcribed into mRNA which, together with the necessary amino acids, ribosomes, enzymes, tRNA, and so forth, translates this sequence into protein. The evidence indicates that proinsulin is a single polypeptide chain which is cleaved and folded after synthesis to make the two chains of insulin. It is thus presumably the product of a single cistron of some 153 nucleotides, representing only about 0.05 $\mu$m of the total length of human DNA.

All somatic cells are believed to contain all the genetic information of the individual, yet only a very restricted group of cells synthesizes proinsulin. In other cells of the body, the proinsulin cistron is repressed. Knowledge of the mechanism of gene repression in higher organisms is progressing rapidly, and one approach in treating diabetes may lie in learning how to derepress the proinsulin cistron, either in the cells where it is normally produced or in other cells of the body. Once such activation has been accomplished, there remains the problem of conversion of proinsulin to insulin and its release from the cells in which its synthesis is effected. By comparison, this may not be very difficult. But such derepression in somatic cells, even for millions of diabetics, will have no effect in upgrading the human gene pool. This approach would either have to be used in conjunction with some appropriate type of directed recombination, or it would have to be extended in some way to the reproductive cells. This leads us to the third solution, genetic surgery.

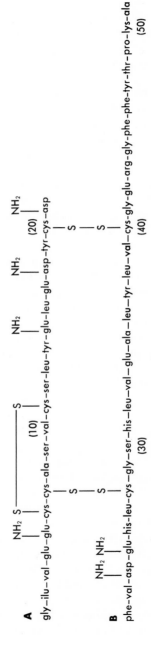

FIGURE 20-4. *Amino acid sequence of the beef insulin molecule, the first protein in which the amino acid sequence was determined. Each molecule consists of an A chain (21 amino acid residues) and a B chain (30 amino acid residues). The A and B chains are joined by disulfide bonds connecting cysteine residues as shown.*

*Genetic Surgery.*  Rather than repression, the problem might be one of a cistron whose nucleotide sequence specifies a "wrong" series of amino acids. Even a single base-pair change—for example, a switch from an adenine-thymine pair to one of guanine-cytosine, or even from an adenine-thymine to a thymine-adenine pair, or the deletion or insertion of one nucleotide pair— can, as we have seen, code for an incorrect amino acid at a given position in the polypeptide chain. The result could be the formation of an aberrant or a nonfunctional protein. This is the sort of change, you will recall, that spells the difference between normal hemoglobin A and the hemoglobin S of sickle-cell disease. Could such defective cistrons be replaced by genetic surgery? In brief, the answer today for human beings is "No, not yet." But it can be done in bacteria and in cell cultures, though we cannot yet control very well which genes are replaced. Only the rashest dogmatism would hold that such a possibility could not be brought to bear in human genetics within the lifetime of today's college student.

As we have noted in earlier chapters, transduction is a process involving transfer of DNA from one cell to another through the mediation of a phage. In the infection of a bacterium by a virulent phage, the vast majority of the new virus particles released upon lysis of the host contain DNA identical to that of the original infecting phage. But a very few contain a segment of bacterial DNA from the host cell, which replaces a corresponding bit of viral DNA. On the other hand, recall that the temperate phages do not regularly lyse and destroy the bacterial cell. Infection of a cell by temperate phage *lambda*, for example, results in incorporation of some of the viral DNA into the bacterial cell's chromosome. The bacterial cell survives and multiplies, some of its descendents containing DNA that includes sequences of nucleotides received from the phage.

The question here is whether this same kind of transfer of genetic material could be effected in the cells of higher organisms. There is evidence to suggest an affirmative answer. Aaronson and Todaro (1969), going beyond earlier suggestions of transformation in cultured mammalian cells (Szybalska and Szybalski, 1962), reported that DNA isolated from simian virus 40 can become established in human fibroblast cells in vitro and appears to express itself in protein synthesis in such cells. SV40 is a small virus which produces tumors in appropriate animal hosts. Human cells in which SV40 DNA has been incorporated undergo certain characteristic changes, including loss of sensitivity to contact inhibition of cell division and the production of SV40-specific mRNA. Such human cells also produce a new protein, the so-called T-antigen, which persists in clonal cells. Aaronson and Todaro conclude their report with these words: "There is considerable evidence [to show] that SV40 DNA can become a permanent part of the host cell genome. Most of the SV40 DNA in transformed cells is associated with the chromosomes . . . However, if the viral DNA's ability to integrate into the human cell genome can be separated from its [tumor producing property], it may then be possible to use 'integrating' viral DNA to insert specific information into human cells." The important point here for our purposes is the incorporation and persistence of viral DNA in the human gene complement and its subsequent manifestation in specific new protein synthesis.

Three additional discoveries of tremendous significance (two of which we have already referred to in Chapters 14 and 18) complete the groundwork, although their application to human genetic surgery must still hurdle some problems. But, by comparison, these by no means appear insurmountable. Although it is, of course, risky to speculate, timetables for discoveries and their utilization are frequently much too conservative. To address ourselves to the question of human genetic modification, rather than hope to come upon a convenient transducing virus carrying, for example, a cistron for proinsulin, it might be far more practical to make it to order.

You will recall the isolation of the 4,700 nucleotides of the operator, promoter and z cistron of the lac operon of *Escherichia coli* by Beckwith and his colleagues (Shapiro et al., 1969, and Chapter 18) and the synthesis of biologically active, normal DNA of phage $\phi$X-174 by Kornberg and his associates (Goulian, et al., 1967, and Chapter 14). This artificially synthesized single-stranded DNA of some 6,000 nucleotides was found to be infective for the usual host (*E. coli*), and the virus particles resulting from infection with it were completely indistinguishable from wild type phage.

Finally, Osterman, Waddell, and Aposhian (1970) have reported that infection of cultured mouse kidney cells by polyoma virus results in production not only of normal polyoma virus progeny but also of **pseudoviruses**. These consist of *fragments of host cell DNA* contained within normal polyoma virus protein coats. The pseudovirus particles, they found, are adsorbed to host cells of secondary cultures and uncoated by them, *apparently in the host cell* (though this, they point out, remains to be tested further). The Aposhian group is currently at work on the question of whether the genetic information of the pseudovirus is expressed in the host cell. At the speed with which discoveries are being made in this area of molecular genetics, the answer could well be determined before these words can appear in print.

To summarize, prospects look promising that we may one day have the capability of isolating and synthesizing cistrons coding for almost any trait, of packaging these in protein coats and, hopefully, of finding that they will express themselves in the recipient cells by the usual biological mechanism of protein synthesis. Once the original isolation and syntheses have been accomplished, they will be done for all time; following Kornberg's methods, they can be copied accurately forever. If the question of "whether" seems answerable in the affirmative, what about the question of "when?" Fleming (1969), although acknowledging that "gene manipulation and substitution in human beings . . . is the remotest prospect of all" in the biological revolution of which he writes, does suggest its feasibility "maybe by the year 2000."

By these techniques and processes, then, any faulty or undesirable gene could be changed, first in the somatic cells of individuals requiring such genetic surgery, and next in the reproductive cells, for there are, of course, two facets to the task here. It is one thing to modify the genetic material of the somatic cells, but to exercise a quality control over human evolution, such modification will also have to be made in the sex cells. We are, however, still left with the problem of defining *desirability* in the genome; that is, desirability from whose viewpoint? The argument is sometimes advanced that discoveries so fraught with the possibility of misuse or misapplication ought not to be made or, having been made, the data should be destroyed or kept hidden. But the compelling duty of scientists is to continue ceaselessly to push back the boundaries of the unknown and to seek out the truth, wherever the search may lead. However, it is just as important a duty of the scientist to point out the consequences of the use or misuse of new discoveries. No scientist should ever withhold new facts or techniques because of fear of what their use might hold for mankind. But he should always be ready to alert the nonscientific community to potential dangers of misapplication. Wilson (1970), a scientist-novelist, puts it succinctly: " . . . because of the scientist's inability to look over the walls of history and foresee what subsequent generations will do with the fruits of his discovery, society today blames the scientist for what it wrenched from his hand and turned into engines of evil. . . . The scientist is bewildered to find himself considered the villain. . . . The very scientists who are being considered the bogeymen are the ones who must still be called upon to use their ingenuity to help undo the damage which society has done to itself."

If a few small cistrons can one day be synthesized, next will come the possibility of replicating the entire human DNA complement, literally making human beings to order with almost any set of predetermined characteristics. Combine, if you will, this kind of genetic surgery with the glass womb, and man will, indeed, then control his own evolution, shaping it to suit whatever the need, good or evil. And he *will* be able to do so in the foreseeable future.

## CONCLUSION

Although the successful application of these approaches still lies largely in the future, the future quickly becomes the present, and it is not at all unlikely that they will one day be possible, and sooner rather than later. Man's capacity for good or ill will thereby be immeasurably increased. How wisely he uses these new powers depends on how carefully he plans now. As Rosenfeld (1965, 1969) has said so well, "It may be comforting to know that the statesmen and the philosophers and the scientists are worrying about all these things, but we cannot let them do all the worrying for us. The time ahead is wild and uncharted. No one has been there, so there are no experts. Each of us, whose body or brain may be modified or whose descendants' characteristics may be predetermined, has a vast personal stake in the outcome. We can guarantee that good will be done only by looking to it ourselves."

## REFERENCES

AARONSON, S. A., and G. J. TODARO, 1969. Human Diploid Cell Transformation by DNA Extracted from the Tumor Virus SV40. *Science*, 166:390–391.

BOUÉ, J. G., A. BOUÉ, and P. LAZAR, 1967. Les Aberrations Chromosomique dans les Avortements. *Ann. Génétique*, 10:179–187.

BURNS, G. W., 1970. Tomorrow—or the Day After. *Ohio Jour. Sci.*, 70:193–198.

CAIRNS, J., 1963. The Chromosome of *Escherichia coli*. *Cold Spring Harbor Symposia Quant. Biol.*, 28:43–45.

DAVIS, B. D., 1970. Prospects for Genetic Intervention in Man. *Science*, 170: 1279–1283.

EDWARDS, R. G., P. C. STEPTOE, and J. M. PURDY, 1970. Fertilization and Cleavage *in vitro* of Preovulator Human Oocytes. *Nature*, 227:1307–1309.

ETZIONI, A., 1968. Sex Control, Science, and Society. *Science*, 161:1107–1112.

FLEMING, D., 1969. On Living in a Biological Revolution. *The Atlantic Monthly*, 223:64–70.

GERMAN, J., 1970. Studying Human Chromosomes Today. *Amer. Scientist*, 58: 182–201.

GOULIAN, M. A., A. KORNBERG, and R. L. SINSHEIMER, 1967. Enzymatic Synthesis of DNA, XXIV. Synthesis of Infectious Phage $\phi$X-174 DNA. *Proc. Nat. Acad. Sci. (U.S.)*, 58(6):2321–2328.

HELLER, J. H., 1969. Human Chromosomal Abnormalities as Related to Physical and Mental Dysfunction. *Jour. Hered.*, 60:239–248.

JAROFF, L., ed., 1971. Man into Superman; the Promise and Peril of the New Genetics. *Time*, April 19, 1971, 33–52. Chicago, Time, Inc.

MACINNES, J. W., and R. B. URETZ, 1966. Organization of DNA in Dipteran Polytene Chromosomes as Indicated by Polarized Fluorescence Microscopy. *Science*, 151:689–691.

MCKUSICK, V., 1971. The Mapping of Human Chromosomes. *Sci. Amer.*, 224: 104–113.

MULLER, H. J., 1965. Means and Aims in Human Genetic Betterment. In T. M. Sonneborn, ed., *The Control of Human Heredity and Evolution*. New York, The Macmillan Co.

OSTERMAN, J. V., A. WADDELL, and H. V. APOSHIAN, 1970. DNA and Gene Therapy: Uncoating of Polyoma Pseudovirus in Mouse Embryo Cells. *Proc. Nat. Acad. Sci. (U.S.)*, 67:37–40.

ROBERTS, D. F., J. CHAVEZ, and S. D. M. COURT, 1970. The Genetic Component in Child Mortality. *Arch. Dis. Childhood*, 45:33–38.

ROSENFELD, A., 1965. Will Man Direct His own Evolution? *Life Magazine*, 59(14), Oct. 1, 1965. Chicago, Time, Inc.

ROSENFELD, A., 1969. *The Second Genesis*. Englewood Cliffs, N.J., Prentice-Hall.

ROSLANSKY, J. D., ed., 1966. *Genetics and the Future of Man*. New York, Appleton-Century-Crofts.

SHAPIRO, J., L. MACHATTIE, L. ERON, G. IHLER, K. IPPEN, and J. BECKWITH, 1969. Isolation of Pure *Lac* Operon DNA. *Nature*, **224**: 768–774.

SONNEBORN, T. M., ed., 1965. *The Control of Human Heredity and Evolution*. New York, The Macmillan Co.

SONNEBORN, T. M., 1968. H. J. Muller, Crusader for Human Betterment. *Science*, **162**: 772–776.

SZYBALSKA, E. H., and W. SZYBALSKI, 1962. Genetics of Human Cell Lines, IV. DNA-Mediated Heritable Transformation of a Biochemical Trait. *Proc. Nat. Acad. Sci. (U.S.)*, **48**: 2026–2034.

WILSON, M., 1970. On Being a Scientist. *The Atlantic Monthly*, **226**: 101–106.

# APPENDIX A
# Answers to Problems

**Chapter 2**

**2-2.** *cc*.

**2-3.** (a) 1. *aa*; 2. *Aa*; 3. *aa*; 4. *A–*.
   (b) 1:1.

**2-4.** (a) 25%.
   (b) 50%.
   (c) Probably zero; evidence *suggests* girl is homozygous normal.

**2-5.** (a) Incompletely dominant as relates to chloride excretion.
   (b) Recessive lethal.

**2-6.** (a) None.
   (b) Yes; this couple's children have a 50% probability of being heterozygotes. If one of such heterozygotes marries another, *their* children (grand-children of the original couple) have a 25% chance of having the disease.

**2-7.** (a) Purple is heterozygous; blue is homozygous.
   (b) Purple.

**2-8.** Hornless is the dominant character. Hornless animals producing horned offspring are heterozygotes; any that do so should not be bred. Since he needs to get rid of a recessive, and cattle usually produce but one offspring per year, the problem is not going to be solved quickly. On the other hand, red animals are homozygous, so roans and whites can be excluded from the breeding program.

**2-9.** (a) *hh*.      (e) *h*.
   (b) *HH*.     (f) *Hh*.
   (c) *H*.      (g) *Hhh*.
   (d) *h*.      (h) *hh*.

**2-10.** Curly is the heterozygous expression of a recessive lethal; 341:162 is a close approximation of a 2:1 ratio.

**2-11.** *ff*; *Ff*; *ff*; *Ff*; *ff*.

**2-12.** Testcross.

**2-13.** *Aa*; *Aa*; *aa*.

**2-14.** On the basis of her daughter, III-4, who has to be *aa*, inheriting one *a* from each parent.

**2-15.** *Hh*; *HY*; *Hh*.

**2-16.** There is a 50% chance she is *Hh*; in that case, her sons would each have a 50% chance of being hemophilic but all daughters would be phenotypically normal. If she is *HH*, she and a normal man cannot have hemophilic children. The genotype of V-2 cannot be determined with certainty.

**2-17.** (a) $\frac{1}{2}$. (b) $\frac{1}{4}$.

**2-18.** No; the transfused blood does not affect the recipient's genotype.

**2-19.** Recessive.

**2-20.** (a) $\frac{2}{3}$ (*not* $\frac{1}{4}$ because his normal phenotype rules out the possibility that he might be homozygous recessive for PKU).

(b) Probably none; it appears highly likely that the girl is homozygous dominant for normal.

**2-21.** (a) $(\frac{2}{3})^2 = \frac{4}{9}$.

(b) $\frac{1}{9}$.

(c) $\frac{1}{4}$.

## Chapter 3

**3-1.** (a) 48.     (e) 48.

(b) 24.     (f) 24.

(c) 48.     (g) 12.

(d) None.    (h) 12.

**3-2.** (a) 40.

(b) 40.

(c) 40.

**3-3.** (a) 80.

(b) 160.

**3-4.** (a) 20.     (e) 10.

(b) 10.     (f) 10.

(c) 30.     (g) 20.

(d) 10.

**3-5.** (a) 1.     (d) 4.

(b) 2.     (e) 2.

(c) 2.     (f) 32.

**3-6.** (a) $(\frac{1}{2})^{30}$.

(b) $[(\frac{1}{2})^{30} \times (\frac{1}{2})^{30}]$.

**3-7.** (a) 33.

(b) Irregularities of pairing at synapsis lead to defective gametes having more or less than one complete set of chromosomes.

**3-8.** Prophase longest, next telophase, next metaphase, and anaphase shortest; why?

**3-9.** 7.

**3-10.** $(\frac{1}{2})^7$.

**3-11.** $+ + + + yyyy$ indicates segregation of the alleles at the first meiotic division, hence no crossing-over; $+ + yy + + yy$ indicates second division segregation, hence crossing-over.

**3-12.** (a) Yes.

(b) Crossing over between the two pairs of genes.

**3-13.** 0.005.

## Chapter 4

**4-1.** (a) $\frac{3}{16}$.     (c) $\frac{2}{16}$.

(b) $\frac{3}{16}$.     (d) $\frac{1}{16}$.

**4-2.** (a) 8.

(b) $2^{12}$.

**4-3.** (a) $1:1$.

(b) $1:1:1:1:1:1:1:1$.

**4-4.** (a) 4.          (c) 16.

(b) 8.          (d) $2^n$.

**4-5.** $2^5 = 32$.

**4-6.** $3^5 = 243$.

**4-7.** Letting $Y$ represent red, and $y$ yellow, the parental genotypes are $Yyh_1h_2 \times Yyh_1h_2$ (red, scattered hairs).

**4-8.** (a) Cream.

(b) $\frac{9}{16}$.

**4-9.** 9 normal:7 deaf.

**4-10.** (a) $9:7$.

(b) $A$–$B$–.

(c) $AaBb$.

(d) $AAbb \times aaBB$.

**4-11.** (a) $aabb$.

(b) $AaBb$.

(c) anything *except aabb*.

**4-12.** 9 black:3 brown:4 albino.

**4-13.** (a) 2.

(b) $AaBb$.

(c) purple, $A$–$B$–; red $A$–$bb$; white $aa$––, if one assumes gene $A$ is responsible for the enzyme converting colorless precursor to cyanidin, and $B$ for the enzyme converting cyanidin to delphinidin.

**4-14.** 9 both enzymes : 3 enzyme #1 only : 3 enzyme #2 only : 1 neither enzyme.

**4-15.** $aaBB \times AAbb$; $aaBb \times Aabb$.

**4-16.** Four: red long, red round, white long, and white round.

**4-17.** (a) $3:6:3:1:2:1$.

(b) $1:2:1$.

**4-18.** (a) Let $A$ represent a color inhibitor gene, $a$ the gene for color, $B$ yellow, $b$ green. Then $A$––– is white, $aaB$– yellow, and $aabb$ green.

(b) P: $AAbb$ (white) $\times$ $aaBB$ (yellow)

$F_1$: $AaBb$

$F_2$: $9\ A$–$B$– $\Big\}$ white
  $3\ A$–$bb$

 $3\ aaB$– yellow

 $1\ aabb$ green.

**4-19.** (a) Disk $C$–$D$–, sphere $C$–$dd$ and $ccD$–, elongate $ccdd$.

(b) P: $CCdd \times ccDD$

$F_1$: $CcDd$

$F_2$: $9\ C$–$D$– disk

 $3\ C$–$dd$ $\Big\}$ sphere
  $3\ ccD$–

 $1\ ccdd$ elongate.

**4-20.** (a) 8.
     (b) 1.
     (c) 24.

**4-21.** (a) 9.
     (b) $\frac{108}{256}$

**4-22.** (a) red $R–S–$; sandy $rrS–$ and $R–ss$; white $rss$.
     (b) case 1 $RRSS \times RRSS$.
          case 2 $RrSS \times RrSS$, or $RRSs \times RRSs$, or $RrSs \times RrSS$, or $RrSs \times RRSs$.
          case 3 $RRSS \times rss$.
          case 4 $rrSS \times RRss$.
          case 5 $rrSs \times Rrss$.

**4-23.**
| | *Genotypic:* | *Phenotypic:* |
|---|---|---|
| (a) | 1:2:1:2:4:2:1:2:1 | 9:3:3:1 |
| (b) | 1:2:1:2:4:2:1:2:1 | 3:6:3:1:2:1 |
| (c) | 1:2:1:2:4:2:1:2:1 | 1:2:1:2:4:2:1:2:1 |
| (d) | 1:2:1:2:4:2 | 3:1 |
| (e) | 1:2:1:2:4:2 | 1:2:1 |
| (f) | 1:2:2:4 | all alike. |

**4-24.** 3 red : 6 purple : 3 blue : 4 white.

## Chapter 5

**5-1.** (a) $(\frac{1}{2})^3$, or $\frac{1}{8}$.
    (b) $\frac{3}{8}$.

**5-2.** $\frac{1}{2}$.

**5-3.** $\frac{1}{2}$.

**5-4.** (a) $\frac{1}{16}$.
    (b) $\frac{1}{36}$.
    (c) $\frac{1}{6}$.

**5-5.** (a) $\frac{3}{4}$.
    (b) $\frac{1}{4}$.

**5-6.** (a) $\frac{4}{16}$.    (c) $\frac{9}{16}$.
    (b) $\frac{1}{16}$.    (d) $\frac{3}{16}$.

**5-7.** (a) $\frac{1}{8}$.
    (b) $\frac{1}{4}$.
    (c) 6.

**5-8.** $\frac{270}{32,768}$, or about 1 in 121.

**5-9.** $\frac{243}{32,768}$, or about 1 in 135.

**5-10.** $\frac{24}{81}$, or roughly 3 in 10.

**5-11.** (a) 1 in 31.6.
     (b) About 1 in 16.

**5-12.** P lies between 0.5 and 0.3 ($\chi^2 = 0.9927$).

**5-13.** (a) P is between 0.20 and 0.05 ($\chi^2 = 2.0$).
     (b) P is between 0.80 and 0.70 ($\chi^2 = 0.1269$).

(c) No.

(d) Either accept results as a better reflection of a 9:7 expectancy, or obtain a larger sample.

**5-14.** (a) $P < 0.01$ ($\chi^2 = 20.0$).

(b) P lies between 0.30 and 0.20 ($\chi^2 = 1.270$).

(c) Yes; significant for a 1:1 expectancy.

(d) The larger the sample the greater the usefulness of the chi-square test.

**5-15.** (a) $\chi^2 = 0.015$; $P = 0.80 - 0.95$; not significant.

(b) $\chi^2 = 0.451$: $P = 0.50 - 0.70$; not significant.

(c) $\chi^2 = 0.563$; $P = 0.30 - 0.50$; not significant.

(d) $\chi^2 = 0.618$; $P = 0.80 - 0.95$; not significant.

## Chapter 6

**6-1.** (a) *wo dil o aw*.

(b) Double (or any even number of) crossovers are not detected in genes as far apart as *wo* and *aw* are here. The more accurate *wo-aw* distance is 22 map units, i.e., $9 + 6 + 7$.

**6-2.** (a) *jvl fl e*.

(b) Double crossovers are missed in a dihybrid cross involving only *jvl* and *e*.

**6-3.** It could be either to the "left" of *jvl* or to the "right" of *e*.

**6-4.** To the "right" of *e*.

**6-5.** (a) Yes.

(b) 0.77%.

**6-6.** 4.

**6-7.** Because genes for each of the seven characters happened to be on a different one of the seven pairs of chromosomes of the pea.

**6-8.** (a) 12.

(b) 12.

(c) 23.

(d) 24 since the X and Y chromosomes are only partly homologous.

**6-9.** (a) 4.

(b) 2.

**6-10.** (a) 8 (2 noncrossover, 4 single crossover, 2 double crossover).

(b) 2.

**6-11.** 0.5.

**6-12.** Yes. Normal beaked plants are doubly homozygous recessive; in this cross, with unlinked genes, about 6% ($= \frac{1}{16}$) of the progeny should have this phenotype. The number actually observed is about 3.68 times greater than is to be expected with unlinked genes.

**6-13.** (a) Data indicate *cis* linkage (*Cu Bk/cu bk*) in each parent and that the frequency of *cu bk* gametes in each was 0.48 ($= \sqrt{0.2304}$).

(b) Crossover gametes were then produced with a frequency of 0.02 each, so the genes are 4 map units apart.

**6-14.** 0.4 *Pl Py*; 0.4 *pl py*; 0.1 *Pl py*; 0.1 *pl Py*.

**6-15.** 16%.

**6-16.** 9%.

**6-17.** 34%.

**6-18.** (a) *h fz eg*; *h-fz*, 14 map units; *fz-eg*, 6 map units.

(b) 0.238.

**6-19.** (a) *d* + + and + *m p*.

(b) *p d m*.

(c) *p-d*, 4.5 map units; *d-m*, 4.5 map units.

(d) Yes; coincidence = 0.5.

**6-20.** (a) *R Ro* and *r ro* each 0.4375; *R ro* and *r Ro* each 0.0625.

(b) 0.1914.

(c) 0.6912.

**6-21.** (a) 0.85.

(b) 0.05.

(c) 0.10.

(d) None.

**6-22.**

|  | (a) | (b) |
|---|---|---|
| + + + | 0.4275 | 0.42625 |
| $pg_{12}\,gl_{15}\,bk_2$ | 0.4275 | 0.42625 |
| + $gl_{15}\,bk_2$ | 0.0225 | 0.02375 |
| $pg_{12}$ + + | 0.0225 | 0.02375 |
| + + $bk_2$ | 0.0475 | 0.04875 |
| $pg_{12}\,gl_{15}$ + | 0.0475 | 0.04875 |
| + $gl_{15}$ + | 0.0025 | 0.00125 |
| $pg_{12}$ + $bk_2$ | 0.0025 | 0.00125 |

**6-23.** (a) 0.485.

(b) 0.015.

**6-24.** (a) 88.2%.

(b) 0.2%.

**Chapter 7**

**7-1.** No.

**7-2.** $c^{ch}c \times c^h c$.

**7-3.** (a) 3.

(b) Superdouble, double, single.

(c) One parent heterozygous for superdouble and single, the other heterozygous for double and single.

**7-4.** Alexandra, normal, Blue Moon, Primrose Queen.

**7-5.** 4.

**7-6.** 1.

**7-7.** 3.

**7-8.** All black.

**7-9.** 3 dark-bellied:1 black.

**7-10.** One parent heterozygous for white-bellied and dark-bellied, the other either the same or heterozygous for white-bellied and plain black.

**7-11.** White-bellied > dark-bellied > black-and-tan > plain black.

**7-12.** 20.

**7-13.** 210.

**7-14.** 8.

**7-15.** 16.

**7-16.** 48.

**7-17.** 162.

**7-18.** Yes.

**7-19.** Yes; accused man cannot be the father.

**7-20.** Yes.

**7-21.** No.

**7-22.** Yes; child cannot be theirs.

**7-23.** No. The claimant's M-N type should not be possible with the purported parentage.

**7-24.** Children numbers 4, 5, and 6 cannot be those of the husband, #4 on the basis of *NS/Ns*, #5 on the basis of *cde/cde* and *MS/NS*, #6 on the basis of all three tests, even allowing for a very low frequency of recombination. Morover, it appears that more than one additional man was involved; numbers 4 and 5 could have been produced by the same man (but not the husband), and number 6 by a third man.

**Chapter 8**

**8-1.** Intelligence, height, skin color, eye color.

**8-2.** Any parental genotypes that can produce at least some $F_1$ genotypes with a greater number of contributing alleles than they themselves have are possible, e.g., *AaBbCcDd* × *AaBbCcDd*, *AaBbccdd* × *aabbCcDd*, etc.

**8-3.** (a) $\frac{1}{4,096}$.

  (b) 13.

  (c) $\frac{924}{4,096}$.

**8-4.** 8 polygenes (4 pairs); 3inches per contributing allele.

**8-5.** 10 polygenes (5 pairs); 4.8 inches per contributing allele.

**8-6.** $\frac{1}{4,096}$.

**8-7.** *AaBbCcDd* × *AaBbCcDd*.

**8-8.** Any in which each parent is homozygous effective for 2 of the 4 pairs, e.g., *AABBccdd* × *aabbCCDD*, etc.

**8-9.** 769. ($\frac{3}{4}$ of 1,024 which are S—————, or 768, plus 1 which is *ssaabbccdd*.)

**8-10.** 8.

**8-11.** (a) 25 and 5 cm.

  (b) 15 cm.

  (c) 1 (25):4 (20):6 (15):4 (10):1 (5).

**8-12.** (a) 15 and 5 cm.

  (b) 15 cm.

  (c) 9 (15):6 (10):1 (5).

**Chapter 9**

**9-1.** 23.0 (actually, 23.04).

**9-2.** 4.478.

**9-3.** 68.26%, or about $\frac{2}{3}$.

**9-4.** 0.895.

**9-5.** 0.9544.

**9-6.** 1.201.

**9-7.** 0.6826, or about 2 chances in 3.

**9-8.** No; $S_d$ = only $(\bar{x}_1 - \bar{x}_2)$, and to be significant $S_d$ must exceed $2(\bar{x}_1 - \bar{x}_2)$.

**9-9.** 8.

**Chapter 10**

**10-1.** (a) Metafemale      (d) Intersex.

      (b) Metamale.      (e) Female (tetraploid).

      (c) Metafemale.

**10-2.** (a) Female.      (d) Male.

      (b) Male.      (e) Male.

      (c) Female.

**10-3.** 9 normal monoecious : 3 pistillate (ears terminal and lateral) : 3 staminate : 1 pistillate (ears terminal only); i.e., 9 monoecious : 3 staminate : 4 pistillate.

**10-4.** $\frac{1}{4}$.

**10-5.** 3 male : 1 female.

**10-6.** (a) $bW$ (or simply $b$).      (c) $BW$ (or $B$)

      (b) $B-(BB$ or $Bb$).      (d) $bb$.

**10-7.** 0.1.

**10-8.** 45% (20% XX + 25% XXY).

**10-9.** (a) $\frac{1}{4}$.

      (b) $\frac{1}{4}$.

      (c) $\frac{1}{3}$.

**10-10.** (a) white.

       (b) red.

**10-11.** $\frac{1}{3}$ male, $\frac{2}{3}$ female.

**10-12.** From the theoretical standpoint several alternative explanations are possible. Among the most likely are:

    (a) nondisjunction of Y in the second meiotic division in spermatogenesis;

    (b) nondisjunction in the first meiotic division in spermatogenesis, giving rise to an XY sperm which fertilizes an X egg;

    (c) first or second division nondisjunction in either spermatogenesis or oogenesis, producing either O sperm or egg which then fuses with an X gamete from the other sex. The XXY condition could also arise through nondisjunction in the first cleavage division of a normal XY zygote whereby one daughter cell receives XXY, and the other (nonviable) OY.

**10-13.** Most likely by lagging of an X in early mitoses of an XX zygote.

**10-14.** Man. Single genes (*Asparagus*) are subject to mutation which could result in a sex imbalance in small populations or a lethal condition, but in man there appear to be many genes governing sex on the X and Y chromosomes. Furthermore, the occasional "male × male" crosses that occur in *Asparagus* increase the likelihood of homozygosity of deleterious genes in the progeny. Also, a 1 : 1 sex ratio in Asparagus occurs only in populations where "males" are heterozygous.

## Chapter 11

**11-1.** 1 bent tail female : 1 normal male.

**11-2.** 50% probability that any girls will be heterozygous (slight nystagmus) and 50% chance that any boys will have severe nystagmus.

**11-3.** Sex-linked recessive.

**11-4.** 1 barred rose male : 1 nonbarred rose female.

**11-5.** $\frac{6}{16}$; equally divided between male and female.

**11-6.** 1 barred : 1 nonbarred; 3 rose : 1 single.

**11-7.** No chance that any children of the boy will develop the disease as long as he marries a $+ +$ girl; each girl has a probability of 0.5 of being heterozygous and, therefore, transmitting the trait to half her sons.

**11-8.** Sex-linked recessive lethal.

**11-9.** 2 female : 1 male, all normal.

**11-10.** $\frac{1}{2}$.

**11-11.** $\frac{3}{64}$.

**11-12.** (a) 0.      (c) $\frac{1}{4}$.
          (b) $\frac{1}{8}$.    (d) $\frac{1}{2}$.

**11-13.** (a) early bald.
          (b) nonbald.
          (c) 9 early bald : 3 late bald : 4 nonbald.
          (d) 12 nonbald : 3 late bald : 1 early bald.

**11-14.** Female.

**11-15.** Male.

**11-16.** Sex-limited.

**11-17.** All males yellow; females 3 white : 1 yellow.

**11-18.** Sex-linked recessive may appear in either sex, but much more frequently in males; it is often transmitted from father to half the grandsons via a female. Holandric genes appear only in the male sex and are transmitted directly from father to all his sons.

**11-19.** Traits determined by holandric genes appear only in the heterogametic sex; these normally cannot be heterozygous.

**11-20.** Sex-linked dominants may be transmitted directly from an affected mother to her sons; they cannot be transmitted from father to son (why?).

**11-21.** All boys will have hairy ears; none of the girls will.

**11-22.** *HhZW* × *hhZZ*, or *hhZW* × *HhZZ*.

**11-23.** I-1, II-3, II-9, III-2, III-4, III-5, III-8.

**11-24.** $\frac{1}{2}$.

**11-25.** It would be possible, but very unlikely. It *appears* that all of the persons listed were free of the gene for hemophilia; if this is so, then Elizabeth II is homozygous normal. Under those circumstances, only a mutation, such as apparently occurred with Queen Victoria, could produce the defect in any children of Elizabeth.

## Chapter 12

**12-1.** *DDDD*.

**12-2.** *DD*.

**12-3.** *DDdd.*

**12-4.** 1 *DD* : 4 *Dd* : 1 *dd.*

**12-5.** (Auto)tetraploids.

**12-6.** *DDd.*

**12-7.** Those having 28 represent diploids; 56, tetraploids; 70, pentaploids; 84, hexaploids.

**12-8.** A different series of chromosomal aberrations in each species, so that normal meiotic pairing is impossible. Translocations are probably the most frequent of these aberrations.

**12-9.** Yes, by creating an allotetraploid hybrid.

**12-10.** Euploidy.

**12-11.** 13.

**12-12.** 12 (dodecaploid).

**12-13.** (a) 1 *P* : 2 *p* : 2 *Pp* : 1 *pp.*
  (b) 1 *P* : 2 *p.*
  (c) 1 *P* : 1 *PP.*
  (d) all *P.*
  (e) 2 *P* : 1 *p.*

**12-14.** (a) 15 purple : 3 white (=5 purple : 1 white).
  (b) 11 purple : 1 white.
  (c) 12 purple : 6 white (=2 purple : 1 white).

**12-15.** (a) 3 normal : 1 eyeless.
  (b) 11 normal : 1 eyeless.
  (c) 35 normal : 1 eyeless.

**12-16.**

**12-17.** *AAA/AA* between heterozygous ultrabar and homozygous ultrabar; *AAAA/AAA* below homozygous ultrabar.

**12-18.** (a) Deletion (deficiency).
  (b) Deletion loop in salivary gland chromosomes.

**12-19.** Yes; it appears that breaks may be induced by LSD. Consequences of breakage might be deletions or other types of chromosomal aberrations, some of which might well produce malformations or be lethal and others result in decreased fertility (why?).

**12-20.** Autosomal monosomy probably constitutes a lethal genic imbalance.

**12-21.** Trisomy for other chromosomes appears to produce a lethal imbalance.

**12-22.** Farther from the centromere which has an interfering effect on crossing over.

## Chapter 13

**13-1.** *M*, 0.5; *N*, 0.5.

**13-2.** *M*, 0.546; *N*, 0.454.

**13-3.** $M$, 0.19; $N$, 0.81.

**13-4.** $T$, 0.6; $t$, 0.4.

**13-5.** (a) 48.

(b) 36.

**13-6.** About 1.4%, or 1 in 70 persons.

**13-7.** 1 in 500.

**13-8.** $I^A$, 0.3; $I^B$, 0.1; $i$, 0.6.

**13-9.** $I^A I^A$, 0.04; $I^A i$, 0.28; $I^B I^B$ 0.01; $I^B i$, 0.14; $I^A I^B$, 0.04; $ii$, 0.49.

**13-10.** Deviation is significant (chi-square = 35.69).

**13-11.** A, 39.36%; B, 8.76%; AB, 2.88%; O, 49.0%.

**13-12.** (a) 5.76%.

(b) 8.4%.

**13-13.** 0.00004.

**13-14.** (a) 0.0198, or approximately 0.02.

(b) 0.0001.

**13-15.** 0.35.

**13-16.** Decrease the frequency of $Hb^s$.

**13-17.** Deterioration.

**13-18.** 0.25.

**13-19.** (a) 0.048.

(b) the 199th generation.

**13-20.** 0.22.

**13-21.** 0.267.

**13-22.** 0.8.

**13-23.** 0.04.

**13-24.** (a) 1,500 years.

(b) Probably not, because of mutation from dominant normal to recessive lethal.

**13-25.** (a) $p^2$.

(b) $p^4$ ($=p^2 \times p^2$).

(c) $2pq$.

(d) $4p^2q^2$ ($=2pq \times 2pq$).

(e) $4pq^3$ ($=2(2pq \times q^2)$).

(f) $p^4 + 4p^3q + 6p^2q^2 + 4pq^3 + q^4$, calculated as follows:

$AA \times AA = p^4$, i.e., $p^2 \times p^2$.

$AA \times Aa = 4p^3q$, i.e., $2(p^2 \times 2pq)$.

$AA \times aa = 2p^2q^2$, i.e., $2(p^2 \times q^2)$.

$Aa \times Aa = 4p^2q^2$, i.e., $2pq \times 2pq$.

$Aa \times aa = 4pq^3$, i.e., $2(2pq \times q^2)$.

$aa \times aa = q^4$, i.e., $q^2 \times q^2$.

**13-26.** (a) $p^2 + 2pq$.

(b) $q^2$.

**13-27.** (a) $p^2q^2 + 2pq^3 + q^4$.

(b) $0.0625 + 0.125 + 0.0625 = 0.25$.

## Chapter 14

**14-1.** Dominance, epistasis, sex linkage.

**14-2.** T, T, G, C, A, T, G, A, C, G.

**14-3.** 68 $\mu$m.

**14-4.** (a) 135.     (c) 111.
       (b) 126.     (d) 151.

**14-5.** (a) 251.     (c) 227.
       (b) 242.     (d) 267.

**14-6.** (a) 329.     (c) 305.
       (b) 320.     (d) 345.

**14-7.** About $1.3 \times 10^8$.

**14-8.** One per minute.

**14-9.** $2 \times 10^5$.

**14-10.** Thymine 20%, cytosine and guanine 30% each.

**14-11.** No; why?

**14-12.** (a) $A/T = G/C = 1.00$.
        (b) That it is double stranded.
        (c) This DNA is the replicative form.

**14-13.** This suggests the possibility that not all gene function in this organism is nuclear in nature. This matter is explored in Chapter 19.

**14-14.** 31.6%.

**14-15.** (a) $4.15 \times 10^6$.
        (b) About 1,400 $\mu$m.

## Chapter 15

**15-1.** No. Why?

**15-2.** Yes.

**15-3.** No.

**15-4.** Strain 1.

**15-5.** Enzyme "a."

**15-6.** Enzymes "a" and "b."

**15-7.** 1, + + +; 2, $a$+ +; 3, +$b$+; 4, $ab$+.

**15-8.** G U C U U U A C G C U A.

**15-9.** 200.

**15-10.** (a) 343.4.
        (b) 0.03434 ($=101 \times 34 \times 10^{-5}$; use 101 instead of 102 because there are $n - 1$ interbase spaces.)

**15-11.** (a) 80.
        (b) 0.027.

**15-12.** (a) UAC.
        (b) TAC.

**15-13.** Transcription: formation of mRNA from a DNA template. Translation: formation of a particular polypeptide chain consisting of specific amino acid residues in a specific sequence as determined by the sequence of mRNA codons.

### Chapter 16

**16-1.** (a) Methionine, alanine, leucine, threonine.

(b) Methionine, tryptophan, glycine, alanine, proline, leucine, leucine, end chain.

(c) DNA trinucleotide TAC transcribes into AUG of mRNA which could serve as a "start-chain" codon.

**16-2.** Methionine, proline, end chain.

**16-3.** It differs by one amino acid; the second is now proline instead of alanine. Sense is restored starting with the third amino acid.

**16-4.** (a) $\frac{6}{216}$, or $\frac{1}{36}$.

(b) $\frac{27}{216}$, or $\frac{1}{8}$.

**16-5.** At GCU, an mRNA codon for alanine. tRNA-mRNA pairing is determined by anticodon-codon complementarity, not by the amino acid.

**16-6.** Tryptophan; it has only one codon, whereas arginine has six.

**16-7.** A-14 mutant has undergone a base change in the second base of the isoleucine codon (AUU, AUC, or AUA) to one coding for threonine (ACU, ACC, or ACA); Ni-1055 mutant has undergone a change in the third base of AUU, AUC, or AUA (coding for isoleucine) to AUG (coding for methionine).

**16-8.** In A446, UAU or UAC has been changed to UGU or UGC (second base); in A187, GG— has been changed at the second position to GU—. These represent base changes at positions 2 and 17, respectively, of the stretch of mRNA involved.

**16-9.** 288 ($= 4 \times 4 \times 1 \times 6 \times 3$).

**16-10.** (a) represents degeneracy.

(b) represents ambiguity.

**16-11.** (a) nonsense.

(b) missense.

(c) degeneracy.

(d) missense.

### Chapter 17

**17-1.** Mate variant animal to normals. If the character appears in the $F_1$, it may be assumed to be due to a dominant gene. If it does not appear in the $F_1$, then $F_1$ animals may be backcrossed to the variant parent. If the new trait appears in the backcross progeny, it may be assumed to be due to a recessive gene. If two animals were available, they should also be crossed to check on dominance. If the trait does not appear through repeated matings of these several kinds, then the character is either environmentally induced or due to more complex genetic mechanisms than can be identified by these tests.

**17-2.** Phenylalanine is coded before deamination; leucine will be coded after deamination.

**17-3.** 1,500.

**17-4.** (a) *AT.*      (d) Both.

(b) *AT.*      (e) Both.

(c) *CG.*

**17-5.** 267, exclusive of initiating and terminating codons.

**17-6.** 801, exclusive of initiating and terminating codons.

**17-7.** Because of the present impossibility of developing specific mutations; one simply takes what he gets in induced mutations. Techniques for directed mutation are not yet adequate.

**17-8.** Short-term effects include radiation sickness, surface and deep tissue burning, loss of hair, etc. Longer-term effects include an increased incidence of leukemia.

**17-9.** (a) 2.

   (b) white → red → blue.

   (c) (1) *AaBb*.

   (c) (2) $A - B -$.

   (d) (1) $A - bb$.

   (d) (2) $aa - -$.

   (e) The $A - a$ pair.

**17-10.** (a) $5 \times 10^9 \left( = 2 \dfrac{\text{molecular weight}}{650} \right)$.

   (b) $5 \times 10^9$.

   (c) $1.7 \times 10^6$ ( = number nucleotide pairs $\times 34 \times 10^{-5}$).

   (d) $8.33 \times 10^8 \left( = \dfrac{\text{number nucleotide pairs}}{3} \right)$.

   (e) $2.78 \times 10^6 \left( = \dfrac{\text{number of codons}}{300} \right)$.

## Chapter 18

**18-1.** They are similar in presumably being composed of a given segment of DNA nucleotides, and each exerts regulatory control over cistrons. On the other hand, no demonstrable product of operators has yet been established.

**18-2.** See text.

**18-3.** (a) Inductive.          (d) Absent.

   (b) Constitutive.          (e) Constitutive.

   (c) Constitutive.

**18-4.** Possibly a chain-initiating triplet.

**18-5.** See text, especially Chapters 14–18, and references.

## Chapter 19

**19-1.** Sex-linked recessive traits show a characteristic inheritance sequence from affected father to "carrier" daughter to about half her sons; sex-linked dominants are transmitted by an affected mother ( × normal father) to about half her sons and half her daughters or by an affected father ( × normal mother) to all his daughters and none of his sons. Purely maternal effects are transmitted from mother to all her progeny but do not persist in certain nuclear genotypes. Extranuclear genetic systems would ordinarily operate through the maternal line. If the trait is repeatedly transmitted through backcrosses of $F_1$ individuals with maternal parent but not with paternal parent, an extranuclear genetic system may be involved. It should be identified and located, and such guiding criteria as those listed at the outset of this chapter applied.

**19-2.** Any genotype will have the phenotype determined by the maternal genotype (a maternal effect).

**19-3.** (a) All normal.

(b) 1 : 1 petite : normal.

**19-4.** (a) In substrain C, between *lys* + *met* and *gal*; in substrain H, between *pil* and *pyr B*.

(b) In C, *muc*; in H, *thr*.

**19-5.** See text and references.

**19-6.** See text and references.

**19-7.** See text and references.

**19-8.** See references, especially Raven (1970) and Margulis (1970).

# APPENDIX B
# Selected Life Cycles

## 1. Bacteria

Bacteria reproduce asexually by cell division, but may also engage in a type of "sexual" reproduction called conjugation. Mating types $F^-$ ("female" or, better, "receptor") and $F^+$ or $Hfr$ ("male" or, better, "donor") are required. Conjugation of $Hfr \times F^-$ includes the following steps and is diagrammed in Fig. B-1:

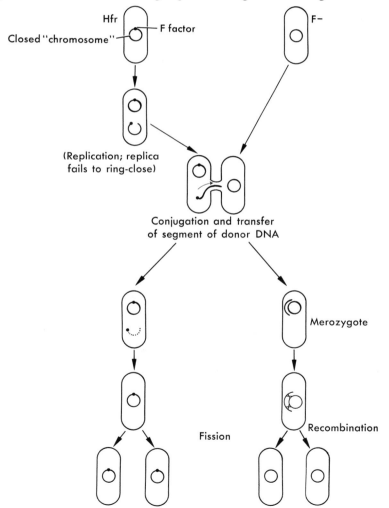

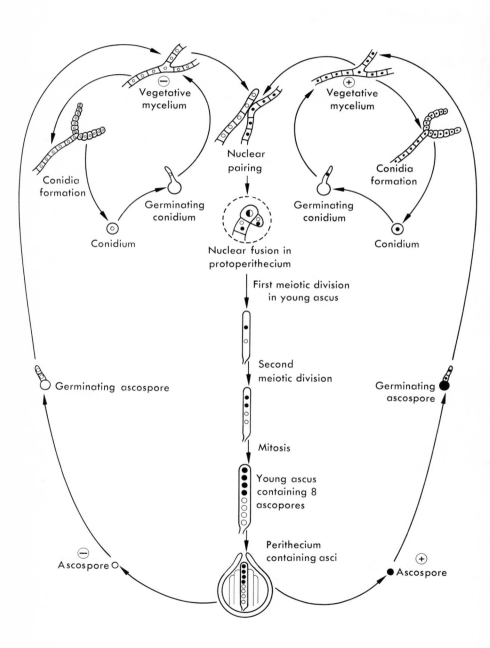

Vegetative mycelium

Vegetative mycelium

Conidia formation

Conidia formation

Germinating conidium

Germinating conidium

Nuclear pairing

Conidium

Conidium

Nuclear fusion in protoperithecium

First meiotic division in young ascus

Germinating ascospore

Second meiotic division

Germinating ascospore

Mitosis

Young ascus containing 8 ascopores

Ascospore

Perithecium containing asci

Ascospore

(a) Replication of donor chromosome; replica fails to undergo ring closure.

(b) Chance collision of *Hfr* and *F⁻*.

(c) Attachment of *Hfr* and *F⁻* cells in pairs by formation of connecting bridge.

(d) Transfer of open, replicated, donor chromosome to *F⁻* cell; generally only a relatively small segment is so transferred.

(e) Partial diploidy of receptor cell (merozygote).

(f) Reproduction of both donor and receptor cells by division after separation of the conjugants.

(g) Regaining of monoploidy by *F⁻* cells.

In $F^+$ cells the fertility factor is not integrated into the chromosome. In $F^+ \times F^-$ conjugation a previously replicated fertility factor is usually the only DNA donated to the $F^-$ cell which, thereby, becomes $F^+$. The original $F^+$ donor, retaining an F factor, remains $F^+$. On the other hand, with $Hfr \times F^-$ conjugation, the *Hfr* donor remains *Hfr*, but a very few $F^-$ receptors will be converted to donors on rare occasions when all of the *Hfr* open, replicated chromosome is transferred.

## 2. Neurospora

Like most fungi, *Neurospora* produces large numbers of asexual spores (here called conidia), but also reproduces sexually if + and − mating strains come into contact. In *Neurospora*, as in many fungi, pairing of nuclei of sex cells does not result in immediate syngamy. The nuclei that ultimately fuse are daughter nuclei of the original pairing nuclei. The essential steps are diagrammed in Fig. B-2 and include:

(a) Contact between filaments (hyphae) of + and − strains.

(b) Pairing (not fusion) of + and − nuclei.

(c) Development of the "fruiting body" (ascocarp), called a perithecium, which consists of $n^+$, $n^-$, and dikaryon $(n^+/n^-)$ hyphae.

(d) Development of large numbers of elongate, saclike sporangia called asci (sing., ascus) in the perithecium.

(e) Fusion in the young asci of a + and a − nucleus which were derived through several mitoses from the original pairing nuclei, thus forming a diploid zygote.

(f) Meiosis of zygote soon after formation, in the developing ascus, to form four meiospores.

(g) Mitosis of the four meiospores to form eight (monoploid) spores called ascospores. Four of these will give rise to + mating strain plants, the other four to − strain plants.

(h) Release of ascospores and their germination to form new adults.

## 3. Saccharomyces (Yeast)

Yeasts are one-celled ascomycete fungi. Multiplication is by "budding," in which the nucleus divides by mitosis. In the full life cycle, however, morphologically identical diploid and monoploid generations alternate as shown in Fig. B-3. The life history consists of the following steps:

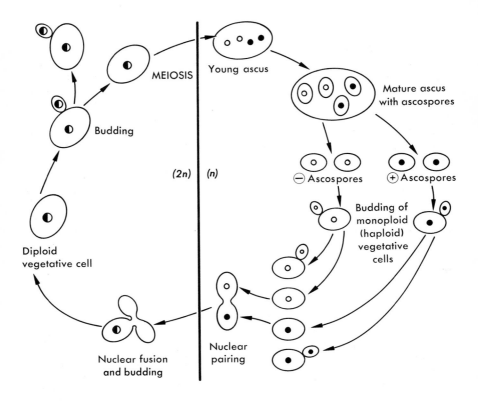

(a) Diploid adults multiply by "budding" but, under certain environmental conditions, undergo meiosis to form four monoploid meiospores within the old cell wall.

(b) Maturation of the four meiospores to become four ascospores (baker's yeast) or, in some other species, mitosis of each of the four meiospores to form eight ascospores.

(c) Liberation of ascospores from ascus (old vegetative cell wall).

(d) Germination of ascospores to form monoploid adult cells. Half the ascospores from any one ascus give rise to + mating strain adults, and half to − mating strain.

(e) Multiplication of monoploid + and − adults by "budding."

(f) Contact between + and − cells.

(g) Formation of intercellular cytoplasmic bridge.

(h) Fusion of + and − nuclei (each monoploid cell in the pair furnishes a single gamete).

(i) Formation of diploid vegetative cell, often from the cytoplasmic bridge.

### 4. Chlamydomonas

The small, unicellular, motile, green alga *Chlamydomonas* reproduces freely by cell division (mitosis and cytokinesis). The vegetative cells are monoploid (haploid).

In sexual reproduction, the vegetative cell functions as a gametangium, its protoplast dividing mitotically to produce 4, 8, 16, or 32 gametes. These sex cells are morphologically similar to the vegetative cells, but smaller in size. In many species the gametes are identical in appearance, hence may be referred to as isogametes. In other species varying degrees of morphological differentiation of gametes occur. Chemical differences among gametes, and the cells producing them, occur and mating strains are designated as $+$ and $-$. Gametes of opposite mating strain come into contact at their flagellar ends; the protoplasts fuse to form a four-flagellate zygote. The zygote soon loses its flagella, develops a wall, and becomes dormant. Germination of the zygote begins with meiosis of its diploid nucleus and ends with liberation of biflagellate zoospores from the old zygote wall. In some species only four zoospores are thus formed, but in others meiosis is followed by one or more mitoses so that 8, 16, or more zoospores are produced. Zoospores resemble the vegetative cells into which they will develop, and of the number produced from a single zygote, half are of each mating strain. The process is diagrammed in Fig. B-4.

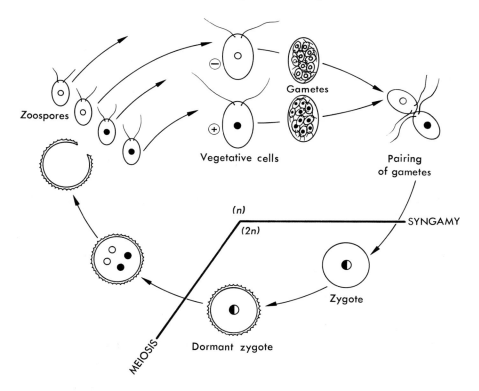

### 5. Sphaerocarpos (Liverwort)

Vegetative plants are small, thin, and lobed; these are monoploid (haploid), unisexual gametophytes (gamete-producing plants). Males produce motile sperms in antheridia; females develop one egg in each of several archegonia. Syngamy occurs when liquid water (from rain or dew) is present, allowing sperms to swim to the archegonia. The resulting zygote develops into a small, multicellular sporophyte (spore-bearing plant), which remains permanently attached to the parent gameto-phyte. It ultimately protrudes from the remains of the archegonium and produces internally a large number of diploid sporocytes which undergo meiosis to produce four meiospores each. Two of each of these will produce male gametophytes, and two female. The life cycle is diagrammed in Fig. B-5.

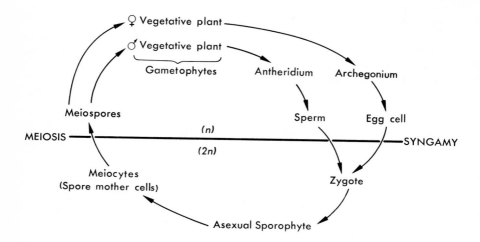

### 6. Flowering Plants (Class Angiospermae, Phylum Tracheophyta)

The plant we recognize by name in the angiosperms is the diploid sporophyte. The monoploid (haploid) gametophyte is microscopic and contained almost entirely within various floral structures. A (usually) triploid food storage tissue, the endo-sperm, also occurs and is cytologically unique to the angiosperms. The life cycle of a representative angiosperm is diagrammed in Fig. B-6 and consists of the following structures and steps:

(a) Production of flowers by the sporophyte.
(b) Meiosis of microsporocytes (pollen mother cells) in anthers of stamens to form four functional, uninucleate microspores each.
(c) Development of young male gametophyte by mitosis of the microspore nucleus within the microspore wall, inside the anther. This two-nucleate structure (tube nucleus and generative nucleus) is sometimes called a pollen grain.
(d) Transfer of pollen grains to stigmas of the pistils where each grain produces a tubular outgrowth, the pollen tube, which grows down through structures of the pistil to the ovule, which it enters via the micropyle.
(e) Development in each ovule of a megasporocyte, which then undergoes meiosis to form four megaspores, three of which degenerate.

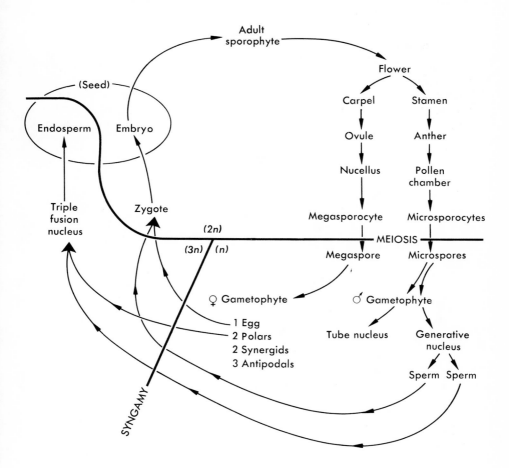

(f)  Development of the female gametophyte by mitosis from the one functional megaspore. In the classical case, the mature female gametophyte consists of eight nuclei (1 egg, 2 polars, 2 synergids, 3 antipodals) in a common cytoplasm within each ovule, and contained within the ovary of the pistil.

(g)  Mitosis of generative nucleus to form two sperms in the pollen tube.

(h)  Entry of the pollen tube into the embryo sac.

(i)  Fusion of egg and sperm to form the zygote.

(j)  Fusion of the second sperm with the two polars to form the triploid triple fusion nucleus.

(k)  Degeneration of synergids and antipodals.

(l)  Development of multicellular embryo from the zygote.

(m) Development of endosperm from the triple fusion nucleus. In some plants this tissue is absorbed by the cotyledons of the embryo during the latter's development.

(n)  Development of seed coat, primarily from the integuments of the ovule.

(o)  Development of a fruit from the ovary.

### 7. Paramecium

Paramecia are elongate ciliates of the phylum Protozoa. Each animal contains a large macronucleus, which exerts phenotypic control for that individual, and two micronuclei which function in the sexual process. The macronucleus is polyploid, the micronucleus diploid in the vegetative animal. Paramecia increase in number only by fission; other processes, important in genetics, also occur and are as follows:

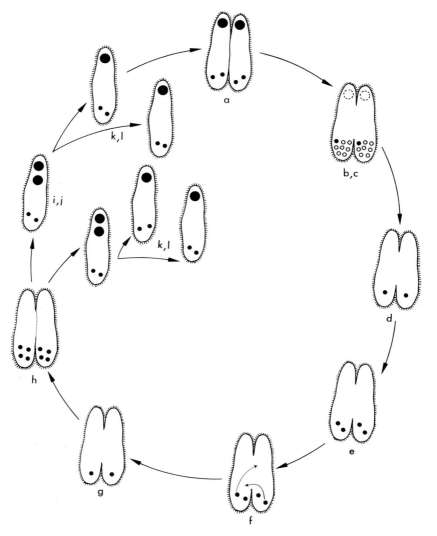

**Fig. B-7**

# FISSION

(a) Mitosis of micronuclei.
(b) Constriction of macronucleus to form two.
(c) Movement of one macronucleus and one micronucleus to each end of the animal, which then constricts in the middle to form two new individuals.

## CONJUGATION (FIG. B-7)

(a) Pairing of two animals (conjugants) and formation of intercellular bridge.
(b) Disintegration of macronucleus.
(c) Meiosis of each of the two micronuclei.
(d) Disintegration of seven of the eight products of meiosis.
(e) Mitosis of the remaining monoploid nucleus to form two.
(f) One of the two monoploid nuclei of each conjugant passes through the connecting bridge to the other animal (reciprocal transfer).
(g) Fusion of the two monoploid nuclei in each conjugant, restoring the diploid condition.
(h) Two mitoses of the fertilization nuclei, resulting in four diploid nuclei per conjugant.
(i) Separation of the conjugants, which are now genetically alike.
(j) Two of the four nuclei in each ex-conjugant become macronuclei, two become micronuclei.
(k) Distribution of two macronuclei to each daughter cell at next fission.
(l) Mitosis of the two micronuclei at next fission, two being distributed to each daughter cell.
(m) Conjugation is usually a short-term event with little cytoplasmic transfer. Under certain conditions, the intercellular connection may persist for a longer period, allowing exchange of considerable cytoplasm.

## AUTOGAMY (FIG. B-8)

This is a type of internal self-fertilization, resembling somewhat the events of conjugation but involving only a single animal. It results in homozygosity of the individual undergoing the process.

(a) Macronucleus behaves as in conjugation.
(b) Meiosis of the two micronuclei and disintegration of seven of the eight resulting nuclei as in conjugation.
(c) Mitosis of the remaining monoploid nucleus to form two.
(d) Fusion of the two monoploid nuclei resulting from step (c).
(e) Restoration of micronuclei and the macronucleus as for conjugation.

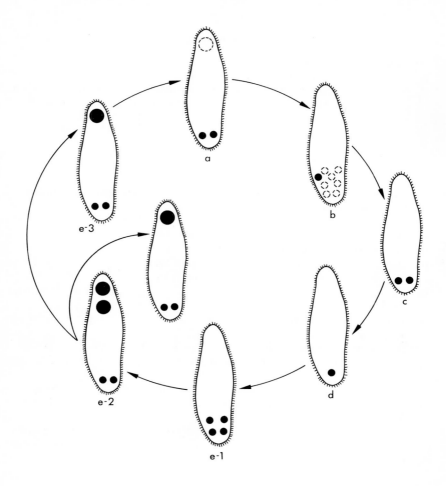

**Fig. B.-8**

### 8. Mammals

In mammals, the somatic cells (except for some, such as liver cells, which may be polyploid) are diploid, meiosis immediately preceding the formation of gametes. The diploid condition is restored at syngamy (Fig. B-9). The following steps are involved in the male:

(a) Development of diploid primary spermatocytes.
(b) Meiosis. The two monoploid products of the first meiotic division are called secondary spermatocytes. The four cells resulting from the second meiotic division are called spermatids.
(c) Maturation of spermatids into sperms.

In the female:

(a) Development of diploid primary oocytes.

(b) Meiosis. The first division produces two unequal cells, a smaller first polar body and a larger secondary oocyte. The second division produces two second polar bodies from the first polar body and, from the secondary oocyte, a third second polar body and a larger ootid.

(c) Maturation of one egg from the ootid; degeneration of the three second polar bodies.

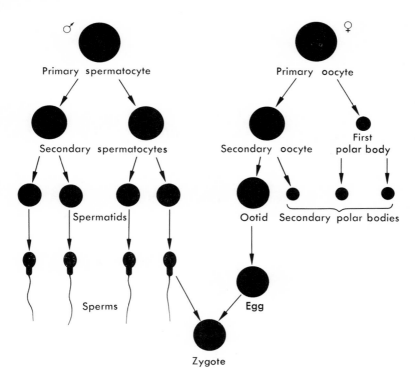

**Fig. B.-9**

# APPENDIX C[1]

# The Biologically Important Amino Acids

**Alanine (ala)**

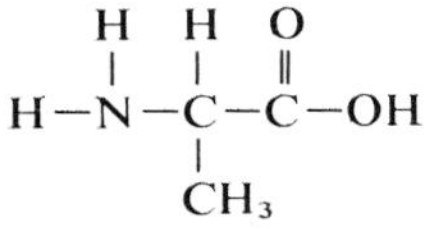

$$
\begin{array}{ccc}
H & H & O \\
| & | & \| \\
H-N-&C-&C-OH \\
& | & \\
& CH_3 &
\end{array}
$$

**Arginine (arg)**

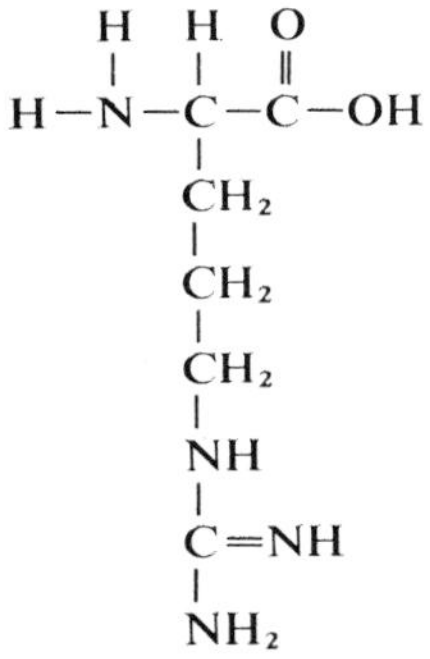

$$
\begin{array}{ccc}
H & H & O \\
| & | & \| \\
H-N-&C-&C-OH \\
& | & \\
& CH_2 & \\
& | & \\
& CH_2 & \\
& | & \\
& CH_2 & \\
& | & \\
& NH & \\
& | & \\
& C=NH & \\
& | & \\
& NH_2 &
\end{array}
$$

**Asparagine (asn)**

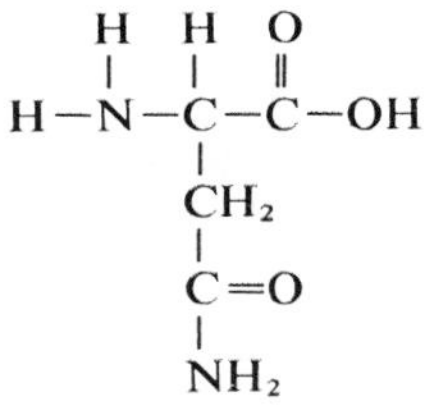

$$
\begin{array}{ccc}
H & H & O \\
| & | & \| \\
H-N-&C-&C-OH \\
& | & \\
& CH_2 & \\
& | & \\
& C=O & \\
& | & \\
& NH_2 &
\end{array}
$$

**Aspartic Acid (asp)**

$$
\begin{array}{ccc}
H & H & O \\
| & | & \| \\
H-N-&C-&C-OH \\
& | & \\
& CH_2 & \\
& | & \\
& C=O & \\
& | & \\
& OH &
\end{array}
$$

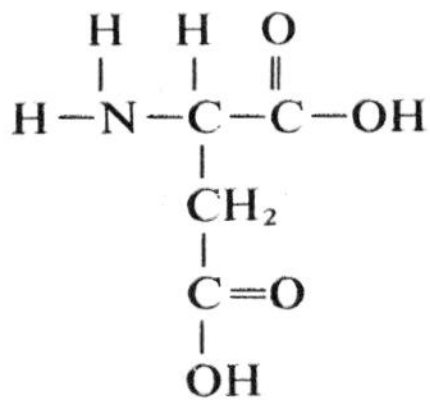

[1] Amino acids marked * are required in the diet of mammals.

**Cysteine (cys)**

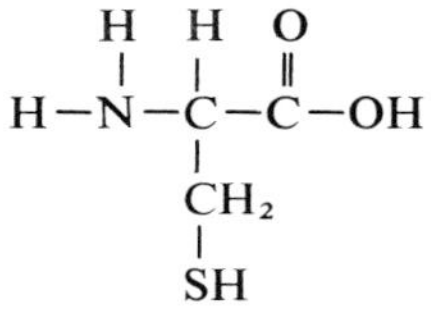

```
        H   H   O
        |   |   ||
   H — N — C — C — OH
            |
           CH₂
            |
           SH
```

**Glutamic Acid (glu)**

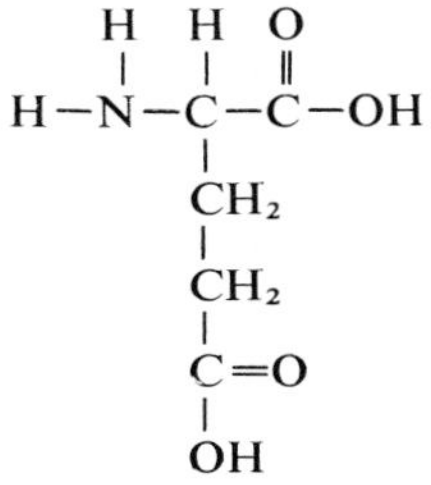

```
        H   H   O
        |   |   ||
   H — N — C — C — OH
            |
           CH₂
            |
           CH₂
            |
           C=O
            |
           OH
```

**Glutamine (gln)**

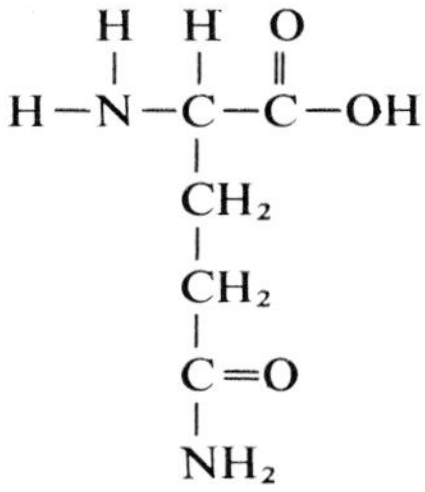

```
        H   H   O
        |   |   ||
   H — N — C — C — OH
            |
           CH₂
            |
           CH₂
            |
           C=O
            |
           NH₂
```

**Glycine (gly)**

```
        H   H   O
        |   |   ||
   H — N — C — C — OH
            |
            H
```

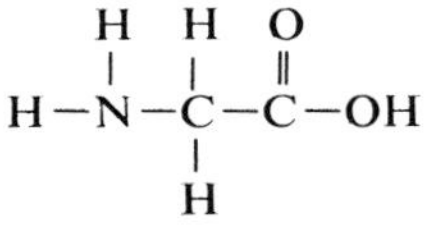

**Histidine (his)**

```
        H   H   O
        |   |   ||
   H — N — C — C — OH
            |
           CH₂
            |
           C ═══ CH
           |      |
      H — N        N
            \     /
              C
              |
              H
```

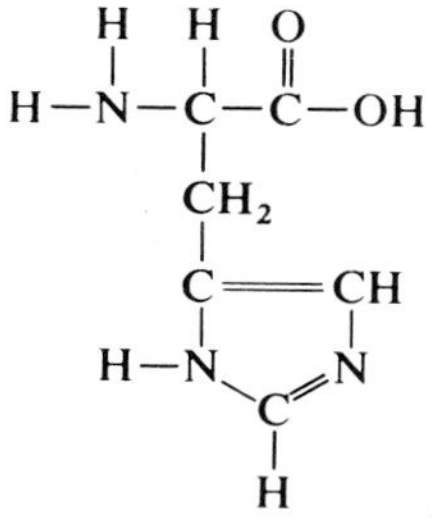

**\*Isoleucine (ilu)**

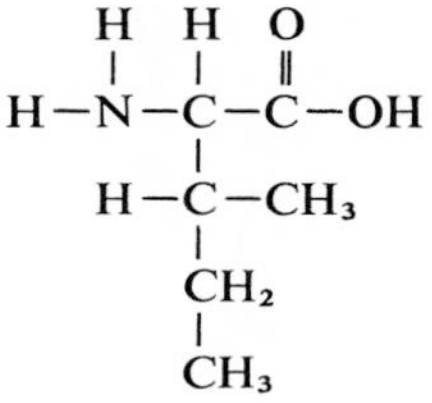

```
           H   H   O
           |   |   ‖
     H — N — C — C — OH
               |
           H — C — CH₃
               |
              CH₂
               |
              CH₃
```

**\*Leucine (leu)**

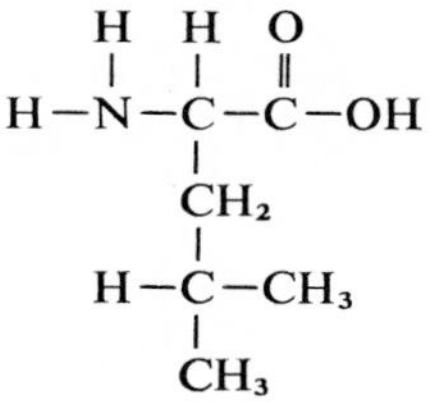

```
           H   H   O
           |   |   ‖
     H — N — C — C — OH
               |
              CH₂
               |
           H — C — CH₃
               |
              CH₃
```

**\*Lysine (lys)**

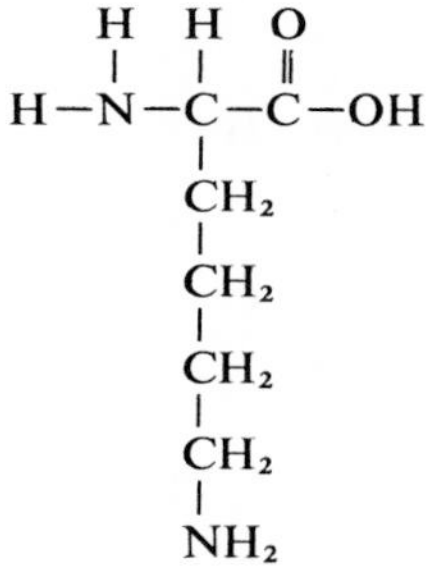

```
           H   H   O
           |   |   ‖
     H — N — C — C — OH
               |
              CH₂
               |
              CH₂
               |
              CH₂
               |
              CH₂
               |
              NH₂
```

**\*Methionine (met)**

```
           H   H   O
           |   |   ‖
     H — N — C — C — OH
               |
              CH₂
               |
              CH₂
               |
               S
               |
              CH₃
```

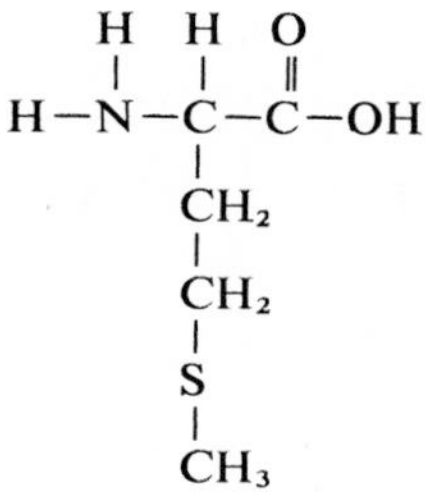

**\*Phenylalanine (phe)**

```
           H   H   O
           |   |   ‖
     H — N — C — C — OH
               |
              CH₂
               |
```

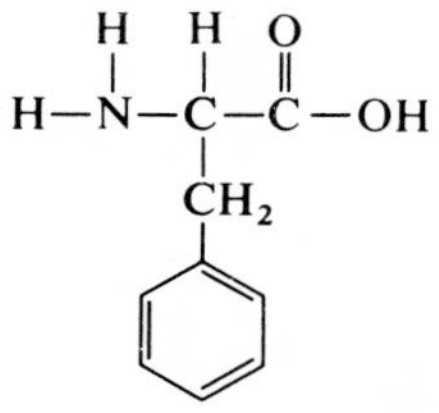

**Proline (pro)**

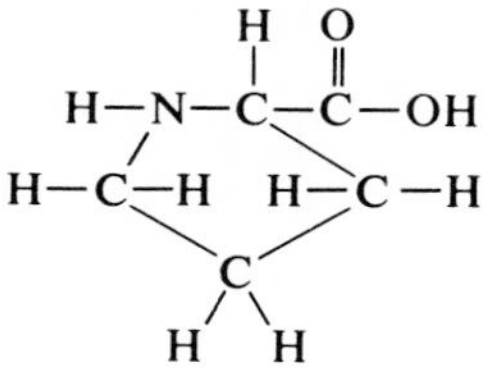

$$
\begin{array}{c}
\underset{|}{H} \quad \overset{O}{\overset{\|}{C}} \\
H-N-\overset{|}{C}-C-OH \\
H-\overset{|}{C}-H \quad H-\overset{|}{C}-H \\
\overset{|}{C} \\
H \quad H
\end{array}
$$

**Serine (ser)**

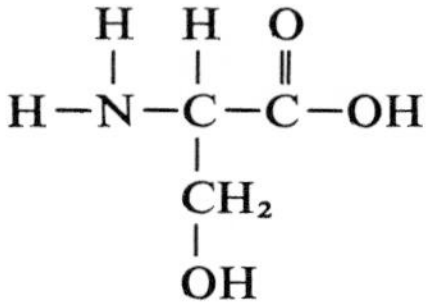

$$
\begin{array}{c}
\underset{|}{H} \quad \underset{|}{H} \quad \overset{O}{\overset{\|}{C}} \\
H-N-\overset{|}{C}-C-OH \\
\overset{|}{CH_2} \\
\overset{|}{OH}
\end{array}
$$

***Threonine (thr)**

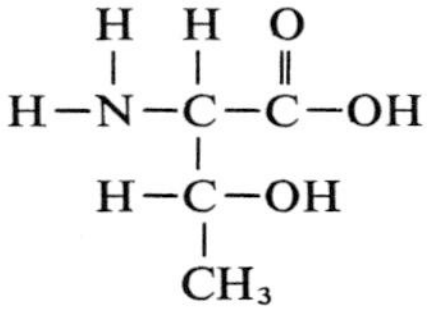

$$
\begin{array}{c}
\underset{|}{H} \quad \underset{|}{H} \quad \overset{O}{\overset{\|}{C}} \\
H-N-\overset{|}{C}-C-OH \\
H-\overset{|}{C}-OH \\
\overset{|}{CH_3}
\end{array}
$$

***Tryptophan (try)**

$$
\begin{array}{c}
\underset{|}{H} \quad \underset{|}{H} \quad \overset{O}{\overset{\|}{C}} \\
H-N-\overset{|}{C}-C-OH \\
\overset{|}{CH_2} \\
C=C-H \\
NH
\end{array}
$$

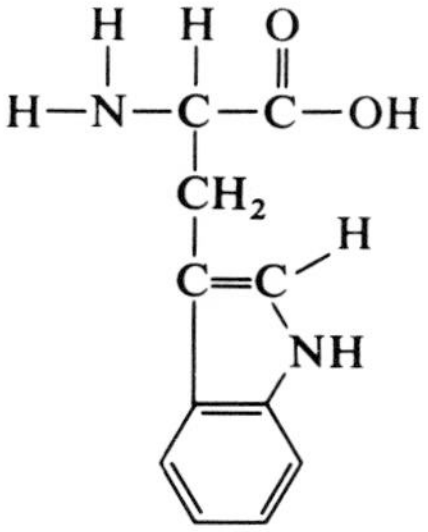

**Tyrosine (tyr)**

$$
\begin{array}{c}
\underset{|}{H} \quad \underset{|}{H} \quad \overset{O}{\overset{\|}{C}} \\
H-N-\overset{|}{C}-C-OH \\
\overset{|}{CH_2} \\
\end{array}
$$

OH

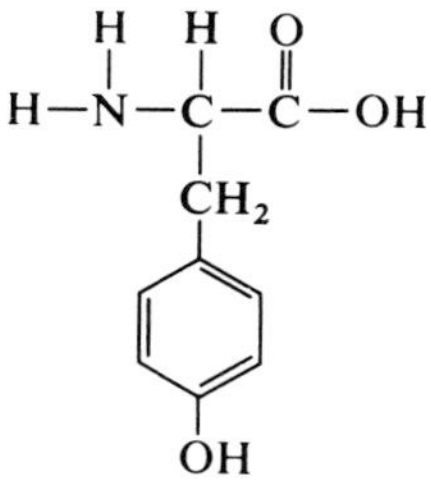

\*Valine (val)

$$
\begin{array}{c}
\text{H} \quad \text{H} \quad \text{O} \\
| \qquad | \qquad \| \\
\text{H}-\text{N}-\text{C}-\text{C}-\text{OH} \\
| \\
\text{H}-\text{C}-\text{CH}_3 \\
| \\
\text{CH}_3
\end{array}
$$

# APPENDIX D
# Useful Formulas, Ratios, and Statistics

| | |
|---|---|
| 3:1 | Monohybrid phenotypic ratio produced by $Aa \times Aa$. |
| 1:2:1 | Monohybrid genotypic ratio produced by $Aa \times Aa$; monohybrid phenotypic and genotypic ratio produced by $a_1a_2 \times a_1a_2$. |
| 1:1 | Monohybrid testcross phenotypic and genotypic ratio produced by $Aa \times aa$. |
| 2:1 | Monohybrid lethal genotypic and phenotypic ratio produced by $a_1a_2 \times a_1a_2$ where either $a_1a_1$ or $a_2a_2$ is lethal; also sex ratio produced by $Aa \times AY$ where $a$ is a sex-linked recessive lethal. |
| "1:0" | Monohybrid lethal phenotypic ratio produced by $Aa \times Aa$ where $aa$ or $A-$ is lethal; also monohybrid testcross phenotypic and genotypic ratio produced by $AA \times aa$. |
| 9:3:3:1 | Dihybrid phenotypic ratio produced by $AaBb \times AaBb$ where phenotypes may be represented as 9 $A-B-$, 3 $A-bb$, 3 $aaB-$, 1 $aabb$; note epistatic possibilities producing "condensations" of this ratio (e.g., 9:7, 9:6:1). |
| 1:1:1:1 | Dihybrid testcross genotypic and phenotypic ratio produced by $AaBb \times aabb$ where there is no linkage. |
| 3:6:3:1:2:1 | Dihybrid phenotypic ratio produced by $Aab_1b_2 \times Aab_1b_2$. Note that dihybrid and polyhybrid ratios are products of their component monohybrid ratios and may be combined in any way. |
| $2^n$ | Number of gamete genotypes and progeny phenotypes where $n =$ the number of pairs of heterozygous genes with complete dominance. |
| $3^n$ | Number of zygote genotypes under the above conditions. |
| $4^n$ | Number of possible zygote combinations under the above conditions, and yielding $3^n$ zygote genotypes. |
| $\dfrac{n}{2}(n+1)$ | The chance of selecting at random any two items in pairs (e.g., the number of possible genotypes for $n$ multiple alleles in a series). |

$(a + b)^n$

Expansion of the binomial provides probability determinations where $n$ = the number of independent events and the choices are two.

$(p + q)^2 = 1$

Binomial whose expansion permits calculation of the frequency of each member of a pair of alleles.

$(p + q + r)^2 = 1$

Trinomial whose expansion permits calculation of the frequency of each of three multiple alleles.

$(\frac{1}{4})^n$

In polygene cases, the fraction of the $F_2$ like either **P** is given by this expression where $n$ = the number of pairs of genes in which the parents (**P**) differ.

$(\frac{1}{2})^n$

In polygene cases, the fraction of the $F_2$ like either **P** is given by this expression where $n$ = the number of effective or contributing alleles.

$$x^2 = \Sigma \left[ \frac{(o - c)^2}{c} \right]$$

Consult tables of chi-square for levels of significance (where degrees of freedom equal 1 less than the number of classes —but see page 252). In general, a value of chi-square $\geq$ than that for **P** = 0.05 is regarded as significant; i.e., there is significant evidence against the hypothesis. A value of chi-square showing a level of **P** = 0.05, for example, does *not* mean that a deviation as large or larger will *not* occur by chance alone under the hypothesis adopted, but it is likely to in only 5 trials out of 100. This is considered too few; at this level, the chance of rejecting a right hypothesis is only 1 in 20.

$$\bar{x} = \frac{\Sigma fx}{n} \quad \text{or} \quad \frac{\Sigma x}{n}$$

The sample mean is self-explanatory.

$$s = \sqrt{\frac{\Sigma f(x - \bar{x})^2}{n - 1}}$$

The standard deviation measures the variability of the sample; in a normal distribution, 68.26% of the sample will lie in the range $\bar{x} \pm s$, and 95.44% will fall in the range $\bar{x} \pm 2s$. Used with normal distributions.

$$s_{\bar{x}} = \frac{s}{\sqrt{n}}$$

The standard error of the sample mean indicates the degree of correspondence between $\bar{x}$ and $\mu$; there is 68.26% probability that $\mu = \bar{x} \pm s_{\bar{x}}$ by chance alone, and 95.44% confidence that $\mu = \bar{x} \pm 2s_{\bar{x}}$ by chance alone.

$$S_d = \sqrt{(s_{\bar{x}_1})^2 + (s_{\bar{x}_2})^2}$$

The standard error of the difference in means is useful in comparing two samples to determine whether the difference in their means is significant. If $(\bar{x}_1 - \bar{x}_2) > 2S_d$, the difference in sample means is considered significant and the two samples to represent two different populations.

$$s = \sqrt{\frac{pq}{n}}$$

The standard deviation ($s$) of a simple proportionality such as heads ($p$) versus tails ($q$) for $n$ trials.

$$s = \sqrt{\frac{pq}{2N}}$$

The standard deviation of gene frequencies where $N$ represents the number of *diploid* individuals, and $p$ and $q$ represent the frequency of each of a pair of alleles.

$$n = \frac{R^2}{8(s^2_{F_2} - s^2_{F_1})}$$

The number of pairs of polygenes ($n$) is calculated from this equation where $R$ is the maximum quantitative range between phenotypes, $s^2_{F_2}$ is the variance of the $F_2$, and $s^2_{F_1}$ is the variance of the $F_1$.

$$q_n = \frac{q_0}{1 + nq_0}$$

The frequency of a recessive lethal ($q_n$) after $n$ additional generations equals the initial frequency of the gene ($q_0$) divided by 1 plus the product of the number of additional generations ($n$) times the initial frequency of the gene.

$$n = \frac{1}{q_n} - \frac{1}{q_0}$$

The number of additional generations ($n$) required to reduce the frequency of a gene from its initial value ($q_0$) to any particular value ($q_n$) is given by this equation.

$$W = 1 - s,$$
$$\text{and } s = 1 - W$$

The adaptive value of a genotype ($W$) is 1 minus its selection coefficient ($s$), and the selection coefficient is 1 minus the adaptive value of the genotype.

$$q_1 = \frac{q_0 - s(q_0)^2}{1 - s(q_0)^2}$$

The equation for determining the frequency of a gene after one generation under selection ($q_1$) when its selection coefficient ($s$) and its initial frequency ($q_0$) are known.

$$q_1 - q_0 = \frac{-sq_0^2(1 - q_0)}{1 - sq_0^2}$$

Change in frequency of a recessive gene under partial selection in one generation.

# APPENDIX E

## Useful Metric Values

| Name | Numerical Value (m) | Power of 10 | Symbol | Synonym |
|---|---|---|---|---|
| Meter | 1.0 | | m | |
| Decimeter | 0.1 | $10^{-1}$ | dm | |
| Centimeter | 0.01 | $10^{-2}$ | cm | |
| Millimeter | 0.001 | $10^{-3}$ | mm | |
| Micrometer | 0.000 001 | $10^{-6}$ | $\mu$m | micron ($\mu$) |
| Nanometer | 0.000 000 001 | $10^{-9}$ | nm | millimicron (m$\mu$) |
| | 0.000 000 000 1 | $10^{-10}$ | | Angstrom unit (Å) |

# APPENDIX F
# General References

With the rapid expansion of molecular genetics, a flood of journal articles and books, many of the latter excellent and inexpensive paperbacks, becomes available each year. Although, therefore, any list is at once out of date and incomplete, those given below will serve as suggestions for further reading. Special attention is directed to the collections of reprints on a given topic, many from less readily obtainable journals. (* Indicates paperback book.)

**Books**

*ADELBERG, E. A., ed., 2nd ed., 1966. *Papers on Bacterial Genetics*. Boston, Little, Brown. Most of the recent significant papers are included, but see also the first edition.

BEADLE, G. W., and M. BEADLE, 1966. *The Language of Life*. Garden City, N.Y., Doubleday. A fascinatingly written overview of genetics written by a top geneticist and his journalist wife.

BOYER, S. H. IV, ed., 1963. *Papers on Human Genetics*. Englewood Cliffs, N.J., Prentice-Hall. A short collection of significant papers on human genetics with emphasis on the biochemical-molecular.

CROW, J. F., and J. V. NEEL, eds., 1967. *Proceedings of the Third International Congress of Human Genetics*. Baltimore, The Johns Hopkins Press. A record of the symposia of the Third International Congress of Human Genetics, covering late developments in human genetics: clinical, molecular, cytogenetics, biochemical, immunogenetics, population genetics, computer processing, and implications for the future of human evolution. Authoritative and current.

*DEBUSK, A. G., 1968. *Molecular Genetics*. New York, The Macmillan Co. Condensed but excellent account of structure, function, and mutation of DNA at the molecular level as well as of gene regulation, recombination, and fine structure.

*DUPRAW, E. J., 1970. *DNA and Chromosomes*. New York, Holt, Rinehart & Winston. Unusually clear and complete account of DNA and the ultrastructure of chromosomes, much of it based on the author's own research.

*FRASER, D., 1967. *Viruses and Molecular Biology*. New York, The Macmillan Co. Good account in brief style of viral life cycle and genetics.

*HARTMAN, P. E., and S. R. SUSKIND, 2nd ed., 1969. *Gene Action*. Englewood Cliffs, N.J., Prentice-Hall. Condensed and compact member of this publisher's *Foundations of Modern Genetics* Series.

*HERSKOWITZ, I. H., 1967. *Basic Principles of Molecular Genetics*. Boston, Little, Brown. Excellent summary.

*INGRAM, V. M., 1965. *The Biosynthesis of Macromolecules*. New York, W. A. Benjamin. Lucid account by one of the pioneers in this area.

KENDREW, J. C., 1966. *The Thread of Life*. Cambridge, Mass., Harvard University Press. "An introduction to molecular biology, based on a B.B.C. television lecture series." Quick and easy reading.

*KING, R. C., 1968. *A Dictionary of Genetics*. New York, Oxford University Press. Invaluable reference for terms and concepts in genetics; includes a chronology of genetics, 1590–1966, and other useful appendices.

*LOOMIS, W. F., JR., ed., 1970. *Papers on Regulation of Gene Activity during Development*. New York, Harper & Row. Collection of reprints of the important papers dealing with this topic.

MCKUSICK, V. A., 2nd ed., 1968. *Mendelian Inheritance in Man*. Baltimore, The Johns Hopkins Press. A catalog of more than 1,500 autosomal dominant, autosomal recessive, and sex-linked traits in man, together with key literature references. An invaluable reference for anyone concerned with human genetics.

*MCKUSICK, V. A., 2nd ed., 1969. *Human Genetics*. Englewood Cliffs, N.J., Prentice-Hall. A survey of the subject encompassing a large amount of material in condensed but clear and highly readable fashion.

*METTLER, L. E., and T. G. GREGG, 1969. *Population Genetics and Evolution*. Englewood Cliffs, N.J., Prentice-Hall. Experimental and theoretical aspects of population genetics; a lucid summary.

*PETERS, J. A., ed., 1959. *Classic Papers in Genetics*. Englewood Cliffs, N.J., Prentice-Hall. All the foundation papers of the science from Mendel to Benzer, including several not readily available elsewhere.

ROMAN, H. L., ed., 1967—. *Annual Review of Genetics*. Palo Alto, Calif., Annual Reviews, Inc. Annually appearing collections of critical reviews in all phases of genetics; an indispensable aid in keeping abreast of developments.

ROSLANSKY, J. D., ed., 1966. *Genetics and the Future of Man*. New York, Appleton-Century-Crofts. Record of a symposium at Gustavus Adolphus College on this very real problem.

SAGER, R., and F. J. RYAN, 1961. *Cell Heredity*. New York, John Wiley & Sons. Not recent as this topic goes, but excellent and extensive reports (much of it original) on the cytological bases of genetics.

*SONNEBORN, T. M., ed., 1965. *The Control of Human Heredity and Evolution*. New York, Macmillan. Record of a symposium at Ohio Wesleyan University, bringing together a number of Nobel laureates, it is well worth reading and pondering.

*SPIESS, E. B., ed., 1962. *Papers on Animal Population Genetics*. Boston, Little, Brown. Good collection of reprints important in population genetics.

*STENT, G. S., ed., 2nd ed., 1965. *Papers on Bacterial Viruses*. Boston, Little, Brown. Most of the recent important papers are included, but see also the first edition.

STURTEVANT, A. H., 1965. *A History of Genetics*. New York, Harper & Row. A live account by one who participated actively in the development of the science.

SUTTON, H. E., 1965. *An Introduction to Human Genetics.* New York, Holt, Rinehart & Winston. A concise appetizer covering the application of many recently developed topics to human genetics.

*SWANSON, C. P., T. MERZ, and W. J. YOUNG, 1967. *Cytogenetics.* Englewood Cliffs, N.J., Prentice-Hall. Structure and behavior of chromosomes as related to genetics; detailed, compact, and highly useful.

*TAYLOR, J. H., ed., 1965. *Selected Papers on Molecular Genetics.* New York, Academic Press. Selection of historic papers in the field, made even more useful by the editor's discerning commentaries.

*WATSON, J. D., 2nd ed., 1970. *Molecular Biology of the Gene.* New York, W. A. Benjamin. A nearly 700-page paperback by half the Watson-Crick team, it is packed with information and diagrams.

*WOESE, C. R., 1967. *The Genetic Code.* New York, Harper & Row. A concise, historical account of the development of the code in its larger biological context.

YČAS, M., 1969. *The Biological Code.* (Volume 12 of *Frontiers of Biology,* edited by A. Neuberger and E. L. Tatum.) New York, American Elsevier. Detailed, modern, and highly readable account of the nature, operation and possible universality of the code with an up-to-date description of protein biosynthesis and extensive literature references.

*ZUBAY, G. L., ed., 1968. *Papers in Biochemical Genetics.* New York, Holt, Rinehart & Winston. Reprints of the major original papers in the field covering the period 1953 to 1967; valuable introductory commentary before each section by the editor.

### Selected Journals

*Advances in Genetics*
*American Journal of Human Genetics*
*Annals of Human Genetics* (formerly *Annals of Eugenics*)
*Biochemical Genetics*
*Cytogenetics*
*Genetica*
*Genetical Research*
*Genetics*
*Genetics Abstracts*
*Hereditas*
*Heredity*
*Journal of Genetics*
*Journal of Heredity*
*Journal of Medical Genetics*
*Journal of Molecular Biology*
*Molecular and General Genetics*
*Nature*
*Proceedings of the National Academy of Science (U.S.)*
*Science*
*Scientific American*

## Symposia and Reviews

*Advances in Genetics* (M. Demerec, ed.), Academic Press.
*Brookhaven Symposia in Biology*
   No. 8.  Mutation (1955)
   No. 9.  Genetics in Plant Breeding (1956)
   No. 12. Structure and Function of Genetic Elements (1959)
*Cold Spring Harbor Symposia on Quantitative Biology*
   Vol. 9.  Genes and Chromosomes (1941)
   Vol. 11. Heredity and Variation in Microorganisms (1946)
   Vol. 16. Genes and Mutations (1951)
   Vol. 20. Population Genetics (1955)
   Vol. 21. Genetic Mechanisms (1956)
   Vol. 23. Exchange of Genetic Material (1958)
   Vol. 26. Cellular Regulatory Mechanisms (1961)
   Vol. 28. Synthesis and Structure of Macromolecules (1963)
   Vol. 29. Human Genetics (1964)
   Vol. 31. The Genetic Code (1966)
   Vol. 33. Replication of DNA in Micro-Organisms (1968)
   Vol. 34. The Mechanism of Protein Synthesis (1969)
*Oak Ridge Symposia in Biology* (Supplements to *Journal of Cellular and Comparative Physiology*)
   1948. Radiation Genetics. *Jour. Cell. Comp. Physiol.*, **35**, Suppl. 1.
   1954. Genetic Recombination. *ibid.*, **45**, Suppl. 2.
   1964. Molecular Aspects of Mutagenic Agents. *ibid.*, **64**, Suppl. 1.

# GLOSSARY

**Acquired character.** An alteration in function or form resulting from a response to environment; it is not heritable.

**Acridine dye.** Organic molecules that produce mutations by binding to DNA and causing insertions or deletions of bases.

**Acrocentric.** A chromosome with a nearly terminal centromere.

**Adaptation.** Adjustment in some way to the environment.

**Adaptive value.** The proportion of the progeny of a given genotype surviving to maturity (relative to that of another genotype) is its adaptive value (also called *fitness*). Expressed as a pure number between 0 and 1. Thus, if only 60 per cent of the progeny of genotype *aa* survive, whereas 100 per cent of those genotype *A–* survive, the adaptive value of *aa* is 0.6.

**Adenine.** A purine base occurring in DNA and RNA. Pairs normally with thymine in DNA.

**Agglutinin.** An antibody which produces clumping (agglutination) of the antigenic structure.

**Albino.** An individual characterized by absence of pigment. Ordinarily applied to animals where skin, hair, and eye are unpigmented and whose skin and eyes are pinkish because of the blood vessels showing through. Also used to describe plants in which a particular pigment (usually the chlorophylls) is absent.

**Aleurone layer.** Outermost layer of endosperm in some seeds, rich in aleurone (proteinaceous) grains; typically triploid cells.

**Allele** (also **allelomorph**; adj., **allelic** or **allelomorphic**). One member of a pair or a series of genes that can occur at a particular locus on homologous chromosomes.

**Allopolyploid.** A polyploid having whole chromosome sets from different species.

**Alternation of generations.** The regularly occurring alternation of monoploid (gametophyte) and diploid (sporophyte) phases in the life cycle of sexually reproducing plants.

**Ambiguity.** The coding for more than one amino acid by a given codon. See also *genetic code*, and *codon*.

**Amino acid.** A class of chemicals containing an amino ($NH_2$) group and a carboxyl (COOH) group, plus a side chain; the basic constructional unit of proteins.

**Amino group.** The $—NH_2$ chemical group.

**Amphidiploid.** A tetraploid individual having two sets of chromosomes from each of two known ancestral species. An allotetraploid in which the species source of the two different genomes is clearly known. See also *allopolyploid*.

**Anaphase.** The stage of nuclear division characterized by movement of chromosomes from spindle equator to spindle poles. It begins with separation of the centromeres and closes with the end of poleward movement of chromosomes.

**Aneuploidy.** Variation in chromosome number by whole chromosomes, but less than an entire set; *e.g.* $2n + 1$ (trisomy), $2n - 1$ (monosomy).

**Angstrom unit** (Å). A measurement of length or distance, often used in describing intra- or intermolecular dimensions; equal to $1 \times 10^{-10}$ meter and $1 \times 10^{-1}$ nanometer (which see).

**Anther.** The microsporangium of flowering plants; distal part of the stamen in which microspores and, later, pollen grains are produced.

**Antibiotic.** Any chemical substance, elaborated by a living organism (usually a microorganism), that kills or inhibits growth of bacteria.

**Antibody.** A substance that acts to neutralize a specific antigen in a living organism.

**Anticodon.** The group of three nucleotides in transfer RNA which pairs complementarily with three nucleotides of messenger RNA during protein biosynthesis.

**Antigen.** Any substance, usually a protein, that causes antibody production when introduced into a living organism.

**Ascospore.** One of the asexual, monoploid (haploid) spores contained in the ascus of ascomycete fungi such as *Neurospora* and the yeasts.

**Ascus** (pl., **asci**). The generally elongate, saclike meiosporangium in which ascospores are produced in ascomycete fungi.

**Asexual reproduction.** Any process of reproduction that does not involve fusion of cells. Vegetative reproduction, by portions of the vegetative body, is sometimes distinguished as a separate type.

**ATP.** Adenosine triphosphate, an energy-rich compound participating in energy-storing and energy-using reactions in the cell.

**Attached-X.** A strain of *Drosophila* in which the two X chromosomes of the female are permanently attached (symbolized $\widehat{XX}$) so that only $\widehat{XX}$ and O eggs are produced.

**Autopolyploid.** A polyploid all of whose sets of chromosomes are those of the same species.

**Autosome.** A chromosome not associated with the sex of the individual and therefore possessed in matching pairs by diploid members of both sexes.

**Auxotroph.** An individual unable to carry on some particular synthesis, hence requiring supplementing of minimal medium by some growth factor.

**Backcross.** The cross of a progeny individual with one of its parents. See also *testcross*.

**Bacteriophage.** See *phage*.

**Balbiani ring.** An RNA-producing puff in the polytene chromosomes (which see) of the dipteran *Chironomus*.

**Barr body.** The inactive, densely staining, condensed X chromosome, generally found next to the nuclear membrane, in nuclei of somatic cells of XX females. The number of Barr bodies in such nuclei is one less than the total number of X chromosomes.

**Base analog.** A slightly modified purine or pyrimidine molecule which may substitute for the normal base in nucleic acid molecules.

**Bivalent.** A pair of synapsed homologous chromosomes.

**Carboxyl group.** An acidic chemical group, $-\text{COOH}$.

**Cartenoid.** Any of a group of yellow, orange, or red pigments associated with chlorophylls in plants, and in animal fat.

**Carrier.** A heterozygous individual, ordinarily used in cases of complete dominance.

**Cell culture.** A growth of cells in vitro.

**Cell-free extract.** A fluid extract of soluble materials of cells obtained by rupturing the cells and discarding particulate materials and any intact cells.

**Centimeter (cm).** $1 \times 10^{-2}$ meter.

**Centriole.** The central granule in the *centrosome* (which see).

**Centromere.** The region of spindle fiber attachment in a chromosome, appearing as a clear area in specially stained preparations. *Synonym, kinetochore.*

**Centrosome.** A self-propagating cytoplasmic body present in animal cells and some lower plant cells, consisting of a centriole and astral rays at each pole of the spindle during nuclear division.

**Chiasma,** (pl., **chiasmata**). The visible connection or crossover between two chromatids seen during prophase-I of meiosis.

**Chi-square test.** A statistical test for determining the probability that a set of experimentally obtained values will be equalled or exceeded by chance alone for a given theoretical expectation.

**Chloroplast.** Cytoplasmic organelle containing several pigments, particularly the light-absorbing chlorophylls, and also DNA and polysomes (which see).

**Chromatid.** One of the two identical longitudinal halves of a chromosome which shares a common centromere with a sister chromatid; results from the replication of chromosomes during a nuclear division.

**Chromatin.** Nuclear material comprising the chromosomes; the DNA-histone complex.

**Chromomere.** Small, stainable thickenings arranged linearly along a chromosome.

**Chromonema** (pl., **chromonemata**). One of the delicate, helically coiled, threadlike filaments composing a chromosome.

**Chromosome.** Nucleoprotein structures, generally more or less rodlike during nuclear division, the physical sites of nuclear genes which are arranged in linear order. Each species has a characteristic number of chromosomes, although individuals with fewer or more than this characteristic number occur, especially in plants.

***Cis* arrangement.** Linkage of the dominants of two or more pairs of alleles on one chromosome, and the recessives on the homologous chromosome. Also known as *coupling.*

**Cistron.** A segment of DNA specifying one polypeptide chain in protein synthesis. Under the concept of a triplet code, one cistron must contain three times as many nucleotide pairs as amino acids in the chain it specifies.

**Clone.** A group of cells or organisms, derived from a single ancestral cell or individual and all genetically alike.

**Code.** See *Genetic code.*

**Codominance.** The condition in heterozygotes where both members of an allelic pair contribute to phenotype, which is then a *mixture* of the phenotypic traits produced in either homozygous condition. In cattle the cross of red $\times$ white produces roan offspring whose coat consists of both red hairs and white hairs. Codominance differs from incomplete dominance.

**Codon.** A set of nucleotides that is specific for a particular amino acid in protein synthesis; generally agreed to consist of three nucleotides, the last of which, in the case of some amino acids, may be any of the four nucleotides.

**Coincidence.** The observed frequency of double crossovers, divided by their calculated or expected frequency. Expressed as a pure number; a measure of interference. In *positive* interference the coincidence is <1; in *negative* interference the coincidence is >1.

**Col factors.** Cytoplasmic particles in bacteria conferring ability to produce colicins (antibiotic lipocarbohydrate-proteins).

**Colinearity.** Said of a genetic code (which see) in which the sequence of nucleotides corresponds to the sequence of amino acid residues in a polypeptide.

**Commaless.** Said of a genetic code (which see) in which successive codons (which see) are contiguous and not separated by noncoding bases or groups of bases.

**Complementation.** The ability of linearly adjacent segments of DNA to supplement each other in phenotypic effect. Complementary genes, when present together, interact to produce a different expression of a trait.

**Conjugation.** Side by side association of two bodies, as of synapsed chromosomes in meiosis, or of two organisms during sexual reproduction.

**Constitutive enzyme.** A continuously produced enzyme.

**Crossing-over.** A process whereby genes are exchanged between nonsister chromatids of homologous chromosomes. *Unequal crossing-over* may occur, with the result that one chromatid receives a given gene twice, while the other chromatid lacks that gene entirely. Chiasmata (which see) are visible evidences of crossing-over.

**Crossover.** Said of a chromatid resulting from crossing-over.

**Crossover unit.** A crossover value of 1 per cent between linked genes. See also *map unit*.

**Cross reacting material (CRM).** A defective protein produced by a mutant gene, enzymatically inactive but antigenically similar to the wild type protein.

**C-terminus.** That end of a peptide chain carrying the free alpha carboxyl group of the last amino acid in the sequence; written at the right end of the structural formula.

**Cytogenetics.** Study of the cellular structures and mechanisms associated with genetics.

**Cytokinesis.** The division of the cytoplasm during cell division.

**Cytology.** The study of the structure and function of cells.

**Cytosine.** A pyrimidine base occurring in DNA and RNA. Pairs with guanine in DNA.

**Deficiency.** The loss of a part of a chromosome involving one or more genes.

**Deficiency loop.** The loop of the nonsynapsing portion of an unaltered chromosome caused by a deficiency in the homologous chromosome.

**Degeneracy.** Said of a genetic code (which see) in which a particular amino acid is coded for by more than one codon (which see).

**Deletion.** See *deficiency*.

**Deoxyribonucleic acid (DNA).** A usually double-stranded, helically coiled, nucleic acid molecule, composed of deoxyribose-phosphate "backbones" which are connected by paired bases attached to the deoxyribose sugar; the genetic material of all living organisms and many viruses.

**Deoxyribonucleoside.** Portion of a DNA molecule composed of one deoxyribose molecule plus either a purine or a pyrimidine.

**Deoxyribonucleotide.** Portion of a DNA molecule composed of one deoxyribose phosphate bonded to either a purine or a pyrimidine.

**Deoxyribose.** The 5-carbon sugar of DNA.

**Deviation.** A departure from the expected or from the norm.

**Dihybrid.** An individual heterozygous for two pairs of alleles; also said of a cross between individuals differing in two gene pairs.

**Dioecious.** Individuals producing either sperm or egg, but not both. In dioecious species, the sexes are separate. Compare with *monoecious*.

**Diploid.** An individual or cell having two complete sets of chromosomes.

**Disjunction.** The separation of homologous chromosomes during anaphase-I of meiosis.

**DNAase.** Any enzyme which hydrolyzes DNA.

**DNA polymerase.** An enzyme catalyzing the formation of DNA from deoxyribonucleotides, using one strand of DNA as a template.

**Dominance.** That situation in which one member of a pair of allelic genes expresses itself in whole (complete dominance) or in part (incomplete dominance) over the other member.

**Dominant.** An adjective applied to that member of a pair of alleles which expresses itself in heterozygotes to the complete exclusion of the other member of the pair. The term is also applicable to the trait produced by a dominant gene.

**Drift** See *genetic drift*.

**Duplication.** A chromosomal aberration in which a segment of the chromosome bearing specific loci is repeated.

**Dysgenic.** Any effect or situation that is or tends to be harmful to the genetics of future generations.

**Embryo sac.** The female gametophyte of a flowering plant. A large, thin-walled cell within the ovule, containing the egg and several other nuclei, within which the embryo develops after fertilization of the egg.

**Endoplasmic reticulum.** A double membrane system in the cytoplasm, continuous with the nuclear membrane and bearing numerous ribosomes.

**Endosperm.** A polyploid (in many species, triploid) food storage tissue in many angiosperm seeds formed by fusion of two (or more) female cells and a sperm. In gymnosperms, endosperm is the old female gametophyte, hence monoploid (haploid).

**Enzyme.** Any substance, protein in whole or in part, that regulates the rate of a specific biochemical reaction in living organisms.

**Episome.** A genetic element that may be present in a given cell, either on a chromosome or separately in the cytoplasm. The *F*, or fertility factor, in *E. coli* is an example.

**Epistasis.** The masking of the phenotypic effect of either or both members of one pair of alleles by a gene of a different pair. The masked gene is said to be hypostatic.

**Equatorial plate.** The figure formed at the spindle equator in nuclear division.

**Eukaryote (eucaryote).** Any organism or cell with a structurally discrete nucleus. Contrast with *prokaryote*.

**Euploidy.** Variation in chromosome number by whole sets or exact multiples of the monoploid (haploid) number—e.g., diploid, triploid. Euploids above the diploid level may be referred to collectively as polyploids.

**F factor.** The fertility factor in the bacterium *Escherichia coli*; it is composed of DNA and must be present for a cell to function as a "male" or donor in conjugation. See also *episome*.

**F$_1$.** The first filial generation; the first generation resulting from a given cross.

**F$_2$.** The second filial generation; the second generation resulting from interbreeding or selfing members of the F$_1$.

**Fertility factor.** See *F factor*.

**Fitness.** See *adaptive value*.

**Fixation.** Attainment of a gene frequency of 1.0.

**Frame shift (reading frame shift).** The shift in code reading that results from addition or deletion of nucleotides in any number other than 3 or multiples thereof.

**Gamete.** A protoplast which, in the process of sexual reproduction, fuses with another protoplast.

**Gametophyte.** In plants, the phase of the life cycle reproducing sexually by gametes and characterized by having the reduced (usually monoploid or "haploid") chromosome number.

**Gene.** The particulate determiner of a hereditary trait; a particular segment of a DNA molecule, generally located in the chromosome. See also *cistron*, *muton*, and *recon*.

**Gene frequency.** The proportion of one allele of a pair or series present in the population or a sample thereof; that is, the number of loci at which a gene occurs, divided by the number of loci at which it could occur, expressed as a pure number between 0 and 1.

**Gene pool.** The total of all genes in a population.

**Genetic code.** The collection of base triplets of DNA and RNA carrying the genetic information by which proteins are synthesized in the cell.

**Genetic drift.** Changes in gene frequency due to chance fluctuations.

**Genetic equilibrium.** Constancy of a particular gene frequency through successive generations.

**Genetic load.** The proportional reduction in average fitness, relative to an optimal genotype; the average number of lethals per individual in a population.

**Genome.** A complete set of chromosomes, or of chromosomal genes, inherited as a unit from one parent.

**Genotype** (adj., **genotypic**). The genetic makeup or constitution of an individual, with reference to the traits under consideration, usually expressed by a symbol—e.g., "+," "*D*," "*Dd*," "*str*." Individuals of the same genotype breed alike. See *phenotype*.

**Guanine.** A purine base occurring in DNA and RNA. Pairs normally with cytosine in DNA.

**Gynandromorph; gynander.** An individual, part of whose body exhibits male sex characters and part female characters.

**Haplo-.** A prefix before a chromosome number denoting an individual whose somatic cells lack one member of that chromosome pair.

**Haploid.** An individual or cell having a single complete set of chromosomes. Synonym, *monoploid*.

**Hemizygous.** An individual having but one of a given gene; or a gene present only once. Designates either a monoploid organism, a sex-linked gene in XY males (or an XY individual with regard to a particular X-linked gene), or an individual heterozygous for a given chromosomal deficiency.

**Hemoglobin.** An iron-protein pigment of blood functioning in oxygen–carbon dioxide exchange of living cells.

**Hemophilia.** A metabolic disorder characterized by free bleeding from even slight wounds because of the lack of formation of clotting substances. It is associated with a sex-linked recessive gene.

**Heterogametic sex.** That sex having either only one, or two different sex chromosomes, as XO, XY, or ZW. The heterogametic sex thus produces two kinds of gametes with respect to sex chromosomes—e.g., X and Y sperms in human beings.

**Heteroploidy.** Change in number of whole chromosomes. See also *aneuploidy* and *euploidy*.

**Heterospory.** In higher plants, the production of two kinds of meiocytes (megasporocytes and microsporocytes) which give rise to two different kinds of meiospores. Compare with *homospory*.

**Heterozygote** (adj., **heterozygous**). An individual whose chromosomes bear unlike genes of a given allelic pair or series. Heterozygotes produce more than one kind of gamete with respect to a particular locus.

**Histone.** Any of several proteins that can complex with DNA.

**Holandric gene.** A gene located only on the Y chromosome in XY species.

**Homogametic sex.** That sex possessing two identical sex chromosomes (XX or ZZ). Gametes produced by the homogametic sex are all alike with respect to sex chromosome constitution.

**Homolog.** See *homologous chromosomes*.

**Homologous chromosomes.** Chromosomes occurring in pairs, one derived from each of two parents, normally (except in case of chromosomes associated with sex) morphologically alike and bearing the same gene loci. Each member of such a pair is the *homolog* of the other.

**Homospory.** In plants, the production of but one kind of meiocyte which gives rise to meiospores morphologically indistinguishable from each other.

**Homozygote** (adj., **homozygous**). An individual whose chromosomes bear identical genes of a given allelic pair or series. Homozygotes produce only one kind of gamete with respect to a particular locus and, therefore, "breed true."

**Hybrid.** An individual resulting from a cross between two genetically unlike parents.

**Hypha** (pl. **hyphae**). One of the filaments of a mycelium in fungi.

**Idiogram.** A diagrammatic representation of the complete chromosome set of an individual, arranged according to (decreasing) size and/or accepted numbering system. Idiograms may be drawn from suitable microscope preparations, or these may be photographed and the various chromosomes arranged in order (and in homologous pairs in diploid organisms).

**Imperfect flower.** One lacking either stamens or pistil.

**Incomplete dominance.** The condition in heterozygotes where the phenotype is intermediate between the two homozygotes. In some plants the cross of red × white produces pink-flowered progeny. Incomplete dominance differs from codominance.

**Incompletely sex-linked genes.** Genes located on homologous portions of the X and Y (or Z and W) chromosomes.

**Independent segregation.** The random or independent behavior of genes on different pairs of chromosomes.

**Inducer (effector).** Substance inactivating a repressor.

**Inducible enzyme.** An enzyme that is synthesized only in the presence of an inducer (which see).

**Interference.** The increase (*negative interference*) or decrease (*positive interference*) in likelihood of a second crossover closely adjacent to another. In most organisms interference increases with decreased distance between crossovers. See *coincidence*.

**Interphase.** The stage of cell life during which that cell is not dividing.

**Intersex.** An individual showing secondary sex characters intermediate between male and female or some of each sex.

**Inversion.** Reversal of the order of a block of genes in a given chromosome. PQ*UTSR*VWX would represent an inversion of genes *RSTU* if the normal order is alphabetical.

**Inversion loop.** The loop configuration in a pair of synapsed, homologous chromosomes, caused by an inversion in one of them.

**In vitro.** Experimental induced biological processes outside the organism (literally, "in glass").

**In vivo.** Experimentally induced biological processes within the organism.

**Isogametes.** Gametes not differentiated as to sex. Fusing isogametes are physically similar but, in some species, are chemically differentiated.

**Karyokinesis.** The division of the nucleus during cell division.

**Karyolymph.** A clear fluid material within the nuclear membrane; "nuclear sap."

**Karyotype.** The size and shape appearance of metaphase somatic chromosomes; often used to refer to photomicrographs of such chromosomes arranged as in an idiogram (which see).

**Kinetochore.** See *centromere*.

**Lampbrush chromosome.** A chromosome having paired loops extending laterally, occurring in primary oocyte nuclei; they represent sites of active RNA synthesis.

**Lethal gene.** A gene whose phenotypic effect is sufficiently drastic to kill the bearer. Death from different lethal genes may occur at any time from fertilization of the egg to advanced age. Lethal genes may be dominant, incompletely dominant, or recessive.

**Life cycle.** The entire series of developmental stages undergone by an individual from zygote to maturity and death.

**Linkage.** The occurrence of different genes on the same chromosome.

**Linkage group.** All of the genes located physically on a given chromosome.

**Linkage map.** A scale representation of a chromosome showing the relative positions of all its known genes.

**Locus** (pl., **loci**). The position or place on a chromosome occupied by a particular gene or one of its alleles.

**Lysis** (n.) (v.i. or vt., **lyse**). Disintegration or dissolution; usually, the destruction of a bacterial host cell by infecting phage particles.

**Lysogenic bacteria.** Living bacterial cells harboring temperate phages (viruses).

**Map unit.** A distance on a linkage map represented by one per cent of crossovers (recombinants), that is, by a recombination frequency of one per cent.

**Mean.** The arithmetic average; the sum of all values for a group, divided by the number of individuals. Symbolized by $\bar{x}$ (sample), or by $\mu$ (population).

**Median.** The middle value of a series of readings arranged serially according to magnitude.

**Megasporocyte.** In plants, the meiocyte that is destined to produce megaspores by meiosis. Synonym, *megaspore mother cell*.

**Meiocyte.** Any cell that undergoes meiosis.

**Meiosis.** Nuclear divisions in which the diploid or somatic chromosome number is reduced by half. In the first of the two meiotic divisions, homologous chromosomes first replicate, then pair (synapse), and finally separate to different daughter nuclei, which thus have half as many chromosomes as the parent nucleus, and one of each kind instead of two. A second division, in which chromosomal replicates separate into daughter nuclei, follows so that meiosis produces four monoploid daughter nuclei from one diploid parent nucleus.

**Meiospore.** In plants, one of the asexual reproductive cells produced by meiosis from a meiocyte.

**Meristem.** An undifferentiated cellular region in plants characterized by repeated cell division.

**Merozygote.** A partially diploid receptor bacterial cell that results from conjugation.

**Messenger RNA.** Ribonucleic acid conferring amino acid specificity on ribosomes; complementary to a given DNA cistron.

**Metacentric.** A chromosome with a centrally located centromere.

**Metafemale** (also **superfemale**). Abnormal females in *Drosophila*, usually sterile and weak, with an overbalance of X chromosomes with respect to autosomes; X/A ratio greater than 1.0.

**Metamale** (also **supermale**). Abnormal males in *Drosophila* with an overabundance of autosomes to X chromosomes; X/A ratio less than 0.5.

**Metaphase.** That stage of nuclear division in which the chromosomes are located in the equatorial plane of the spindle prior to centromere separation.

**Micrometer ($\mu$m).** A commonly employed unit of measurement in microscopy, it equals $1 \times 10^{-6}$ meter or $1 \times 10^{-3}$ millimeter. Synonym, *micron ($\mu$)* in older usage.

**Micron.** See *micrometer*.

**Microspore.** In plants, the meiospore that gives rise to the male gametophyte and sperms.

**Microsporocyte.** In plants, a cell that is destined to produce microspores by meiosis. Synonyms, *microspore mother cell* and *"pollen mother cell."*

**Millimeter (*mm*).** A unit of distance measurement equal to $1 \times 10^{-3}$ meter.

**Missense.** A mutation by which a particular codon is changed so as to incorporate a different amino acid, often resulting in an inactive protein. A *missense codon* results when one or more bases of a *sense codon* (which see) are changed so that a different amino acid is coded for.

**Mitochondrion** (pl., **mitochondria**). Small cytoplasmic organelle where cellular respiration occurs.

**Mitosis.** Nuclear division in which a replication of chromosomes is followed by separation of the products of replication and their incorporation into two daughter nuclei. Daughter nuclei are normally identical with each other and with the orginal parent nucleus in both kind and number of chromosomes. Mitosis may or may not involve cytoplasmic division.

**Mode.** The numerically largest class or group in a series of measurements or values.

**Monoecious.** Individuals producing both sperm and egg.

**Monohybrid.** The offspring of two homozygous parents that differ in only one gene locus or in which only one such locus is under consideration.

**Monohybrid cross.** A cross between two parents that differ in only one heritable character or in which only one such character is under consideration.

**Monoploid.** An individual having a single complete set of chromosomes. Also the fundamental number of chromosomes comprising a single set. Synonym, *haploid*.

**Monosomic.** An individual lacking one chromosome of a set ($2n - 1$).

**Morphology.** The study of form and structure in organisms.

**Mosaic.** An individual, part of whose body is composed of tissue genetically different from the other part.

**Multiple alleles.** A series of three or more alternative alleles any one of which may occur at a particular locus on a chromosome.

**Multiple genes.** See *polygenes*.

**Mutagen.** Any agent that brings about a mutation.

**Mutation.** A sudden change in genotype having no relation to the individual's ancestry. Used for changes in a single gene itself ("point mutations") and for chromosomal aberrations.

**Muton.** The smallest segment of DNA or subunit of a cistron that can be changed and thereby bring about a mutation; probably as small as one nucleotide pair.

**Mycelium.** The threadlike filamentous vegetative body of many fungi.

**Nanometer** (*nm*). A unit of distance equal to $1 \times 10^{-9}$ meter. Synonym, *millimicron* (*m$\mu$*).

**Nondisjunction.** The failure of homologous chromosomes to separate at anaphase-I of meiosis. *Primary nondisjunction* may occur in an XX female, leading to production of XX or O eggs (in addition to the normal X eggs); or it may occur (first

division) in an XY male, resulting in XY and O sperm or (second division) in XX and O or YY and O sperm (in addition to normal Y or X sperms). *Secondary nondisjunction* may occur in an XXY female giving rise to eggs with XX, XY, X, or Y chromosomal combinations.

**Nonsense.** A codon that does not specify any amino acid in the genetic code.

**Normal curve.** A smooth, symmetrical, bell-shaped curve of distribution.

**N-terminus.** The amino ($-NH_2$) end of a peptide chain, by convention written as the left end of the structural formula.

**Nucleolus.** Deeply staining body containing both RNA and protein within the nucleus.

**Nucleoside.** Portion of a DNA or RNA molecule composed of one deoxyribose molecule (in DNA), or ribose (in RNA), plus a purine or a pyrimidine.

**Nucleotide.** Portion of a DNA or RNA molecule composed of one deoxyribose phosphate unit (in DNA), or one ribose phosphate unit (in RNA), plus a purine or a pyrimidine.

**Nullisomic.** A cell or organism lacking both members of a given chromosome pair ($2n - 2$).

**Oligonucleotide.** A linear sequence of a few (generally not over 10) nucleotides.

**Ontogeny.** The complete development of the individual from zygote, spore, etc., to adult form.

**Oocyte.** The diploid cell that will undergo meiosis (oogenesis) to form an egg.

**Oogenesis.** Egg formation.

**Operator site.** A segment of DNA in an operon that affects activity or nonactivity of associated cistrons;

it may be combined with a repressor and thereby "turn off" the associated cistrons.

**Operon.** A system of cistrons, operator and promoter sites, by which a given genetically controlled, metabolic activity is regulated.

**Ovary.** The female gonad in animals or the ovule-containing portion of the pistil of a flower.

**Ovule.** Structure within the ovary of the pistil of a flower, which becomes a seed. It represents a megasporangium, together with some overgrowing tissue (integuments), and ultimately contains the female gametophyte (embryo sac), one of whose nuclei is an egg.

**P.** The parental generation in a given cross.

**Parameter.** Actual value of some quantitative character for a population. Compare *statistic*.

**Parthenogenesis.** Development of a new individual from an unfertilized egg.

**Pedigree.** The ancestral history of an individual; a chart showing such history.

**Peptide bond.** A chemical bond (CONH) linking amino acid residues together in a protein.

**Perfect flower.** One having both stamen(s) and pistil(s).

**Petite.** A slow growing strain of yeast (*Saccharomyces*) lacking certain respiratory enzymes and forming unusually small colonies on agar. *Segregational petites* bear mutant nuclear gene(s), whereas *neutral petites* (sometimes called *vegetative petites*) bear mutant mitochondrial DNA.

**Phage.** A virus that infects bacteria.

**Phenotype** (adj., **phenotypic**). The appearance or discernible character of an individual which is dependent upon its genetic makeup, usually expressed in words—e.g., "tall," "dwarf," "wild type," "prolineless." Identical phenotypes may not necessarily breed alike.

**Phylogeny.** The evolutionary development of a species or other taxonomic group.

**Pistil.** The entire part of the flower that produces megaspores (which, in turn, produce eggs). Sometimes, and *incorrectly*, referred to as a female floral part.

**Plaque.** Clear area on culture plate of bacteria where these have been killed by phages.

**Plasmagene.** A self-replicating, cytoplasmically located gene.

**Pleiotropy.** The influencing of more than one trait by a single gene.

**Polar body.** One of the three very small cells produced during meiosis of an oocyte, containing a monoploid nucleus but little cytoplasm. It is nonfunctional in reproduction.

**Pollen.** The young male gametophyte of a flowering plant, surrounded by the microspore wall.

**Polygenes.** Two or more different pairs of alleles, with a presumed cumulative effect, governing such quantitative traits as size, pigmentation, intelligence, among others. Those contributing to the trait are termed contributing (effective) alleles; those appearing not to do so are referred to as noncontributing or noneffective alleles.

**Polymer.** A chemical compound composed of two or more units of the same compound.

**Polynucleotide.** A linear sequence of many nucleotides.

**Polypeptide.** A compound containing amino acid residues joined by peptide bonds. A protein may consist of one or more specific polypeptide chains.

**Polyploid.** An individual having more than two complete sets of chromosomes—e.g., triploid (3*n*), tetraploid (4*n*).

**Polyribosome.** See *polysome*.

**Polysome.** A group of ribosomes joined by a molecule of messenger RNA.

**Polytene chromosome.** Many-stranded giant chromosomes produced by repeated replication during synapsis in certain dipteran larval tissues. Synonym, *giant chromosome*.

**Population.** An infinite group of individuals, measured for some variable, quantitative character, from which a sample is taken.

**Position effect.** A phenotypic effect dependent upon a change in position on the chromosome of a gene or group of genes.

**Probability.** The likelihood of occurrence of a given event. Usually expressed as a number between 0 (complete certainty that the event will *not* occur) and 1 (complete certainty that the event *will* occur).

**Progeny.** Offspring individuals.

**Prokaryote.** A cell or organism lacking a discrete nuclear body (also *procaryote*).

**Promoter site.** Site on DNA at which mRNA synthesis is initiated in an operon. May be combined with a repressor protein to inhibit mRNA synthesis by associated cistrons.

**Prophase.** The first stage of nuclear division, including all events up to (but not including) arrival of chromosomes at the equator of the spindle.

**Protoplast.** A structural unit of protoplasm; all the living (protoplasmic) material of a cell. The two principal parts are nucleus and cytoplasm.

**Prototroph.** An individual able to carry on a given synthesis; a wild type individual able to grow on minimal medium.

**Pseudoalleles.** Nonalleles so closely linked as often to be inherited as one gene, but shown to be separable by crossover studies.

**Pseudodominance.** The expression (apparent dominance) of a recessive gene at a locus opposite a deficiency.

**Punnett square.** A "checkerboard" grid designed to determine all possible genotypes produced by a given cross. Genotypes of the gametes of one sex are entered across the top, those of the other down one side. Zygote genotypes produced by each possible mating are then entered in the appropriate squares of the grid.

**Pure line (pure breeding line).** A strain of individuals homozygous for all genes being considered.

**Purine.** Nitrogenous base occurring in DNA and RNA; these are adenine and guanine.

**Pyrimidine.** Nitrogenous base occurring in DNA (thymine and cytosine) or RNA (uracil and cytosine).

**Recessive.** An adjective applied to that member of a pair of genes which fails to express itself in the presence of its dominant allele. The term is also applicable to the trait produced by a recessive gene. Recessive genes express themselves ordinarily only in the homozygous state.

**Reciprocal cross.** A second cross of the same genotypes in which the sexes of the parental generation are reversed. The cross *AA* (♀) × *aa* (♂) is the reciprocal of the cross *aa* (♀) × *AA* (♂).

**Reciprocal translocation.** The exchange of segments between two nonhomologous chromosomes.

**Recombinant.** An individual derived from a crossover gamete.

**Recombination.** The new association of genes in a recombinant individual, arising either from independent assortment of unlinked genes or from crossing over between linked genes.

**Recon.** The smallest segment of DNA or subunit of a cistron that is capable of recombination; probably as small as one nucleotide pair.

**Reduction division.** See *meiosis.*

**Regulator gene.** A gene responsible for production of a repressor protein (which see).

**Replicate.** To form replicas from a model or template; applies to synthesis of new DNA from preexisting DNA as part of nuclear division.

**Repressor.** A protein produced by a regulator gene that can combine with and repress action of an associated operator gene.

**Resistance transfer factor (RTF).** Possibly an episome conferring multiple resistance to several drugs which can be transferred between certain genera of bacteria.

**Ribonucleic acid (RNA).** A single-stranded nucleic acid molecule, synthesized principally in the nucleus from deoxyribonucleic acid, composed of a ribose-phosphate backbone with purines (adenine and guanine) and pyrimidines (uracil and cytosine) attached to the sugar ribose. RNA is of several kinds and functions to carry the "genetic message" from nuclear DNA to the ribosomes.

**Ribonucleoside.** Portion of an RNA molecule composed of one ribose molecule plus either a purine or a pyrimidine.

**Ribonucleotide.** Portion of an RNA molecule composed of one ribose-phosphate unit plus a purine or a pyrimidine.

**Ribose.** The 5-carbon sugar of ribonucleic acid.

**Ribosomal RNA.** That ribonucleic acid incorporated into ribosomes; it is nonspecific for amino acids.

**Ribosome.** Cytoplasmic structure, usually adherent to the endoplasmic reticulum, which is the site of protein synthesis.

**RNAase.** An enzyme which hydrolyzes RNA.

**RNA polymerase.** An enzyme catalyzing the formation of RNA from ribonucleotides (which see) using one strand of DNA as a template.

**Sedimentation coefficient.** The rate of sedimentation of a solute in an appropriate solvent under centrifugation. An $s$ value of $1 \times 10^{-13}$ second is set as one *Svedberg unit.*

**Selection coefficient.** The measure of reduced fitness of a given genotype; it equals one minus the adaptive value (which see) of that genotype.

**Self-fertilization.** Functioning of a single individual as both male and female parent. Plants are "selfed" if sperm and egg are supplied by the same individual.

**Semiconservative.** Replication of DNA in which the two sugar-phosphate "backbones" become separated, each being conserved as one of the two strands of two new DNA molecules.

**Sense codon.** A codon (which see) specifying a particular amino acid in protein synthesis.

**Sex chromosomes.** Heteromorphic chromosomes not occurring in identical pairs in both sexes in diploid organisms; in man and fruit fly these are designated as X and Y chromosomes.

**Sex-influenced trait.** One in which dominance of an allele depends on sex of the bearer; e.g., pattern baldness in humans is dominant in males, recessive in females.

**Sex-limited trait.** One expressed in only one of the sexes; e.g., cock-feathering in fowl is limited to normal males.

**Sex-linked gene.** A gene located only on the X chromosome in XY species (or on the Z chromosomes in ZW species).

**Siblings** (also **sibs**). Individuals having the same maternal and paternal parents; brother-sister relationship.

**Significance.** In statistical treatments, probability values of >0.05 are termed *not significant*, those ≤0.05 but >0.01 are *significant*, those ≤0.01 but >0.001 are *highly significant*, and those ≤0.001 are *very highly significant*. Significant probability values indicate that the results, although possible, deviate too greatly from the expectancy to be acceptable when chance alone is operating.

**Soma** (adj., **somatic**). The body, cells of which in mammals and flowering plants normally have two sets of chromosomes, one derived from each parent.

**Spermatid.** The monoploid cells, resulting from meiosis of a primary spermatocyte, which will mature into sperms.

**Spermatocyte.** The cell that undergoes meiosis to produce four spermatids.

**Spermatogenesis.** Development of sperms.

**Spore.** An asexual reproductive protoplast capable of developing into a new individual. See also *meiospore*.

**Sporocyte.** In plants, a meiocyte.

**Sporogenesis.** Formation of spores.

**Sporophyte.** In plants, the phase of the life cycle reproducing asexually by meiospores and characterized by having the double (usually diploid) chromosome number.

**Stamen.** That part of a flower producing microspores (which, in turn, produce sperms). Sometimes, and *incorrectly*, referred to as a male floral part.

**Standard deviation.** A measure of the variation in a sample. Symbolized by $s$.

**Standard error of difference in means.** Measure of the significance of the difference in two sample means. Symbolized by $S_d$.

**Standard error of sample mean.** An estimate of the standard deviation of a series of hypothetical sample means, serving as a measure of the closeness with which a given sample mean approximates the population mean. Symbolized by $s_{\bar{x}}$.

**Statistic.** Actual value of some quantitative character for a sample from which estimates of parameters may be made.

**Stigma.** The pollen receptive portion of the pistil of a flower.

**Structural gene.** A cistron.

**Svedberg unit.** See *sedimentation coefficient*.

**Synapsis** (v.i., **synapse**). The pairing of homologous chromosomes occurring in prophase-I of meiosis.

**Syngamy.** The union of the nuclei of sex cells (gametes) in reproduction.

**Tautomer.** An alternate molecular form of a compound, characterized by a different arrangement of its electrons and protons as compared with the common form of the molecule.

**Taxon.** A taxonomic group of any rank.

**Taxonomy.** The study of describing, naming, and classifying living organisms, and the bases on which resultant classification systems rest.

**Telocentric.** A chromosome having a terminal centromere.

**Telophase.** The concluding stage of nuclear division characterized by the reorganization of interphase nuclei.

**Temperate phage.** A phage (bacterium-infecting virus) that invades and multiplies in, but does not ordinarily lyse its host.

**Template.** A model, mold, or pattern; DNA acts as a template for RNA synthesis.

**Testcross.** The cross of an individual (generally of dominant phenotype) with one having the recessive phenotype. Generally used to determine whether an individual of dominant phenotype is homozygous or heterozygous, or to determine the degree of linkage.

**Tetrad.** The four monoploid (haploid) cells arising from meiosis of a megasporocyte or microsporocyte in plants; also, a group of four associated chromatids during synapsis.

**Tetraploid.** A polyploid cell tissue, or organism having four sets of chromosomes (4n). See also *polyploid, allopolyploid,* and *autopolyploid.*

**Three-point cross.** A trihybrid testcross (e.g., *ABC/abc* × *abc/abc,* etc.) used primarily in chromosome mapping.

**Thymine.** A pyrimidine base occurring in DNA. Pairs normally with adenine.

**Totipotency.** The property of a cell (or cells) whereby it develops into a complete and differentiated organism.

**Trans arrangement.** Linkage of the dominant allele of one pair and the recessive of another on the same chromosome. Also known as *repulsion.*

**Transcription.** Synthesis of messenger RNA from a DNA template.

**Transduction.** Recombination in bacteria whereby DNA is transferred by a phage from one cell to another.

**Transfer RNA.** Amino acid-specific RNA which transfers activated amino acids to mRNA where protein synthesis takes place. Sometimes referred to as *soluble RNA.*

**Transformation.** Genetic recombination, particularly in bacteria, whereby naked DNA from one individual becomes incorporated into that of another.

**Transgressive variation.** Appearance in progeny of a more extreme expression of a trait than occurs in the parents. Assumed to result from cumulative action of polygenes, but careful testing of variation in parental lines is necessary for verification.

**Transition.** The substitution in DNA or RNA of one purine for another, or of one pyrimidine for another.

**Translation.** The process by which a particular messenger RNA nucleotide sequence is responsible for a specific amino acid residue sequence of a polypeptide chain.

**Translocation.** The shift of a portion of a chromosome to another part of the same chromosome or to an entirely different chromosome. (See also *reciprocal translocation.*)

**Transversion.** The substitution in DNA or RNA of a purine for a pyrimidine or vice versa.

**Trihybrid.** An individual heterozygous for three pairs of genes.

**Triplet.** A group of three successive nucleotides in RNA (or DNA) which, in the genetic code (which see), specifies a particular amino acid in the synthesis of polypeptide chains.

**Triplo-.** Prefix denoting a trisomic individual where the identity of the extra chromosome is known—e.g., triplo-IV *Drosophila,* or triplo-21 human beings.

**Triploid.** A polyploid cell, tissue or organism having three sets of chromosomes (3n).

**Trisomic.** An individual having one extra chromosome of a set (2n + 1).

**Universal donor.** A person with group O blood, whose erythrocytes therefore bear neither A nor B antigens, and whose blood can be donated to members of groups O, A, B, and AB if necessary.

**Universal recipient.** A person of blood group AB who can receive blood from members of groups AB, A, B, or O if necessary.

**Uracil.** A pyrimidine base occurring in RNA.

**Virulence.** The ability to produce disease.

**Virulent phage.** A phage (virus) that destroys (lyses) its host bacterial cell.

**Wild type.** The most frequently encountered phenotype in natural breeding populations; the "normal" phenotype. ¦ *Dominate*

**Wobble hypothesis.** The partial or total lack of specificity in the third base of some triplet codons (which see) whereby two, three, or four codons differing only in the third base may code for the same amino acid. See Table 16-1.

**Zygote.** The protoplast resulting from the fusion of two gametes in sexual reproduction; a fertilized egg.

# Index